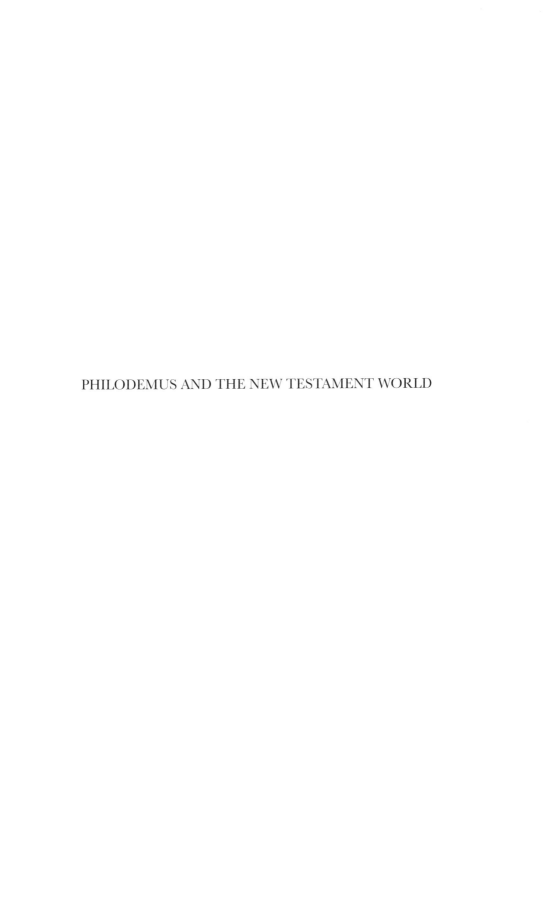

PHILODEMUS AND THE NEW TESTAMENT WORLD

SUPPLEMENTS TO
NOVUM TESTAMENTUM

VOLUME CXI

PHILODEMUS AND THE NEW TESTAMENT WORLD

EDITED BY

JOHN T. FITZGERALD
DIRK OBBINK
GLENN S. HOLLAND

BRILL
LEIDEN · BOSTON
2004

This book is printed on acid-free paper.

Library of Congress Cataloging-in-Publication Data

Philodemus and the New Testament world / edited by John T. Fitzgerald, Dirk Obbink, and Glenn S. Holland.
    p. cm. — (Supplements to Novum Testamentum, ISSN 0167-9732 ; v. 111)
    Includes bibliographical references and indexes.
    ISBN 90-04-11460-2 (hb : alk. paper)
    1. Philodemus, ca. 110-ca. 40 B.C. 2. Bible. N.T. Epistles—Criticism, interpretation, etc.
    I. Fitzgerald, John T., 1948- II. Obbink, Dirk. III. Holland, Glenn Stanfield, 1952- IV. Series.

B598.P44P48 2003
187—dc22
                                      2003060804

ISSN   0167-9732
ISBN   90 04 11460 2

PRINTED IN THE NETHERLANDS

CONTENTS

Preface vii

List of Contributors xi

Abbreviations xiii

Introduction: Philodemus and the Papyri from
Herculaneum 1

PART ONE

PHILODEMUS' ETHICAL, THEOLOGICAL,
RHETORICAL, AESTHETIC, AND HISTORICAL WORKS

DAVID ARMSTRONG
All Things to All Men: Philodemus' Model of Therapy
and the Audience of *De Morte* 15

DISKIN CLAY
Philodemus on the Plain Speaking of the Other
Philosophers 55

DIRK OBBINK
Craft, Cult, and Canon in the Books from Herculaneum 73

DAVID SIDER
How to Commit Philosophy Obliquely: Philodemus' Epigrams
in the Light of his *Peri Parrhesias* 85

L. MICHAEL WHITE
A Measure of *Parrhesia*: The State of the Manuscript
of PHerc. 1471 103

PART TWO

PHILODEMUS' THOUGHT WITHIN
THE CONTEXT OF THE GRECO-ROMAN WORLD

ELIZABETH ASMIS
Epicurean Economics 133

DAVID L. BALCH
Philodemus, "On Wealth" and "On Household Management:"
Naturally Wealthy Epicureans Against Poor Cynics 177

ROBERT N. GAINES
Cicero, Philodemus, and the Development of Late Hellenistic
Rhetorical Theory 197

PAMELA GORDON
Remembering the Garden: The Trouble with Women in the
School of Epicurus 221

GLENN S. HOLLAND
Call Me Frank: Lucian's (Self-)Defense of Frank Speaking
and Philodemus' Περὶ Παρρησίας 245

PART THREE

PHILODEMUS AND THE NEW TESTAMENT WORLD

BENJAMIN FIORE
The Pastoral Epistles in the Light of Philodemus'
"On Frank Criticism" 271

J. PAUL SAMPLEY
Paul's Frank Speech with the Galatians and the
Corinthians 295

BRUCE W. WINTER
Philodemus and Paul on Rhetorical Delivery (ὑπόκρισις) 323

JOHN T. FITZGERALD
Gadara: Philodemus' Native City 343

Index of Ancient Authors and Texts 399

Index of Modern Scholars 426

PREFACE

This volume has its origins in the work of the Hellenistic Moral Philosophy and Early Christianity Section of the Society of Biblical Literature. The group itself was first established as a consultation of the SBL at its annual meeting in 1990. It was created to address topics— that is, philosophical τόποι—that were of common concern both to the moral philosophers of the late Roman republic and early empire and to the leaders of the early Christian movement. The membership of the group has included both New Testament scholars and classicists, with the intention of promoting cooperation and conversation between two interconnected, but too often disciplinarily exclusive, fields of inquiry.

Beginning in 1991 with the Annual Meeting of the Society of Biblical Literature in Kansas City, Missouri, the group focused its attention on the τόπος of friendship as it was addressed by the moral philosophers on the one hand and the authors of the New Testament books on the other. The group's continuing discussion has produced two earlier collections of essays, both edited by John T. Fitzgerald: *Friendship, Flattery, and Frankness of Speech: Studies on Friendship in the New Testament World*, SuppNT 82 (Leiden: Brill, 1996), and *Greco-Roman Perspectives on Friendship*, SBLRBS 34 (Atlanta: Scholars, 1997). The former volume featured an essay on "Frank Speech, Flattery, and Friendship in Philodemus" by Clarence E. Glad, as well as a section of four essays examining "Παρρησία in the New Testament," including essays by David E. Fredrickson (writing on the Pauline epistles), S. C. Winter (Acts), Alan C. Mitchell, S. J. (Hebrews), and William Klassen (the Johannine corpus).

The interest among the members of the Hellenistic Moral Philosophy and Early Christianity Group in the work of Philodemus, and more particularly their concentration on his treatise Περὶ παρρησίας, clearly arose specifically out of their concern with the τόπος of friendship and its attendant virtues. At the same time, the group's work has produced specific benefits for all those interested in Philodemus' work, most notably the first modern-language translation of Περὶ παρρησίας. Members of the group first undertook translation of Philodemus' treatise in 1993; the final translation was published in 1998 as

Philodemus: On Frank Criticism (David Konstan, Diskin Clay, Clarence E. Glad, Johan C. Thom, James Ware, trans., SBLTT 43, Graeco-Roman 13 [Atlanta: Scholars, 1998]). The present volume is something of a companion to that translation, and the editors hope it will prove of interest to classicists and biblical scholars alike.

In the Introduction that follows this preface, John T. Fitzgerald discusses the renaissance of scholarly interest in Epicureanism in general and the works of Philodemus in particular, and provides some of the pertinent bibliography on other authors whose work is found among the Herculaneum papyri.

The volume's fourteen essays are divided among three major sections. The first is devoted to Philodemus' ethical, theological, rhetorical, aesthetic, and historical works. Here the reader will find David Armstrong's essay on Philodemus' treatise *De Morte*, Diskin Clay's examination of the relationship of Philodemus' *On Frank Criticism* to his histories of the Academic and Stoic philosophers, Dirk Obbink's article on the distinctions between Epicurean philosophical communities and religious cults as revealed in the books from Herculaneum, and David Sider's essay on Philodemus' philosophical epigrams. Also included here is L. Michael White's essay on the physical state of the manuscript of Περὶ παρρησίας (PHerc. 1471).

The second section is concerned with Philodemus' thought and works within the context of the Greco-Roman world. Elizabeth Asmis discusses the topic of wealth in the work of Philodemus and among the Epicureans, while David Balch compares the Epicureans' attitudes towards wealth with those of the Cynics. Robert Gaines addresses the development of rhetorical theory in the works of Cicero and Philodemus, while Pamela Gordon investigates the role of women in the Epicurean community, and Glenn S. Holland exposes Lucian of Samosata's appropriation of philosophical παρρησία as a license and rationale for his satirical attacks against the philosophical schools of his day.

The third section addresses Philodemus and the New Testament world. Benjamin Fiore traces the recommended use of παρρησία in the Pastoral epistles. J. Paul Sampley deals specifically with Paul's use of παρρησία in his letters to the churches in Galatia and in Corinth, and Bruce Winter writes on Philodemus and Paul on rhetorical delivery (ὑπόκρισις). Finally, John T. Fitzgerald provides an overview of Gadara of the Decapolis, that places Philodemus' native city—a largely Gentile enclave in Syria—in its historical, cultural, and religious context.

The editors would like to express their gratitude to the editorial board and especially to Margaret M. Mitchell and David P. Moessner, the executive editors of the series Supplements to Novum Testamentum at E. J. Brill for their assistance and support, and for including this volume in that series. We wish also to thank them for their patience and understanding in awaiting this volume, which has taken an unduly long time to prepare, and we extend the same thanks to all of the volume's contributors, who likewise have been patient and supportive while this volume was in preparation. Finally, the editors trust that readers from a variety of backgrounds and academic orientations will find this collection useful and illuminating, and that it will contribute to a better understanding both of Epicurean philosophy in general, and the work of Philodemus in particular

GLENN S. HOLLAND

LIST OF CONTRIBUTORS

David Armstrong
Professor of Classics
The University of Texas at Austin
Austin, Texas

Elizabeth Asmis
Professor of Classics
The University of Chicago
Chicago, Illinois

David L. Balch
Professor of New Testament
Brite Divinity School
Texas Christian University
Fort Worth, Texas

Diskin Clay
RJR Nabisco Professor of Classical Studies
Duke University
Durham, North Carolina

Benjamin Fiore, S.J.
Professor of New Testament
Canisius College
Buffalo, New York

John T. Fitzgerald
Associate Professor of New Testament
University of Miami
Coral Gables, Florida

Robert N. Gaines
Associate Professor of Communication
University of Maryland
College Park, Maryland

Pamela Gordon
Associate Professor of Classics
University of Kansas
Lawrence, Kansas

Glenn S. Holland
Bishop James Mills Thoburn Professor of Religious Studies
Allegheny College
Meadville, Pennsylvania

Dirk Obbink
Fellow and Tutor in Greek
Christ Church
University of Oxford
Oxford, England

J. Paul Sampley
Professor of New Testament and Christian Origins (ret.)
Boston University
Boston, Massachusetts

David Sider
Professor of Classics
New York University
New York, New York

L. Michael White
R. N. Smith Professor of Classics
Director, Institute for the Study of Classics and Christian Origins
The University of Texas
Austin, Texas

Bruce W. Winter
Director, Institute for Early Christianity in the Greco-Roman World
Tyndale House
University of Cambridge
Cambridge, England

ABBREVIATIONS

AB	Anchor Bible
ABD	*Anchor Bible Dictionary*
ADAJ	*Annual of the Department of Antiquities of Jordan*
AJP	*American Journal of Philology*
ANRW	*Aufstieg und Niedergang der römischen Welt*
Anth. Pal.	*Palatine Anthology*
AV	Authorized Version
BAG²	Walter Bauer, ed., *A Greek-English Lexicon of the New Testament and Other Early Christian Literature*, trans. William F. Arndt and F. Wilbur Gingrich, 2nd ed., 1958
BAR	*British Archaeological Reports*
BASP	*Bulletin of the American Society of Papyrologists*
BDF	F. Blass, A. Debrunner, and R. W. Funk, *A Greek Grammar of the New Testament*
BJS	Brown Judaic Studies
CA	*Classical Antiquity*
CErc	*Cronache Ercolanesi*
CIL	*Corpus inscriptionum latinarum* (1863–)
ClAnt	*Classical Antiquity*
CP	*Classical Philology*
CQ	*Classical Quarterly*
CR	*Classical Review*
DCH	D. J. A. Clines, ed., *Dictionary of Classical Hebrew* (Sheffield, 1993–)
DDD	*Dictionary of Deities and Demons*, ed. K. van der Toorn, B. Becking, and P. W. van der Horst, 2nd ed., 1999
DNP	*Der neue Pauly: Enzyklopädie der Antike*
EDNT	*Exegetical Dictionary of the New Testament*
EPRO	Etudes preliminaries aux religions orientales dans l'empire Romain
FGrHist	F. Jacoby, *Die Fragmente der griechischen Historiker* Berlin-Leiden, 1923–
GRBS	*Greek, Roman, and Byzantine Studies*
HThR	*Harvard Theological Review*
IEJ	*Israel Exploration Journal*
IG	*Inscriptiones graecae*
IGRom	*Inscriptiones graecae ad res Romanas pertinentes*, ed. R. Cagnat et al. (1906–27)
JAAC	*The Journal of Aesthetics and Art Criticism*
JBL	*Journal of Biblical Literature*
JEA	*Journal of Egyptian Archaeology*
JHS	*Journal of Hellenic Studies*
JNTS	*Journal for the Study of the New Testament*
JQR	*Jewish Quarterly Review*
JRS	*Journal of Roman Studies*
JSJ	*Journal for the Study of Judaism in the Persian, Hellenistic and Roman Period*
KD	Κύριαι Δόξαι ("Authoritative Opinions")
LCL	Loeb Classical Library
LRB	*London Review of Books*
LSJ	H. G. Liddell, R. Scott, Henry Stuart-Jones, eds., *A Greek-English Lexicon*, 9th ed. (Oxford: Clarendon, 1940)

LXX	Septuagint
MD	*Materiali e discussioni per l'analisi dei testi classici*
NAB	New American Bible
NovTSup	Supplements to Novum Testamentum
NRSV	New Revised Standard Version
NTS	*New Testament Studies*
ÖBS	*Österreichische biblische Studien*
*OCD*¹	*Oxford Classical Dictionary*, 1st ed., 1949
*OCD*²	*Oxford Classical Dictionary*, 2nd ed., 1970
*OCD*³	*Oxford Classical Dictionary*, 3rd ed., 1996
OGIS	*Orientis graeci inscriptions selectae*
OSAPh	*Oxford Studies in Ancient Philosophy*
PBACAP	*Proceedings of the Boston Area Colloquium in Ancient Philosophy*
PCG	*Poetae comici Graeci*, eds. Rudolf Kassel and Colin Austin (Berlin: W. de Guyter, 1983–91)
PHerc	Herculaneum Papyrus (now in the Biblotheca Nazionale, Naples)
POxy.	Oxyrhynchus Papyrus
PP	*La Parola del passato*
QUCC	*Quaderni urbinati di cultura classica*
RA	*Revue d'assyriologie et d'archéologie orientale*
RAC	*Reallexikon für Antike und Christentum*
RE	*Realencyclopädie der classischen Altertumswissenschaft*
RhM	*Rheinisches Museum für Philologie*
*RGG*⁴	*Religion in Geschichte und Gegenwart*, 4th ed. (1998–)
RRW	George Kennedy, *The Art of Rhetoric in the Roman World* (Princeton: Princeton University Press, 1972)
RSR	*Recherches de science religieuse*
SBL	Society of Biblical Literature
SBLDS	Society of Biblical Literature Dissertation Series
SBLTT	Society of Biblical Literature Texts and Translations
ScrHier	Scripta hierosolymitana
SEG	*Supplementum epigraphicum Graecum* (1923–)
SIG	*Sylloge inscriptionum graecarum*
SJLA	Studies in Judaism in Late Antiquity
SNTSMS	Society for New Testament Studies Monograph Series
StPB	Studia Post Biblica
Supp. JRA	Supplements to the Journal of Roman Archaeology
SV	Vatican Sayings
SVF	Hans Friedrich August von Arnim, ed., *Stoicorum Veterum Fragmenta*, vols. 1–4, (Leipzig: B. G. Teubner, 1903–24)
TAPA	*Transactions of the American Philological Association*
TLS	*Times Literary Supplement* (London)
TrGF	*Tragicorum Graecorum fragmenta*, eds. Bruno Snell and Richard Kannicht (Göttingen: Vandenhoeck & Ruprecht, 1983–86[?])
TSAJ	Texts and Studies in Ancient Judaism
U	Hermann Usener, ed., *Epicurea* (Leipzig: B. G. Teubner, 1887)
ZDPV	*Zeitschrift des deutschen Palästina-Vereins*
ZPE	*Zeitschrift für Papyrologie und Epigraphik*

INTRODUCTION:
PHILODEMUS AND THE PAPYRI
FROM HERCULANEUM

John T. Fitzgerald

Scholarly assessments of Philodemus in the late nineteenth and early twentieth centuries were often sharply negative. Domenico Comparetti and Giulio De Petra, for example, described him in 1883 as "an obscure, verbose and unauthoritative Epicurean of the days of Cicero."[1] Sir John Pentland Mahaffy, writing in 1906, contemptuously dismissed him as "a very tenth-rate pupil" of Epicurus and condemned him as being "morally as bad as bad could be."[2] A similar verdict about Philodemus' works was given in 1908 by Ethel Ross Barker, who said that they were "quite third-rate in character" and thus "of little or no value as philosophy or as literature."[3]

This generally low appraisal of Philodemus,[4] which was often accompanied by a hostile attitude toward the Epicurean tenets which he espoused,[5] began to change during the course of the twentieth

---

[1] Domenico Comparetti and Giulio De Petra, *La Villa ercolanese dei Pisoni: I suoi monumenti e la sua biblioteca. Ricerche e notizie* (Turin: E. Loescher, 1883; repr. Naples: Centro Internazionale per lo Studio dei Papiri Ercolanesi, 1972), 79: "un oscuro, verboso, non autorevole epicureo dei tempi ciceroniani." This assessment is quoted with approval by Charles Waldstein and Leonard Shoobridge, *Herculaneum: Past, Present, and Future* (London: Macmillan, 1908), 83.

[2] John Pentland Mahaffy, *The Silver Age of the Greek World* (Chicago: University of Chicago Press; London: T. Fisher Unwin, 1906), 161 and 255.

[3] Ethel Ross Barker, *Buried Herculaneum* (London: Adam and Charles Black, 1908), 82 and 118.

[4] Not all treatments of Philodemus from this period are as negative as those given in the text. A much more balanced assessment is provided by Franz Susemihl, *Geschichte der griechischen Litteratur in der Alexandrinerzeit*, 2 vols. (Leipzig: Teubner, 1891–92), 2:267–78, who argues that Cicero's depiction of Philodemus as an educated man (*Pis.* 68–70) is richly confirmed by his works (268). The most lavish praise of this period is bestowed on Philodemus' poetry, often at the expense of his prose works. For example, Alfred Körte, *Hellenistic Poetry* (New York: Columbia University Press, 1929), 402, praises Philodemus as "the finest of the later epigrammatists" yet thinks that his philosophical writings "are of little significance" in terms "both of style and of content."

[5] See, for example, Mahaffy, *The Silver Age of the Greek World*, 158, whose low estimate of Philodemus is connected with his contempt for Epicureanism as a "very demoralising theory."

century.[6] By the century's end a more positive estimate of Philodemus had emerged among most scholars.[7] This heightened current appreciation is the result of at least four converging factors. First, contemporary scholars, building upon the work of their predecessors, have a generally better understanding of Epicureanism and often are more sympathetic toward it.[8] The school was much more diverse and innovative than most previous scholars had imagined,[9] and this new perspective on Epicureanism is partly the result of paying greater attention to Philodemus' works, which reveal several important internal debates within the school[10] and "contain a wealth of information about Epicureanism as practiced among the Greek-speaking inhabitants of Italy in the first century B.C.E."[11]

Second, some of Philodemus' works are largely transcripts of lectures

---

[6] See, for example, the brief comments by Piero Treves, "Philodemus," *OCD¹* (1949): 681–82 and *OCD²* (1970): 818–19. Although he disparaged Philodemus' prose as "dull and colourless," Treves also referred to the "taste and ingenuity" of Philodemus' epigrams and called his theory of art "particularly remarkable." Of course, purely negative statements about Philodemus' works continued to be made. Raleigh Trevelyan, for example, in 1976 called Philodemus' *On Music* "a ridiculous diatribe." See his *The Shadow of Vesuvius: Pompeii A.D. 79* (London: Michael Joseph, 1976), 47.

[7] For an example of this new appreciation of Philodemus, see esp. Michael Erler, "Die Schule Epikurs," *Die hellenistische Philosophie*, ed. H. Flashar, Grundriss der Geschichte der Philosophie, Die Philosophie der Antike 4.1 (Basel: Schwabe, 1994), 289–362, esp. 337–43. I gratefully acknowledge here my great indebtedness to Erler's work on Philodemus and other members of the Epicurean school. His discussions and bibliographies are utterly indispensable for research on any member of the Garden and especially for those whose writings are preserved among the Herculaneum papyri.

[8] On ancient Epicureanism, see esp. the studies produced by members of the Association Guillaume Budé and published in the *Actes du VIIIᵉ Congrès (Paris, 5–10 avril 1968)* (Paris: Société d'édition "Les Belles Lettres," 1969), the essays in Jean Bollack and André Laks, eds., *Études sur l'Epicurisme antique*, Cahiers de philologie 1 (Lille: Publications de l'Université de Lille III, [1976]), and the studies in Gabriele Giannantoni and Marcello Gigante, eds., *Epicureismo greco e romano: Atti del congresso internazionale, Napoli, 19–26 maggio 1995*, Elenchos 25, 3 vols. (Naples: Bibliopolis, 1996). On Roman Epicureanism, see John Ferguson and Jackson P. Hershbell, "Epicureanism under the Roman Empire," *ANRW* 2.36.4 (1990): 2257–2327, and Catherine J. Castner, *Prosopography of Roman Epicureans from the Second Century B.C. to the Second Century A.D.*, Studien zur klassischen Philologie 34 (Frankfurt: Peter Lang, 1988).

[9] On tradition and innovation in Epicureanism, see the studies published in *Greek, Roman, and Byzantine Studies* 30 (1989): 144–335.

[10] The importance of Philodemus' writings for intramural debates within Epicureanism was recognized by earlier scholars, but this information was seldom exploited in depictions of the school. See, for example, Friedrich Überweg and Karl Praechter, Grundriss der Geschichte der Philosophie, vol. 1: *Die Philosophie des Altertums*, 12th rev. ed. (Berlin: Mittler, 1926), 444.

[11] Pamela Gordon, "Epicureanism," *Encyclopedia of Classical Philosophy*, ed. D. J. Zeyl (Westport, CT: Greenwood, 1997), 208–14, esp. 212.

(σχολαί) given by his teacher Zeno of Sidon,[12] who was "probably the most important Epicurean philosopher after Epicurus" himself.[13] Of particular importance is the work *On Signs*, which Philodemus compiled from two or three sets of lecture notes.[14] A work of logic, it "is one of the most interesting documents in the history of scientific method" and "may be regarded as the first systematic defence of induction."[15]

Yet Philodemus' significance is not due simply to his transmission of Zeno's thoughts. A third factor in the rise of a more just assessment of Philodemus is the growing awareness that in his own writings he not only "greatly surpassed the average literary standard to which most Epicureans aspired" but also developed certain original ideas, especially in the theory of art.[16] His epigrams were particularly noteworthy, so much so that he is now regarded as "one of the finest epigrammatists of antiquity."[17]

Fourth, there is an increasing recognition of Philodemus' importance for understanding the intellectual, cultural, social, and theological world of his day. A man of wide-ranging interests and intellectual curiosity,

---

[12] On Zeno of Sidon, see the texts assembled by Anna Angeli and Maria Colaizzo, eds., "I frammenti di Zenone Sidonio," *CErc* 9 (1979): 47–133. For discussion, see Gregory Vlastos, "Zeno of Sidon as a Critic of Euclid," *The Classical Tradition: Literary and Historical Studies in Honor of Harry Caplan*, ed. L. Wallach (Ithaca: Cornell University Press, 1966), 148–59; Kurt von Fritz, "Zenon von Sidon," *RE* 10 A (1972): 122–38; Adele Tepedino Guerra, "Zenone di Sidone," ΣΥΖΗΤΗΣΙΣ: *Studi sull'epicureismo greco e romano offerti a Marcello Gigante*, Biblioteca della Parola del Passato 16, 2 vols. (Naples: G. Macchiaroli, 1983), 2:551–52; and Erler, "Die Schule Epikurs," 268–72. The lectures of Zeno are mentioned in the subscripts of PHerc. 1003, 1389, and 1471.

[13] Elizabeth Asmis, "Philodemus' Epicureanism," *ANRW* 2.36.4 (1990): 2369–2406, esp. 2371.

[14] This work (preserved in PHerc. 1065) draws on the lecture notes of both Zeno and Bromius (*On Signs* 27); it also incorporates an account by Demetrius of Laconia (*On Signs* 45), which probably also derives from Zeno's lectures (so Asmis, "Philodemus' Epicureanism," 2381).

[15] Elizabeth Asmis, "Philodemus," *Encyclopedia of Classical Philosophy*, 381–82, esp. 382. On the topic of Epicurean methodology in scientific investigation, see Asmis' *Epicurus' Scientific Method*, Cornell Studies in Classical Philology 42 (Ithaca: Cornell University Press, 1984).

[16] Piero Treves and Dirk Obbink, "Philodemus," *OCD*³ (1996): 1165–66, esp. 1165.

[17] Richard Janko, ed. and trans., *Philodemus, On Poems, Book 1*, Philodemus: The Aesthetic Works 1.1 (Oxford: Oxford University Press, 2000), v. Thirty-five of the epigrams included in the *Palatine Anthology* are attributed to Philodemus, and POxy. 54.3724 (a late first-century C.E. papyrus roll, edited by Peter Parsons), which is an incipit list of epigrams chiefly by Philodemus, proves that a collection of Philodemus' epigrams circulated in Roman Egypt. On the latter, see David Sider, "Looking for Philodemus in POxy. 54.3724," *ZPE* 76 (1989): 229–36, and Alan Cameron, *The Greek Anthology from Meleager to Planudes* (Oxford: Clarendon, 1993), 379–87.

he was "highly regarded in educated Roman circles"[18] and influenced a number of writers, especially poets. Indeed, allusions to and imitations of his poems are found in Catullus,[19] Horace,[20] Propertius,[21] Vergil,[22] Ovid,[23] and perhaps others,[24] and his *On Poems* is now widely

---

[18] Michael Erler, "Philodemus," *Routledge Encyclopedia of Philosophy*, ed. E. Craig, 10 vols. (London: Routledge, 1998), 7:365–67, esp. 365. For Philodemus' success in influencing eminent Romans, see also Susemihl, *Geschichte der griechischen Litteratur*, 2:267–68, and Treves and Obbink, "Philodemus," 1165. Among those mentioned by name in the fragments of Philodemus are Plotius Tucca, Lucius Varius Rufus, Vergil, and Quintilius Varus Cremonensis. See Alfred Körte, "Augusteer bei Philodem," *Rheinisches Museum* 45 (1890): 172–77; Walter Wimmel, "Der Augusteer Lucius Varius Rufus," *ANRW* 2.30.3 (1983): 1562–1621, esp. 1567; Castner, *Prosopography*, 45–46, 62, 73–74; and Marcello Gigante, *Philodemus in Italy: The Books from Herculaneum*, trans. Dirk Obbink, The Body, In Theory: Histories of Cultural Materialism (Ann Arbor: University of Michigan, 1995), 47. Varius wrote a hexameter poem on death (*De morte*), apparently written with the Epicurean aim of freeing humans from the fear of death. Edward Courtney, ed., *The Fragmentary Latin Poets* (Oxford: Clarendon, 1993), 271–75, esp. 275, dates it to 44/43 B.C.E., "exactly the date of Philodemus' work" *De morte*.

[19] L. Landolfi, "Tracce filodemee di estetica e di epigrammatica simpotica in Catullo," *CErc* 12 (1982): 137–43.

[20] Horace's acquaintance with Philodemus' poems is beyond dispute; he not only mentions Philodemus by name (*Sat.* 1.2.121) but also addresses throughout his poetry the same group of friends as Philodemus does in his works; see esp. David Armstrong, "The Addressees of the *Ars poetica*: Herculaneum, the Pisones, and Epicurean Protreptic," *Materiali e discussioni per l'analisi de testi classici* 31 (1993): 185–230, esp. 197–98. Philodemus' understanding of frank speech is especially discernible in Horace's *Satires*; see, for example, N. W. De Witt, "Parrhesiastic Poems of Horace," *CP* 30 (1935): 312–19, and Kirk Freudenburg, *The Walking Muse: Horace on the Theory of Satire* (Princeton: Princeton University Press, 1993), 88–90. That Philodemus and Horace were personally acquainted is highly probable; for a succinct statement of the evidence in support of a direct contact between the two, see Steven Oberhelman and David Armstrong, "Satire as Poetry and the Impossibility of Metathesis in Horace's *Satires*," in *Philodemus and Poetry: Poetic Theory and Practice in Lucretius, Philodemus, and Horace*, ed. Dirk Obbink (New York: Oxford University Press, 1995), 233–54, esp. 235–36. Less certain is the hypothesis that Horace was Philodemus' student; for a recent denial of this widespread supposition, see Anastasia Tsakiropoulou-Summers, "Horace, Philodemus and the Epicureans at Herculaneum," *Mnemosyne* 51 (1998): 20–29. See also the latter's "Philodemus' *Peri poiematon* and Horace's *Ars poetica*: Adapting Alexandrian Aesthetics to Epicurean and Roman Traditions" (Ph.D. Diss., University of Illinois at Urbana-Champaign, 1995).

[21] See, for example, Joan Booth, "Moonshine: Intertextual Illumination in Propertius 1.3.31–3 and Philodemus, *Anth. Pal.* 5.123," *CQ* 51 (2001): 537–44.

[22] Vergil was a student of the Epicurean philosopher Siro, who resided in Naples and was a friend of Philodemus. The latter mentions Siro in PHerc. 312 (see also Cicero, *Fin.* 2.119), and Vergil is one of the young Roman poets to whom Philodemus dedicates at least three books of his *On Vices and Virtues*. See Marcello Gigante and M. Capasso, "Il ritorno di Virgilio a Ercolano," *Studi Italiani di Filologia Classica* 7 (1989): 3–6; Marcello Gigante, "Virgilio e i suoi amici tra Napoli e Ercolano," *Atti e memorie dell'Accademia Virgiliana di Mantova*, n.s. 59 (1991): 87–125; David Sider, "The Epicurean Philosopher as Hellenistic Poet," in *Philodemus and Poetry* 42–57, esp. 43–44; and Janko, *Philodemus* 6.

[23] Treves and Obbink, "Philodemus," 1165.

[24] See, in general, Jane Isabella Marion Tait, *Philodemus' Influence on the Latin Poets*

regarded as "a major source on Hellenistic poetics."[25] In terms of philosophy, he was not, to be sure, a conspicuously original thinker, but he was certainly the leading Epicurean philosopher of his day and was already recognized as such by Asconius in the mid-fifties of the first century C.E.[26] Indeed, it is virtually certain that Cicero, who knew Philodemus (*Fin.* 2.119; *Pis.* 68–72) and had frequently heard Zeno, Philodemus' teacher, lecture (*Nat. d.* 1.59; *Tusc.* 3.38), made use of Philodemus' *De pietate (On Piety)* in writing Book 1 of his *De natura deorum*, especially 1.25–41.[27] In writing this work Cicero may also have drawn on Book 3 of Philodemus' *De dis (On the Gods)*.[28] Similarly, it has been suggested that Philodemus may have been one of Cicero's sources for Book 1 of his *De finibus*.[29] That Seneca was acquainted with some of Philodemus' epigrams as well as certain of his philosophical treatises, such as *De morte*, is also a distinct possibility.[30]

[](Ph.D. Diss., Bryn Mawr College; Ann Arbor: Edwards Brothers, Inc. Lithoprinters, 1941), who thinks that, in addition to the poets mentioned above, both Tibullus and Martial were also influenced by Philodemus' poetry.

[25] Erler, "Philodemus," 366. On this topic, see esp. the essays in *Philodemus and Poetry*.

[26] Asconius (3–88 C.E. or 9 B.C.E.–76 C.E.) wrote his commentaries on Cicero's speeches in the years 55–57 C.E. In commenting on Cicero's *In Pisonem* 68, Asconius says that Cicero "means Philodemus, who was the most distinguished (*nobilissimus*) Epicurean of that age." For text and translation of Asconius' commentaries, see Simon Squires (ed. and trans.), *Asconius Pedianus, Quintus: Commentaries on Five Speeches of Cicero* (Bristol: Bristol Classical Press; Wauconda, IL: Bolchazy-Carducci, 1990); for an analysis, see Bruce A. Marshall, *A Historical Commentary on Asconius* (Columbia: University of Missouri Press, 1985). It should be noted that Lucretius was Philodemus' younger contemporary and exerted much greater influence on posterity through his *De rerum natura* than did his more prolific fellow Epicurean. But during the first century B.C.E. Philodemus appears to have been regarded as the more significant of the two.

[27] For a convenient list of the correspondences between Philodemus' *De pietate* and Cicero's *De natura deorum*, see Hermann Diels, *Doxographi graeci* (Berlin: G. Reimer, 1879), 529–50. For a recent discussion, see Dirk Obbink, "De livre du *De natura deorum* de Cicéron et le *de pietate* de Philodème," *Cicéron et Philodème: Le polémique en philosophie*, ed. C. Auvray-Assayas and D. Delattre, Études de literature ancienne 12 (Paris: Éditions Rue d'Ulm, 2001), 203–25. It should be noted, however, that some scholars think in terms of a common source used by both Cicero and Philodemus rather than literary dependence. For this viewpoint, see Joseph B. Mayor, *M. Tulli Ciceronis De Natura Deorum Libri Tres, with Introduction and Commentary*, 3 vols. (Cambridge: Cambridge University Press, 1880–85), xlii–lii, and Erler, "Die Schule Epikurs," 328.

[28] G. Arrighetti, "Filodemo, De dis III, col. X–XI," *Studi classici e orientali* 7 (1958): 83–99; idem, "Filodemo, De dis III, col. XII–XIII,20," *Studi classici e orientali* 10 (1961): 112–21; and Paul MacKendrick, *The Philosophical Books of Cicero* (New York: St. Martin's Press, 1989), 182.

[29] Rudolf Hirzel, *Untersuchungen zu Cicero's philosophischen Schriften*, 3 vols. in 4 (Leipzig: S. Hirzel, 1877–83), 2:689–90, and Moses Hadas, *Hellenistic Culture: Fusion and Diffusion* (New York: Columbia University Press, 1959), 113.

[30] Marcello Gigante, "Seneca, ein Nachfolger Philodems?" in *Epikureismus in der*

This new evaluation of Philodemus has arisen particularly in the last thirty years, when there has been a strong resurgence of interest by classicists and literary critics in his works. Credit for this contemporary appreciation must be given, above all, to the late Professor Marcello Gigante in Naples, Italy, who, together with his students, took the lead in editing or re-editing many of the papyrus texts that contain Philodemus' works.[31] These papyri were discovered more than two centuries ago—in 1752–1754 to be precise—at several locations within a villa in the city of Herculaneum, which was destroyed along with Pompeii when Mt. Vesuvius erupted in 79 C.E.[32] Owing to the papyrus rolls found there, this house is commonly known as The Villa of the Papyri.[33] Its owner, often identified as Lucius Cal-

---

späten Republik und der Kaiserzeit, ed. M. Erler, Philosophie der Antike 11 (Stuttgart: Steiner, 2000), 32–41.

[31] Gigante served as the secretary of Centro Internazionale per lo Studio dei Papiri Ercolanesi from its creation in 1969 until his death in 2001. See esp. his *Scetticismo e Epicureismo: Per l'avviamento di un discorso storiografico*, Elenchos 4 (Naples: Bibliopolis, 1981); *Ricerche filodemee*, 2d ed., Biblioteca della Parola del Passato 6 (Naples: G. Macchiaroli, 1983); *Cinismo e Epicureismo*, Memorie dell'Istituto Italiano per gli Studi Filosofici 23 (Naples: Bibliopolis, 1992); *ATAKTA: Contributi alla papirologia ercolanese*, Biblioteca della Parola del Passato 17 (Naples: G. Macchiaroli, 1993); *Philodemus in Italy; Altre ricerche filodemee*, Biblioteca della Parola del Passato 18 (Naples: G. Macchiaroli, 1998); and *Filodemo nella storia della letteratura greca*, Memorie dell'Accademia di archeologia lettere e belle arti in Napoli 11 (Naples: Accademia di archeologia, lettere e belle arti, 1998). For a recognition of Gigante's importance to the Philodemean renaissance, see Don Fowler, "Sceptics and Epicureans: A Discussion of M. Gigante, *Scetticismo e Epicureismo,*" *Oxford Studies in Ancient Philosophy* 2 (1984): 237–67, esp. 238.

[32] An indispensable bibliographical guide to scholarship on all aspects of Herculaneum is provided by I. C. McIlwaine in her *Herculaneum: A Guide to Printed Sources*, 2 vols. (Naples: Bibliopolis, 1988) and "Herculaneum: A Guide to Printed Sources. Supplement," *CErc* 20 (1990): 87–128.

[33] See esp. Maria Rita Wojcik, *La Villa dei Papiri ad Ercolano: Contributo alla ricostruzione dell'ideologia della nobilitas tardorepubblicana*, Ministero per i Beni Culturali ed Ambientali; Soprintendenza archeologica di Pompei, Monographie 1 (Rome: "L'Erma" di Bretschneider, 1986). For a detailed review of Wojcik's work, see Richard Neudecker in *Gnomon* 61 (1989): 59–64. In addition to the famous papyri, the villa contained numerous bronze and marble statues and busts. Two important studies of the villa's art collection and display are Dimitrios Pandermalis, "Zur Programm der Statuenausstattung in der Villa dei Papiri," *Mitteilungen des Deutschen Archäologischen Instituts, Athenische Abteilung* 86 (1971): 173–209, and Gilles Sauron, "Templa Serena. À propos de la 'Villa des Papyri' d'Herculanum: les Champs-Elysées épicuriens. Contribution à l'étude des comportements aristocratiques romains à la fin de la République," *Mélanges d'Archéologie et d'Histoire de l'École française de Rome, Antiquité* 92 (1980): 277–301. For a comparison with other Roman galleries, see Thuri Lorenz, *Galerien von griechischen Philosophen- und Dichterbildnissen bei den Römern* (Mainz: P. von Zabern, 1965). For Gigante's attempt to relate the papyri to the decorative program of the villa, see his *Philodemus in Italy*, 1–13. For important reservations on the current tendency to

purnius Piso Caesoninus, *cos.* 58 (the father-in-law of Julius Caesar),[34] had an enormous library consisting of some 1000 books.[35] The papyri contain not only the works of Philodemus but also those of other Epicurean philosophers, including Epicurus[36] and his close friend

---

interpret the villa's statues in terms of content and an all-embracing program, see Richard Neudecker, "The Roman Villa as a Locus of Art Collections," *The Roman Villa—Villa Urbana*, ed. A. Frazer, University Museum Monograph 101, Symposium Series 9 (Philadelphia: The University Museum, University of Pennsylvania, 1998), 77–91.

[34] This attribution appears to have been initially advanced by Domenico Comparetti in *La Villa de' Pisoni in Ercolano e la sua biblioteca* (Naples: F. Giannini, 1879) and then elaborated by Comparetti and De Petra in *La Villa ercolanese dei Pisoni*, 1–53, esp. 1–32. As the frequent reference to the house as the "Villa of the Pisones" suggests, this is now the *communis opinio*. It is defended by major scholars such as Gigante, *Philodemus in Italy*, 13, but it is by no means uncontested. For example, Wojcik (*La Villa dei Papiri*, 276–84) conjecturally identifies the family of the Appii Claudii Pulchri as the Republican owners of the villa. (On this family, see esp. T. P. Wiseman, "Pulcher Claudius," *Harvard Studies in Classical Philology* 74 [1970]: 207–21.) There is inscriptional evidence that this family was involved in local patronage; Ap. Claudius Pulcher (*cos.* 38), for example, is credited with building the Herculaneum theater (*CIL* 10.1423f.). But there is nothing explicit that links this family with the Villa of the Papyri. Therefore, while her arguments against the Pisones as owners have convinced some scholars (such as Neudecker in *Gnomon* 61 [1989]: 64 and Jean Ch. Balty in *L'Antiquité Classique* 58 [1989]: 559–61), her own thesis has found few supporters. It is rejected by Jean-Michel Croisille in *Latomus* 49 (1990): 912–13 (esp. 913: "une hypothèse mal fondée") and by Eleanor Winsor Leach in *American Journal of Archaeology* 92 (1988): 145–46 (esp. 146); the latter points out, *contra* Wojcik, that the presence of the Pisones in Herculaneum is confirmed by a bust of Piso Pontifex (*cos.* 15) that derives from the town. For a photograph of the bust and a discussion of Piso Pontifex, see Sir Ronald Syme, *The Augustan Aristocracy* (Oxford: Clarendon, 1986) frontispiece, 329–45. This Piso (the son of Piso Caesoninus) may well be the one who is responsible for the villa's decorative display of art. For this thesis, see Pandermalis, "Programm der Statuenausstattung," 196–97.

[35] For an orientation to the papyri, see Mario Capasso, *Manuale di papirologia ercolanese*, Università degli Studi di Lecce, Departimento di Filologia Classica e Medioevale, Testi e studi 3 (Galatina: Congedo, 1991). The precise number of books originally recovered from the Villa of the Papyri is unclear; the figures given in contemporary scholarly literature vary considerably; see, for example, Janko, *Philodemus*, 4 ("between 800 and 1,100 books"), and Obbink, "Preface," viii ("over a thousand papyrus rolls"). Some works are preserved in only one papyrus roll, whereas numerous papyrus rolls are devoted to other works. For an invaluable inventory, which has more than 1800 entries, see M. Gigante, ed., *Catalogo dei Papiri Ercolanesi* (Naples: Bibliopolis, 1979), cited hereafter as *Catalogo*. See also the supplement to the *Catalogo* by Mario Capasso, "Primo Supplemento al *Catalogo dei Papiri Ercolanesi*," *CErc* 19 (1989): 193–264, cited henceforth as "Primo Supplemento."

[36] Numerous papyrus fragments of Epicurus' thirty-seven-volume treatise *On Nature* are preserved and perhaps also a fragment from an unidentified work (PHerc. 996; see *Catalogo*, 211–12, and "Primo Supplemento," 232). In addition, the Herculaneum papyri not only contain references to Epicurus' letters and other works but also important quotations from them. Philodemus' *Memoires* (PHerc. 1418), for instance, is an especially valuable source for Epicurus' letters. On Epicurus and his writings,

Metrodorus of Lampsacus[37] as well as other Epicureans from later
periods, including Colotes of Lampsacus,[38] Carneiscus,[39] Polystratus,[40]

---

see esp. Michael Erler, "Epikur," *Die hellenistische Philosophie*, 29–202. For fragments of
his works and letters, see the editions of Graziano Arrighetti, ed., *Epicuro, Opere*, 2d
ed., Biblioteca di cultura filosofica 41 (Turin: G. Einaudi, 1973), and Carlo Diano, ed.,
Epicuri Ethica et Epistulae (Florence: Sansoni, 1974), a reprint of three works published
1946–48. On Epicurus' letters in the Herculaneum papyri, see now Anna Angeli,
"Frammenti di lettere di Epicuro nei papiri d'Ercolano," *CErc* 23 (1993): 11–27.

[37] PHerc. 200 contains a fragment of Metrodorus' *On Wealth* (see *Catalogo*, 103,
and "Primo Supplemento," 217). For a brief synopsis of the life and writings of
Metrodorus (ca. 331–278 B.C.E.), see Erler, "Die Schule Epikurs," 216–22. For *On
Wealth*, see frgs. 16–19 in Alfred Körte, *Metrodori Epicurei Fragmenta* (Leipzig: Teubner,
1890), reprinted in *Epicureanism: Two Collections of Fragments and Studies*, Greek and
Roman Philosophy 16 (New York: Garland, 1987), 547–48, and Adele Tepedino
Guerra, "Il PHerc. 200: Metrodoro, sulla ricchezza," *Actes du XVe Congrès interna-
tional de papyrologie*, ed. Jean Bingen and Georges Nachtergael, 4 vols., Papyrologia
Bruxellensia 16–19 (Brussels: Fondation égyptologique Reine Élisabeth, 1979),
3:191–97. For the possibility that the Herculaneum papyri contain remnants of
another work by Metrodorus, either his *Against the Dialecticians or Against the Sophists*
(Diog. Laert. 10.24), see Emidio Spinelli, "Metrodoro contro i dialettici?," *CErc* 16
(1986): 29–43, Capasso, *Manuale*, 193 n. 219, and Adele Tepedino Guerra, "Metrodoro
'Contro i Dialettici'?," *CErc* 22 (1992): 119–22. Some of the anonymous letters
quoted in the papyri may well be those of Metrodorus. David Sedley, for example, credits him with being the author of two letters quoted in Philodemus' *Negotia*
(PHerc. 1418 col. 20); see his "Epicurus and the Mathematicians of Cyzicus," *CErc*
6 (1976): 23–54, esp. 29–30. For a recent contribution, see Adele Tepedino Guerra,
"La scuola di Epicuro: Metrodoro, Polieno, Ermarco," *CErc* 30 (2000): 35–44.

[38] Fragments of both his *Against Plato's Euthydemus* (PHerc. 1032; see *Catalogo*
236–37, and "Primo Supplemento," 238) and *Against Plato's Lysis* (PHerc. 208; see
Catalogo, 105, and "Primo Supplemento," 217) are preserved and were edited by
Wilhelm Crönert in *Kolotes und Menedemos: Texte und Untersuchungen zur Philosophen- und
Literaturgeschichte*, Studien zur Palaeographie und Papyruskunde 6 (Leipzig: E. Avenarius,
1906; repr. Amsterdam: Hakkert, 1965), 162–72. On Colotes (ca. 310–260 B.C.E.)
and these two works, see Erler, "Die Schule Epikurs," 235–40, and Adele Concolino
Mancini, "Sulle opere polemiche di Colote," *CErc* 6 (1976): 61–67. For his impor-
tance in shaping the Epicurean response to Academic skepticism, see Paul A. Vander
Waerdt, "Colotes and the Epicurean Refutation of Skepticism," *Greek, Roman, and
Byzantine Studies* 30 (1989): 225–67. See also Plutarch's *Adversus Colotem* and the commentary on this work by Rolf Westman, *Plutarch gegen Kolotes: Seine Schrift "Adversus
Colotem" als philosophiegeschichtliche Quelle*, Acta philosophica Fennica 7 (Helsinki: A. G.
der Finnischen Literaturgesellschaft, 1955); on the latter, see the review by Phillip
De Lacy in *American Journal of Philology* 77 (1956): 433–38. See now Giovanni Indelli,
"Colote di Lampsaco, il bersaglio polemico di Plutarco, e Polistrato, il terzo capo
del Giardino," *CErc* 30 (2000): 45–52.

[39] Carneiscus (late 4th–early 3rd century B.C.E.) wrote a work on friendship
(*Philistas*) that dealt particularly with the death of a friend. In it he not only pre-
sented Philistas as a model Epicurean but also criticized the Peripatetic philosopher
Praxiphanes. Fragments are preserved in PHerc. 1027 (see *Catalogo*, 235–236, and
"Primo Supplemento," 238; see also PHerc. 440 and 1115 in *Catalogo* 149, 271–72,
and "Primo Supplemento," 225, 244). See Crönert, *Kolotes und Menedemos*, 69–72,
179; Fritz Wehrli, *Die Schule des Aristoteles: Texte und Kommentar*, Heft IX: *Phainias von
Eresos, Chamaileon, Praxiphanes*, 2d ed. (Basel: Schwabe, 1969), 93–96, 107–08; Erler,

Demetrius of Laconia,[41] Lucretius,[42] and perhaps even Lucius Manlius Torquatus (praetor 49 B.C.E.), the spokesman for Epicureanism in

---

"Die Schule Epikurs," 241–43; Mario Capasso, "Per una nuova edizione del *Filista* di Carneisco (*PHerc.* 1027)," *Atti del XVII Congresso internazionale di papirologia*, 3 vols. (Naples: Centro Internazionale per lo Studio dei Papiri Ercolanesi, 1984), 2:405–17, and idem, ed. and trans., *Carneisco, Il secondo libro del Filista (PHerc. 1027). Edizione, traduzione e commento*, La Scuola di Epicuro 10 (Naples: Bibliopolis, 1988).

[40] Polystratus (flourished mid-third century B.C.E.) was head of the Epicurean school in Athens following the death of Hermachus (Diog. Laert. 10.25). For an overview of his life and writings, see Erler, "Die Schule Epikurs," 247–50. Fragments of two of his writings are preserved among the Herculaneum papyri. The first is *On Irrational Contempt* (PHerc. 336/1150; see *Catalogo*, 128–30, and "Primo Supplemento," 221–22), a polemical work which, as its full title indicates, is directed "against those who irrationally despise popular beliefs." The standard critical edition is that of Giovanni Indelli, ed. and trans., *Polistrato, Sul disprezzo irrazionale delle opinioni popolari. Edizione, traduzione e commentio*, La Scuola di Epicuro 2 (Naples: Bibliopolis, 1978). See also his "Polistrato," ΣΥΖΗΤΗΣΙΣ, 2:525–27. For text and an English translation of 23.26–26.23, see A. A. Long and D. N. Sedley, *The Hellenistic Philosophers*, 2 vols. (Cambridge: Cambridge University Press, 1987), 1:35–37; 2:29–30. For text and an English translation of col. 5b 9–7a 8 Wilke, see Phillip De Lacy, "Limit and Variation in the Epicurean Philosophy," *Phoenix* 23 (1969): 104–13, esp. 105. See also the comments on Polystratus in P. H. De Lacy and E. A. De Lacy, eds. and trans., *Philodemus, On Methods of Inference*, rev. ed., La Scuola di Epicuro 1 (Naples: Bibliopolis, 1978), 191–93, and Thomas Cole, *Democritus and the Sources of Greek Anthropology*, American Philological Association Monograph Series 25 (Cleveland: Western Reserve University Press, 1967; repr. Atlanta: Scholars Press, 1990), 77–79. The identity of Polystratus' opponents is vigorously debated, with some scholars seeing several schools criticized. Indelli (*Polistrato*, 55–82), for example, believes that Cynics, Pyrrhonists, Stoics, and Megarians are criticized on various grounds. Others think that a specific group is in mind. Robert Philippson, for example, identifies them as Cynics. See his "Polystratos' Schrift über die grundlose Verachtung der Volksmeinung," *Neue Jahrbücher* 12 (1909): 487–509, which is reprinted in his *Studien zu Epikur und den Epikureern*, ed. C. Joachim Classen, Olms Studien 17 (Hildesheim: Olms, 1983), 4–26. That the Cynics are the chief opponents is also the view of Gigante, *Cinismo e Epicureismo*, 83. David Sedley, on the other hand, thinks that Academic skeptics are the target of Polystratus' polemic. See his review of Indelli's *Polistrato* in *Classical Review* 97 (1983): 335–36. Erler, "Die Schule Epikurs," 248–49, believes that Polystratus is attacking skepticism as a philosophical movement, not engaging in polemics against a single group of opponents. The second preserved work is Polystratus' *On Philosophy* (PHerc. 1520; see *Catalogo*, 351–52, and "Primo Supplemento," 257), which Crönert, *Kolotes und Menedemos*, 35–36 and 178, viewed as a polemical work directed at the Cynics, especially the followers of Bion of Borysthenes. But Mario Capasso has argued persuavively that it, like Aristotle's *On Philosophy*, was a protreptic work. See his "L'opera polistratea sulla filosofia," *CErc* 6 (1976): 81–84.

[41] Demetrius of Laconia (ca. 100 B.C.E.) was the contemporary of Zeno of Sidon, the teacher of Philodemus. For treatments of his life and writings, see Costantina Romeo and Enzo Puglia, "Demetrio Lacone," ΣΥΖΗΤΗΣΙΣ, 2:529–49, and Erler, "Die Schule Epikurs," 256–67. In PHerc. 1012 (col. 44 Puglia) Demetrius refers to Zeno as "dearest" (φίλτατος), and the close relationship of Demetrius and Zeno helps to explain why more of Demetrius' treatises have been preserved among the Herculaneum papyri than those of any other Epicurean, save Philodemus. His works

Cicero's *De finibus*.[43] Other Epicurean writers are also represented in the Herculaneum papyri, though their identity is unknown.[44] There

were edited by Vittorio De Falco, *L'epicureo Demetrio Lacone* (Naples: A. Cimmaruta, 1923; repr. in *Epicureanism: Two Collections of Fragments and Studies*, Greek and Roman Philosophy 16 [New York: Garland, 1987]), but the edition is problematic and is gradually being replaced; see the reviews by E. Bignone in *Rivista indo-greco-italica di Filologia, Lingua, Antichità* 7 (1923): 181–86, and Robert Philippson in *Philologische Wochenschrift* 44 (1924): 313–30, 648.

Major works partially preserved include the following: 1) *Quaestiones convivales* (PHerc. 1006); see *Catalogo*, 216–17; "Primo Supplemento," 234; and De Falco, *Demetrio Lacone*, 59–61; 2) *On the Puzzles of Polyaenus* (PHerc. 1083, 1258, 1429, 1642, 1647, 1822); see *Catalogo*, 263, 294, 328–29, 372–73, 399; "Primo Supplemento," 242, 247, 252, 259–60, 263; and De Falco, *Demetrio Lacone*, 97–107; 3) *On Geometry* (PHerc. 1061); see *Catalogo*, 250–51; "Primo Supplemento," 240–41; De Falco, *Demetrio Lacone*, 96–98; and Anna Angeli and Tiziano Dorandi, "Il pensiero matematico di Demetrio Lacon," *CErc* 17 (1987): 89–103 (which also deals with the preceding work on Polyaenus' puzzles); 4) *On Poems* (PHerc. 188 and 1014); see *Catalogo*, 101, 224–25; "Primo Supplemento," 217, 235–36; De Falco, *Demetrio Lacone*, 80–96; the new edition by Costantina Romeo, ed. and trans., *Demetrio Lacone, La poesia (PHerc. 188 e 1014. Edizione, traduzione e commento*, La Scuola di Epicuro 9 (Naples: Bibliopolis, 1988); and Nicola Pace, "La rivoluzione umanistica nella scuola epicurea: Demetrio Lacone e Filodemo, teorici di poesia," *CErc* 30 (2000): 71–79; 5) an untitled work preserved in PHerc. 1786; see *Catalogo*, 394; "Primo Supplemento," 262; De Falco, *Demetrio Lacone*, 54–57; and the edition by Enzo Puglia, "Nuove letture nei *PHerc.* 1012 e 1786 (Demetrii Laconis opera incerta)," *CErc* 10 (1980): 25–53, esp. 49–52); and 6) another untitled work preserved in PHerc. 124; see *Catalogo*, 80; "Primo Supplemento," 213; and De Falco, *Demetrio Lacone*, 57–58.

On internal and other grounds, Demetrius is the most likely author of five additional works: 1) *On the Size of the Sun* (PHerc. 1013); see *Catalogo*, 223–24; "Primo Supplemento," 235; De Falco, *Demetrio Lacone*, 61–65; and the new edition of Costantina Romeo, "Demetrio Lacone sulla grandezza de sole [PHerc. 1013]," *CErc* 9 (1979): 11–35; 2) *On Fickleness* (PHerc. 831); see *Catalogo*, 190–91; "Primo Supplemento," 229; Körte, *Metrodori Epicurei Fragmenta*, 571–91; and esp. Robert Philippson, "Papyrus Herculanensis 831," *American Journal of Philology* 64 (1943): 148–62 = *Studien zu Epikur und den Epikureern*, 284–98; 3) an untitled work preserved in PHerc. 1012, which deals with issues of textual criticism (including scribal errors) in the exegesis of Epicurus' writings; see *Catalogo*, 222–23; "Primo Supplemento," 235; De Falco, *Demetrio Lacone*, 20–54; the new edition by Enzo Puglia, ed. and trans., *Demetrio Lacone, Aporie testuali ed esegetiche in Epicuro (PHerc. 1012). Edizione, traduzione e commentio*, La Scuola di Epicuro 8 (Naples: Bibliopolis, 1988), which also contains Gigante's collection of testimonia to Demetrius; and Matilde Ferrario, "La nascita della filologia epicurea: Demetrio Lacone e Filodemo," *CErc* 30 (2000): 53–61; 4) an untitled theological work (perhaps *On the Gods* or *On the Form of God*) in support of Epicurus' understanding of the gods as anthropomorphic, defending this view against objections to it raised by Bion of Borysthenes and others; preserved in PHerc. 1055; see *Catalogo*, 246–48; "Primo Supplemento," 240; De Falco, *Demetrio Lacone*, 65–80; this work was earlier edited by Enrico Renna, "Nuove letture nel PHerc. 1055 (Libro incerto di Demetrio Lacone)," *CErc* 12 (1982): 43–49, and has now been re-edited, with an Italian translation and full commentary, by Mariacarolina Santoro, *[Demetrio Lacone], [La forma del dio] (PHerc. 1055)*, La Scuola di Epicuro 17 (Naples: Bibliopolis, 2000); and 5) an untitled rhetorical work preserved in PHerc. 128; see *Catalogo*, 81, and "Primo Supplemento," 213.

are also a few non-Epicurean works,[45] including two or three treatises by the Stoic philosopher Chrysippus,[46] a Latin hexameter poem

---

[42] Knut Kleve, "Lucretius in Herculaneum," *CErc* 19 (1989): 5–27.

[43] For the possibility that Torquatus is mentioned in the subscript of PHerc. 1475, see Felice Costabile, "Opere di oratoria politica e giudiziaria nella biblioteca della Villa dei Papiri: i *PHerc.* latini 1067 e 1475," *Atti del XVII Congresso internazionale di papirologia*, 3 vols. (Naples: Centro Internazionale per lo Studio dei Papiri Ercolanesi, 1984), 2:591–606. On Torquatus, see Cicero, *Brutus* 265 and Pliny, *Ep.* 5.3.5 (here identified as a writer of poems); see also Catullus 61, where he is apparently the addressee. For other aspects of his life, see F. Münzer, "Manlius (Torquatus)," *RE* 14:1 (1928): 1203–7, and the studies mentioned in Castner, *Prosopography*, 40–42.

[44] PHerc. 176 is an example of a work written by an unidentified Epicurean. See *Catalogo*, 94–95; "Primo Supplemento," 215–16; Erler, "Die Schule Epikurs," 336–37; and the edition by Anna Angeli, "La scuola epicurea di Lampsaco nel PHerc. 176 (fr. 5 coll. I, IV, VIII–XXIII)," *CErc* 18 (1988): 27–51.

[45] In addition to the presence of non-Epicurean authors in the library, the villa's art gallery included numerous statues and busts of non-Epicureans. One is a small bronze bust inscribed with the name Zeno (Naples Museum Inventory Nr. 5468). Whereas some earlier scholars (such as Comparetti and De Petra, *La Villa ercolanese*, 263) understood this to be a portrait of Philodemus' teacher Zeno, contemporary scholars believe it is Zeno of Citium, the founder of Stoicism. See Gisela M. A. Richter, *The Portraits of the Greeks*, 3 vols. (London: Phaidon, 1965), 2:187–88, 251, and figure 1089, and Pandermalis, "Programm der Statuenausstattung," 197–98.

[46] The first of Chrysippus' partially preserved two or three works is his *Logical Questions*, contained in PHerc. 307. On this papyrus, see *Catalogo*, 123–24; "Primo Supplemento," 220–21; *SVF* 2, frg. 298a; and the new edition by Livia Marrone, "Le Questioni logiche di Crisippo (*PHerc.* 307)," *CErc* 27 (1997): 83–100. See also her "La logica degli epicurei e degli stoici: Filodemo e Crisippo," *CErc* 30 (2000): 111–18. For the text of col. 1–2 and an English translation, see David Sedley, "The Negated Conjunction in Stoicism," *Elenchos* 5 (1984): 311–16, esp. 314–15; for col. 9.7–12, see Long and Sedley, *Hellenistic Philosophers*, 1:224, 229; 2:225. For discussion, see Wilhelm Crönert, "Die Λογικὰ Ζητήματα des Chrysippos und die übrigen Papyri logischen Inhalts aus der herculanensischen Bibliothek," *Hermes* 36 (1901): 548–79; Livia Marrone, "Nuove letture nel PHerc. 307 (*Questioni logiche* di Crisippo)," *CErc* 12 (1982): 13–18; idem, "Il problema dei 'singolari' e dei 'plurali' nel *PHerc.* 307," *Atti del XVII Congresso internazionale di papirologia*, 3 vols. (Naples: Centro Internazionale per lo Studio dei Papiri Ercolanesi, 1984), 2:419–27; and Jonathan Barnes, "ΠΙΘΑΝΑ ΖΥΝΗΜΜΕΝΑ," *Elenchos* 6 (1985): 453–67, esp. 461–62. The second work is his *On Providence*, preserved in PHerc. 1038 and 1421 (see *Catalogo*, 238, 315; "Primo Supplemento," 239, 250; Alfred Gercke, "Chrysippea," *Jahrbücher für classische Philologie*, Suppl. 14 [1885]: 689–780, esp. 704–14; *SVF* 1, p. vi). A third work, most likely by Chrysippus, is preserved in PHerc. 1020; see *Catalogo*, 231; "Primo Supplemento," 237; H. von Arnim, "Über einen stoischen Papyrus der herculanensischen Bibliothek," *Hermes* 25 (1890): 473–95; *SVF* 2, frg. 131; A. A. Long, "Dialectic and the Stoic Sage," *The Stoics*, ed. J. M. Rist, Major Thinkers Series 1 (Berkeley and Los Angeles: University of California Press, 1978), 101–24, esp. 108–10 and 123 n. 20–21 (on cols. 1 and 4); and Long and Sedley, *Hellenistic Philosophers*, 1:255, 257–59; 2:256–57 (text and translation of parts of cols. 1 and 4). For the suggestion that Philodemus' *On Piety* preserves a reference by Chrysippus to the moon-god Men, see Eugene N. Lane, "Chrysippus, Philodemus, and the God Men," *ZPE* 117 (1997): 65–66.

on events following the battle at Actium (including Octavian's capture of Pelusium in 30 B.C.E., Cleopatra's lethal experiments on criminals, and the encampment of the Roman army before the walls of Alexandria),[47] a fragment of Book 6 of Ennius' *Annales*,[48] and some lines from the comedian Caecilius Statius' *The Money-Lender*.[49]

Students of Second Temple Judaism,[50] Hellenistic Judaism,[51] and early Christianity[52] increasingly have begun to take a lively interest in this Philodemean renaissance. The publication of this collection of essays in a series devoted to the investigation of the New Testament within its ancient context is a reflection of this growing interest, and the editors as well as contributors hope that these studies will lead to a greater awareness of Philodemus and his importance for the New Testament world.

---

[47] The poem is the *Carmen de bello Actiaco* (or *Aegyptiaco*), preserved in PHerc. 817. Some have attributed it to the epic poet Gaius Rabirius, whereas others have suggested that it may be part of Cornelius Severus' *Res Romanae*. Still others, such as Gigante, "Virgilio," 87–125, have attributed it to Lucius Varius Rufus. It is also sometimes dated to the Neronian period, which, if correct, would make it one of the latest additions to the villa's library. See *Catalogo*, 186–89; "Primo Supplemento," 228–29; Henry Bardon, *La Littérature latine inconnue*, 2 vols. (Paris: C. Klincksieck, 1952–56), 2:73–74, 136–37; and the edition by Giovanni Garuti, *C. Rabirius, Bellum Actiacum e papyro Herculanensi 817* (Bologna: Zanichelli, 1958). See also Courtney, *The Fragmentary Latin Poets*, 334–40, and Gerrit Kloss, "Die dritte Kolumne des *Carmen de bello Actiaco* (PHerc. 817)," *ZPE* 116 (1997): 21–27. A composite text and English translation is given by Herbert W. Benario, "The 'Carmen de bello Actiaco' and Early Imperial Epic," *ANRW* 2.30.3 (1983): 1656–62, esp. 1659–62. A facsimile of col. 6 of the poem is available in Sir Edward M. Thompson, *An Introduction to Greek and Latin Palaeography* (Oxford: Clarendon, 1912), 276.

[48] Knut Kleve, "Ennius in Herculaneum," *CErc* 20 (1990): 5–16. See also Gigante, "Ennio tra Ercolano e Pozzuoli," in *Ennio tra Rudiae e Roma*, Associazione italiana di cultura classica; Università degli studi di Lecce (Galatina: Congedo, 1994), 123–38.

[49] Knut Kleve, "How To Read an Illegible Papyrus. Towards an Edition of PHerc. 78, Caecilius Statius, *Obolostates sive Faenerator*," *CErc* 26 (1996): 5–12.

[50] See, for example, Shaye J. D. Cohen, "The Beauty of Flora and the Beauty of Sarai," *Helios* 8 (1981): 41–53.

[51] See, for example, Martin Hengel, *Judaism and Hellenism: Studies in their Encounter in Palestine during the Early Hellenistic Period*, 2 vols. (Philadelphia: Fortress, 1974), 1:86, 109. See also Everett Ferguson, "The Art of Praise: Philo and Philodemus on Music," in *Early Christianity and Classical Culture: Comparative Studies in Honor of Abraham J. Malherbe*, ed. John T. Fitzgerald, Thomas H. Olbricht, and L. Michael White, NovTSup 110 (Leiden: Brill, 2003), 391–426.

[52] See, for example, Abraham J. Malherbe, *Paul and the Thessalonians: The Philosophic Tradition of Pastoral Care* (Philadelphia: Fortress, 1987), 84–87, and esp. Clarence E. Glad, *Paul and Philodemus: Adaptability in Epicurean and Early Christian Psychagogy*, NovTSup 81 (Leiden: Brill, 1995).

PART ONE

PHILODEMUS' ETHICAL, THEOLOGICAL,
RHETORICAL, AESTHETIC, AND
HISTORICAL WORKS

ALL THINGS TO ALL MEN: PHILODEMUS' MODEL OF THERAPY AND THE AUDIENCE OF *DE MORTE*

David Armstrong

Abstract

Philodemus' *De Morte* is clearly addressed (unlike most of his more technical treatises) to a mixed audience, containing Epicureans and members of other philosophical sects and non-philosophers alike. It is epideictic at least in the sense that it shows what Epicureanism can do to combat the fear of death, and though it is undeviating and merciless in its insistence that death is the end, it is undogmatic about other points that Epicureanism taught just as firmly, and refers to other philosophers and even figures in ancient history who were not philosophers as heroic examples of fearlessness on a par with the standard heroes of the school like Metrodorus and Epicurus. As well, the treatise takes seriously and sympathetically the more natural fears of humanity confronted with death—probably at least partly because of the tactics necessary in addressing a mixed audience—and if studied seriously along with the more familiar sayings of Epicurus and Lucretius on death would necessitate a radical revision of the criticisms of their approach in modern secondary literature as unsympathetic and facilely eudaimonistic.

τοῖς πᾶσιν γέγονα τὰ πάντα, ἵνα πάντως τινὰς σώσω. καὶ τοῦτο ποιῶ διὰ τὸ εὐαγγέλιον, ἵνα συγκοινωνὸς αὐτοῦ γένωμαι.

I am made all things to all men, that I might by all means save some. And this I do for the gospel's sake, that I might be fellow-partaker thereof (1 Cor. 9:22b–23 [AV]).

In these famous words, which are cited at the opening of Clarence Glad's *Paul and Philodemus: Adaptability in Epicurean and Early Christian Psychagogy*,[1] Paul concludes a splendid rhetorical period in which he describes the adaptability of his own preaching:

---

[1] Clarence Glad, *Paul and Philodemus: Adaptability in Epicurean and Early Christian Psychagogy*, (Leiden: Brill, 1995), 1. I must thank John Fitzgerald for help in orienting me to the vast literature on 1 Cor. 9:19–23: besides what is said in the standard commentaries, such treatments as David Daube's comments in *The New Testament and Rabbinic Judaism* (London: Athlone, 1956) 336–51, esp. 336–41 on the similar economies practiced by Hillel and other rabbis toward their converts; Günther

> For though I be free from all men, yet have I made myself servant
> unto all, that I might gain the more. And unto the Jews I became as
> a Jew, that I might gain the Jews; to them that are under the law, as
> under the law, that I might gain them that are under the law; to them
> that are without law, as without law (being not without law to God,
> but under the law to Christ) that I might gain them that are without
> law. To the weak became I as weak, that I might gain the weak: I
> am made all things to all men, that I might by all means save some
> [1 Cor. 9:19–22 (AV)].

As Glad notes, Paul has been compared to Odysseus in his versa-
tility and resourcefulness—and also accused, like Odysseus, of hypocrisy
for his adaptability.[2] But his adaptability to different audiences, Jews
and pagans as well as convinced Christians, and to different moral
capacities, to "the weak" as well as the strong, springs from a more
honorable source: the desire to bring the faith to and share it with
many different people on their own terms, in the conviction that
Christ died for all, by finding the way to influence their souls in
their actual present state. Paul submerges his own convictions in
favor of theirs, to the extent his conscience and commitment allows
him, to exercise what Glad calls "psychagogy."

Glad believes that Paul in this followed the therapeutic style of
Hellenistic philosophy, especially that of the Epicureans, and more
particularly Philodemus' prescriptions in the treatise *On Frank Criticism*,
which is gaining more and more attention in studies of the psychology of therapy in ancient philosophy and religion.[3] Here rules

---

Bornkamm, "The Missionary Stance of Paul in I Corinthians 9 and in Acts," *Studies
in Luke-Acts*, ed. Leander E. Keck and J. Louis Martyn (Nashville: Abingdon, 1966)
194–207 (Bornkamm even admits a certain coherence between this passage and
the portrait of Paul in Acts, especially Acts 21:17–26, 204–205); Peter Richardson,
"Pauline Inconsistency: I Corinthians 9:19–23 and Galatians 2:11–14," *NTS* 26
(1980) 347–62; W. Willis, "An Apostolic Apologia? The Form and Function of
1 Cor. 9," *JNTS* 24 (1985) 33–48; and especially Abraham J. Malherbe, "Determinism
and Free Will in Paul: The Argument of 1 Corinthians 8 and 9," *Paul in Hellenistic
Context*, ed. Troels Engberg-Pedersen (Minneapolis: Fortress, 1995), 231–55.

[2] Glad, *Paul and Philodemus*, 1. Glad refers specifically to W. B. Stanford, *The
Ulysses Theme: A Study in the Adaptability of a Traditional Hero*, 2nd rev. ed. (New York:
Barnes and Noble, 1968) 9 and Malherbe, *Paul and the Popular Philosophers* (Minneapolis:
Fortress, 1989), 100–101.

[3] It is fortunate that we now have *Philodemus: On Frank Criticism*, trans. David
Konstan, Diskin Clay, Clarence E. Glad, Johan C. Thom, James Ware, SBLTT
(Atlanta: Scholars, 1998). See my review in *RSR*, 25 (1999) 88; also, my review
article on R. Ancona, *Time in the Odes of Horace*, R. O. A. M. Lyne, *Horace: Behind
the Public Poetry*, and *Horace 2000: Essays for the Bimillennium*, *Phoenix* (1988) 237–45,
and my review of Susanna Morton Braund and Christopher Gill, eds., *The Passions
in Roman Thought and Literature*, *Bryn Mawr Classical Review* (1998) 5.10, in which I

are laid down for the treatment of the psychological and moral problems of those who have submitted themselves to the Epicurean discipline, both individually and in groups. These rules are exemplified in various other ethical discourses of Philodemus—especially *On Anger*, which explicitly refers to *On Frank Criticism* as part of its assumed background reading, and gives directions for the philosopher's attitude toward anger which seem to be consistent with that treatise's precepts.[4] Glad argues throughout his book that Philodemus' and his teacher Zeno's model of suiting therapeutic speech to the problems of the individual or individuals addressed was an important influence on Paul's own *parrhesia* to his Christian communities and a primary source of their practices, instilled by him, of "mutual exhortation, edification and correction."[5] Glad argues that Paul's παρρησία resembles the Philodemean model more than has been previously appreciated, and more, indeed, than the model of psychotherapy and instruction found in any other ancient philosophical literature.

How true this is I leave to others to decide, as far as concerns Paul's authentic writings and his precepts to the communities he addresses there. There is another aspect of the words in 1 Cor. 9:19–23 that all readers used to think of, and many readers who are not professional New Testament scholars probably still do when they read them. This is the lively and imaginative picture given in many passages of the book of Acts of Paul's preaching, not to the communities of the faithful that he has founded, but to hostile Jews and to unconvinced pagans and other non-Christian audiences such as the Athenian Stoics and Epicureans of Acts 17 or the Roman officials and Jewish royalty of Acts 26. This picture of Paul's preaching seems intended to exemplify just precisely the flexibility and adaptability he displays in addressing all kinds of audiences. The situation in Pauline studies is

---

recommend Philodemus' and Plutarch's conception of *parrhesia* as vital to the understanding of Horace's and Seneca's relationship to their addressees. I hope that much more will be done in this field, now that a text and English translation of Philodemus' treatise is at last readily available.

[4] One should put vices before one's pupils' eyes like a doctor describing the horrors of disease (*On Anger* col. 4); thus Stoic diatribe is not useless (cols. 1–2). Part of the imitation-Stoic diatribe in the *De Ira* is addressed directly to pupils in Philodemus' school (col. 18.35–col. 21). One excuse for the apparent irascibility of a wise man may be his desire to help others with therapeutic discourse of the aggressive or severe kind (36.24f., where Philodemus expressly refers the reader to the treatise *On Frank Criticism* for further definitions), which Philodemus calls τὸ σκληρὸν τῆς παρρησίας εἶδος (*On Frank Criticism* fg. 7, 9–11).

[5] Glad, *Paul and Philodemus*, 335.

easily summarized: "most scholars agree that Acts must be excluded
entirely as a source for the contents of Paul's preaching,"[6] and Glad
duly leaves these famous speeches aside, along with the whole question
of Paul's adaptability to the unconverted and hostile among his audiences, for which Acts is the only source. It seems a pity, for whatever
the historical truth of Acts, these brilliant and daring speeches, full
of *parrhesia* and adaptability at once, will always be part of the Western
world's picture of the Apostle to the Gentiles. And Paul's method
in Acts is at least commensurate with that of Paul in the letters.

As for Philodemus, we already know at least one important area
of his writings in which he was happy to abandon his usual bitter,
combative and sectarian style in discussing the views of philosophical opponents and appeal to a general audience. This was in his
works on the history of philosophy, in which his biographical and
doxographical learning is displayed for once without rancor and without sarcasm and in which his point of view is wholly neutral.[7] I
would like to argue that we have another example, and a very important one in many different ways, of Philodemus' adaptability to non-
Epicurean audiences: the striking and beautiful fragment of his treatise
On Death, marked in the papyrus as being the end of book IV of
that treatise, and most probably the grand rhetorical conclusion of
the whole as well.

Although it has never yet reached the audience it deserves,[8] Philo-

---

[6] Victor Paul Furnish, in Eldon Jay Epp and George W. MacRae, eds., *The New Testament and Its Modern Interpreters* (Atlanta: Scholars, 1989), 331. See also the remarks of Charles Talbert, 311: "Research on the speeches has moved from taking them as sermons of Peter and Paul, through taking them as examples of the earliest *kerygma*, to taking them as Lucan [i.e., Luke's own] compositions."

[7] See the comments of Tiziano Dorandi, "Filodeino storico del pensiero antico" (*ANRW* 2.36.4, 1992), 2407–2423, and Richard McKirahan, "Epicurean Doxography in Cicero, *De Natura Deorum* book I," in *Epicureismo Greco e Romano*, ed. Gabriele Giannantoni and Marcello Gigante (Naples: Bibliopolis, 1996) 2:865–878.

[8] It is so far available to the public as a whole only in the text and commen-
tary with Dutch translation of Taco Kuiper (*Philodemus over den dood*, [Amsterdam: H. J. Paris,1925]), itself not in every large library, and in earlier Greek texts even less accessible, like Domenico Bassi's (*Herculanensium Voluminum Collectio Tertia*, I [Milan: U. Hoepli, 1914]) and Walter Scott's (*Fragmenta Herculanensia* [Oxford: Clarendon, 1885]), of both of which the most that can be said is that the reader in the United States can find them here and there with effort, and neither of which offers a translation even into Latin. There are excellent editions, easily available, of the very fragmentary opening columns (1–9) and the well- preserved last three (37–39), with translation and commentary in Italian, by Gigante, "L'inizio del quarto libro 'della Morte' di Filodemo" and "La chiusa del quarto libro 'della Morte' di Filodemo," in *Ricerche Filodemee* 2 (Naples: G. Macchiaroli, 1983), 115–162, 163–234. The reader

demus' fragmentary treatise *On Death* is at any rate often noticed by
the specialists who have studied it as a striking exception to his usual
style, so often complained of as obscure and formless, almost impro-
visational in its long, sprawling sentence-structures. Indeed, even in
On Death Philodemus' writing avoids just as militantly as elsewhere
the conventional rhetorical shapes given by anthesis, parallelism, and
periodic subordination to the prose of even the lesser writers of classical Attic Greek. Its only conventionally elegant formal characteristic
here as elsewhere is the avoidance of hiatus. But since this is equally
characteristic of Philodemus' writing even in the most abstruse and
technical of his compositions, for example the fairly well-preserved
text of the treatise on pure logic *On Signs and Inferences*, it would be
reasonable to conjecture that this easy trick was simply an automatic
habit with Philodemus whenever he wrote or spoke to an audience
(as with many writers of Greek prose after Demosthenes had made
it fashionable).[9] On the other hand, there is a warmth, enthusiasm,
and humanity in *On Death*, combined with a lively vivid humor in
many passages, a lack of embittered controversy with the views of
other schools, and a surprisingly liberal view of the integrity of ordinary, unphilosophical human fears of death and ordinary human grief,
which sets the treatise apart from almost all the other philosophical
literature on the fear of death and the consolation of grief in antiquity. Most of all, in the concluding pages, Philodemus achieves a
solemn, religious eloquence—unconventional, original, and deeply
emotional, yet consciously literary and (as we shall see) full of self-
referential tricks more like those of Hellenistic poetry than those of
philosophical prose—that has impressed every careful reader so far
as something extraordinary and far superior to his ordinary manner
and style.[10] It is as though this peroration were a sudden and extra-

---

will see that I have tentatively offered a conjecture or two in the texts I quote. I
have given longer excerpts in this paper than I would otherwise have done to make
at least a fairly reliable version of the text more readily available.

[9] For a brief but comprehensive survey of what can be said about Philodemus'
style and its characteristics, with a review of previous scholarship, see Dirk Obbink,
Philodemus on Piety, Part 1: Critical Text with Commentary (Oxford: Clarendon, 1996), 86–88.

[10] The appreciations of this passage are confined, as so often in Philodemus' secondary literature, to the few who have worked with it in detail, but they are eloquent. See for example the appreciative comments of Kuiper, 107ff., Gigante "La
Chiusa," 162–180, esp. 163–164 with note 1, and 180, and Philippson, *RE*
"Philodemus" 2476 (he praises esp. col. 38 and also cites an unusually beautiful
sentence in praise of Epicurus from fr. 8 of the *On Epicurus* as being elevated above
Philodemus' normal style). Barbara Wallach, in *Lucretius and the Diatribe Against the*

ordinary exception to his usual stock in trade, violent controversy with opponents, adamant adherence to his own and his master Zeno of Sidon's version of Epicureanism, and determined scholastic exposition in defense of all the minutiae of this version against all comers within the school or without. Here Philodemus makes a sudden and successful excursion into the heights of that epideictic prose that he considers in his *On Rhetoric* to be the essence of rhetoric, above all mere political and forensic ends, and gives us for once an example of what he could do in prose, if he tried, to equal the literary heights he achieved in his poetic epigrams.[11]

It can, I think, be shown that these unusual rhetorical splendors result from the effort to attract and impress a mixed audience, containing philosophers of other schools than the Epicurean and also laypersons—probably, in this age of the Roman Republic, both men and women[12]—with the unique power of the school's psychological consolations for the fear of death and for grief over the death of friends and family members. Whether Philodemus actually delivered this peroration before such an audience is not an important issue, but it can be shown that the reader is asked to imagine one. It can also be argued that this is the probable reason why, of all surviving Epicurean arguments against the fear of death, this treatise is the most humane and liberal, sympathizing with and allowing for ordinary human pain and fear at the thought of death, what Philodemus calls its φυσικὸν δῆγμα or "natural sting." His apparent understand-

---

Fear of Death (Leiden: Brill, 1976), 8 et passim, does not seem to differentiate between the rather commonplace diatribe against anger in the *De Ira* and the masterpiece that is the peroration of *On Death*, calling both "Bionean," but does underline the stylistic difference of the two passages from the rest of Philodemus' work.

[11] For these, see the new commentary of David Sider, *The Epigrams of Philodemus: Introduction, Text, and Commentary* (New York: Oxford University Press, 1997). The best previous edition (with translation) was in A. S. F. Gow and Denys Lionel Page's *The Greek Anthology: The Garland of Philip, and some contemporary epigrams* (London: Cambridge University Press, 1968).

[12] A mixed audience of men and women is not to be excluded, both because Roman audiences contained more women than Greek ones and because of the surviving evidence about Philodemus' work. None of Philodemus' surviving dedications are to women, but there is a striking passage on how to teach philosophy to women in the school without wounding their sensitivities about their inferior educational opportunities or making them burst into tears in *On Frank Criticism*, col. 22. I have given what I think is conclusive evidence that Calpurnia, the wife of Caesar, and her circle shared her father's Epicurean convictions in my article, "The Addressees of the *Ars Poetica*: Herculaneum, Epicurean Protreptic and the Pisones," *MD* 31, 1994, 185–230 (200 n. 29).

ing of ordinary human pain in this treatise goes far beyond anything
in, for example, Lucretius' diatribe on death[13] or for that matter
Philodemus' own words in other, more sectarian treatises such as
"On Choices and Avoidances," so well edited and presented recently
by Voula Tsouna and Giovanni Indelli.[14] Many passages cannot be
made sense of fully, unless the audience is more like that for Paul's
speech on the Areopagus—containing Stoics as well as Epicureans,
members of other schools, and also ordinary people eager to hear
"something new"—than scholars have previously imagined. That in
turn motivates Philodemus, while never departing from the strict
Epicurean denial of every possibility of life after death in any form,
to make a significant concession to his audience in the hope of winning their assent. He admits that the very "blessed Nature," ἡ μακαρία
φύσις, that the Epicureans thought worthy of thanks for making pleasure and happiness possible, also motivates at least and makes under-
standable even in the best of us the more noble aspects of our
frustrated desire to live and not die. In many situations, we find, the
Epicurean philosopher will simply allow tears and anguish their full
course, without any hint that his pupil is yielding to "womanish" or
unphilosophical emotions, before he tries to go further—and that
not merely with lay people but with the wise. Of course he will
retain his confidence that the pain his patient feels is curable, brief in
duration, and not a major impediment to the happiness of the wise

---

[13] Philosophers as such are of course committed to taking Lucretius at his word
and examining what he gives as arguments against the fear of death in and for
themselves. It is therefore Lucretius 3.830–1094 that figures almost exclusively in
modern discussions of the Epicureans' arguments against the fear of death. Of course
the larger imaginative perspective of Charles Segal's *Lucretius on Death and Anxiety*
(Princeton: Princeton University Press, 1990), has not yet affected these discussions
as it deserves to, because it has so far been treated as mere literary criticism. This
is a book in which the whole poem, its terrifying conclusion as the present text
gives it included, is treated as a *consolatio mortis* still more large-minded and humane
than anything I argue for in Philodemus, and from that perspective Segal makes
us see the tirade against the fear of death in a much larger and nobler context. I
think the re-entrance of Philodemus' point of view into the discussion will make
this perspective on Lucretius necessary even in philosophical argument. But perhaps it will also make it possible to see less discord than Segal sees between Lucretius
as poet and as philosopher.

[14] *[Philodemus] [On Choices and Avoidances]*, ed. Giovanni Indelli and Voula Tsouna-
McKirahan, La Scuola di Epicuro,15 (Naples: Bibliopolis, 1995). The brackets
express that strictly speaking neither the author nor the name of the treatise is
known, but the conjecture seems well founded to the editors; see the editors' remarks
at the end of their preface, 66–70. Cf. Gigante, "Filodemo quale autore dell'Etica
Comparetti," *Richerche Filodemee* 2, 245–76.

Epicurean. But pain it will be nonetheless, and this concession adds a new and crucial dimension to our understanding of the Epicurean therapy for the fear of dying.

Our surviving portion of *On Death* disposes of one or two ancillary topics, before turning to its principal argument (cols. 12–39). These are the refutation, or, where Philodemus considers refutation irrelevant or unsympathetic, the sympathetic consolation of various objections to specific kinds of deaths: dying young, dying friendless, dying unjustly at the hands of a tyrant or a tyrannical democracy like Zeno the Eleatic or Socrates, dying unburied or at sea, and so on. Before we come to this sections, cols. 1–3 refute the idea that one loses some possible good by dying: anyone who has achieved true happiness has had all the happiness that eternity itself has to offer. In cols. 4–10 Philodemus is evidently discussing the possibility that at least some deaths, if not all, involve no very violent pain, or are even pleasurable,[15] and also argues that even violent deaths so thin out the faculty of perception that it is doubtful the dying person continues to perceive much. What sort of transition was made to the principal argument in col. 11 is unknown: it is nearly illegible, at least so far as available texts show. These earlier columns are quite fragmentary, and yet here and there enough survives to show the striking attractiveness and unconventionality of Philodemus' style and presentation:

```
. . . ]ε ταλ[α]ίπωρος ἐποι[μώζει                    30
οἵω]ν ἐστέρηται διαλελυ[μένος τὸ
σῶμ]α ὑπάρχων. ἐπιχεώμ[εθα . . .
. εἰ]ρημένοις Διὸς σωτῆρ[ος διότι
τὴν ἡ]δονὴν ὁπόσος χρόνος τῶι ἀ[ν-
θρώπῳ]¹⁶ παρασκευάζειν πέφυκεν ὅτ[αν    35
τις αὐ]τῆς καταλάβη[ι] τοὺς ὅρους τό
θ᾽ ἅμ]α τὸ σάρκινον εὐθὺς ἀπολα-
βεῖν τ]ὸ μέγεθος τῆς ἡδονῆς ὅπε[ρ
καὶ ὁ] ἄπειρος χρόνος περιεποίη[σεν ‖
ἴσον]
```

. . . and in his wretchedness laments over what things he has been deprived of when he exists with his body dissolved. But let us pour

---

[15] A commonplace in the literature of consolation, cf. Cicero, *Tusculans* 1.82 and the parallels (starting with Plato, *Timaeus* 81e) in Max Pohlenz's note *ad loc.*, *De Ciceronis Tusculansis disputationibus* (Göttigen: W. F. Kaestner, 1909).

[16] Following Kuiper's restoration of τῶι ἀ[νθρώπῳ)] in preference to Gigante's ἅ[παντι], though the sense remains much the same.

[libations] to Zeus Soter,[17] (for the) reasons stated, because any amount of time is of the nature to provide pleasure to a man,[18] when a person understands the limits of it (pleasure), and the fact, also, that human flesh speedily achieves the exact same intensity of pleasure that eternity itself has ever encompassed . . .[19] (3.30–4.1)
(Col. 8)

       [συμβή-
σεταί τε κατὰ τὸν λό[γον τούτων μετ᾽
ἄ[κ]ρων ἀλγηδόνων ἐ[πιγίνεσθαι τὰς
τελευτάς, ἀξιούντω[ν ἀ]δύν[ατον εἶναι
τὴν ἀνυπέρβλητον λύεσθαι συ[μφυί-
αν μὴ μετ᾽ ὀχλήσεω[ς] ἀνυπερβ[λήτου.   5
Φήσομέν γε τὴν συμπάθ<ε>ιαν πρ[ὸς τὸ
σῶμα τῆς ψυχῆς, εἰ καὶ τὰ πολλὰ ν[όσου
[[μετ]] <τῆς> ὀχλήσεως αἰτίας [οὔση]ς ἢ π[υ]κ[νού-
σ]ης ἀσυμμέτρως τὰ μ[έλη τ]ῶν ζώ[ιων
ἢ διϊστανούσης, ἀλλ᾽ οὐ φ[αμέν] γε ἀδ[ύνα-   10
τον λυθῆναί ποτ᾽ αὐτὴν [ἄλλ]ης τυχο[ῦσαν
. . .] ἑτεροιώσεως ἥτις καὶ [ἐσ]τί τινος
ἀ]λγ[ηδό]νος α[ἰ]τία.[20] λ[επ]τομερὲς γὰρ
σῶμ]α καὶ τελέως εὐκίν[ητον ἡ] ψ[υ]χὴ κα[ὶ
δι]ὰ τοῦτ᾽ ἐκ μικροτάτ[ω]ν σ[υν]έστηκ[ε   15

---

[17] Gigante well compares the libations of the two philosophical martyrs Seneca and Thrasea Pactus at their deaths to Jupiter Liberator, Tacitus *Ann.* 15.63, 16.35 (the only time this title for Jupiter occurs in Latin).

[18] Or τῶι ἄ[παντι] (Gigante), "to every man." As Philodemus most often uses διότι after a vowel and to avoid hiatus (cf. Obbink, *Philodemus on Piety*, 87), line 33 might be better as . . . σωτῆρ[ος, ὅτι πᾶ-lσαν ἡ]δονὴν, or some other adjective, e.g. τελείαν, ἄφατον (conjectures for which I thank Jeffrey Fish): "because any amount of time is of the nature to provide every (perfect, indescribable) pleasure to a man." Cf. Epicurus, KD 19 (= SV 22), "limited time and infinite time provide equal pleasure, if a man measures its limits by reasoning," and 20, "The flesh believes the limits of pleasure unlimited and that unlimited time is required to acquire it, but the understanding, taking into account the end and limits of the flesh, and dissolving its fears concerning eternity, prepares the perfect life, and has no longer need of unlimited time; but neither refuses pleasure nor troubles itself about its departure from life, as if it died lacking something of the best life." Philodemus here attempts not unsuccessfully to imitate these sayings with a new eloquence of his own.

[19] Cf. Epicurus, SV 33, "The voice of the flesh is for not being hungry, not being thirsty, not being cold, and a man that has these things and can expect to keep having them could contest even with <Zeus> in happiness." For further parallels cf. Gigante *ad loc.*, "L'Inizio" 131–139.

[20] Kuiper *ad loc.* suggests [ἄλλ]ης τυχο[ῦσαν] ἑτεροιώσεως ⟨ἢ⟩ ἥτις κα[μόν]τι τινὸς [ἦν] [ἀ]λγ[ηδό]νος αἰτια, "finding some other change than that which was indeed the cause of pain to the sick man." This gives something more like what must have been the sense, though the hiatus before ἥτις is improbable. I have assumed the pain was meant to be small in my translation.

καὶ λει]οτάτων καὶ περιφε[ρε]στά[τ]ων,
διε]σ[παρ]μένη καὶ παρὰ τοῦτο πολλὴν
εὐ]πορία[ν π]αρέ[χ]ουσα[[ι]], πῶς οὐ[κ] ἐξίπτα-
ται δ[ιὰ τῶν ἑτοίμ]ων πόρων ἐν τῇ σα[ρ-
κὶ π[λεόνων] ἢ μ[υρίω]ν; [ἐ]κ τίνος [δὴ] κἂν   20
εἴπ[ωμ]ε[ν ἀλγηδόν]ο[ς] αἰτία[ν εἶναι
τὴ[ν τῶν τοιούτων διά]κρισιν λί[αν δε-
δοίκα[σιν, ἧς τάχιστ᾿ ἀ]ποτετελεσ-
μέ[νης ἀναισθητήσομεν; . . .] αμ [. . .
συν[. . . . .]ων τ[. . .]ν   25
α[. . . . . τέ]ρψεως α-
. . . .]ακα[. . .
τοὺς ἀπ[οσπασμοὺς] συμβα[ίν]ει
κατα [. . . . . .]αιπερ [. . .]ρους δ[ι]ὰ
.]υρου[. . . . . κ]ἂν εἴ τις ἐπειδήπερ [ἐκ   30
τῶν] τοιούτω[ν] συνέστηκεν [ἀ]ξιώιη δ[ὴ
ταρ]αττόντων κατὰ τὴν σύνκρισ[ιν
οὕ]τως μεθ᾿ ἡδονῆς γίν[εσθαι τὰς
τε]λευτάς, οὐκ ἂν ἀπίθαν[ον λέγοι, κατὰ τοῦ]το μὲν συμβαίνε[ι λύεσθαι
τὴν] ἀνυπέρβλητον κοινω[νίαν μεθ᾿ ἡδο-   35
νῆς] κα[ὶ τ]έρψεως. καὶ γὰ[ρ . . . .
. . γερό]ντων μετ[βολ . . . .
(Col. 9)
με]τὰ τινας μέθας καὶ κώ[μους χω-
ρὶς] πόνου [κα]θάπερ ἐπὶ τῆς α[ὐξήσεως
τῆς] ἀπο τῶν παιδίων ἐπὶ τὴ[ν ἀκ]μὴ[ν
καὶ] τῆς ἀπ[ά]σης ἀπο τῶν ἄκ[ρ]ων φθί-
σεως] ἐπὶ τὸ γῆρας. γίνονται δὲ νεανι-   5
ῶν] μεταβολαὶ καὶ δι᾿ ἀσυμμέτρων
κινη]μάτων ὥσπερ εἰς ὕπνον τοῦ
μηκ]ωνίου. πλὴν καὶ τὸ βιαίου[ς γί]νεσ-
θαι τ]οὺς ἀποσπασμοὺς τῆς ψυχῆς ἀπὸ
τοῦ σώ]ματος καὶ διὰ τοῦτο τὴν μεγίσ-   10
την ἑτ]εροίωσιν [ἐπ]ακολουθεῖν. ἀ[ρα]ιώ[σει
τὴν αἰσθη]τικ[ὴ]ν ἕ[ξι]ν. οὐ [γὰ]ρ ἐξ ἀνάγκης
πίπτειν οὐ]δὲ κ[ατὰ τὴ]ν ὥ[ραν] ἔτου[ς ὡ]ς καρ-
πους ἀπὸ τῶ]ν δένδρω[ν——] ἀλλα (. . .)

8. . . . and it will result according to their argument that all deaths are
accompanied by extreme pain, since they claim it is impossible that
this, the height of all natural unions, can be dissolved without the
height of all anguish. But we shall say of that sympathy of the soul
with the body, that even if for the most part sickness is the cause of
pain, as it either abnormally condenses or swells the limbs of living
things, [10] still we say that it is not impossible that this sympathy
should somehow be dissolved by coming to some different alteration,

which is (indeed) the cause of some (minor) pain. For the soul is a body that consists of tiny particles, and is exceedingly mobile, and thus is composed of the smallest and smoothest and roundest atoms. And it is scattered (throughout the body), and because of this can easily do so;[21] so why does it not just fly out through the pores in the flesh that are there ready for it, more than ten thousand of them? For what reason, indeed, even if we admit that the separation of such elements is a cause of pain, do men fear it excessively, since the minute this separation has been accomplished [we shall be unconscious?][22] . . . [with] enjoyment . . . (c. 13 lines unintelligible)

. . . these tearings-apart (?) happen to be . . . Indeed, if, since the soul is made up of such things, a person should even claim that when things disturb (them) in their union in this manner, our deaths come with pleasure, he would say nothing unpersuasive, and then on the one hand it would happen that this height of all unions dissolves with pleasure and enjoyment, and in fact . . . the departure of the old . . .

9. [or of the dissolute?] after certain drunkennesses and banquets comes about as painlessly as our growth from children to maturity and our entire gradual decline from maturity to old age. And sometimes young men suffer the change (from life to death) through irregular motions as if (sinking) into a sleep produced by poppy-flower.[23] But in fact even the occurrence of violent separations of soul from body, and the very great alteration following because of it, will [thin out] the faculty of perception; for this does not occur from necessity or in its due season of year, as when fruits fall from the trees, (but) . . . (8.1–9.14)

In this second passage both the eloquence and the informality are even more on show than in the first. One need only consider the startling anacoluthon created by the resumptive οὔ φαμεν after φήσομέν γε in 8.6–10 (which I have tried to reproduce in my translation) for the informality, and the last three sentences (8.30–10.14) with their loose casual connectives and crowded rush of brilliant imagery, for both the informality and the eloquence at once.[24] Thus even through

---

[21] πολλὴν | εὐ]πορία[ν π]αρέ[χ]ουσα in Greek (Gigante's reading, after Hayter) appears to be a pun on the following allusion to the body's many πόροι.

[22] And therefore, of course, we must logically feel less and less as it advances. Philodemus does not believe that the moment of death itself is or can be particularly painful.

[23] μηκ]ώνιον is used rather of the poppy-flower than opium: cf. LSJ s.v. To translate it just "opium" here spoils Philodemus' imagery, which goes back to the famous image in Homer of Priam's son Gorgythion sinking "like a poppy flower" under an ax-blow (*Il.* 8.306–308). The supplement is Gomperz' (Hayter's ὀψ]ωνίου, "tidbits of food," does not convince). See also Gigante, "L'Inizio" 158.

[24] Other features of Philodemus' style are illustrated here too: note the hyperbatic placement of ταρ]αττόντων in 8.32, exemplifying one of the few striking characteristics

the damaged state of the text one can see that this is rhetoric, not just argument, that Philodemus is trying to appeal to the emotions as well as the reason. We can say that his style exemplifies the kind of epideictic rhetoric, the belletristic striving for pure beauty in language that, he argues in *On Rhetoric*, constitutes the archetype of rhetorical style.[25] And yet it derives its beauty and power precisely from the air of sincerity and emotional earnestness that comes from the *avoidance* of artificial and obvious rhetorical devices such as Isocratean balance, antithesis and symmetry, relying instead on originality of thought and on poetic imagery. Or in philosophical terms, we can say that his style is protreptic, a rhetoric to convince potential initiates, like the contemporary poetry of Lucretius[26]—a style the Epicureans only used with caution, arguing as they usually did that sober and ana-lytic prose, not elegant rhetoric and still less poetry, was best fitted to convey truth. Epicurus himself seems not to have used rhetoric at all, but Philodemus argued that the use of protreptic rhetoric to put things "before the eyes," πρὸ ὀμμάτων (*On Anger* 4.16) and make them more accessible to the imagination could have medical value and so was worth borrowing even from the Stoics (*On Anger* 4.4–24 Indelli); this attitude makes his manner here more explainable.

In the only other example we have of Philodemus' resorting to extensive rhetorical heightening to make his points in the course of an ethical treatise, it seems that he first apologizes at length for the usefulness of rhetoric and emotional heightening to disgust the pupil with the effects of anger (*De Ira* col. 1–8.8). He then gives his presum-ably delighted and amused pupils an extended parody or imitation of how the Stoic diatribe style of vivid denunciation and ridicule of the angry could be used in Epicurean terms to discourage anger (8.20–31.24).[27] The minute he has finished he recurs to his usual cold, ana-

---

of his style besides the avoidance of conventional balance, his love of hyperbaton. The casual way in which he frequently uses μέν . . . δέ contrasts, avoiding cut-and-dried antithesis, is well illustrated by the way in which the μέν of 8.32 is appar-ently answered, if it is answered at all, by πλὴν καί in 9.8.

[25] For this aspect of Philodemus' rhetorical theory, G. M. A. Grube, *The Greek and Latin Critics* (London: Methuen, 1965), 200–206, is still the most easily avail-able exposition in English.

[26] On Lucretius' use of poetry and poetic style to make Epicureanism appealing to non-Epicureans, cf. Carl Joachim Classen, "Poetry and Rhetoric in Lucretius," *Probleme der Lukrezforschung*, (Hildesheim: G. Olms, 1983), 331–73 = *TAPA* 1968 77–118, and the chapter "Lucretius and the Reader" in Diskin Clay, *Lucretius and Epicurus* (Ithaca: Cornell University Press, 1993), 256–309.

[27] The uniqueness of the rhetorical disquisitions in *On Anger* and *On Death* com-pared to Philodemus' usual manner is noticed by Wallach, 8.

lytic and sarcastic argumentative style for the rest of the treatise.[28]

In *On Death*, so far as we know, the epideictic style prevailed from beginning to end of the treatise; it certainly pervades all the surviving columns of book IV. And there is no apology for the use of rhetoric, either, as in *On Anger*. The treatise ends, uniquely in our surviving Philodemean literature (and we have ends of many books, if beginnings of very few), in a perfect blaze of unapologetic rhetorical magnificence and poetic artifice. Philodemus' usual manner is to end undramatically (as in *Poetics* V or *De Musica* IV or *De Ira*) with a series of tidyings-up of minor objections and lesser points. Nor does the subject of death move Philodemus elsewhere to any special eloquence just as a subject. A fine comparison in a treatise clearly addressed to fellow Epicureans is the section on death and its impact on the fool compared to the wise man that concludes [*On Choices and Avoidances*] (to give that treatise the editors' title, cf. note 14, above), cols. 17–23. Here, the argument that most of the confusion, pain and useless greed and ambition of fools' lives comes from the fear of death—a topic that inspired Lucretius to high poetry, e.g. *DRN* 3.41–93—and that the wise man's plans by contrast are always moderate and rational and take death fully into account, is put in Philodemus' grayest utilitarian prose from beginning to end. The concluding sentence reads equally like an anticlimax in the Greek and the editors' translation ("And feeling confidence against illness and death, he endures with strength the therapies that can remove them," [*On Choices and Avoidances*] 23. 9–12).[29] By contrast, *On Death* employs, as we shall see, every sort of rhetorical and poetic artifice, and especially in the fine peroration at the end, to persuade its audience.

It is only, however, in the longer passage arguing against objections to dying that occur in particular cases, such as when someone dies young, that we find evidence of who the intended audience for this epideictic rhetoric is. The audience of *On Anger* is certainly Epicurean and probably members of Philodemus' own school at Naples, for a long section in the middle is addressed directly to members of the school and pictures vividly how the individual's lessons in school and

---

[28] For the unique and startling character of the diatribe section and its striking difference in style from the rest of the treatise, cf. *Filodemo: de l'Ira: edizione, traduzione e commento*, ed. Giovanni Indelli, La Scuola di Epicuro 5 (Naples: Bibliopolis, 1988), 24–28.

[29] "Alleviate them," as suggested by Dirk Obbink in his review, *OSAPh* 15 (1997) 280 n. 69, would of course be more logical.

the life of the school as a whole can be disturbed by unrestrained anger (18.34–21.40). The later, argumentative sections argue fairly abstrusely for the Epicureans'—or rather the Zenonian Epicureans', as Philodemus is arguing also against other Epicureans here—strict definition of what sort of anger is a virtuous emotion. By contrast, the impact of the arguments in *On Death* nowhere depends on acceptance of any technical position in Epicureanism, though of course the speaker himself assumes some of them, especially the absolute mortality of the human soul. Many passages are deliberately couched so as to appeal to any person interested in philosophy, and praise the instinct of ordinary people in certain matters as being *pro tanto* as right as any philosopher's. Other passages praise philosophers who are not Epicurean or atomist, along with and beside Epicureans and atomists, in a way not usual with Philodemus. Although these features all have parallels in other ancient treatises on death and the fear of death, some other references seem to me to show decisively that Philodemus is addressing an audience which contains members of other philosophical schools, and also Romans as well as Greeks.

An example of *On Death*'s unusual liberalism towards the virtues of ordinary men and philosophers of other schools is found in the splendid conclusion of Philodemus' argument that one should not fear to die unjustly at the hands of a tyrant, whether a monarch or a tyrannical democracy, such as killed Socrates (cols. 34–35). This, as we will see below, is one of those cases that give "natural pain" even to the wise, but a pain that can be endured, in this case because of one's conviction of innocence. A good man will not be troubled by the thought that he alone has suffered injustice, says Philodemus ironically in conclusion,

καὶ
γὰρ μυρίους οἶδε καὶ τῶν ἐπιφανεστά-
των φθόνωι καὶ διαβολῆι περιπεσόν-
τας [ἔ]ν τε δήμοις καὶ παρὰ δυνάσταις,
ὑπὸ δὲ τυράννων καὶ τοὺς ἀρίστους
μάλιστα καὶ βασιλεῖς ὑπὸ βασιλέων,   5
πείθεται δὲ καὶ τοὺς καταγνόντας ἔν
τε τῶι παντὶ βίωι τετιμωρῆσθαι πρὸς
τῆς ἐν αὐτοῖς κακίας καὶ δι᾽ αὐτὸν με-
ταμελείαις πολλαῖς ὀδυνήσεσθαι δυσχερέστε-   10
ρον ὑπ᾽ ἄλλων. ἐγὼ δὲ θαυμάζω τῶν
ἀβίωτον ἡγουμένων τὸ καταγνωσ-

θῆναι καὶ ταῦτ' οὐχ ὑπὸ σπουδαίων, ἀλ-
λ᾿ ὑπὸ χειρίστων ἀνθρώπων, μᾶλλον
δὲ θη[ρ]ίων, εἰ μακαρίως ἡγοῦ[ν]ται βε-
βιωκέναι καὶ βιώσεσθαι τοὺ[ς] παμπο-
νήρο[υ]ς μέν, ἀπολυομένους δὲ διαβο-
λῶν ἢ μηδόλως διαβαλλομ[έ]νους
παρὰ τοῖς τοιούτοις, ἔτι δ᾿ εἰ μὴ νομί-
ζουσιν [κ]α[ὶ] τῶν φρονιμωτά[των] τὸν   20
βίον εἶ[αι] ταλαίπωρον, εἴπερ ἔσ[τι] συμ-
φορὰ τ[ὸ γί]νεσθαι περιπετῆ τοῖ[ς] τοιούτοις, προλαμβ[ά]νοντας ἴσως ἔσε[σ]θαι καὶ
περὶ ἑα[υ]τ[οὺς], ἐπειδὴ τύχης εἰ[σὶ]ν ἔρ-
γον. οὕ[τω] δ᾿ἐστὶ πιστὸν τὸ γεν[ν]αίως   25
δύνασθαι [φ]έ[ρε]ιν τὰ τοιαῦτα το[ὺ]ς ἀρε-
τ[η]φόρους τῶν [ἀ]νδρῶν, ὥστε κα[ὶ] τῶν
ἰδιωτῶ[ν] πάρ[εσ]τιν θεωρ[εῖν τ]ιν[α]ς οὐ-
κ εὐλόφως μόνον ὑ[π]οφέροντα[ς], ἀλλὰ καὶ κ[α]τανωτιζομένους τῶν δι-
ατιθέντων· [ἔ]α γὰρ ε[ἰ] Σωκράτης καὶ Ζή-
νων ὁ Ἐ[λ]εάτη[ς] καὶ Ἀγ[ά]ξαρχος, ὥς τινες
ἱστ[ο]ροῦ[σι], κα[ὶ τ]ινες ἄλλοι τῶν φιλοσο-
φησάντων.

For in fact he knows of ten thousands of the most excellent who fell
by envy and slander, both in democracies and at the courts of princes;
and by tyrants' hands the best men more than any, and kings by the
hand of kings, and has faith too that those who condemned him are
punished already throughout their own life out of the evil inside themselves, and on his account will be anguished with many a pang of
repentance, and probably also will themselves later be hurt yet more
horribly by others. But I am amazed at them, who think it unendurable to be condemned, and that not by good men, but by the
worst of them, beasts rather; if they think that those live happily and
will live happily, who are very evil, but acquitted of slanders, or not
slandered at all among such men as these; and then, if they do not
think the life even of the most intelligent of us to be wretched, if in
fact it is a misfortune to become vulnerable to such men.[30] But perhaps they anticipate that this will happen to themselves also, since they
are (?)[31] the work of chance. But it is so certain that the standard-
bearers of virtue among men can endure such things nobly, that one

---

[30] Another striking example of the improvisatory structure of Philodemus' periods, and of his overuse of double negatives and litotes.

[31] Or possibly the scribe wrote εἰσιν by error for ἐστιν, "since this is the work
of chance."

can see even ordinary men not just enduring with neck unbowed, but displaying the profoundest contempt for those who put them there, let alone Socrates,[32] and Zeno the Eleatic,[33] and Anaxarchus as historians tell us, and others of the philosophers. [34.37–35.30]

So also in col. 29.10–12, Philodemus remarks that most of the philosophers, "not just Epicurus and Metrodorus," have lived as glorious lives and died as edifying a death as any warrior on the battlefield; and at 31.1 he says that Epicurus *and Plato* were both greater men than Alexander's magnificently entombed friend Hephaestion (as part of the argument that to be buried humbly or not at all is nothing to be feared). Does this unusual liberalism on his part indicate a mixed audience of Epicureans and non-Epicureans? I think this is certain from a significant phrase at col. 32.24–31:

τίς, ἂν δ[ὴ μ]ετὰ
ταῦτα διά τιν[ος] αἰτίας γυμ[ν]ωθῆ<ι>   25
τὰ λείψα[ν]ά τ[ιν]ος, ὃ πολλάκ[ι]ς [οἴ]δα-
μ[ε]ν γεγ[ονός], ο[ἰκ]τρὸν ἡγήσεται τὸν
οὐκ ὄντ[α]; τ[ίς δ' ο]ὐκ ἂν πεισθε[ί]η [κ]α[ὶ]
τοὺς πε[ριε]σταλμένους καὶ [τοὺς ἀ-]
τάφους [εἰ]ς ἅ πο[τ]ε νομίζει σ[τοιχ]εῖ-   30
α πάντας ἀναλυθήσεσθαι;

Who, if indeed at some later time for some reason some dead person's bones do get exposed, as we know has often happened, will consider this non-existent person pitiable? Who would not be persuaded, that both those who are properly laid out and those who are not buried at all will dissolve *into whatever he may believe to be the elements into which all men dissolve?*[34]

---

[32] It is important to note that Philodemus elsewhere—speaking to Epicureans in his normal voice—takes the doctrinaire point of view that Socrates' condemnation is not an illustration of the power of rhetoric to overcome virtue, because not being an Epicurean he had not the right virtues anyway (*Rhetoric* VII, cols. XXIX–XXX Sudhaus I pp. 265–7). See the comments on this passage by Eduardo Acosta Méndez and Anna Angeli, *Filodemo, Testimomianze su Socrate*, La Scuola di Epicuro 13 (Naples: Bibliopolis, 1992), 243–49. Here, therefore, he may well be conciliating his audience by speaking with more admiration of Socrates than he would have used in addressing an audience composed only of other Epicureans.

[33] Zeno the Eleatic, and Anaxarchus the Democritean, the teacher of Pyrrho, the founder of Skepticism, died violently at the hands of tyrants; above, in col. 34.1–3, Philodemus gave Socrates as an additional example, and also the Homeric hero Palamedes, and Alexander's unjustly executed friend Callisthenes.

[34] It reinforces this point, I think, that Philodemus has said, in discussing pain at the prospect of one's body corrupting in the grave, that all men σκελετοὶ γίνονται, τὸ δὲ πέρας εἰς τὰς πρώτας ἀναλ[ύ]ονται φύσεις, "become skeletons, then dissolve into their primal *natures*," 30.3—here too apparently using φύσεις as a neutral word for "elements" that will not entail the doctrine of atoms.

If there is any non-negotiable point in Epicureanism, it is what the elements consist in, namely the atoms. Consequently, it seems to me, the audience cannot be composed of doctrinaire Epicureans. But the audience is also not all lay people, since those would have no special beliefs about the minima of matter. The audience must include philosophers of various schools, with various different beliefs about them, but who all accept that bodies buried or unburied dissolve into at least some kind of elements. I take this sentence to be conclusive proof that Philodemus was addressing this treatise both in its spoken and its written version to a mixed audience of Epicureans and believers in other schools, and probably also believers in none.

Many details of Philodemus' presentation become much clearer if this is understood. A wise youth like Pythocles, he says in col. 19, has enjoyed all the happiness there is in life, and though there is no reason not to live longer, he loses nothing by dying. "But the fool will have no happiness worthy of consideration to forget, not even if he lasts out the years of Tithonus,[35] nor is it more alien to his nature to depart hence, once he is born, by the swiftest road and right now, than to leave life more slowly—even if we would not advise him thus" (19.33–20.1). Surely, the artistic effect here is that Philodemus pretends for a moment to forget that the Epicureans counseled in all circumstances against suicide, even for fools, and then rights himself by pretending to remember "our" doctrine just in time—a charming rhetorical effect, which would be lost on an audience of fellow-believers, and also lost without an audience containing people who knew their philosophy well enough to appreciate the joke.

But perhaps what becomes clearer on this supposition is not only the rhetorical tone of the treatise but the reasons for the style and manner of the philosophy of death Philodemus gives us here. We will see that the most complete section we have is a peroration; it is also a reply, in its way, to objections that people still make to the Epicurean theory of death and dying—and no doubt, therefore, it preempts objections people made even then. In particular, we may note that Philodemus has a reply (or at least an implied reply) to give to both of the two objections which seem to have pre-empted most of the voluminous modern debate about Epicurus' arguments on death and dying.[36]

---

[35] The mythological lover of the Dawn, who gave him eternal life, but not eternal youth, so that he lives on forever feeble and senile.

[36] For a good overview of this debate, see the chapter on Lucretius' view of

First, much of this literature deals with Epicurus' and Lucretius' doctrine that the indifference with which we regard time after our death
and the events to come in it should be equal to that which we undeniably regard the time before we were born—the "symmetry argument," as it is called. Philodemus unfortunately does not confront
the possible objections to this argument head on in our surviving
texts. But in fact his reply to them is implied in much that he says.

One way of stating the symmetry argument which would command ready assent even from a modern person is the following case.
It is no more a matter of concern to an individual that she should
live to see the Big Crunch or the Big Fadeout, whichever is to end
the universe, than that she missed the Big Bang. Perhaps most peo-

---

death in Martha Nussbaum's *The Therapy of Desire: Theory and Practice in Hellenistic
Ethics* (Princeton: Princeton University Press, 1994), 192–239, itself based on her
earlier "Mortal Immortals: Lucretius on Death and the Voice of Nature," *Philosophy
and Phenomenal Research* 50, 1989, 303–351. Some chief contributions: "The Makropulos
Case: Reflections on the Tedium of Immortality," in Bernard Williams, *Problems of
the Self* (London: Cambridge University Press, 1973); F. Miller, "Epicurus on the
Art of Dying," *Southern Journal of Philosophy* 14 (1976), 169–77; Thomas Nagel,
"Death" in *Mortal Questions* (London: Cambridge University Press, 1979); Harry
Silverstein, "The Evil of Death," *The Journal of Philosophy* 77 (1980), 401–424; "Harm
and Self-Interest," in Joel Feinberg, *Rights, Justice and the Bounds of Liberty* (Princeton,
Princeton University Press, 1980); Ernest Partridge, "Posthumous Interests and
Posthumous Respect," *Ethics* 91 (1981), 243–64; O. H. Green, "Fear of Death,"
Philosophy and Phenomenal Research 43 (1982), 99–105; Amélie Rorty, "Fearing Death,"
Philosophy 58 (1983), 175–88; George Pitcher, "The Misfortunes of the Dead," *American
Philosophical Quarterly* 21 (1984), 183–88; Anthony L. Brueckner and John Martin
Fischer, "Why is Death Bad?," *Philosophical Studies* 50 (1986), 213–27; David Furley,
"Nothing to Us?" in *The Norms of Nature: Studies in Hellenistic Ethics*, ed. Malcolm
Schofield and Gisela Striker (Cambridge: Cambridge University Press, 1986), 75–91;
Steven Luper-Foy, "Annihilation," *Philosophical Quarterly* 37 (1987), 233–52 (an espe-
cially brilliant piece on whose arguments Philodemus' *On Death* could have shed
much light); Palle Yourgrau, "The Dead," *Journal of Philosophy* 84 (1987), 84–101;
F. M. Kamm, "Why is Death Bad and Worse than Pre-Natal Non-Existence?,"
Pacific Philosophical Quarterly 69 (1988), 161–64; Philip Mitsis, "Epicurus on Death
and Duration," *PBACAP* 4 (1988), 303–322; Fred Feldman, "On Dying as a Process,"
Philosophy and Phenomenological Research 50 (1989), 375–89; Ishtiyaque Haji, "Pre-Vital
and Post-Vital Times," *Pacific Philosophical Quarterly* 72 (1991), 171–80; Brueckner
and Fischer, "Death's Badness," *Pacific Philosophical Quarterly* 74 (1993), 37–45; Walter
Glannon, "Epicureanism and Death," *The Monist* 76 (1993), 222–34. Except for
Stephen Rosenbaum's brilliant defenses of Epicurus' positions in detail, "How to
Be Dead and Not Care: a Defense of Epicurus," *American Philosophical Quarterly* 23
(1986), 217–25, "The Symmetry Argument: Lucretius Against the Fear of Death,"
Philosophy and Phenomenological Research 50 (1989), 353–73, "Epicurus and Annihilation,"
Philosophical Quarterly 39 (1989), 81–90, "Epicurus on Pleasure and the Complete
Life," *The Monist* 73 (1990), 21–41, most of these articles would have needed rad-
ical revision had Philodemus' *On Death* been part of modern scholarship's apparatus of Epicurean texts.

ple would agree that what is to happen many generations from now after many human lifetimes have expired matters almost as little. The fact that I will not see 2300 c.e. is not a great concern to me, no more than that I did not see the world of 1600 c.e. But the nearer we get to our own time the less this symmetry seems to apply. I was born in 1940, and am perfectly content to apprehend the 1930's (no halcyon era anyway!) from films and books, but decades that could potentially belong to my life and probably will not I am indeed somewhat afraid to miss. But here the reason seems fairly clear: I had no personal interests and connections with the progress of things in the 1930's, but I do now, connections with people and interests that will continue then in my absence. So if I regret that I won't live till 2050 or near it, what I regret is the breaking off of all sorts of stories and interests in which I am personally involved.

It seems as if it were a major argumentative mistake on Lucretius' part, which modern writers justly reproach, to introduce this so-called symmetry as a consolation for not being there tomorrow, or the next decade—even though I think most could agree the more time I add, a hundred years perhaps, the less pressing the need to survive must become. The closer I get to my own times and to the length of a plausible human life, the less impressive the argument from symmetry becomes. But this must be because my unconsciousness in death will be breaking off relationships, plans, involvements, everything that constitutes my life in society, in a way that my unconsciousness of everything before birth right up to the moment before did not.

Philodemus seems to have intuited this distinction. The one time, at any rate, he brings up the annihilating thought of the vast abyss of time before and after our birth, and of the mortality of the universe itself, he does so only as a conclusion to one of his topics, as a sort of *reductio ad absurdum* when he has already dealt with the meaning of loss in the present context. In cols. 35–36 he is arguing against the pain of fearing one will be forgotten—one more of his many (he concedes) φυσικὰ δήγματα, natural pains, that death carries, but in this case probably the reward of evil: "in many cases this is the result of a friendless life, that is," he adds bitingly, "one that has had nothing good about it" (35.36–39). If a good man has lost the friends who should remember him before dying he will "in the large picture lose nothing he needs, for we need these things not for their own sake, but that of the approved life which it is their nature to accompany; and so when that life is completed what anxiety will come to us for that which is nothing to us nor even in our mind?" (35.39–36.8). It is only after this that he adds that no one will be remembered, nor should want to be remembered, literally forever:

ἀλλὰ μὴν εἰ συμφορὰ [τὸ] μὴ μνημονε[ύ-]
εσθαι, τοὺς [π]λείστους ἡ[γ]ητέον οἰκτροὺ[ς
γεγονένα<ι> τῶν ὑπαρξά[ν]των ἀφ᾿ ο[ὗ δή-]
πο]τ[ε] χρόνο[υ] μ[ν]ήμης ἠ̣ξιώθη [τι ὑ-]
πάρχον, ἅπ[α]ντας δὲ τ̣ο[ὺς] πρότερο̣[ν], ἐ-
πει]δήπερ [οὐδ]εὶς οὐδὲ[ν ἱσ]τόρ[η]σεν [ὑπὲ]ρ
αὐ]τῶν· οὐ[κ] ἂν φθάνο[ι]μεν δὲ κ[αὶ π]άγ-
τ]ας ἁπ[λῶς] τοὺς γεγον[ότα]ς ἢ[καὶ] γε-
ν]ησομ[έ]ν̣ο[υς] ἐν τῶι κό[σ]μωι, φ[θαρ]έν-
τ]ο̣ς γὰρ [ο]ὐδ[εὶ]ς μνημο[ν]εύ[σει, πᾶς ἐξώ-][37]
λης [γάρ].

But in fact if it's a misfortune not to be remembered, we must think most men who have lived since that time when some remembrance came to be thought worthy of preservation, and all men who lived before it, to have become wretched, since nobody has told any story about any of them. Or why should we hesitate to call simply everybody that's been born and everybody that will be born in the whole universe such, since when that falls apart nobody will remember them, for it will (all?) be out of existence? (36.17–25)

Philodemus' main concern is in fact with the breaking off of good things in life, that is, with the loss to the dead person of those things that he planned to, or might potentially, have done. Even if he or she does not feel this loss it remains a loss, just as the secret enmity or contempt of our friends is an evil to us even if we do not know of it.[38] Philodemus' response is threefold, and only one part of it is common in other Epicurean literature and figures in modern discussions of Epicurean attitudes to death. This is the first part, the argument that (as we have already seen him say) pleasure once fully experienced is not time-dependent, and is completely fulfilling. Once we have experienced even for a short time the same pleasure as the gods— that is, fulfillment of basic needs and freedom from the fear that this will not continue—we can depart after that, having missed nothing of a full life *for ourselves as individuals*. Modern critics are at least aware

---

[37] Kuiper prints this conjecture of his father W. Kuiper, which is *spatio longius*, but it would work just as well without πᾶς.

[38] As Nagel first argued in "Death," n. 36 above, 404, a point much discussed in the succeeding literature.

of this argument, although it does not figure largely in their discussion. It is not exclusive to Philodemus, but merely common Epicurean doctrine, grounded in the master's own surviving writings.[39]

The other two, however, are not found in other surviving Epicurean literature, and have been ignored in modern discussion, presumably because the text was considered barely available, too difficult without a translation (or with only the Dutch one available), or too problematic. It is my contention that they are drawn out of Philodemus by the desire to convince an audience of skeptics. But it also seems not improbable they were advanced long before him in lost writings of the school, because their rhetorical and emotional value is more universal and less dependent on the particular Epicurean doctrine of pleasure. These are, that (1) while a desire for more pleasure in length of life for oneself and *simpliciter* is either irrelevant (for we have had it fully already) or brings one down again to the consideration of trivial and unnecessary pleasures, one must acknowledge that the prospect of death as an interruption of one's virtuous and benevolent plans for friends and for the survival of one's good name among them is "naturally painful," indeed, causes us pain intended by nature as a motivation to stay alive. This is a pain that *should* be felt by a wise person—indeed by wise persons more than others, since their plans are the best grounded in reason and thus the most compelling to them. Though it can be consoled by reason, it must and should be felt. This concession alone is enough to throw a monkey wrench into most of the modern discussion of Epicurean views of death, because it is assumed, since no other surviving text says this, that an Epicurean cannot make such a concession consistently with the school's doctrine of happiness; but in fact, as we shall see, he can.

The other argument, which forms the basis of Philodemus' extraordinary peroration at the end, is again new, though equally consistent with the school's basic doctrine. It is held in reserve against the possible objection that the sage in that case, since he is exposed by nature to real mental pain at the thought of the ruin of his plans and his reputation by death, is not really happy. This is (2) that being wise entails the firm and permanent contemplation of death as part of life, the knowledge that the surprise, as Philodemus argues, is not that we should die but that given the universality and

---

[39] Again, see Gigante's excellent note on 3.32–39, "L'Inizio," 118.

omnipresent possibility of death the surprising thing is life. Once we realize this we are no longer so much afraid of death as we are both much more thankful for life and for every day of it we are improbably given, and able to accept death at any and every moment as a thing already taken into account and expected. Again, it seems that the parallel for this is not so much to be sought in the literal arguments about death given by Epicurus and Lucretius, but in what Philodemus implies in the grandiose rhetoric of his peroration is the whole tenor and example of Epicurus' life, and in what Segal has shown is the whole tenor of Lucretius' poem—particularly the famous and paradoxical conclusion of book VI, the portrayal of human life as exposed at every point to natural disaster and plague. Only by accepting nature's *memento mori* as a permanent background to the enjoyment of life can true enjoyment be secured.

Philodemus begins his discussion of possible objections to death with what clearly to him is the most important, objections to dying young (cols. XII–XX.1), which he discusses at length. He gives arguments which for the most part rely on the first contention, that to experience true philosophical happiness is to be fulfilled, however short one's life thereafter:

> ἐ[ξὸν δὲ
> ἐμποσῶι χρόνωι τὸ μέγιστον αὐ[τῶν]
> καὶ περιποιήσασθαι κα[ὶ] ἀπολαῦσαι κ[α-
> θάπερ ὑπέδειξ[α], ὀ[ρέξ]ε[τα]ι νέος τις ὁ [μὴ
> μα[ιν]όμενος ἔτ[ι] το[ύ]το⟨υ⟩⁴⁰ καὶ τῆς ἀπε[ι]
> ρίας, οὐχ ὅ[τι] τῆς τοῦ γέροντος προσ[ποι-
> ήσεται ζω[ῆ]ς; ἔτι δὲ μειράκιον ἄφθ[ο-
> να περι[ποιήσ]εται τού[τ]ων ὥστε γε-
> γανωμένος ἀπέρχεσθαι κἂν ῾ρηθῆν[αι
> πλέ[ο]ν βεβιωκέναι τῶν ἀναπολαύσ-
> τ]ων [ὅσα διέ]ζων ἔτη. σιωπῶ γὰρ ὅ-
> τι] πολλάκι πολλοῖς τ[ῶ]ν ἀφρόνω[ν] τὸ
> νέ]ου[ς τελ]ε[υ]τῆσαι λυσ[ιτελέ]στερον
> φα]ίν[εται καὶ μ]ὴ κατὰ τὴν ἡλικίαν
> ε]ὐθ[ηνοῦσι] τραφῆν[αι οἴ]κοις, ἐν
> ἀ]δε[ίαι δὲ τρο]φῆς ἀ[φθονί]αν μ[. . .

But, it being possible in a certain limited amount of time to acquire for oneself the greatest of these good things and to enjoy it, as I have

---

⁴⁰ Bassi reads ἐπ[ὶ] το[ῦ]το.

shown, will any young man in his senses desire any longer[41] even time
without end, not to speak of aiming at the old man's (length of) life?
Even as a youth he will acquire such abundance of these (good things)
as to depart glowing with joy, and as one who can be said to have
been (truly) alive, far longer than those who never enjoyed any of the
years they (merely) lived through. For I say nothing of the fact that,
in many instances, dying young would seem more profitable for many
of the foolish, and not in their childhood to have been brought up in
such flourishing households and in no fear about abundance of nour-
ishment. . . . (13, 3–18)

For foolish people, of course, no length of time avails to produce joy
that will fulfill one in life, and indeed we might argue that they would
be better off dying younger and experiencing still less confusion and
evil. This sounds like the usual Epicurean severe line but in fact it
is not, because Philodemus makes an unusual concession even here.
This is that it is reasonable to be frustrated about having begun to
be philosophical about life and not having completed the process
because of an early death. The frustration of virtuous plans to study,
contemplate and be wise is a pain with which the Epicurean can
and should sympathize, though Philodemus has no sympathy with
the objection that death interrupts some plan merely to acquire more
knowledge:

τὸ δὲ ζητεῖν π[αρὰ ταύ]την
τὴν αἰ]τίαν ὡς [π]λεῖστον [χ]ρό[ν]ον ζῆν
εὔλο]γον καί τι[να]ς νέους τελευ-
(Col. 14)
τῶντας διὰ τοῦτο δυστυ[χ]εῖς νομίζειν. τὸ μὲν γάρ, ἵνα συντελέσηταί τ[ις
τὰς συνγ[ε]νικὰς καὶ φυσικὰ[ς] ἐπιθυμία[ς
καὶ πᾶσαν ἀπολάβη⟨ι⟩ τὴν ο[ἰ]κειοτάτην
ἢ] ἐνδέ[χ]εται διαγωγήν, ὀρέγεσθαι προσ-
βι]ῶναί τινα χρόνον, ὥστε πληρ[ω]θῆ-
ναι] τῶν ἀγαθῶν καὶ πᾶσα[ν] ἐκβαλεῖν
τὴ]ν κατὰ τὰς ἐπιθυμίας ὄ[χ]λησιν ἠ-
ρεμ]ίας μεταλαμβάνοντα, νοῦν ἔχον-
τός ἐ]στιν ἀνθρώπου· τὸ δ᾽ ἵνα τῆς
ἱστορ]ίας, πόσα δή ποτέ τις [π]ροσ[βιώσε-
τ᾽ ἔτη] κα[θ]άπερ ἐξὸν ταμ[ι]εῖον τοῦ
νοῦ παρ]α[π]λησίως τὸν ἀπέρ[αντον
κόσμ]ον σ[υμπεριέχε]ιν.

_____

[41] Or (Bassi) "in addition to this."

But attempting for this cause[42] to live as long as possible is reasonable and also to think of some that die young as unfortunate for this reason. For the wish (to live a while longer) that one may fulfill one's innate and natural desires and design an entire way of life as perfect for oneself as is possible, so as to be filled with good things and cast out all the trouble given by one's desires, receiving peace of mind in its place, is proper for an intelligent human being. But (to want this) in order that (we may fulfill a desire) for knowledge! How many extra years would a person need to live, as if it were possible anyway to hold the whole limitless cosmos in the storehouse (so to speak) of one's mind? (13.36–14.14)

Thus we see in a first instance what Philodemus will and will not admit as a legitimate and natural cause of pain in death. A desire to satisfy further one's greed for knowledge, which cannot humanly be entirely fulfilled—a desire belonging to the class of limitless desires which Epicurus deprecates like the desire for more sex or more power—is not to be acknowledged by the wise man. But that one has to die, and so break off one's studies before one has attained full philosophical happiness, is a cause of pain and can reasonably be called ill-fortune. Philodemus hopes that he knows the consolation here.

[ὧι]
δ'], ὥσπερ [ἐ]ξ[ὸν παρ]αμένοντ[α προκό]ψ[αι]
κ]ατὰ φιλοσοφία[ν] γ' ἁρπάζεσθαι δ[ει]-
νόν], φυσικ[ὸν] μὲν τ[ὸ ν]ύττες[θ]α[ι τ]ὸν το[ι]-   35
οῦ]τον· ὅτ[ι δ' ἄ]λλο[ι]ς εὐλογίαν παρα-
διδοὺς τοῦ [ὁμοίω]ς κατὰ φιλοσοφίαν
π[ρ]οκόψει[ν βεβίωκε], θαυμά[ζεθ' ὡς] ἀ-
γαθο[ῖς ἐντυχὼν πο]λὺ μείζο[σι, διδάσ-

(Col. 18)
καλ[ός τ' ἐκλή]θ[η] μυ[ρί]ων, ἀ[πίθ]ανον
δὲ ἐ[πιδεκ]τικὴν μακαρ[ίας] διαθέσ[ε-
ως ψυ[χὴν] μὴ τοιαύτην ε[ὐθέ]ως ὑπά[ρ]-
χειν ὥ[σ]τε [τοῖ]ς ἀξιολόγοις ἀ[γαθο]ῖς ἡ[ρ]μα-
τίσθαι, γεγ[ομέ]νην δὲ δὴ [τῶν] ἐκ φι-   5
λοσοφίας [λόγ]ων [ἴδριν] καὶ π[α]ντελῶς
οὐχ οἷόν τε [μὴ] περιδεδράχθαι θαυμά-
σιον ἀγαθό[ν, ὥ]στε γαυριάματος ἀπιέναι
μεστόν. πο[λὺ μ]ὲν οὖν κρεῖττο[ν] ἦν προ-
βάντα σοφ[ῶς νέ]ον ἀξίως τῆς φύ[σ]εως συν-   10
αυξηθῆν[αι καὶ] ἀ[π]ολαῦσαι τῆς δυνα-

---

[42] I.e., to enjoy wisdom, not merely to study for the sake of additional knowledge.

τωτάτω[ς ἐχούσης] εὐετηρ[ία]ς. ἀλλὰ
καὶ τὸ γει[τνιῶ]ν [χάριτος ἄ]ξιον πολ-
λῆς, καὶ τὰ τ[οιαῦτ᾿⁴³ οὐ] διαχ[εῖ]σθαι δ[ύνα]-⁴⁴
ται] τῶ <ι> χρόνῳ<ι> [ἀλλ᾿ ἀεί τ᾿ ἐπι]πολά-   15
ζει.

But as for the person to whom being taken away is a fearsome thing,
because he envisions the possibility of progress in philosophy, it is on
the one hand natural for such a one to feel pain.⁴⁵ But because, on
the other hand, he has lived handing along to others the confidence
to imitate his progress in philosophy, he is to be admired as achieving much greater good, and is to be called the teacher of myriads.
Nor is it probable, that a soul so capable of a blessed disposition does
not become strong enough immediately to be firmly grounded on all
the goods worthy of valuing, and indeed, having become experienced
in the arguments of philosophy, quite utterly incapable of any but a
complete grasp of so wondrous a joy in life, as to depart greatly exult-
ing. So therefore it is much better for a young man who has made
progress in wisdom to have matured in a way worthy of his nature
and to have enjoyed that happiness which is the most powerful that
there can be. But even a happiness less perfect⁴⁶ is worth great gratitude, and such things cannot be annihilated by time but keep their
value forever . . . (17.32–18.16)

Once more we can see the powerful rhetorical and emotional tone
as well as the avoidance of formal structure (especially in the casu-
ally constructed double negatives: "*Nor* is it probable, that a soul so
capable of a blessed disposition *does not* become strong enough . . . ").
As for the life of fools, he adds, it is miserable whether they die
young or old and might as well never have begun, and would be
better ended as quickly as possible—not, as we saw above, that the
Epicureans would ever advise suicide.

Again, Philodemus says (taking up the triumph one's inability to
defend oneself after death will give enemies), they give us a natural
pain—the pain he defines as anger, and considers a virtuous emotion if not accompanied by pleasure in revenge, in *de Ira*—while

---

⁴³ Bassi prints (and Scott's engraving clearly shows) τατ where Kuiper's conjecture requires τοι (in τοιαῦτ᾿).
⁴⁴ Diels, *spatio longius*; so I have shortened the line with οὐ for Kuiper's οὐκέτι.
⁴⁵ Again the idea of the natural pain, φυσικὸν δῆγμα, this time as νύττεσθαι, "to
be pricked, stabbed."
⁴⁶ Lit., "the neighboring thing," either as I translate with Kuiper, a less than
perfect happiness, or the "second prize" of being an inspiration to others; the text
as it stands is ambiguous.

alive, but in the first place we will not feel it, and in the second no one who knows a good man is his enemy, and it is only those who know us whose hatred is worth considering in any larger context than the here and now.

Next, he discusses the pain of dying childless and without heirs to perpetuate our memory, which he dismisses as unworthy of a wise person without difficulty. But, he adds, with startling emphasis, that does not mean we should be indifferent to the damage our family and friends may suffer from our loss. Indeed, "leaving behind parents or children or a spouse or others who are close to us, who will be in straits because of our death or even deprived of life's necessities, I admit brings with it a truly natural pang and can rouse flows of tears especially and like nothing else from a man of understanding mind . . .":

τὸ τοίνυν κα-
ταλείπειν γονεῖς ἢ παῖδα[ς] ἢ γα[μ]ε-
τὴν ἢ τινας ἄλλους τῶν ἐ[πι]τηδε[ί]-
ων, ἐν συμφο[ρ]αῖς ἐσομένο[υς] διὰ [τ]ὴν   5
καταστροφὴν ἡμῶν ἢ καὶ τ[ῶ]ν ἀν[αγ-
καίων ἐλλείψοντας, ἔχει μ[ὲ]ν ἀμέ-
λει φυσικώτατον δηγμὸν κα[ὶ δ]α[κ]ρύ-
ων προέσεις ἐγείρει τῶι νοῦν ἔχοντ[ι
μόνον ἢ μάλιστα. (25.2–10)

This time the bite, the δηγμός, is not only natural but "most natural," φυσικώτατος. It is in fact hard to see what more Philodemus could have said without abandoning a central position of Epicureanism, that serious evil does not happen to the wise, only endurable evil.[47] The tone of sympathy goes so far that I am not certain whether we can construe the νοῦν ἔχων, the man of understanding mind, to be the philosopher as well as the pupil. He might very well share his pupil's tears as well as condoning them, before attempting the consolation. A suggested consolation evidently followed,[48] but the text of the rest of col. 25 is too uncertain in my opinion to see quite

---

[47] This is concisely stated by Philodemus in *de Ira*: he is arguing that the wise man's anger, since he necessarily and naturally feels it—it too is natural, φυσική— cannot be a great evil to him. There *cannot* be a μέγα κακὸν καὶ τοῖς σοφοῖς . . . ὑπομενητόν, a non-trivial evil that even the wise must endure (*De Ira* 39.31–33).
[48] A δέ, that is, to answer the μέν in line 7.

what it was; clarity resumes only in the last line as Philodemus changes the topic to "pain over dying among foreigners."

Here too it turns out (col. 26) that this thought is naturally painful:

. ὅ]-
ταν δ᾽ ἐπὶ ξένης, φυσ[ικὸν] δη[. . . -
(Col. 26)
καὶ⁴⁹ φιλολόγοις κα[ὶ] μάλιστ᾽ ἐὰ[ν] γονεῖς
ἢ συγ[γ]ενεῖς ἄλλους ἐπὶ τῆς πατρίδος
ἀπολε[ί]πωσιν, ἀλλ᾽ ὥστε νύττειν μό-
ν]ον, ο[ὐ]χ ὥστε λύπην καὶ μεγάλην
ταύτην ἐπιφέρειν [κ]αταφερομένους
ἐπὶ τὰς ἐν τῶι ζῆν [πα]ρακολουθούσας
ἐ]πι ξένης [γῆ]ς δ[υ]σχρ[ησ]τίας.

> Now, when death occurs in a foreign land, it is natural . . . even for learned men⁵⁰ to feel a pang, and most of all if they leave parents or other family members at home, but only a pang, not such as to bring them in addition as they lie dying something that could truly be called a great grief, over and above the other difficulties that follow upon life in a foreign country. (25.37–26.6)

Here Philodemus is on less risky ground: he is certain that the "natural pang" in this case can be described as trivial and non-threatening to the wise person's happiness. He concludes eloquently (col. 27) that though it is better for the intellectual's reputation after death to have died in his city among friends as did the founders of the School, "yet even this belongs rather to people who debase themselves far enough to believe in the myths, unless indeed they are to believe that they will end up too far from the place allotted them in Hades."

In all these cases it important to see that the phrase "natural pang" is not thrown away. It is occasionally doubted that the Epicurean system could ascribe purpose to natural feelings without touching on the kind of teleology it rejected; but we need not doubt that the pain of illness, which makes us seek a doctor, the "natural pain" we

---

⁴⁹ Kuiper has δη[χθῆ-] ναι? At the end of col. 25, line 38, and beginning of col. 26, line 1; however, Bassi's picture of the papyrus (and his text) quite clearly shows col. 26 beginning with καὶ, not ναι.

⁵⁰ Kuiper's emendation would be brilliant if 26.1 did not in fact begin with KAI, so that we must read something like φυσ[ικὸν] δὴ [τοῦτο] καὶ φιλολόγοις and understand συμφοράζειν from the previous passage with τοῦτο. But certainly the notion of the φυσικὸν δῆγμα is present here also. By the *philologoi* Philodemus means people like himself, intellectuals living among the "barbarians" (as he later ventures to call his Roman audience; cf. n. 60 below).

should feel in anger (as opposed to the unnatural pleasure Aristotle was too willing to accept in it), which we feel in order to motivate the removal of wrong or injustice, and the pain caused by the "natural" aversion to death, which I would assume is there to keep us alive and must be taken account of even when death can no longer be avoided, are good things and natural in the sense that they are not alien to the good life.

Fortunately a text that perfectly explains "natural" as Philodemus and other Epicureans use it of emotions has been highlighted in recent discussion. In discussing the "natural anger" of *On Anger* cols. 39–40, John Procopé usefully cites the definitions of "natural" given by Philodemus' older contemporary Demetrius Laco:[51]

> φύσει γὰρ λέγεται ὁ ἄνθρωπος ποριστικὸς εἶναι τρο] φῆς,
> ἐπειδήπερ ἀδιαστρόφως, φύσει δὲ πόνων εἶναι δεκτικός,
> ἐπειδὴ κατηναγκασμένως, φύσει τὴν ἀρετὴν διώκειν,
> ἐπεὶ συμφερόντως, φύσει δὲ τὰς πρώτας τῶν ὀνομάτων
> ἀναφωνήσεις γεγονέναι λέγομεν, καθὸ [. . . (col. 67)

> . . . for "by nature" man is said to find himself food, since he does so by unperverted instinct, "by nature" to suffer pain, since it is compulsory; by nature to pursue excellence, since it is to our benefit, and "by nature" we say the first utterances of names occurred, since . . . (my translation)

The names were given "by nature" because they had "a direct, one-to-one correspondence with their objects,"[52] as we may infer from the *Letter to Herodotus*, 75f. The last three senses, Procopé argues, are obviously present in Philodemus' conception of "natural anger," φυσικὴ ὀργή, and he adds the first "may also have had its uses."[53] It seems just as necessary that all four should apply also to what Philodemus sympathetically and emphatically calls the various φυσικὰ δήγματα the wisest feel at the approach of death. Our instinct, compulsion, the true nature of the situation, and most of all our own

---

[51] John Procopé, "Epicureans on Anger," *Philanthropia kai eusebeia: Festschrift für Albrecht Dihle zum 70 Geburtstag*, ed. Glenn W. Most, Hubert Petersmann, Adolf Martin Ritter (Göttingen: Vandenhoeck & Ruprecht, 1993), 363–86 (372–73). Procopé cites *Demetrio Lacone: Aporie testuali ed esegetiche in Epicuro*, ed. Enzo Puglia, Marcello Gigante (Naples, Bibliopolis, 1988), 182f., col. 67. This quotation meets the objection that a "natural" emotion that serves for self-preservation, like anger and the fear of death, would imply an inappropriate and un-Epicurean teleology in nature like that of Aristotle or the Stoics.

[52] Procopé, 373.

[53] Procopé, 373 n. 39.

good—for our projects are good, and the fear of breaking them off serves as usefully to keep us alive and more as anger that enables us to repel insult—all conspire to justify "natural" grief.

The topics of pain at dying without winning glory in battle, but merely passively from disease (cols. 28–9), of pain at one's body suffering corruption in death (29–30), of pain at not being buried with the distinction due to one's rank or not being buried at all, for instance because one drowns at sea (30–33), by contrast do not call forth any sympathy from Philodemus. He treats them with humor and satire instead. But, as we saw, he sympathizes with the "natural distress" of those who are pained at the thought of death by unjust condemnation (33 fin.-35), a passage in which again he shows his consciousness of a mixed audience, for the proper stance of a wise man before tyrants or unjust judges was more the preserve of the Stoics. Philodemus is at pains, as we saw, to evolve a stance with which the wise man can defy his tormentors, but in thought only, without resorting to the Stoic but un-Epicurean device of taking refuge in suicide. Yet once more, we find that there is a φυσικὸν δῆγμα (π]άλιν δὴ συν[γ]νωστὸν ἂν δόξειε[ν] εἶναι τὸ λυπεῖσθαι, 33.36–34.1: "here again to be in pain is forgivable") in unjust condemnation, with which Philodemus expresses fiery sympathy. The wise man will find his consolation in his utter contempt for his judges, in his own perfect innocence, and in the thought of many before him who have borne injustice without fear, both famous philosophers and ordinary people. But there is no hint of the Stoic doctrine that suicide is always an option.

Philodemus' last topic among the fears of death is the fear that one will be forgotten, another φυσικὸν δῆγμα (these exact words are used, 35.36), 35 fin.-36. But here the "natural pang" is suffered only or mostly by fools, for it comes from a wasted life, that is, one without friends. The man who has had good friends will in the final analysis be able to die without them round him, for they are necessary for a good life, not a good death.

We see, therefore, that Philodemus has preempted the objection that he is unsympathetic to the breaking off of the plans and affections of a good human life by representing them as an evil which the Epicurean can admit and mitigate with argument. Evils occur in a good person's death, but no unendurable evil occurs. However, since Philodemus has conjured up so many deaths which have to be endured alone, without the philosopher's or any other friends' consolation and help, he concludes with a peroration, the finest thing in the treatise and (many have thought) in his entire surviving work, on the spirit in which such a lonely death is to be endured. He might have been expected to dwell on the familiar Epicurean consolation, the reflection on past pleasures which cannot be taken away but will always have happened. This is the theme on which Epicurus dwelt in his famous last letter, in which he told his friends he balanced his past pleasure in their company against the tortures of strangury which were killing him and found them endurable because of that thought.[54] In a different key it is used by Horace to describe to Maecenas how a man endures disaster, and it is interesting that Horace recommends daily contemplation:

> *Ille potens sui*
> *laetusque deget, cui licet in diem*
> *dixisse, "Vixi, cras vel atra*
> *nube polum pater occupato*
>
> *vel sole puro, non tamen irritum*
> *quodcumque retro est efficiet, neque*
> *diffinget, infectumque reddet*
> *quod fugiens semel hora vexit."*

He can spend his life self-possessed and happy, who can say day by day, "I have lived (today); tomorrow let the Father cover the pole with dark clouds or pure sunlight, nonetheless he cannot make vanish that which is past or render undone what the fleeting moment has once brought me." (*Carm.* 3.29.41–48)

Philodemus also has a theme of daily contemplation to recommend. He begins his peroration with a contrast between the fool and the wise person, which has been the theme also of everything that preceded in the discussion of objections to death: the fool's objections are always trivial, the wise man's important but capable of consolation. Thus he sums up everything we have from cols. 12–36:

> . .] πόλιν καὶ ἀσημόνως γε λυπούμενος
> πρὶν ἢ δυνατὸν εἴη ταῦτ' ἀναμαχέσα-
> σθαι, καὶ καθ' ἔσκατον χρόνον "εἰ τοῦτ' ἐ-
> πιδὼν γενόμενον, ἀπέθνη<ι>σκον, οὐκ ἂν
> ἐπεστρεφόμην τῆς τελευτῆς" λέγων,
> κἂν, εἰ θέλει τις, ὁ μετ' ὀλοφυρμοῦ βοῶν
> "ἐγὼ μὲν ἐκ τῶν ζώτων αἴρομαι, καὶ

---

[54] Diogenes Laertius 10.22.

πολλάκις ἀγαθὰ τοσαῦτ᾽ ὦ ἔχων καὶ δυ-
νάμενος ἀπολαύειν, ὁ δεῖνα δὲ καὶ ὁ δεῖ-
ν]α περιέσται." καὶ γὰρ βλέπεται δι᾽ ὧν   10
ὁ μὲν τεύξεται παραμυθίας, ὁ δ᾽ οὐδὲ
προσφωνήσεως ἀξιωθήσεται.

... and city, and with confused voice[55] lamenting that before he
could win these things back[56] (he was to die), and saying on
every occasion "If I were dying having seen this accomplished, I
would not be trying to avoid my end;" and then (compare with
him) if you like the person wailing and sobbing that "I am being
taken away from among the living, and that when I have many
times as many goods (sc. as this fellow or that) and can still
enjoy them, and this fellow or that will survive me;" and indeed
one can see the ways in which the one will find his consolation,
and the other be considered not even worthy of talking to. (37.1–12)

Clearly "the one" was a man with plans for "(his friends or family
and) city," though the beginning of the sentence is lost with the last
few lines of col. 46, and we finish the discussion of objections with
the general comment that all wishes to continue virtuous relationships and plans are worth consoling—and can be consoled. But
Philodemus' transition is to a much more original line of thought,
at least so far as we know, though of course Epicurus or Metrodorus
may have taken this stance in works now lost. He claims that the
real tower of strength for the wise person is *the day-by-day religious
contemplation of death itself*, kept up so energetically that it becomes the
foundation of a life in which every waking in the morning is a resurrection from the grave:

συνελόν-
τ[ι] δ᾽εἰπεῖν, ἀ[ν]ειρημένων τῶν μάλιστα
λυ]πεῖν ε[ἰ]θισ[μ]ένων, οὐδὲν κατ[[ατ]]επεί-
γ]ει τὰς τῶν παντοδαπῶς ἀδημονούν-   15
των καὶ ῥιπταζομένων προφάσεις
ἐκπεριοδε[ύ]ειν, εἰ κα[ὶ κ]ατὰ τὸ π[α]ραπῖ-
π[τ]ον ἀξιοῦνται λόγο[υ]. τὸ τοίνυν συν-
α[ρ]πάζεσθα[ι] θανάτου προσπίπτον-
τ[ο]ς, ὡς ἀπροσ[δο]κήτου τινὸς καὶ π[α]ρα-   20
δόξου συνα[ν]τῶντο[ς], ἡ[μεῖ]ν [μὲ]ν

---

[55] Gigante defends the text, but there are attractions to Gomperz' ἀσ⟨χ⟩ημόνως,
"gracelessly"—even given that this is said of the person Philodemus sympathizes
with, a relatively wise man in comparison with "the other."

[56] Or "made this loss good," "undone this damage" (LSJ s.v. ἀναμάχομαι).

οὐχί, γί]νετα[ι δ]ὲ περὶ τοὺς πλείστ[ου]ς
ἀγνοοῦν[τ]ας, ὅτι πᾶς ἄνθρωπος κ[ἂ]ν
ἰσ[χ]υρότερος ἦ[ι] τῶν Γιγάντων ἐφ[ήμ]ε-
ρός [ἐσ]τι πρὸς ζωὴν καὶ [τε]λευτήν, καὶ   25
ἄδ[ηλ]όν ἐ[στι]ν οὐ τὸ αὔ[ρι]ον μόν[ο]ν,
ἀλλὰ καὶ [τὸ αὐ]τίκα δή· [πά]ντες γὰ[ρ] ἀ-
τ<ε>ί[χισ]τον [πόλι]ν πρὸς θάνατον οἰκοῦ-
μεν [κ]αὶ πάν[τα] γέμει πο[ι]ητικῶν α[ὑ-
τοῦ παρά τε τ[ὴ]ν φυσικὴν σύστασι[ν, ἡ-]   30
μῶν οὕτως ἀ[σ]θενῶν ὄντων, κα[ὶ τ]ῆς
ψυχῆς ἑτοι[μο]τάτους π[ό]ρους εἰς [ἐ]κ-
πνοὴν ἐχούσ[ης] καὶ τοῦ [π]εριέχοντος
ἅμα τῆι τύχηι διακρίσεως ἡμων ἀ-
μύθητα <ὅσα ποιητικά> γεννῶντος καὶ πολλάκις ἅμα   35
νο[ή]ματι, καὶ πονηρίας ἀνθρώπων καὶ
ταῦ[τ]α καὶ πα[ρ’ αὐ]τοὺς δυ[σ]τόπαστα καὶ
πάμπολλ’ ὅσ[α] προσεπεισφερούσῃ[ς
ὥστ’, εἰ μή τίς ἐ[σ]τιν [ε]ὐτελέστατος, π[αρ-
άλ]ογον ἡγεῖσθαι κα[ὶ π]αράδοξ[ο]ν οὐ-   40
(Col. 38) κ εἰ τε[λ]ευτᾶ<ι> τις, ἀλλ’ εἰ διαμένει πρὸς
ποσὸν χρόνον, τὸ δὲ καὶ μέχρι γήρως
καὶ τερατωδέστατον. ἔνιοι δ’ οὕτως
εἰσὶν τὸν ἀνθρώπινον βίον παρω<ι>κηκό-
τες, οὐ χυδαῖοι μόνον, ἀλλὰ καὶ τῶν φι-   5
λοσοφεῖν δὴ λεγομένων, ὥστε καὶ δι-
α<τά>ττονται τοσαῦτα μὲν ἔτη διατρεί-
ψειν Ἀθήνησιν φιλομαθοῦντες, το[σ]αῦ-
τα δὲ τὴν Ἑλλάδα καὶ τῆς βαρβάρου
τὰ δυνατὰ θεωροῦντες, τοσαῦτα δὲ   10
οἴκοι διαλεγόμενοι, τὰ δὲ λοιπὰ με-
τὰ τῶν γνωρίμων· "ἄφνω δ’ ἄφαντον
προσέβα μακρᾶς ἀφαιρούμενον ἐλπίδας τὸ Χρεών." ὁ δὲ νοῦν ἔχων ἀπει-
ληφὼς ὅ[τι] δύναται πᾶν περιποιῆσαι   15
τ]ὸ πρὸς εὐδαίμονα βίον αὔταρκες, εὐ-
θὺς ἤδη τὸ λοιπὸ[ν] ἐντεταφιασμένος περιπατεῖ κα[ὶ] τὴν μίαν ἡμέραν
ὡς αἰῶνα κερδα[ί]νει, παραιρουμένης
δὲ οὔτε [σ]τενάζων, εἰ[ι] οὕτως ἐλλείπων   20
τι τοῦ κ[ρ]ατίστου β[ί]ου συνακολουθεῖ προ-
θα[νοῦσ]ι καὶ τὴν ἐκ τοῦ χρ[ό]νου προσθή-
κ]ην ἀξιο[λόγ]ως ἀ[π]ολαβὼν ὡς παραδό-
ξω<ι> συνκε[κ]υρηκὼς εὐτυχία[ι κ]αὶ κα[τ]ὰ
τ[ο]ῦτο το[ῖς] πράγμασιν εὐχα[ρ]ιστεῖ.

So to put it briefly, since the things that customarily give the most pain have been discussed, there is no urgent need for a complete sur-

vey of the excuses of men in every kind of way tormented and thrash-
ing about, though they may occasionally be worthy of notice. But at
any rate, to be caught unprepared when death comes upon us by
chance, as though it were meeting us as a thing unexpected and paradoxical, does not happen to us[57] but does happen to most men, ignorant as they are that every human being, were he stronger even than
the Giants, is an ephemeral creature in his life and his death, and it
isn't just tomorrow that is uncertain but the right-here-and-now. For
we all inhabit "an unwalled city"[58] where death is concerned and all
things are full of its causes, both according to our physical makeup,
since we are so weak, and our soul has so many passages by which
to breathe out and leave us, and because the world around us gen-
erates innumerable causes of dissolution that attack us as swift as chance
and frequently as swift as thought,[59] and there is the wickedness of
mankind that brings on us in addition both these roads to death and
others impossible for themselves to guess at and innumerable; so that
unless a person is the greatest of fools, he might well think the absurd
and paradoxical thing to be not that one should die, but that he should
stay here some little while, and his lasting it out to old age a wonder
and a miracle. But some have dwelt in human life as such aliens in
it, not just ordinary men but some at any rate called philosophers,
that they draw up plans to spend so many years at Athens in the pursuit of learning, so many years seeing Greece and what is accessible
of barbarian lands,[60] so many years back at home in philosophical dialogue and the rest with their circle of friends—"and suddenly, unnoticed," Necessity "comes forward, cutting off our long hopes."[61] But

---

[57] Epicureans and philosophical people in general.

[58] A quotation from Epicurus (or Metrodorus): see Gigante's excellent note, "La
chiusa" 194–97.

[59] ἅμα νοήματι, the usual Epicurean phrase for instantaneous events like the
"atomic swerve" (*Ep. Herod.* 61). It is sometimes used just to mean "quickly" or
"instantly" (e.g. *Ep. Herod.* 83), but I like the more dramatic implication here: death
can be as instantaneous as the atomic swerve, itself in Epicurean dogma an event
taking the smallest conceivable instant of time. Of course only an Epicurean would
appreciate the full meaning.

[60] A pleasant joke aimed at his Roman audience; Philodemus is describing his
own life-story, which took him from Athens to the "barbarians" of Italy and left
him resigned to dying among them; see n. 49 above. For this use of the word "barbarian" to refer to Roman audiences listening to Greek works of literature, my col-
league Timothy Moore compares this usage in Plautus, e.g. *As.* 11, *Tri.* 19, *Mi.*
211; cf. Gonzalez Lodge, *Lexicon Plautinum* (Leipzig: B. G. Teubner, 1924–1930,
reprint: Hildeshim, NY: G. Olms, 1971), s.v. *barbarus*.

[61] From some verses from an unknown tragedy, recited by the actor Neoptolemus
before Philip II of Macedon not long before his murder (*ap.* Diodorus Siculus
16.92.3):

φρονεῖτε νῦν αἰθέρος ὑψηλότερον
καὶ μεγάλων πεδίων ἀρούρας,
προνεῖθ᾽ ὑπερβαλλόμενοι

the man of sense, when he has come to understand that he can attain
that which is self-sufficient to a happy life, from that point on walks
about as one already laid out for burial in his shroud (ἐντεταφιασμένος)
and enjoys every single day as if it were a whole era, and when that
is taken from him, goes forth (to die) not mourning, that thus, having somehow missed something that belongs to the best possible life,
he joins the company of those who have died before. And all supplement to his time, he receives as in reason, he ought, as one who
has lighted upon an unexpected piece of good fortune, and gives thanks
accordingly to—the facts (τοῖς πράγμασιν εὐχαριστεῖ).[62] (37.12–38.25)

θεῶν δόμους, ἀφροσύνα
πρόσω βιοτὰν τεκμαιρόμενοι·   5
ὃ δ᾽ ἀμφιβάλλει ταχύπουν
κέλευθον ἕρπων σκοτίαν,
ἄφνω δ᾽ἄφαντος προσέβα
μακρὰς ἀφαιρούμενος ἐλπίδας
θνατῶν πολύμοχθος ῞Αιδας.   10
[4 F. G. Schmidt: δόμων δόμους MSS, νόμους R. Methner]

Think now things higher than highest heaven,
aspire to boundless plains of earth,
think, rising in pride above
the gods' own houses, in folly
judging your life extended far:
yet He ambushes you, swiftly
walking His shadowy path,
and suddenly, unnoticed, arrives,
cutting off our long hopes,
the Woe of mortals, Hades. (Nauck adesp. 127 = Snell *TrGF* II.127).

Philodemus as an Epicurean substitutes Necessity (τὸ Χρέων) for Hades in his quotation. But the text is difficult, and Gigante reconstructs 3–6 as

προνεῖθ᾽ ὑπερβαλλόμενοι
δόμοις δόμους ("trying to excel houses with houses"), ἀφροσύνα
πρόσω βιοτὰν τεκμαιρόμενοι·   5
⟨τ⟩ὸ δ᾽ ἀμφιβάλλει ταχύπουν ⟨Χρέων⟩
("but swift-footed Necessity ambushes him")
κέλευθον ἕρπον σκοτίαν

so that both subjects, Necessity and Hades, will be present in the original ("La
Chiusa" 206–211, with a valuable commentary on the fragment and Horatian parallels which seem to show that Horace knew the passage well, perhaps through
Philodemus). Perhaps the way in which the article, adjective and noun "surround"
the verb in line 6 in Gigante's reading in pictorial word arrangement argues for
it, as does the more regular distribution of the two adjectives between Necessity
and the path.

[62] For thanksgivings to Nature, if not to the gods, the model for the school was
Epicurus: "Thanks be to blessed Nature, because she has made what is necessary
easy to supply and what is not easy unnecessary." Fr. 67 Bailey = fr. 22.1 Arr.[2]
(χάρις τῇ μακαρίᾳ Φύσει ὅτι τὰ ἀναγκαῖα ἐποίησεν εὐπόριστα, τὰ δὲ δυσπόριστα οὐκ
ἀναγκαῖα). I assume that by τὰ πράγματα here Philodemus means the same thing
as ἡ φύσις, i.e., "external reality."

This is an amazing passage: for Philodemus, the Epicurean man or woman achieves, because of his or her exact awareness of death, a daily resurrection from the dead. The religious imagery of death and resurrection, which was popular in mystery religions to describe the initiatory experiences of new adherents and which Christians later used to assert their convictions about the unique eschatological experience of Jesus of Nazareth, is seized upon by Philodemus to portray what the Epicureans can experience on a daily basis. It is to go to bed as if wrapped in one's shroud (ἐντεταφιασμένος) every night, and wake up resurrected every day. It is a secular, and yet equally religious, counterpart to Paul's "always bearing about in the body the death (νέκρωσιν) of Jesus, that also the life of Jesus in our body might be made manifest" (2 Cor. 4:10–11).[63]

These long, sure-footed rhetorical periods are unique in Philodemus' surviving work, and so is the sustained, profound and tranquil emotion they convey. Philodemus now pours one last vial of scorn on the fool, who ignores the nature of things and his own death, and is always making futile plans to the last minute, pushing away and ignoring his intuitions (ἐπιβολαί, 39.7) of the dreadful truth till too late. But this contrast is merely to heighten his final definition of wisdom and religious courage in the face of death—and a still greater rhetorical and poetic triumph:

οἱ δὲ φρενήρεις κ[ἄν] δ[ι]ά τι-	15
νος αἰτίας ἀναγκαίας ἀν[υπο]νόητοι	
γένωνται τοῦ τάχ᾽ ἤδη σ[υ]γκυρή[σ]ειν	
τὴν τοῦ β[ί]ου παραγραφήν, [ὅ]ταν ἐν ὄμ-	
ματι γένεται, περ[ι]οδεύσαντες ἀρρή-	
τως τοῖς ἀ[γ]νοοῦσιν ὀξύτα[τ]α καὶ τὸ	
πά]ντων ἀπολε[λ]αυκέν[αι] καὶ τὸ	20
τ[ε]λέαν αὐτοὺς ἐπιλαμβάνειν ἀναισ-	
θ[ησ]ίαν οὕτως ἀκαταπλήκτως ἐκπνέ-	
ο[υσι]ν, ὡς ε[ἰ] μηδὲ τὸν ἐλάχιστον χρό-	
ν[ον] ἐγλείπουσαν ἔσχον τ᾽ν ἐπιβολήν.	25

ΦΙΛΟΔΗΜΟΥ ΠΕΡΙ ΘΑΝΑΤΟΥ
ΤΟ Δ᾽

---

[63] I must thank John Fitzgerald for reminding me of this parallel and pointing me to his excellent discussion of it in his *Cracks in an Earthen Vessel: An Examination of the Catalogues of Hardships in the Corinthian Correspondence*, SBL Dissertation Series 99 (Atlanta: Scholars, 1988).

But with persons of stable mind, even if through some unavoidable cause they were unsuspecting in advance of the fact that already the *paragraph and limit* of their life was approaching, when it comes into actual view, they *summing up in one period systematically*, and with keenest vision (in a way that is a mystery unexplainable to the ignorant),[64] their own complete enjoyment of life and the utter unconsciousness that is to come over them, breathe their last as calmly, as if they had never put aside their view[65] for an instant of time.

PHILODEMUS ON DEATH BOOK FOUR

Here Philodemus gives his audience one last surprise. He has shown them that he can compose rhetorical periods the equal of any rhetorician's in support of his grand idea, and rising to its religious dignity in structure. This time, in finishing off the explanation of his idea of the right religious attitude to death with a reference to Epicurean philosophy as itself the true religious mystery and initiation, he brings in two new elements, one a necessary reference to the technicalities of Epicurean philosophy (yet one couched in terms easily intelligible to the whole audience), and the other a brilliant piece of self-reference characteristic of the higher reaches of Hellenistic poetry, although not so much of prose.

The technicality is the reference to the φανταστικὴ ἐπιβολὴ τῆς διανοίας, which is the Epicurean equivalent of what old-fashioned Catholics used to call an "act of attention." If not Epicurus himself, who used the words in nearly this sense, then certainly his followers (and among them Philodemus) made this "act of attention or concentration of the mind upon a notion" exactly parallel in the sensual world with fixing one's eyes carefully upon an object and observing it accurately, a criterion of truth.[66] It seems, from a par-

---

[64] Notice the characteristic Epicurean metaphor, so common in Lucretius, of clear mental presentation throughout this sentence, contrasted with the dim and confused grasp of the common man of the images that he chooses to focus on in his dishonesty and fear; also the imagery of religious initiation. This of course is already in Epicurus, for whom the philosophy he preaches is an initiation (*Epistle to Herodotus* 36: a person who knows the philosophy perfectly is "an initiate in its mysteries," ὁ τετελεσιουργημένος, 83: a person making progress in it is ἀποτελούμενος . . . πρὸς γαληνισμόν, "being initiated . . . toward calm of mind").

[65] To the concept "death." One brings things up in mind by an "imaginative act of attention" (φανταστικὴ ἐπιβολὴ τῆς διανοίας), according to the Epicureans.

[66] Diogenes Laertius 10.31 says that later Epicureans added this to the criteria of truth, and sure enough Philodemus (*On Signs and Inferences* fr. 1 De Lacey) lists it among them. A classic discussion is Cyril Bailey, *Epicurus: the Extant Remains* (Oxford: Clarendon Press, 1926), 259–74. It is relevant to our passage that one of the chief contexts for the use of this criterion is religious, the contemplation of the

allel passage in Philodemus' *De Dis*, to have been *when directed to spiritual truths* an important spiritual act, for "the most continual focusing, (συνεχεστάτη ἐπιβολή) on goods past present and to come" is there apparently said to be a support to the wise man's piety (*De Dis* 3, col. 2.23–27). This "most continual focusing" is what Philodemus describes again here—a focusing on the truth of death that even when left aside for a time is so effective that when death itself appears it is as if its contemplation had never been suspended. The fool's ἐπιβολαί or "focusings" on death were only such as all of us have, momentary and such as he could push away (ἀπωθεῖν); the wise man willingly takes the contemplation of death into himself permanently, and is fortified and made happy. When death comes, it is as if his clear contemplation had never been suspended at all; for μηδὲ τὸν ἐλάχιστον χρόν[ον] ἐγλείπουσαν, "never suspended for the least instant of time" and συνεχεστάτη in *De Dis* 3, "most continual" mean the same thing. Those who knew the Epicurean system would have seen exactly what Philodemus meant. But for those of his audience who did not know the technical term, the description of continual, unbroken, intense "attention" (for that is what the word means in ordinary Greek also) as opposed to uneasy apprehensions we push away would have been quite enough.

But to Philodemus' solemn theme of the contemplation of death, since he says it leads to lightheartedness and enjoyment of life, it is fitting that a note of amusement and wit should be added, just to prove he smiles while he says this. And this is the second original note struck here: the daring, self-referential Hellenistic literary joke of the last sentence. My emphasis in the translation makes clear the puns. If the man sees approaching the παραγραφή, that is, (a) the circumscription and close of his own life and (b) the end of the paragraph *and* the treatise as well as (c) the *paragraphé* mark the scribe is

---

gods as they actually are and must be, and that Lucretius uses the Latin translation *animi iactus* to describe the bold adventure of contemplating the infinity of the universe outside our cosmos: *De rerum nat.* 2.1044–47, cf. on the same subject Cicero *Nat. D.* 1.54 *se iniciens animus et intendens* (derived from Philodemus). Modern literature tends to deal with the logic of *prolepsis* by preference and leave the question of "focusing" a little to the side. Cf. A. A. Long and D. N. Sedley, *The Hellenistic Philosophers* (Cambridge: Cambridge University Press, 1987), 1.88–90, where "focusing" is glossed rather unexcitingly, "that we can test a theory about external objects *merely* by closing our eyes and examining them" (90; authors' italics). Bailey seems to me to have shown conclusively that a more intense act of intellection and understanding than that is intended.

about to put at the end of this treatise along with the subscription, then he can (a) look systematically round his life and (b) sum up his life in one periodic sentence (as Philodemus is doing)—περιοδεύω also can mean either thing. One imagines Philodemus holding up his manuscript smiling and pointing, to the blank at the bottom of the page, the symbol of the blankness of death.[67]

We can be sure that is what he is doing, because not only do other authors follow him in this, he does it in his own poetry. My friend Jeffrey Fish pointed out Seneca *Ep.* 77.20, where he concludes the epistle with a similar joke about the *clausula* or concluding periodic rhythm both of a sentence and a life:

> *quomodo fabula, sic vita non quam diu, sed quam bene*
> *acta sit, refert; nihil ad rem pertinet, quo loco desinas;*
> *quocumque voles desine; tantum bonam clausulam impone.*

> As in a play, so in life, not how long but how well acted is the point; it is nothing to the point in which place/passage you stop; stop where you like; only give it a good concluding rhythm.

And indeed Seneca does, because *clausulam impone* gives us the favorite of all concluding rhythms in formal prose, cretic + iamb. (There is a similar joke about *clausula* and death at *Ep.* 66.48.) Of course Horace, Philodemus' admirer, has his own version: the brilliant concluding line of *Ep.* 1.16:

> *hoc ait, moriar: mors ultima linea rerum*

> He means, I think, "I can die": death is the final limit.

But Philodemus himself, in an epigram probably placed at the end of a book of love poems (AP 11.41 = 4 Sider), plays the same trick with the *coronis* or final mark at the end of a book. "Seven years are added to my thirty pages (σέλιδες) already torn out of my life; now the white locks cover my head, Xanthippe, the messengers of adult age. Yet here I am still with singing gossip and revels, and

---

[67] In a similar way William Empson arranged in his *Collected Poems* (NY: Harcourt Brace, 1949, 60–61) that his 21-line poem "Ignorance of Death" should be printed across two facing pages, so that the last stanza,

> Otherwise I feel very blank upon this topic,
> And think that though important, and proper for anyone to bring up,
> It is one that most people should be prepared to be blank upon.

stands above six-sevenths exactly of a blank page.

fire rages still in my unquenchable heart; but Muses, write the *coro-nis* itself right away, the *coronis*, my Ladies, of my folly:"

αὐτὴν ἀλλὰ τάχιστα κορώνιδα γράψατε, Μοῦσαι,

ταύτην ἡμετέρης, δεσπότιδες, μανίης (7–8).[68]

Instead of writing in the easy way he usually did to address his audience of believers, Philodemus accepted the difficulties of casting his thoughts into protreptic rhetorical form so he could be "all things to all men" and convince them that Epicureanism offered the best therapy for the fear of death. By so doing, he actually brought himself into a better and more convincing line of argument than even Lucretius himself discovered in his diatribe on death in book 3. It is one that would have answered almost all of objections of the modern writers on "Epicurus and Lucretius on death:" that the school's arguments are based too much on the symmetry topos; that they leave too little room to risk one's happiness in concern and love for friends, family and country; that they discourage caring about or planning for what is to follow after death for one's loved ones; and especially that they are unsatisfying in regard to one's own selfish desires for permanence on earth. Philodemus spurns the symmetry argument as poor therapy and only usable in an ancillary role. He considers that one's natural involvement with family, friends and country are meant to keep one alive and that the pain at breaking them off is natural and right. As for the protest that none of this satisfies our individual desire merely to keep existing, he offers an impressive solution, with every emotional decoration of poetry and rhetoric he can contrive, although modern minds might think it too religious and contemplative in tone. This is the argument that the continual *meditatio mortis* he recommends is the only attitude that can give to the experience of life itself true, reliable and intense joy.

Nor has Philodemus departed at all from what is suggested by the (for him) sacred text of Epicurus himself. After all, what does the train of thought I have described do, except flesh out some suggestions

---

[68] Several of these parallels arc already cited by Gigante *ad loc.* ("La chiusa" 233) and by Kaibel in his edition of "Philodemus" epigrams, and Kuiper before him. Cf. also W. Schmid, "Contritio und 'ultima linea rerum' in neuenepikureiscen Texten," *RhM* 100 (1957) 301–327. Sider's commentary and translation take Xanthippe "herself" (αὐτήν) to be "this coronis," which may be right but does not affect my point. See also Obbink, *Philodemus: On Piety*, pt. 1, 90–94.

that are already there in Epicurus' surviving writings? Epicurus himself says that the wise man will feel grief and mental pain at his
own death and his friends' deaths. All this is in the three words,
λυπηθήσεσθαι τὸν σοφόν (Diogenes Laertius 10.119). He also says that
the wise man "will be more susceptible of emotions [presumably the
natural emotions as we have just defined them] than other men; but
that will be no hindrance at all to his wisdom" (117). In other words,
the truer his vision of life, the more deeply and authentically he will
grieve for whatever damage his friends' death and his own does to
their sacred κοινωνία, their communion in friendship, love and projects, and the more complete his human happiness and wisdom will
be nonetheless.[69] And as for the continual religious meditation on
death making life more joyous and worthwhile, that is merely a more
emotional and emphatic way of saying what is already in the *Epistle
to Menoeceus* (124): συνέθιζε δὲ ἐν τῷ νομίζειν μηδὲν πρὸς ἡμᾶς εἶναι τὸν
θάνατον . . . ὅθεν γνῶσις ὀρθὴ τοῦ μηθὲν εἶναι πρὸς ἡμᾶς τὸν θάνατον·
ἀπολαυστὸν ποιεῖ τὸ τῆς ζωῆς θνητόν, "*practice yourself in/accustom yourself to* the belief that death is nothing to us . . . for right knowledge
that death is nothing to us makes the very mortality of life an enjoy-
able thing." It seems that the modern debate about Epicurean views
of death has been so far quite impoverished without Philodemus'
brilliant sermons on these simple texts from Epicurus.

---

[69] One might say that this way of describing the mental pain that is a natural
qualification of the wise man's happiness is the parallel of the better known contention that he is "happy" even in extreme physical pain: "Even on the rack the
wise man is happy . . . however, when on the rack he will give vent to both cries
and groans." Mental pain is also "natural" in the sense that it arises from an unper-
verted instinct and by compulsion, and does good, since it gives relief and is perfectly in correspondence with the situation.

PHILODEMUS ON THE PLAIN SPEAKING
OF THE OTHER PHILOSOPHERS[1]

Diskin Clay

Abstract

Philodemus was the author of a history of philosophy entitled *The Ordering of the Philosophers*. Histories of the Academic and Stoic Philosophers are a part of this larger work. He was also the author of sharply polemical treatises against other philosophers, among which *On the Stoics* stands out for its hostile engagement and partisan sarcasm. Since Domenico Comparetti's edition of Philodemus' history of the Stoic philosophers, the contrast between his treatment of the Stoics in these two treatises has been well appreciated. What has not been appreciated is the explanation of this contrast. I argue that Philodemus' twin treatises, *Academicorum Historia* and *Stoicorum Historia*, lack the polemical engagement and vigor of a work like *On the Stoics* because they reflect his interest in philosophical proselytizing and education so impressively displayed in his *On Frank Criticism* (Περὶ παρρησίας). This essay probes into the connections between this work and Philodemus' histories—not of Academic and Stoic philosophy—but of the Academic and Stoic philosophers as educators and practitioners of the art of παρρησία.

---

[1] Texts: Philodemus, *The Stoics*: Tiziano Dorandi, "Filodemo, Gli Stoici (PHerc. 155e 339)," *CErc* 12 (1982) 91–133; *Academicorum Historia*: Siegfried Mekler, *Academicorum philosophorum index Herculanensis* (Berlin: Widemann, 1902; repr. 1958); Konrad Gaiser, *Philodems Academica: Die Berichte über Platon und die Alte Akademie in zwei herkulanensischen Papyri* (Stuttgart: Bad Connstatt: Fromman-Holzboog, 1988; Tiziano Dorandi, *Filodemo, Storia dei Filosofi: Platone e l'Academia (PHerc. 1021 e 164)*, La Scuola di Epircuro 12 (Naples: Bibliopolis, 1991); *Stoicorum Historia*: Domenico Comparetti, "Papiro ercolanese inedito," *Rivista di Filologia e di Istruzione Classica* 3 (1875): 449–555; Wilhelm Crönert, *Kolotes und Menedemos* (Munich: Müller, 1906; repr. Amsterdam: Hakkert, 1965); Augusto Traversa, *Index Stoicorum Herculanensis* (Genoa: Instituto di filologia classica, 1952); Tiziano Dorandi, *Filodemo, Storia dei Filosofi: La Stoá da Zenone a Panezio (PHerc. 1018)*, Philosophia antiqua 60 (Leiden: Brill, 1994); *On Plain Speaking*: (*Philodemi* Περὶ παρρησίας *libellus*) ed. Alexander Olivieri (Leipzig: Teubner, 1914). I cite Philodemus on "Gli Stoici," the Academic, and Stoic philosophers in the editions of Dorandi; *On Plain Speaking* in the edition of Olivieri, helped by the joint work of David Konstan, Diskin Clay, Clarence E. Glad, Johan C. Thom, and James Ware, *Philodemus On Frank Criticism* SBLTT 43 (Atlanta: Scholars, 1998)—all translations of Περὶ παρρησίας are from this version; *De Ira: Filodemo, L'ira*, ed. Giovanni Indelli, La Scuola di Epicuro 5 (Naples: Bibliopolis, 1988).

Philodemus' Ordering of the Philosophers
(ἡ τῶν φιλοσόφων Σύνταξις)

Other than his epigrams, which Cicero mentions admiringly in his speech against Piso (*In Pisonem* 68–72), and which bear an attribution to Philodemus in the *Palatine Anthology*, the only work for which Philodemus was known in antiquity and in early modern Europe was a work of at least ten books entitled ἡ τῶν φιλοσόφων Σύνταξις.[2] Since the painful and sometimes destructive sectioning and unrolling of the papyri of the library of the Villa dei Papiri, other works unmentioned by later authors have become better known than this work, which we shall entitle *The Ordering of the Philosophers*.[3] Philodemus' *Rhetoric* and *On Methods of Inference* have been well studied and recently his *On Death, On Poems*, and *On Music* have been the subject of intense interest.[4] Interest in the philosophical part of Philodemus' *On Piety* will dramatically increase now that Dirk Obbink has restored the ordering of the columns of the two sections into which the original papyrus was divided and presented the text in an admirable edition, translation, and commentary.[5]

Yet an understanding of the organization and scope of *The Ordering of the Philosophers* has remained out of reach. Tiziano Dorandi, who has edited two of the books that must have belonged to it and Philodemus' polemical treatise *On the Stoics*, which he rightly thinks did not, has clearly set out the history and the problems of recovering the plan of the work as a whole from the evidence of the

---

[2] Diog. Laert. 10.3, who cites book 10 as containing evidence for Epicurus having inspired (αὐτῷ προτρεψαμένῳ) his three bothers to join his philosophical community. Cicero's remarks come in *In Pisonem* 70–71. Twenty-nine epigrams are collected in Denys Lionel Page, *Epigrammata Graeca* (Oxford: Clarendon, 1975), 291–300. Some were edited by Marcello Gigante in *Filodemo: Epigrammi scelti* (Naples: Bibliopolis, 1970; 2nd ed. Naples: Bibliopolis 1989). They are now edited as a whole and translated by David Sider, *The Epigrams of Philodemos* (Oxford: Oxford University Press, 1997).

[3] It has long gone under the Italian title "La rassegna ['muster' or 'review'] dei filosofi di Filodemo."

[4] The recent interest in these is well documented in *ANRW* 2.36.4 (1990), both in Tiziano Dorandi, "Filodemo: gli orientamenti della ricerca attuale" (2329–68) and Elizabeth Asmis, "Philodemus' Epicureanism" (2369–2460). To these one should add the collection of essays in *Philodemus & Poetry: Poetic Theory & Practice in Lucretius, Philodemus, & Horace*, ed. Dirk Obbink (Oxford: Oxford University Press, 1995), and the important edition of Philodemus' *On Poems* V to which many of these essays are indebted, Cecilia Mangoni, *Filodemo: Il quinto libro della Poetica (PHerc. 1425 e 1538)*, La scuola di Epicuro 14 (Naples: Bibliopolis, 1993).

[5] Dirk Obbink, *Philodemus: On Piety, Part 1* (Oxford: Oxford University Press, 1996).

Herculaneum papyri. His conclusion: its plan remains an enigma.[6]

Two observations need to be made both on the Σύνταξις and on the scholarship devoted to it. As for the work itself, as we know it best from Philodemus' twin histories of the Academic and Stoic philosophers, it is most remarkable for its conspicuous lack of polemic and partisan zeal. Domenico Comparetti, who edited Philodemus' history of the Stoic philosophers in 1875, justly observed that it shows no signs of having been written by an Epicurean.[7] Both Theodor Gomperz and Siegfried Mekler, who edited Philodemus' history of the Academic philosophers under the title *Academicorum Index Herculanensis*, note the dispassionate and "colorless" character of Philodemus' treatment of both Academic and—more surprisingly—Stoic philosophers.[8] As for the scholarship devoted to *The Ordering of the Philosophers*, it is equally remarkable that it has concentrated on associating the papyri that might have been a part of this ambitious work but has left those papyri deemed ineligible for consideration in its penumbra. That is, Philodemus' history of the Academic and Stoic philosophers has not been integrated into his fuller production as a philosopher and historian of philosophy and education in philosophy. It is true, as Marcello Gigante has suggested, that Philodemus' large aim in these histories of philosophy was to integrate Epicurean philosophy into the long history of Greek philosophy and to present it in this context to his own age and to the elite of his adopted country.[9] In this, his project coheres with the nearly contemporaneous projects of Lucretius and Cicero, who saw themselves as the first Romans to convey to their fellow Romans in adequate Latin the message of Epicurean and Greek philosophy. The result of both the disengaged attitude of the author of these histories and the concentration of

[6] In "Filodemo storico del pensiero antico," *ANRW* 2.36.4 (1990) 2407–23, giving a summary of an earlier characterization in *Rendiconti dell'Accademia di Archeologia, Lettere e Belle Arti di Napoli* 55 (1980) 31–49. Elizabeth Asmis also gives a catalogue of the works she takes to belong to the Σύνταξις in "Philodemus' Epicureanism," *ANRW* 2.36.4 (1990) 2374 n. 20, as does Michael Erler in "Epikur," *Die Philosophie der Antike*, 4.1: *Die hellenistische Philosophie*, ed. Hellmut Flashar, Grundriss der Geschichte der Philosophie (Basel: Schwabe, 1994), 297–301.

[7] "Papiro ercolanese inedito," 471.

[8] Gomperz in *Jenaer Literaturzeitung* 2 (1875): 604 (as reported by Dorandi, "Filodemo storico del pensiero antico," 2422); Mekler in *Academicorum Index*, xxxi–xxxii. The observation is made once again by Asmis, "Philodemus' Epicureanism," 2376.

[9] *Philodemus in Italy*, trans. Dirk Obbink (Ann Arbor: University of Michigan Press, 1987) 40; cf. Dorandi, "Filodemo storico del pensiero antico," 2422–43.

scholars on the other writings of Philodemus only as these might be seen as part of the Σύνταξις is that the character and purpose of this history have still to be fully understood.

I do not claim to understand the structure and contents of the Σύνταξις as a whole. We have significant evidence for Philodemus' histories of only two schools, which pick up, as is usual for the Herculanean papyri, only well into the argument. Nor do I claim to understand fully Philodemus' motives for composing this history—not of Greek philosophy—but of Greek philosophers. But a reading and review[10] of Dorandi's scrupulous new editions of Philodemus' histories of the Academic and Stoic philosophers suggests that these works lack the polemical edge found, for example, in his tract *On the Stoics*, his treatment of the *Politeiai* of Zeno of Kition and Diogenes of Sinope. The histories lack this polemical character precisely because they were part of an educational project visible in *On Frank Criticism* (Περὶ παρρισίας), his biography of Epicurus, his tract *On Anger*, his treatise *On Flattery*,[11] and in his *Philosophy in Action*, a work I have referred to—with due reverence—as Philodemus' "Acts of the Epistle."[12] In this case study of philosophy as it manifests itself not in theory but in action, the epistles in question are the letters of Epicurus.[13] The inclusion of letters as evidence for a philosopher's life and philosophy as his philosophy exhibits itself in action might, as Graziano Arrighetti has suggested,[14] be Philodemus' contribution to the tradition initiated in Peripatetic biography. In this biographical mode, the subjects of biography are pressed into service to provide the biographer with the evidence for their own lives. In a sense, such biography is autobiographical. In this study, I will focus on Philodemus' treatments of Academic and Stoic philosophers and their relation to

---

[10] Review of Tiziano Dorandi, *Filodemo, Storia dei Filosofi: La Stoá da Zenone a Panezio (PHerc. 1018)* in *AJP* 118 (1996): 146–49.

[11] Studied by Tristano Gargiulo, "PHerc. 222: Filodemo sull'adulazione," *CErc* 11 (1981): 103–27, Francesca Longo Auricchio, "Sulla concezione filodemea dell'adulazione," *CErc* 16 (1986): 79–92, and Clarence E. Glad, "Frank Speech, Flattery, and Friendship in Philodemus," in *Friendship, Flattery, and Frankness of Speech*, ed. John T. Fitzgerald, NovTSup 82 (Leiden: Brill, 1996), 23–29.

[12] Diskin Clay, "A Lost Epicurean Community," in *Tradition and Innovation in Epicureanism*, ed. Paul A. Vander Waerdt (1989), 324. Usually, it is referred to simply as the *Tractatus*. It is edited anew by Luigi Spina, "Il trattato di Filodemo su Epicuro e altri (PHerc. 1418)," *CErc* 7 (1977): 43–83.

[13] C. Militello, *Filodemo: Memorie Epicuree (PHerc 1418e310)* (Naples: Bibliopolis, 1997) and Spina, "Il trattato di Filodemo su Epicuro."

[14] Graziano Arrighetti, *Dieci anni di Papirologia ercolanese* (Naples: Società nazionale di scienze, lettere e arti in Napoli, 1982), 17.

his treatise *On Plain Speaking*, or, to give it the title of a recent translation into English, *On Frank Criticism*.[15]

The title Dorandi has given Philodemus' treatments of the Academic and Stoic philosophers is *Storia dei Filosofi*. In want of a subscription to PHerc. 1021, Philodemus' history of post-Platonic philosophy has gone under the uninformative title Mekler chose for it at the beginning of this century, *Academicorum philosophorum index Herculanensis*.[16] The problem is that the word σύνταξις occurs in neither of Philodemus' companion treatises on the history of the Academic and Stoic philosophers. The word which comes closest to giving us a title for these histories is συνα[γωγή at the end of Philodemus' *Academicorum Historia* (Col. XXXVI.19 Dorandi). No title is preserved in the subscription to PHerc. 1018, which gives us Philodemus' history of the Stoic philosophers.

In the *Catalogo dei papiri ercolanesi*,[17] the title of this treatise is given as [Φιλοδήμου | Περὶ τῶν ἀπὸ Ζήνωνος Στωικῶν καὶ αἱρέ | σεων ἁπάντων | σ]τ[ί]χ[οι . . . .] | Συ[ντάξεως τῶν φιλοσόφων | βίβλος.] This is approximately the title Augusto Traversa gave the work in his edition, *Index Stoicorum Herculanensis*.[18] The reader will appreciate how ambitious Traversa's supplements are. The near inspiration for his heavily reconstructed title comes from the title Domenico Comparetti first gave its companion work (PHerc. 1021) on the Academic philosophers, Φιλοδήμου Σύνταξις τῶν φιλοσόφων. Comparetti's inspiration was, of course, the notice in Diogenes Laertius, who, as we have seen, cites the tenth book of Philodemus' ἡ τῶν φιλοσόφων σύνταξις— a book obviously devoted to the school of Epicurus and his inspiration to the life of philosophy (10.3). The word that deserves the stress is "philosophers"—not philosophy. Philodemus' twin histories follow the pattern of another work usually referred to as Τὰ Χρονικά (*The Chronicles*) of Apollodorus of Athens, but also known as ἡ χρονικὴ Σύνταξις (*The Chronological Ordering*).[19]

---

[15] Already the subject of the first three essays included in *Friendship, Flattery, and Frankness of Speech*: Konstan, "Friendship, Frankness and Flattery" (7–19); Glad, "Frank Speech, Flattery and Friendship in Philodemus" (21–59); and Troels Engberg-Pedersen, "Plutarch to Prince Philopappus on How to Tell a Flatterer from a Friend" (61–79); see n. 11.

[16] See n. 1.

[17] Marcello Gigante, ed., *Catalogo dei papiri ercolanesi*, Centro internazionale per lo studio dei papiri ercolanesi (Naples: Bibliopolis, 1979), 229.

[18] See n. 1.

[19] As it is described by Diodorus Siculus, XIII 103.4 (*Fragmente der griechischen*

One way of illustrating the character of Philodemus' histories of the Academic and Stoic philosophers, both in their successions and in their students, is to observe that in it Philodemus evinces virtually no interest in the doctrines maintained or rejected by his philosophers. His is not the kind of work attributed to (the other) Apollodorus of Athens by Diogenes Laertius. It is not a συναγωγὴ τῶν δογμάτων. This Apollodorus is evidently the "tyrant of the Garden" who assumed leadership of the Epicurean school in Athens in around 150 B.C.E.[20] In his *Academicorum Historia*, Philodemus mentions the progress made in geometry in the age of Plato and in the Academy (Col. Y.3–1.7 Dorandi) and in *Stoicorum Historia* he mentions Ariston of Chios' doctrine on indifference in passing (Col. X.8–10 Dorandi). The strange lack of interest in "philosophy" in a history of philosophers contrasts with Philodemus' vivid and mordant interest in doctrine (*dogma*) in the case of a work such as *On the Stoics*. When he comes to mention the Epicureans in these histories of Academic and Stoic philosophers, there is no hint of Philodemus' allegiance to this school. He speaks for instance of Metrodorus of Stratonikeia as having once "listened [to the lectures] of the Epicureans" before turning to the Academy of Carneades (*Academicorum Historia*, XXIV.9–12 Dorandi). At the end of his history of the Stoics, Philodemus says that he knew Panaetius' pupil Thibron (Col. LXXVI.6–7) and he speaks of another pupil, Apollonius of Ptolemais, as "our friend" (*Stoicorum Historia*, Col. LXXVIII.3 Dorandi).

On the Stoics

What is it that makes the Stoics of Philodemus' history of the Stoics exempt from the criticism he mounts against them in *On the Stoics*? The contrast becomes evident in the points of contact between Philodemus' *On the Stoics* and, for want of a better title, his *Stoicorum Historia*. Philodemus' *Academicorum Historia* begins with Plato and Eucleides of Megara and their pupils and clearly envisages a sequel in a history of the other schools (Col. XXXI.15–19 Dorandi). But let us first consider Philodemus' two very different treatments of the

---

Historiker 244 fr. 35). Apollodorus of Athens is an important source for Philodemus in both his histories; Felix Jacoby, *Apollodors Chronik: Eine Sammlung der Fragmente*, Philologische Untersuchungen 16 (Berlin, Weidmann, 1902), *FGrHist* 244, and note 36 below.

[20] Diog. Laert. 7.181; the scant details appear in M. Erler, "Epikur," 280–81.

Stoics. Here the contrast in treatment can be seen at its starkest. Zeno is a figure central to both works. In *On the Stoics*, he is mockingly praised as the "chorus leader" and "founder" of the Stoic school in order to daub his followers with the stain of the outrageous doctrines of his Republic (Πολιτεία).[21] These followers are called "these noble men," these "paradigms of sanctity," and their doctrines—derisively—as "noble."[22]

Irony gives way to abuse, and Philodemus brings out the Cynic character of Diogenes' *Politeia* by speaking of the Stoics who were pleased to adopt the life of dogs and commit the outrageous acts that he discovers in the *Politeiai* of both Zeno and the Cynic Diogenes of Sinope—open homosexuality, a community of wives and "children," cannibalism, parricide—to name a few of his damning particulars (Cols. XVIII.1–XXI Dorandi).[23] It is abundantly apparent from *On Frank Criticism* that Philodemus espouses the constructive παρρησία the philosopher addresses to his pupil. But, as he views them in *On the Stoics*, the founders of the Stoic school will say anything and everything. They know no restraint.[24] A remark at the conclusion of this tract reveals that Philodemus' polemic was provoked by Stoic attacks on the Epicureans, a hostility already apparent in Philodemus' reference to the Epicureans expelled from Phalannai and Messene because of their doctrine of pleasure (Col. III.6–8 Dorandi): "But we [Epicureans] have long ago purged our ears and mind and do not come into contact with this most grievous slander, as we have shown" (Col. XXII.5–10 Dorandi). Nonetheless, *uritur et loquitur*.

---

[21] Ὁ κορυφαῖος, α[ὐτῶν], Col. XIII.24, τῆς ἀγωγῆς Ι ἀρχηγέτην, Col. XIV.21–22. He is "filled with disgraceful teachings" (ἀνάμεστος αἰσχρῶν δογμάτων, Col. XIV.23).

[22] τοὺς γενναίους, Col. XV.2; τοῖς παναγέσι, Col. XVIII.5; τὰ καλὰ τῶν [ἀνθρ]ώπων, Col. XVIII.1.

[23] We are reminded of how shocking these doctrines were both in Philodemus' Roman context and in imperial times by Miriam Griffin and David Krueger. See their contributions to *The Cynics: The Cynic Movement in Antiquity and Its Legacy*, ed. Robert Bracht Branham and Marie-Odile Goulet-Cazé (Berkeley and Los Angeles: University of California Press, 1996): Griffin, "Cynicism and the Romans: Attraction and Repulsion" (191–92); Krueger, "The Bawdy and Society: The Shamelessness of Diogenes in Roman Imperial Culture" (222–39).

[24] Dorandi's characterization of Philodemus' argument and his tactic of pairing Stoic and Cynic is telling: "Cinici e Stoici vivono alla maniera dei cani, abusano la *parrhesia*, indossano un mantello doppio, sequono considerazioni che scadono su un piano per lo più sessuale" ("Cynics and Stoics live like dogs and abuse their right to speak freely. They wear a folded cloak, and they pursue topics that descend to the level of graphic references to sex;" "Gli Stoici" 94).

Stoicorum Historia

The contrast with Philodemus' very different treatment of Stoic philosophers in his *Stoicorum Historia* requires an explanation. Here too, Philodemus speaks of Zeno and his *Politeia*, in a context where he describes the unease of some Stoics over the proposals of Zeno's political philosophy and his youthful *Politeia* as being "in some manner stitched together" (Col. IV.4–5 Dorandi). He also repeats the phrase from *On the Stoics*—"a finger demonstrates it" (Col. IV.5–7 Dorandi; cf. "On the Stoics," Col. III.13 Dorandi) to convey the fact that, despite the embarrassing doctrines it puts forth, it cannot be attributed to any thinker other than Zeno. Since we have focused on Zeno and the two very different treatments of his *Politeia* in Philodemus' two treatises on the Stoics, we might continue with Zeno to observe the contrast between Philodemus' polemical engagement in *On the Stoics* and his strange disengagement from polemic in his *Stoicorum Historia* before considering an explanation for the contrast.

In his history of the Stoic philosophers from Zeno to his own contemporaries, Philodemus is interested in character and the lives of the Stoics. Philodemus' deepest engagement in the thought of his subjects might come in his remark on Ariston of Chios, "who declared indifference as the end of life" (Col. X.8–10 Dorandi).[25] What attracts notice about Philodemus' treatment of the Stoics (and the Academics as well) is that there is no hint of sectarian hostility to them, although Philodemus does betray some irritation at the anonymous eulogy of Zeno treated in Cols. VI and VII. Occasionally, he gives dramatic scenes from the lives of his Stoics and the actual words of the dialogues in which his philosophers engaged. The first and most striking scene involves Zeno: envoys from Antigonus Gonatas reach Zeno in Athens. The Macedonian king was considering which position to offer Zeno and told him through his envoys: "A person as bad as you will not even be able to scold bath attendants!" To which Zeno replied: "You say . . ." (Col. VIII Dorandi). We have lost his riposte. It must have been clever, biting, and philosophical. But the theme of the Stoics and their relations to dynasts is important to Philodemus, especially in the cases of zeno's students, Perseus (Cols. XIII–XVI Dorandi) and Panaetius (Col. LXVIII Dorandi), as is the theme of the character

---

[25] James Porter addresses this passage in his "The Philosophy of Ariston of Chios," *Cynics* 166–67, and explores the meaning of indifference in Ariston's thought.

of the Stoics (and Academics) as teachers. Diogenes Laertius preserves what at first seems a very different account of Zeno's relations with Antigonus and reproduces a letter of extreme politeness in which Zeno declines the king's invitation to join him in Pella. In his place, Zeno sent Perseus and Philonides of Thebes.[26] But the next column in Philodemus' treatment of Zeno makes it clear that Antigonus was merely teasing the old philosopher and that he treated Zeno "as his equal and peer" (Col. VIII.2 Dorandi). Philodemus' interest, clearly, is in Zeno's frankness before a powerful figure like Antigonus.[27]

This side of Philodemus' history of the philosophers reminds us both that one of the meanings of φιλοσοφία is a way of life (as it is for Epicurus in his last will and testament, Diog. Laert. 10.17) and that Philodemus was the author of the fascinating treatise *On Frank Criticism* (Περὶ παρρησίας). In *Stoicorum Historia*, Cleanthes provides a dramatic case-study in tolerance—not of the plain speaking of the philosopher, but of public abuse. Cleanthes shows us the restraint Philodemus recommended in a teacher who would employ plain speaking with discretion as well as firmness in his treatment of two poets who were his students. One, the comic poet Baton, who has left us some interesting popular philosophical disquisitions—excerpted precisely because they were popular philosophy—insulted Cleanthes in a comedy.[28] Arcesilaus resented the insult and wanted to remove Baton from the Stoa. After a short tonic dialogue with Arcesilaus on what is most important to human happiness, Cleanthes allowed Baton to stay (Cols. XXII–XXIII Dorandi), only to have to face the abuse of another student, the tragic poet, Sositheos, who mocked Cleanthes' style of speech in a satyr play (from which we have the quotation in Col. XXIV.3–9).[29]

The point is that the philosopher will both employ and endure plain speaking in—and even abuse from—his students. Rather than expelling the offenders, Cleanthes allows them to remain in the Stoa,

---

[26] Diog. Laert. 7.6–9. Diogenes reproduces the letters from Apollonius of Tyre's tract on Zeno.

[27] An account of their relationship is to be found in William Woodthorpe Tarn, *Antigonos Gonatas* (Oxford: Clarendon, 1913; repr. Chicago: Argo, 1969) 29–36. In view of the evidence, Tarn states: "if we seek the bond of union between these two opposite natures, we shall probably find that it consisted in a kind of savage honesty common to both, a desire for the thing as it really is" (35).

[28] *PCG*, IV.T.4 (p. 28) Kassel-Austin.

[29] This attack was known to Diogenes Laertius, 7.173 (*SVF* 1 603 and *TrGF* 199 fr. 4, p. 272).

gradually to win them over (Col. XXV.1–3 Dorandi). In his treatise on "How to Distinguish a Flatterer from a Friend," Plutarch
recalls the incident that involved Cleanthes and Baton: "When he
wrote a line insulting Cleanthes in a comedy, Arcesilaus read him
out of the school. But, when Baton won Cleanthes over and repented
of what he had done, Arcesilaus made peace with him" (*Moralia*
55C). This anecdote from Plutarch puts the anecdote in Philodemus'
Stoicorum Historia squarely in the context of plain speaking. Oddly,
we hear of Cleanthes and his stern frankness in *On Frank Criticism*—
a treatise devoted almost entirely to the moral education of the
Epicureans. Here Philodemus is discussing the tactic of an audacious
use of frankness and says that those who employ it will not diverge
from the paradigm of two masters: Metrodorus of Lampsacus and
Cleanthes: ". . . so that they [will employ frankness] aggressively in
regard to [laziness and] procrastination. Therefore, they [will be]
rather too strict {in the application of frankness} if they were born
in want of things conducive to [good will] and friendship and toward
the long-term imitation of those who taught {them} . . . [in] the
process of teaching or moments of teaching they will in no way differ
from Cleanthes or Metrodorus, for it is obvious that an attentive
{teacher} will employ a more abundant {frankness}" (Cols. Va and
Vb Olivieri). In sequel, Philodemus stresses how the dosage of medicinal plain speaking must be adjusted to the character of the individual student (Col. VIa Olivieri).

A large collection of curt responses—usually directed at dull young
men and one directed at Antigonus Gonatas—formed around Cleanthes
after his death.[30] As for Metrodorus of Lampsacus, we know from
the immediate sequel that he recognized that his associate and peer,
Polyaenus, "often insinuated himself into conversation and was quite
sociable."[31] Metrodorus is also mentioned later in *On Frank Criticism*,
as Philodemus quotes his renegade brother Timocrates saying "that
he both loved his brother as no one else did and hated him as no
one else" (Col. XXb.1–5 Olivieri). This remark might derive from
a letter Metrodorus wrote his older brother Metrodorides about their
rift; Metrodorus also wrote a polemical tract against his brother, as
did Timocrates against Metrodorus.[32]

---

[30] *SVF* 1 597–619, especially the replies given in 597 (to Antigonus Gonatas),
605 (to Arcesilaus), and 605–617 (his sharp and clever responses to stupid questions).
[31] Col. VIa.11–14 (*Metrodori Epicurei Fragmenta* fr. 45 Koerte).
[32] Philodemus, *On Anger* Col. XII 26–29 Indelli and *Metrodori Epicurei Fragmenta*
XXI Koerte.

Academicorum Historia

We can now return to Plato and the Academy, with which Philodemus began. Once again, the relation between the philosopher and the man of power is a matter of great interest to Philodemus. In the case of the Stoics, Philodemus' attention is trained on Zeno in his relation to Antigonus, the political career of Perseus, and the involvement of Panaetius in the affairs of both Athens and Rhodes, where he was given the title "the second founder;" each of these cases illustrates the intimate connections between philosophers and dynasts— or cities.[33] Indeed, one of the Stoics attempted to become a dynast. In the course of his discussion of Perseus, Philodemus mentions the treatise of Hermippus of Smyrna on just this subject: "On those who abandoned philosophy for political power."[34]

One could well expect that Philodemus would be interested in the relations between Plato and the court of Syracuse, because it is in such contacts as these that a philosopher's autonomy and freedom of speech are tested and vindicated. In the *Academicorum Historia* Plato naturally plays a large role. Philodemus gives a sketch of the literature on Plato's early life and of the moment when, after spending time with the Pythagoreans of Italy, he arrived at the court of Dionysius I in Syracuse. His description of this first encounter of philosopher and dynast recalls that earlier and paradigmatic meeting of Solon and Croesus in Lydia: "Dionysius showed himself to be ill at ease in response to Plato's forthrightness (παρρησία[ν]), because, when Plato was asked who he thought was more blessed than others, Plato did not say Dionysius" (Col. X.11–15 Dorandi). The crucial term is not "blessed" but "forthrightness," παρρησία. In the context of the confrontation of philosopher and tyrant we cannot translate the term as "frank criticism." That Philodemus' (and his teacher Zeno of Sidon's) interest was fixed on this philosophical honesty, which is the beginning of an openness to philosophy and moral reformation, is suggested by a fragmentary passage from his *On Frank Criticism*, where he seems to return to Plato, the proverb "a second tack," and the

---

[33] Zeno and Antigonus, the passages reviewed from Cols. VIII and IX; Perseus' relations with Antigonus and his αὐλικὸς βίος are taken up in Cols. XIII–XVII; Panaetius is called the "second founder" (δεύτερος κτίστης) of Rhodes, Col. LXXII.5; cf. Plutarch, "Precepts for Governing a Republic," *Moralia* 18.814D.

[34] *Stoicorum Historia* XVI 2 Dorandi. The title of this work seems to have been Περὶ τῶν ἀπὸ φιλοσοφίας εἰς δυναστείας μεταστάντων; see Dorandi ad loc., *Storia dei Filosofi: Platone e l'Academia* 91 n. 350 and Hermippus, fr. 90, Fritz Wehrli, *Die Schule des Aristoteles: Supplementband* (Basel: Schwabe, 1974).

relation between Plato and Dionysius II, who could not bear the
frank speech of the philosopher who was his inferior—in station and
in power (Cols. XVb–XVIa Olivieri). We will return to this passage
as we come to Philodemus' *On Frank Criticism*.

The long section on Polemon reflects a number of the themes
shared by Philodemus' histories of the Academic and Stoic philosophers and his treatment of plain speaking (in *On Frank Criticism*),
which is mainly but not entirely devoted to the first generation of
the Epicurean school in Athens, as "those who led the way" (οἱ καθηγημόνες, οἱ καθηγησάμενοι) provide models for the philosopher in
therapy for his pupils. Polemon's youthful excesses were notorious
in the biographical tradition on which Philodemus depended.[35] He
clearly depended on the *Lives* of Antigonus of Carystus.[36] But his
attention fastens on both the austere and tough character of Polemon
after his conversion and his relation to the philosopher who converted him to philosophy, Xenocrates. After troubles with the law
and a life of public drunkenness and lasciviousness, Polemon decided
to leave Athens to live just outside its walls in the Academy, where
many in the Academy built reed huts to keep him company. "He
seems to have nurtured a youthful admiration for Xenocrates and
this admiration resulted in his constant praise [of the philosopher]
and the fact that he emulated his conduct in everything"—ἐμιμεῖτο
π[άντο]θεν τὰ περὶ αὐτοῦ (Col. XIV.41–45 Dorandi). This emulation
is familiar to Philodemus from the example of those Epicureans who
engaged in "the long-term imitation of those who taught {them}"
(*On Frank Criticism* Va Olivieri). Among the Academics, Philodemus
also records the case of Charmadas' emulation of Agathocles of Tyre
(*Academicorum Historia*, XXIII.8 Dorandi).

For there to be an emulation of a teacher on the part of the
pupil, the pupil has to come to admire his teacher. In the case of
Xenocrates and Polemon, this admiration did not come about auto-
matically or through Polemon's simply listening to Xenocrates' lectures. Polemon was *hunted* by Xenocrates. Philodemus' words are:
"But once he had been hunted down by Xenocrates and introduced
to him, he transformed his life to such an extent that he never

---

[35] Cols. IV.25–XV. The testimonia for Polemon and fragments relative to his
career are collected by Gigante, *Polemonis Academici fragmenta* (Naples: Accademia di
archeologia, lettere e belle arti, 1977).

[36] Gaiser (*Philodems Academica* 129–31) includes Antigonus of Carystus' *Life of Polemon*
in his elaborate reconstruction of Philodemus' sources and their sources.

relaxed the expression of his face or changed his posture or altered the tone of his voice" (θηραθεὶς δ᾽ὑπὸ Ξενοκράτους καὶ συστα[θε]ὶς αὐτῷ, τοσοῦτο μετήλ[λ]αξε κατὰ τὸν βίον, ὥστε μηδέποτε τὴν τοῦ προσώπου φαντασίαν δια[λῦ]σαι καὶ σχέσιν ἀλλοιῶσ[αι] μ[ή]τε τόν τ[ό]νον τῆς [φωνῆς] . . ., *Historia Academicorum*, Col. XIII.10–18 Dorandi). Proof of this is the attack of the mad dog that terrified his companions and left Polemon with a wound in the groin but impassive (Col. XIII.20–27 Dorandi). The metaphor of the philosopher's hunt for the young is as old as Plato's *Sophist*, where the sophist is described as a "paid hunter of the young" (*Sophist* 231D).[37] At the end of his history of the Academic philosophers, Philodemus mentions a pupil of Carneades, Phanostratus of Trachis. He is notable for his expert and refined investigation of all methods of winning pupils over (εὖ πρὸς [π]ᾶ[σα]ν ψυχαγωγίαν ἠκ[ριβ]ωμ[ένος, col. XXXVI 4–5 Dorandi). Philodemus' *On Frank Criticism* is Epicurean counterpart of this enterprise.

On Frank Criticism

PHerc. 1471 preserves in fragmentary form the title of Philodemus *On Frank Criticism*: ΦΙΛΟΔΗΜ[ΟΥ] ΤΩΝ ΚΑΤ ΕΠΙΤΟΜΗΝ ΕΞΕΙΡ ΓΑΣΜΕΝΩΝ ΠΕΡΙ ΗΘΩΝ ΚΑΙ ΒΙΩΝ ΤΩΝ ΖΗΝΩΝ[Σ ΣΧΟ]ΛΩΝ. The title is fuller and better preserved than most, but it presents a problem. It is clear from the syntax of this work and the accusative + infinitive constructions dependent on "he [Zeno] said" that Philodemus depends on the lectures he heard Zeno of Sidon give and which he tran- scribed. We in turn are dependent on Philodemus for the abbrevi- ated discussion of characters and ways of life and their bearing on the question of how the philosopher should approach the student he believes needs correction and improvement. Like some of the devoted students he describes in his histories of the Academic and Stoic philosophers, Philodemus preserved the lectures of his teacher. We know from his history of the Stoics the very different fates of two of Carneades' students who prepared versions of his lectures. One, Zeno of Alexandria, was exposed to humiliation by the master in front of his fellow students; the other, Hagnon of Tarsus, won his favor (*Academicorum Historia*, XXII.35–XXIII.7).

---

[37] This theme is pursued by Wolfgang Schmid, "Die Netze des Seelenfängers: Zur Jagdmetaphorik im philosophischen Protreptikos des Demetrios Lakon (Pap. Herc. 831)," *Parola del Passato* 10 (1955): 44–47; reprinted in *Ausgewälte philologische Schriften* (Berlin: W. de Guyter, 1984), 48–55.

Philodemus' abridgment of Zeno's lectures creates a dependency that makes a judgment about the treatise *On Frank Criticism* a delicate matter: are we hearing only the abbreviated speech of Zeno, or is the voice of Philodemus also audible?[38] The same dilemma faces us in an evaluation of his works on the Academic and Stoic philosophers. Clearly in his *Academicorum Historia*, Philodemus owes a great deal to Apollodorus of Athens, the "chronographer;" and he owes something to this "man of letters" (and poet of comic trimeters) in his *Stoicorum Historia*. He is not reticent about his debts.[39]

Whatever Philodemus owes on credit, his spending habits are apparent in his two histories of the philosophers and in his *On Frank Criticism*. There are obvious differences between these histories and Philodemus' presentation of Zeno's lectures on frank criticism. The first proceed in chronological sequence, and sometimes provide *archon* years, in the manner of Apollodorus of Athens. Zeno's lectures pursue a variety of topics and are structured on Philodemus' summary of Zeno's responses to at least fourteen questions concerning the range of reactions to frank criticism. Most of these questions (described as ζητούμενα or τόποι) concern the sage or philosopher (σοφός); a few concern his pupils.[40] For his histories, Philodemus relied on a variety of sources; for *On Frank Criticism* he relied on Zeno. The histories concentrate first on Academic and then on Stoic philosophers in chronological sequence from Plato and Zeno to Philodemus' own

---

[38] David Sedley has ventured that "it seems not over-bold to suggest that many of his works should be thought of in some ways comparable in content to Arrian's transcripts of Epictetus' teaching." See his "Philosophical Allegiance in the Greco-Roman World," in *Philosophia Togata: Essays on Philosophy and Roman Society*, ed. Miriam Griffin and Jonathan Barnes (Oxford: Clarendon, 1989), 104. My own sense of the matter is that Philodemus' interests and philosophical personality are also expressed by the choices made in the abridgement (κατ᾽ ἐπιτομήν).

[39] Philodemus actually quotes sections from Apollodorus in his history of the Academic philosophers, XXVI.35–44; XXVII.1–12; XXVII.32–XXVIII.16; XXVIII.35–XXIX.16; XXIX.39–XXX.11; XXXI.1–12; XXXI.34–XXXII.10; XXXII.14–16. These passages appear in *FGrHist* 224 as frs. 47, 52–60. The conspectus provided by Dorandi for Philodemus' dependencies in both works is synoptic: *Storia dei Filosofi: Platone e l'Academia* 83–99; *Storia dei Filosofi: La Stoá da Zenone a Panezio* 32–35. In the history of the Stoics, Apollodorus is referred to as "the man of letters"—ὁ γραμματικός (Col. LXIX.4–5 Dorandi). Gaiser provides a more elaborate conspectus and stemmata in his discussion of the sources of Philodemus' history of the Academics, *Philodems Academica* (1988): 87–133.

[40] Frs. 5.6–8; 53.2–6; 67.9–11; 70.5–7; 74.3–10 (four questions, apparently on the sons of wealthy fathers); 81.1–4 (explicitly concerning the σοφός); 88.1–4 (on students); Col. Ia.1–4; IIIa.3–5 (οἱ σοφοί); XIXa.5–8; XXIA.1–5; XXIb.12–15; XXIIb.10–13; and XIVa.7–9.

contemporaries; *On Frank Criticism* concentrates on the first generation of the Epicureans in Athens and is extremely general in its
description of philosophical education. Thus, only Epicureans of the
first generation of the school are actually named in *On Frank Criticism*:
Epicurus first and foremost, then his associates Apollonides, Hermarchus, Idomeneus, Leonteus, Metrodorus, Polyaenus, Pythocles, and
Timocrates, the renegade brother of Metrodorus. We have noticed
the single case of a Stoic named by Philodemus, Cleanthes (Col.
Vb.2 Olivieri).

But the interests that all three works share in common are also apparent. Like Zeno of Sidon, Philodemus is more concerned in these three
treatises with character, the choice and condition of life, and with
education, rather than doctrine. Philodemus is also interested in the
theme of the philosopher and his ambiguous and dangerous relation
to the powerful. The relation between Plato and the court of Syracuse
is treated in Philodemus' history of the Academic philosophers. I
would suggest that it is also glanced at in *On Frank Criticism*.

The topos of the confrontation of tyrant and philosopher is as old
as Herodotus' account of the meeting between Solon and Croesus
(*Histories* I.30–33). It is also one of the questions Philodemus addresses
in a specific form at the end of *On Frank Criticism*: "Why is it that,
when other things are equal, those who are illustrious both in resources
and reputations abide {frank criticism} less well {than others}?" (Col.
XXIIb.10–13 Olivieri). The possible reference to Plato occurs in the
context of the question: "Will philosophers diverge from one another
in their frankness?" (Col. IIIa.3–5 Olivieri). In Col. XVb, Philodemus
seems to be treating the philosophers who have erred in their use
of forthright criticism and are forced to take "another tack." The
expression "second sailing" is proverbial in Greek, and Plato seems
to recognize it as he describes his second trip to Sicily and his attempt
to influence Dionysius II of Syracuse.[41] Olivieri thought that we might
have here a reference to Plato; Philippson thought not.[42]

Plato's encounters with Dionysius, father and son, were notorious,
and Plutarch, in his treatise on "How to Distinguish a Flatterer from a
Friend," twice cites Plato's diplomatic tact in handling Dionysius II.[43]

---

[41] Letter 7.337E (ἡ ... δευτέρα πορεία τε καὶ πλοῦς). Plato evokes the proverb in
Phaedo 99D, *Statesman* 300C, and *Philebus* 19C.
[42] Olivieri in his note *ad loc.*; Philippson in his review of Olivieri, *Berliner Philologische
Wochenschrift*, 27 (May 1916) 688.
[43] *Moralia* 7.52F and 26.67C–E.

The text of Philodemus can be read to continue: "when he encountered {him, i.e., Dionysius II}, he {Plato} missed the mark in the
exercise of plain speaking, but he [set] no value on those very persons who best recognize what concerns them" (Col. XVIa.1–5 Olivieri).
There are others who faced Plato's difficulties in the court of
Syracuse—to name only the Socratic Aeschines and the lyric poet
Philoxenus.[44] The other instance of plain speaking with the great is
an anecdote concerning Alexander the Great and the people who
asked him whether they should address him in a Greek or a barbarian fashion (fr. 24.8–12 Olivieri).

The best known passage in Philodemus' *On Frank Criticism* does
not concern criticism only; it also reflects the allegiance Epicureans
of his day swore to Epicurus: ". . . we shall admonish others with
great confidence, both now and when those {of us} who have become
offshoots of our teachers have become eminent. And the encompassing and most important thing is, we shall obey Epicurus, according to whom we have chosen to live" (fr. 45.1–11 Olivieri). Such
obedience makes the cases of apostasy Philodemus considers in the
works we have reviewed all the more relevant to the Epicurean: the
case of Dionysius "the renegade" (ὁ μεταθέμενος) in his history of
the Stoics and the painful case of Timocrates in his *On Frank Criticism*.[45]
But what impresses more is Philodemus' sense of his own authority: καὶ νῦν διαπρέψαντες οἱ καθ[ηγη]τῶν οὕτως ἀπότομοι γενηθέντες.
Philodemus' debt to his sources and to those who led the way before
him is great, but the project he undertook in his histories of the
Academic and Stoic philosophers is very much his own. It is also a
part of still other projects that deal with the education of the philosopher by the philosopher. When Philodemus speaks of Epicurus as
the philosopher "according to whom we have chosen to live," his

---

[44] The difficulties of Aeschines are recognized in Plutarch, *Moralia* 26.67C–D
(Gabriele Giannantoni, *Socratis et Socraticorum Reliquiae* VIA 11 [Naples: Bibliopolis,
1990]). Diodorus Siculus XV.6 is our source for the anecdotes concerning Philoxenus
of Cythera and Dionysius I. Summaries of the traditions concerning Plato's deal-
ings with the court in Syracuse can be found in Alice Swift Reginos, *Platonica: The
Anecdotes concerning the Life and Writings of Plato*, Columbia Studies in the Classical
Tradition 3 (Leiden: Brill, 1976), 70–85; Mekler (1902): 6–7 and François Lasserre,
De Léodamas de Thasos à Philippe d'Oponte, Témoinages et fragments (1987): 669–72.
[45] Sedley, "Philosophical Allegiance," well demonstrates the importance of *On
Frank Criticism* for the question of philosophical allegiance in the Greco-Roman world.
We have noted the reference to Timocrates; Dionysius is mentioned in *Stoicorum
Historia* (1994) Cols. X.48 and XXIX.5 Dorandi.

word (ἡ<ι>ρήμεθα) suggests the word for a philosophical sect (αἵρεσις). His project of treating the role of frank criticism in his presentation of Zeno's lectures on frank criticism and its role in the education of the philosopher explains why Philodemus is so non-sectarian in his histories of the other philosophers, the Academics and the Stoics.[46]

---

[46] A version of this essay has appeared as Chapter 6 of *Paradosis and Survival: Three Chapters in the History of Epicurean Philosophy* (Ann Arbor: University of Michigan Press, 1998).

CRAFT, CULT, AND CANON IN THE BOOKS
FROM HERCULANEUM

Dirk Obbink

Abstract

Some have argued that the Epicureans might have constituted something like a Hellenistic cult or religion. Although the Epicureans would
cite authoritative teachers, most notably Epicurus himself, and showed
concern for establishing a canon of Epicurean authorities, Philodemus
in his treatises does not appeal to those authorities in the deferential
way that a member of a cult or religion would appeal to the cult's
deity or leader. Moreover, the selection of works in the Herculaneum
library gives no indication of any attempt to gather a collection of
authoritative canonical texts, but rather an interest in the pressing
issues of a particular period in the history of Hellenistic philosophy.

Much discussion has been given to the possibility that the Epicureans,
who not only rejected the theology of pagan myths but also were
so unorthodox as to admit women and educate their slaves,[1] might
have constituted something like a Hellenistic cult or religion, organized along the lines of, for example, certain early Christian groups.

   In what follows I will argue against this view, in particular its
most coherent, recent formulation by David Sedley.[2] Sedley focuses

---

[1] Unorthodox, that is, in organization. But where doctrine was concerned,
Epicureans toed the line, at least in adhering to expressed positions of the founder
of the school. Though Epicurus claimed to have had no teacher, he took up lines
of inquiry laid down by Plato and the pre-Socratics. While the Epicureans rejected
the value of traditional παιδεία, they held knowledge of grammar to be a *sine qua
non* of doing philosophy. Leontion is one example among many of the women
among the Epicureans. According to Cicero in *De natura deorum* she became too
outspoken as a result; see Pamela Gordon's contribution in this volume. In Philodemus'
poetry, women are occasionally represented discussing philosophical themes. Epicurus'
learned slave Mus studied with him, according to Diogenes Laertius. In addition,
Epicurus in the *Kyriai Doxai* emphatically says that it is never too late to start study-
ing philosophy, which suggests that the Garden operated like a modern academic
extension division in admitting non-traditional students.
[2] David Sedley, "Philosophical Allegiance in the Greco-Roman World," in Miriam
Griffin and Jonathan Barnes, eds. *Philosophia Togata: Essays on Philosophy and Roman
Society* (Oxford: Clarendon, 1989), 97–119.

on the Epicurean books recovered from a Roman villa on the Bay
of Naples destroyed in the eruption of Vesuvius in 79 C.E. and excavated in the eighteenth century.[3] Seeking an explanation for why the
books from Herculaneum (mostly the writings of the first century
B.C.E. Epicurean philosopher Philodemus) so closely follow the example set by the school's founder, and therefore lack the sort of original philosophical argumentation or speculation we would expect
from Aristotle or modern analytic philosophers, Sedley argues that
what gives these works "their cohesion and identity is less a disin-
terested common quest for the truth than a virtually religious commitment to the authority of a founder figure."[4]

I argue in response that the Epicureans, while claiming the authority of a famous teacher, made no more of a religious commitment
to that authority than do scholars in modern university settings to
their own teachers and intellectual forebears. An alternative explanation must instead be sought for similarities between the organization and procedure of Epicurean groups and that of other Hellenistic
groups. These may instead be due to those groups' emulation of certain features of the Hellenistic philosophical schools.

The books from Herculaneum have long been known. Already in
the early nineteenth century it could be complained of them that
they had lain idle since their discovery in the eighteenth, "ignored
by the unlearned, and regretted by the learned."[5] The difficulties of
these texts, due to their carbonized state of preservation, have blocked
their use as evidence for Hellenistic philosophy and religion. The
Greek in which they are written is so esoteric that it would be difficult
to control and translate if they had come down to us in perfect condition. But there are indications that this situation is starting to
change. New recent work on the papyri in Italy, where they are housed
at Naples in the Bibliotheca Nazionale, together with an NEH-funded

[3] See "Guide to Editions and Translations," in Marcello Gigante, *Philodemus in Italy: The Books from Herculaneum*, trans. Dirk Obbink, 2nd ed. (Ann Arbor: University of Michigan Press, 2002), 115–26; "Classified Bibliography," in Dirk Obbink, ed., *Philodemus and Poetry: Poetic Theory and Practice in Lucretius, Philodemus, and Horace* (Oxford: Oxford University Press, 1995) 270–81; *Catalogo dei papiri ercolanesi* (Naples: Bibliopolis, 1979), with updates in *CErc* 19 (1989): 193–264, and *Indice dei papiri ercolanesi in "Cronache ercolanesi" 1971–1995*, 3rd supplement to *CErc* (Naples: Macchiaroli, 1995).
[4] Sedley 97.
[5] William Drummond and Robert Walpole, *Herculanensia; or Archeological and Philological Dissertations, containing a Manuscript Found among the Ruins of Herculaneum* (London: T. Cadell & W. Davies, 1810), ii.

project to edit and translate the papyri, are rapidly supplying reliable editions of the fragmentary books, equipped with modern translations. The new work utilizes electronic microscopes making it possible to read many previously intractable passages. We now have whole books of Epicurus' magnum opus *On Nature* (of which Epicurus' *Letter to Herodotus* and Lucretius' *De rerum natura* are summaries). Several books with titles like *On Epicurus* and *Records of the School* survive to document the organization and instructional methodology of the Epicureans during the first three centuries before Christ.[6] Numerous ethical works,[7] including *On Anger* (available with an Italian translation in the edition of G. Indelli)[8] and *On Death*[9] treat the psychology of the emotions. Another important treatise, *On Frank Criticism*, treats the subject of frank speech (*parrhesia*), and more broadly issues of interpersonal relations between the members of the school and between members and outsiders.[10] Philodemus also wrote *On Piety*[11] and *On Gods*,[12] as did the second-century Epicurean Demetrius Laco.[13]

The last two topics throw into sharp relief the interest that the books from Herculaneum hold for students of Hellenistic religion. I will return to their content after first characterizing the philosophical discourse, and its connections with cult and religion, to be found in the books from Herulaneum.

---

[6] New edition, translation, and commentary by C. Militello, *Memorie Epicuree* (PHerc. 1418 e 310), La Scuola di Epicuro 16 (Naples: Bibliopolois, 1997).

[7] PHerc. 1251, for example, is a practical introduction to Epicurean ethics; see the new edition with commentary and English translation: [*Philodemus*], [*On Choices and Avoidances*] eds. Giovanni Indelli and Voula Tsouna-McKirahan, La Scuola di Epicuro 15 (Naples: Bibliopolis, 1995), with my review article, "The Mooring of Philosophy," *OSAPh* 15 (1997): 259–81.

[8] See my review, *BASP* 28 (1991): 89–90; a new English translation by David Armstrong is forthcoming.

[9] Taco Kuiper, ed., *Philodemus Over den Dood* (Amsterdam: H. J. Paris, 1925) with Dutch translation; forthcoming English translation by David Armstrong.

[10] New English translation by David Konstan, Diskin Clay, Clarence E. Glad, Johan C. Thom, James Ware, *Philodemus: On Frank Criticism*, SBLTT 43 (Atlanta: Scholars Press, 1998).

[11] Obbink, ed. *Philodemus On Piety*, Part 1: Critical Text with Commentary (Oxford: Oxford University Press, 1996); new edition of Part 2 forthcoming.

[12] New edition of book 1 in progress by Pål Tidemandsen (University of Oslo) incorporating the unpublished work of Knut Kleve; forthcoming edition of book 3 by Holgar Essler.

[13] PHerc. 1055: Vittorio De Falco, *L'epicureo Demetrio Lacone* (Naples: A. Cimmaruta, 1923), 9f., 18, 58, 65–80, with the corrections of E. Renna, *CErc* 12 (1982): 43–9. A new edition by Mariacarolina Santoro is expected shortly.

Apart from intense allegiance to the school's founders and their teachings, the books show the Epicureans as existing in highly organized, specifically structured, yet avowedly egalitarian, communities.[14] As might be expected at a time of Hellenistic diaspora, the communities were scattered, separated by vast stretches of land and water, held together by an epistolary literature exchanged, memorized and circulated among members of satellite communities visited periodically by itinerant, ambulatory leaders of the school from an intellectual center, Athens. The satellite communities contributed (at Epicurus' own request) annual dues (συντάξεις) of two hundred drachmas to belong to this community of like-minded thinkers. In return they would receive letters from the Master and the other scholarchs (leaders of the school, whom Philodemus refers to now as οἱ ἄνδρες, "The Masters," now as καθηγέμονες, "teachers"). They could also expect the occasional visit. An incident in which Epicurus was shipwrecked en route to Lampsacus[15] provided in many a letter opportunity for reflection on the nature of mortality and death, in anticipation of the Master's grateful appearance. The books assume (whether in fact or as a rhetorical topos) that the Epicureans, like some Jewish and Christian groups, were charged by their opponents with atheism, misanthropy, social irresponsibility, sexual immorality, and gross hedonistic pursuit of pleasure. In the Herculaneum library, whole treatises may be structured as detailed responses to such charges, a convenient manner of doctrinal exposition, to be sure, but for that reason no less committed, as far as we can tell, to setting the record straight.

In making his case for religious authority in the books, Sedley not only points out that the Epicureans advocated a kind of "therapy of the word,"[16] but also draws attention to the strict doctrinal unity

---

[14] The work by Norman De Witt on this subject (especially the article "Organization and Procedure in Epicurean Groups") has been deservedly discredited and should be ignored. See however the excellent treatment by Abraham Malherbe, "Self-Definition among Epicureans and Cynics," in Ben F. Meyer and E. P. Sanders, eds. *Jewish and Christian Self-Definition*, vol. 3, *Self-Definition in the Greco-Roman World* (Philadelphia: Fortress, 1982), 46–59. For further information in relation to Hellenistic religious groups see Henry A. Fischel, *Rabbinic Literature and Greco-Roman Philosophy: A Study of Epicurea and Rhetorica in Early Midrashic Writings*, Studia Post-Biblica 21 (Leiden: Brill, 1973), and H. Reiche's illuminating article "Myth and Magic in Cosmological Polemics," *RhM²* 114 (1971): 296–329.

[15] See Diskin Clay, *Paradosis and Survival: Three Chapters in the History of Epicurean Philosophy* (Ann Arbor: University of Michigan Press, 1998), chapter 3: "Sailing to Lampsacus."

[16] Gigante, "'Philosophia medicans' in Filodemo," *CErc* 5 (1975): 53–61. Martha

observed by their Epicurean authors. The requirement of orthodoxy was, to varying degrees, imposed by all the Hellenistic philosophical schools, if less so by the Stoics, as Sedley emphasizes. This was due in part to the fact that the Epicureans were largely ruled by a set of canonical texts (which accounts for the preservation among the books of the Herculaneum library of books of the second century B.C.E. by Demetrius Laco and of the third by Epicurus and Colotes). Similarly, Plato's books were inherited by his successors in the Academy, whose work for several generations consisted solely in the guarded study of the founder's dialogues.

The Aristotelians of the Peripatos seem at first sight exceptional in this respect, insofar as Theophrastus followed Aristotle closely, but his successor Strato did not. The latter didn't even manage to retain for the school the manuscripts of Aristotle's own works. The result is highly instructive, as Sedley points out: from the beginning of Strato's headship (267 B.C.E.) the school rapidly declined in importance and re-emerged only during the course of the second century under the headship of Critolaus. As Aristotle's esoteric works became unavailable the school floundered virtually to the point of extinction. "It was arguably only the belated establishment of a set of canonical school texts by Andronicus in the late first century B.C. that Aristotelianism was able to become once again a major presence on the philosophical stage. Thus the Peripatos' fall from prominence under Strato serves to re-emphasize the indispensable cohesive force exerted by a school's commitment to its scriptures. Without them there was no school."[17]

The discovery of a philosophical library at Herculaneum seemed therefore to point to the existence there of just such a school, loyal to its Athenian roots in the Epicurean Garden. Some of the books it contained were standard textbook surveys, from an Epicurean point of view, of philosophical positions of the day. Ethics seemed to be

---

Nussbaum's article "Therapeutic Arguments: Epicurus and Aristotle" in Malcolm Schofield and Gisela Striker, eds. *Norms of Nature: Studies in Hellenistic Ethics* (Cambridge: Cambridge University Press, 1986), 31–74 may be usefully consulted, though she mischaracterizes the Epicurean approach to persuasion as appealing primarily to the irrational. See also her edited collection *Poetics of Therapy* (special issue of the periodical *Apeiron*) and *The Therapy of Desire: Theory and Practice in Hellenistic Ethics* (Princeton: Princeton University Press, 1994), with the glowing review by Sedley in *TLS*; more to the point is Bernard Williams, "Do Not Disturb," *LRB* (20 Oct. 1994), 25–26. A recent treatment of Hellenistic philosophical therapy is that of S. White in J. G. F. Powell, ed., *Cicero The Philosopher* (Oxford: Oxford University Press, 1995).
   [17] Sedley 100.

stressed over physics, with the latter being represented in the books on theology, since the Epicureans were materialists (they eschewed logic and dialectic).[18] Philodemus' interest in ethics and character-development is apparent, for example, from his treatise *On Household Management* (Περὶ οἰκονομίας). It treated the question of whether the philosopher will own and manage property. The treatise was book 9 of his larger work *On Vices and Virtues*. The elegantly displayed subscription reads Φιλοδήμου | Περὶ κακιῶν καὶ τῶν | ἀντικειμένων ἀρετῶν | καὶ τῶν ἐν οἷς εἰσι | καὶ περὶ ἅ θ', in the attenuated style of Hellenistic philosophical book-titles: *Philodemus' [treatise] Concerning Vices and their Corresponding Virtues and the People in Whom They Occur and the Situations in Which They are Found, book 9.* Philodemus' answer is that the philosopher will own property, in order to receive enough income to be happy; it is clear, however, that one's dependants will do the actual managing.

Some of Philodemus' writings are in fact the writing up of the lecture notes he took at Zeno's classes in Athens. His book *On Frank Criticism* (Περὶ παρρησίας), dealing in particular with the topic of master-pupil relationships, is subtitled as being ἐκ τῶν Ζήνωνος σχολῶν, i.e., based on notes "from Zeno's classes." Others show clear dependence on Zeno, especially *On Signs*, which is a report on a debate over logical inference from observation (or what we might call scientific method) between Stoics and Epicureans in the late second century B.C.E. Philodemus transcribes his own notes on Zeno's lectures, plus those of his fellow pupil Bromius (who Philodemus tells us had attended a different set of lectures from his own), together with the Epicurean Demetrius of Laconia's very similar account of the same debate. Philodemus has no personal involvement in the debate, as Sedley notes: "not only Zeno's arguments, but also the Stoic ones to which they are rejoinders, are known to Philodemus from those classes in Athens."[19] Sedley usefully suggests that some of Philodemus' works should be thought of as in some ways comparable in content

---

[18] The demotion of physics to a back-seat position in the writings of Philodemus is an unexplained mystery. Though the library contained a complete copy of Epicurus' *On Nature*, it is almost never cited. An exception that proves the rule is Philodemus' fairly technical discussion of the formation and dissolution of the atoms of the soul in *On Death* 4 (only the fourth book survives). The connections with the discussion of death and the fifty proofs why the soul cannot be immortal in the third book of Lucretius are too obvious to miss. Not surprisingly, the only Herculaneum treatises to quote from Epicurus' *On Nature* are *On Death* and *On Piety*.

[19] Sedley 104.

to Arrian's transcripts of Epictetus' teaching. Arrian revered Epictetus and was totally devoted to his teachings, as Philodemus was to Epicurus', with his own teacher Zeno serving as intermediary. In *Against the* [the rest of the title is lost], Philodemus says that he was a devoted ἐραστής (a word with erotic connotations) of Zeno while he lived, and now that he is dead Philodemus is an indefatigable encomiast (ὑμνητής) of him.

As Sedley notes,[20] there is no solid evidence that the works of Philodemus were themselves, strictly speaking, published. They may well have been produced purely for private use or teaching purposes. Diogenes Laertius cites Philodemus' *History of Philosophers* (in ten books), but apart from Philodemus' racy poems (preserved in the Greek anthology),[21] no other work of Philodemus is attested as having circulated. A native of Gadara in Syria who came to Italy via Athens in the early first century B.C.E., Philodemus was known principally for his elegant poetry and his works of philosophical historiography.[22] According to Sedley, "It is at least easy to see why an Epicurean working in Italy might be nervous about developing doctrinal ideas for himself, in isolation from the current climate of thought in the Garden at Athens, and why secondary literary activities like philosophical biography should be for him the much less hazardous option."[23] Sedley is thinking of the ancient Greek tradition that philosophers might be prosecuted for impiety for their beliefs. But in fact there is no evidence of this practice post-dating the middle of the fourth century, and none that Philodemus was ever faced with such a hazard—intellectual persecution at the hands of the authorities— as envisaged by Sedley.[24] More likely we have a situation in which Philodemus reproduced the basic tenets of the school for the benefit of his wealthy but (according to Cicero) philosophically recalcitrant patron Piso. These works were published, as far as we know, by neither Piso nor Philodemus. Rather Piso invited his circle of friends

---

[20] Ibid.

[21] New edition, translation, and commentary: David Sider, *The Epigrams of Philodemus* (Oxford: Oxford University Press, 1997). The poems circulated in Egypt in the first century C.E.: *The Oxyrhynchus Papyri*, vol. LIV (London: Egypt Exploration Society, 1987) no. 3724.

[22] See Sider, *Epigrams of Philodemus*, 227–34 for a partial collection of testimony (his T8, 231 should be discarded, as having no demonstrable connection with Philodemus of Gadara).

[23] Sedley 105.

[24] Obbink, "The Atheism of Epicurus," *GRBS* 30 (1989): 187–223.

in to make use of them as they would in his vacation villa on the sunny Bay of Naples. On certain occasions Philodemus was invited to give a demonstration of the Epicurean approach to currently fashionable topics, such as how traditional poetry might be read to provide an acceptable philosophical education,[25] and so be useful to the potential Republican ruler, an aristocratic would-be king.

The Library offers a glimpse of the school's concern for establishing a canon of Epicurean authorities:[26] (1) by branding of certain works as heretical; (2) through textual scholarship: Demetrius of Laconia, at any rate, was prepared to posit scribal error in cases of discrepancies between the scholarchs' transmitted words and coherent or valid argument; (3) by correction: Epicurus himself had said explicitly that some of his own and his colleagues' work had been mistaken. Philodemus' teacher Zeno "looked into the matter" of parts of certain treatises, attributed to Epicurus' early associates (Metrodorus is specifically named), whose authenticity was suspect on stylistic grounds.[27] One potential result would be to exclude the discredited texts from the canon.

Does this then add up to religious commitment to the authority of a founder figure? Did the later Epicurean groups constitute cults and conventicles ("cells," according to one recent, hostile critic) or a school of philosophy? Philodemus and other later Epicureans certainly did venerate Epicurus and offer him (and the other early Scholarchs) cultic veneration.[28] Does this mean they constituted a religion, or at least functioned as a religious community? Or is this simply a continuation, within a philosophical corporation organized along family lines, of the extremely widespread Greek and Athenian practice of offering cultic veneration to dead members of one's household?

Philodemus' treatise *On Piety*, virtually unexploited for this question to date, shows that the Epicureans did engage in philosophical

---

[25] Or the seeds thereof. This allows us to assimilate to the pattern of the Library Philodemus' treatise *On the Good King according to Homer*, for which special exception must be made by Sedley; he disallows it as "outside Philodemus' philosophical activities" (105 n. 24). Edited with Italian translation by Tiziano Dorandi (Naples: Bibliopolis, 1982); English translation by Elizabeth Asmis, "Philodemus' Poetic Theory and *On the Good King According to Homer*," *ClAnt* 10 (1991): 1–45; a new edition with English translation and commentary is forthcoming by Jeffrey Fish.

[26] Sedley 106–7.

[27] See on *On Piety* 705–6 (Obbink).

[28] Especially Clay, "The Cults of Epicurus," *CErc* 16 (1986): 11–28; more broadly, William Scott Ferguson, "The Cult of Heroes," *HThR*.

disputation of the day, offered rhetorical proofs (πίστεις) for the gods'
existence, defended their philosophy and the cult of its founder as
a kind of θεραπεία conducive to ethical and psychological well-being.
Philodemus claims that the Epicureans credit "not only all the gods
of the Greeks, but many more besides" (a remarkable thought), to
which he contraposes the Stoics' reduction of the elements to "one
universal god" and their failure to acknowledge "all the gods that
common report [ἡ κοινὴ φήμη] has handed down. With these we
[Epicureans] concur."[29] As a result, he says, piety is "virtually the
same thing as justice," which offers social security and so is cultivated by the Epicurean as a craft (τέχνη) of living, susceptible of
general principles, and teachable.[30] "No one," says Philodemus, "has
ever succeeded in producing absolutely certain proofs [ὑποδείξεις]
for the existence of the gods; nevertheless we believe in them and
worship then, as do all humans, with the exception of certain mad-
men [τινες παράκοποι]."[31]

The difference between this approach and a "virtually religious
commitment to the authority of a founder figure" is that Philodemus
offers arguments, in refuting his opponents point for point, for why
the Epicureans believe in and worship gods. There is no appeal *per
se* to the founder's words or opinions as authoritative, except insofar as they provide demonstrative argument for the positions held.
And in general, I argue, it is this feature that distinguishes the
Hellenistic philosophical schools largely from the broader complex
social and theological movements we call Hellenistic religions: in the
latter a founder's words or actions alone may serve, without proof,
to define membership, allegiance, authority, persuasion, and power.
As Sedley himself notes "only the Pythagorean sect stooped to that."[32]

A similar pattern may be observed elsewhere in the composition
of the books of the library, i.e., in Philodemus' sparring partners,
Epicurean and non-Epicurean alike, the objects of his polemic. In
such cases Philodemus often does not even bother to name names.
But when he does so, we meet not figures of authority invested with
power and charisma, but shadowy, unattested types, philosophers

---

[29] *On Piety*, PHerc. 1428 col. 10, 8–11, 5 in Albert Henrichs, *CErc* 4 (1974):
20–21.
[30] *On Piety* 2260–5 (Obbink 260).
[31] *On Piety* 640–57 (Obbink 150).
[32] Sedley p. 102.

and grammarians by profession who never quite made the transition to the codex apart from the odd dictionary entry or mention in somebody else's book. Lack of authority here is sometimes frustrating. It is sufficiently annoying that Philodemus often does not dignify his opponents by mention of their names. But when he obliges it seems like downright impertinence for it to turn out to be Pausimachos or Herakleodoros or Andromenides (some of the κριτικοί attacked in *On Poems*), just nobody really, had his name not been accidentally dropped in Hesychius' entry on Ἐνοδία.[33] About such figures we cannot even claim to be tolerably well informed by Philodemus. As κριτικοί go, Crates and Aristo are well enough known. But Demetrius of Byzantium, Karneiskos, Philista, Tisamagora(s) are ciphers to us. Dionysius of Cyrene, a Stoic, recently surfaced repeatedly in new fragments from Philodemus' *On Gods*. He was otherwise mentioned only by Tertullian (*Adv. nat.* 2.2) and Isidorus (*Etym.* 8.6,18), and, of course, by Philodemus. He was probably known to Varro,[34] and seems to have been Philodemus' principal opponent in *On Gods*. In *On Piety*[35] Philodemus tosses off the name Philippos as a standard example of a notorious atheist. He sounds like someone we should know, but we don't, apart from his mention here.[36]

Of course there is no lack of philosophical luminaries among the papyri. Epicurus figures in a big way: there was apparently a complete Περὶ φύσεως in the Villa's library, some books in multiple copies in

---

[33] Pausimachos is a complete cipher to us outside of Philodemus' *On Poems*; see Richard Janko's edition and translation of *On Poems* 1–2, (Oxford: Oxford University Press, 2001); edition and translation of *On Poems* 1–2 (Oxford: Oxford University Press, 2001); Janko, "Philodemus Resartus: Progress in Reconstructing the Philosophical Papyri from Herculaneum," *PBACAP* 1991 vol. 7 (1993): 271–308, 299–302 (on Pausimachus); Constantina Romeo, *Demetrio Lacone: Sulla Poesia*, La Scuola di Epicuro (Naples: Bibliopolis, 1988), 57–65 (on Demetrios of Byzantium and Pausimachos). Herakleodoros is known only from Philodemus' references in *On Poems* 5; see Cecilia Mangoni, *Filodemo, Il quinto libro della poetica*, La Scuola di Epicuro 14 (Naples: Bibliopolis, 1993), 275–77, with Italian translation. Andromenides makes a brief appearance in the Hesychius entry Ἡνοδία· "Αρτεμις· καὶ κυνηγετικά, ὡς Ἀνδρομενίδης, which at least shows he had an interest in glossing poetic epithets of the gods; see Romeo 45–50; Mangoni, 277–79.

[34] Cf. Isid. *Etym.* 8.6, 21..On Dionysios of Cyrene see Hermann Diels, *Philodemus über die Götter, Erstes Buch*, Abhandlungen der Königlich Preussischen Akademie der Wissenschaften 1916, Philosophisch-historische Klasse Nr. 7 (Text und Erläuterung), 55–57. On the new fragments of *De dis*, Knut Kleve, "The Unknown Parts of Philodemus, *On the Gods*, Book I," in *L'Epicureismo Greco e Romano, Atti del Congresso Internazionale*, vol. 2 (Naples: Bibliopolis, 1996), 671–81.

[35] PHerc. 1428 col. 12, 8–12 in Albert Henrichs, *CErc* 4 (1974): 22.

[36] Unless he is Philip of Opus, who makes an appearance in Philodemus' *Index Academicorum* (see the chapter of Clay in this volume). But he doesn't seem to fit the description of someone who explicitly denied the existence of the gods.

old manuscripts dating back at least to the second century B.C.E., though little evidence in the rest of the papyri that they were much read.[37] In spite of Lucretius' encomium of Epicurus as a god in the proem of *De rerum natura* 5, the words of the founder were no sacred scripture. The works of Epicurus and the early founders of the school, Hermarchus, Metrodorus, and Polyaenus are of course cited frequently, as are non-Epicurean philosophers, if not exactly the ones we would expect. Plato is occasionally mentioned, and there were at Herculaneum copies of books by the early Epicurean scholarchs (Colotes and Polyaenus) attacking dialogues of Plato and Aristotle by name. There is even a copy of a treatise on logic by the Stoic philosopher Chrysippus, and there may have been more non-Epicurean books. Even the extant papyri are full of holes, into which interstices fall the names of philosophers and their books, as well as their arguments.

We might have expected prosopographical potpourri from the works of an author who, like Philodemus, was preserved at random and was not subject to the same criteria of selection for transmission as our canonical authors and texts.[38] But if we ask who is most often discussed in the philosophical library from Herculaneum, it may occasion some surprise that the most frequently discussed figure by far in the Herculaneum papyri (after Epicurus himself) is not Plato or Aristotle, nor any of Epicurus' pupils, nor Crates, nor any of the founders of Stoicism. It is Diogenes of Babylon, the second century Stoic champion of Chrysippus, who himself came to Rome in 155 B.C.E.[39]

It is tempting to ascribe some of Diogenes' prominence in the books from Herculaneum to the pivotal position he occupied in the transmission of Greek philosophical and literary culture to Republican Rome. This is at least suggested by the common interest in him exhibited him by Cicero and the resident alien Philodemus. Diogenes himself had visited Rome within recent historical memory, an event alluded to more than once by Cicero.[40]

---

[37] See above, n. 18.

[38] See *BASP* 28 (1991): 89–90.

[39] This can be gauged from a mere glance at the exhaustive philosophical prosopography, compiled by Tiziano Dorandi, of the Herculaneum library which appears in *Corpus di papiri filosofici*, vol. 1 (Firenze: Olshiki, 1989), 38 on Diogenes, for whom over a hundred entries are recorded, thus exceeding the number of mentions of Epicurus' favorite pupils, including Hermarchos and Metrodoros, and exceeded only by those for Epicurus himself.

[40] See Obbink and P. A. Vander Waerdt, "Diogenes of Babylon: The Stoic Sage in the City of Fools," *GRBS* 32 (1991): 355–96, esp. 389–96.

The books from Herculaneum may turn out to be as interesting for the intellectual world they document as for the principal author they preserve. Philodemus' works in this respect provide a valuable control. While he moved in the same circles as canonical authors, wrote on the same subjects, read the same books, and tapped into the same system of patronage, his works were ultimately preserved at random. They did not depend for transmission upon the process of selection and canonization of later antiquity or the tastes of the Renaissance Humanists. The prominence of Diogenes of Babylon in Philodemus' writings suggests the former's pivotal importance at a time when the Stoa was about to undergo radical changes. This was a time that coincided with the transmission of much of Greek philosophy to Roman culture, including the model for a philosophical school sensitive to the persuasiveness of the word, but distinct from the affairs of cult.

HOW TO COMMIT PHILOSOPHY OBLIQUELY: PHILODEMUS' EPIGRAMS IN THE LIGHT OF HIS *PERI PARRHESIAS*

David Sider

Abstract

Philodemus occasionally fashioned a persona for himself in his epigrams that differs from that of the serious voice he uses in his prose treatises, in that his poetic self often falls short of the aims set by his prosaic self. This essay looks closely at two of these epigrams in order to show both how they accord with Philodemus' Περὶ παρρησίας, and how the particular technique of speaking frankly therein derives from poetic and Platonic models.

If, as seems to be the case, Philodemus believed that poetry was not the medium for rational argument, which could properly be conveyed only via prose,[1] there would be sufficient reason to exclude his epigrams from any account of his philosophy. And even if the epigrams are found to be (in some way) consistent with Philodemus' Epicurean views, they could still, as indeed they very largely have been, be ignored in a straightforward philosophical analysis. But if, as I hope to show, the epigrams are not merely consistent with but are intended to illustrate doctrines found in his prose, they become more philosophically interesting in themselves.

As may be seen in greater detail in my edition of his epigrams,[2] Philodemus is not in these short poems primarily concerned with

---

[1] See further below, and cf. Elizabeth Asmis, "Philodemus's Poetic Theory and *On the Good King According to Homer*," *CA* 10 (1991): 1–45; Asmis, "Epicurean Poetics," in *Philodemus and Poetry*, Dirk Obbink, ed. (New York: Oxford University Press, 1995), 15–34; David Sider, "The Epicurean Philosopher as Hellenistic Poet," *Philodemus and Poetry* 42–57. The title of my essay owes something to P. Mitsis, "Committing Philosophy on the Reader: Didactic Coercion and Reader Autonomy in *De Rerum Natura*," *MD* 31 (1993): 111–28.

[2] Sider, *The Epigrams of Philodemos: Introduction, Text, and Commentary* (New York: Oxford University Press, 1997); cf. 34, 36f., 40, 187f.

providing us with autobiographical information (although there may be some), nor does he care to portray an authorial persona that is consistent with his "historical" self, at least not uniformly, although he may choose to do so when it suits his poetic purposes. Indeed, what we find is that in several of the epigrams he presents a narrator who falls short of the Epicurean goals for ethical behavior and thought which in his prose he lays out presumably for himself as well as for his reader.

Since these epigrams were in the first instance almost certainly recited by Philodemus during dinner parties to a group of like-minded Greek and Roman friends in the vicinity of Naples,[3] it was then and remains now easy to attach the name "Philodemus" to the first-person narrator, provided we (his audience then and now) recognize that "Philodemus" does not necessarily equal Philodemus.[4]

In this essay I shall present the case for reading two of Philodemus' epigrams as illustrations of views presented in his Περὶ Παρρησίας, which in turn should be seen as themselves summing up some earlier examples of frank criticism as seen both in poetry and Plato. The two poems are *Anth. Pal.* 9.570 and 9.512 (3 and 29 in my new numeration):[5]

3

—Ξανθὼ κηρόπλαστε μυρόχροε μουσοπρόσωπε,
  εὔλαλε, διπτερύγων καλὸν ἄγαλμα Πόθων,
ψῆλόν μοι χερσὶ δροσιναῖς μύρον· ἐν μονοκλίνῳ
  δεῖ με λιθοδμήτῳ δεῖ ποτε πετριδίῳ
εὕδειν ἀθανάτως πλουλὺν χρόνον. ᾆδε πάλιν μοι,   5
  Ξανθάριον, ναὶ ναὶ τὸ γλυκὺ τοῦτο μέλος.
—οὐκ ἀίεις, ὤνθρωφ' ὁ τοκογλύφος; ἐν μονοκλίνῳ
  δεῖ σε βιοῦν αἰεί, δύσμορε, πετριδίῳ.

Anth. Pal. 9.570 [14 Gow-Page]

<Man:> Xantho—formed of wax, with skin smelling of perfume, with the face of a Muse, of splendid voice, a beautiful image of the double-winged Pothoi—
pluck for me with your delicate hands a fragrant song: "In a solitary rocky bed made of stone I must surely someday

---

[3] Cf. Alan Cameron, *Callimachus and his Critics* (Princeton: Princeton University Press, 1995), ch. 3, "The Symposium."

[4] The scholarly literature on such fictional personae is large; in addition to those authors cited below, cf. also *The Poet's I in Archaic Greek Lyric*, ed. S. R. Slings (Amsterdam: VU University Press, 1990).

[5] Since the text is fairly secure, the critical apparatus may be safely omitted here.

sleep a deathlessly long time." Yes, yes, Xantharion, sing again for me
this sweet song.

<Xantho:> Don't you understand, man, you accountant you? You
must live forever, you wretch, in a solitary rocky bed!

29

—ἤδη καὶ ῥόδον ἐστὶ καὶ ἀκμάζων ἐρέβινθος
καὶ καυλοὶ κράμβης, Σώσυλε, πρωτοτόμου
καὶ μαίνη σαλαγεῦσα καὶ ἀρτιπαγὴς ἁλίτυρος
καὶ θριδάκων οὔλων ἀφροφυῆ πέταλα·
ἡμεῖς δ᾽ οὔτ᾽ ἀκτῆς ἐπιβαίνομεν οὔτ᾽ ἐν ἀπόψει   5
γινόμεθ᾽ ὡς αἰεί, Σώσυλε, τὸ πρότερον·
—καὶ μὴν Ἀντιγένης καὶ Βάκχιος ἐχθὲς ἔπαιζον,
νῦν δ᾽ αὐτοὺς θάψαι σήμερον ἐκφέρομεν.

Anth. Pal. 9.512 [20 Gow-Page]

<Philodemus:> Already the rose and chickpea and first-cut cabbage-
stalks are at their peak, Sosylus,
and there are sautéed sprats and fresh cheese curds and tender curly
lettuce leaves.
But we neither go on the shore nor are we on the promontory, Sosylus,
as we always used to.
<Sosylus:> Indeed, Antigenes and Bakkhios were playing yesterday,
but today we carry them out for burial.

As printed here, each poem is in dialogue form.[6] Gow and Page,
however, following the lead of Kaibel, stripped the first of its final
distich, believing it to be a Byzantine addition.[7] And the second poem
appears as a dialogue for the first time in my edition, all earlier
editors content to follow the (not entirely dependable) manuscripts
in printing the entire epigram as if spoken by one voice.[8]

It is important to note that these two poems are part of a larger
group of epigrams in which the author puts himself forward as the

---

It is available in Sider, *Epigrams of Philodemos*, 3–4, 164. Hereafter, all epigrams of
Philodemus will be identified first by my numbers.

[6] *Epigram* 20 (*Anth. Pal.* 5.46) is a dialogue between a streetwalker and her cus-
tomer; on this form in general, cf. Wilhelm Rasche, *De Anthologiae Graecae epigram-
matis quae colloquii formam habent* (Munich: Aschendorff, 1910).

[7] Georg Kaibel, "Sententiarum liber primus," *Hermes* 15 (1880): 459f.; Andrew
Sydenham Farrar Gow and Denys Lionel Page, *The Greek Anthology: The Garland of
Philip* (Cambridge: Cambridge University Press, 1968), 2:384. The authenticity of
the last distich is well defended by Wolfgang Schmid, "Philodem als Dichter und
als Philosoph: Über eine Athetese Kaibels in AP 9.570," *Acta Conventus XI Eirene,
21–25 Oct. 1968* (Warsaw: Ossolinuem, 1971), 201–207 = Schmid, *Ausgewählte
Philologische Schriften* (Berlin: W. de Gruyter, 1984), 267–74.

[8] The καὶ μήν of line 7 is best understood as "inceptive-responsive," when "a
person who has been invited to speak expresses by the particles his acceptance of the
invitation;" John Dewar Denniston, *The Greek Particles* (Oxford: Clarendon, 1934), 355.

persona of the narrator. Most of them are linked by the name
Xanthippe, which may be abbreviated to Xantho, Xanthion, or
Xantharion.[9] In *Epigram* 5 (*Anth. Pal.* 5.112) the narrator would like
to turn from manic love to a life governed more by mature and
rational thought. *Ep.* 6 (*Anth. Pal.* 11.34) contrasts two symposia as
metaphors for wild living and marriage, respectively. *Ep.* 4 (*Anth. Pal.*
11.41), in obvious parallel with 5 and 6, also looks to a new way
of living. As I argue in my edition (34–38), these poems can be seen
as part of a cycle in which the narrator marries Xanthippe and plans
to live a life of reason, in contrast with his previous style of living.
Since there is some evidence that, among his friends at least,
Philodemus could be called by the nickname Socrates,[10] Xanthippe,
Socrates' wife, becomes an obvious namesake for a woman (real or
fictitious) who is to play the role of wife to this philosopher.

Turning first to *Epigram* 3, we note that the narrator asks Xantho to
console him as he grieves at the thought of his own death. Since this
is an Epicurean subject we know well from Lucretius' discussion and
from Philodemus' own *De Morte*,[11] it is easy to see that the speaker
of lines 1–6, whom I regard as a persona of Philodemus, here fails
to maintain the required *sang-froid* in the face of his mortality. Even
were we to agree with Kaibel and Gow-Page in secluding the last
two lines we would still have a poem in which Philodemus' audience
(originally a live audience of friends) would be treated to the amus-
ing sight of someone, dispassionate in his prose on the subject of

---

[9] In *Ep.* 3 (*Anth. Pal.* 9.570), Philodemus addresses the same woman once as
Xantho (v. 1) and again as Xantharion (v. 6; see the commentary in my edition
ad. loc.). It cannot be proven that the two other names mentioned refer to the
same woman, but this is a reasonable assumption in light of the fact that the use
of such nicknames was a commonplace in Hellenistic epigram and in Latin love
elegy, which was greatly influenced by the former.

[10] Catullus 47 begins with an address to Porcius and Socration, whom he identifies
as two associates of Piso. I follow (with further argument) G. Friedrich, *Catulli
Veronensis Liber* (Leipzig: Teubner, 1908), 228, in identifying Socration as Philodemus
and Piso as L. Piso Caesonius, who seems to have acted as Philodemus' patron
and who is the best candidate for owner of the Villa dei Papiri, where all of
Philodemus' (et aliorum) prose was found. Sider, "The Love Poetry of Philodemus,"
AJP 103 (1982): 208–213. Nicknames were common in Philodemus' circle. Vergil,
for example, was called Parthenias (= *virgo*; cf. Donatus, *Vita Verg.* 11) and Philodemus'
fellow Epicurean Siron was called Silenus (*Schol. ad Verg. Ecl.* 6.10, 13).

[11] On the former see Barbara Price Wallach, *Lucretius and the Diatribe against the
Fear of Death: De Rerum Natura III 830–1094* (Leiden: Brill, 1976); Charles Segal,
Lucretius on Death and Anxiety (Princeton: Princeton University Press, 1990). On the
latter see Marcello Gigante, *Ricerche filodemee*, 2nd ed. (Naples: G. Macchiaroli, 1983),
115–234, and the essay by David Armstrong in this volume.

death, now almost quaking at the thought that he too must die. At the end of its sixth line, however, the poem lacks closure, closure provided by the last two lines, Xantho's response, as she sharply repeats his words to remind him that death is indeed an eternal sleep which, since he will never wake from it, need not concern him.

This is closely paralleled by the dramatic situation of *Epigram* 29, where once again it is easy to imagine the first voice belonging to Philodemus,[12] who begins by alluding to the foods of the season, but whatever good feeling this may have evoked before is tempered by the remark that "we do not go as usual down to the shore." Why this is so is explained in the last distich, probably delivered by Sosylus, not only reminding Philodemus (and hereby telling us) that they must take part in the funeral for two friends who died (perhaps together in a boating accident), but also hinting that Philodemus' maudlin tone is inappropriate. Their deaths have to be accepted, just as we must accept the thought of ourselves someday dying. Compare Epicurus *SV* 66, συμπαθῶμεν τοῖς φίλοις οὐ θρηνοῦντες ἀλλὰ φροντίζοντες ("let us sympathize with our [dead] friends not by lamenting but by meditation"), *Rat. Sent.* 40, πληρεστάτην οἰκειότητα ἀπολαβόντες οὐκ ὠδύραντο ὡς πρὸς ἔλεον τὴν τοῦ τελευτήσαντος προκαταστροφήν ("having derived the greatest closeness, they [i.e., those with an Epicurean cast of mind] do not grieve over someone who has died before them as though it were something pitiable"). Note that Lucretius too sets up a dialogue on the subject of the right attitude towards death, but that unlike Philodemus he is to be seen not at all in the man in fear of death (3.904–11). Lucretius' righteous persona is that of the narrator of didactic epic best illustrated by Hesiod but also seen in Empedocles.[13]

Epigrams 3 and 29 thus appear to be remarkably similar in form and content: In each Philodemus allows himself to drift from Epicurean

---

[12] In general I take the position that unless there are clear signs to the contrary (such as those epigrams written by men in the persona of a woman), all first-person narratives in epigrams and elegy are to be understood as a persona of the author, who is free to embellish or belittle himself. That the persona of this poem is Philodemus is argued by Gigante, *Philodemus in Italy*, trans. Dirk Obbink (Ann Arbor: University of Michigan Press, 1995), 55–59, who further (but to my mind not convincingly) sets the poem at the belvedere belonging to the villa in Herculaneum where the texts of Philodemus' prose treatises were found. For my arguments against Gigante's interpretation of this poem, see my commentary ad *Ep.* 29.5.

[13] Cp. Mitsis, who shows how much of Lucretius' critical tone is deflected from the reader to the foolish Memmius; cf. esp. 122f.

orthodoxy on the subject of death, and in each he is called back, none too politely, to his senses by someone who must be accounted a friend in both the ordinary sense and in the special sense accorded the word φίλος by the Garden. That both poems are concerned with death we may consider an accident; the similarity of form seems far more interesting, illustrating as it does the way in which one Epicurean can speak frankly with another in the way Philodemus describes in his Περὶ Παρρησίας.[14]

Παρρσηία, that is παν + ῥῆσις, originally was a typically Athenian characteristic (praiseworthy or blameworthy, depending on one's point of view), meaning not necessarily that one did in fact say everything but that the citizen was *able* to "say everything;" cf. Aristoph. *Thesm.* 540–541: εἰ γὰρ οὔσης | παρρησίας κἀξὸν λέγειν . . . ("for if there is *parrhesia* and it is possible to speak . . ."). Here is Socrates on the onset of the democratic polity: οὐκοῦν πρῶτον μὲν δὴ ἐλεύθεροι, καὶ ἐλευθερίας ἡ πόλις μεστὴ καὶ παρρησίας γίγνεται, καὶ ἐξουσία ἐν αὐτῇ ποιεῖν ὅτι τις βούλεται ("First, then, the men become free, and the city comes to be full of freedom and frank speech, and it is possible to do whatever one wants in it," *Rep.* 557b).[15] It is important to note, however, that although this Athenian frankness had a clear political component, it was from the very first a quality the Athenians admitted and admired in their daily lives.[16]

But since implicit in the Athenian political ideal of παρρησία is the notion that the citizen is free to stand up in the assembly and freely state his views on how the state should best proceed, the word came to have this same idea of improvement now directed towards a single auditor (although one would not learn this from reading LSJ s.v. παρρησία, which fails to cite texts where this word is regarded

---

[14] Alexander Olivieri, ed., *Philodemi: De libertate dicendi* (Leipzig: B. G. Teubner, 1914), on which see Clarence E. Glad, *Paul and Philodemus: Adaptability in Epicurean and Early Christian Psychagogy*, NovTSup. 81 (Leiden: Brill, 1995); Glad, "Frank Speech, Flattery, and Friendship in Philodemus," in John T. Fitzgerald, ed., *Friendship, Flattery, and Frankness of Speech*, NovTSup 82 (Leiden: Brill, 1996); Gigante, *Philodemus in Italy*, 38–39. It has now been translated by David Konstan, Diskin Clay, Glad, Johan C. Thom, and James Ware, *Philodemus: On Frank Criticism*, SBLTT 43 (Atlanta: Scholars, 1998).

[15] For a brief overview of the political aspect of this word, cf. Kurt Raalflaub, "Des freien Bügers Recht der freien Rede: Ein Beitrag zur Begriffs- und Sozialgeschichte der athenischen Demokratie," in Werner Eck et al., eds. *Studien zur antiken Sozialgeschichte: Festschrift Friedrich Vittinghoff* (Cologne: Böhlau, 1980); David E. Fredrickson, "Παρρησία in the Pauline Epistles," in Fitzgerald 165–68. The *locus classicus* for the hostile view of Athenian free speech is provided by Ps.-Xenophon, *Ath.* passim.

[16] Cf. Eur. *Ba.* 668, Plato, *Symp.* 222c, *Phdr.* 240d.

as a component of ethical virtue). Thus, as the ameliorative sense shifts from the public to the private sphere, it becomes appropriate to discuss the circumstances that call for its use. When, that is, and towards whom is it appropriate to use παρρησία as a means of correcting an individual's faults?

For παρρησία, it seems, requires great care in its use. Much as a physician (a favorite metaphor of Philodemus in this context)[17] must be careful not to cause harm when he applies his healing instruments, so too the one who would apply "biting" words must be careful lest he be thought merely insulting: τῆς πικρᾶς πα[ρρησίας] ὁμοιότητα πρὸς τὴν [λοι]δορίαν ἐχούσης, ὡς λοιδορούμενοι καὶ δυσνοίας ("keen frankness is similar to insult, so as for one to think that they insult even with ill will;" fr. 60.4–7).[18]

One must, therefore, take into account the status of the individual before the application of stinging but healing words. Women, famous men, the rich, and the old, for example, are particularly sensitive to criticism: women because they think that they deserve pity and pardon more than ridicule and contempt (col. XXIb–XXIIb), illustrious men because they believe envy to be behind all criticism (col. XXIIb–XXIVa), and the old simply because they would like to believe that with age comes intelligence (col. XXIV).

The situation is obviously more favorable for παρρησία between teacher and student, although here too one must exercise care since some students are "imperfect," that is, not yet in command of the Epicurean doctrines that would prepare their disposition to receive frank criticism. See, for example, fr. 10.3–7 ἀλλά ποτε καὶ ἁ[πλ]ῶς ποήσεται τὴν παρ[ρη]σίαν, παρακινδυνευτέ[ον ε]ἶναι νομίζων, ⟨ἐὰν⟩ ἄλλως μὴ ὑπ[α]κούωσι[ν ("but on occasion he [i.e., the teacher] will employ frankness because he thinks it worth the risk, [whenever] they [i.e., students] otherwise pay no attention"). But some students cannot endure receiving such criticism from their teachers, however much it is motivated by good intentions (fr. 31). Giving in to one's disposition to speak frankly can spell ruin (ἀ[π]ώλογτο, strong language) if one addresses the wrong people (fr. 72). One should not

---

[17] At one point he compares παρρησία to an enema (Philod. Περὶ παρ. fr. 64.5–7 Oliveri); cf. Glad, *Paul and Philodemus*, 133–37.

[18] All translations of Greek in this essay are my own, but in the case of Περὶ Παρρησίας I wish to acknowledge guidance by a penultimate version of the translation prepared by Konstan, Glad, et al.

therefore employ frankness in every case, but only when necessary (col. IIb), and of course when appropriate.

The best circumstances for employing frank criticism would seem to be when the one who chastises and the one chastised are of equal or nearly equal status, each having been trained in the teachings of Epicurus, who offers the finest example in this as in all ethical behavior: καὶ τὸ συνέχον καὶ κυριώτ[α]τον, Ἐπικούρῳ, καθ᾽ ὃν ζῆν ᾑρήμεθα, πειθαρχήσομεν ("What is basic and of utmost importance is that we shall follow Epicurus, according to whom we have chosen to live," fr. 45.7–10). Epicurus and Metrodorus both spoke frankly to their friends, that is, their fellows in the Garden (fr. 15). There is thus no shame if an Epicurean requires an occasional rebuke, for none of us is perfect; nor will he take offense even if the language is harsh, for he knows that it is for his own good. Since, furthermore, friendship is reciprocal, neither will he withhold criticism from a fellow student of Epicureanism: ἀλλ᾽ ἀναγκαίως τό τε λαθραιοπραγεῖν ἀ[φ]ιλώτατον δήπουθεν ὁ δὲ μὴ προσα[ν]αφέρων φανερός ἐστιν περιστέλλων καὶ ταῦτα τῶν φίλων τὸ[ν ἐ]ξοχώτατ[ον·] καὶ π[λ]ε̣ῖο̣ν ο̣[ὐ]δὲν ἔσται κρύπτοντος ("But to act in secret is surely most unfriendly. The person who does not bring the matter up will clearly be concealing these things from the most excellent of his friends; nor will the one concealing gain anything from it," fr. 41).

Although the statements quoted above are isolated from an already disjointed text, enough is clear to justify our using them to illuminate *Epigrams* 3 and 29. Both Xantho and Sosylus fit the profile for Epicurean friends in that they feel free to use language that to an outsider might well appear harsh, but which is necessary in order to restore Philodemus to a proper Epicurean state of mind. This third person, however, διά[β]ολόν τε γὰρ ο[ὐ]χ ἡγήσετ[α]ι τὸν ἐπιθυμοῦντα τὸν φίλον τυχεῖν διορθώσεως, ὅταν μὴ τοιοῦτος ᾖ τις, ἀλλὰ φιλόφιλον ("... will not think that the person desiring his friend to obtain correction is insulting him, when he is not such a person, but rather that he is his friend's friend;" fr. 50.3–8).[19] These two

---

[19] "Friend to one's friend" is clearly preferable in this Epicurean context than LSJ's (s.v. φιλόφιλος) "loving one's friend." Philodemus uses the word again in fr. 85, interestingly of the teacher's disposition towards his students. Cf. *Epigram* 7 (*Anth. Pal.* 5.4.5), where Philodemus refers to Xantho as his φιλεράστρι᾽ ἄκοιτις, which I argue in my commentary (*Epigrams of Philodemos*, 88–89) is to be understood as both "lover to a friend" and "friend to a lover," where again "friend" is to be understood in its Epicurean sense.

poems, then, illustrate Epicurean παρρησία in action; in particular that kind practiced between two friends.[20]

It is important to keep in mind, furthermore, that the person on the receiving end of the criticism is the author himself. By this device, Philodemus avoids writing poetry that would substitute itself for philosophical discourse, a project which Philodemus thinks is doomed to failure in his Περὶ Ποιημάτων, book 5, where the essence of poetry is defined almost exclusively in formalist aesthetic, not ethical, terms.[21] A particular poem may contain true statements or valid thought (διάνοια) which may contribute to its overall success, but it is *how* these are expressed rather than their truth value that is important. However much one may appreciate Nicander's didactic *Alexipharmaka*, a person bitten by a snake will doubtless choose a more prosaic source of information to cure himself. Similarly, ethical advice is best sought in prose treatises on the subject. An important corollary of this is that a poem may be judged good even if its facts (or its morality, theology, etc.) are wrong. Note in particular Philodemus' Περὶ Ποιημάτων, Book 5, col. 5.6–18 Mangoni, where Philodemus argues that a poet is free to write without any intention of benefiting his audience, and that someone (we do not know who) is wrong to burden the poet with having exact knowledge. Put even more strongly, even bad men can produce good literature: ὄν[τ]ες πονηροί, τ[ε]χνῖται [δὲ] ὅμως οὐ κωλύονται δ[ιαφορ]ώτατοι π[ά]ν[τ]ων ὑπ[άρχ]ειν ("they may be wicked, but they are not hindered from being the most skilled technicians;" *Rhet.* 2.226 Sudhaus, col. 21.12–5).

This is not to say that poems must be bereft of all ideas, such as seems to have been argued by Crates of Mallos, for whom euphony was paramount.[22] Philodemus seems to have argued for some middle ground where the excellence of a poem is a product of its poetic

---

[20] For the use of παρρησία in Latin poetry, see Norman W. DeWitt, "Parresiastic Poems of Horace," *CP* 30 (1935): 312–19; Agnes Kirsopp Michels, "Παρρησία and the Satire of Horace," *CP* 39 (1944): 173–77. On the relationship between Philodemus and Horace, see Jane Isabella Marion Tait, *Philodemus' Influence on the Latin Poets* (Ph.D. diss. Bryn Mawr, 1941), 64–76; Q. Cataudella, "Filodemo nella Satira I 2 di Orazio," *PP* 5 (1950): 18–31; Marcello Gigante, *Orazio. Una misura per l'amore: Lettura della satira seconda del primo libro* (Venice: Edizioni Osanna Venosa, 1993).

[21] See the essays by Asmis ("Epicurean Politics," 15–34), Sider ("The Epicurean Philosopher as Hellenistic Poet," 42–57), and Michael Wigodsky ("The Alleged Impossibility of Philosophical Poetry," 58–68) in *Philodemus and Poetry*.

[22] For Philodemus' criticism of Crates, see Asmis, "Crates on Poetic Criticism," *Phoenix* 46 (1991): 138–69.

values and the ideas expressed, which need not be true, and if true
need not (indeeed cannot) be pitched at the highest level; see
Philodemus' Περὶ Ποιημάτων, Book 5, col. 26.5–8, where it is said
that the thought contained in a poem should occupy some middle
ground between the wise man and the ordinary person.

How, then, do Philodemus' poems fit into this scheme? In a broad
sense they do so simply by providing their audience with a pleasurable
experience, most likely during the symposium part of the evening,
when friends amuse each other with discourse and other pleasing
activities. Some of Philodemus' poems, moreover, including the two
under review here, by alluding to philosophical ideas of Epicurus
and others, were specifically designed for Philodemus' audience of
Greeks and Romans, all of whom, whether Epicurean or not, were
well-versed in Greek philosophical texts, and hence especially pleased
to recognize oblique allusions to the arguments of Epicurus, Plato,
and Aristotle.

In the case of *Epigrams* 3 and 29, the pleasure derives in part from
a *Schadenfreude* as someone else is chided for a philosophical failing.
But this pleasure is tempered by the fact that the apostate is also
the author/narrator as well as their friend, who, since he is in control of the words of the poem, is therefore also determining their
reaction. The philosophical "message," such as might be found in a
prose treatise or didactic poem, is thus deflected from the putative
audience back to the speaker. One is free, perhaps one is expected, to
take the point to heart, but there is no direct moral suasion—only
the example of a situation in which the speaker of the poem might
be expected to take the point to heart.

Here then is an oblique method of imparting ethical guidance:
Criticize someone else by criticizing yourself.[23] It would be surprising if Philodemus were the first to think of this; and in fact he could

---

[23] This does not exhaust the possibilities. One can also criticize another by pretending to criticize a third person, as in Sophocles' *Aias*, first when Menelaos, arguing with Teucer, invents someone else to criticize (ἤδη ποτ' εἶδον ἄνδρ' ἐγώ, 1142),
whom he then likens to Teucer (οὕτω δὲ καὶ σέ, 1147); and next when Teucer, in
obvious imitation of Menelaos, also claims to have seen a fool (ἐγὼ δὲ γ' ἄνδρ' ὄπωπα
μωρίας πλέων, 1150): "And then someone seeing him, someone like me and equally
angry, said something like the following: . . ." (1152–53). In a passage in Sophocles'
Antigone (688–700) cited by Arist. *Rhet.* in illustration of this very point, Haemon
reports the general discontent of the citizens with Creon's actions rather than criticize his father directly, but he may do this because their discontent carries greater
weight than his own; see also below, n. 37.

draw from models in both poetry and philosophical prose, as appropriate for a philosophical poet. Perhaps the most straightforward example is in Solon's *Salamis*, when, in a successful attempt to stir his fellow Athenians to fight on behalf of this island, he describes the shame he would feel should Athens lose the island:

εἴην δὴ τότ' ἐγὼ Φολεγάνδριος ἢ Σικινήτης
  ἀντί γ' Ἀθηναίου πατρίδ' ἀμειψάμενος·
αἶψα γὰρ ἂν φάτις ἥδε μετ' ἀνθρώποισι γένοιτο·
  "Ἀττικὸς οὗτος ἀνήρ, τῶν Σαλαμιναφετέων."

("Would I were then a citizen of Pholegandros or Sicinos [two obscure towns], having given up my Athenian citizenship. For [otherwise] this might soon be said of me: 'This man is Attic, one of those who lost Salamis;'" fr. 2 West.) In other words, "*I* would be a fool" readily translates into "*You* would be foolish." According to Diogenes Laertius, our source for this fragment, it was these very lines of the poem that most moved the Athenians to action.[24]

A more complex but equally transparent attempt to guide another by one's own mistaken action can be found in Phoenix' speech to Achilles in *Iliad* 9. By unnecessarily (as it seems) mentioning his youth, Phoenix gives himself the opportunity to recount an episode with obvious relevance to Achilles (9.448–493, in abbreviated and annotated paraphrase):

> Hated by my father [cp. Agamemnon; in the *Iliad*'s concern with ranking, fathers, rulers, and elders are roughly equivalent] because of a woman [cp. Chryseis and Briseis], I intended to cut him down but was checked by a god [cp. Athena's restraining of Achilles, 1.188–221]. Isolated and supplicated [cp. Achilles], I ran away but lost my station in life [which you, Achilles, should avoid].

A more elaborate parallel follows, in which the story of Meleager is presented in such a way as to serve even more powerfully as a negative exemple, but many of the elements in this latter story were prefigured in Phoenix' autobiographical account, in which he was willing to cast himself in an unfavorable light in order to nudge

---

[24] Diog. Laert. 1.47. Cp. Solon 33 W, where Solon gives voice to the mockery of the crowd for his failing to avail himself of the riches available to one in his position of power: οὐκ ἔφυ Σόλων βαθύφρων οὐδὲ βουλήεις ἀνήρ . . . ἤθελον γάρ κεν κρατήσας . . . ἀσκὸς ὕστερον δεδάρθαι κἀπιτετρίφθαι γένος ("Solon was not born a deep thinker or man of good counsel . . . I wish I had his power and could be king for a day. I'd let myself be flayed alive and give up my family.")

Achilles in the right direction.[25] Note how beautifully Phoenix' speech illustrates Περὶ Παρρησίας fr. 9.6–9: ἐπεὶ καὶ μετάξει ποτ᾽ ἐφ᾽ ἑαυτὸν ὁ σοφός θ᾽ ἁμάρτημ᾽ ἄνετον ἐν τ[ῇ] νεότητι γε[γ]ονέ[ν]αι, "since the wise man will on occasion transfer an intemperate misdeed onto himself, (saying) that it occurred when he was young."

One could also point to passages in Pindar where he chides himself in such a way that his primary audience, the commissioner of the ode, could be expected to see the relevance to his own situation. In *Pyth.* 3.61 sq. μὴ φίλα ψυχά, βίον ἀθάνατον | σπεῦδε ("Don't, my soul, strive for immortal life"), for example, the soul addressed is clearly, at least in the first instance, his own.[26] The message, however, not to be eager for immortal life, has far greater relevance for the ailing Hieron to whom the poem is addressed. Here it is Pindar chiding his own soul, that is, himself, rather than another person, but the result remains that of one person accepting a rebuke (which he has himself composed) obliquely directed at another. Pindar, in Protean fashion, creates shifting personae for himself that, fleetingly and allusively, assimilate themselves to that of the *laudandus*. In his use of the words σοφία and σοφός, for example, he often refers both to the poetic craft as practiced by himself and to the more general wisdom found in wise rulers such as Hieron.[27] The result is that any statement that seems to offer advice to the poet has potential application to the *laudandus*.

These poetic examples are clearly relevant to Philodemus, but perhaps the closest parallel to his portrayal of himself as one in need of frank criticism is offered by Sappho 1:

---

[25] It should be clear from the above that I do not agree with John Bryan Hainsworth's comment that Phoenix' autobiography is (only) "to establish Phoenix' credentials" (119), or that it is "rather inconsequential" (121); *The Iliad: A Commentary.* Vol. III: *Books 9–12* (Cambridge: Cambridge University Press, 1993). For an interpretation of this section of Phoenix' speech along the lines outlined above, see Ruth Scodel, "The Autobiography of Phoenix," *AJP* 103 (1982): 128–36, who notes that "by leaving the argument veiled entirely in narrative, Phoenix succeeds in presenting his message far more tactfully than even the celebrated Odysseus" (136).

[26] So Gildersleeve ad loc., Slater s.v. φίλος 1 b; cp. also *Ol.* 1.4 εἰ δ᾽ ἄεθλα γαρύεν ἔλδεαι, φίλον ἦτορ ("If you desire to sing of athletic games, my heart").

[27] See *N.* 7.17–20; for the best treatment of the intentional ambiguity between poet and patron, see Thomas K. Hubbard, "The Subject/Object Relation in Pindar," *QUCC* 22 (1986): 52–72. See further David C. Young, *Three Odes of Pindar: A Literary Study of Pythian 11, Pythian 3, and Olympian 7* (Leiden: Brill, 1968), 44 n. 1, 58ff.; J. M. Bremer, "Pindar's Paradoxical ἐγώ and a Recent Controversy about the Performance of his Epinicia," in Slings 41–58, esp. 47.

ποικιλόθρον᾽ ἀθανάτ᾽ Ἀφρόδιτα,
παῖ Δίος δολόπλοκε, λίσσομαί σε,
μή μ᾽ ἄσαισι μηδ᾽ ὀνίαισι δάμνα, πότνια, θῦμον,

ἀλλά τυίδ᾽ ἔλθ᾽, αἴ ποτα κἀτέρωτα
τὰς ἔμας αὔδας ἀίοισα πήλοι
ἔκλυες, πάτρος δὲ δόμον λίποισα χρύσιον ἦλθες

ἄρμ᾽ ὑπασδεύξαισα· κάλοι δέ σ᾽ ἆγον
ὤκεες στροῦθοι περὶ γᾶς μελαίνας
πύκνα δίννεντες πτέρ᾽ ἀπ᾽ ὠράνω αἴθερος διὰ μέσσω·

αἶψα δ᾽ ἐξίκοντο· σὺ δ᾽ ὦ μάκαιρα,
μειδιαίσαισ᾽ ἀθανάτῳ προσώπῳ
ἦρε᾽ ὄττι μοι δηῦτε πέπονθα κὤττι δηῦτε κάλημμι

κὤττι μοι μάλιστα θέλω γένεσθαι
μαινόλᾳ θύμῳ· "τίνα δηῦτε πείθω
... σάγην† ἐς σὰν φιλότατα; τίς σ᾽, ὦ Ψάπφ᾽, ἀδίκησι;

καὶ γὰρ αἰ φεύγει, ταχέως διώξει,
αἰ δὲ δῶρα μὴ δέκετ᾽, ἀλλὰ δώσει,
αἴ δὲ μὴ φίλει, ταχέως φιλήσει κωὐκ ἐθέλοισα."

ἔλθε μοι καὶ νῦν, χαλέπαν δὲ λῦσον
ἐκ μερίμναν, ὄσσα δέ μοι τέλεσσαι
θῦμος ἰμέρρει, τέλεσον, σὺ δ᾽ αὔτα σύμμαχος ἔσσο.

"Dapple-flowered, immortal Aphrodite, daughter of Zeus, weaver of wiles, I beseech you, mistress, not to overcome me and my spirit with worry and woe; but come here if ever before you hearkened to my voice from afar and yoked your father's chariot and came here. And swift sparrows would guide you with wings aflutter from heaven through midair all round the dark earth. They came quickly. And you, my blessed one, with a smile on your immortal face, asked what again had I suffered and why was I again calling and what again was my and my heart's greatest wish. 'Whom am I again to persuade . . . to your love? Who wrongs you, Sappho? If in fact she flees, very soon she will be in pursuit; if she now does not receive your gifts, she will be offering gifts; and if she does not love, she will very soon be loving, however unwilling.' Come to me also now, release me from harsh cares, and accomplish all that my heart wishes to accomplish; and you yourself become my ally."

Here we have precisely those points noticed above in Philodemus' two epigrams: the poet presents a persona for him/herself asking for comfort (Sappho in the form of a hymn, Philodemus in colloquy with friends) but actually more in need of instruction, which the poet him/herself provides in the form of a mocking second voice. Sappho's

lyric form allows for greater sophistication than is found in Philodemus'
epigram. Note in particular how Sappho shifts from the indirect to
the direct form of Aphrodite's questions.[28] It may also be relevant
that Philodemus was convinced that both Sappho and epigram could
convey the values of ποίησις.[29] As Page notes, "Aphrodite smiles for
a most obvious reason: because she is amused . . . And we must not
forget that the smile and speech of Aphrodite are given to her by
Sappho: it is Sappho who is speaking, and the smile must be Sappho's
too, laughing at herself even in the hour of her suffering."[30]

While there is reason to believe that Sappho 1 is among Philodemus'
poetic models, he would also have been aware of Socrates' frequent
use of this same device to deliver tactfully what could otherwise be
regarded as harsh criticism.[31] Note, for example, how Socrates, when
dealing with the rather dense Hippias, reaches a point beyond which
politeness will not succeed, especially as Hippias, a lover of long prepared speeches, is disinclined to pursue the discussion in Socrates'
preferred fashion. Socrates now "remembers" a discussion he had
on this same matter (περί γε ἐπιτηδευμάτων καλῶν, "about fine practices," *Hippias Major* 286a) with some other, unnamed person who
"threw me into *aporia* in a very insulting fashion" (ὑβριστικῶς, 286c).
It is largely with this other person(a) that Socrates conducts the
Socratic dialogue that follows.[32]

Similarly, when Agathon, only slightly more intelligent than Hippias,
begins to flag and, admitting that he can no longer follow the argument, says that he will accept Socrates' (incomplete) account of love,
Socrates is forced to invent a conversation with Diotima, who (like

---

[28] For the mockery inherent in the goddess' δηὖτε, see Denys Lionel Page, *Sappho
and Alcaeus: An Introduction to the Study of Ancient Lesbian Poetry* (Oxford: Clarendon,
1955), 14; Sarah Tolle Mace, "Amour, Encore! The Development of δηὖτε in Archaic
Lyric," *GRBS* 34 (1993): 335–64.

[29] Phil. Περὶ Ποιημάτων Book 5, col. 38.7–10 Mangoni, on which see Gigante,
"Filodemo e l'epigramma," *CErc* 22 (1992): 5–8; my edition, 28–31.

[30] Page 15–16. See further on this point, John J. Winkler, "Double Consciousness
in Sappho's Lyrics," in his *Constraints of Desire: The Anthropology of Sex and Gender in
Ancient Greece* (New York: Routledge, 1990), 162–87, esp. 166–76.

[31] Although I shall ignore the fact that the Socrates of the dialogues is himself
but a refraction of the persona of Plato, what is said here about the former could
also be applied to the latter. That is, the occasional harshness of tone is not felt
by the reader to be directed in his or her direction.

[32] That this splitting of Socrates into two is somehow relevant to the idea adum-
brated in the dialogue that τὸ καλόν is a harmony of disparate elements need not
be pursued here; cf. Sider, "Plato's Early Aesthetics: The *Hippias Major*," *JAAC* 25
(1977): 465–70.

the hostile stranger in *Hippias Major*) will take over the discussion (*Symposium* 201cd). For me, the surest sign that their conversation never took place (that is, the astute reader is expected to infer that within the dramatic frame it is fictitious) is that, supposedly, Socrates had been arguing then exactly as Agathon is now, that Eros was a great god and the god of beautiful things, and that Diotima refuted Socrates with exactly the same argument Socrates has just been using on Agathon.[33] It seems unlikely that Socrates ever repeated dialogues in this way, for if they could be duplicated they could just as well be written down, whereas, as *Phaedrus* (also a dialogue about love) makes clear, what is "written" down in the soul is living, and hence unique—and writing is not at all a conveyance of true philosophy.

In *Crito*, Socrates assimilates himself to Crito ("if while *we* are preparing to run away," 50a) so that he can have the personification of the laws of Athens criticize Socrates himself (εἰπέ μοι, ὦ Σώκρατες, τί ἐν νῷ ἔχεις ποιεῖν; 50c; this vocative is repeated several times throughout the speech) when of course their objections are to the position occupied only by Crito. Socrates invites Crito to help him answer (τί ἐροῦμεν, ὦ Κρίτων; 50b, c), but against such an assault by an angry parent, Crito can not begin to argue (54d).

The last example from Plato is the speech of the personified Logos which chides both Socrates and Protagoras for having switched sides in the argument over whether virtue can be taught (ὥσπερ ἄνθρωπος ... εἰ φωνὴν λάβοι, "as though human ... if it could speak," *Prot.* 361a). It might seem that here at least Socrates does deserve some of the blame dished out by the Logos, were it not altogether likely that Socrates has maneuvered the argument to just this point in order to show, first, that the matter is far from settled, and, second and more important, that if this is the case the young Hippocrates should clearly not be putting himself into the care of Protagoras. That this impasse is entirely to Socrates' liking is shown by the fact that he chooses this moment to leave on the grounds of an appointment (362a), although immediately afterwards—as we read in the

---

[33] 201e, σχεδὸν γάρ τι καὶ ἐγὼ πρὸς αὐτὴν ἕτερα τοιαῦτα ἔλεγον οἷάπερ νῦν πρὸς ἐμὲ Ἀγάθων, ὡς εἴη ὁ Ἔρως μέγας θεός, εἴη δὲ τῶν καλῶν· ἤλεγχε δή με τούτοις τοῖς λόγοις οἷσπερ ἐγὼ τοῦτον, ὡς οὔτε καλὸς εἴη κατὰ τὸν ἐμὸν λόγον οὔτε ἀγαθός. Whether Diotima herself is, as I believe, also a fiction does not matter here; for a review of the scholarship on this issue, cf. David M. Halperin, "Why is Diotima a Woman?" in his *One Hundred Years of Homosexuality and Other Essays on Greek Love* (New York: Routledge, 1990), 119–24.

opening of the dialogue—he sits down with a friend who asks him
to narrate an account of his meeting with Protagoras, "if there is
nothing to prevent you" (310a). This strongly suggests that this is a
chance meeting, that is, that Socrates' excuse to Protagoras of a
meeting was fabricated to end the discussion where it did.[34] The criticism of the Logos, therefore, is directed primarily to Protagoras,
secondarily to Hippocrates, and not at all to Socrates.

For this oblique means of criticizing another there seems to be
no name and only general recognition. David Young suggests that
when Pindar addresses himself in a way calculated to include the
addressee of the poem as well, this technique "might be called the
'first-person indefinite,'"[35] but this label does not seem adequate even
for Pindar's usage, let alone the more general topos we have been
discussing here. Aristotle notices that one may have another voice
speak one's own displeasure with a person's behavior in order to
avoid blame: "Since, when one speaks of one's own ethical character one is open to envy, charges of long-windedness, or contradiction, and when speaking of another's to charges of abuse or rudeness,
it is necessary to make another person speak [i.e., in one's place]."[36]
As his examples from Isocrates and Archilochus show, however,
Aristotle is thinking of situations like that of Sophocles' *Aias*,[37] where
the person criticized remains the same, rather than what we have
found in Philodemus and others, the substituting of oneself for the
person criticized. Ps.-Demetrius, *De Elocutione*, 287–94, a work dependent on Aristotle's *Rhetoric* III, also discusses covert and ambiguous
ways of censuring people, but none is of the precise sort Philodemus
uses, and the closest *Eloc.* comes to a label is (τὸ ἐσχηματισμένον ἐν
λόγῳ), a rather vague expression which is regularly translated as
"covert allusion."[38]

---

[34] I owe this observation to Elinor West.
[35] Young 58.
[36] εἰς τὸ ἦθος, ἐπειδὴ ἔνια περὶ ἑαυτοῦ λέγειν ἢ ἐπίφθονον ἢ μακρολογίαν ἢ ἀντιλογίαν
ἔχει, καὶ περὶ ἄλλου ἢ λοιδορίαν ἢ ἀγροικίαν, ἕτερον χρὴ λέγοντα ποιεῖν, *Rhet.* 3.1418b24.
[37] See note 23 above.
[38] Note in particular c. 292, where we are instructed how to be circumspect
when trying to get powerful people to change their ways: "We shall not speak
directly, but either blame others who have acted the same way . . . or praise others who have acted the opposite way." Cp. Philostratus *VS* 2.1, Quintilian 9.2.66f.
See also Wilmer Cave Wright, trans., *Philostratus and Eunapius*, LCL (Cambridge:
Harvard University Press, 1989), 570n. I owe the references to Demetrius and those
in this note to John T. Fitzgerald.

However unrecognized or nameless as a topos, the technique of Philodemus' *Epigrams* 3 and 29 would seem to be a successful blending of poetic and philosophic models designed in equal measure to amuse—because the author invites us to join him in making fun of himself—and to illustrate the particular form of παρρησία that Epicureans—such as Philodemus himself and the audience for his poems—are expected to exercise with each other should one of them go astray.

A MEASURE OF *PARRHESIA*: THE STATE OF THE MANUSCRIPT OF PHERC. 1471

L. Michael White

Abstract

A description of the physical state of the manuscript of Philodemus' *On Frank Criticism* (Περὶ παρρησίας) not only illustrates the problem of restoring the text, but also provides insight into the character and social context of a private library in antiquity. An analysis of the scrolls gives valuable information regarding the process of transcribing, preserving, and reading manuscripts in a philosophical school.

The state of the manuscript of Philodemus' work *On Frank Criticism* (Περὶ παρρησίας) is of interest to New Testament scholars for several reasons. The principal one, naturally, is the restoration of the text itself, allowing production of a critical edition and providing a base for translation and literary analysis.[1] But the peculiar nature of the papyri from Herculaneum gives us other insights as well. It is one of the few cases where we can actually see physical evidence for the character of a private library in antiquity. The historical circumstances of the destruction of the Villa of the Papyri, as it is usually called, and the preservation of its scorched contents yield a *terminus ante quem* and archaeological context for dating and study. Also, analysis of the scrolls gives valuable information regarding the social context of ancient literature and the people who produced and read it. In the case of Περὶ παρρησίας we are able to see evidence of text authorship and transmission through several stages as well as evidence for manuscript production and use within the context of a philosophical school.

---

[1] It was this concern that gave rise to the present discussion when the Hellenistic Moral Philosophy and Early Christianity Group decided to undertake a translation of the work. Those efforts have now been published as *Philodemus, On Frank Criticism*, trans. David Konstan, Diskin, Clay, Clarence E. Glad, Johan C. Thom, James Ware, SBLTT 43 (Atlanta: Scholars, 1998). I must express gratitude to several scholars, specialists on the Herculaneum papyri, who were generous in sharing their knowledge with me: Richard Janko, Dirk Obbink, and David Armstrong.

The Text and Its School Context

The title and authorship of the work Περὶ παρρησίας (also known by the Latin title *De libertate dicendi*) is confirmed from the *subscriptio* of the papyrus, which describes it as a work "of Philodemus, being an accurate rendering in epitome from the classes of Zeno On Character and Life, which is On Frank Criticism."[2] Philodemus was born c. 110 B.C.E. in Gadara of the Decapolis and studied with Zeno of Sidon while the latter was head of the Epicurean school at Athens. Zeno was born c. 150 B.C.E., and Cicero reports having heard lectures of Zeno, "a testy old man" (*acriculus . . . senex*), while with Atticus in Athens, probably c. 79–78 B.C.E.[3] It appears that Zeno died within that decade, but Philodemus continued to be a "singer of praises" (ὑμνητής) for Zeno after his death.[4] Several other of Philodemus' works found at Herculaneum are based on the lectures of Zeno.[5] Thus, the class lectures that formed the basis for Περὶ παρρησίας date to his earlier Athenian period but were likely epitomized in the period after Zeno's death. Whether they were first committed to writing in Greece or Italy is not known. A number of Philodemus' larger works show stages of authorial reworking. Marcello Gigante dates the Περὶ παρρησίας between 75–50 B.C.E., when Philodemus was beginning to work out more speculative and creative applications

---

[2] The *subscriptio* appears after Column 24 (according to the present numbering of the text in critical editions): ΦΙΛΟΔΗΜΟ[Υ] ‖ ΤΩΝ ΚΑΤ ΕΠΙΤΟΜΗΝ ΕΞΕΙΡ ‖ ΓΑϹΜΕΝΩΝ ΠΕΡΙ ΗΘΩΝ ΚΑΙ ΒΙ ‖ ΩΝ ΕΚ ΤΩΝ ΖΗΝΟΝΟ[Ϲ | *vac.* | Ο ΕϹΤΙ ΠΕΡΙ ΠΑΡΡ[Η]ϹΙΑΣ. On the rendering of the term παρρησία with "frank criticism" or "frank speech" instead of "freedom of speech" (*vel sim.*) see Clarence E. Glad, "Frank Speech, Flattery, and Friendship in Philodemus," in *Friendship, Flattery, and Frankness of Speech: Studies on Friendship in the New Testament World*, ed. John T. Fitzgerald, NovTSup 82 (Leiden: Brill, 1997), 30–31.

[3] *Tusculan Disputations* 3.38; *De finibus* 1.16.

[4] PHerc. 1005, col. 14.8–9 (Angeli). See Anna Angeli, *Agli amici di scuola (PHerc. 1005)*, La Scuola di Epicurus 7 (Naples: Bibliopolis, 1988); Angeli reconstructs the damaged title of this work as "*To the Friends of the School*", dating from c. 50 B.C.E. For a complete listing of the texts see Marcello Gigante, *Catalogo dei Papiri Ercolanesi* (Naples: Bibliopolis, 1979), 45–52.

[5] At least two other works also carry the phrase "from the classes of Zeno" in the title, PHerc. 1003 and 1389. See Gigante, *Philodemus in Italy: The Books from Herculaneum*, trans. Dirk Obbink (Ann Arbor: University of Michigan Press, 1995) 25; Glad, "Frank Speech, Flattery, and Friendship," 30. The treatises *On Piety* (*De pietate*) and *On Signs* (*De signis*) also seem to be based on the lectures of Zeno. See Obbink, *Philodemus, On Piety*, Part 1: Critical Text with Commentary (Oxford: Clarendon, 1996), 18.

of the Epicurean school tradition based on his studies with Zeno.[6]

Philodemus might have come to Italy as early as 70 or as late as 55 B.C.E., under the patronage of L. Calpurnius Piso Caesoninus, the father-in-law of Julius Caesar.[7] According to Cicero, Piso's bitter rival, Philodemus had become acquainted with Piso while the latter was a young man (*adulescentem*), perhaps while traveling in Greece about the same time as Cicero.[8] This led to Piso's relationship as his student, friend, and, eventually, patron. Piso, a noted philhellene, later served as proconsul of Macedonia in 57–55 B.C.E. and reportedly[9] returned with sculptures and other Greek treasures for his houses, presumably including the villa at Herculaneum. Piso's relationship with Philodemus has also been confirmed within the Herculaneum library by the closing dedication of Philodemus' work *On the Good King according to Homer*.[10]

On one of his visits to Greece, it would seem, Piso convinced Philodemus to move to Italy and take up teaching the doctrines of Epicurus there. Philodemus thus became part of a thriving Italian school of Epicureanism, centered in Rome and Campania. Lucretius, also a Campanian, died in 55 B.C.E., and Philodemus' work on poetry shares some themes.[11] A copy of Lucretius' *De rerum natura* has recently

---

[6] Gigante, *Philodemus in Italy*, 24.

[7] See the discussion of the dates by Elizabeth Asmis, "Philodemus' Epicureanism," *ANRW* 2.36.4 (1990): 2371 who argues for the earlier date in contrast to Robert Philippson, "Philodemos (5)," *RE* 19.2 (1938): 2444–45, who argued for the later date based on Piso's term as *imperator* of Macedonia in 57–55 B.C.E. Gigante, *Philodemus in Italy*, 64 and Tiziano Dorandi, "Filodemo: gli orientamenti della recerca attuale," *ANRW* 2.36.4 (1990): 2330–32 follow the later dating. A number of the references above come from Asmis.

[8] *In Pisonem* 68.

[9] Cicero, *Pro Sestio* 94, cf. 19; *De provinciis consularibus* 6–7; *In Pisonem* 85. See also Gigante, *Philodemus in Italy*, 49 and Herbert Bloch, "L. Calpurnius Piso Caesoninus in Samothrace and Herculaneum," *AJA* 44 (1940), 485–93.

[10] PHerc. 1507: [εἰ δέ τινας παραλελοί ‖ παμε]ν τῶν ἀφ[ορμῶν], ὦ] Πει ‖ σω[ν], ἃς ἔστι παρ᾽ Ὁμήρου [λ]α ‖ βεῖν εἰς ἐπανόρθωσιν δ[υ] ‖ να(σ)τε[ιῶν], καὶ τ[ῶν] πα[ρα ‖ δε[ιγμά]των [. . . ("If, O Piso, I have treated some of the starting points that one can take from Homer for the correct reform of monarchies . . ."; trans. Obbink in Gigante, *Philodemus in Italy*, 64. For this restoration of the text see Dorandi, *Filodemo, Il buon re secondo Omero*, La Scuola di Epicuro 3 (Naples: Bibliopolis, 1982), 42, 109, 208.

[11] A personal connection between Lucretius and Philodemus, while not unlikely given their circles of influence, is not demonstrable from the texts; so Gigante, *Philodemus in Italy*, 36. See David Armstrong, "The Impossibility of Metathesis: Philodemus and Lucretius on Form and Content in Poetry," in *Philodemus and Poetry: Poetic Theory and Practice in Lucretius, Philodemus, and Horace* (Oxford: Oxford University Press, 1995), 210–32. See also nn. 17 and 19 below.

been confirmed to be among the scrolls at the villa in Herculaneum.[12] In addition to Philodemus' groups at Rome and Herculaneum, there was also a conventicle at Naples under the tutelage of another Epicurean teacher, Siro.[13] Siro and Philodemus were friends; they socialized together in Campania and even shared students.[14] Beginning about 48 B.C.E. when he was 21, Virgil apparently spent some six years in this company.[15] Philodemus' treatise *On Calumny* (PHerc. Paris 2, Περὶ διαβολῆς/*De calumnia*), which comes from this period,[16] was dedicated to Virgil, Varius, Plotius Tucca, and Quintilius Varus.[17] This Varius may well be L. Varius Rufus, poet and friend of both Virgil and Horace,[18] who, like Philodemus, authored a work *On Death*.[19] Philodemus' interactions with these same individuals may also be inferred from other references in his works.[20] Also named among this group was Horace, whose Epicurean influences and relationship with Philodemus are noteworthy.[21] Another member of this younger

---

[12] PHerc. 1829 contains fragments of *De rerum natura* 5.1301 and 1509. It was unrolled in 1988; see Knut Kleve, "Lucretius in Herculaneum," *CErc* 19 (1989): 5–27 and Gigante, *Philodemus in Italy*, 2, 6 and fig. 6.

[13] See John Ferguson, "Epicureanism under the Roman Empire," *ANRW* 2.36.4 (1990): 2265; Asmis, "Philodemus' Epicureanism," 2372–74.

[14] For Philodemus referring to Siro, see PHerc. 312, fr. 1, col. 4.

[15] This assumes that the *Catalepton* is correctly attributed to Virgil, as is stated by Suetonius in *Vita Vergili* 18. In *Cat.* 5.2 the author refers to himself as *docta dicta Sironis*. In *Cat.* 8 the poem refers to Siro's villa as the author's abode. Ancient commentators on Virgil also state that he studied with Siro; thus, Donatus, *Vita Verg.* 79 and Servius, *In Ecl. Verg.* (on 6.13). See Asmis, "Philodemus' Epicureanism," 2373 n. 17.

[16] See n. 45 below.

[17] So Gigante, *Philodemus in Italy*, 44, 47 and fig. 15. Gigante (44–45) also argues that Philodemus' *De morte* was composed after the death of Lucretius (perhaps along with other notables of the time) and should be read in the context of book 3 of the *De rerum natura*. See also Gigante, *Ricerche Filodemee*, 2nd ed. (Naples: Gaetano Macchiaroli, 1983), 147 and the forthcoming text and translation of the *De morte* by David Armstrong. A preliminary version of portions of this translation appear in Armstrong's article in this volume.

[18] Virgil, *Eclogues* 9.35f.; Horace, *Satires* 1.10.43f.; *Odes* 1.6.

[19] Gigante, *Philodemus in Italy*, 44; Ferguson, "Epicureanism under the Roman Empire," 2265–68. See also W. Wimmel, "Der Augusteer Lucius Varius Rufus," *ANRW* 2.30.3 (1983): 1567–68.

[20] See PHerc. 1082 (Περὶ κολακείας/*De garulitate*) col. 11.1–7 and in PHerc. 253 (Περὶ κακιῶν/*De vitiis*) fr. 12.4–5; so Asmis, "Philodemus' Epicureanism," 2373, n. 18.

[21] See Ferguson, "Epicureanism under the Roman Empire," 2268–69. In particular, connections have been suggested between Horace's poetics and those of Philodemus, as well as Horace's adoption of παρρησία as a stylistic mode in his satirical works. See Gigante, *Philodemus in Italy*, 26–7, 75–6, 86–7 and Steven Oberhelman and David Armstrong, "Satire as Poetry and the Impossibility of Metathesis in Horace's *Satires*," in *Philodemus and Poetry*, 233–54. See also David Armstrong, "The Addressees of the *Ars Poetica* of Horace: Herculaneum, Epicurean

circle was Caius Maecenas, Horace's intimate friend and literary patron.[22] An equestrian, he was a trusted aide and adviser to Augustus; together with Horace and Virgil they formed an Epicurean literary and social inner circle to the emperor, despite philosophical differences.[23] Maecenas reportedly left his estates to Augustus and in the will stipulated, "Remember Horatius Flaccus as you remember me."[24]

As Gigante has shown, the intimate character of the teacher's relationship to his circle of students/friends can also be glimpsed from one of the many epigrams of Philodemus preserved from his salon in Rome. In one he invites "(my) dearest friend, Piso" (φίλτατε Πείσων) to join his circle of "truest companions" (ἑτάρους . . . παναληθέας) for a banquet.[25] Philodemus concludes his poetic invitation, "If, in any case, you should also turn kindly eyes on us, Piso, we shall celebrate

---

Protreptic and the Pisones," in *Mega Nepioi: The Adressees of Ancient Didactic Poetry*, ed. A. Schiesaro (special issue of *Materiali e Discussioni* 31 [1994]), 185–230.

[22] Horace dedicated the books of his *Odes* and *Epodes* to him (1.1.1 and 1.1 respectively); cf. *Epistles* 1.1. *Ode* 1.20 is an invitation from Horace to Maecenas to come for drinks; compare the dinner invitation of Philodemus below, nn. 25–6. *Ode* 2.17 was addressed to Maecenas on the subject of death, and there Horace referred to him as "the great beauty and crown of my existence" (lines 3–4: *mearum | grande decus columenque rerum*) and "one half of my own soul" (lines 5–6: *te meae . . . partem animae . . . [ego] altera*). The sentiment throughout was Maecenas' despair that Horace might die before him, to which Horace replied that their destiny was one and he would not live on without him. Maecenas died 59 days before Horace in 8 B.C.E., and the two were buried nearby one another on the Esquiline; see Suetonius, *Vita Horati*.

[23] See Ferguson, "Epicureanism under the Roman Empire," 2263–4. Virgil dedicated his *Georgics* to Maecenas (*Georgics* 1.1; cf. Suetonius, *Vita Vergili* 20). Suetonius also reports that Virgil had a house on the Esquiline "near the Gardens of Maecenas" (*iuxta hortos Maecenatianos*), even though he usually lived in Campania or Sicily (*Vita Verg.* 13). For Maecenas' dealings with Augustus, see Velleius Paterculus, *Hist.* 2.88 and Cassius Dio, *Hist.* 55.7.

[24] Suetonius, *Vita Horati*: "*Horati Flacci ut mei esto memor.*" Suetonius also reports that Maecenas diplayed his affection for Horace in an epigram that runs: "If more than my own innards, Horace, / I love thee not, then should you your soul-mate / witness emaciated in the extreme" (*Ni te visceribus meis, Horati, | Plus tam diligo, tu tuum sodalem | Nimio videas strigiosiorem*). (In line 3 I have restored the original reading of the ms. (*nimio* or *ninio*) over against proposed editorial emendations.) The word plays are hard to carry over into English. For *sodalis* (literally, "intimate, booncompanion," l. 2), therefore, I have used a modern colloquialism to capture the "visceral" character of the imagery, remembering that the soul is also one of the internal organs. For a similar theme in poems of love and friendship compare Catullus, *Carm.* 14: *Ni te plus oculis meis amarem . . .* (cf. *Carm.* 82).

[25] Some 30 epigrams of Philodemus are extant in the *Palatine Anthology*. See now also the edition of David Sider, *The Epigrams of Philodemos: Introduction, Text, and Commentary* (New York: Oxford University Press, 1997). The dinner invitation is *Anth. Pal* 11.44 = *Epigram* 27 Sider; quotations above are from lines 1 and 5. (NB: The reference is mistakenly cited as 9.44 in Gigante, *Philodemus in Italy*, 79. Alas, Philodemus, a case of *metathesis* in the transcription of Roman numerals.) For a similar dinner invitation in poetic form compare Catullus, *Carm.* 13.

the twentieth not simply but richly" (ἢν δέ ποτε στρέψῃς καὶ ἐς ἡμέας ὄμματα, Πείσων, | ἄξομεν ἐκ λιτῆς εἰκάδα πιοτέρην).[26] The occasion for this dinner fellowship was one of the regular commemorations of the death of Epicurus, held on the twentieth of each month and celebrated annually on his birth date, the twentieth of Gamelion.[27] At least some of these banquets were probably held at the villa in Herculaneum.[28] The common meal[29] of this society of friends was also the school of the master, Epicurus. As we learn from Philodemus' treatise, frank speech was to be cultivated among the interactions of the group both as an expression of friendship and for the betterment of self and others; it was a well-known topic among these Epicurean conventicles.[30]

Production and Deposition of the Scroll

In addition to these social and psychogogical functions, another important aspect of Philodemus' school at Herculaneum was the transcribing and copying of the books in the library. Apparently Philodemus

---

[26] *Anth. Pal.* 11.44, lines 7–8; cf. Gigante, *Philodemus in Italy*, 80. It sounds as though Philodemus is also asking Piso to act in his capacity as patron in blessing the dinner not only with his presence but also with more sumptuous fare. It is also possible that Horace used this epigram as a model for a similar poetic invitation addressed to his patron and friend, Maecenas (*Odes* 1.20); cf. n. 22 above and Gigante, *Philodemus in Italy*, 87–9.

[27] Approximately February 6. Cicero, *De finibus* 2.101 shows knowledge of the practice based on the will of Epicurus, which gives a slight variation on the report of Diogenes Laertius, *De clar. phil. vit* 10.18; however, the *Chronology* of Apollodorus, *apud* Diogenes Laertius 10.14 says that he was born on the seventh (or the seventeenth) of Gamelion, 341 B.C.E. See Gigante, *Philodemus in Italy*, 80–81; cf. Asmis, "Philodemus' Epicureanism," 2372. For other connections to the family of Piso see also Armstrong, "The Addressees of the *Ars Poetica*," 185–230; see 200–201 and n. 29 specifically on the twentieth as a special commemorative date among these Roman Epicureans.

[28] Gigante, *Philodemus in Italy*, 53–9 argues that Philodemus' epigram in *Anth. Pal.* 9.512 (= *Epigram* 29 Sider) was set at the villa, at the overlook on the west end of the garden, called in the poem the "belvedere" (ἄποψις). Notably, the epigram opens with a reflection on garden vegetables of past springs; it is not only a reminiscence on the pleasures of seasons and dinners past, but also a reflection on the passing away of some friends from the circle.

[29] Another epigram of Philodemus (*Anth. Pal.*11.35 = *Epigram* 28 Sider) celebrates the contributions made by several friends, including Philodemus himself, to an upcoming dinner. See Gigante, *Philodemus in Italy*, 59–60.

[30] See Gigante, "Filodemo sulla Libertà di Parola," 75–6; cf. *Philodemus in Italy*, 26–7; Glad, "Frank Speech, Flattery, and Friendship," 30–41.

brought with him from Athens a library of works by various philosophers, chief among them those of Epicurus himself.[31] Also in the library were the works of later Epicureans such as Demetrius of Laconia, the second century B.C.E. commentator on Epicurus.[32] Works of earlier Latin writers, such as the poets Ennius and Caecilius Statius, were also found in the library.[33] These earlier texts were then studied for accuracy and copied; they thereby became the core of the library at Herculaneum. Philodemus' own works, including both epitomes of Zeno and further elaborations of his own, made up a large portion of the library. The treatise Περὶ παρρησίας was cited intertextually in the works Περὶ ὀργῆς (PHerc. 182, *De ira*) and Περὶ κολακείας (PHerc. 1082, *De garulitate* or *De adulatione*).[34] The work Περὶ σημειώσεων (PHerc. 1065, *De signis*) comes at the end of this process; it also relied on the lectures of Zeno, but seems to have been produced (or revised) ca. 40 B.C.E., not long before Philodemus' death.[35]

This order of composition is also supported in part by the paleography of the manuscripts. All of the present texts are scribal copies rather than Philodemus' autographs. In some cases both earlier drafts and final versions of the same work are found at Herculaneum.[36]

---

[31] See Gigante, *Philodemus in Italy*, 18. A total of 25 scrolls from Herculaneum may contain books (or parts of books) of Epicurus' Περὶ φύσεως. PHerc. 154 and 1042 both carry the *subscriptio*: Ἐπικούρου || Περὶ φύσεως || ια᾿ (Epicurus' *On Nature*, book 11).

[32] For example, the *subscriptio* of PHerc. 1786 is restored as [Δημητ]ρίου Λάκω[νος || Περὶ τι]νω[ν Ἐπι]κ[ούρου | δοξῶ]ν ὅ ἐστι . . . ("Demetrius of Laconia On Certain Doctrines of Epicurus, which is . . ."). See Gigante, *Philodemus in Italy*, 19–20. For the listing of works by other authors see Gigante, *Catalogo dei Papiri Ercolanesi*, 53–5.

[33] In 1990 PHerc. 21 was identified as containing book 6 of Ennius' *Annales*. See Gigante, *Philodemus in Italy*, 6 and fig. 5; Knut Kleve, "Ennius in Herculaneum," *CErc* 20 (1990): 5–16. These works were not necessarily part of Philodemus' own library, but likely were used in studies on poetry. Both were known for their Greek influences.

[34] Gigante, *Philodemus in Italy*, 25. So see *De Ira* col. 36.24–5 (Indelli): περὶ παρρησίας λόγος; PHerc. 1082, col. 1.1–7: περὶ παρρησίας πραγματεία. See also *De rhetorica* 2.1 (Sudhaus): τὸ τάγμα τῆς παρρησίας, and Περὶ εὐσεβείας (*De pietate*) col. 75, lines 2175–6 (Obbink): τῆς παρρησίας φιλοσόφῳ πρεπούσης. See also Glad, "Frank Speech, Flattery, and Friendship," 30.

[35] The dating is based on the reference in col. 2.15–18 ("the pygmies that Antony just now brought from Syria"); see Asmis, "Philodemus' Epicureanism," 2372 following H. M. Last, "The Date of Philodemus' *De Signis*," *CQ* 16 (1922): 177–80. But see also below at n. 52, since this may apply only to the text of PHerc. 1065.

[36] Gigante, *Philodemus in Italy*, 17. For example, in Philodemus' *History of the Academy* (part of his Σύνταξις τῶν φιλοσόφων) PHerc. 1021 is the draft and PHerc. 164 the final version. In the case of the volumes of *De rhetorica*, PHerc. 1674 and 1506 are drafts, while PHerc. 1672 and 1426 respectively are the final versions. See also below nn. 39–40.

Yet, despite being scribal copies, the scrolls were direct products of Philodemus' authorial activities, and the transcriptions were made under his own supervision. Often a large complete work or a group of related works was assigned to a single scribe for copying, and the same scribe made corrections.[37] Generally scribes were paid a fixed amount per one hundred lines copied, and the total lines were calculated for each work. Paleographically Guglielmo Cavallo identified a total of sixteen distinctive groups of scribal hands among the Herculaneum papyri; from these he postulated a total of thirty-four different scribes who may be identified on the basis of stylistic and morphological features of the handwriting.[38]

Unfortunately, the names of these scribes are not usually recorded, with one possible exception. About 50 B.C.E. the same scribe who transcribed PHerc. 182, containing Περὶ ὀργῆς (De ira), also transcribed a preliminary draft (ὑπομνηματικόν) of two scrolls of De rhetorica (PHerc. 1506 and 1674).[39] Later, after it was emended and corrected, four other scribes working closely together and with similar handwriting were assigned the task of producing the final version (ὑπόμνημα) of De rhetorica, comprising twenty-two scrolls in all. Seven scrolls of this later version were copied by a scribe whose name is possibly preserved as Ποσειδώνακτος τοῦ Βίτωνος ("Poseidonactus, son of Biton").[40] Cavallo dates this copy on paleographic grounds between 50–25 B.C.E.[41]

---

[37] Gigante, Philodemus in Italy, 25, 29; the four books of De Musica are by a single scribe. By contrast, the De rhetorica seems to have been composed over a long period of time and reflects a number of scribal hands. Recently Dirk Obbink has shown that a single scribe produced the text of De Pietate (343 columns in two scrolls) and also made the emmendations and corrections (Philodemus, De Pietate, 61–72, 76).

[38] Guglielmo Cavallo, Libri scritture scribi a Ercolano, Supplements to Cronache ercolanesi 13 (Naples: Gaetano Macchiaroli, 1983), 28–46.

[39] Cavallo's Scribe IX (from group F); so Libri scritture scribi, 33, 45, 51. The term ὑπομνηματικόν (meaning "notes" or "draft") is used in the subscriptio of PHerc. 1506 (Cavallo, 65).

[40] This possibility is based on the occurrence of this name at the lower margin below the subscriptio of one of the scrolls (PHerc. 1426). The same scribe, Cavallo's Scribe XXII (Libri scritture scribi, 25–6), who belongs to hand-group N (Cavallo, 39–40), also produced PHerc. 240, 421, 467, 1095, 1101, and 1633, all of which are from the De rhetorica. Cavallo's Scribes XX, XXI, and XXIII also belong to this hand-group, and all four worked on parts of De rhetorica. Among the four the handwriting is very similar with only small but consistent variations in a few letters. See Cavallo, Libri scritture scribi, 39–40, 63–4. The term ὑπόμνημα (meaning "treatise") is used in the subscriptio of PHerc. 1427, which comes from Scribe XX working on the final edition.

[41] Libri scritture scribi, 63.

Using the paleographic analysis of Cavallo, Gigante dates the composition of Περὶ παρρησίας to between 75–50 B.C.E., but perhaps toward the end of this period (see Table 1).[42] It appears that the same scribe who produced Περὶ παρρησίας (contained in one scroll, PHerc. 1471) also produced PHerc. 1003, another work of Philodemus based on the lectures of Zeno ("book 3"), and two texts of Demetrius of Laconia (PHerc. 831 and 1006).[43] The *subscriptio* to PHerc. 1471 indicates that this treatise was part of a larger multi-volume work, "On Character and Life" (Περὶ ἠθῶν καὶ βίων).[44] The work "On Character and Life" might have contained the volume *On Calumny* (Περὶ διαβολῆς, PHerc. Paris 2), dating after 48 B.C.E., that was addressed to Virgil and other students.[45] Not long after the scroll of Περὶ παρρησίας was transcribed, another copyist (Scribe XXIV) ca. 50 B.C.E. produced two scrolls on moral *topoi*: PHerc. 57, containing Philodemus' work Περὶ μανίας (*De insania*) and PHerc. 97, containing part of the work Περὶ πλούτου ("On Wealth").[46] About this same time Scribe IX was at work on PHerc. 182, containing Περὶ ὀργῆς

---

[42] Gigante, *Philodemus in Italy*, 25, based on Cavallo, *Libri scritture scribi*, 54. This is Cavallo's hand-group M (PHerc. 1471, 1003, 1538, 831, 1006). It should be noted, however, that Cavallo does not assign a distinctive scribal identity to any of the scrolls in this group. Cavallo also notes that there are some chronological difficulties in the comparanda to this hand type, since it betrays something of an Egyptian-Greek morphology. The scroll may, therefore, be later. Nonetheless, Gigante, following Cavallo, assumes that the date of the production of the scrolls was in effect identical with the date of the composition by Philodemus. Whether this assumption is justified is yet to be confirmed or disconfirmed on internal evidence of the scrolls, but there are logical objections; cf. Asmis, "Philodemus' Epicureanism," 2373 n. 15.

[43] In the *subscriptio* of PHerc. 1003 the attribution to Zeno is secure, but the actual title of the work is uncertain; it reads: Φιλοδήμου ‖ Περ[ὶ τ]ῶν Ζ[ή]νων[ος σχολῶν] | γʹ. The other text which carries a similar attribution to the lectures of Zeno, PHerc. 1389, belongs to Cavallo's hand-group I and dates to "the first half of the century" (*Libri scritture scribi*, 35, 52). Morphologically this hand is similar to that of several of the other ethical treatises that come from this period, including the *De Morte* (PHerc. 1050) and *De signis* (1065), which appear to have been copied ca. 40 B.C.E.

[44] Compare also the title of PHerc. 168: [ΦΙΛΟΔΗΜΟΥ ‖ . . . ΠΕΡΙ ΒΙ]Ω[Ν ΚΑΙ] ‖ ΗΘ[ΩΝ Η ΠΕΡΙ ΤΟΥ ΜΗ(?) ΚΑΤΑ Τ]Α Τ[ΥΧ]ΟΝ[ΤΑ] ΖΗ[Ν] | ΥΠ[Ο]ΜΝΗΜΑΤ[ΩΝ] | Αʹ. Cavallo does not discuss the hand of this ms. Wilhelm Crönert in *Kolotes und Menodemos* (Munich: Müller, 1906; repr. Amsterdam: Hakkert, 1965), 127 n. 534 proposes to find a further reference to the work "On Character and Life" in PHerc. 1082 (Περὶ κολακείας/*De garulitate*); cf. Gigante, *Philodemus in Italy*, 26. The latter work clearly does refer to Περὶ παρρησίας (see n. 34 above).

[45] See n. 17 above. The conjecture of Gigante (*Philodemus in Italy*, fig. 15) is supported by the fact that slanderous speech shows up in conjunction with Philodemus' discussion of frank speech; see Περὶ παρρησίας fr. 17.7, 50.3, 51.7–8.

[46] Cavallo, *Libri scritture scribi*, 40, 45, 54. This is Cavallo's hand-group O, within which the two scrolls 57 and 97 are quite distinctive.

(*De ira*).[47] This work on anger (Περὶ ὀργῆς) appears to be part of larger, multi-volume work "On the Passions," including perhaps Περὶ μανίας (PHerc. 57, *De insania*).[48] Based on these ethical works, Philodemus also undertook an even more extensive multi-volume project, which went under the main title "On Vices and their Corresponding Virtues" (Περὶ κακιῶν καὶ τῶν ἀντικειμένων ἀρετῦων) containing ten to fourteen distinct works[49] (see Table 1). Ten of these scrolls were produced by a single copyist (Group P, Scribe XXV) with some affinities to that of Scribe XXIV, who produced PHerc. 57 and 97 that likely belong to this same larger collection "On Vices and their Corresponding Virtues."[50] These scrolls were probably produced between 50 and ca. 40 B.C.E.[51]

During the last decade of his life it seems that Philodemus continued to revise his previous works while also producing new ones. His corpus of ethical works, then, basically falls into three main groups, with Περὶ παρρησίας probably being one of, if not the earliest (see Table 1).[52] Based on Cavallo's dating of the scribal hands,

---

[47] See above n. 39.

[48] PHerc. 182: [ΦΙΛΟΔ]Η[ΜΟΥ | ΠΕΡΙ ΗΘΩΝ Ο ΕCΤΙ ΠΕ]ΡΙ ΟΡΓΗC. The *subscriptio* clearly gives us the title *On Anger*, but the rest was restored by C. Wilke, *Philodemi de ira liber* (Leipzig: Teubner, 1913). Gigante (*Philodemus in Italy*, 25) follows Wilke in assuming that it was part of the same larger work "On Character and Life" which also contained Περὶ παρρησίας. In his more recent edition, however, G. Indelli thinks that it was part of another larger work entitled *On Passions* (Περὶ πάθων); see G. Indelli, *Filodemo: L'ira*, La scuola di Epicuro 5 (Naples: Bibliopolis, 1988), 35–6 and the translator's note in Gigante, *Philodemus in Italy*, 25. The suggestion that the *De insania* was also part of the same larger work *On the Passions* is supported by Cavallo's dating of the two hands, see nn. 39 and 46 above.

[49] See Gigante, *Philodemus in Italy*, 38–39. These include *On Household Management* (*De oeconomia*, PHerc. 1424), which contains the main title and designates the scroll as book 9 (θ΄), as well as *On Flattery* (Περὶ κολακείας/*De gratulite*; PHerc. 222, plus 223, 1082, 1089, 1457, 1675), *On Death*, book 4 (Περὶ θανάτου δ΄/*De morte*; PHerc. 1050, plus 189, 807?), *On Vices* (Περὶ κακιῶν/*De vitiis*; Pherc. 253, 1457), *On Arrogance*, which is *On Vices, book 10* (Περὶ κακιῶν ι΄/*De vitiis*; PHerc. 1008), and *On Greed* (Περὶ φιλαργυρίας/PHerc. 465 and 1613).

[50] These include PHerc. 1017, 1025, 1678, and 1414 (see Table 1); Cavallo, *Libri scritture scribi*, 41.

[51] Cavallo (55) simply says that the hand is late in the first century B.C.E. (ca. 50–25); however, since one of the scrolls (PHerc. 671) from Scribe XXV is part of the work *De signis*, it would appear that the whole collection must come from ca. 40 or after (see n. 35 above), unless it could be determined that PHerc. 671 is an earlier version of the same work which was emended and recopied later by the scribe of PHerc. 1065, which Cavallo similarly dates to ca. 50–25, but without identifying a discrete scribe from other works in hand-group I. In this event, the production of the seventeen scrolls from Scribe XXV would date to between 50–40.

[52] This is Gigante's view of the dating; however, the title of PHerc. 168: Περὶ

it would appear that the period from ca. 50 b.c.e. to the death of Philodemus (after ca. 40 b.c.e.) was a flurry of copying activity in the library at Herculaneum. How long it continued is not clear; however, it does appear that the library was kept intact for over a century thereafter, until the villa was buried in the eruptions of 79 c.e.[53]

Discovery and Restoration of the Scroll

The single known manuscript of Περὶ παρρησίας (PHerc. 1471) was recovered with the cache of nearly 1800 papyrus scrolls and fragments found at the Villa from 1752–54. It was first unrolled and given its numerical designation among the Herculaneum papyri by Francisco Casanova in 1808, when the *Officina* was under the direction of Carlo Maria Rosini. The process of unrolling used was that of Father Piaggio's machine, rather than the earlier procedure of *scorziatura*; the latter involved cutting away the outer layers in sections and then pulling the sheets apart. As a result, the integrity of those portions of the scroll that remain is much greater.[54] The condition of PHerc. 1471 is reported as "not crumbled, legible, and in good condition."[55] These remains were then conserved in glass frames (Latin *tabulae*, Italian *cornici*), and the physical state of the papyrus (with the legible portions of text) reproduced by drawings.[56] These hand copies or apographs (Italian *disegni*) then became the basis for the first printed versions of the text.[57] The *editio princeps* of the PHerc. 1471, containing

βίων καὶ ἠθῶν, ἢ Περὶ τοῦ μὴ (or μάτην?) κατὰ τὰ τυχόντα ζῆν ὑπομνημάτων αʹ (*On Not Living According to Chance*, book 1) may suggest another early volume in the larger work *On Character and Life*.

[53] For the disposition of the scrolls after the eruption and the implications for their prior storage see Gigante, *Philodemus in Italy*, fig. 1; Mario Capasso, *Manuale di papirologia ercolanese*, Studi e Testi 3 (Lecce: Congedo Editore, 1991), 65–84; and Francesca Longo Auricchio and M. Capasso, "I rotoli della villa ercolanesi: dislocazione e ritrovamento," *CErc* 17 (1987): 47.

[54] For the history of the discoveries see Capasso, *Manuale di papirologia ercolanese*, 87–116. Capasso (100–102) calls this "the golden age of the Piaggio method." For the problems of reconstruction posed by the earlier *scorziatura* method, see the discussion by Dirk Obbink, *Philodemus: On Piety*, 37–53 and Richard Janko, "A First Join between PHerc. 411+1583 (Philodemus, *On Music* IV): Diogenes of Babylon on Natural Affinity and Music," *CErc* 22 (1992): 123–29.

[55] Gigante, *Catalogo*, 335.

[56] For examples of the process, see Mario Capasso, *Storia fotografica dell' Officina dei Papiri Ercolanesi* (Naples: Bibliopolis, 1983) passim; for examples of *disegni* drawn before photography was regularly employed, see 136–41.

[57] As numerous scrolls were unrolled in this period, some *disegni* were drawn in

the ninety-four Fragments and the twenty-four Columns from the Neapolitan apographs, was published in two parts in *Voluminum Herculanensium* V (1835 and 1843).[58] Alexander Olivieri produced the critical Teubner edition in 1914 from reexamination of the actual papyrus.[59] He took Fragments 1–88 (*cornici* 1–13), as stored in the Naples collection of the Bibliothecae Herculanensis, along with the 24 Columns (*cornici* 17–21) to produce his main text. He also included an appendix comprised of fourteen previously unedited fragments, designated A–N (from *cornici* 14–16).[60] Olivieri's readings have to date formed the standard critical edition of the text, but have been supplemented by the work of Robert Philippson and Marcello Gigante. Philippson[61] provided a critical review of Olivieri using the original *disegni* copies of the text and further supplemented and corrected many of Olivieri's readings. More recently Gigante[62] has provided many new readings and/or confirmations from the text, which can now be studied with enhanced light techniques, microscopy, and photography. The new edition of the work in the Society of Biblical Literature's Texts and Translations (SBLTT) series is based essentially on Olivieri's text, but it incorporates many of the corrections, emendations, and supplements of Philippson, Gigante, and some other scholars. It also contains the six Neapolitan apographs (N. 77, 79, 84, 87, 91, and 93) omitted by Olivieri.[63]

Oxford (designated O) at the Bodleian Library, and the rest in Naples (designated N). All the *disegni* of PHerc. 1471 were drawn in Naples. For the technical data on PHerc. 1471 see Gigante, *Catalogo*, 335–38.

[58] Vol. V.1 (1835) 1–48; vol. V.2 (1843): 1–168. See Gigante, *Catalogo*, 336; and his "Filodemo sulla Libertà di parola," in *Richerche Filodemee*, 57.

[59] *Philodemi ΠΕΡΙ ΠΑΡΡΗΣΙΑΣ Libellus*, ed. Alexander Olivieri (Leipzig: Teubner, 1914).

[60] These seem to be dissociated fragments from the section comprising Fragments 1–88 (*Cornici* 1–13).

[61] Robert Philippson, "Review of *Philodemi Περὶ παρρησίας Libellus*. Ed. Alexander Olivieri. Leipzig 1914, Teubner. X, 83S. 8. 2 M. 40," *Berliner Philologische Wochenschrift* 22 (27 May 1916), 677–88.

[62] Gigante's readings were published in stages as "Filodemo sulla Libertà di Parola," in *Actes du VIIIᵉ Congrès Association G. Budé* (Paris, 1969), 196–217; *CErc* 2 (1972): 59–65; *CErc* 4 (1974): 37–42; and *CErc* 5 (1975): 53–61. These were collected together into his article in *Richerche Filodemee*, 55–113.

[63] *Philodemus, On Frank Criticism*, vii–viii.

Reconstructing the Shape of the Scroll

On the basis of the extensive conservation and editing work it is possible to draw some conclusions about the shape of the original text. As with most of the Herculaneum papyri, the text is better preserved toward the end rather than the beginning, since the scrolls were typically rolled from right to left, that is with the end of the scroll placed on the *umbilicus* first. Thus, the title or *subscriptio*, which comes after the last section of text (Column XXIV), is well preserved.[64] Due to the scorching of the scrolls in the pyroclastic flow that inundated the villa, the outer layers tend to be burned away, and only the center portions are preserved. Hence, in the case of PHerc. 1471, the 24 Columns represent the center (Italian *midollo* or "marrow") of the scroll, while the 88 (or 94) Fragments represent the remaining outer layers (Italian *scorzi*) that were not burned away. In turn, these Fragments actually represent some segment from the middle of the text, since the outermost layers of the original scroll, which contained the beginning of the text, were burned away. In attempting to reconstruct the text, then, the principal questions are: How was the text formatted on the scroll? What proportion of the original text is represented by the preserved sections? How do they fit together?

The basic layout of PHerc. 1471 can best be ascertained from the twenty-four Columns in comparison with other known works from the library. The Herculaneum scrolls typically were produced on rolls of papyrus measuring from 6–9 meters in length, but a few exceeded 10–12 meters. The normal height was ca. 19–20 centimeters, while some range up to 22 cm or more.[65] The text was copied in columns measuring ca. 15–18 cm in height and ca. 5–6 cm in width, with ca. 1 cm between columns. Each column contained 30–40 lines of text, with each line containing 17–25 letters.[66] The two longest single scrolls that can be confirmed contained 204 columns with 33 lines of 16–20 letters per column (PHerc. 1426, *De*

---

[64] For the text see n. 2 above. The *subscriptio* appears in the upper half of the scroll after a blank space nearly two columns wide, or approximately in what would be the position of "Column XXVIIa," relative to the present text numbering in critical editions. For a photograph of Col. 22–24 and the *subscriptio*, see Capasso, Manuale di papirologia, fig. L11.

[65] See Cavallo, *Libri scritture scribi a Ercolano*, 14–16; Capasso, *Manuale di papirologia*, 204–205

[66] Olivieri, *Philodemus*, iv.

rhetorica, book 3) and 245+ columns with 36 lines of 16–20 letters per column (PHerc. 1425, *De poemata*, book 5) of text respectively.[67] These two scrolls were produced by two scribes (XIX and XXII, respectively) both from Cavallo's group N.

The columns of PHerc. 1471 are barely 5 cm wide with ca. 1 cm (or slightly less) between columns, both slightly narrower than usual; top and bottom margins were also closer than usual to the edge of the papyrus, an attempt perhaps to squeeze the text onto a single scroll. Yet the morphology of this scribal hand (Group M) is large and at times elaborate, especially at the beginning of a line. Each line typically contains ca. 17–23 letters, but the most common for this text seems to be 18–20 letters (i.e., one-half of a hexameter-length line or a little more). The columns seem to be ca. 30–33 lines long. Cavallo estimates the overall size of the scroll of PHerc. 1471 as ca. 11.50 meters in length, ca. 21 cm in height, and containing ca. 200–205 columns.[68] At this scale, it was one of the larger scrolls, and Philodemus' treatise Περὶ παρρησίας, one of the longest single-volume works in the entire collection.[69]

The actual portions of the text as preserved can be analyzed according to these general patterns. Columns I–XXIV show consistent damage at the top and bottom of the scroll, but more at the top (see Table 2). Also, the *midollo* of the scroll was broken in half, causing a lacuna of two to three lines (or 1–1.5 cm) in the middle of each column.[70] The largest preserved section of the text in height appears in Col. I–III (height 18.5 cm, not counting the broken portion in the middle and the edges are not extant). In some sections, notably

---

[67] See Obbink, *Philodemus: De Pietate*, 70; Cavallo, *Libri scritture scribi*, 16, plus plates XLIII and XXXIX respectively.

[68] Cavallo, *Libri scritture scribi*, 16; cf. Capasso, *Manuale dei papirologia*, 205. Olivieri (*Philodemus*, iv) estimated the total number of (half-)lines at 6767, which (at 33 lines per column) equals approx. 205 total columns. We shall reevaluate these calculations below.

[69] For the sake of comparison, the scroll of *De Ira* (PHerc. 182, ed. Indelli) contains ca. 2500 total lines in 124 columns of 40 lines each (or a total of 4960 half-lines, and coheres with the scribal notation in the *subscriptio*, which gives 2385 total lines). *De Morte* (PHerc. 1050) carries a scribal notation of 4436 total lines in its *subscriptio*. The scroll shows columns containing 39 lines with ca. 22–25 letters per line (see Cavallo, *Libri scritture scribi*, Pl. XXVIII = PHerc. 1050 *cornice* 10, measuring 23.4 × 18.5 cm). From the same scribal group (I) comes PHerc. 1065, which was formatted with 38 lines per column and 22–24 lettes per line (see Cavallo, Pl. XXIX = cornice 10, measuring 29 × 21.1 cm). *De Pietate*, as recently restored by Obbink (*Philodemus: De Pietate*, 70) comprised a total of 343 columns on two scrolls.

[70] For this reason, Olivieri's text is divided into sections, viz. Col. Ia and Ib, etc.

in Col. II–III,[71] it would appear that some of the bottom margin of the papyrus is preserved, while in Col. XXIV, no more than one or two lines are lost at the top.[72] With 27 lines extant (not counting the lacuna in the middle), Col. XVII (a+b) is the closest to a fully preserved column in the text. Thus, given the possibility of a missing 1–2 lines at the top and 2–3 lines in the middle of the text, it would appear that PHerc. 1471 was formatted with either 30 or 33 lines per column and averaging 18–20 letters per line.[73]

Because of joins in the sections of papyrus within each *cornice*, the order of Col. I–XXIV is, for the most part, secure; each one represents a single, nearly complete column of the original text (see Table 2).[74] Also, on the basis of stichometric notations made by the scribe in the left intercolumnar margin of the text (see Table 3),[75] it is possible to calculate the scribe's method of recording the number of lines copied. Since the last four of these occur in Col. I–XXIV, they appear to give a solid reading of the overall length of the text. The final notation (K) occurs at Col. XXIVb, line 9 and represents a second time through the alphabet. Prior to that H, Θ, I occur in order and at regular intervals of about six columns.[76] At 30 or 33 lines per column, this would represent a count of 180 or 200 lines of the text per letter of the alphabet, where each line of text is being counted by the scribe as one-half στίχος (i.e., one half of a hexameter-length line; see Table 4).[77] On the basis of this system

---

[71] Each of these contain 14 lines in the lower (or b) portion of the column. Cf. Col. XXIIIb, which contains 15 lines, even though a clear bottom margin is not visible. For a photograph of *Cornice* 17 (Col. I–II) see Cavallo, *Libri scritture scribi*, pl. xxxvi.

[72] Col. XXIVa contains 14 lines with what may be a top margin.

[73] Olivieri (*Philodemus*, iv) assumes 33 lines per column in his calculations.

[74] Note that due to the unrolling process, it was possible to keep the Columns in their proper order as they were taken off the scroll. These were then sectioned and the top and bottom half of each section situated in its own *cornice*. See Table 2 for the location, order, and size of remaining sections.

[75] These are recorded in Olivieri's critical edition, in their original positions and discussed on p. vi. The SBLTT text and translation of Konstan, et al., however, does not include these marginal notations.

[76] See Table 3. On the basis of study of the photographs (see n. 71 above) I have provisionally restored a Z in Col. IIa, line 2 (what would be line 1 of Olivieri's text, but there are other readable letters on the papyrus). This interval is consistent with the later ones in Olivieri.

[77] See Cavallo, *Libri Scritture scribi*, 14–16. This should be roughly 36 letters (16 syllables). So at exactly 18 letters per line, 200 lines equals 100 *stichoi*. At 20 letters per line, 180 lines equals 100 *stichoi*. But these numbers also yield some variables for counting the number of columns needed. Olivieri's calculations are based on 200 lines and 33 lines per column. See Table 4.

of reckoning the scribe's work, Olivieri calculated that the text of
Περὶ παρρησίας contained a total of 6767 half-lines (3383 lines), which
would yield a total of 205 columns at 33 half-lines per column.[78]
Working backward from the stichometric notation of Col. VIIb, line
6 (*H*), and assuming each letter represents about 6 columns, then it
yields 187 columns (i.e., letters A–Ω plus A–H) up to that point and
a total of 204 columns plus a few lines by the end of Col. XXIV
(see Table 4). Following Olivieri's calculations, then, Cols. I–XXIV
represent roughly the last 11.75% of the original scroll, while the
Fragments would represent the extant remains of the first 180 columns
of the original scroll.

Ordering the Fragments

The more difficult portion of the text to evaluate is that contained
in the Fragments, and the other unedited material, from *cornici* 1–16.
In form, at least, each of the ninety-four Fragments (plus the fourteen items labeled A–N from Olivieri's Appendix) represents a portion of one column. In reading the text, it is clear that there is often
little continuity between the Fragments. Ranging from six to fourteen lines each, they represent less than half (from 18–42%) of a
column of thirty-three lines. Nor is it always clear how each of these
108 fragmentary columns should go together.

On the one hand, within each *cornice* the sections of text are laid
out in linear strips, along the top and bottom half of the tray. In
many cases, each of these strips has enough joins to suggest that we
have a horizontal, linear section through a continuous sequence of
columns. So, for example, in *Cornice* 4,[79] the section in the upper

---

[78] Olivieri, *Philodemus*, vii. Philippson, "Review of Olivieri," 680 notes the problems with Olivieri's counting; cf. note the cautionary comment of Obbink, *Philodemus:
De Pietate*, 70 n. 4.

[79] I have had a limited view of the actual papyrus remains of PHerc. 1471 in
Naples. This analysis is based on careful study of published photographs. The photo
of this *cornice* is published in Gigante, *Catalogo dei Papiri Ercolanesi*, pl. 6 (between
320–21). In the caption it is recorded as *Cornice 7, frr. 8–15*. Careful study of the
photograph confirms that these are, indeed, the same as Olivieri's Frags. 8–15,
which he places in *Cor.* 4. But there is another discrepancy in the recording, since
the measurements of the preserved papyrus materials as reported by Olivieri and
Gigante respectively, do not match. Coincidentally, the measurements of Gigante's
Cor. 7 are correct for these two sections of papyrus, and match closely with those
reported by Olivieri for *Cor.* 4 (as noted in Table 2). Moreover, Gigante's measurements differ significantly from Olivieri's for each of the *cornici* from 1–16 in a

part of the tray (measuring 39.5 cm according to Olivieri) shows a clear run of seven consecutive columns each containing 9–11 lines of text (ca. 7.5 cm in height). These are published as only six Fragments (8–13) in Olivieri's text, and there is no mention of the relative linear sequence. Unfortunately, Olivieri makes no mention that there is another portion of a column preserved, with joins on both sides, between his Frag. 12 and 13. Also, in the lower part of the same tray, the section of papyrus (measuring 30.7 × 7 cm according to Olivieri) preserves five more consecutive columns, which include Olivieri's Frag. 14 and 15, and one from his Appendix (labeled simply as *post* Frag. 15).[80] But unreported by Olivieri is the presence of two more column fragments with left and right margins intact that join this lower section of *Cor.* 4; one is before Frag. 14 and the other is after Frag. 15 but before Olivieri's "post-Frag. 15" scrap. Then there is yet another detached fragment at the end of this section that represents another portion of a column, presumably from the same section of the papyrus.[81] Olivieri also locates two more different, dissociated fragments (I and J in his Appendix) with this same portion of the text.[82]

Thus, in this section of the text, the eight Fragments (8–15) presented by Olivieri actually reflect two discrete horizontal sections across continuous columns of the papyrus running seven and five (or six?) columns respectively (all in *Cor.* 4 [7]), with possibly two more proximate columns (from Olivieri's Appendix). Given the way that these sections of papyrus were numbered when they were originally unrolled and drawn, it appears that they should be understood as a continuous linear section through 12–15 consecutive columns of the original scroll.[83] A good comparative measure for further study may

---

pattern that is consistent with that for Olivieri's *Cor.* 4 = Gigante's *Cor.* 7, at least for *Cor.* 1–13. It seems possible that Olivieri has given the numbers of the *cornici* in a different order than Gigante. If so, it may have implications for the ordering of material in the text, even though the basic sequence of Fragments 1–88 (94N) is likely to remain the same. These difficulties can only be noted in the present study and must await further analysis of the actual papyrus for clarification.

[80] Olivieri, *Philodemus*, 67.

[81] This fragment has only a right margin preserved; therefore, it might be either part of Olivieri's "post-Frag. 15" scrap (which it follows in the *cornice*), or a part of a separate column.

[82] Olivieri, *Philodemus*, 66–7. These are not the same as the ones noted above from the photograph of *Cor.* 4 [7]. Here note Philippson's criticism of Olivieri, *Berliner Philologische Wochenschrift*, 679.

[83] It is also possible that Casanova and the original *disegnatori* meant for the two

be gained from the foregoing analysis: a continuous linear strip of papyrus from PHerc. 1471 measuring ca. 40 cm in length should normally contain seven consecutive columns of text and their inter-columnar margins. Hence, as with *Cor.* 4 [7], a number of the sec-tions of papyrus contained in *Cornici* 1–13 actually preserve more columns of text than reported by Olivieri or the Neapolitan *disgeni* (see Table 2, column 3 and note e).

On the other hand, other materials in *cornici* 1–13 do not seem to fit together in this fashion. While sections of text within a *cornice* may come from one area of the scroll, the relations of the materi-als from different *cornici* are not so clear. For example, Frag. 20, line 6 (Olivieri's *Cor.* 5) contains the stichometric notation Υ while the small scrap that occurs in Olivieri's *Cor.* 4 post-Frag. 15 contains the notation I. If these readings are correct,[84] the interval between these notations should be some 66 columns (instead of the five in Olivieri). The physical character of these materials is a key to the problem (see Table 2).

The total amount of papyrus material preserved, as reported by both Olivieri and Gigante (see Table 2), is far more than the 88–104 edited fragments. Laid end-to-end (in the manner suggested above for the two strips in *Cor.* 4) the preserved sections (as reported by Olivieri) in *Cornici* 1–16 measure 10.529 meters (or enough to con-tain 175.5 columns of text). When combined with the material in *Cornici* 17–21 (Cols. I–XXIV), this yields a total length of 12.045 meters (or enough for 200.75 columns of text).[85]

Close examination of the materials reveals that there are many sections that contain legible written remains but were either too small or too corrupt to be edited. Yet they often contain enough legible

---

strips in each *cornice* to be understood as a section of a top and bottom portion of the scroll that were *approximately* from the same area of the text. In this case *Cor.* 4 [7] would represent a continuous run across only seven columns. For further thoughts on these possibilities see below at n. 89.

[84] I have studied the photograph of *Cor.* 4 [7] (containing the notation post-Frag. 15), and it appears to be an I, although it might be a T. (For the photograph, see n. 79 above. See also the comment of Philippson, *Berliner Philologische Wochenschrift*, 680 n. 3.) If it were the latter, it would be the appropriately preceding section of text before that found in *Cor.* 5. But such readings can only be confirmed on the basis of microscopic analysis of the actual papyri. It will require careful analysis of the order of fragments as stored in the *cornici*; cf. n. 79 above and Table 2.

[85] Olivieri (*Philodemus*, vi) reported the total of all the sections laid end-to-end as 11.85 m, but the actual total of the measurements he published is 12.045 m (see Table 2).

text to discern the configuration of the column. For example, in *Cor.* 1 (containing only Frag. 1–2 in Olivieri's edition), the total extent of linear papyrus material preserved is 61 cm (Olivieri), enough for 10 columns. Similarly, in *Cor.* 2 (containing only Frag. 3), the total amount of preserved linear papyrus material is another 72 cm (Olivieri), or another 12 columns. The largely unedited material in *Cor.* 14–16 (presented only as the 14 items A–N in Olivieri's Appendix) preserves a total of 207.8 cm of linear papyrus in six sections of material, enough for over 34.5 columns of text. What this means, is that overall, a substantial proportion of the total scroll was actually preserved, even though Olivieri estimated that the total amount of extant readable text was only one-sixth of the complete work.[86]

There are, then, basically two ways that the Fragments and Appendix sections may be understood to fit together. The first is that they represent a substantial portion of the entire scroll running in some consecutive order. Since the tops of these fragments tend to show more damage than the bottoms, they could then be expected to represent a section near the bottom half of the scroll, comparable in height to the bottom section of Columns I–XXIV. Intriguing as this might be, several factors make it unlikely.[87] Chief among them is that there is far too much papyrus material preserved. With a total length of ca. 11.80–12.045 m of papyrus material extant (or enough for over 200 columns) we would possess parts of all but the first three columns of the text. Few of the Herculaneum scrolls suffered so little damage to the outer layers. Also, between Frag. 20, line 6 and Col. VIIb, line 6 the stichometric notations (from Φ–H, see Table 3) would necessitate 66 intervening columns; however, the number of column fragments and columns preserved between these two points is over 81.[88] Moreover, Olivieri's Frag. 88 (= 94 in the Neapolitan *disegni*) clearly does not join directly to Col. I, so there is even more material that needs to be factored into the equation.

---

[86] Olivieri, *Philodemus*, vii. On this point see Philippson's criticism, *Berliner Philologische Wochenschrift*, 680.

[87] Compare Olivieri, *Philodemus*, iv.

[88] Following the Neapolitan *disegni*, (but excluding the material in *Cor.* 14–16) this would still total 81 columns, if tallied this way. Five of Olivieri's Appendix items (K–N) also come from this area of the text, in his view; therefore, the number goes to 86. Also, it is Olivieri's contention that other material from *Cor.* 14–16 was originally distributed across the text, i.e., that it should be interspersed in relationship with material in *Cornici* 1–13.

Consequently, this suggests a second, more likely arrangement, namely that some of the Fragments represent top portions of original columns in the scroll, while others represent bottoms.[89] Like the section in Col. I–XXIV, then, it may be assumed that this portion of the scroll was at some point broken in half and the two halves unrolled separately. In the case of the 24 Columns, the original *disegnatori* were able to ascertain the corresponding order of tops and bottoms by working backward from the end of the scroll and matching up the sections of tops and bottoms. But in the earlier sections of the text, lacunae made it impossible to match up tops and bottoms, even though individual sections of papyrus preserved continuous horizontal column order over limited stretches. If such is the case, then there are two possibilities for the relationships of various sections of Fragments:

(1) If the two linear sections preserved in each *cornice* were arranged by the original *disegnatori* so that a portion from the top half of the scroll was placed with a portion from the bottom half from *approximately* the same area of the text, then the order of Fragments 1–88 (94) must be broken up into units of material by *cornice* location and studied for these approximate relationships. The challenge here is determining which of the two sections in each *cornice* should be the top and locating a vertical join from which to establish relative positions for the remaining columns fragments above and below.[90]

---

[89] See Philippson, *Berliner Philologische Wochenschrift*, 679: "Wie seine Wiedergabe von Fragmenten sind auch seine Mitteilungen über die Fragmente mangelhaft. Auf S. III der Praefatio gibt er [Olivieri] nur an, welche seiner Fragmente auf den einselnen Tafeln enthalten sind, nicht wie viel diese außerdem enthalten, bezw. ob seine Fragmente unmittelbar aufeinanderfolgen, oder ob solche und wie viele zwischen ihnen auf den Tafeln noch vorhanden sind. Auch im Texte bringt er keinerlei Angabe darüber. Der Appendix enthält einige von den Neaplern übergangene Fragmente, nach Tafeln gerdnet und mit den Ziffern, die sie dort tragen, aber mit wenigen Ausnahmen ohne Angabe, wie sie sich in die Fragmente der Neapler und seiner Ausgabe einordnen. So trägt das erste Fragment des Appendix die Bezeichnung Tab. I fr. 2; wie verhält sich dieses zu seinem Fragment 2, das auch auf Tab. I steht? Ebenso macht er keine Angabe, ob die Fragmente oberen oder unteren Seitenrand enthalten; man muß die Neapler Ausgabe aufschlagen, um sich darüber zu belehren. Und doch sind alle diese Tatsachen für das Verständnis der Bruchstücke sehr wichtig. Denn nach der erhaltenen Stichometrie scheinen die Fragmente auf den Tafeln ziemlich in der ursprünglichen Reihenfolge angebracht zu sein. Man muß also diese kennen, um ihren Gedankenzusammenhang zu erkennen. Außerdem gehört der Papyrus zu denen, die wagerecht durchschnitten sind; man könnte also nach dem etwa erhaltenen Rande bestimmen, ob die Fragmente zum unteren oder oberen Teile einer Kolumne, ob zwei vielleicht zu derselben gehören."

[90] Taking *Cor.* 4 [7] for example, based on the discussion above (n. 79), Olivieri's Frag. 8–13 (and one unedited column) would then represent a top half, while his

(2) If the two linear sections preserved in each *cornice* appear to be consecutive columns from adjacent sections of the text, then it is likely that some entire *cornici* would be all tops, while others are all bottoms. If this is the case, then future analysis will need to consider whether and which *cornici* might be considered running horizontal sections of scroll tops and which others are bottoms. Then, can the two be matched together at any points?

Even if we conceive of the material in this way, a substantial proportion of the scroll has been preserved.[91] As it is, it appears that Olivieri's arrangement of the eighty-eight fragments will not allow for them to be ordered relative to one another, or to the twenty-four columns (see Table 4). Only further analysis of the papyri and the text will shed new light on these questions.

Conclusion

There is still much to be learned about this important work of Philodemus. Since it was one of the earliest works in his ethical corpus, it seems to have served as a foundation for later writings. It also served as a guide for day-to-day activities and interactions among members of the Epicurean community.

It is possible that the lost sections at the beginning of the text contained the philosophical and ethical preamble to these more practical guidelines. It might have been based on commentary and questions drawn from Epicurus' own letters or other writings, as allusions

---

Frag. 14–15 plus the "post-Frag. 15" scrap (and two or three unedited column fragments) would represent a bottom. If aligned in this way, it might be possible to propose a join by "sliding" the two sections laterally to establish a vertical ordering. In this instance, the order might be read as Frag. 9 + 14 followed by 10 + 15 then 11 (a top), or 10 + 14 followed by 11 + 15, then 12 (a top). If the tops and bottoms were inverted, then the likely ordering would be something like Frag. 8 (a bottom) followed by 14 + 9, then 15 + 10, or Frag. 9 (a bottom) followed by 14 + 10 then 15 + 11.

[91] For example, if we were to take a clear point of disjuncture in the existing text, as between Frag. 43 and 44, where there is also a break between *cornici*, one can get a sense of the scale of the remaining text. Thus, if *Cor.* 1 & 2 represent the outer, most damaged sections of the text, and *Cor.* 3–7 (Frag. 4–43 plus unedited sections = 319.9 cm) represents all tops of columns while *Cor.* 8–13 (Frag. 44–88/94N, = 357.9 cm) represents all bottoms, we would still have well over 50 columns of text preserved. When combined with Columns I–XXIV plus the Olivieri's Appendix items and the unedited material in *Cor.* 1, 2, and 14–16, there is still perhaps as much as 55–70% of the total scroll preserved. This crude estimate is not meant to be a proposed reconstruction; it is meant to give a sense of scale only. Any future reconstructions of the text must await results of direct analysis of the papyri in Naples.

within the treatise presuppose.[92] On the other hand, it might have
begun with the traditional Athenian *topos* on tyranny, and the role
of frank speech as an antidote.[93] This possibility is given circumstantial
support by the fact that Philodemus also wrote a treatise *On the Good
King according to Homer*,[94] and the use of the term παρρησία has now
been confirmed within this text.[95] But these conjectures must await
further analysis of the scroll for definitive answers. What is clear is
the complex and multi-layered process of authorship, production,
and transmission of these materials: from the traditions and writings
of Epicurus, to the lectures and commentary of Zeno of Sidon, to
the epitomizing and elaboration of Philodemus, to the transcription
of an unnamed scribe, to the use and storage at the Villa, and finally
to the modern efforts to restore both the scroll and the text.

[92] See Frag. 9, 15, 20.

[93] It should be noted that Clarence Glad ("Frank Speech, Flattery, and Friendship
in Philodemus," 31–2) argues that by the Hellenistic period παρρησία had largely
lost this meaning and only referred to interpersonal relationships. I am not fully
convinced. I wonder whether inklings of the older usage from the Athenian political realm are not still to be heard even though the context has changed. For Greeks
now forced to deal with Romans of power and wealth, there are still some points
of contact, such as we see later during the second sophistic in Dio Chrysostom's
treatises on kingship and tyranny. Plutarch also notes that Ptolemy, Antony, and
Nero succumbed to the deleterious effects of flattery (*Quomodo adulator* 56E–F). Indeed,
during the second sophistic it became a typical rhetorical trope to eschew any
appearance of flattery in panegyrics toward Rome and its emperors. So see the
opening sections of Aelius Aristides, *Roman Oration*. I suspect this is a subject that
needs further investigation. For a contemporaneous comments on tyranny from the
Republican period compare Cicero, *De officiis* 3.36 (which says that tyranny and
greed for power come from delusion) and 3.84 (which quotes from Accius the maxim
that tyrants have few true friends, in contrasting tyranny with a free state).

[94] PHerc. 1507 (see n. 10 above); it was produced by Scribe XXVIII (Group Q)
who also produced a copy of *De Poemata*; cf. Cavallo, *Libri scritture scribi*, 43. It should
also be noted that Plutarch's *How to Tell a Flatterer from a Friend* (*Mor.* 48E–74E) was
addressed to his friend and protegé "King" Philopappos and opens with a reference to Plato, *Laws* 731D–E, a passage dealing with "great men." Since it also
mentions issues like calumny and vice, it reflects some of the standard *topoi* that
might also have been considered by Zeno of Sidon, and so also by Philodemus.

[95] This has been reported to me by Jeffrey Fish, who is now producing a new
critical edition of the text. The relevant passage (from Col. 23, lines 17–18) reads:
καὶ παρρησίας ἄπειρον ἰ‖σηγόρου ("had no experience of frank speech with equals").
The reference is to the young Telemachus before he has journeyed abroad and
seems to refer to the rights of frank speech among members of the assembly. I
wish to thank Dr. Fish for sharing this information with me.

Table 1: *Philodemus' Ethical Works*

1. *Treatises on Character and Life* (Περὶ ἠθῶν καὶ βίων)

a. *those attested with* Περὶ ἠθῶν καὶ βίων *in the title*

PHerc.°	TITLE	HAND	SCRIBE	DATE*
1471	Π. η. καὶ β., ὅ ἐστι Περὶ παρρησίας (*On Frank Criticism*)	M	?	75–50
168	Π. β. καὶ η., ἢ Περὶ τοῦ μὴ (*or* μάτην?) κατὰ τὰ τυχόντα ζῆν ὑπομνημάτων α′ (*On Not Living according to Chance*, book 1)	?	?	75–50?

b. *probably part of the same work*

Paris 2	Περὶ διαβολῆς (*On Calumny*)	?	?	post 48[1]

c. *others related works on ethics*

1050	Περὶ θανάτου δ′ (*On Death*, book 4)	I	?	post 40[2]
189	Περὶ θανάτου ?	?	XXXIII	50–25?
807	Περὶ θανάτου ?	L	XVIII ?	ca. 50±
873	Περὶ ὁμιλίας (*On conversation*)	L	XVIII	ca. 50±
163	Περὶ πλούτου α′ (*On wealth*, book 1)	I	?	post 40
97	Περὶ πλούτου (*On wealth*)	O	XXIV	ca. 50±
312	Περὶ γάμου (*On marriage*) ?	?	?	?
1251	Περὶ αἱρέσεων καὶ φυγῶν (*On Choices and Avoidances*)? [also known as *The Comparetti Ethics*]	N	?	50–25
346	[A Protreptic Treatise: *Tractatus (on Epicurean Ethics)*]	?	?	?

° All reference numbers and titles for Herculaneum papyri are taken from Marcello Gigante, *Catalogo dei Papiri Ercolanesi* (Naples: Bibliopolis, 1979); cf. Mario Capasso, *Manuale di papirologia ercolanese*, Studi e Testi 3 (Lecce: Congedo Editore, 1991).

* The columns for Hands, Scribes, and Dates are based on Guglielmo Cavallo, *Libri scritture scribi a Ercolano*, Supplements to *Cronache ercolanesi* 13 (Naples: Gaetano Macchiaroli, 1983), 28–46, for all cases where Cavallo offers analysis or unless otherwise noted. The Date refers to the production of the scroll itself. All dates are B.C.E.

2. Treatises on the Passions (Περὶ πάθων); *texts possibly from this larger work*

PHerc.	TITLE	HAND	SCRIBE	DATE
182	Περὶ ὀργῆς (*On Anger*)	F	IX	ca. 50±
57	Περὶ μανίας (*On Insanity*)	O	XXIV	ca. 50±
353	Περὶ μανίας ?	?	?	
1384	Περὶ ἔρωτος (*On Sexual Passion*) ?	?	?	?

3. *Treatises on Vices and their Corresponding Virtues*
(Περὶ κακιῶν καὶ τῶν ἀντικειμένων ἀρετῶν)

PHerc.	TITLE	HAND	SCRIBE	DATE
1424	Περὶ οἰκονομίας (*On Household Management*) [Full title: Περὶ καιῶν καὶ τῶν ἀντικειμένων ἀρετῶν καὶ τῶν ἐν οἷς εἰσι καὶ περὶ ἃ θ΄ . . . (*On Vices and their corresponding Virtues and the People and Situations in which they occur, book 9: . . .*)	P, a	XXV	50–25[3]
1675	Περὶ καιῶν καὶ τῶν ἀντικειμένων ἀρετῶν καὶ τῶν ἐν οἷς εἰσι καὶ περὶ ἃ (*On Vices and their corresponding Virtues and the People and Situations in which they occur*)	P, a	XXV	50–25
222	Περὶ καιῶν καὶ τῶν ἐν οἷς εἰσι καὶ περὶ ἃ ζ΄ ὅ ἐστι περὶ κολακείας (*On Vices and the People and Situations in which they occur, book 7: On Flattery*)	P, a	XXV	50–25
1082	Περὶ κολακείας (*On Flattery*)	P, a	XXV	50–25
1089	Περὶ κολακείας (*On Flattery*) ?	P, a	XXV	50–25
1457	Περὶ κακιῶν (*On Vices*)	P, a	XXV	50–25
253	Περὶ κακιῶν (*On Vices*)	P, a	XXV	50–25
1008	Περὶ κακιῶν ι΄ (*On Vices*, book 10: On arrogance?*)	P, a	XXV	50–25
465	Περὶ φιλαργυρίας (*On Greed*) ?	P, a	XXV	50–25
1613	Περὶ φιλαργυρίας (*On Greed*) ?	P, a	XXV	50–25
1017	Περὶ ὕβρεως (*On Pride*)	P, c[4]	¤	50–25
1025	Περὶ φιλοδοξίας (*On Love of Fame*)	P, c	¤	50–25
1678	Περὶ ἐπιχαιρεκακίας (*On Spitefulness*)	P, c	¤	50–25
1414	Περὶ χάριτος (*On Gratitude*)	P, c	¤	50–25

[1] Based on the fact that Virgil joined the school of Siro in 48, and this work names him along with others in the dedication. See John Ferguson, "Epicureanism under the Roman Empire," *ANRW* 2.36.4 (1990): 2265.

[2] Cavallo (52) dates this hand between 50–25, but one of the other scrolls in this group (PHerc. 1065, *De signis*) may be dated to after 40 B.C.E. based on internal references to historical events; see Elizabeth Asmis, "Philodemus' Epicrueanism," *ANRW* 2.36.4 (1990): 2372 following H. M. Last, "The Date of Philodemus' *De Signis*," *Classical Quarterly* 16 (1922): 177–80.

[3] Cavallo (55) dates this hand to between 50–25, but the range may likely be narrowed on other grounds to between ca. 48 to ca. 40±, based on the other literary activities of the library in this period (cf. Cavallo, 63).

[4] The following four scrolls were all produced by closely related, if not the same, scribal hand, which is in turn part of the hand-group (P) from which Scribe XXV came. For this reason, it would appear that these last four scrolls go with the larger work *On Vices and their Corresponding Virtues*, even though some of the topics would go equally well with the collection of treatises *On the Passions*.

Table 2: *PHerc. 1471—Order and Disposition of Extant Material*

Cornice # (Olivieri)	Text Contained (Olivieri) [+ Neapolitan *disegni*]	Columns Reported | (possible)	Papyrus Material (number of sections)	Measurements (by section, in *cm*)	
				Olivieri[a] top/bottom of tray	Gigante[b] top/bottom of tray
1	Frag. 1, 2	2|(6) |(4)	1 (2) / 1 (2)^dd	36 × 6.5 / 25 × 7	^1 24.4 × 10 ^2 11.4 × 6.2/ ^3 17.3 × 6.2 ^4 18.8 × 9
2	Frag. 3	1|(6) | (6)	1/ 1	36 × 7.5 / 36 × 7	^1 37 × 8.5 / ^2 34.5 × 7.6
3	Frag. 4–7	4|(6) |(5)	1/ 1	36.5 × 7 / 31 × 8	23.6 × 8.4 / 29.2 × 7
4^c	Frag. 8–12, [+1 uned*], 13/ [+1*],14,15, [+1*],[+1 (=O's Append.)], [+1*]	6|(7) 2|(5)	1/ 1	39.5 × 7.5 / 30.7 × 7^d	36.5 × 7 / 35 × 6.2
5	Frag. 16–24	9|(5) |(4)	1 / 1	31 × 6.5 / 23.5 × 7	35 × 6.2 / 24 × 6.7
6	Frag. 25–33	9|(5.5) |(6)	1 / 1	32.5 × 6.5 / 36 × 7	36.6 × 6.5 / 31 × 7.1
7	Frag. 34–43	10|(4.75) |(5)	1 / 1	27 × 7 / 28.6 × 7	39 × 7 / 30 × 6.3
8	Frag. 44–52	9|(5) |(5)	1 / 1	28.5 × 7 / 29 × 7	30 × 6 / 23 × 6.8
9	Frag. 53–65	13|(5.75) |(7)	1 / 1	34 × 7 / 39.5 × 7	32.2 × 6.6 / 35.4 × 6.7
10	Frag. 66–74	9|(5.75) |(3)	1 / 1	34.5 × 7.5 / 18 × 7	26.8 × 6.5 / 28.5 × 6.5
11	Frag. 75, 76,[77N], 77,[79N]	5|(7) |(6.5)	1 / 1	39.5 × 11 / 38.5 × 10	28.5 × 7 / 28.5 × 6.8
12	Frag. 78, 78, 80,81,[84N], 82	6|(7) |(6)	1 / 1	41 × 11 / 37 × 10.5	34.3 × 7 / 39.5 × 7
13	Frag. 83, [87N],84,85, 86,[91N], 87,[93N],88,	9|(5.75) | (5)^c	1 / 1	34.5 × 10.5 / 30 × 10	34.1 × 6.8 / 17.1 × 6.8
14	Appendix (frs. A-N) + unedited frs.	?|(4) |(5)	1 / 1	23.5 × 10 / 29 × 7.5	38.5 × 10 / 39 × 9.5
15	Appendix + unedited frs.	?|(7) |(6.75)	1 / 1	40 × 10.5 / 38.5 × 10	30 × 9.8 / 37.5 × 9
16	Appendix + unedited frs.	?|(6) |(6)	1 / 1	37.3 × 10 / 35 × 8	33.7 × 9.5 / 29.1 × 9.2
17	Col. I–III	3|(3)	1 / 1	17.5 × 18.5	17.7 × 9 / 16.5 × 7.1
18	Col. IV–IX	6|(5.5)	2 / 1	33 × 17	^1 17 × 7.9 ^2 17.7 × 8.4 / ^3 33.7 × 9.5
19	Col. X–XV	6|(5.5)	1 / 1	32.3 × 17	33.6 × 8 / 32 × 7.6
20	Col. XVI–XXI	6|(5.5)	1 / 1	32.8 × 17.7	33.5 × 8.3 / 32.5 × 7.5
21	Col. XXII–XXIV + *subscriptio*	3^+|(3^+)	1 / 1	33 × 17	31.5 × 8.4 / 28.5 × 7.2
□ Totals		118|(168)^f	45	1204.50 cm	1180 cm

Table 3: *PHerc. 1471—Stichometric Notations in the Papyrus*

Location (Cornice #) (per Olivieri)	Position in Text per Olivieri) [all are in left margin]	Marginal Notation	Numerical order	Olivieri's prior cols. (act.)| lines (extant)	Intervals prior columns (conjectured)
2	extra fr. 8, line 1 (= Appendix)	$\bar{H}$	7	?	A–H = 42 ?
4^g	extra fr. after Frag. 15, line 2 (= Appendix)	$\bar{I}$	9	?	Θ–I = 12 ?
5	Frag. 20, line 6	$\bar{Y}$	20	?	K–Y = 66 ?
17	Col. II^a, line 2 ? [provisional reading by LMW]^h	Z ?	[30]		[Φ–Z = 60]
18	Col. VII^b, line 6	$\bar{H}$	31	[6 | 109]	Φ–H = 66 ?
19	Col. XIII^b, line 7	$\bar{Θ}$	32	6 | 134	
20	Col. XIX^b, line 9	$\bar{I}$	33	6 | 150	
21	Col. XXIV^b, line 9	$\bar{K}$	34	5 | 121	
21	[Col. XXIV^b, remainder]			+ 4 lines	
				Total 203 cols. + 4 lines & *subscr.*	

Table 4: *PHerc. 1471—The Stichometry of the Text: Variable Calculations*

1 Lines/Col.| Lines/100 *stichoi*	2 No. of Cols. per stichometric letter	3 Total no. of Half-Lines^i (Lines)	4 Total no. of Columns^j	5 No. of Cols. of Fragments^k	6 Total at Col. XXIV^l
30 | 180	6.0	6094 (3047)	203.13	179	203
33 | 180	5.45 (= 5 cols. + 15 lines)	6109 (3054.5)	185.12	161.95	185.95
30 | 200	6.66 (= 6 cols. + 20 lines)	6754 (3377)	225.13	199.45	223.45
33 | 200	6.06 (= 6 cols. + 2 lines)	6769 (3383.5)	205.12	180.86	204.86

^{a} *Philodemi* ΠΕΡΙ ΠΑΡΡΗΣΙΑΣ *Libellus*, ed. by Alexander Olivieri (Leipzig: Teubner, 1914), iii–iv.

^{b} Marcello Gigante, *Catalogo dei Papiri Ercolanesi* (Naples: Bibliopolis, 1979), 355.

^{dd} See note d below.

^{c} See above n. 79. I have analyzed the published photograph of this *cornice* from Gigante, *Catalogo dei Papiri*, Pl. 6 (between 320–21). The contents noted in column 2 are based on these observations; * designates unedited fragmentary columns not reported by Olivieri or the Neapolitan *disegni*. In like manner, column 3 summarizes for each *cornice* the number of fragments (or columns) reported by Olivieri [plus extra Neapolitan *disegni*] compared with the number of columns possible calculated on the basis of the amount of papyrus material preserved (per Olivieri's measurements, see col. 5). NB: Whereas Olivieri designates it as *Cornice* 4, Gigante labels it *Cornice* 7 (see the following note).

ᵈ The measurements given by Gigante for *Cornice* 7 also match those reported by Olivieri for *Cornice* 4. Nor is this a random discrepancy. It must be noted that the measurements for the papyrus sections from *Cornici* 3–13 in Olivieri's number match very closely with those for *Cornici* 6–16 respectively in Gigante's numbering. Some of these are rather distinctive measurements, as marked by the lines above; so note Olivieri *Cor.* 5 → Gigante *Cor.* 8 and Olivieri *Cor.* 10 → Gigante *Cor.* 13. Close comparison of these measurements further suggests that Olivieri's *Cor.* 1–2 match Gigante's *Cor.* 5–6, while Olivieri's *Cor.* 14, 15, 16 actually resemble the measurements in Gigante's *Cor.* 3, 1, 2 respectively. All of this seems to suggest that Olivieri has, without any explanation, reordered the *Cornici* numbers, at least by moving the complex and largely unedited material in his *Cor.* 14–16. While this analysis maintains the basic numerical order of the materials in Fragments 1–88 (94), it does call into some question the way that Olivieri made his determinations. It also leaves some uncertainty concerning the relationship between Frag. 88 (= 94N) and Col. I.

ᵉ The subtotal for *Cor.* 1–13 equals: 94 | (144). *Cor.* 5, 7, 9, and 10 (plus 4, as corrected) and *Cor.* 17–21 show the proper number of columns for the amount of papyrus material preserved. The remainder (*Cor.* 1–3, 6, 8, 11–13, plus 14–16) report less columns than should be possible for the amount of material preserved.

ᶠ Totals in column 3 do not include the material in *Cornici* 14–16, which represents an additional 14 reported column fragments (Olivieri's Appendix) but 34.75 possible columns.

ᵍ See note c above.

ʰ This is a tentative suggestion based on study of the published photograph of *Cornice* 17 (Col. I–III) as found in Guglielmo Cavallo, *Libri scritture scribi a Ercolano*, Supplements to *Cronache ercolanesi* 13 (Naples: Gaetano Macchiaroli, 1983) Plate XXVI.

ⁱ The calculation is the number of stichometric letters times the number of lines per 100 *stichoi* (= 1 stichometric letter), but with the qualification that the last letter (K) contains only 5 columns of text (see Table 3, s.v. *Cornice* 21). Thus, the equation is $(33 \text{ [A-}\Omega\text{+A-I]} \times \Delta) + (5 \times \Theta \text{ [K]} + 4)$ = total number of half-lines in the text, where (based on the information in column 1 of the table) Δ = number of lines of text per 100 *stichoi* (180 or 200) and $\Theta = 5 \times$ number of lines per column (5×30 or 33, i.e., 150 or 165).

ʲ Number of lines (col. 3) divided by number of columns per stichometric letter (column 2).

ᵏ Based on the stichometric notation in Col. VII, line 6 (H = 31 stichometric letters) and subtracting 7 to yield the number of columns before Col. I. Cf. Table 3, s.v. *Corniche* 18.

ˡ Total of Fragments (column 5) + 24 Columns.

PART TWO

PHILODEMUS' THOUGHT WITHIN THE CONTEXT
OF THE GRECO-ROMAN WORLD

EPICUREAN ECONOMICS

Elizabeth Asmis

Abstract

This paper offers an analysis of Philodemus' views on wealth in the context of Epicurean economic theory in general. The discussion is in three parts. The first part offers a survey of the relationship of Epicureans to the rest of society. It is argued that, instead of forming separate social and economic enclaves, the Epicureans were closely integrated in their daily lives with the rest of society. The second part examines the basic doctrines of Epicurean economics. Beginning with the concept of "natural wealth," the discussion moves from the evidence about Epicurus to Philodemus' *On Wealth* and *On Household Economics*. The question is now raised: to what extent does Philodemus reshape the economic views of Epicurus and Metrodorus? The third part of the paper attempts to assess Philodemus' own contribution in *On Household Economics*. Philodemus, it is argued, revises Epicurean economics to suit the circumstances of Roman aristocrats. Elaborating the view that it is preferable to have much rather than just a little, Philodemus offers a new evaluation of lives: best is the life of the philosopher that is shared with others; second best is that of the comfortably-off landowner, who shares his resources with his friends. While admiring the frugal life of Epicurus and his associates, Philodemus also envisions a more comfortable life, in which philosophers such as himself share their insights with Roman landowners.

Epicurus begins his *Letter to Menoeceus* (122), a summary of his ethics, by urging both young and old to do philosophy (φιλοσοφεῖν). It is never too early or too late, he points out, to secure mental health—in short, to be happy. Suppose a person agrees: how does a person go about earning a living while doing philosophy? This paper will examine how a person combines the need to earn a living with the choice to be an Epicurean. It will do so in three parts. The first section will set out a context by surveying the relationship of Epicureans to the rest of society. Next is a discussion of the philosophical principles that govern a person's economic life. Third, we turn to ways of earning and managing an income. The paper will focus increasingly on Philodemus' *On Household Economics* (περὶ οἰκονομίας).

Epicureanism and Society

Epicureanism differs in important respects in its relationship to society from other ancient philosophical movements. In the first place, it is anti-elitist. Epicurus addressed his message to all individuals, regardless of age, sex, education, economic circumstances, or social station. He viewed traditional education as an outright hindrance. In a letter, Epicurus congratulated a new student, Apelles, for coming to philosophy "pure of all education."[1] Similarly, he advised the young Pythocles to "flee all education."[2] The only true education, Epicurus held, is Epicurean philosophy. Epicurus designed his teaching in such a way that not just the affluent, but the most lowly working person, including even the slave, would have enough time to do philosophy. Young and old, male and female, educated and uneducated, poor and rich, all were invited to become Epicureans.[3]

At the same time, Epicureanism is not addressed to the masses. Epicurus was as contemptuous of the crowd as any other ancient philosopher.[4] He took great care to distinguish his teaching from demagoguery. The wise man, he said, will found a school, but not in such a way as to "draw a crowd," nor will he give public addresses.[5] Epicurus aimed to convert individuals. He sought to do so by engaging the intellectual assent of each person. Philosophical doctrines must be firmly rooted in each individual's own understanding in order to have the appropriate effect, and this comes about through reasoning, not through momentary enthusiasm. Even though Epicurus

---

[1] U 117.

[2] U 163, cf. 164. The only concession Epicurus made to traditional education is that there is a benefit in knowing the rudiments of grammar—that is, in knowing how to read and write. A wise person, he said, must know letters (Sextus Empiricus, *Against the Grammarians* 49).

[3] The only known restrictions occur in this text (Diogenes Laertius 10.117 = U 226): "[Epicurus held] that one cannot become wise on the basis of every condition of the body, nor in any race" (οὐδὲ μὴν ἐκ πάσης σώματος ἕξεως σοφὸν γενέσθαι ἂν οὐδ' ἐν παντὶ ἔθνει). Presumably, Epicurus held that severe physical handicaps, such as serious deficiencies in sense perception and debilitating illness, will prevent a person from becoming wise. Interestingly, the statement contains no mention of intellectual prerequisites as such. The reference to "race" is intriguing. Allegedly, Epicurus also said that only Greeks can philosophize (U 226). A related claim is that not every race of human beings was able to form social compacts so as to develop a system of justice (KD 32).

[4] U 187; SV 29, 45, 81.

[5] Diogenes Laertius 10.120: σχολὴν κατασκευάσειν, ἀλλ' οὐχ ὥστ' ὀχλαγωγῆσαι; and οὐ πανηγυριεῖν.

used memorization as a fundamental teaching method for both novices and advanced students, he insisted that memorization must be accompanied by a personal evaluation of the evidence.

While opposing traditional values, Epicureanism does not remove the individual from the rest of society. It keeps a person integrated in the daily routine of ordinary life while shifting his or her aims away from those of the rest of society. Epicureans form a close community with one another; but they also adapt themselves to the institutions of the larger community. There is ample margin for happiness within social constraints. A striking example is the participation of Epicureans in public religious events. Epicureans may join religious festivities so long as they keep pure of wrong beliefs. Epicurus himself is said to have taken part "in all the traditional festivals and sacrifices," and to have used the common oaths.[6] He proclaimed that the wise man enjoys the sights and sounds of Dionysiac rites as much as anyone.[7] Epicurus sought to elevate people from all ranks of society to the heights of happiness by having them accept social institutions while rejecting conventional beliefs.

The Epicureans in general, and especially Epicurus and his immediate friends, cultivated close personal relationships with one another. However, the picture that has been painted of Epicureans as living in alternative communities, separate from the rest of society, needs to be corrected. About 307/6 or 305/4 b.c.e., Epicurus purchased a house in a district called Melite, which became the headquarters of Epicureanism in antiquity. Cicero reports that, even though the house was "small" (*angusta*), it held large companies of close friends.[8] Epicurus also acquired grounds outside the city called the "Garden," which gave its name to his philosophical school.[9] The house and Garden were passed on from one head of school to another. Epicurus' closest philosophical associates in Athens included his three brothers; a slave called Mys ("Mouse"); the other three main founders of the school, Metrodorus, Polyainos, and Hermarchus; Leontion, a woman who lived with Metrodorus and wrote an Epicurean philosophical treatise; and

---

[6] Philodemus *On Piety* 1, 790–840 (Obbink); partly at U 169.

[7] U 20.

[8] Cicero *On Ends* 1.65.

[9] R. E. Wycherley argues, against the prevailing opinion, that the garden was close to the house within the city ("The Garden of Epicurus," *Phoenix* 13 (1959): 73–77). This proposal is intended in part to explain the fact that the philosophical activities in the Garden and house were closely connected.

students such as Nicanor, Pythocles, and Colotes.[10] In his will, Epicurus describes Hermarchus and Nicanor as being among those who "grew old in philosophy" with him.[11] Epicurus was especially close to Metrodorus, who died seven years before him. Metrodorus is called "almost another Epicurus" by Cicero.[12] Epicurus paid him the honor of calling him a wise man.[13] The joint monthly celebration in honor of both Epicurus and Metrodorus, for which Epicurus made provision in his will, attests to the special intimacy between the two men.[14]

Friends are said to have come from everywhere to "live with him [Epicurus] in the Garden."[15] It has been conjectured rather fancifully that Epicurus' followers took up residence in "hutments" in the garden (as Farrington puts it).[16] There is no evidence, however, that the garden grounds contained residential quarters. Nor is there any reason to suppose that Epicurus and his friends needed to share the same residential quarters in order to share a philosophical life. In his will, Epicurus stipulated that Hermarchus and "those who philosophize with him" should have the Garden, on the one hand, "to spend time in (ἐνδιατρίβειν) philosophically" and the house in Melite, on the other hand, "to live in" (ἐνοικεῖν). The Garden was to be as "secure" as possible. Epicurus singled out two persons to share the house with Hermarchus: the son of Metrodorus, and the son of Polyainos, whose care was entrusted to Hermarchus.[17]

---

[10] At 10.10, Diogenes Laertius mentions that Mys was the "most distinguished" of the slaves who did philosophy with Epicurus. In addition to Leontion, other *hetairai* who are said to have associated with Epicurus and Metrodorus are Mammarion, Hedeia, Erotion, and Nicidion (Diogenes Laertius 10.7); see the article by Pamela Gordon in this volume.

[11] Diogenes Laertius 10.20–21.

[12] Cicero *On Ends* 2.92. The two men, it is said, never parted during their acquaintance, except for a six months' trip by Metrodorus (Diogenes Laertius 10.22).

[13] Cicero *On Ends* 2.7 (U 146). Cicero mentions that Metrodorus did not want to refuse the honor, but that he did not himself claim to be a wise person. Cicero also asserts that Epicurus considered himself alone a wise person.

[14] See below, n. 26.

[15] Diogenes Laertius 10.10.

[16] Benjamin Farrington, *The Faith of Epicurus* (London: Weidenfeld & Nicholson, 1967), 12. Norman De Witt (cf. "Epicurean Contubernium, *TAPA* 67 [1936]: 55–63, "Organization and Procedure in Epicurean Groups," *CP* 31 [1936]: 205–211, *Epicurus and his Philosophy*, Minneapolis: University of Minnesota Press, 1954, 95–96) is primarily responsible for the prevailing view that the Epicureans went to school in residential communities. He is followed by Martha C. Nussbaum (*The Therapy of Desire* [Princeton: Princeton University Press, 1994], 117–19).

[17] Diogenes Laertius 10.17–19, including (17): ἐν ᾧ ἂν τρόπῳ ἀσφαλέστατον ᾖ. Epicurus also provides for the daughter of Metrodorus, with the injunction that she should be obedient to Hermarchus. He does not specify whether she will also live in the house.

These arrangements indicate that the Garden was used as a place for meetings, whereas the house was the residence of the head of the school and a few close associates. There is nothing unusual about the provision for the security of the Garden. Apart from financial security, we would expect the maintenance of the Garden to include physical means of protection, such as a wall and a gate-keeper. There is no support whatsoever for the suggestion that students would give up their worldly possessions in order to live in the Garden.[18] We are told that, contrary to Pythagoras, Epicurus did not think it right for people to hold their property in common.[19] The "small" house in Melite could accommodate only a small number of permanent occupants and their guests. This would not preclude large numbers of guests coming to stay with Epicurus successively for varying periods of time. Before Metrodorus' death, we may suppose that the house regularly accommodated Epicurus, Metrodorus and Leontion with their two children, a few slaves, and a steady stream of guests.

Seneca stresses the importance of communal life in Epicureanism when he says, "what made Metrodorus, Hermarchus, and Polyainos great is not Epicurus' school, but their life together (*contubernium*)."[20] Plutarch likewise draws attention to the communal meals and gatherings of Epicurus and his friends.[21] Epicurus is said to have spent "an entire mina" (one hundred drachmas) a day on food.[22] It has been estimated that this amount could feed from one to two hundred people.[23] The figure is suspect, however, since it comes from a vehement

---

[18] Nussbaum (*Therapy of Desire*, 118) conjectures that a student would give up her property and probably her children, so as to be supported from a central fund while residing in the Garden. This seems to me contrary to what we know about Epicurus' attitude towards property and towards children.

[19] Diogenes Laertius 10.11. The reason given by Epicurus is that this would be a sign of mistrust, and so incompatible with friendship.

[20] *Epistle* 6.6: Metrodorum et Hermarchum et Polyaenum magnos viros non schola Epicuri sed contubernium fecit. De Witt points out that in the period of the Roman Republic the term *contubernium* "was restricted to denote the cohabitation of slaves and the use of common quarters by soldiers in service" and that later it came to signify common life in general ("Epicurean Contubernium," 59). On the close personal relations of Epicurus and his friends, see esp. Diskin Clay ("Individual and Community in the first Generation of the Epicurean School," in ΣΥΖΗΤΗΣΙΣ: *Studi sull' Epicureismo greco e romano offerti a Marcello Gigante* (Naples: G. Macchiaroli, 1983), 255–79, esp. 266–78) and Francesca Longo Auricchio, "La Scuola di Epicuro," *CErc* 8 (1978): 21–37.

[21] *Live unknown* 1129a.

[22] Diogenes Laertius 10.7.

[23] Horst Steckel, "Epikuros," in *Paulys Realencyclopädie der classischen Altertumswissenschaft*, suppl. vol. 11 (Stuttgart: Alfred Druckenmüller, 1968), 585.

attack on Epicurus by Timocrates, brother of Metrodorus and a one-time follower who ended up bitterly recanting his Epicureanism.[24] If the sum is right, then Epicurus did attract a surprisingly large number of people to his garden, though not nearly as many as the two thousand people that Theophrastus is alleged to have attracted to his lectures.[25] Even though the number who visited Epicurus' Garden may have reached two hundred in a day, there is no evidence that this group formed a self-sufficient economic enclave.

In his will, Epicurus allocated part of his revenues toward funeral rites for his parents and brothers, an annual day of celebration on his birthday, a gathering in honor of himself and Metrodorus on the twentieth day of each month, and two annual days of celebration for his brothers and for Polyainos respectively.[26] Among those who were invited to these events were well-disposed non-Epicureans. We have a text in which Epicurus is cited as inviting "all in the house" as well as "outsiders who have good will toward him and his friends." Epicurus adds that this is not demagoguery.[27]

These celebrations constitute a kind of "religious calendar," as Clay has shown.[28] Despite the veneration of Epicurus by his followers,[29] however, there are fundamental differences between Epicureanism and religious cults. Unlike religious groups, such as the, ὀργεῶνες (sacrificial associates, to whom Epicurean communities have been compared), the Epicureans did not have a secret doctrine.[30] Some

---

[24] After recanting his Epicureanism, Timocrates attacked Epicurus vehemently in his book Εὐφραντά (*Merriment*). Timocrates (or perhaps Diogenes Laertius) supports the figure of one mina by saying that Epicurus himself mentioned it in two letters. In view of Timocrates' hostility and the serious distortions in his other accusations, the figure is suspect, at least as a daily sum.

[25] See Diogenes Laertius 5.37. Steckel makes this comparison, ("Epikuros," 585).

[26] Diogenes Laertius 10.18. Clay has gathered the testimonies for these events in "The Cults of Epicurus," *CErc* 16 (1986): 11–28.

[27] PHerc. 1232 fr. 8 col. 1, quoted and discussed by Clay, "Cults of Epicurus" 13–18. Clay argues that the event is a celebration in honor of Epicureans who have died.

[28] Clay, "Individual and Community," 274–79, and "Cults of Epicurus," 25.

[29] The incident of Colotes embracing the knees of Epicurus is often cited in this connection (U 141). On a lighter note, Cicero (*On Ends* 5.3) speaks of the portraits of Epicurus in drinking cups and on rings. On portraits of Epicurus see also Pliny, *Natural History* 35.5.

[30] Ὀργεῶνες met regularly to sacrifice to a hero or god (William Scott Ferguson, "The Attic Orgeônes," *Harvard Theological Review* 37 [1944]: 61–140). The Epicureans have also been compared to members of a type of religious community called *thiasos* (so Clay, "Individual and Community," 275–79). Like the Epicureans, members of these groups function as ordinary members of society while forming clubs that meet regularly and impose dues. A crucial difference, however, between the religious

ancient critics charged that Epicurus escaped prosecution for impiety only because his philosophy went unnoticed.[31] This inconspicuousness was intentional, but it is not the same as an attempt at secrecy. It is the meaning of Epicurus' well-known saying: λάθε βιώσας, "do not attract notice to your life."[32] Epicurus neither concealed his doctrines nor broadcast his views to the public at large. Non-Epicurean friends were freely invited to Epicurean events. Epicurus' policy was to accept social conventions while preserving philosophical integrity.

The money for Epicurean communal events came from gifts and fees. Philodemus quotes Epicurus as soliciting an annual contribution of the relatively small sum of one hundred and twenty drachmas. The same text mentions another yearly assessment sent to Epicurus on behalf of a man and his father.[33] Contributions of food were also sent to Epicurus. In one letter, Epicurus asked for a "little pot of cheese, so that when I wish I can have a luxury."[34] Like the contributions, the expenditures were modest. In general, Epicurus and his friends lived frugal lives. They are said to have drunk mostly water and just a little wine. Epicurus himself wrote that he was content with water and plain bread.[35] About the middle of the first century

---

groups and the Epicureans is that the former are bound by an obligation for secrecy. As Walter Burkert points out, "The main obligation was not propagating a faith, but withholding the central revelation" (*Ancient Mystery Cults* [Cambridge: Harvard University Press, 1987], 45–46). See further Michael Erler's criticisms, *Die Hellenistische Philosophie, Grundriss der Geschichte der Philosophie: Die Philosophie der Antike*, eds. Michael Erler and Hellmut Flashar, 4.1 (Basel: Schwabe, 1994), 206–207.

[31] Philodemus *On Piety* part 1, lines 1402–12 (Obbink).

[32] See U 551.

[33] Philodemus PHerc. 1418 ("Treatise On Epicurus and Others") col. 30 (Luigi Spina, "Il trattato di Filodemo su Epicuro e altri (PHerc. 1418)," *CErc* 7 (1977): 62). See also the new edition by C. Militello, *Memorie Epicuree (PHerc. 1418 e 310)*, La Scuola di Epicuro (Naples: Bibliopolis, 1997). There is also mention of a third contribution having to do with income derived from hiring out slaves. It is highly unlikely that Philodemus' *On Frank Criticism* fr. 55 says anything at all about contributions; the general sense requires an application of a remedy, not a contribution of money. This fragment is cited by De Witt as showing that Epicurus accepted contributions even though he did not exact fees ("Epicurean Contubernium," 57, n. 10); the latter claim is contradicted by PHerc. 1418, col. 30.

[34] Diogenes Laertius 10.11 (U 182); also U 183.

[35] Diogenes Laertius 10.11. At U 181, Epicurus writes that he "exults" in plain water and bread, while "spitting on" the pleasures of luxury—not because of themselves, but because of the troubles that follow. Seneca (*Epistle* 18.9) shows that Epicurus did not practice stark frugality continually, but on a regular basis on set days. He says that Epicurus set aside certain days on which he satisfied his hunger "stintingly" (*maligne*) in order to see if this would detract from his having full pleasure.

B.C.E., Philodemus invited his prominent friend Piso to dinner on the twentieth in a poem that provides a unique insight into this Epicurean event. Philodemus playfully observes that the meal will be modest unless Piso enriches it.[36]

From the time of Epicurus, then, people came to learn, talk, and eat together in the Garden in the pursuit of philosophy. This is not a welfare society, even though, as friends, Epicureans were expected to help one another.[37] Those who could afford it were expected to make contributions. With the exception of the occupants of the house, the Epicureans lived and worked in the larger community. They blended in with the rest of society: they dressed in the same way, performed similar jobs, and dwelt alongside others.[38] The life that they shared with other Epicureans was especially important; it was, in a sense, the only real life. Yet there was also a life, however attenuated, outside the Garden, and Epicurus gave instructions on how to cope with it.

Epicurus kept in touch by letter with other groups of Epicureans that sprang up around the Aegean. He himself founded schools in Mytilene and Lampsacus before he set up his school in Athens, and he continued to have especially close relations with his friends in Lampsacus.[39] There is no evidence that any of these schools were residential, although it would not be surprising if some Epicureans lived together, in emulation of Epicurus' own house in Athens.

For the period after Epicurus, we have very little evidence about Epicurean communities until the end of the second century B.C.E. Philodemus provides information about dissident schools at Rhodes and Cos about the end of the second century and beginning of the

---

[36] *Palatine Anthology* 11.44 = no. 27 in David Sider, *The Epigrams of Philodemus* (Oxford: Oxford University Press, 1997). On the meals held on the twentieth of each month, see also Cicero *On Ends* 2.101.

[37] In the text sometimes cited in support of a welfare policy, PHerc. 1418 col. 12 (Spina), Epicurus simply advises Timocrates to help certain people not only because they are close to him but also because of their character. This text appears to deal with Timocrates' personal relationships. It does not show that more affluent Epicureans were regularly expected to contribute to the livelihood of the more needy.

[38] Anthony Long throws doubt on the traditional picture of Epicureans living in alternative communities, even though he accepts it for the purpose of his argument. Long undertakes to show (rightly, I think) that the Epicureans did have a concern for people in the wider community ("Pleasure and Social Utility—The Virtues of Being Epicurean," *Aspects de la Philosophie hellénistique*, 283–316, esp. 286–87, 293).

[39] Diogenes Laertius 10.15.

first century B.C.E.[40] He also provides a general account of the relationship between teachers and students in his treatise *On Frank Criticism* (Περὶ παρρησίας). Whereas the four founders of Epicureanism (Epicurus, Metrodorus, Hermarchus, and Polyainos) were regularly called "leaders" (καθηγημόνες), as well as "the men" (οἱ ἄνδρες), other teachers were called "guides" (καθηγηταί, καθηγούμενοι).[41] The students were called "those who receive preparation" (οἱ κατασκευαζόμενοι).[42] There is no evidence that schools were organized with different ranks of teachers.[43] We hear of an Epicurean school founded by Siro at Naples, which included Vergil among its students.[44] Possibly this was a residential school; and there may have been others. But the evidence suggests that residential communities (such as Epicurus' "small" house in Athens) contained just a tiny fraction of Epicureans.

Teachers of Epicureanism appeared in Italy in the second century B.C.E. Among them, the first Epicurean reported to have had an important influence is Amafinius, whose simple-minded writings, Cicero alleges, moved the multitude. After him, according to Cicero, many other Epicureans "took all of Italy by storm" by their many writings.[45] Cicero says nothing about any of the converts attending school. As he puts it, the Epicureans gathered ignorant villagers to their cause.[46] Notwithstanding Cicero's verdict, many politically prominent Romans were swayed by Epicureanism in the late Republic. Cassius, one of the murderers of Caesar, was an Epicurean; so were many members of

---

[40] Francesca Longo Auricchio and Adele Tepedino Guerra, "Aspetti e Problemi della Dissidenza Epicurea," *CErc* 11 (1981): 29–38; and David Sedley, "Philosophical Allegiance in the Greco-Roman World," *Philosophia Togata: Essays on Philosophy and Roman Society*, eds. Jonathan Barnes and Miriam Griffin (Oxford: Oxford University Press, 1989), 112–17.

[41] *On Frank Criticism*, fr. 8.6–7, 42.10, etc; see Longo Auricchio, "La Scuola di Epicuro," 22–23.

[42] *On Frank Criticism*, frs. 2.3, 25.6–7; etc.

[43] De Witt's reconstruction ("Organization and Procedure," also *Epicurus*, 94) of an Epicurean campus community, with different grades of professors, has been shown to be without foundation by Marcello Gigante, "Filodemo sulla libertà di parola," *Ricerche Filodemee* (Naples: Gaetano Macchiaroli, 1969), 55–113; 110–13.

[44] See Erler, "Die Hellenistische Philosophie," 370–71.

[45] *Tusculan Disputations* 4.6–7: Italiam totam occupaverunt. Cicero speculates that the writings of Amafinius caught on because they were very easy to understand, or because of the appeal of pleasure, or because there was nothing better. See also *Academica* 1.5 and *Tusculan Disputations* 2.6–8.

[46] *On Ends* 2.12.

the Caesarian party.[47] In his writings, Cicero shows us a number of Roman aristocrats who were converted to Epicureanism, including Torquatus, spokesman for Epicurean ethics in book 1 of *On Ends*, and Velleius, spokesman in book 1 of *On the Nature of the Gods*. Some, if not all, of these Romans had the benefit of private instruction. Philodemus, who studied with Zeno, head of the Epicurean school in Athens, moved to Rome where he became a close friend of the aristocrat L. Piso Caesoninus. Lucretius dedicated his poem to another member of the aristocracy, Gaius Memmius. The Roman Epicureans clearly looked to Epicureanism for guidance on how to fashion the careers that they were traditionally expected to follow.

As Epicureanism spread throughout the Hellenized East and to the Roman world, the Epicurean community as a whole was no longer as tightly knit as in the first generation. The relationship of Epicureans to the rest of society, however, remained basically the same. From the very beginning, Epicureans from all ranks of life worked alongside others in the community. Epicurus' ethics was designed to provide guidelines on how to sustain a philosophical life amid the rest of society. While drawing fixed boundaries on how to achieve happiness, Epicurus offered considerable flexibility to his followers on how to adapt to their social and economic circumstances.

In a light-hearted saying, Epicurus sums up his advice as: "One should laugh, philosophize, budget (οἰκονομεῖν), arrange all other personal affairs, and never stop uttering the correct philosophy."[48] More precise instructions appear throughout his ethical writings as well as in two works (not extant), *On Wealth* (περὶ πλούτου) and *On Lives* (περὶ βίων), which dealt specifically with the question of how to manage an income. Metrodorus also wrote a book titled *On Wealth*. This book too is not extant. Fortunately, however, we have papyri remains of two works by Philodemus, *On Wealth* and the so-called *On Economics*. In both of these works, Philodemus draws on Metrodorus. While all of these works offer guidance on how to arrange one's economic

---

[47] See Arnaldo Momigliano, "Review of Benjamin Farrington's *Science and Politics in the Ancient World*," *Journal of Roman Studies* 31 (1941): 149–57; 151–57; and David Sedley, "The Ethics of Brutus and Cassius," *Journal of Roman Studies* 87 (1997): 41–53; 41, 46–47.

[48] SV 41: γελᾶν ἅμα δεῖν καὶ φιλοσοφεῖν καὶ οἰκονομεῖν καὶ τοῖς λοιποῖς οἰκειώμασι χρῆσθαι καὶ μηδαμῇ λήγειν τὰς ἐκ τῆς ὀρθῆς φιλοσοφίας φωνὰς ἀφίεντας. De Witt ("Epicurean Contubernium," 59) suggests that this advice applied to "lay members" who needed to organize their own households. This distinction between lay members and residents of a school is untenable.

life, they are intent on distinguishing this advice from technical advice. The Epicureans did not consider any profession worthwhile except that of the philosopher. Life is worthwhile only insofar as it is shaped in accordance with philosophical principles. The economic advice of the Epicureans aims to show how to make and spend money philosophically, not just how to make money.

Putting a Limit to Wealth

This section will examine the Epicurean notion of the proper range of wealth. We shall first gather the evidence concerning Epicurus' own teaching, then turn to Metrodorus and Philodemus.

(a) *Epicurus on Natural Wealth*

The basic concept of Epicurean economics is that of "natural wealth."[49] Epicureans shared with other ancient philosophers the principle that the right way to live is to live naturally. Epicurus gave his own interpretation to this principle: to live naturally is to live pleasantly. We have a natural instinct, which is present from birth in all living beings, to pursue pleasure and avoid pain. Pleasure serves as a measuring-stick (κανών) for everything we do. The aim of human life, therefore, is to live pleasantly. The achievement of this natural aim makes us happy.[50]

In order to attain this goal, we must make a number of distinctions. There are two kinds of pleasure: the absence of pain, which is called "katastematic" and consists in the painless functioning of body and soul; and pleasant stimuli, or "kinetic" pleasures. The height of pleasure is the absence of pain. Kinetic pleasures bring variation, but do not increase the amount of pleasure.[51] Consequently, while a

---

[49] This is called ὁ φυσικὸς πλοῦτος, ὁ πλοῦτος ὁ κατὰ φύσιν, etc. Aristotle previously associated natural wealth with the household and set limits to it (*Politics* 1.9, esp. 1257b19–58a18).

[50] See esp. *Letter to Menoeceus* 128–29.

[51] See esp. KD 3 and 18, and U 408–28. I agree, for the most part, with John M. Rist (*Epicurus: An Introduction* [Cambridge: Cambridge University Press, 1972], 100–122) and Phillip Mitsis (*Epicurus' Ethical Theory* [Ithaca: Cornell University Press, 1988], 11–51); see also the alternative views of Jean Bollack, ed. (*La pensée du plaisir. Epicure: textes moraux, commentaires* [Paris: Éditions de Minuit, 1975], 149–56, 184–87) and J. C. B. Gosling and C. C. W. Taylor (*The Greeks on Pleasure* [Oxford: Clarendon Press, 1982], 365–96).

person should try to maximize pleasure by removing pain, he or she must not seek out kinetic pleasures over and above the absence of pain unless no pain is associated with this pursuit.[52] A person must always calculate the amount of pain attending a prospective pleasure in order to make sure that no more pain will ensue than pleasure.[53] This hedonistic calculus demands a distinction between present and future. In addition, we must distinguish between bodily and mental pleasures. Even though we aim for both bodily and mental well-being and even though all mental pleasure is ultimately dependent on the body, mental pleasure contributes much more to happiness than bodily pleasure, for the mind has control over the body.[54] Even if a person is tortured on the rack, he or she can be perfectly happy by focusing the mind's attention on a past or future pleasure.[55]

Having pleasure requires some material resources. A person may have little or much, but there are limits to both how little and how much one should have. These limits are based on a distinction among three kinds of desires: natural and necessary; natural and unnecessary; and unnatural and unnecessary.[56] The last are "empty," for they are due to the empty opinion that there will be pleasure when it is reasonable to expect that there will be no more pleasure than pain. Necessary desires are of three types: necessary for happiness, necessary for bodily absence of pain, and necessary for life. Desires that are both unnecessary and natural are optional: a person will satisfy these desires, but only if they do not require an intense effort. If the effort is intense, the desired pleasure is not attained and the desire belongs to the third kind.[57] Epicurus illustrated the first kind by the desire for water and plain bread. Water and bread "yield the highest pleasure

---

[52] One of the problems of Epicurean ethics is what motivation there is for a person to enjoy a kinetic pleasure when she has already attained the maximum of pleasure through the removal of pain. (Cicero raises this problem in *On Ends* 2.29.) The answer appears to be that all pleasures are desirable, even if they only vary the feeling of pleasure; hence they are to be chosen unless they are outweighed by pain. In itself, the desire for pleasure is infinite; but it has a limit imposed on it by the calculation of the mind, which balances pleasure against pain (see KD 18 and 20).

[53] *Letter to Menoeceus* 129–30.

[54] U 429–39.

[55] Diogenes Laertius 10.118 (U 601).

[56] *Letter to Menoeceus* 130 and U 456.

[57] KD 30. The claim that an intrinsically natural desire may, under some circumstances, be unnatural is in agreement with the claim that pleasure, which is naturally good, is bad if it leads to more pain than pleasure (*Letter to Menoeceus* 129–30).

when they are taken by someone who needs them."[58] The second kind may be illustrated by the desire for some wine and cheese, and the third by the desire for unlimited wine and delicacies.[59] Whereas the first two kinds of desire have a limit, the third has no limit. Unnatural desires can never be satisfied; a person always wants more.

The distinction among the three kinds of desires applies to wealth, just as to any other object that we seek for the sake of pleasure. In the following maxim, Epicurus distinguishes "natural wealth" from the imaginary wealth that is the object of empty opinions:

> Natural wealth is both limited and easy to obtain. But the wealth [that is the object] of empty opinions goes on to infinity.[60]

"Empty opinions" about wealth make us seek ever more wealth. Just like all desires, the desire for wealth has a natural limit that sets it off from the empty craving for infinitely more. In addition to being limited, natural wealth is easy to obtain. For, as Epicurus maintains, "everything natural is easy to obtain, whereas everything empty is difficult to obtain."[61]

The claim that natural wealth is easy to obtain raises problems. Are we to understand that it easy to obtain sufficient wealth to satisfy not only the necessary desires, but also unnecessary natural desires? Epicurus blocks this interpretation in another saying:

> Thanks be to blessed nature, because it has made what is necessary easy to obtain, and what is difficult to obtain unnecessary.[62]

In the light of this text, we must suppose that although natural wealth corresponds to the entire range of natural desires, the wealth that is easy to obtain is only the bare minimum of natural wealth. This is the wealth required to satisfy the necessary desires. The two attributes, being easy to obtain and being limited, apply to opposite ends

---

[58] *Letter to Menoeceus* 131.

[59] A scholion on Aristotle's *Nicomachean Ethics* (U 456) uses the examples: food and clothing for necessary desires; sex for natural and unnecessary desires; and a certain kind of food, clothing, or sex for unnecessary desires. The scholiast on KD 29 gives the examples: drink (when thirsty) for necessary desires; sumptuous food for natural and unnecessary desires; crowns and the dedication of statues for unnatural desires.

[60] KD 15: ὁ τῆς φύσεως πλοῦτος καὶ ὥρισται καὶ εὐπόριστός ἐστι. ὁ δὲ τῶν κενῶν δοξῶν εἰς ἄπειρον ἐκπίπτει.

[61] *Letter to Menoeceus* 130: τὸ μὲν φυσικὸν πᾶν εὐπόριστόν ἐστι, τὸ δὲ κενὸν δυσπόριστον.

[62] U 469: χάρις τῇ μακαρίᾳ φύσει, ὅτι τὰ ἀναγκαῖα ἐποίησεν εὐπόριστα, τὰ δὲ δυσπόριστα οὐκ ἀναγκαῖα. At KD 21, Epicurus asserts that "it is easy to obtain that which removes pain due to want and that which makes one's whole life complete."

of the range of natural wealth: there is both a threshold that is easy
to attain and an upper limit beyond which we must not strive. This
interpretation of "easy to obtain" is confirmed by numerous testimonies, including Cicero's report that natural wealth is easy to obtain
because "nature is satisfied with just a little."[63]

How easy is it, however, to have enough resources to satisfy the
necessary desires? The necessary desires include the desire for happiness,
as well as the desire for absence of bodily pain and the desire for
life itself. These three types of desire are ranked in descending order
of difficulty of attainment. Even though we need just a little to be
happy, provided we have a philosophical attitude, we may question
how easy it is for a slave toiling in the mines, to take an extreme
case, to obtain the bare minimum required to eliminate bodily pain
and achieve happiness? We may perhaps make sense of Epicurus'
confident claim by taking it as a broad generalization: by and large,
natural wealth is easy to come by, for we require very little to satisfy
all the necessary desires. This is true for slaves, among others. At the
same time, the amount of natural wealth available to a slave will
normally be much smaller than that possessed by the owner of a
slave. It follows that the same type of desire is natural for the owner,
but unnatural for the slave.

Epicurus and his followers were intent on using terms in their
ordinary sense. However, this does not prevent a word from being
assigned a new, philosophical meaning. In the ordinary sense, the
person who has just enough to satisfy the necessary desires is poor.
By philosophical reasoning, on the other hand, this person is naturally
wealthy. Epicurus proposes this semantic shift in the following maxim:

> When measured by the goal of nature, poverty is great wealth; un-
> bounded wealth is great poverty.[64]

It was a philosophical commonplace that the person who lives in the
right way is rich, even if poor.[65] Epicurus interprets this principle in

---

[63] *On Ends* 2.91; see also U 470. Cicero also associates natural wealth with the
necessary desires at *Tusculan Disputations* 5.93 (U 456). At U 471 natural wealth is
said to be made up in full (συμπεπλήρωται) by bread, water, and any type of shelter. The verb signifies that this is all the wealth we need in order to have a full
complement of pleasure.

[64] SV 25: ἡ πενία μετρουμένη τῷ τῆς φύσεως τέλει μέγας ἐστὶ πλοῦτος. πλοῦτος δὲ
μὴ ὁριζόμενος μεγάλη ἐστὶ πενία.

[65] It may be traced back to Xenophon's *Oeconomicus* 2.1–4, where Socrates claims
that he is sufficiently rich, whereas Critoboulos is poor, even though he possesses

his own way by identifying the "goal of nature" with the absence of bodily and mental pain. So long as poverty is sufficient to remove bodily pain and it is joined by the proper mental attitude, it is an abundance of riches; for it suffices to make a person happy. By contrast, the failure to draw boundaries to one's wealth is a great destitution, for it removes happiness. The paradox was a much publicized principle of Epicurean ethics, repeated in many variations.[66] Epicurus gives it particular application in a letter to his friend Idomeneus: "If you wish to make Pythocles wealthy, don't add possessions, but take away desire."[67]

No matter how little he has, the person who is content with just a little has enough not only for himself, but also for others:

> Even when reduced to necessity, a wise person knows better how to give than to take; for so great is the treasure of self-sufficiency that he has found.[68]

Self-sufficiency is never selfish; it distributes its riches to others. Most important, it makes a person free: "the greatest reward of self-sufficiency is freedom."[69] Great wealth, on the other hand, is incompatible with freedom:

> A free life cannot acquire many possessions, because this is not easy to do without fawning upon the crowd or the powerful, but it possesses all things in continuous lavishness. If by chance it obtains many possessions, it would easily distribute them so as to obtain the good will of associates.[70]

Whereas it is easy to have enough and be free, it is not easy to acquire a large amount of wealth without incurring political obligations to either the crowd or the powerful and so forfeiting one's freedom. A free person always has enough to be lavish with. This applies to

---

a hundred times more. Philodemus gives an Epicurean interpretation to this text by asking whether five minas is enough for Socrates' "necessary and natural requirements" (*On Household Economics* col. 5.4–14).

[66] See, for example, U 202, 471, 477. At SV 81, Epicurus points out that the greatest wealth does not remove anxiety, any more than does fame or any other object of indiscriminate desire.

[67] U 135.

[68] SV 44: ὁ σοφὸς εἰς τὰ ἀναγκαῖα συγκαταθεὶς μᾶλλον ἐπίσταται μεταδιδόναι ἢ μεταλαμβάνειν. τηλικοῦτον αὐταρκείας εὗρε θησαυρόν.

[69] SV 77.

[70] SV 67: ἐλεύθερος βίος οὐ δύναται κτήσασθαι χρήματα πολλὰ διὰ τὸ τὸ πρᾶγμα ⟨μὴ⟩ ῥᾴδιον εἶναι χωρὶς θητείας ὄχλων ἢ δυναστῶν, ἀλλὰ ⟨σὺν⟩ συνεχεῖ δαψιλείᾳ πάντα κέκτηται. ἂν δέ που καὶ τύχῃ χρημάτων πολλῶν, καὶ ταῦτα ῥᾳδίως ἂν εἰς τὴν τοῦ πλησίον εὔνοιαν διαμετρήσαι.

a slave as well as a legally free person. If great wealth happens to
come one's way, it is easy to mete it out to those who will be disposed
to return the favor. This is not a crassly calculating move. Rather,
ordinary social bonds are replaced by bonds among friends who,
however poor they may be, have enough to share with one another.
"One must release oneself," Epicurus said, from the "prison of ordinary affairs and politics."[71]

Even though Epicurus stressed that one needs only enough to satisfy the necessary desires, he also held that one should not live at the
very edge of necessity. In his work *On Lives*, Epicurus said that the
wise person "will not be a Cynic . . . or beg."[72] The Cynic lives from
moment to moment. By contrast, the wise person "will take fore-
thought for possessions and the future."[73] Instead of seeking only a
bare minimum, the wise person will try to secure a margin of safety.

Along with having an economic safety net, a person should practice a simple life for the most part. In the *Letter to Menoeceus*, Epicurus
lists the advantages of a simple life style:

> Being used to a simple, inexpensive way of life provides full health,
> makes a person unhesitating in the face of life's necessities, makes us
> stronger when we approach occasional luxuries, and makes us fearless
> of fortune.[74]

Epicurus does not recommend the simple life as the only way to live:
we are to become accustomed to it so that we may both contemplate
a life of necessity without apprehension and enjoy occasional luxuries
without being mastered by them. Epicurus himself lived frugally on
the whole while enjoying occasional luxuries.

Self-sufficiency does not require that one must always live simply.
Rather, one should always be prepared to have just a little:

> We think self-sufficiency a great good, not in order that we may in
> every case use just a little, but so that if we do not have much, we
> may use just a little in the genuine persuasion that those who least
> need extravagance enjoy it with the greatest pleasure . . .[75]

---

[71] SV 58: ἐκλυτέον ἑαυτοὺς ἐκ τοῦ περὶ τὰ ἐγκύκλια καὶ πολιτικὰ δεσμωτηρίου.

[72] Diogenes Laertius 10.119: οὐδὲ κυνιεῖν . . . οὐδὲ πτωχεύσειν.

[73] Diogenes Laertius 10.120: . . . καὶ κτήσεως προνοήσεσθαι καὶ τοῦ μέλλοντος.

[74] *Letter to Menoeceus* 131: τὸ συνεθίζειν οὖν ἐν ταῖς ἁπλαῖς καὶ οὐ πολυτελέσι διαίταις
καὶ ὑγιείας ἐστὶ συμπληρωτικὸν καὶ πρὸς τὰς ἀναγκαίας τοῦ βίου χρήσεις ἄοκνον ποιεῖ
τὸν ἄνθρωπον καὶ τοῖς πολυτελέσιν ἐκ διαλειμμάτων προσερχομένους κρεῖττον ἡμᾶς
διατίθησι καὶ πρὸς τὴν τύχην ἀφόβους παρασκευάζει.

[75] *Letter to Menoeceus* 130: καὶ τὴν αὐτάρκειαν δὲ ἀγαθὸν μέγα νομίζομεν, οὐχ ἵνα

The attitude of being content with just a little affords the greatest enjoyment of luxuries when they are available. Epicurus implies that a person will accept kinetic pleasures when they are easy to obtain, thus varying his pleasure even though not increasing it. The quoted text is designed to set the Epicurean way of life apart from that of the Cynics. The Cynics practiced the self-sufficiency of always living as simply as possible. A diet of bread and water was not optional for them, but a requirement. Epicurus agrees with the Cynics that self-sufficiency is a great good, but he claims that this does not require restricting the desires in every case to those that are necessary.[76]

In sum, Epicurus demarcated a permissible range of income by setting it off both from extreme poverty and from great wealth. This range is natural, for it corresponds to our natural desires. It extends from the poverty of having just a little to a comfortable way of life that is mostly quite simple but includes occasional luxuries. A lot of money is not a good thing to cultivate; if a lot of money comes one's way, it is best to give it to others. Epicurus does not draw precise distinctions within the permissible range. What matters, after all, is the precision of the philosophical boundaries. On the whole, he demarcates a middle range of income against the harshness of destitution and the luxury of great wealth.

(b) *Metrodorus and Philodemus on Poverty and Wealth*

Philodemus' *On Wealth* (περὶ πλούτου) and *On Household Economics* provide further evidence about Epicurus' concept of natural wealth. In his treatise *On Household Economics*, Philodemus mentions that he followed the "leaders" in expounding the philosophical "measure of wealth" in his *On Wealth*.[77] We have only remains of the latter part of book 1 of Philodemus' *On Wealth*. In these very fragmentary columns,

---

πάντως τοῖς ὀλίγοις χρώμεθα, ἀλλ᾽ ὅπως ἐὰν μὴ ἔχωμεν τὰ πολλά, τοῖς ὀλίγοις χρώμεθα, πεπεισμένοι γνησίως ὅτι ἥδιστα πολυτελείας ἀπολαύουσιν οἱ ἥκιστα ταύτης δεόμενοι . . .

[76] For a comparison of Cynic and Epicurean self-sufficiency, see Gigante, *Cinismo e Epicureismo*, Memorie dell'Instituto Italiano per gli Studi Filosofici 23 (Naples: Bibliopolis, 1992) 48–53. On Cynic self-sufficiency, see further Audrey N. M. Rich, "The Cynic Conception of AUTARKEIA," *Mnemosyne* 9 (1956): 23–29.

[77] *On Household Economics*, col. 12.19–22. Philodemus' *On Wealth* is therefore earlier, as Tepedino Guerra points out ("Il primo libro 'Sulla Ricchezza' di Filodemo," *CErc* 8 [1978]: 52–95; 53), contra Tiziano Dorandi ("Filodemo: gli orientamenti della ricerca attuale," *Aufstieg und Niedergang der römischen Welt* 2.36.4, ed. W. Haase [Berlin: Walter de Gruyter, 1990], 2359).

Metrodorus is cited five times.[78] He is, therefore, a major source. The title of Philodemus' *On Household Economics* is a modern conjecture, plausibly based on Philodemus' own reference to his book as being περὶ οἰκονομίας.[79] The papyrus has the title: Book Theta (9) of "On vices and the opposing virtues, and the persons in whom they are, and the situations in which they are found."[80] *On Household Economics* is much better preserved than *On Wealth*. The extant portion consists of approximately the last thirty columns. Philodemus cites Metrodorus as the author of arguments showing that Cynic poverty is to be rejected in favor of a more affluent way of life. The section devoted to these arguments is substantial, consisting of approximately ten columns (12.5–22.16). They form the central section of what remains of *On Household Economics*. This part of the paper will examine the fragments of *On Wealth* and this central section of *On Household Economics*.

One of the questions raised by these texts is to what extent Philodemus may have departed from Metrodorus or Epicurus, despite his assurances that he is following them. We may expect that Epicurus and Metrodorus were more or less of one mind concerning the limits of poverty and wealth. Philodemus, on the other hand, belongs to a very different society; he is at home among aristocrats in Rome in the first century B.C.E. As an Epicurean, Philodemus is obligated to follow the leaders, and he does so with enthusiasm. This does not mean, however, that he does not exercise considerable freedom in interpreting Epicurus' doctrines. Philodemus' teacher, Zeno, as well

---

[78] *On Wealth*, cols. 24.35, 37.11–15, 41.5 and 12–13, and 47.34. The text (PHerc. 163) has been edited by Tepedino Guerra, "Il primo libro."

[79] *On Household Economics* col. 27.20. The title has commonly been translated as "On Household Management." Voula Tsouna McKirahan ("Epicurean Attitudes to Management and Finance" in *Epicureismo greco e romano*, ed. G. Giannantoni and M. Gigante [Naples: Bibliopolis, 1996], 2:701–714) translates as "On Property Management," which corresponds to Philodemus' definition of his topic at col. 12.8–10. My translation "On Household Economics" attempts to reflect Philodemus' focus on personal property throughout his treatise. Tsouna McKirahan proposes that Philodemus differed from Metrodorus by making a systematic use of the concept of a skill (τέχνη) and by directing attention away from the concept of the right measure and use of wealth to the topic of administration.

[80] Περὶ οἰκονομίας (PHerc. 1424) was edited by Christian Jensen, *Philodemi Περὶ οἰκονομίας qui dicitur libellus* (Leipzig: Tuebner, 1906). A new edition by Tsouna McKirahan and G. Indelli is in progress. The treatise has received a very useful commentary by Renato Laurenti, *Filodemo e il pensiero economico degli Epicurei*, Testi e Documenti per lo Studio dell'Antichità 39 (Milan: Istituto Editorale Cispalpino-la Goliardica, 1973), which is reviewed by Matilde Ferrario, "Una nuova edizione dell' opera filodemea sull' economia," *CErc* 6 (1976): 92–95.

as Philodemus, were remarkably innovative in their exegesis of Epicurus. Philodemus was intent on adapting Epicurean teachings to Roman conditions.[81] He mentions the Romans once in passing in *On Household Economics*.[82] We need to ask, therefore, to what extent he had them in mind in the rest of his discussion.

Let us turn, first, to *On Wealth*. An issue that pervades the fragments is whether poverty and wealth are good, bad, or indifferent. Philodemus states that neither poverty nor wealth is "once and for all" good or bad or indifferent. Rather, they are good, bad, or indifferent for some people, but not for others.[83] In *On Household Economics*, Philodemus points out that wealth does not appear to be harmful in itself but "because of the wickedness of those who use it."[84] Whether poverty or wealth is good, bad, or indifferent, therefore, depends on how people use it. Thus, either poverty or wealth is good for a person who uses it to secure pleasure; either is bad for someone who derives pain from it; and either is indifferent for someone who derives neither pleasure nor pain.

At the same time, extreme deprivation is unconditionally bad. Some followers of Epicurus, Philodemus tells us in *On Wealth*, call "poverty" bad, on the grounds that Epicurus himself often said so. What they mean by "poverty," Philodemus explains, is "having nothing" (ἀνύπαρ-ξις), not "having a little" (ὀλίγων ὕπαρξις).[85] The former is a state of mendicancy. Having a little can be good, whereas being a beggar is simply bad.[86] This is clearly a reference to the Cynic way of life. Along with Epicurus and his other followers, Philodemus rejects the

---

[81] For example, in *The Good King according to Homer*, see Elizabeth Asmis, "Philodemus's Poetic Theory and *On the Good King According to Homer*," *Classical Antiquity* 10 (1991): 1–45.

[82] *On Household Economics* col. 25.38.

[83] *On Wealth*, col. 51.2–10. Similarly, Diogenes Laertius (10.120) reports that "health is good for some, indifferent for others." This report is somewhat surprising in view of Epicurus' claim that happiness consists in bodily health and mental tranquillity (*Letter to Menoeceus* 128). However, if we understand that health is indeed indifferent to someone like Epicurus who can disregard bodily suffering, then we can reconcile these claims. Health is a constituent of the good, but it is not absolutely necessary. Unlike health, wealth and poverty are not themselves constituents of the good (or bad), but only insofar as they are used to produce pleasure (or pain).

[84] *On Household Economics* col. 14.8–9; and see below, n. 106.

[85] *On Wealth*, cols. 42.31–43.7, 45.15–38, 46.31–34, and 48.18–24.

[86] At *On Wealth* cols. 47.9–11, someone is said "in his second book" to "consider the poverty of the leader good." It is possible that this is a comment by Metrodorus on the poverty of Epicurus.

economic deprivation of the Cynic. At the same time, Philodemus offers a clarification of the term "poverty." Whereas some Epicureans, and possibly Epicurus himself at times, stretched the term to refer to the condition of "having nothing," Philodemus uses it consistently to signify "having a little."

In support of the claim that wealth and poverty are not good or bad absolutely, Philodemus adduces the argument that whereas there is a big difference between good and bad, there is "not much difference [διαφορά]" between wealth and poverty.[87] Wealth has a "small superiority" ([μι]κρὰν . . . ὑπεροχήν) over poverty.[88] This small superiority, however, makes no difference to happiness. In the same column in which he presents the argument that there is "not much difference," Philodemus cites Metrodorus as follows:

> All accusations made against poverty as falling short of wealth are truly falsehoods, as Metrodorus said.[89]

Even though wealth has a "small superiority," this must not be taken to mean that poverty "falls short" in any way with respect to happiness. The term "superiority" is morally neutral. The small advantage makes no difference to happiness, for a person "derives equal pleasures from poverty as from wealth."[90] This claim is in agreement with the Epicurean doctrine that unnecessary natural pleasures bring no increase in pleasure. Although there is a small difference between poverty and wealth in the production of pleasure, this difference is, strictly speaking, something indifferent. As Philodemus observes, "the change from wealth to poverty is indifferent."[91] As a result, a person will not fear the trouble that attends a change from wealth to poverty.[92] This sense of security is especially important since wealth is "easily destroyed."[93] Philodemus concludes the book by offering advice to

---

[87] *On Wealth*, col. 41.35–37. A related argument is (col. 41.32–34): "When many bad things are put together, they do not make a good, but poverty makes wealth." This argument rests on the premise that many small possessions make up wealth. Seneca (*Epistle* 87, 38 = SVF Antipater 3.54) mentions that this claim is a sophism that was bandied about by all the dialecticians and refuted by the Stoic Antipater.

[88] *On Wealth*, col. 51.27–30.

[89] *On Wealth*, col. 41.9–14: πάνθ' [ὅ]σα κατηγ[ο]ρεῖται πενίας ὡς ἐλλειπούσης πλούτου, ταῖς ἀληθείαις, ὡς ὁ Μητρόδωρος ἔφη, καταψεύσματ' ἐστί.

[90] *On Wealth*, col. 56.4–8.

[91] *On Wealth*, col. 53.3–5.

[92] *On Wealth*, col. 36.12–14.

[93] *On Wealth*, col. 54.7–10; cf. col. 55.10.

both the poor and the rich. If we are rich, he says, "we will not on that account despise those who are not, nor will we give up our soul because of a desire for wealth."[94]

The threefold distinction of good, bad, and indifferent is a prominent feature of Stoic ethics. The Stoics held that only virtue (or what partakes of it) is good, only vice (or what partakes of it) is bad, and that everything else is indifferent. In short, only what is morally good is good, only what is morally bad is bad. However, there is a difference among so-called "indifferents" (ἀδιάφορα): some are preferred, some are dispreferred, and some are neither. Preferred indifferents have "much value" (although they are immeasurably inferior to the only truly valuable thing, the good); they include wealth, health, a good reputation, and so on. Dispreferred things have "much disvalue;" they include poverty, illness, a bad reputation, and so on.[95] Under ordinary circumstances, a person will select what is preferred and decline what is dispreferred; under special circumstances, he may select what is dispreferred and decline what is preferred.[96] Chrysippus went so far as to say it is madness to consider wealth, health, and so on, as "nothing" and not to "hold on" to them.[97] To select preferred things is a duty (καθῆκον); but it is a so-called intermediate duty, not a perfect duty. Perfect duty consists in selecting things virtuously.[98] One reason for selecting preferred things, such as wealth, is that they provide larger scope for the exercise of virtue than their opposites.[99]

It is possible that Metrodorus himself used the Stoic distinction between good, bad, and indifferent to present Epicurus' position. But it is much more likely that Philodemus did so in a later period, after Stoic terminology came to be used widely by the Epicureans in their debates with Stoics and others. This trend is exemplified especially

---

[94] *On Wealth*, col. 58.4–9. His advice to the poor is not preserved.

[95] SVF 1.190, 192, etc.

[96] Despite their preference for wealth, the Stoics had much respect for Cynicism. One of the Stoics, Apollodorus, called Cynicism a "short path to virtue" (Diogenes Laertius 7.121). The Stoics reportedly held that the wise person "will be a Cynic" (Diogenes Laertius 7.121), but another source explains this as meaning that if the wise man is already a Cynic he will remain one, but he will not start out to become one (SVF 3.638). As Cicero indicates (*On Ends* 2.68, SVF 3.645), these testimonies may be reconciled with the general Stoic position on wealth by taking the Cynic way of life as an exception that falls under the rubric of κατὰ περίστασιν, "in special circumstances."

[97] Plutarch *Stoic Refutations* 1047e (= SVF 3.138).

[98] SVF 3.494–96.

[99] Seneca, *On the Happy Life* 21–22.

by Philodemus' teacher Zeno. Philodemus, it is plausible, interpreted Metrodorus' claim that poverty does not "fall short" of wealth by saying that the change of the one to the other is "indifferent." Philodemus agrees with the Stoics that poverty and wealth are strictly indifferent. Because he takes "poverty" to mean "having a little," his exegesis is responsible for the claim that wealth has only a "small superiority." At first sight, this assessment seems to be in conflict with the Stoic view that wealth has great selective value and poverty great selective disvalue. However, the Stoics held in effect that the difference is tiny, since it is morally irrelevant. That wealth has a "small superiority" corresponds roughly to the joint Stoic claim that wealth is indifferent and that it has great selective value.

Nonetheless, there is a significant difference between the Epicurean and Stoic views. The Stoics proposed wealth, along with health, and so on, as aims to be attained even for the wise person. It is the duty of everyone, under normal circumstances, to choose wealth, health, and so on. What really matters is whether this aim is pursued virtuously; still, a person should make an effort to obtain preferred things. In the second century B.C.E., the Stoic Antipater stressed this effort by saying that it is the goal to "do everything in one's power, continuously and without divergence, to obtain the primary things according to nature."[100] By contrast with the Stoics, the Epicurean is relaxed about being wealthy; he cares just a little.

When Philodemus, therefore, points out that wealth has just a "small superiority," he is concerned to emphasize that wealth is worth just a little effort. One should not think of it, as the Stoics did, as being greatly preferable. It helps just a little toward attaining happiness, even though it is not necessary for happiness and makes no difference to how happy one is.

Philodemus considers further the permissible range of income in his *On Household Economics*. The treatise is in two parts: (I) a refutation, directed against Xenophon's *Oeconomicus* (cols. 1–7.37), then the Peripatetic *Oeconomica*, which Philodemus ascribes to Theophrastus (cols. 7.37–12.2); and (II) an exposition of Epicurean doctrine. The second part is divided into two clearly demarcated sections. The first section (IIA) begins with a definition of "household economics" (οἰκονομία) and is a treatment of the limits of poverty and wealth

---

[100] SVF Antipater 3.57.

(cols. 12.5–22.16). In the second section (IIB), Philodemus proposes to add details about the sources and management of income (col. 22.17 to end). It has traditionally been agreed that in the first section (IIA) Philodemus follows Metrodorus closely, whereas in the second section (IIB) he speaks in his own voice.[101] In the following examination, an attempt will be made to determine whether there is any difference in position between Metrodorus and Philodemus. We will first examine section IIA on the limits of poverty and wealth.

After defining his topic as the philosophical "use and preservation of possessions" (col. 12.5–25), Philodemus immediately invokes the authority of Metrodorus. He will cite, he says, the sort of arguments offered by Metrodorus in his book *On Wealth*

> in response to those who will say perhaps that the Cynics have chosen by far the lightest and easiest way of life by stripping away everything of theirs as much as possible that does not make life inexpensive, so that it is lived peacefully and most calmly, with the least concern and trouble.[102]

Metrodorus agreed with the Cynics that the best life is one that is most tranquil and trouble-free. However, he argued,

> this goal does not appear to come about if we flee everything whose presence occasionally brings us trouble and contention. For many things engender some pain by their presence, but disturb more by their absence.[103]

Analogously, it causes some trouble to be healthy; but we suffer terribly if we lack good health. Likewise, a trustworthy friend may cause

---

[101] Siegfried Sudhaus ("Eine erhaltene Abhandung des Metrodor," *Hermes* 41 (1906): 45–58, esp. 56) argued that these columns (12.45–21.35) are an extract from Metrodorus' lost work *On Wealth*, and that subsequently Philodemus "speaks in his own name" (as indicated by οἶμαι in col. 24.35). Sudhaus supports his view with a stylistic analysis (see below, n. 122) along with other arguments. Renato Laurenti 151–53) proposes that Philodemus is following Metrodorus not only in this section, but also in the subsequent section on the sources of income (cols. 22.17–23.36). After this, Laurenti holds, Philodemus finishes the book "con le sue forze" (169).

[102] *On Economics* col. 12.29–38: . . . π[ρὸς τ]οὺς ἐροῦντας ἴσως ὅ[τι πολ]ὺ κουφοτάτην καὶ ῥά[ι]σ[τη]ν οἱ Κυνικοὶ διαγωγὴν [ᾕρην]ται πᾶν αὐτῶν περιε[ιρηκό]τες εἰς τὸ δυνατόν, ὃ μ[ὴ γ᾽εὐ]τελῆ παρέχει βίον εἰρη[ναίω]ς τ]ε καὶ μάλιστ᾽ ἀθορύβ[ω]ς [καὶ μετὰ τῆ]ς ἐλαχίστη[ς] φρο[ντίδος κ]αὶ πραγματε[ί]ας [δια]νυ[ό]μενον.

[103] Col. 13.3–11: οὐ μὴν οὕτω γε φαίνεται τοῦτο γίνεσθαι τὸ τέλος, ἂν πάντα φύγωμεν ὧν ὑπαρχ[όν]των κἂν πράγματά ποτε σχῶμεν κἂν ἀγωνιάσαιμεν. πολλὰ γὰρ τῶν πραγμάτων ἐνποεῖ μέν τινας λύπας ὑπάρχοντα, πλείω δ᾽ὀχλεῖ μὴ παρόντα.

pain at times, but not having one brings more trouble.[104] In the same way, we must "accept" wealth if it is less of a burden in the long run when it is present—a person must always consider one's whole life, not just the moment. One should not use as a "measuring stick" (κανών) whether wealth brings toil; for even one's daily needs require toil. What matters is whether wealth makes a contribution "for the most part" to the best kind of life.[105] Wealth "does not appear to bring on profitless troubles by itself, but because of the wickedness of those who use it."[106]

The argument proceeds tentatively and cautiously. After indicating that wealth need not be bothersome, Philodemus indicates that wealth, so long as it does not go beyond the bounds set by nature, may indeed be much preferable to poverty:

> The care and preservation [of wealth] that suits someone who takes care of it properly does not afford greater trouble than the provision of daily needs, and even if it affords more trouble, this is not more than the difficulties from which it releases us, unless someone shows that natural wealth does not provide a much greater balance of rewards over toil than [does] the life of little means, which he will be very far from showing.[107]

The sentence is very carefully worded. Through double negatives, the suggestion is made that wealth, so long as it is naturally limited, may bring a much greater balance of rewards over toil than a life of having just a little. The negative wrapping of the suggestion helps to blunt the contrast between natural wealth and the poverty of having just a little. Nonetheless, the contrast is a surprise. Epicurus stressed that natural wealth includes the condition of having just a little. The argument here is carefully presented in such a way that it does not contradict this basic doctrine. The point is that wealth, so long as it is naturally limited, may be much preferable to the condition of having just a little. Thus the opposition is, strictly, between wealth and poverty, not between natural wealth as such and poverty.

---

[104] Col. 13.11–19.

[105] Cols. 13.34–14.5.

[106] Col. 14.5–9: οὐ φαίνεται δ᾽ ὁ πλοῦτος ἐπιφέρειν ἀλυσιτελεῖς δυσχερείας παρ᾽ αὑτὸν ἀλλὰ παρὰ τὴ[ν] τῶν χρωμένων κακίαν.

[107] Col. 14.9–23: ἡ γὰρ ἐπιμέλεια καὶ τήρησις, ὅση πρέπει τῶι κατὰ τρόπον αὐτοῦ προεστῶτι, παρέχει μέν τιν᾽ ἐνίοτ᾽ ὄχλησιν, οὐ μὴν πλείω γε τοῦ κατὰ τὸν ἐφήμερον [πο]ρισμόν, ἂν δὲ καὶ πλείω, τῶν ἄλ[λ]ων ὧν ἀπαλλάττει δυσχερῶν [ο]ὐ πλεῖον᾽, ἂν μ[ὴ] δείξῃ τις, ὡς οὐκ ἀποδί[δω]σιν ὁ φυσικὸς πλοῦτος [πο]λλῶ[ι] μείζους τὰς ἐπικαρπίας ἢ τοὺς πόνους τῆς ἀπ᾽ [ὀ]λίγων ζωῆς, ὃ πολλοῦ δεήσε[ι] παρ]ιστάνε[ιν].

Nonetheless, wealth is picked out from the range of natural wealth as possibly much preferable to poverty, and this opposition is not found in the fragments of Epicurus.

Philodemus immediately hedges this possibility by setting out conditions for the possession of wealth. A person must not become distressed when it is lost or pursue it with relentless effort. One must not pile up money or seek to get as much as possible.[108] A person who is "relaxed" about these matters will satisfy his daily needs more easily than the person who has nothing to spare.[109] The wise person will not take great pains to preserve wealth; for he can be content with just a little, even though he prefers a more affluent way of life:

> A temperate man is not distressed by, and is confident for the future in, a lowly and poor way of life, knowing that what is natural is managed also by this, but he inclines in his wishes rather toward a more affluent (ἀφθονωτέραν) way.[110]

Again, the words are chosen very carefully: the person who is content with little "inclines in his wishes" toward a "more affluent" existence. The Epicurean will not strain to acquire wealth, but he has an inclination toward affluence as making a slight contribution to happiness. Being "temperate," he knows that poverty suffices for happiness.

In addition to being relaxed about wealth, a wise person will share it with others. The confidence that comes from knowing that poverty is sufficient makes a person "share everything."[111] A person who has a "moderate and common life" and a "sound and true account [λόγος]" will not be bad at finding what is sufficient.[112] Philodemus here sums up in effect two main principles of Epicurean economics: setting a limit to wealth by the use of reason, and sharing it with friends. The latter principle becomes increasingly prominent in the remainder of the treatise. What reason teaches is:

> One should accept more, if it comes about without harm and easily, but one should not suffer because of this.[113]

---

[108] Col. 14.23–46.

[109] Col. 15.21–26 (including ἀνειμένος at line 24).

[110] Cols. 15.45–16.6: οὔτε γ[ά]ρ ἀσχαλᾶι σώφρων ἀνὴρ καὶ πρὸς τὸ μέλλ[ον εὐ]θ[α]ρρὴς τῆι ταπεινῆι καὶ πενιχρᾶι διαίτηι, τὸ φυσικὸν εἶδος καὶ ὑπὸ ταύτης διοικούμενον, ῥέπει δὲ τῆι βουλήσει μᾶλλον ἐπὶ τὴν ἀφθονωτέραν.

[111] Col. 18.2–7; cf. col. 18.34–35.

[112] Col. 16.8–10, including: βίος μέτριός τε καὶ κοινὸς καὶ λόγος ὑγιὴς καὶ ἀληθινός.

[113] Cols. 16.44–17.2: τὸ [δὲ π]λεῖον, ἂ[ν ἀ]βλ[α]βῶς καὶ [εὐ]πόρως γίνηται, δεκτέ[ον, τὸ] δὲ κακοπαθ[ε]ῖν κατ᾽ α]ὐτὸ τοῦτο μή.

As he continues the argument, Philodemus restates this hypothetical state of affairs in the form of an exhortation:

> Let us not say that if we remove the burden from the possession of wealth, we will also remove wealth. For it is possible to leave this without adding the other ... The preservation of wealth can come about also without futile toil.[114]

Philodemus ends by encouraging others to accept wealth whenever it comes without undue pain.

In conformity with Epicurus' teachings, Philodemus is careful to set off the right way not only from the extreme poverty of the Cynics, but also from the pursuit of great wealth. "Great toil" is involved in trying to get as much wealth as possible, as quickly as possible. This is the way of the professional manager or money-maker. Using tentative language again, Philodemus suggests that the wise person "must perhaps not be said to be an expert and businessman who makes much money quickly."[115] He concludes that ordinary know-how is sufficient. For "it appears" that, just as in other activities, so everyone has sufficient economic skill to attend to his needs. As everyone knows enough to prepare food without being a professional cook, so "it appears to be like this" about keeping one's belongings. Many people, including the good man, "seem altogether not bad" about finding what they need.[116] People who are intent on making money think that poverty is troublesome, even though "nature shows, if one pays attention to her, that it is easily satisfied with using just a little."[117] This is, once again, canonical Epicurean doctrine.

Philodemus closes the entire section of argument (IIA) with a lengthy table of contents, preceded by a reference to Metrodorus as having refuted Aristotle's claim that the good person is also a good money-maker.[118] The table of contents is as follows: (1) how much one should take care of; (2) what and what sort of thing economics is understood to be; (3) how, and how not, the wise man is a good manager, and

---

[114] Col. 18.7–20: μὴ δὴ λέγωμεν ὡς, εἰ περιαιρήσομεν τὸ βάρος αὐτοῦ κατὰ τὴν κτῆσιν, ἀφελούμεθα καὶ τὸ πλουτεῖν. ἔστι γὰρ μὴ προσόντος ἐκείνου τοῦτο καταλείπειν ... ἡ δὲ σωτηρία δύν[ατ]αι γίνεσθαι καὶ χωρὶς τῶν [μ]αταίων πόνων.

[115] Col. 17.2–6.

[116] Col. 17.14–40.

[117] Col. 19.4–19, including (18–19): καὶ τοῖς ὀλίοις εὐκόλ[ω]ς χρήσεθ᾽.

[118] Cols. 21.28–22.6. Philodemus treats the topics roughly in this order: (2) at col. 12.5–25, (1) at cols. 12.25–17.2, (3) and (4) together at cols. 17.2–18.2, and (5) at cols. 18.2–21.35.

likewise a good money-maker; (4) what type of management is an expertise (τέχνη) and what type is not, and that ordinary know-how is advantageous whereas expert management is not; and (5) how one must be disposed in attitude (πῶς διακείμενον) in taking care of one's possessions. The elaborate table of contents suggests that Philodemus was following a larger, more detailed exposition, divided into precisely demarcated sections. Just before turning to his own follow-up discussion (IIB), Philodemus mentions that "he," that is, Metrodorus, showed extensively that "occasional troubles, worries, and bother are much more profitable for the best way of life than the opposite course."[119] The "opposite course" is Cynicism. From the beginning to the end of his arguments, it appears, Philodemus has been drawing on Metrodorus' extensive refutation of Cynic poverty.

Even though Philodemus' exposition is based solidly on Epicurus' own teachings, there is something new in his presentation. The whole thrust of his discussion is to show that it is preferable to be wealthy rather than poor. After arguing against the Cynics, Philodemus takes the discussion in the direction of showing that it is better to have more rather than less. Instead of arguing simply against the extreme poverty of the Cynics, Philodemus argues for limited wealth. In this progression, he appears to skip a step. Instead of reminding the reader that it makes no difference to happiness whether one has a little or a lot, he focuses on the advantages of having a lot, then goes back to saying that, after all, it is sufficient to have just a little.

Philodemus emphasizes that the rich person must not grab; he accepts. This contention is reminiscent of Epicurus' own claim that a person will accept occasional luxuries. But there is a difference. Philodemus has a person accept wealth on a continuous basis, on the ground that it tends to be less trouble than being poor. Epicurus is more comfortable with giving away wealth than keeping it. In a variation on Epicurus' recommendation, Philodemus has the rich man share with others while keeping his wealth. This is not to say that there is a change of doctrine. Everything Philodemus says is compatible with Epicurus' own teachings. But there is a change of emphasis. Whereas Philodemus offers a defense of wealth, Epicurus' economic advice appears, on the whole, a consolation for poverty.

Since we do not have Metrodorus' books, we cannot check whether this emphasis is already in Metrodorus. Speaking generally, it

---

[119] See note 150.

is unlikely that Metrodorus differed as much from Epicurus as Philodemus' presentation suggests.[120] Philodemus' language may provide a clue. A striking feature of the entire section of argument is the frequent occurrence of the terms "perhaps" and "appears."[121] The use of these qualifying expressions is in contrast with Philodemus' highly assertive style later in the treatise and elsewhere in his writings. One might suppose, therefore, that Philodemus has taken these terms from Metrodorus.[122] As a faithful defender of Epicurus' doctrines, Metrodorus could be expected to hedge any apparent change of emphasis by the use of qualifying expressions. On the other hand, it seems equally possible that Philodemus used tentative expressions to hedge his own interpretation of Metrodorus' arguments. On the whole, it is reasonable to suppose that if Metrodorus already emphasized the advantages of wealth more than Epicurus did, Philodemus reinforced this shift in his own selective presentation of Metrodorus' arguments. Again, there need not be any incompatibility of doctrine. Philodemus' statement that the temperate man "inclines" toward affluence is compatible with everything that he reports about Metrodorus in *On Wealth*, and it may indeed be a direct quotation from

---

[120] F. Castaldi ("Il concetto della ricchezza in Epicuro," *Rendiconti, Accademia dei Lincei, classe di scienze morali, storiche, e filologiche*, 6, 4 [1928] 287–308: 305) mentions briefly that Metrodorus' notion of poverty is "confused" and that Metrodorus departs from Epicurus in supposing that poverty is something bad. According to Castaldi, Philodemus returns to Epicurus' position. As Laurenti points out (*Filodemo e il pensiero economico*, 139), the text cited by Castaldi (col. 19 of *On Household Economics*) fails to support his view of Metrodorus. On the other hand, Castaldi is right to notice a difference in Philodemus' discussion. Following d'Amelio (1926, whose book I have not been able to check), Reimar Mueller (*Die epikureische Gesellschaftstheorie*, Schriften zur Geschichte und Kultur der Antike 5, [Berlin: Walter De Gruyter, 1972] 25–28) takes Philodemus to present the position of Metrodorus, whose position he takes to be the same as that of Epicurus. Mueller puts Philodemus' arguments in the context of fourth and third-century economics, in which there was a polarization of income, attended by rapid changes. The poor became poorer, Mueller points out, whereas those in the middle range could amass much wealth, but just as quickly lose it again.

[121] "Perhaps" (ἴσως, which may also be translated as "presumably") occurs at cols. 12.29 (as cited), 17.5 (as cited), 18.40, and 19.44. "Appears" (φαίνεται) occurs at cols. 13.3 (as cited), 14.5 (as cited), 17.15 (as cited), and 17.29–30 (as cited). In addition to φαίνεται, ἔοικε ("seems," "is likely"), or the plural form, is used at cols. 10.43–44, 17.38 (as cited), and 21.13. Outside this section, "perhaps" occurs at col. 2.17, "appear(s)" at cols. 11.18–19 and 22.28 (cited below), and "seem" at col. 22.36–37 (cited below).

[122] Sudhaus does not include these expressions in his analysis of Metrodorus' style ("Abhandlung," 45–46). Among the linguistic features that he attributes to Metrodorus are: the use of hiatus at cols. 12.46, 14.38, 17.31, 20.13, 20.33, and 22.41 (contrasting with Philodemus' avoidance of hiatus); and the vulgar form ὅλιος at cols. 13.34, 18.5, and 19.19.

Metrodorus. The expression is also compatible with Epicurus' own inclination to enjoy occasional luxuries. Whether or not Philodemus took this expression from Metrodorus, nothing prevents him from using it to shape a position of his own.

In order to assess Philodemus' own contribution more precisely, we need to put the section that we have just examined in the context of his entire work *On Household Economics*. The work as a whole moves from a refutation of previous treatments of economics to the establishment of an Epicurean position by means of a refutation of Cynic poverty. The section on the limits of poverty and wealth (IIA) is embedded in the larger project of delineating an Epicurean economics as a counterpart to traditional economics. In this project, the discussion of the sources and management of income (IIB) is of crucial importance. We have a report on what Epicurus himself said about how a wise person earns money. We shall examine this information first, then return to Philodemus' more elaborate treatment in *On Household Economics*. We will then be in a position to draw some conclusions about the evolution of Epicurean economic thought.

Acquiring and Managing an Income

(a) *Epicurus on the Wise Person*

Epicurus reportedly said that the wise person "will make money if he lacks resources, but only from his wisdom."[123] Accordingly, the wise person will make money only if he lacks it and only on the basis of his wisdom. Epicurus did not specify how the wise person will use his wisdom to make money, but his list of activities that are permitted to the wise person suggests a number of possibilities. Since the wise person will found a school,[124] we expect that, in case of need, he will impose a fee for his teaching. Also, since the wise person "will serve a king upon occasion," he will presumably sometimes derive an income from a king.[125] We may assume, too, that the wise

---

[123] Diogenes Laertius 10.120: χρηματιεῖσθαί τε ἀλλ᾽ ἀπὸ μόνης σοφίας ἀπορήσαντα.
[124] Diogenes Laertius 10.120.
[125] Diogenes Laertius 10.120: καὶ μόναρχον ἐν καιρῷ θεραπεύσειν. Philonides, an Epicurean who lived in Antioch in the first half of the second century B.C.E., did just that. He is said to have converted Demetrius I Soter (160–152 B.C.E.) to Epicureanism (Michael Erler, "Epikur," *Die Hellenistische Philosophie*, ed. Hellmut Flashar, Grundriss der Geschichte der Philosophie: Die Philosophie der Antike, Bd. 4 [Basel: Schwabe, 1994] 252).

person may draw on the resources of his friends, for "friendship [comes about] because of need."[126] In all these cases, the wise person shares his wisdom with those who remunerate him.

Epicurus himself derived an income from his teaching. The bequests he made in his will show that he was not poor. The qualification "when lacking resources" (ἀπορήσαντα) may, therefore, be understood in a fairly broad sense to accommodate a modest level of affluence.[127] The wise person needs sufficient resources to run a school. If he lives very frugally, as Epicurus did, this income may be quite substantial even if modest. On the other hand, the condition "when lacking resources" indicates a clear difference from the Stoic position. Whereas the Stoic wise person normally aims to be wealthy, Epicurus has the wise person make money only exceptionally, when he is in need.

Importantly, the Epicurean wise person does not retreat into solitary contemplation. He or she will perform the social duty of teaching others by founding a school. This activity may be viewed as taking the place of engaging in politics. As Seneca reports, Epicurus held that the wise person will not do politics "unless something intervenes." Seneca opposes this position to the Stoic doctrine that a person should pursue politics except under special circumstances.[128] In general, the Epicurean will not engage in politics. There are exceptions, however, as we have just seen. Occasionally, the wise person may serve a king, although this service is probably best regarded as a kind of education rather than as a form of political activity.[129] It should be emphasized that, in Epicureanism, political inactivity goes along with being a law-abiding citizen. As part of his duties as a citizen, the wise person will, for example, act as a member of a jury.[130]

---

[126] Diogenes Laertius 10.120: καὶ τὴν φιλίαν [γίνεσθαι] διὰ τὰς χρείας.

[127] As D. P. Fowler has argued ("Lucretius and Politics," *Philosophia Togata*, eds. Jonathan Barnes and Miriam Griffin [Oxford: Oxford University Press, 1989] 120–50: 130–31), there are no grounds for changing the manuscript reading to εὐπορήσαντα, as proposed by Gigante in *Diogene Laerzio, Vite dei Filosofi*, 2nd ed. (Bari: Laterza, 1976), 439, 574 n. 94, and "Atakta V," *CErc* 14 (1984): 125–33, 125.

[128] Seneca *On Leisure* 3.2 (= U 9); the phrase "nisi si quid intervenerit" corresponds to κατὰ περίστασιν ("under special circumstances").

[129] Diogenes Laertius 10.119 reports that the wise person will "not engage in politics or be a tyrant" (οὐδὲ πολιτεύσεσθαι . . . οὐδὲ τυραννεύσειν). The prohibition against tyranny is in itself a kind of qualification: the wise person may engage occasionally in a benign form of politics, though never in autocratic rabble-rousing.

[130] Diogenes Laertius 10.120 (δικάσεσθαι).

The three Epicurean ways of earning money suggested above invite comparison with the three "leading" (προηγούμενοι) ways of life proposed by the Stoics: (a) royal (βασιλικόν), (b) political (πολιτικόν), and (c) having knowledge (ἐπιστημονικόν). Correspondingly, the Stoics proposed, a person will make money by: (a) ruling as king or deriving an income from a king; (b) participating in politics; or (c) exacting fees for teaching.[131] These sources of income are summed up as making money "from politics and from prominent friends." As for all duties, there are exceptions. A person will live with a king who shows a good nature and a love of learning; and he will not participate in politics if he is not going to help the country but foresees serious dangers coming from the state.[132]

In a variation on the three sources of income, Chrysippus specified that a wise person may earn money from a king, from friendship, and from imparting his wisdom through instruction (σοφιστεία).[133] Presumably, friendship overlaps with politics as a source of income. With respect to the first way of life, Chrysippus noted that if a wise person cannot be king himself, he will live with a king and go on expeditions with him.[134] As a source of income, the life of knowledge coincides with the life of instruction. Following the lead of Protagoras, Chrysippus worked out a precise policy about how a wise person should exact a fee: he advised him either to take the money in advance or to contract to have the student pay after a period of time.[135]

The main difference between the Stoics and Epicureans is that whereas the Stoics recommended politics and teaching equally as ways of earning an income, the Epicureans advised against politics as a source of income. Even if a person counsels a king, he does so as a philosophical teacher, not as a political ally. The Epicureans recognized just one best way, which may be practiced in a variety

---

[131] Arius Didymus in *Stobaeus Eclogae* 2 (= SVF 3.686). According to Diogenes Laertius (7.130), the Stoics distinguished among three kinds of life: theoretical, practical, and rational (λόγικον), of which the last is to be chosen since "a rational creature" is intended for contemplation and action. It appears that the rational life combines the first two. In addition, it appears that the royal, political, and knowledgeable lives are all subdivisions of the rational life.

[132] Arius Didymus in *Stobaeus Eclogae* 2 (= SVF 3.690).

[133] Plutarch *Stoic Refutations* 1043e (= SVF 3.693).

[134] Ibid. 1043b–c (= SVF 3.691).

[135] Ibid. 1043e–44a, 1047f. Protagoras devised the policy of having the student either pay the amount asked for or deposit in a temple what he thought the instruction was worth (Plato *Protagoras* 328b–c).

of settings: imparting wisdom through teaching. At the same time, there is something that the Stoics and Epicureans have in common: the imposition of fees for teaching. Plato prohibited the taking of fees as a sophistic practice. Both the Stoics and the Epicureans regard it as entirely honorable. Some of the Stoics, including Chrysippus, made clear their opposition to Plato by using the term "sophistry" (σοφιστεία, also σοφιστεύειν) to designate instruction by a wise person, as the sophists originally conceived of their teaching. Other Stoics continued to use the term in a derogatory sense.[136] The Epicureans generally used the term "sophist" in a pejorative sense, but they too thought it proper to receive an income for instruction.[137]

(b) *Philodemus' New Economics*

In *On Household Economics*, Philodemus is concerned not only with the occupation of being a wise person, but with the entire range of occupations suitable for persons who live philosophically. All of these people are "philosophers" in a broad sense. In the strict sense, as Philodemus points out, a philosopher does not engage in business dealings at all.[138] In a broad sense, a philosopher is anyone who does philosophy, even if he has just a little time for philosophical study. In *On Household Economics*, Philodemus shows how to combine earning a living with doing philosophy. It is in this sense that Epicurus invites anyone at all, both young and old, to do philosophy.

Let us first go back to Philodemus' definition of his topic in *On Household Economics*. After criticizing Xenophon's *Oeconomicus* and the Peripatetic *Oeconomica*, Philodemus introduces the Epicurean position

---

[136] SVF 3. 686.

[137] Some Epicureans, who claimed to be genuine Epicureans, branded others as sophists (Diogenes Laertius 10.26). There has been much debate on who these "sophists" were; see esp. Longo Auricchio and Tepedino Guerra, "Aspetti e Problemi della Dissidenza Epicurea," *CErc* 11 (1981): 25–40. The following people, described by Philodemus (*To friends of the school*, col. 2.8–17; Anna Angeli, ed., *Filodemo, Agli amici de scuola (PHerc. 1005)*, La Scuola di Epicuro, 7 [Naples: Bibliopolis, 1988]), fit the description: "Some of those called Epicureans say and write many things gathered [from Epicurean writings], as well as many things that are peculiar to them and in disagreement with our enterprise, some of which have been torn away superficially and quickly from it" (. . . τῶν χρηματιζόντων τινὰς Ἐπικουρείων πολλὰ μὲν συμφορητὰ καὶ λέγειν καὶ γράφειν, πολλὰ δ'αὐτῶν ἴδια τοῖς κατὰ τὴν πραγματείαν ἀσύμφωνα, τινὰ δ'ἐκεῖθεν ἐσπαραγμένα φλοιωδῶς καὶ ταχέως . . .). Among Roman Epicureans, Amafinius and his successors, as described by Cicero, also appear to be candidates (see n. 45 above).

[138] *On Household Economics*, col. 11.16–17.

by first distinguishing the Epicurean notion of economics from that of others:

> We will speak not about how one can live nobly in a house, but how one must be set up concerning the acquisition and preservation of possessions, which is the proper sense of *oikonomia* and *oikonomikos*.[139]

The definition of *oikonomia* is one of the topics that Philodemus includes in his table of contents for the middle section (IIA). We may attribute it, therefore, to Metrodorus. In Xenophon's *Oeconomicus*, the good *oikonomos* was defined by Socrates' interlocutor as someone who "inhabits well (εὖ οἰκεῖν) his own house (οἰκίαν)."[140] Typically, Socrates understands "well" in a moral sense. In his criticism of Xenophon, Philodemus responds to this definition by saying that "well" can mean one of two things: very beneficially and happily, or making a lot of money.[141]

In denying now that his topic is "how to live nobly in a house" (ἐν οἴκωι καλῶ[ς] . . . βιοῦν), Philodemus implies that he will not deal simply with ethics. As he goes on to say, he will deal specifically with the income that is appropriate for a philosopher. There is a "measure of wealth" for the philosopher. His precise topic, therefore, will be the acquisition and preservation of possessions within philosophically set limits.[142] Instead of writing a purely ethical treatise or a technical tract on how to make a lot of money, Philodemus will deal with the practical problem of how a person living a philosophical life will manage an income.

The choice of topic puts Philodemus, along with Metrodorus, in a long tradition of philosophical investigation. While Socrates focused exclusively on the morality of household management, others, including

---

[139] *On Household Economics*, col. 12.5–12: διαλεξόμεθα τ[ο]ίνυν οὐχ ὡς ἐν οἴκωι καλῶ[ς] ἔστιν βιοῦν, ἀλλ᾽ ὡς ἵστασθαι δεῖ περὶ χρημάτων κτήσεώς τε καὶ φυλακῆς, περὶ [ἃ] τὴν οἰκονομίαν καὶ τὸν οἰκονομικὸν ἰδίως νοεῖσθαι συμβέβηκεν.

[140] At *Oeconomicus* 1, 2, Critoboulos offers the definition εὖ οἰκεῖν τὸν ἑαυτοῦ οἶκον, which is emended by Socrates to include other households. Philodemus cites the emended definition at col. 1.6–8 as: [ε]ὖ οἰκεῖν τὸ[ν] ἴδιον οἶκον καὶ τὸ ποιεῖν τὸν ἀλλότριον εὖ οἰκεῖσθαι.

[141] *On Household Economics*, col. 1.4–21. At col. 20.16–32 Philodemus assigns the same two possibilities of meaning to the expression "good money-maker" (χρηματιστής). He objects here that, instead of showing how a wise person handles money in an advantageous way, other philosophers force the meaning of the expression by simply foisting the title of good money-maker on the good person (cols. 20.45–21.12). Philodemus singles out Aristotle as guilty of this practice (col. 21.28); the same charge might be made against the Stoics.

[142] *On Household Economics*, col. 12.15–25.

Xenophon, Aristotle, and pseudo-Theophrastus, sought to give economic advice that was consistent with philosophical principles. Even
though Philodemus argues that Xenophon and pseudo-Theophrastus
failed in this purpose, his treatise shares their general aim.

There is, however, an important difference. Traditionally, the
household was viewed as the basic unit from which society is built
up. Aristotle developed this view in detail: the household, composed
of father, mother, children and slaves, forms the smallest governing
unit and is governed in turn by the city, which is composed of households. By contrast, the Epicureans did not privilege the household
as the foundation of social or moral life. They rejected the family,
just as they did political life. Epicurus held that the wise person will
not marry or have children except in special circumstances.[143] This
is directly opposed to the Stoic view, which continues the Aristotelian
tradition, that a person will marry and have children except under
special circumstances.[144]

In his criticisms of Xenophon and pseudo-Theophrastus, Philodemus
has already indicated a shift from taking the household as the basic
social and economic unit to treating the individual as an autonomous
member of society. Whereas pseudo-Theophrastus endorses Hesiod's
advice to "acquire a house and a wife first," Philodemus objects that
life can be happy without a wife.[145] He also questions whether, as
Hesiod and pseudo-Theophrastus supposed, it is necessary in every

---

[143] U 526. Epictetus points out that the Epicurean wise person will not raise children or participate in politics (*Discourses* 1.23) and that in a hypothetical Epicurean
city there will be no marriage, no rearing of children, and no political participation (3.7.19). At Diogenes Laertius 10.119, the manuscripts state that the wise person "will marry and have children, as Epicurus says in his *Problems* and in the books
On Nature, but that under special circumstances he will marry at some time in his
life" (καὶ μὴν καὶ γαμήσειν καὶ τεκνοποιήσειν τὸν σοφόν . . . κατὰ περίστασιν δέ ποτε
βίου γαμήσειν). The other testimonies, together with the expression κατὰ περίστασιν
and adversative δέ, seem to me to demand the addition of a negative in the first
clause. Jean Bollack (*La pensée du plaisir. Epicure: textes moraux, commentaires*, ed. Jean
Bollack [Paris: Éditions de Minuit, 1975] 40) suggests that the text can stand as it
is in the sense that the wise person "pourra se marier." The Epicurean position
does not, of course, mean that a person who becomes an Epicurean will abandon
spouse or children, nor will he or she necessarily remain unmarried. Rather, if a
person has a choice, he or she will not marry or have children. Epicurus himself
was unmarried and childless. His close friend Metrodorus was not married, but
lived with a woman, Leontion, and had children.
[144] Diogenes Laertius 7.121, and SVF 3.494, 616, and 686.
[145] *On Household Economics* col. 9.1–3.

case that the wife should be a virgin.[146] He proposes that the steward and laborer need not be slaves; both can be free persons.[147] Philodemus rejects at length pseudo-Theophrastus' discussion of the relationship of the household to the city on the grounds that this topic is irrelevant, obvious, or wrong.[148]

Even though he provides only a few indicators, Philodemus thus offers the option of a domestic arrangement without wife or children, with domestic help that may consist of free persons. Although Philodemus does not explicitly endorse this option, he undermines conventional assumptions. Consequently, when Philodemus comes to announce that he will not treat "how to live nobly in a house," but will discuss how to manage possessions, there is a hint that he will ignore the traditional household as an economic unit and focus instead on the individual as shaping his own life. There is no explicit rejection of the traditional household or family, but rather an assumption that they are incidental to one's goal as an individual.[149]

It is fitting, therefore, that Philodemus should begin his exposition of Epicurean economics with a refutation of the Cynic life. The Epicurean, too, is on his own. He does not, however, reject wealth. Although his economic activity is not embedded in a family or city structure, he makes use of the existing social and economic structure in order to secure a livelihood. As we have seen, Philodemus follows Metrodorus in arguing that the Epicurean will make some effort to obtain some wealth. Philodemus draws this middle section of his treatise to a close by offering a detailed table of contents, as cited earlier. Then, starting a new paragraph, Philodemus makes the following transition to a new discussion:

> It is possible to take up some things both about the sources from which (πόθεν) and about how (πῶς) one should procure and preserve [possessions]. His extended discussion was principally concerned with showing that occasional troubles, worries, and bother are much more

---

[146] *On Household Economics* col. 9.7–9.
[147] *On Household Economics* col. 9.16–20.
[148] *On Household Economics* cols. 7.45–8.18
[149] Similarly, Carlo Natali ("Oikonomia in Hellenistic Political Thought," *Justice and Generosity*, ed. Malcolm Schofield and Andre Laks, [Cambridge: Cambridge University Press, 1995] 95–128: 110) points out that, in contrast with Aristotle, "Philodemus eliminates the section on social, affectionate and hierarchical relationships within the household, and restricts the 'economic' discussion to the single point of wealth."

profitable for the best way of life than the opposite course. But let us
say, following [his lead], that to think that the best procurement and
use is by the spear belongs to people who court fame in accordance
with neither wisdom.[150]

As Sudhaus and Laurenti have argued, the pronoun "his" (αὐτῶι)
refers to Metrodorus, the source of the preceding arguments.[151] It is
opposed to "we," Philodemus himself. Metrodorus offered an extended
refutation of the Cynic way of life (the "opposite course"), which
Philodemus has just reviewed. Philodemus now proposes to add some
material on the sources of income and how to manage it. His previous table of contents did not include sources of income, but it did
include "how" one must be mentally disposed in managing an income.
In "taking up" some things, Philodemus promises to focus on two
issues that were not treated at length by Metrodorus. He says that
he will "follow." We expect that he will follow Metrodorus, but,
interestingly, he does not say so explicitly.[152] The grammatical impre-
cision, together with the emphatic "we," suggests that Philodemus is
now intent on pursuing a course of his own. For this very reason,
he needs to mention that he is still following the authority of others.
There is no reason to suppose that he will no longer use the text of
Metrodorus that he has been following all along. But Philodemus now
stresses that he will speak in his own voice. If he is still using a text
of Metrodorus, he will not simply report it; he will build on it a
position of his own.

In his new discussion of the sources of income (cols. 22.17–23.36),
Philodemus first rejects occupations praised by others, then advances
rhetorically from second and third best to the best way of life. He
plunges immediately into his topic by dismissing one candidate: making money from warfare. Philodemus' examples are all taken from
Greek history: Gellias the Sicilian, Scopas the Thessalian, and the

---

[150] Col. 22.6–26: ἔστιν δ' ἀνελέσθαι τι[νὰ] καὶ πρὸς τὸ πόθεν καὶ πῶς πορίζεσθαι
δεῖ καὶ φυλάττειν. ἡ συνέχουσα μέντοι γ᾽ἀνάτασις αὐτῶι γέγονεν πρὸς τὸ μακρῶι μᾶλλον λυσιτελεῖν τὰς ποτὲ γινομένας ὀχλήσεις καὶ φροντίδας καὶ πραγματείας τῆς ἐναντίας
αἱρέ[σ]εως εἰς διαγωγὴν τὴν ἀρίστην. ἡμε[ῖς] δὲ [λ]έγωμεν ἀκολοθοῦντες [τὸ] μὲν
ο[ἴεσ]θαι πορισμὸν ἄ[ριστο]ν εἶναι τὸν δορίκτητον κα[ὶ χ]ρῆσιν ... δοξοκόπων ἀνθρώπων
εἶναι κατὰ σοφίαν οὐδετέραν.

[151] See note 101 above.

[152] As Sudhaus (47) notes, this omission is "strange." Sudhaus suggests the emendation ἀκολουθούντῳ[ς]. However, the grammar is not so strange as to require
emendation; and the proposed change goes against the evidence of the transcriptions which show E or C after ἀκολουθούντ.

Athenians Cimon and Nicias. He adds a short essay on the difference between the political or practical life and the theoretical life. The latter consists in having the leisure to investigate the truth. In a last use of the tentative "appear" and "seem," Philodemus notes that those who praise the military life "appear" to assign success only to the practical life and "seem" to detach noble deeds from the theoretical life.[153] This is a traditional contrast, previously developed in detail by Aristotle.[154] The tentative wording, the Greek examples, and the allusive homage to Cynicism as a kind of "wisdom" (alongside Epicureanism) all point to the presence of Metrodorus in Philodemus' discussion.

Still staying within a Greek context, Philodemus next rejects four occupations in quick succession. It is "ridiculous," he says, to earn an income from horsemanship, it is "not fortunate" to do mining by using slaves, and it is "mad" to make money "from both, working oneself."[155] Still proceeding at top speed, Philodemus ends his list of rejected occupations with the life of the working farmer, then makes a quick reversal:

> It is burdensome to make money by farming oneself, so as to do the work oneself, but [having] others [do the work], while possessing the land, is appropriate to a good person.[156]

In Xenophon's *Oeconomicus*, Socrates put forward the life of the farmer as the best life, regardless of whether he works the land himself or supervises others.[157] This portrait is balanced by a description of the life of a gentleman farmer later in the *Oeconomicus*.[158] The gentleman farmer supervises others and has time to go to town in the mornings. Philodemus dismisses the life of the working farmer summarily as "burdensome." His clipped style suggests not only that he is impatient to get on with his choice of lives, but also that he has a

---

[153] *On Household Economics* cols. 22.28–41.

[154] Aristotle's argument at *Politics* 7.3 (1325b14–23) is especially pertinent. Here Aristotle proposes that the theoretical life is much more a life of action than the so-called practical life. It seems to me quite possible that Metrodorus (whom Philodemus mentions at col. 21.34–35 as refuting Aristotle) had this text of Aristotle before him.

[155] *On Household Economics* col. 23.1–7.

[156] *On Household Economics* col. 23.7–11: ταλαίπωρον δὲ καὶ τὸ γεωργο[ῦν]τ᾽ αὐτὸν οὕτως ὥστε αὐτουργεῖν. τὸ δ᾽ ἄλλων ἔχοντα γῆν κατὰ σπουδαῖον.

[157] *Oeconomicus* 5.1–17 and 6.8–11. Similarly, the Peripatetic *Oeconomica* (1, 1343a25–26) states that farming is "prior by nature."

[158] Ischomachus describes his daily routine as a gentleman farmer at *Oeconomicus* 11.14–18.

text before him. The vigorous use of the terms "ridiculous" and "mad" is a tell-tale mark of Philodemus' own style.[159] The curtness of the language signals a clash between Philodemus' source and his response to it. He is now imposing his own preferences on his text.

As soon as Philodemus has mentioned the life of the gentleman farmer, he becomes expansive again. This type of life

> least has intrigues against men, from which much unpleasantness comes about. It [provides] a delightful way of life, a leisurely retreat with friends, and an income that is most seemly among [temperate] people.[160]

Philodemus adds briefly:

> Nor is it unseemly to make money from a tenement and the experience or expertise of slaves, so long as this is in no way indecent.[161]

But these two lives—that of the gentleman farmer and the entrepreneur—are only second and third best respectively:

> It is first and finest to receive a share of gratitude (εὐχάριστο[ν]), along with full respect, in return for philosophical discourses shared with receptive men, as happened to Epicurus. These discourses are, for the rest, true, free from strife, and, in general, without disturbance, whereas [earning money] by sophistic and contentious discourses is no better than [earning it] by the discourses of demagogues and informers.[162]

The best way to earn an income is that of the philosopher, imparting words of truth to men who are grateful for them and respect their author. Just as Epicurus demanded, these words must not be rabble-rousing. Using the word "sophistic" in a pejorative sense, Philodemus points out that, unlike contentious sophistic speeches, philosophical discourses are free from discord. They differ in this

---

[159] See, for example, the use of γελοῖος at cols. 26.20 and 34.28–29 of *On Poems* 5, and μανικός at col. 35.17 of *On Poems* 5.

[160] *On Household Economics* col. 23.11–18 (following immediately upon the text cited in n. 156): ἥκιστα γὰρ ἐπιπλοκὰς ἔχει πρὸς ἀνθρώπους, ἐξ ὧν ἀηδίαι πολλαὶ παρακολουθοῦσι, καὶ διαγωγὴν ἐπιτερπῆ καὶ μετὰ φίλων ἀναχώρησιν εὔσχολον καὶ παρὰ τοῖς [σώφροσι]ν εὐσχημονεστάτην πρόσοδον.

[161] *On Household Economics* col. 23.18–22 (following immediately upon the preceding text): ο[ὐκ ἄ]σχ[η]μον [δ᾽ο]ὐδὲ ἀπὸ συνοικία[ς τε] καὶ δούλων ἐμπειρίας ἢ καὶ τέχνας ἐχόντων μηδαμ[ῶς] ἀπρεπεῖς.

[162] *On Household Economics* col. 23.23–36: πρῶτον δὲ καὶ κάλλιστον ἀπὸ λόγων φιλο[σό]φων ἀνδράσιν δεκτικοῖς μεταδιδομέν[ων] ἀντιμεταλαμβάνειν εὐχάριστο[ν ἅμ]α μετὰ σεβασμοῦ παντ[ός], ὡς ἐγένετ᾽ Ἐπικο[ύ]ρωι, λο[ιπὸ]ν δὲ ἀληθινῶν καὶ ἀφιλο[ν]ε[ί]κων καὶ [σ]υ[λ]λήβδη[ν] εἰπεῖν [ἀτ]αράχων, ὡς τό γε διὰ σοφ[ιστι]κῶν καὶ ἀγωνιστι[κ]ῶν ο[ὐδέν] ἐστι βέλτιον τοῦ διὰ δη[μοκ]οπικῶν καὶ συκοφαντικ[ῶν].

respect also from political speeches that rouse the mob or plant legal accusations against individuals.[163]

Philodemus cites Epicurus as an example, but he is surely also thinking about himself. The term "philosophical" includes not only the discourses of a wise person, such as Epicurus, but also of his philosophical followers, such as Philodemus. Philodemus previously defined a "philosopher" in the strict sense as someone who does not engage in business activities at all. The best life belongs to this kind of philosopher. The second and third best lives belong to persons who conduct their business activities philosophically.

There is a long tradition in Greek literature of ranking lives. In this tradition, Philodemus' ranking is remarkable in a number of ways. It is hardly surprising that Philodemus puts the philosopher in first place. But this is the first time, as far as I know, in which the occupation of philosopher is put explicitly in first place as a source of income.[164] Philodemus is discreet about the philosopher's income. He only hints at his remuneration in the words "gratitude" and "respect." The philosopher does not peddle his discourses, as Plato accused the sophists of doing, or use them to gain personal power, like the demagogue or informer. Just as he shares his thoughts with others, so others share their gratitude with him.

Further, Philodemus does not simply put lives in ranked order. In his evaluation, the first two kinds of life, the life of the philosopher and the life of the gentleman farmer, combine into a social union. Philodemus envisages the philosopher in the company of friends who honor and respect him. Guided by the philosopher, the gentleman farmer provides a refuge for people who have the leisure to share the pleasure of doing philosophy with each other. If one cannot be a philosopher, it is best to be a landowner and host or, if not that, an entrepreneur, having the leisure to gather with others in the country. Epicurus had said that the wise man "will love the country" (φιλαγρήσειν).[165] Philodemus offers a vivid image of how he will enjoy

---

[163] The three types of speeches that Philodemus rejects are perversions of the three Aristotelian types of rhetoric: panegyric (which came to be associated with sophistic speech-making), deliberative, and forensic. Philodemus takes a more positive view of sophistic rhetoric as a skill (τέχνη) in his *Rhetoric* bks. 1 and 2 (see esp. bk. 1, col. 7).

[164] Philodemus' ranking may be seen as an Epicurean version of Xenophanes' contention that his wisdom is worth more to the city than that of anyone else (Diels-Kranz 21 B 2).

[165] Diogenes Laertius 10.120.

the country. The landowner offers his estate as a retreat, far removed from the turmoil of politics, where the philosopher may impart truthful discourses to a company of friends. The two best ways of life form a new social unit that takes the place of the household as well as the city.

While Philodemus' rural retreat epitomizes Epicurean values, it also accommodates traditional values. After criticizing Xenophon's and pseudo-Theophrastus' gentleman farmer, Philodemus brings him back in second place. In Xenophon's *Oeconomicus*, Socrates contrasted the life of the farmer with that of the manual laborer (the so-called "banausic" person) as "depriving a person least from the leisure of taking care of friends and cities."[166] Subsequently, Aristotle put the working farmer and the banausic laborer in the same category: working farmers, too, lack the leisure to participate in political affairs, so that it is best for their job to be done by slaves.[167] Philodemus shares the aristocratic leanings of Aristotle and pseudo-Theophrastus. Philodemus' reason for having others do the work, however, is crucially opposed to the traditional view: the leisure of the gentleman farmer is not only devoted to philosophy, but also free from politics. Like Aristotle, Philodemus values the contemplative life of the philosopher most highly. In general, then, Philodemus' ranking does not appear so very different from that of his predecessors. But he has changed it radically by stripping away politics along with excess luxury. Instead of having the landowner use his leisure to participate in politics, he has him use it to serve as host for a company of friends doing philosophy together.

This way of life is made possible by "others" working the land. Philodemus accepts a social order in which some people work so that others may enjoy leisure. He mentions the use of slaves explicitly in his third way of life, that of the landlord or industrialist. The use of slaves is not contrary to Epicurus' own practice; he, too, owned slaves. As Philodemus will go on to show, the owner will be kind to his slaves. Presumably, he will give them some leisure to do philosophy. Nonetheless, Philodemus' endorsement of leisurely gentility, together with his brief dismissal of the working life of the farmer, is hardly egalitarian. While accepting traditional economic and social hierarchies, Epicurus opened up hope to the downtrodden. Philodemus

---

[166] *Oeconomicus* 6.9: ἥκιστα ἀσχολίαν παρέχειν φίλων τε καὶ πόλεως συνεπιμελεῖσθαι.
[167] *Politics* 7, 10 (1330a25–26); cf. 7, 9 (1329a25–26).

does not take away that hope, but shows that privilege has a great advantage. Even though, as he will point out at the very end of his book, wealth has just a "small superiority" over poverty, his ranking gives a strong preference to wealth by opposing its comforts to the hardship of being poor.

There are clear signs in Philodemus' text that his evaluation of lives is indebted to Metrodorus. But there are also signs that Philodemus is reshaping the material that he has before him. The gaps, elliptical summaries, and forceful expressions suggest that Philodemus is expressing his own views. Moreover, Philodemus places special emphasis on three lives: the rejected life of the military man, and the first and second place lives of the philosopher and the landowner. This emphasis, together with the rhetorical build-up to the best way of life, appears to be Philodemus' own contribution. Metrodorus presumably adjudicated among different professions. At the same time, we may credit Philodemus with selecting details and ordering them on a scale that highlights certain occupations and is marked by strong contrasts.

While everything that Philodemus says in his ranking fits Metrodorus' Greece, his emphasis is directly relevant to Roman society of the first century B.C.E. One thinks of Piso, Philodemus' rich friend, enjoying his villa in the country and hosting his Epicurean friends. On a more modest scale, there is Horace, enjoying his farm with the help of slaves. One also thinks of Atticus, who ran a book trade by employing slaves. For aristocrats such as Piso, Philodemus' ranking carries a special message. In the first place, Philodemus invites the Roman upper classes to open their estates to philosophy. The settings of Cicero's dialogues illustrate this practice. In addition, it is interesting to note that what Philodemus explicitly rejects about the political life is military activity. All political participation is likely to disturb, but using political office to enrich oneself through war is especially bad. It was the custom among Roman aristocrats to do just that. Philodemus appears to be extending a message to Roman aristocrats and others who have broken into their circle: don't pursue the military life, and avoid political intrigue as much as possible by transforming your estates into philosophical havens for friends.

After ranking the sources of income, Philodemus turns to his second follow-up topic, "how" to manage one's income (cols. 23.36–27.20). He already dealt with this issue in the middle section (IIA), which is closely indebted to Metrodorus. The additional treatment provides a good test of Philodemus' own contribution to the topic of economics.

While it is difficult to disentangle Metrodorus' ranking of lives from that of Philodemus, Philodemus' new comments on the manner of managing an income are marked by clear differences in both style and content from the earlier treatment. These differences, which include the use of the first person pronoun, show that Philodemus is now on his own.[168] The new discussion is blatantly aristocratic in its orientation. After ranking the well-to-do landowner and businessman in second and third place, Philodemus gives them detailed advice on how to administer their wealth.

Philodemus begins his new treatment with an introduction to Epicurean ethics. True to the title of his book, he offers an essay on vices and their corresponding virtues. Forbidden are excessive desires and fears, injustice (ἀδικία), not having friends (ἀφιλία), not being humane (ἀφιλανθρωπία), and harshness (ἀνημερότης). On his previous treatment of "how" a person must be disposed, Philodemus required philanthropy and sharing, and he mentioned friends.[169] Metrodorus led the way, but Philodemus now goes much further. He first lays out a complete foundation of Epicurean ethics, as he prohibits immoderate desires and the fear of death, of the gods, and of pain. Applying Epicurus' general precepts to the aristocrat in particular, he points out that "nothing is accustomed to drain and overturn the most distinguished and wealthiest [houses]" as much as luxuries, womanizing, and the like, along with the aforementioned fears.[170] Philodemus argues that honesty is the best policy, and that having friends and being generous to them is a good investment.[171] The prohibition against being inhumane and harsh implies having power over others.[172] Although Philodemus' advice is relevant to anyone at all, including the circle of Epicurus and Metrodorus in Athens, it is especially appropriate as a code of ethics for the Roman aristocrat.

After his discussion of the five vices and their opposites, Philodemus follows up with "more specialized" advice, as he puts it.[173] This advice is aimed directly at the affluent. Philodemus now depicts in some

---

[168] The first person occurs at cols. 24.35 and 25.32, then repeatedly in the conclusion.

[169] *On Household Economics* col. 18.6–7 and 34–35, and col. 15.6

[170] *On Household Economics* cols. 23.42–24.11.

[171] *On Household Economics* col. 24.11–29.

[172] Epicurus is praised by Diogenes Laertius (10.10) for his mildness (ἡμερότης) to his slaves.

[173] *On Household Economics* col. 24.41: ὡς δ' ἰδιώτερον εἰπεῖν.

detail the economic bonds that unite the rich and their friends. Quoting the Epicurean leader Hermarchus, Philodemus again stresses how advantageous it is to have friends.[174] He encourages people to spend freely in order to get a good return, and mentions that some Romans apportion their income among expenditures, equipment, replenishment, and the "treasury."[175] Transposing a traditional value of Athenian society to Roman society, Philodemus invokes "gentle-manliness," καλοκἀγαθία, as a standard of conduct.[176] A person should not be afraid upon occasion, he says, to take away time even from philosophy in order to attend to business matters.[177] The ownership of slaves again comes up as a matter of concern. On this point, Philodemus simply refers the reader to his previous comments.[178] He returns repeatedly to the topic of friends. One should consult regu-larly with friends on all economic matters.[179] In times of plenty, a person should indulge the harmless desires of oneself and one's friends; in times of austerity, one should be harder on oneself than one's friends.[180] A person should make the same financial provisions for friends as for children.[181]

Completing a circle, Philodemus ends by saying that if there is good advice to be had from Xenophon and Theophrastus, one should not omit to use it. The aristocratic way of life that Philodemus dis-missed at the beginning of his book subsequently insinuated itself increasingly into his discussion of Epicurean economics. It now makes an overt come-back, pruned to be sure, but welcomed in its chas-tened state. Philodemus has constructed a careful progression of argu-ment: he first argued cautiously and with much circumspection, following Metrodorus, that it is better to have more than less, then made this argument concrete by distributing occupations along a scale that favors the rich. Philodemus expresses his own preferences in this scale. After offering a general code of ethics slanted toward the rich, he ends by showing the wealthy how to manage their resources in the company of their friends. The whole offers a counter-

---

[174] *On Household Economics* cols. 24.41–25.4.
[175] *On Household Economics* cols. 25.4–26.1.
[176] *On Household Economics* col. 25.44.
[177] *On Household Economics* col. 26.9–18.
[178] *On Household Economics* col. 26.28–34. The earlier discussion is at cols. 9.26–10.28.
[179] *On Household Economics* col. 26.18–28.
[180] *On Household Economics* col. 26.1–9.
[181] *On Household Economics* col. 27.5–9.

part to traditional aristocratic society: the Epicurean "gentleman" is relaxed about making money and uses it to enjoy philosophical leisure with friends.

Appropriately, Philodemus feels impelled to conclude by offering a word of excuse for writing on economics: he is merely following the example of Metrodorus, he says, who gave quite specific instructions.[182] Philodemus contrasts his treatment with the more detailed treatment of "more satrap-like" philosophers.[183] He has in mind Xenophon and pseudo-Theophrastus, whom he attacked earlier. The person who would accuse him of "saying altogether little on a subject that will help rather much (μ[ε]ιζόνως ὠφελήσοντος)" seems to him "more persuasive." However, his shorter treatment is fitting, Philodemus says, because wealth has only a "small superiority" over poverty.[184] That is why he offers only quite general instructions. For further guidance, he points to other works on ethics. Philodemus realizes that he has been lavishing attention on a wealthy life-style. There is nothing wrong with that, he indicates, for there is a benefit in being moderately wealthy. As a counterpoise, he reminds the reader that it really matters very little whether one is wealthy or not.

Philodemus' economics fits squarely into Epicurean ethics. At the same time, he offers a new vision of an Epicurean society that is suitable for Roman aristocrats. While he reiterates the orthodox Epicurean doctrine that wealth makes no difference to happiness and is just a little preferable to poverty, he comes close in effect to meeting the Stoics in their preference for wealth. The Stoic endorsement of wealth and political leadership had long proved attractive to Roman aristocrats. Proposing Epicureanism as a better option, Philodemus shows the Romans that they can continue to stay wealthy as Epicureans, so long as they do so in moderation. Philodemus inserts this new aristocratic ideal into an Epicurean framework. He does not thereby change the framework. The poor, too, can attain Epicurean happiness; but in his *On Household Economics*, Philodemus focuses on the Roman rich. He offers Roman aristocrats an alternative to their traditional political ambitions, as he invites them to use their wealth for their personal well-being and that of their friends.[185]

---

[182] *On Household Economics* col. 27.20–29.

[183] *On Household Economics* col. 27.30–35.

[184] *On Household Economics*, col. 27.35–46 (including μ[ικ]ρὰν ... ὑπεροχὴν at col. 27.43–45).

[185] I am very grateful to the editors for their astute comments and suggestions, which helped me to rethink some difficulties and remove some obscurities.

PHILODEMUS, "ON WEALTH" AND "ON HOUSEHOLD MANAGEMENT:" NATURALLY WEALTHY EPICUREANS AGAINST POOR CYNICS*

DAVID L. BALCH

Abstract

This article is a study and partial translation of two of Philodemus' tractates, "On Wealth" and "On Household Management." In both works, the Epicurean author mounts a polemic against the Cynics, and some of these arguments can be traced back two and a half centuries to Metrodorus, a founder of the Epicurean school. Philodemus argues for a mean of wealth, so that the extremes of both luxury and Cynic poverty (πτωχεία) are vices. He argues for "natural wealth" and himself lived in the villa of his wealthy patron, while Cynics had nothing and were homeless.

Given the analogous tension within the early Jesus movement between settled householders and wandering mendicants, I argue that the centuries-old debate between Epicureans and Cynics sheds light on Jesus blessing the "poor" (οἱ πτωχοί; Luke 6:20b). It has been argued that this beatitude describes *la condition humaine* as one of poverty, whether or not one is poor economically. But the words he employed mean that Jesus blessed Cynic mendicancy and lived that homeless life style, and that the first beatitude has an irreducible economic element.

> "Blessed are the mendicants" (μακάριοι οἱ πτωχοί; Luke 6:20b).
> ". . . mendicancy . . . the deprivation not of many, but of all things"
> (πτωχεία[ν] . . . τ[ὴ]ν στέρ[ησιν οὐ] πολλῶν, ἀλλὰ πάν[των];
>
> Philodemus, *On Wealth*, col. XLV, line 15).[1]

---

* I offer this essay to my daughter, Christina Irene Balch. When we were discussing whether she had sufficient funds for her study at the University of California, she said, "If I do not have enough money to eat one day, I fast; it's good for my body." I presented this paper at the Studiorum Novum Testamentum Societas meeting in Strasbourg in August, 1996.

[1] Adele Tepedino Guerra, "Il primo libro 'Sulla Ricchezza' di Filodemo," *CErc* 8 (1978) 52–95, 70. Tepedino Guerra's edition includes an introduction (52–57), a table comparing previous editions (58–60), text-critical explanation (60), fragmentary Greek text of columns II–LIX (61–74), Italian translation (75–77), commentary (78–91), Greek index (92–95), and an index of names (95). Cp. Elizabeth Asmis, "Philodemus' Epicureanism," *ANRW* II.36.4 (1990) 2369–2406, at 2385–90, esp.

"You who know, and whose vast knowing
is born of poverty, abundance of poverty—
make it so the poor are no longer
despised and thrown away.
Look at them standing about—
like wildflowers, which have nowhere else to grow." (Rilke)[2]

This article is a study and partial translation of two of Philodemus'
tractates, *On Wealth* and *On Household Management*. Both were papyrus
scrolls in the Greek library of the Villa dei Papiri at Herculaneum.
Nowhere else in the Greco-Roman world may we examine the architecture of a house/villa, interpret the meaning of a sculptural program of ninety pieces, and study a library of 1787 volumes,[3] one of
which discusses how to manage a household and rejects alternative—
luxurious as well as Cynic—ways of life. In both works Philodemus
mounts a polemic against the Cynics,[4] and the polemic sheds light
on the meaning of Jesus' first beatitude.

2387 on the Cynics. She observes (2387, n. 46) that Philodemus, "On Wealth" is
preserved in PHerc. 163, PHerc. 200, and possibly PHerc. 97; Tepedino Guerra's
edition is of PHerc. 163. See Michael Erler, "Epikur," in *Die Hellenistische Philosophie*,
ed. Hellmut Flashar (Grundriss der Geschichte der Philosophie: Die Philosophie der
Antike, Bd. 4; Basel: Schwabe, 1994) 29–490, esp. 289–362 on Philodemus.

[2] "The Book of Poverty and Death," *Rilke's Book of Hours: Love Poems to God*, trans.
Anita Barrows and Joanna Macy (New York: Riverhead, 1996) 3:19, 143, an edited
translation of "Das Stundenbuch," in *Rainer Maria Rilke, Ausgewählte Werke*, (Leipzig:
Im Insel, 1938) 1.9–104. He wrote this final third of the *Book of Hours* in Paris,
where he had gone in 1902 to write on Rodin, discovering also the horrors of
urban poverty. His prose description of this poverty is "Die Aufzeichnungen des
Malte Laurids Brigge," *Ausgewählte Werke* 2.7–212; for this second reference I thank
Hubert Cancik.

[3] Joseph Jay Deiss, *Herculaneum: Italy's Buried Treasure*, rev. ed. (Malibu: J. Paul
Getty Museum, 1989) 68. Eight hundred of the scrolls remain unread (71). Virtually
all are in Greek, with a very few in Latin, so there may be a Latin library as yet
undiscovered. Marcello Gigante, *Philodemus in Italy: The Books from Herculaneum*, trans.
Dirk Obbink (Ann Arbor: University of Michigan, 1995) 47: "Perhaps we can
securely confirm the suspicion of Pandermalis, who recognizes 'in the selection and
groupings of the sculptures . . . the direct influence of the doctrine of Philodemus,
the philosopher of the house. . . .'" Compare F. Gregory Warden and David Gilman
Romano, "The Course of Glory: Greek Art in a Roman Context at the Villa of
the Papyri at Herculaneum," *Art History* 17/2 (June 1994) 228–54. Warden and
Romano's interpretation of the sculptural program, however, does not correspond
to Philodemus' philosophical thoughts on household management as interpreted by
Elizabeth Asmis in this volume.

[4] Marcello Gigante, *Cinismo e Epicureismo* (Memorie dell'Istituto Italiano per gli
Studi Filosofici 23 [Naples: Bibliopolis, 1992]), esp. 32–33, 42–43, 99–113, reviewed
by Michael Erler in *Gnomon* 68/4 (1996) 292–94, who says Gigante has set the

Philodemus, Περὶ πλούτου (On Wealth)

Philodemus, in *On Household Management* XII.21, refers to his own work *On Wealth*, which is therefore earlier.[5] Philodemus produced his first works in the period 75–50 B.C.E., but wrote *On Vices and Virtues* after 50; "the central position to the whole work is occupied by book 9, 'On Household Management,' well preserved in PHerc. 1424 . . ."[6] The wealth defined, debated, and defended in the earlier (more fragmentary) work is the basis for the later one, so I will survey it, translating crucial phrases and sentences.[7] The fragmentary remains of the work make the translation disjointed and discontinuous.

---

direction of future research. Cp. Tepedino Guerra, "Il primo libro" 55 (with n. 25), 78, 79, 86, 89. At col. XXXII, lines 4–5 Crillo conjectures "[Ζη]νων" (cf. Tepedino Guerra, 53, n. 7; also 78–79). The extant fragments of Philodemus' "On Wealth" name the Cynics (col. L, line 7). His *On Household Management* XII. 25ff. names and mounts a polemic against the Cynics.

[5] Christianus Jensen, *Philodemi Περὶ οἰκονομίας qui dicitur libellus* (Leipzig: Teubner, 1906) 38. Cf. the text and translation by Johann Adam Hartung, *Philodems Abhandlungen über die Haushaltung und über den Hochmut und Theophrasts Haushaltung und Characterbilder* (Leipzig: W. Engelmann, 1857). However, Renato Laurenti, *Filodemo e il pensiero economico degli epicurei* (Testi e Documenti per lo Studio dell'Antichita 39 [Milan: Istituto Editoriale Cispalpino-la Goliardica, 1973]) 14 criticizes Hartung for ignoring the acute textual emendations of Leonhard von Spengel in the *Gelehrte Anzeigen* 7 (Königliche bayerische Akademie der Wissenschaften [Munich: 1838]), Nos. 255–56: 1001–07, 1009–16, 1022–23; and 9 (1839) Nos. 193–95: 505–36. See the review of Laurenti by Matilde Ferrario, "Una nuova edizione dell'opera Filodemea sull' Economia," *CErc* 6 (1976) 92–95.

[6] Gigante, *Philodemus* 21, 39. On Cicero's translation about 85 B.C.E. of Xenophon's work of the same title into Latin, see Sarah B. Pomeroy, *Xenophon Oeconomicus: A Social and Historical Commentary with a New English Translation* (Oxford: Clarendon, 1994, 1995) 70. On Philodemus' influence on others see Laurenti, *Filodemo*, 20 n. 22.

[7] Important recent studies of poverty and wealth, however, do not include a reference to Philodemus' treatise *On Wealth*: Hans Dieter Betz, *The Sermon on the Mount* (Hermeneia [Minneapolis: Fortress, 1995]) 110–19 with bibliography; his *Der Apostle Paulus und die sokratische Tradition* BHT 45 (Tübingen: J. C. B. Mohr [Paul Siebeck], 1972) 109–13; and Martin Hengel, *Property and Riches in the Early Church: Aspects of a Social History of Early Christianity* (Philadelphia: Fortress, 1974), a translation of *Eigentum und Reichtum in der frühen Kirche* (Stuttgart: Calwer Verlag, 1973). I know of no New Testament scholar who refers to Philodemus' treatise on wealth, even though some scholars survey Greek discussions and although Philodemus calls πτωχεία evil (XLII.26–35; XLIII.1–8), the condition of persons whom Jesus pronounced "blessed." This failure to consider what Philodemus says has consequences for interpretation, as we shall see. Clarence E. Glad, *Paul and Philodemus: Adaptability in Epicurean and Early Christian Psychagogy*, NovTSup 81 (Leiden: Brill, 1995), clarifies many Philodemian texts but has no occasion to refer to this one.

A. *Philodemus, "On Wealth:" A Translation of Selected Sentences*[8]

Philodemus refers to persons who are:

"procuring the preservation [of wealth] also with anxious pain, and who are so struggling in regard to the loss of property that without property . . ." (ποιούμενοι τὴ[ν φυ]λακὴν καὶ σὺν μερίμναις ἐ[π]ῳδύνοις· καὶ περὶ τῆς ἀποβολῆς οὕτως ἀγωνιῶντες ὡς ἀνυπ[αρξίας . . .] . . .; XXVII, frag. 2, lines 9–10)

". . . when they consider [wealth], they are superior to the indigent and poor and needy . . ." (ὅ[τ]αν δ[ιανοῶν[9]]ται περι[γ]ίνοντ[αι] τῶ[ν] κατὰ [τὴ]ν [ἔ]νδειαν κα[ὶ] πε[νί]αν καὶ δέ[ησι]ν·; XXXIV.4–9)

". . . for worry about an (economic) fall is not worthy of fear . . ." (οὐ [γὰ]ρ ἄξιον φόβου τὸ κατὰ μετάπτωσιν ἐνόχλημα·;[10] XXXVI.10–14)

"It is said that the healing of all bodily pains[11] . . . a good thing . . . someone could say. And he said confidently, as Polyainos[12] said, 'reason heals what it has wounded.' And it does this, as Epicurus said, 'whenever the wise person yields, falling into poverty, [this] one alone is not defeated . . .'" λέγε]σθαι πα[σῶν] τῶ[νδε θεραπ]είαν ἀλγηδόνων, . . . ἀγαθὸν [. . . ἄ]ν τις εἴπειε· καὶ θαρ[ρ]ούντως εἶ[π]ε δὴ καί, καθάπερ ἔφησε Πολύαινος, "ὅπερ ἔτρωσε θεραπεύει [ὁ λό]γος" καὶ το[ῦ]το ποεῖ κ[αθ]άπερ εἶπεν Ἐπίκουρος, [ὅτα]ν παρῆι ποτὲ πεσὼ[ν . . . ὁ σο]φὸς εἰς πενί[αν, μόνον οὐ τρέπεται . . .)'; XL.6–16)

". . . Everything which is charged against poverty on the grounds that it is inferior to wealth is, in truth, as Metrodorus said, a false accusation . . ." (καὶ πάνθ' [ὅ]σα κατηγ[ο]ρεῖται πενίας ὡς ἐλλειπούσης πλούτου, ταῖς ἀληθείαις, ὡς ὁ Μητρόδωρος ἔφη, καταψεύσματ' ἐστί, . . .; XLI.10–15)

". . . many evils together do not make a good, but [many states of] poverty [together make] wealth. There is a great difference between good and evil, but not between wealth and poverty, and wealth is a

---

[8] I thank Professors Ronald F. Hock and Abraham J. Malherbe for substantive assistance with this translation of *On Wealth*, especially Hock for his full translation. I also thank Prof. Voula Tsouna for further suggestions. I remain responsible for the final wording. On Philodemus' difficult Greek, see the comments of Erler, "Epikur" 335–36.

[9] Cirillo's emendation (apud Tepedino Guerra's edition) is δ[ιατριβῶν]ται ("consume"); the sentence might then be ironic.

[10] LSJ 1116 cites the final four words as Epicurus, frag. 154 Usener. LSJ s.v. μεταπίπτω; generally, "change for the worse," ἐξ εὐπορῆς εἰς πενίην, Democr. 101. See Philodemus, "On Wealth" LIII.2–5.

[11] Tepedino Guerra, "Il primo libro," 78; in Philodemus λυπέω refers to suffering of soul, ἀλεγέω to suffering of body.

[12] The same Polyainos whom Seneca (*Ep.* 18.9 = frag. 158 Usener) says wrote to Epicurus (Tepedino Guerra, "Il primo libro," 54 n. 14 and 81 n. 6).

good discussed by philosophers . . ." (κακὰ [πολ]λὰ συν{ι}θέμενα οὐ ποεῖ ἀγαθόν, πεγ[ία] δὲ πλοῦτον· ἀγαθοῦ καὶ κακοῦ μεγάλη διαφορά, πλούτου δὲ καὶ πενίας οὐ μεγάλη, καὶ ἀγαθὸν ὁ πλοῦτος ζητεῖται παρὰ τοῖς φιλοσόφοις; XLI.32–39)[13]

". . . labor . . ." (πόνον;[14] XLII.14)

". . . therefore, since mendicancy is called poverty, whenever the school of Epicurus says that poverty is an evil, they mean this (i.e. mendicancy) . . .; they subscribe to the common and Epicurean use of language . . ." (διότι καὶ τῆς πτωχείας πενίας [καλ]ουμένης, ὅταν οἱ περὶ τ[ὸν] Ἐπί[κουρο]ν κακὸν λέ[γ]ωσι τὴν πενίαν, ταύτην λέγουσιν . . . εἰσὶ καὶ τῆς κοινῆς καὶ τῆς Ἐπικούρου συνηθείας . . . ; XLII.26–35)

". . . They assert that mendicancy alone . . . is said to be an evil . . . Of the subjects [forms of povery] expounded by us, every mendicancy is an evil . . ., called an evil as by the founders . . ." (. . . πτω]χείαν μόν[ην . . . λ]έγεσθαι κακὸν . . . ἀποφαίνονται· κα[κὸν δὲ π]τωχεία τις [πᾶ]σα [τῶν] ὑφ᾽ ἡμῶν ἐκκειμένων . . . κακὸν καὶ λέγεται ὡς τῶν καθηγεμό[νων][15] . . .; XLIII.1–8)

". . . he means that mendicancy . . . is the privation not of many, but of all things . . . This is why some Epicureans are said to use such calculations on behalf of (the notion) that poverty is evil. Epicurus in many other (books) says that poverty is an evil, but in different (writings) that have been collected this is not [his] opinion . . ." (πτωχεία[ν . . . δια]νοεῖ τ[ὴ]ν στέρ[ησι]ν οὐ πολλῶν, ἀλλὰ πάν[των . . .] διὰ [ταῦτ]α [τῶν] Ἐπικουρείων λέγοντα[ί τι]νες ὑπ[ὲρ τ]οῦ κακὸν εἶνα[ι τ]ὴν πε[γ]ίαν [ἐ]πιλογισ[μοῖ]ς χρῆσθαι τοιούτοις· ὁ Ἐπίκουρος ἔν τε ἄλλοις πο[λλ]οῖς φησι τὴν πενίαν κακὸν εἶναι, καὶ ἐν τα[ῖ]σδ᾽ ἑτέραις συναχθείσα[ις] μὴ φέρεσ[θαι]· . . .; XLV.15–40)

---

[13] Tepedino Guerra, "Il primo libro," 88; cf. Seneca, *Ep.* 87.38–39 ("Some arguments in favor of the simple life"): ". . . there is only one knot left for you to untangle . . . 'Good does not result from evil. But riches result from numerous cases of poverty; therefore, riches are not a good.' This syllogism is not recognized by our school, but the Peripatetics both concoct it and give its solution. Posidonius, however, remarks that this fallacy, which has been bandied about among all the schools of dialectic, is refuted by Antipater as follows: "The word poverty is used to denote, not the possession of something, but the non-possession, or, as the ancients have put it, deprivation (for the Greeks use the phrase by deprivation, meaning negatively). Poverty states, not what a man has, but what he has not . . ." (trans. Richard M. Gummere in LCL).

[14] Tepedino Guerra, "Il primo libro," 86; πόνος is a Cynic term; cp. Laurenti 113–14 citing Diog. Laert. 6.71.

[15] Tepedino Guerra, "Il primo libro," 86; Cirillo's text is ὁσίων καθηγεμόνων, which D'Amelio translates "santi maestri." Asmis, following F. Longo Auricchio, "La scuola di Epicuro," *CErc* 8 (1978) 22–23, claims that καθηγημόνες was used of founders, καθηγούμενοι of other teachers/guides.

"... all say that poverty is an evil, although they see what they are saying is an evil (?), but no one dares to say that the possession of few things is evil ..." (τὴν [πεν]ίαν λέγουσιν πά[ντ]ες κακὸν εἶναι, βλέποντες ὅ λέγουσι κακὸν ὑπάρχειν, τὴν δὲ τῶν ὀλίγων ὕπαρ[ξιν] οὐδεὶς [δὴ το]λμήσηι κακὸν εἰπεῖν, ...; XLVI.26–34)

"... for since the Master considers poverty to be a good ..." (... τὴν γὰρ πε[νί]αν τοῦ καθηγεμόνος ἀγαθὸν εἶναι νομίζοντ[ος] ...; XLVII.9–11)

"... although calling it poverty they were not prevented from saying that it has evil,[16] but Metrodorus was therefore able to console those who are grieving at this, in fact, not those who are only grieving at evil, but also those as if they were grieving at evil ..." ([... τὴν πενί]αν ὀνομάζοντες οὐκ ἐκωλύοντο λέγειν κακὸν ἔχε[ιν], ἀ[λ]λ᾽ οὖν [π]αραμυθεῖσθαι τοὺς ἐπὶ ταύτηι λυπουμένου[ς]ἐδύνατο Μητρόδωρος, οὐ δὴ{ι} τοὺς ἐπὶ κακῶι μό[ν]ον λυπουμένους, ἀλλά τε καὶ τοὺς ὡς ἐπὶ κα[κ]ῶι [λυπουμένους ...; XLVII.26–35)

"... not saying that they define poverty in relation to having few things, but as their nonexistence, producing ..." (... μηδ[ὲ φ]ήσ[αν]τες ὅτι κατὰ τῆς τῶν ὀλίγων ὑπάρξεως τ[ιθ]έασι[ν τ]ὴν πενί[αν], ἀλλ᾽ ὡς κατὰ τῆς ἀνυπαρ[ξίας] παριστάμενοι ...; XLVIII.18–24)

"... to dispute concerning language and names ..., both place the possession of few things as characteristic of poverty, which is a good ..." ([... π]ερὶ φωνῆς [καὶ ὀ]νο[μ]άτ[ω]ν [ἀ]μφ[ι]σβ[ητ]εῖν ... [ἀμφ]ότεροι τιθέασι[ν] τὸ [τῆι] πενίαι προσεῖνα[ι] τ[ὴν ὀλ]ίγων [ὕπ]αρξιν, ὅ ἐστιν ἀγαθ[ὸν ...] ...; XLIX.5–12)

"[poverty] ... according to theory and according to ordinary language is an evil ..." (... κακό[ν δὲ] κατὰ τὸ θ[εώ]ρημα λέγεται καὶ κατὰ τὴν [συνήθειαν ...]; XLIX.35–39)

"... just as the Cynics ..." (... κ[α]θάπε[ρ] οἱ Κυνικοί ...; L.5)

"... to set poverty wholly in opposition to wealth, and truly sometimes to call wealth good and great ..." (κα[ὶ τ]ὸ πάντως κα[τ᾽] ἐναντιό[τ]ητα τῶι πλού[τ]ωι τ[ὴ]ν πενίαν τίθεσθαι, καὶ τὸ μὴν [ἐνί]οτε ἀγαθὸν λέγεσθαι τὸν πλοῦτον καὶ μ[έ]γα ...; L.30–38)

"... one could rightly say that poverty is absolutely a good or an evil. But if it is not a good for everyone, it is an evil to some and indifferent to others. But I say that it is neither absolutely a good nor an evil nor something indifferent; nor, by analogy, is wealth. Others have different opinions ..." (... τὴν πενίαν ... ἀγαθὸν [καθάπαξ ἤ κα]κὸν ὀρθῶς [ἄν τις ἔλεγε]· εἰ δ᾽ οὐ πᾶσίν ἐστιν ἀγαθ[όν], ἀλλ᾽ ἐνίοις καὶ κακόν, τισιν

---

[16] Tepedino Guerra, "Il primo libro," 88; some scholars suppose that those who call poverty evil are Platonists and Peripatetics. However, Philodemus' treatise makes it clear that some Epicureans did the same.

δ᾽ ἀδ[ιά]φορον. οὐ καθάπαξ ἀγαθ[ὸν ἢ] κακὸν ἢ ἀδιάθορον, ὡς οὐδὲ τὸν πλοῦ[τον]· τῶν μέντοι γε ἀλλοδόξων . . .; LI.2–11)

". . . the acquisition of wealth which can readily gratify the needs of the body . . ." (τὸ [. . . πλο]ύτου κτ[ῆ]σιν [. . .] δυναμέν[η]ν ἐξ ἑτοίμου τὰς τοῦ σώματος ἐπιτη[δεύσ]εις συμπληροῦν . . .; LII.27–31)

". . . [They say] that the fall from wealth into poverty is something indifferent . . ." ([ἀδιά]φορο[ν μὲ]ν εἶναι τὴν ἐκ πλούτου μετάπτωσιν εἰς πενίαν . . .; LIII.2–5)

LIV and LV are difficult columns:

". . . so that there is almost no bodily suffering. Even if wealth cures, it is not permitted to say that it [wealth] is a great thing. Insofar as it is also easily destroyed and perfectly subject to being taken away, wealth does not permit . . ." (ὥσθ᾽ ὅσον οὐκ ἔστιν ἄλγημα κἂν [θ]εραπεύῃ⟨ι⟩] πλοῦτος, οὐκ ἔ[ξ]εστιν αὐτὸ[17] μέγα λέγειν· ἐπεὶ καὶ καθ᾽ ὅσον [εὔ]φθαρτός ἐσ[τι] καὶ [τελ]έως εὐαφαίρετος ὁ [πλ]οῦτος οὐκ [ἐ]πιτρέπει . . .; LIV.4–10)

"The fact that the sources of wealth are easily destroyed hinders in perfect or even worthy pleasure. For it is not possible, in view of such considerations, to make (pleasure) excessive. Therefore, not great . . ." (. . . πρὸς δὲ τελείαν ἡδονὴν ἢ καὶ ἀξιόλογον ἐμποδίζει τὸ τὰ ποιητικὰ[18] εὔφθαρτα εἶναι· [σ]φοδρὰν γὰρ ο[ὐ δύν]αται παρασκ[ευάζειν τοι]αῦτ᾽ ἐννοού[με]να· [δι]όπερ οὐδὲ μεγάλα . . .; LV.4–14).

"But reason in this situation and henceforth brings the same pleasures from poverty as those from wealth, so that it [poverty] becomes a matter of indifference . . ." ([. . . ὁ μὲν] λό[γος κατὰ] τοῦτο κα[ὶ] κατὰ τὸ λοιπὸ[ν ἐ]κ τῆς πενίας τὰς ἴσ[ας] ἡδονάς κομίζεται τὰς ἐκ πλούτου ὥστ᾽ εἰς ἀδιαθορίαν καθί⟨σ⟩τασθαι . . .; LVI.2–9)

"If we are poor, nor even if we are rich shall we think with pride of such non-things for this reason, nor shall we betray our souls by desire for wealth . . ." (ἐὰν ὦμεν πένητες, οὐδ᾽ ἂν πλουτῶμεν ὑπερφρονήσομεν χάριν τούτου [τῶ]ν μὴ τοιούτων, οὐδ᾽ ἐκ[δ]οθησόμεθα τὴν ψυχὴν ὑπὸ τῆς [ἐ]πιθυμίας τῆς π[ρ]ὸς πλοῦτον . . .; LVIII.3–9)

"We shall admire the discoveries of treasures and the arrangements of livelihoods, but we shall admire the philosophy that prepares for such things" (εὑρέσεις τε θησαυρῶν καὶ διατά[ξ]εις βίων ἀλ[λὰ μὴν κα]ὶ φιλοσοφίαν [θα]υμασόμεθα τὴν τοιούτοις κατασκευάζουσαν; LVIII.26–30). "Philodemus, 'On Wealth,' Book a" (Φιλοδήμου Περὶ πλούτου α᾽; LIX)

---

[17] Ronald F. Hock proposes the emendation αὐτόν, which I accept. This requires emending μέγα to μέγαν.

[18] Ronald Hock proposes ποιητικά, which I accept.

B. *Observations Concerning Philodemus, "On Wealth"*

Philodemus' principal thesis is πλούτου μέτρον, moderation/mean of wealth,[19] neither managing wealth with anxiety nor fearing its loss. Wealth can satisfy the natural necessities of the body, but through λόγος, philosophical reason, the wise person is not defeated by changes in life. The wise Epicurean liberates the soul from passions, consoles, and encourages.[20] Excessive riches bring preoccupation and anxiety; but mendicancy, the privation of everything, is an evil according to both Philodemus and the founder of the school (XLIII.4–8, a polemic against the Cynics).[21] The Master himself said that the wise person will "not turn Cynic (so the second book 'On Life' tells us); nor will he be a mendicant . . . He will have regard to his property and to the future" (οὐδὲ κυνιεῖν . . .; οὐδὲ πτωχεύσειν . . . καὶ κτήσεως προνοήσεσθαι καὶ τοῦ μέλλοντος; Diog. Laert 10.119–120, trans. Hicks [LCL]). Epicurus called Cynics the "enemies of Greece" (Diog. Laert. 10.8).

Philodemus' work reflects a debate over the definition and value of wealth, poverty, and mendicancy that was occurring among Epicureans (cf. XLIX.5–12; XLV.15–40).[22] But all Epicureans mounted polemics against the Cynics (cf. L.5 and "On Household Management," below), who rejected wealth and living in houses that exhibit riches. Philodemus' work reflects various positions within the Garden. Poverty is sometimes called an evil (XLII.26–35; XLIII.1–8; XLVI.26–34; XLVII.26–35), while Metrodorus writes that poverty is not inferior to wealth (XLI.10–15). But elsewhere, neither poverty nor wealth is said to be a good, an evil, or indifferent; pride is the problem

---

[19] Tepedino Guerra, "Il primo libro," 53. Laurenti, *Filodemo* 9 observes that the Aristotelian criterion of μεσότης is omnipresent in Epicurean ethics. Marcello Gigante, *Ricerche Filodemee* (Naples: Gaetano Macchiaroli, 1969; 2nd ed., 1983) 274 cites Philodemus, "On Household Management" XII.17ff. on μέτρον.

[20] Tepedino Guerra, "Il primo libro," 54, n. 21 on βοήθημα and παραμύθιον at XLVI.4–5.

[21] On the topos περὶ πλεονεξίας see Abraham Malherbe, "The Christianization of a Topos (Luke 12:13–34)," *NovT* 38:2 (1996) 123–35. Erler, "Epikur," 321 in view of Philodemus, Περὶ φιλαργυρίας, suggests that avarice is the vice opposed to the virtue of "household management." But compare Philodemus' title: "on vices and the opposing virtues" (n. 27). In the treatise good household management is a *mean* (XII.18–19; see n. 19). The vice at one extreme is indeed greed (XV.20), but the opposite extreme is the vice of Cynic mendicancy (*On Wealth* XLII.26–35, but see *On Household Management* XV.21–26).

[22] See also Aristotle, Politics 5.1303b.15.

(LI.2–11; LVIII.3–9). Yet again, wealth is good and great (L.30–38), but it is also said not to be a good (LIV.4–10). There is anxiety about the loss of property (XXVII, frag. 2.9–10), yet the loss of property is indifferent (LIII.2–5).

In contrast, the Cynics taught simple living, eating necessary food, and wearing only a mantle. "Wealth and fame and high birth they despise . . . Diogenes . . . used to say that it was the privilege of the gods to need nothing and of god-like men to want but little" (πλούτου . . . καταφρονοῦσιν . . . ὀλίγων χρῄζειν; Diog. Laert. VI.104, trans. Hicks in LCL). A fragment of Crates reads: "Crates said he has not considered himself honored in wealth, but in poverty" (Κράτης οὐ τῷ πλούτῳ εἶπεν ἑαυτὸν ηὐδοξηκέναι μεγάλα, ἀλλὰ τῇ πενίᾳ; frag. 38).[23] Most relevant for the present paper, Antisthenes said to Socrates, "I conceive that people's wealth and poverty are to be found not in their real estate [house] but in their hearts (οὐκ ἐν τῷ οἴκῳ τὸν πλοῦτον καὶ τὴν πενίαν ἔχειν ἀλλ᾽ ἐν ταῖς ψυχαῖς; Xenophon, *Symposium* IV.34, trans. Todd [LCL]).[24]

Epicureans and the Cynic Diogenes seem to agree on one definition of poverty (πενία) as a state of having "few things" (Diogenes in Diog. Laert. VI.104, quoted above, and Philodemus, "On Wealth" XLVI.26–34),[25] and that it is a good. They disagree on the value of mendicancy and, very practically, on whether to live in wealthy households—households like the Villa dei Papiri where Philodemus' treatise defending wealth was found, a house so striking that J. Paul Getty spent $17 million recreating it in California.[26] They may agree

---

[23] Tepedino Guerra, "Il primo libro," 55, n. 25 citing Friedrich Wilhelm August Mullach, *Fragmenta Philosophorum Graecorum* (Paris: Didot, 1881; reprint Aalen: Scientia, 1968) 2.338.

[24] Tepedino Guerra, "Il primo libro," 55, n. 25. Antisthenes continues critiquing those who bend their backs to any toil (πάντα πόνον) to increase their holdings. He is able to share his spiritual wealth with his friends (Xenophon, *Sym.* 4.43). See Ulrich von Wilamowitz-Möllendorff, "Der kynische prediger Teles," *Antigonos von Karystos*, Philologische Untersuchungen 4 (Berlin: Weidmann, 1881) 292–319 and *Teles (The Cynic Teacher)*, ed. and trans. Edward N. O'Neil, SBLTT 11, Graeco-Roman Religion 3 (Missoula: Scholars, 1977), diatribes 4A and 4B, "A Comparison of Poverty and Wealth." See also nn. 32–33.

[25] See Diog. Laert. 10.130: Epicurus refers to "being contented with little if we have not much" (trans. Hicks in LCL).

[26] See *The J. Paul Getty Museum Guide to the Villa and its Gardens*, ed. Andrea P. A. Belloli (Malibu: J. Paul Getty Museum, 1988, 1989). See Mario Pagano, *Herculaneum: A Reasoned Archaeological Itinerary* (Naples: T & M srl, 2000).

about the definition of wealth, but disagree about its value: Philodemus affirms that moderate wealth is good, although it is precarious, easily lost, and may be the occasion for worried pain. Cynics absolutely deny its value. Philodemus writes a logical sequel to *On Wealth* in a later treatise concerning how to preserve, manage, and increase household wealth.

Philodemus, Περὶ οἰκονομίας *(On Household Management)*,[27] *including anti-Cynic arguments originally made by Metrodorus c. 300 B.C.E.*

Siegfried Sudhaus argued that cols. XII.45–XXI.35 of Philodemus' work on household management have their source in the thought of Epicurus' friend[28] Metrodorus, and so dates this section c. 300 B.C.E., the time of the founding of the school.[29] Voula Tsouna-McKirahan argues rather that Philodemus directly refers to Metrodorus' earlier work only three times (XII. 17–XIII.29; XXVII.23–29; and XX.45–XXI.35).[30] She observes that Sudhaus' linguistic arguments are weak, since there is no term that could not have been used by Philodemus, but many that are distinctly Philodemean. Moreover, the Cynic way of life was debated in both Metrodorus' and Philodemus' times.

> Perhaps the difference between the two positions should be formulated as follows: Metrodorus says that wealth is a good thing because its presence entails less pain than its absence. Philodemus says that the

---

[27] The title is a modern reconstruction on the basis of the content, which Philodemus describes as being περὶ οἰκονομίας. The subscript of the papyrus shows the title only as book nine of "On Vices and the Opposing Virtues, and the Persons in Whom They Occur and the Situations in Which They are Found" (Asmis 2385, n. 44); cf. Erler, "Epikur" (n. 1) 318–21. This manner of opposing vices and virtues was attributed earlier to Aristotle (cf. Laurenti, *Filodemo*, 18, n. 18).

[28] See Diog. Laert. 10.19.

[29] Siegfried Sudhaus, "Eine Erhaltene Abhandlung des Metrodor," *Hermes* 41 (1906) 45–58, and "Περὶ πλούτου," *Hermes* 42 (1907) 645–47, cited in agreement by Tepedino Guerra, "Il primo libro," 55, n. 27 and Laurenti 108–09: "un frammento genuino di Metrodoro" and a "testimonianze sul cinismo." Cf. Metrodorus, Περὶ οἰκονομίας and Περὶ πλούτου in Alfred Körte, "Metrodori Epicurei fragmenta," *Jahrbuch für classische Philologie*, Suppl. 17 (Leipzig: Teubner, 1890) 527–58; 545–46, 547–48.

[30] Voula Tsouna-McKirahan, "Epicurean Attitudes to Management and Finance," in *Epicureismo Greco e Romano: Atti del Congresso Internazionale, Napoli, 19–26 Maggio 1993* (Naples: Biblopolis, 1996), 2:701–714, esp. 702 n. 6.

presence of wealth is preferable to its absence only if one administers it properly [with the appropriate mental disposition and not as an art].³¹

Diogenes of Sinope (c. 412/403–c. 324/321 B.C.E.) was a Cynic who lived earlier than Metrodorus (c. 331–278 B.C.E.); they expressed contrasting opinions on life style. Diogenes said:

> All the curses of tragedy, he used to say, had lighted upon him.
> At all events he was
> A homeless (ἄοικος)³² exile, to his country dead.
> A wanderer who begs his daily bread (πτωχός, πλανήτης, βίον ἔχων τοὐφ᾽ ἡμέραν (Diog. Laert. 6.38 [LCL]).³³

One of his counter-cultural sayings is recorded in this way: "Someone took him into a magnificent house and warned him not to spit, whereupon having cleared his throat he spat into the man's face, being unable, he said, to find a baser place" (Diog. Laert. 6.32). Martin cites a tradition of the barbarian Scythians: Herodotus says they have no established cities, but carry their houses on wagons

---

³¹ Tsouna-McKirahan, "Epicurean Attitudes," 707 n. 16. My additional explanation in brackets is based on her subsequent arguments.

³² Cf. Diog. Laert. 6.23 and Teles IVA (43H, line 161; ed. O'Neil 44–45), but Teles writes of πενία, never of πτωχός. On the other hand, Diogenes managed the household of Xeniades (Diog. Laert. 6.74). See the debates in pseudo-Socrates, *Epistles* 12–13 and Ronald Hock, "Simon the Shoemaker as an Ideal Cynic," *GRBS* 17 (1976) 41–53, esp. 48–52.

³³ Laurenti 10–11, 108–10, 113–15, who gives the references to Xenophon, Plutarch, and Diogenes Laertius that I cite in below and nn. 32 and 37. Also cited by R. Bracht Branham and Marie-Odile Goulet-Cazé, eds., "Introduction," *The Cynics: The Cynic Movement in Antiquity and Its Legacy* (Berkeley and Los Angeles: University of California Press, 1996) 24; R. Bracht Branham, "Defacing the Currency: Diogenes' Rhetoric and the Invention of Cynicism," in Branham and Goulet-Cazé 81–102, 91; Margarethe Billerbeck, "The Ideal Cynic from Epictetus to Julian," in Branham and Goulet-Cazé 205–221, 214 (she adds that Maximus of Tyre, *Or.* 36, later describes the Cynics as houseless [ἄοικος] and homeless [ἀνέστιος]); and Richard P. Martin, "The Scythian Accent," in Branham and Goulet-Cazé 147, who cites I. Lana, "Tracce di dottrine cosmopolitische in grecia prima del cinismo," *RFIC* 29 (1951) 193–216, 317–38. Martin 147 cites Plutarch, *Banquet of the Seven Sages* 155a: Anacharsis prides himself on being homeless. See also Diog. Laert. 6.71 on Diogenes and πόνος, and the comments of Goulet-Cazé, *L'ascese cynique: Un commentaire de Diogene Laërce VI 70–71* (Paris: Libr. Philosophique J. Vrin, 1986). Cf. Xenophon, *Mem.* 1.5.6 for Socrates' attitude toward money and slavery. Socrates says he has not even an obol and is proud of his poverty (Xenophon, *Symp.* 3.8–9; cp. Diog. Laert. 6.21). Anthony A. Long, "The Socratic Tradition: Diogenes, Crates, and Hellenistic Ethics" in Branham and Goulet-Cazé 28–46, 32 cites a similar tradition of Antisthenes (Xenophon, Sym. 4.34–44).

and thus cannot be cornered or even contacted unless they wish
(Herodotus 4.46.3).[34]

Diogenes also wrote a work concerning wealth (Περὶ πλούτου) and
one entitled *A Mendicant* (Πτωχόν;[35] Diog. Laert. 6.80) expressing such
sentiments. The work on wealth has the same title as the very different
contemporary work by Metrodorus, as well as the one written two
and a half centuries later by Philodemus.

Philodemus begins his work on household management by criticizing others, then discusses the Epicurean view, first presenting
Metrodorus' position, then working out his own over against the
Cynics. Jensen reconstructs only twenty-eight of an estimated original ninety-eight columns. Laurenti outlines[36] the work as follows:

   I. Others' works on household management
       A. Criticism of Xenophon, *Oeconomicus* (Socrates)[37]
       B. Criticism of ps.-Theophrastus (ps.-Aristotle, *Oeconomica* I)
   II. Various problems concerning household management
       A. The philosopher and wealth
       B. Sources of wealth for the wise person

In the first section,[38] Philodemus accuses Socrates of forcing the
meaning of words because he takes "good household manager" to
mean "to manage well one's own house and to cause another's house
to be well managed, in that one understands 'good' to mean what
in a great and blessed way is beneficial" (τὸ [ε]ὖ οἰκεῖν τὸ[ν] ἴδιον
οἶκον καὶ τὸ ποιεῖν τὸν ἀλλότριον εὖ οἰκεῖσθαι ῾λαμβανομένου τοῦ ε[ὖ]
τοῦ μεγαλωστὶ συμφέροντος καὶ μακαρίως; col. I.5–10; cp. Xenonphon,
Oec. I.2–4). The alternative is "to acquire many things and to maintain newly-acquired and pre-existing property, and accordingly to
manage well one's own house and to cause another's house to be
well managed" (τὸ πορίζειν πολλὰ χρήματα καὶ φυλάττειν πῶς διαμενεῖ
τὰ πορισθέντα καὶ προϋπάρχοντα καὶ κατὰ τοῦτο τὸ εὖ [ο]ἰκεῖν τὸν ἴδιον

---

[34] Martin, "The Scythian Accent," 139.

[35] This is the predicate accusative of an unexpressed verb; see Herbert Weir
Smyth, *Greek Grammer* (Cambridge: Harvard University Press, 1920) 362, #1615.

[36] Laurenti 16; also Asmis 2385.

[37] Plutarch, *Reply to Colotes* 1118C and Anna Angeli, "La critica Filodema all'e-
conomico di Senofonte," *CErc* 20 (1990) 39–51.

[38] Karin Lehmeier, who is working on a dissertation with Dieter Lührmann,
wrote a seminar paper (Nov. 1997) critiquing the interpretation of col. I that I had
given in Strassbourg (Aug. 1996). I appreciate her critique and incorporate it into
this paragraph, including her references to Xenophon.

οἶκον καὶ π[οι]εῖν οἰκεῖσθαι τὸν ἀλλότριον; I.11–17). Philodemus takes the second alternative to represent the common meaning of "household manager," one who works to increase property (αὔξειν τὸν οἶκον; Xenopon, *Oec.* I.4). He criticizes Xenophon for going beyond the common use of the term when he includes "what in a great and blessed way is beneficial." Household management concerns acquiring economic resources, not what benefits human domestic relationships.

Philodemus also criticizes both Xenophon and ps.-Theophrastus for the opinion that a wife is necessary for a happy life, an assertion Philodemus denies (II.8–12; IX.1–3). And both earlier philosophers, he says, include more on the subject of wealth than a philosopher needs.

In the second major section of the tractate, Philodemus takes up Epicurean ideas. The following section translates selected Metrodoran/Philodemian sentences from the beginning of this second section. Philodemus' work *On Household Management* is complex. For this article I choose to translate a short section at the beginning of the second major section of the tractate that refers to the earlier work *On Wealth*. This section contains the material which Sudhaus has argued has its source two centuries earlier in Metrodorus. The section also exhibits aspects of the Epicurean debate with the Cynics.

A. *Translation of Philodemus,* Concerning Household Management
XII.2–XVI.12; XXI.28–35; XXVII.42–47, XXVIII.3–5[39]

Now that the views concerning these people [Xenophon (Socrates) and ps.-Theophrastus] have been sufficiently indicated, one must sketch our doctrines in a concise fashion (col. XII.2–5). Accordingly, we will discuss, not how to live nobly in a household, but how one must take a stand regarding the acquisition and preservation of property, with which [the terms] "household management" and "household manager," it is agreed, are strictly concerned, although we do not continue to dispute in any way with those who choose to assign other [concerns] to these terms; and [how one must take a stand] regarding acquisition [of property] that is needed by the philosopher, not just by anybody (XII.5–17).

[39] I thank Stanley K. Stowers for early assistance. Then Ronald F. Hock translated all of cols. XII–XVI. I modified his translation, and Elizabeth Asmis suggested other changes. Their assistance, especially Hock's detailed translation, has been indispensable. I remain responsible for the final wording.

A philosopher has a [moderate] measure of wealth (πλούτου μέ[τρ]ον), a view which we have handed on in accord with our teachers in the book *On Wealth*, so that we might explain the management of the acquisition and preservation of this measure [of wealth]. (XII.17–25). Well then, in Metrodorus' book *On Wealth* this sort of thing is found on the topic in the argument against those who say fairly that Cynic philosophers have chosen a way of life that is much too frivolous and easy. [Cynics] as far as possible remove everything from themselves which does not provide a simple life that ends peacefully and especially without confusion and with the least anxiety and trouble—precisely what the one who merely gathers for himself daily (κ]αθ' η[μέραν) has (XII.25–41). For this also applies to a philosopher, but more than this is already entirely empty (κενόν; XII.41–43). Therefore he [Metrodorus] has written that it is acceptable to say that this life is the best, with which the greatest tranquility and peace as well as the least annoying worry are associated (XII.44–XIII.3).

This does not seem, however, to be the goal, if we should flee everything in relation to whose possession we might at some time have troubles or might be distressed (XIII.3–8). For many of these matters produce some distress (λύπας) when they are possessed, but many more distresses when they are not present (XIII.8–11). Therefore bodily health involves some care and laborious toil (πόνον), terrible distress [in body] nevertheless rather, whenever [health is] absent (XIII.11–15). Similarly the true friend also produces distress (λ[ύ]π[ας]) to some degree when present, but causes more distress when absent (XIII.15–19). In this manner, the earnest person is able to distinguish clearly many things into what is advantageous and disadvantageous and to choose some rather than others. [The earnest person] does this not courteously, not because he is able to live "nobly" [καλῶς (against Socrates; see XII.6–7)] and be in need of many things which, by not possessing, he will live miserably and lacking some he will be distressed (XIII.19–29).

Accordingly one must not flee everything by whose possession it is possible at some time to have troubles, worries and anxieties of such and such a kind, as I have said above (XIII.29–35; cp. XIII.3–8). One must accept some things, among which also is wealth, since one has less misery when it is present, rather for the whole of life but not (only) for some crisis (καιρό[ν]; XIII.35–39). It is not safe to use the same rule with regard to toil (κανόνι τῶι [π]όνους). Indeed, there are toils (πόνοι) for the one who provides for himself daily (καθ' ἡμέραν), and even the one with plenty will have some troubles ([ὀ]χλήσει[ς) at some time (XIII.39–44). Similarly, even for the one who has acquired a moderate amount, it is not just (δίκα[ιον) to reject it on account of such a [possible] change of fortune (XIII.44–XIV.2).

But one must consider this for the most part as contributing to the best way of life (XIV.2–5). Wealth does not seem to produce unprofitable annoyances by itself, but (only) through the evil (κακίαν) of those who use it (XIV.5–9). For the care and preservation [of wealth], as is fitting for one who is customarily in charge, sometimes produces trouble (ὄχλησιν), but not more than occurs with earning a living day by day (XIV.9–15). And even if it [wealth] [produces] more [trouble], it is not more than the others which set free from difficulties (XIV.15–17). If someone cannot show that natural wealth (ὁ φυσικὸς πλοῦτος) does not yield much greater revenues than the toils (πόνους) which derive from a life of little . . . (XIV.17–23).[40]

For I consider that wealth is rightly managed in this way: not to be grieved (λυ[πε]ῖσθαι) by what is lost nor on account of intemperate zeal in matters of profit and loss to be involved with "slave treadmills" by oneself (XIV.23–30). For toil (π[όν]ος) in acquisition involves both dragging oneself by force and being anxious over losses since they will immediately lead to present and expected pain (XIV.30–37). But if someone can remove such difficulties ([δ]υσχ-ηρείας) from himself and neither attempt to accumulate and to gain as much property as possible by toil nor even that authority which wealth provides, nor prepare to preserve money with difficulty (δ[υ]σχηρῶς) or to accumulate easily, the mode of life and readiness for acquisition would be precisely similar to sharing [with others] through it [wealth] (XIV.37–XV.3). For administering these things in this way follows on the fact that the wise person has acquired and is acquiring friends (XV.3–6). Besides, if[41] these things are not disposed in this manner, since, if these things are wasted, although others will not be found, much ease occurs regarding household management; otherwise,[42] for those requiring speech more than the many agonies in war (XV.6–14).

---

[40] The apodosis is not clear.
[41] Supplying ἄν as Jensen proposes in the apparatus.
[42] Again, from this point through XV.21 the translation follows Jensen's apparatus, but even then, the conclusion of the sentence is incomprehensible.

But if they cannot somehow fall into this manner of life since they are unable to have a single friend... (XV.14–21). For it is possible to say that such a person has easier daily acquisition, since he is relaxed in this way about the things said by one who has no money (XV.21–26). For we see that the property preserved by such men is not less than the property of intense people, but if not,[43] it is not thus quickly destroyed and not insecure property (XV.26–31).

Therefore a wise man will at no time be bound by wealth in such a way that he, for the sake of preserving it, endures great toils (πό[γ]ους) that are equivalent to nothing[44] (XV.31–37). For this must cause use [of a property] to be without pain and the delight through this use to be unalloyed, a delight which does not add to the acquisition of wealth an oppressive anxiety for wise men; how will it be possible to be preserved, even when the most perilous times (κ[αιρ]οί) prevail (XV.37–45)? For a person who is prudent and confident about the future is not distressed by a humble and penurious mode of life (ταπεινῆι καὶ πενιχρᾶι διαίτηι), since he knows that the physical [body] is provided for by this [mode of life];[45] and he inclines willingly to the more abundant [mode of life]. Nor is what is sufficient for him to be found to be evil (κ[α]κὸς), the one for whom life is moderate (μέτριός) and ordinary, and speech is healthy and true, even if he does not readily welcome any chance [life that happens to come along] (XV.44–XVI.12).

B. *Observations Concerning Philodemus, On Household Management*

The texts Vesuvius preserved for us in the Villa dei Papyri in Herculaneum are fragmentary, and several have been published in Italian journals. There has been an amazing renaissance of classical studies in Italy in the last decade or two, much of it related to exciting archaeological discoveries, including ongoing work in Pompeii

---

[43] This post-classical combination of particles (εἰ δὲ μή) is rare, and can be added to the examples listed by Margaret E. Thrall, *Greek Particles in the New Testament: Linguistic and Exegetical Studies* (Grand Rapids: Eerdmans, 1962) 9–10.

[44] This translation leaves out πλῆθος.

[45] Karin Lehmeier, "Gemeinschaft nach dem ΟΙΚΟΣ-Modell: Philodem und Paulus im Vergleich," in *Text und Geschichte: Facetten theologischen Arbeitens aus dem Freundes- und Schulerkreis. Dieter Lührmann zum 60. Geburtstag*, ed. S. Maser and E. Schlarb (Marburg: N. G. Elwert, 1999) 107–21, 119 compares Paul at Phil. 4:12.

and Herculaneum.[46] In one bookstore in Rome, I recently counted fourteen *series* of Greek and Latin texts, most with introductions, translations, notes, and bibliography.[47] Philodemus' "On Wealth" is an example of an exciting text that northern European and American scholars have ignored.

At the very least, Philodemus' two treatises *On Wealth* and *On Household Management* show that there was significant conflict both among Epicureans and between Epicureans and Cynics with respect to both the definition of the terms πτωχός (mendicant), πενία (indigent), and πλοῦτος (wealth), and over their evaluation as good (ἀγαθός) or evil (κακός).

The shift from wandering ascetics in the Jesus movement to early Christian households[48] in Jerusalem and Corinth was more than sociological. This change of social location also crossed boundaries that had been philosophically debated and defined, polemically attacked, and apologetically defended by Epicureans and Cynics for three centuries.

Reading these two tractates means further that Jesus' blessing of mendicants belongs within a centuries-old mutual polemic between Epicureans and Cynics, an opposition as old as Epicurus/Metrodorus and Diogenes of Sinope.[49] Hans Dieter Betz observes that the Matthean

---

[46] On the social and religious function of houses in these cities, see Carolyn Osiek and David L. Balch, *Families in the New Testament World: Households and House Churches* (Louisville, KY: Westminster/John Knox, 1997) chap. 1.

[47] The most important of these are the critical editions in the series Lorenzo Valle (Milan: Arnoldo Mondadori); the most extensive series is I Classici della BUR (Biblioteca Universale Rizzoli [Milan: Rizzoli]), most of them published or revised within the last decade.

[48] See Gerd Theissen, *Sociology of Early Palestinian Christianity* (Philadelphia: Fortress, 1977) chaps. 2–3; Malherbe, *Social Aspects of Early Christianity*, 2nd ed. (Philadelphia: Fortress, 1983); Wayne A. Meeks, *The First Urban Christians: The Social World of the Apostle Paul* (New Haven: Yale University Press, 1983) chap. 1; and Luise Schottroff, *Lydia's Impatient Sisters: A Feminist Social History of Early Christianity* (Louisville KY: Westminister/John Knox, 1995), esp. chap. 1.

[49] For a survey of the current discussion see F. Gerald Downing, *Cynics and Christian Origins* (Edinburgh: T & T Clark, 1992). For a critique of Downing, Burton L. Mack, and Eric Leif Vaage, see Hans Dieter Betz, "Jesus and the Cynics: Survey and Analysis of a Hypothesis," *Journal of Religion* 74:4 (1994) 453–75. In various ways those three writers appeal to a "Hellenistic Galilee" which somehow removed Jesus from Judaism, an idea that has a hideous history in Germany earlier in our century. The Pharisees in Jerusalem and Philo in Alexandria were also hellenized, but not therefore less Jewish. For the German Christian appeal to a hellenistic Galilee, see Susannah Heschel, "Theologen für Hitler: Walter Grundmann und das

(5:3) "blessed are the poor *in (the) spirit*," "presupposes reflection and
debate about what Jesus may have meant when he called the poor
blessed."[50] This is a debate that is then, I observe, a later parallel
to the internal Epicurean debate about what Epicurus meant when
he sometimes said that poverty (πενία) is evil, but other times expressed
a different opinion, that poverty is good (Philodemus, *On Wealth*
XLV.15–40 and XLVII.9–11). In contrast to modern assumptions,
"no one [of these thinkers] *dares* to say that the possession of few
things is an evil" (XLVI.30–34). But against the Cynics, Epicureans
defined πτωχός (mendicancy) and homelessness as evil. Both Epicurus'
sayings and Luke's version of the Beatitudes (Luke 6:20–26) juxta-
pose the rich and the poor as good and evil, blessed and cursed,
unlike the Beatitudes as they appear in Matthew (Matt. 5:3–11).

Betz observes, "Indeed, praising the condition of poverty as such
would hardly be conceivable in antiquity, unless it were done as an
act of folly or cynicism."[51] Antisthenes and Xenophon's Socrates,
however, did praise their mendicant life style,[52] and this is precisely
the heated debate between Epicureans and Cynics (with a capital C)
in the two tractates discussed above. With regard to this ancient dispute, Jesus blesses Cynic mendicancy and lives that life style (cf.
Matt. 8:20//Luke 9:58), with or without knowing that the alterna-
tives had philosophical labels and arguments. Betz mistakenly concludes that "while one must take material deprivation seriously, such
conditions as such cannot be the reason for the blessing," assuming
rather that the Sermon on the Mount "has in mind a topos . . .
which addresses the general human condition."[53] Both Epicurus and

---

'Institut zur Erforschung und Beseitigung des jüdischen Einflusses auf das deutsche
kirchliche Leben,'" in *Christlicher Antijudaismus und Antisemitismus: Theologische und kirchliche Programme Deutscher Christen*, ed. Leonore Siegele-Wenschkewitz (Frankfurt: Haag,
1994) 125–70, 154–55; more briefly, S. Heschel, "Nazifying Christian Theology:
Walter Grundmann and the Institute for the Study and Eradication of Jewish
Influence on German Christian Life," *Church History* 63:4 (1994) 587–605. For one
rejection of the thesis of a Cynic Jesus see James Robinson, "The History-of-Religions
Taxonomy of Q: The Cynic Hypothesis," *Gnosisforschung und Religionsgeschichte: Festschrift
für Kurt Rudolph zum 65. Geburtstag*, eds. Holger Preissler and Hubert Seiwert (Marburg:
Diagonal, 1994) 247–65.
  [50] Betz, *Sermon on the Mount*, 113, n. 7.
  [51] Ibid. 114.
  [52] See nn. 23, 33–35 above, including Xenophon, *Mem.* 1.5–6, cited by Betz,
Sermon on the Mount 117, n. 184.
  [53] Betz, *Sermon on the Mount*, 114.

Metrodorus on the one hand and Diogenes on the other understood the human condition. For example, Diogenes wrote works on death and on love (Diog. Laert. 6.80), as did Epicurus (Diog. Laert. 10.27). Nevertheless, Epicurus, Metrodorus, and Philodemus repudiated mendicancy, and the last lived in the villa of his wealthy patron. Socrates and Diogenes repudiated wealth and Diogenes was homeless. Diogenes' wealthy follower Crates sold his lands and gave away the proceeds to his fellow citizens (cp. Mark 10:29//Matt. 19:29//Luke 18:29).[54] He and his wife Hipparchia lived and slept together in public places.[55] Neither Epicurus, Metrodorus, nor Diogenes in their debates, nor Jesus in the first beatitude describes "*la condition humaine* as one of poverty, desertion, and misery."[56] The "humility" which is parallel to poverty is also a social/economic condition, not primarily an "intellectual insight."[57] Diogenes' pupil Monimus does value Socrates' saying "know thyself," but as a "dusty mendicant" (Diog. Laert. 6.83). Socrates takes "pride" in not having a penny (Xenophon, *Sym.* 3.8), but Philodemus writes about "living well," preferably with wealth (*On Household Management* I.5–8; XVI.5–6).

Betz focuses on πτωχός as a metaphor, which would mean that those living inside the wealthy Piso's estate were just as "poor" as homeless Cynics living without an *obol*, an interpretation which makes the mutual polemics between Epicureans and Cynics, their repudiation of each others' economic life styles, irrelevant. Betz's interpretation makes wealth harmless, not an issue, which is not a neutral

---

[54] Long, "The Socratic Tradition," in Branham and Goulet-Cazé 42, citing Gabriele Giannantoni, *Socratis et Socraticorum Reliquiae*, Elenchos 18 (Naples: Biblopolis, 1990) 2:524–28, 540, who cites Diog. Laert. 6.87–88; Origen, *Comm. in Matth.* 15.15; Plutarch, *Can Vice Cause Unhappiness?* (499D); Teles IVA: *A Comparison of Poverty and Wealth* (38, 40, 44 O'Neil).

[55] Branham and Goulet-Cazé 10; Long, "The Socratic Tradition" in Branham and Goulet-Cazé 42–45. Giannantoni 2:531, 533 cites Musonius, Or. 14: Is Marriage a Handicap for the Pursuit of Philosophy?, Sextus Empiricus, Outlines of Pyrrhonism 1.14.153: Diog. Laert. 6.93.

[56] Betz, *Sermon on the Mount* 114–15.

[57] Pace Betz, *Sermon on the Mount* 115–16; cp. the use of the adjective ταπεινός ("humble") by Philodemus, *On Household Management* XVI.2 to refer to *economic* poverty. I discuss urban conflict between rich and poor, proud and humble social groups narrated by the historian Dionysius of Halicarnassus in "Rich and Poor, Proud and Humble in Luke-Acts," *The Social World of the First Christians: Essays in Honor of Wayne A. Meeks*, eds. L. Michael White and O. Larry Yarbrough (Minneapolis: Fortress, 1995) 214–33 and in "Political Friendship in the Historian Dionysius of Halicarnassus, *Roman Antiquities*," in *Greco-Roman Perspective on Friendship*, ed. John T. Fitzgerald (Atlanta: Scholars, 1997) 123–44.

thesis in a modern world society where capitalism has won, where
there is conflict between first and two-thirds world countries. On the
contrary, for Jesus those who are financially wealthy are in mortal
danger (Luke 16:19–31; v. 20 on the mendicant Lazarus). The offense
of Jesus' (and Luke's) challenge cannot be made palatable in Western,
profit-oriented societies.[58]

As a theologian I observe that I and most of Jesus' contemporary
North American and European middle-class followers agree with
Philodemus: it is better to live in a house where health and friend-
ships are more easily maintained, far better than trying to find food
daily whether we are young or old. The difficulty with these obvious assumptions is that Jesus has blessed not us, but those who have
no house, nothing at all (Matt. 5:3, par. Luke 6:20; Matt. 11:5 par.
Luke 7:22; Luke 14:13; Luke 16:20; Mark 10:21 par. Matt. 19:21
par. Luke 18:22). There is no quick solution to the contradiction,
but at a minimum, must not those who are professed followers of
the mendicant Jesus at least be in conversation with those who have
nothing, whether they live in the first or in the two-thirds world?[59]

---

[58] See Ernst Käsemann, "Was ich als deutscher Theologe in fünfig Jahren ver-
lernte [What I Unlearned in Fifty Years as a German Theologian]" in *Kirchlichte
Konflikte* (Göttingen: Vandenhoeck & Ruprecht, 1982) 1.233–44, at 243: "I unlearned
spiritualizing the beatitudes of the Sermon on the Mount. They promise God's kingdom, whose earthly inbreaking exhibits signs and wonders, healing and freedom
from demonic possession. They reclaim God's earth not only from our egotism, our
lethargic hearts and hypocrisy, but also from the tyranny of the enslaving powers.
Every one of us is called into service and given corresponding gifts. Insofar, I am
no longer satisfied with the Augsburg Confession (Article 7); the visible church is
known by the preaching of the gospel and the evangelical administration of the
sacraments, but also by the presence of the poor, with whose blessing Jesus' list of
deeds ends (Matthew 11:6)" (my translation). Gadara, the city where Philodemus
was born and educated, is mentioned in the gospels; the whole town begged Jesus
to leave after he exorcised two demoniacs (Matt. 8:28–34).

[59] For discussion of the relationship between the wealth of the first world and
the poverty of the two-thirds world, see the classic by Frantz Fanon, *The Wretched
of the Earth*, with an introduction by Jean-Paul Sartre (New York: Grove, 1963).

CICERO, PHILODEMUS, AND THE DEVELOPMENT OF LATE HELLENISTIC RHETORICAL THEORY

Robert N. Gaines

Abstract

Philodemus' *On Rhetoric* reflects theoretical tendencies that arose significantly after the beginning of the first century B.C.E. Particularly, along
with Cicero in his *De oratore* and *Orator*, Philodemus addresses the artistic status of rhetoric with a complicated conception of art (τέχνη). In
the process, he emphasizes presentational parts of rhetoric over substantive parts, divides his rhetorical genera into two sets, using the aim
of practical persuasion as a criterion, and makes rhetoric dependent
upon other disciplines for its successful practice. Consistent with these
findings, there can be no doubt that Philodemus was an active participant in the developments that shaped late Hellenistic rhetorical theory.

For a long time the standard view has been that the Epicureans in
general and Philodemus in particular contributed nothing of significance
to the development of rhetorical theory.[1] And there are certain inherent obstacles to any attempt to combat this view. For one thing, we
have little, if any, evidence that our chief source for Epicurean rhetorical thought, Philodemus' *On Rhetoric*,[2] exerted any influence on theories

---

[1] For ancient reflections of the view, see Dion. Hal. *Comp.* 24 and Quint. *Inst.*
2.17.15, 12.2.24; the contemporary view is represented in John L. Stocks, *New
Chapters in the History of Greek Literature* (Oxford: Clarendon, 1921), 22–23, and "Two
Books on Philodemus," *CR* 38 (1924): 32, Wilhelm Kroll, "Rhetorik," *RE*, Suppl.
7, 1083–84, George Kennedy, *The Art of Persuasion in Greece* (Princeton: Princeton
University Press, 1963), 301, and Elizabeth Rawson, *Intellectual Life in the Late Roman
Republic* (Baltimore: Johns Hopkins University Press, 1985), 143, 45–46.

[2] The most recent attempt to reconstruct the text of Phld. *Rhet.* is by Tiziano
Dorandi, "Per una ricomposizione dello scritto di Filodemo sulla Retorica," *ZPE*
82 (1990): 59–87. The best available texts for books of the work are currently as
follows: Bks. 1–2, Francesca Longo Auricchio, ed., Φιλοδήμου Περὶ ῥητορικῆς, *Libros
primum et secundum*, Ricerche sui Papiri Ercolanesi 3 (Naples: Giannini editore, 1977);
book 3, Siegfried Sudhaus, *Philodemi Volumina Rhetorica*, 2 vols. and suppl. (Leipzig:
B. G. Teubner, 1892–96): 2:196–239, and Jürgen Hammerstaedt, "Der Schlußteil
von Philodems drittem Buch über Rhetorik," *CErc* 22 (1992): 9–117 [= Sudhaus
2:139–72]; book 4, Sudhaus 1:147–225; book 5 (?), Sudhaus 1:270–89 and 2:1–64
[= 1:289–325]; book 6 (?), Sudhaus 1:325–85 and Maria Giustina Cappelluzzo,

subsequent to its composition in the mid-first century B.C.E.[3] Moreover, those indications we do have about the intellectual connections of *On Rhetoric* seem to suggest that the work constituted a kind of anachronism, engaging in controversies from previous centuries and attacking opponents whose time of life had long since passed.[4] Given these obstacles, we should hardly wonder that our libraries are not crowded with tributes to the significance of Philodemus' *On Rhetoric*.

Nonetheless, I think it may be insisted that sources and influences are not the only measures of significance for a theoretical work. Accordingly, in this essay I would like to pursue a brief investigation along different lines. In particular, given the conception and treatment of rhetoric that is evident in Philodemus' work on this subject, I shall attempt to show that, whatever else may be true of him, Philodemus was an active participant in the developments that shaped late Hellenistic rhetorical theory. My argument in this connection will be developed in three parts. Within the first I shall very generally sketch the status of rhetorical theory at the turn of the first century B.C.E. Within the second I shall outline the sorts of advancements that appear to represent development in rhetorical theory around the mid-first century B.C.E. Finally, within the third part of my argument, I shall illustrate how Philodemus' *On Rhetoric* exemplifies the sorts of theoretical innovations that were current in his day.

"Per una nuova edizione di un libro della Retorica Filodemea (PHerc. 1004)," *CErc* 6 (1976): 69–76; book 7 (?), Matilde Ferrario, "Frammenti del V libro della 'Retorica' di Filodemo (PHerc. 1669)," *CErc* 10 (1980): 55–124 [= Sudhaus 1:225–28], Sudhaus 1:228–70, Matilde Ferrario, "Verso una nuova edizione del quinto libro della 'Retorica' di Filodemo," *CErc* 4 (1974): 93–96, "Per una nuova edizione del quinto libro della 'Retorica' di Filodemo," *Proceedings of the XVIII International Congress of Papyrology: Athens, 25–31 May 1986*, ed. Vasileios G. Mandelaras, 2 vols. (Athens: Greek Papyrological Society, 1988), 1:167–84, and Sudhaus 2:131–67; cf. Dirk Obbink, "The Books from Herculaneum: A Guide to Editions and Translations," in Gigante, *Philodemus in Italy: The Books from Herculaneum*, trans. Dirk Obbink (Ann Arbor: University of Michigan Press, 1995), 116–17.

[3] See Appendix.

[4] See for example, Stocks, *New Chapters* 23, and "Two Books" 32, Rawson, *Intellectual Life* 144–46. Marcello Gigante places Philodemus' backward-looking tendencies in a favorable light by interpreting *On Rhetoric* as "opera di storiografia letteraria" (*Filodemo in Italia*, Bibliotechina del saggiatore, 49 [Florence: Felice Le Monnier, 1990] 45; cf. 38, 39 = *Philodemus in Italy* 36; cf. 30, 31).

Rhetoric at the Turn of the First Century B.C.E.

At the turn of the first century B.C.E., rhetorical theory was characterized by widespread agreement concerning the nature of rhetoric,
its constituent parts, the kinds of rhetorical discourse, and the relation of rhetoric to other disciplines.[5] This much is clear from con-
certed attempts to portray the status of rhetoric at the time, for
example, in Cicero's *De oratore* and Quintilian's *Institutio oratoria*.[6] But
such agreement is equally clear from the extant rhetorics that represent early first-century thinking—and I mean here not just the
school rhetorics contained in Cicero's *De inventione* and the *Rhetorica
ad Herennium*, but also the Academic rhetoric preserved by Cicero in
his *De partitione oratoria*.[7]

Within each of these treatises, rhetoric, in its nature, is conceived
as an art. And we may take it from all the treatises that the artistic
status of rhetoric was understood as a settled matter. For none of
the treatises actually argues that rhetoric is an art, rather each assumes

[5] Cf. George Kennedy, *The Art of Rhetoric in the Roman World* (Princeton: Princeton
University Press, 1972), 114–26 (hereafter *RRW*).

[6] *De or.* 1.145 (rhetoric as art), 1.142 (five parts), 1.141 (three kinds of rhetorical
discourse), 1.42–44, 46, 85–86, 145 (little relation of rhetoric to other disciplines);
Inst. 2.17.2 (rhetoric as art), 3.3.1 (five parts), 3.3.14–4.1, 4.12–16 (three kinds of
rhetorical discourse), 1.pr.11–17 (little relation of rhetoric to other disciplines).

[7] On the preceptive nature of *De inventione* and *Rhetorica ad Herennium*, see, e.g.,
Kennedy, *RRW* 103–48. The date of *De inventione* very likely falls between 91 and
88 B.C.E. Kennedy, *RRW*, 107–10; cf. Harry M. Hubbell, ed. and trans. *De Inventione,
De optimo genere oratorum, Topica*, by Cicero (Cambridge: Cambridge University Press,
1949), xii. But dates between 85 and 80 have also been suggested; cf. Guy Achard,
ed. and trans., *Cicéron De l'invention* (Paris: Société D'Édition «Les Belles Lettres»,
1994), 6–10, Anton Daniel Leeman, *Orationis Ratio: The Stylistic Theories and Practice
of the Roman Orators, Historians and Philosophers*, 2 vols. (Amsterdam: Adolf M. Hakkert,
1963), 1:92 and Wilhelm Kroll, "M. Tullius Cicero (Rhetorische Schriften)," *RE*,
Neue Bearbeitung (1939): 1093. *Rhetorica ad Herennium* seems to be a work of the
early to middle 80's; cf. Gualtiero Calboli, ed. and comm., *Cornifici Rhetorica ad C.
Herennium*, 2nd ed. (Bologna: Pàtron, 1993), 12–17, Kennedy, *RRW* 113, Leeman,
Ratio 1:25. Dates into the 70's and even the 50's have been entertained, cf. M. I.
Henderson, "The Process 'de repetundis,'" *JRS* 41 (1951): 73 n. 18 (*terminus ante
quem* 75), A. E. Douglas, "Clausulae in the *Rhetorica ad Herennium* as Evidence of its
Date," *CQ* n.s. 10 (1960): 65–78 (c. 50). The composition of *De partitione oratoria*
probably falls during the years 54–52; cf. Brady B. Gilleland, "The Date of Cicero's
Partitiones Oratoriae," *CP* 56 (1961): 29–32; followed by Kennedy, *RRW* 229, and
Leeman, *Ratio* 1:92. On the Academic basis and general nature of *De partitione oratoria*, see Anton D. Leeman, Harm Pinkster, and Jakob Wisse, *M. Tullius Cicero, De
oratore libri III: Kommentar*, vol. 4 (Heidelberg: Universitätsverlag C. Winter, 1996),
99; cf. Wilhelm Kroll, "Rhetorik," 1088–89, "Cicero," 1102–03.

without question that rhetoric holds this status. In fact, *De inventione* unambiguously applies the term *"ars"* to the theory of speaking no less than twenty-six times.[8] Likewise, *"ars"* is used in quite the same way thirty-seven times in *Rhetorica ad Herennium* and three times in *De partitione*.[9] Accordingly, our evidence is that turn-of-the-century rhetoricians felt a confident consensus that rhetoric was an art.

In conceiving the parts of rhetoric, our treatises also generally agree. *De inventione* and *Rhetorica ad Herennium* are nearly identical; both divide rhetoric into invention, arrangement, style, memory, and delivery, and both offer their main advice about speech parts and issues of dispute under the rubric of invention.[10] *De partitione* organizes its conceptual elements somewhat otherwise—dividing rhetoric into the power of the orator, the speech, and the question (including issues of dispute).[11] But its differences from the others are largely cosmetic, since it treats the power of the orator in regard to invention, arrangement, style, memory, and delivery and shows that the principles in other segments of the treatise relate closely to these powers.[12] Yet, however it is that we estimate their differences, the

---

[8] *Inv. rhet.* 1.5 (2), 1.7 (6), 1.8 (4), 1.9 (5), 1.16, 1.50; 2.4, 2.5, 2.6, 2.7, 2.8 (2), 2.11.

[9] *Rhet. Her.* 1.1 (2), 1.3 (2), 1.16; 2.1, 2.7; 3.1, 3.16 (3), 3.17; 4.1 (2), 4.3 (3), 4.4, 4.6 (5), 4.7 (3), 4.8 (4), 4.10 (5), 4.69 (2); *Part. or.* 48, 137, 139.

[10] On the structure of this treatise, see Karl Barwick, "Die Gliederung der rhetorischen τέχνη und die horazische Epistula ad Pisones," *Hermes* 57 (1922) 2–7, Kroll, "Rhetorik," 1098, Friedrich Solmsen, "The Aristotelian Tradition in Ancient Rhetoric," *AJP* 62 (1941): 48–49, Dieter Matthes, "Hermagoras von Temnos 1904–55," *Lustrum* 3 (1958): 109, 115–17, Robert N. Gaines, "On the Rhetorical Significance of *P. Hamb.* 131," *Rhetorica* 7 (1989): 336–37.

[11] *Part. or.* 3. Augustus S. Wilkins, ed., *Brutus, Orator, De optimo genere oratorum, Partitiones oratoriae, Topica*, vol. 2 of *M. Tulli Ciceronis Rhetorica* (Oxford: Clarendon, 1903): C. Quot in partis tribuenda est omnis doctrina dicendi? P. Tris. C. Cedo quas? P. Primum in ipsam vim oratoris, deinde in orationem, tum in quaestionem. ("C. Jun.: Into how many parts ought the theory of rhetoric as a whole be divided? C. Sen.: Three. C. Jun.: Pray tell me what they are. C. Sen.: First, the speaker's personal resources, second the speech, and third the question." Harris Rackham, trans., *De oratore, book III, De fato, Paradoxa Stoicorum, De partitione oratoria*, LCL (Cambridge: Harvard University Press, 1942). The divisions are treated within *Part. or.* as follows: the power of the orator, 3, 5–26; the speech, 4, 27–60; the question, 4, 61–138 (unlimited issues of dispute, 61–68; limited issues of dispute or kinds of causes [= genera], 68–138). Regarding this unusual treatise structure, see Barwick, "Gliederung," 2, Kroll, "Rhetorik," 1098, Solmsen, "Tradition," 50, and Gaines, "Significance," 336.

[12] Although Cicero initially identifies the resources of the speaker as things and words, he quickly turns to speaker functions as the means of analysis to be used in actually explicating the power of the speaker (*Part. or.* 3 [initial analysis of speaker functions], 5–8 [invention], 9–15 [arrangement], 16–24 [style], 25 [delivery], 26 [memory]). On the relations of speaker functions to materials handled under the

three treatises stand in complete agreement on what aspects of rhetoric are most deserving of extended attention. For one thing, *De inventione* and *Rhetorica ad Herennium* state that invention is the most important part of rhetoric (*Inv. rhet.* 1.9; *Rhet. Her.* 2.1). Moreover, in all three treatises, discussion related to the finding of speech materials significantly overshadows treatment of other constituents of the art. As is well known, *De inventione*, which was originally designed to handle the whole of rhetoric, leaves off with the completion of invention alone.[13] So too, *Rhetorica ad Herennium* devotes 48 percent of its space to invention (1.3–3.15 = 89 sections), 37 percent to style (4.1–69 = 69 sections), and 13 percent to the rest (3.16–40 = 25 sections). Finally, *De partitione* devotes 59 percent of its space to finding speech materials (5–8, 61–138 = 82 sections) allocating 29 percent to organizing speech materials (9–15, 27–60 = 41 sections) and only 8 percent to all other elements of rhetoric combined (16–26 = 11 sections).

As for the kinds of rhetorical discourse, our three treatises exhibit a similar level of agreement. *De inventione* and *Rhetorica ad Herennium* are again essentially identical; both recognize exactly three types of rhetorical discourse, namely, those on demonstrative, deliberative, and judicial matters, all of which relate to particular persons and circumstances (*Inv. rhet.* 1.7, *Rhet. Her.* 1.2). Of course, this sort of analysis was inherited from Aristotle and represents a self-conscious movement away from the scheme of Hermagoras, who, in the previous century, had allocated to rhetoric the treatment of matters both limited and not limited to particular persons and circumstances (*Inv. rhet.* 1.8). Particularly in this connection, *De partitione* differs slightly from the other two treatises. For *De partitione* contemplates the rhetorical treatment of unlimited matters, and these of theoretical and practical forms (62–67); still, alongside this treatment of unlimited matters, its conceptualization of limited matters leads to a three-fold account of discursive types: laudatory (which is identical to demonstrative, 69–82), deliberative (83–97), and judicial (98–138). Despite their differences, then, the three treatises may be said to be in unison insofar as all identify, and offer theoretical principles for, exactly three kinds of discourse on limited matters.

---

speech and the question, see, e.g., *Part. or.* 9 (arrangement related to limited and unlimited questions), 9–15 (arrangement related to kinds of causes and speech parts), 68 (unlimited issues of dispute related to invention and arrangement).
[13] Cf. Kroll, "Cicero," 1091–92, Achard, *De l'invention* 5.

Now, on the relation of rhetoric to the other disciplines, it seems
fair to say that with some variation, all our treatises conceive of
rhetoric as largely independent. *Rhetorica ad Herennium* makes this independence fairly explicit. Here the study of rhetoric is twice distinguished from philosophy (1.1, 4.69) and the author makes clear that
the only things a speaker needs for rhetorical mastery are principles
of the art, imitation, and practice (1.1, 1.3, 4.69). Matters are slightly
more complicated in *De inventione*. In this work Cicero declares that
practice of oratory apart from moral study is folly, yet he makes
clear that the admonition is necessary since one can acquire eloquence without such study (1.1). Similarly, he insists that rhetoric is
an essential part of political science, yet he indicates that possession of rhetoric does not include mastery of the whole of political
science (1.6). Again, he observes that the principles of argument
exploited by speakers comprise a part of philosophical logic, but he
is quick to note that the whole of philosophical logic is quite unsuit-
able for speakers (1.33, 77, 86).[14] Accordingly, the overall impres-
sion we get is that while there is a moral requirement for the speaker
as citizen and while rhetoric shares certain principles with political
and logical science, nevertheless, mastery of the rhetorical art *per se*
requires knowledge of the rules of rhetoric and little else. The case
of *De partitione* is somewhat special, in that the work is apparently
the self-conscious product of a philosophical school. Consistent with
our expectations in a work of this sort, we find the admonition that
the divisions of oratory may not be discovered, understood, or used
apart from the instruction of the Academy (139). The reason for
this, as Cicero explains, is that the principles of rhetorical argumentation are shared with dialectic in a broad "art of subtle discussion and copious speaking;" not only that, but a speaker would
be hard pressed to speak with facility about what is good, bad, right,
wrong, useful, useless, moral or immoral without possession of the
moral arts (139). Still, even here a marked degree of independence
is to be recognized. For apart from logic and morals, no other arts
are required of the speaker. And it seems significant that as a kind
of conclusion to the matter, Cicero observes in setting out all the
divisions of oratory, that he has only pointed out the arts apart from

---

[14] Cf. Kennedy, *RRW* 135–38; but in my view Kennedy overestimates the force
of philosophy in Cicero's early rhetorical theory.

rhetoric, suggesting their mastery is something beyond and quite separable from what is required of the speaker (140).

To conclude, then, rhetorical theory around the turn of the first century was marked by general agreements: first, that rhetoric was an art, plain and simple; second, that rhetoric was usefully conceived as containing five parts or powers, among which invention was the most important; third, that rhetoric properly recognized and provided principles for exactly three kinds of speaking on limited matters; and fourth, that mastery of the rhetorical art was independent—or nearly independent—of all the other arts.

Developments in First Century Rhetoric

In regard to these conclusions, I would now like to examine certain of the developments in rhetorical theory which may be noted beginning around the mid-first century B.C.E., particularly those which arise in the mature works of Cicero, namely *De oratore* and *Orator*.[15] I believe that these works are particularly useful in this connection, not only because Cicero's later rhetorics were subsequently recognized as innovative,[16] but because Cicero himself characterized the works as advancements over his own and other theories.[17] Certainly, no one in the first century B.C.E. was better qualified to make such a judgment. Accordingly, in what follows I shall briefly address myself respectively to Cicero's considered views of the artistic status of rhetoric, the parts of rhetoric and their importance, the number and significance of rhetorical genera, and finally the disciplinary relations of rhetoric.

On the problem of whether rhetoric is an art, Cicero's most deliberate view is presented in *De oratore*.[18] Within this work, he treats the problem twice, once in the voice of Crassus (1.99–110) and once in

---

[15] From *Att.* 4.13.2 it is clear that *De or.* was certainly concluded by mid-November of 55; see Leeman and Pinkster, *M. Tullii Cicero, De oratore libri III: Kommentar*, vol. 1 (Heidelberg: Universitätsverlag C. Winter, 1981), 17–21. *Or.* may be dated with some certainty in the latter part of 46; cf. Otto Jahn and Wilhelm Kroll, ed. and comm., *M. Tullii Ciceronis Orator* (Berlin: Weidmann, 1913), 1; Robert Philippson, "M. Tullius Cicero (Philosophische Schriften)," *RE*, Neue Bearbeitung, 1123, 1126.

[16] Cf. Quint. *Inst.* 1.6.18, 3.1.20, 3.6.60 and Tac. *Dial.* 30–32.

[17] For example, in *De or.*, Cicero comments on the superiority of his treatment over *Inv. rhet.* (1.5), Greek rhetorical treatises (1.23), and other writers *de ratione dicendi* (2.11); likewise, in *Orat.*, he stresses his originality in handling prose rhythm (174).

[18] At *Orat.* 113, 122, 145, 147, and 162, Cicero assumes the artistic status of rhetoric and its elements; cf. *Brut.* 25–26, 69, 151, 291.

the voice of Antonius (2.29–33). The upshot of these treatments is that while rhetoric is not an art, if art requires exact knowledge, nonetheless it may be considered an art, if judged by popular opinion or the pragmatic standard, since these require only possession of methods useful for practice (1.107–109, 2.32–33). Cicero's handling of the art problem is easy to underestimate, I think, because it exploits elements that were already known in his day.[19] What such an estimation ignores is the complication generated in Cicero's solution. He is not simply saying that rhetoric is an art, provided you apply the proper definition; rather, when confronted with the question, "Is rhetoric an art?," he answers, "No and yes, for there are two levels of arts." This complication helps not only to explain the nature of rhetoric, but also to elaborate the dispute which had surrounded rhetoric since at least the time of Plato.[20]

In connection with the parts of rhetoric, Cicero's position evolved gradually; in fact, definite stages in his departure from the "standard view" may be noted in *De oratore* and *Orator*. In *De oratore*, books 2 and 3, one of Cicero's admitted objectives was to present a τεχνολογία concerning the art of speaking.[21] In the pursuit of this objective, he gives treatment to all five of the usual parts of rhetoric. Invention, combined with arrangement, comes in for the lengthiest treatment with 251 sections (2.99–349), style takes second place with 194 sections (3.19–212), while delivery and memory occupy a total of only 33 sections (2.350–67, 3.213–227). All of this seems fairly typical. But there are indications that Cicero does not entirely adopt the

---

[19] Cf. Leeman and Pinkster, *De or. Komm.* 1:190–94.

[20] I have argued elsewhere that one of Cicero's aims in *De oratore* is to join in the dispute with philosophy over the artistic status, scope, and utility of rhetoric ("Cicero's Response to the Philosophers in *De Oratore*, book 1," *Rhetoric and Pedagogy: Its History, Philosophy, and Practice: Essays in Honor of James J. Murphy*, ed. Winifred Bryan Horner and Michael Leff [Mahwah, NJ: Lawrence Erlbaum Associates, 1995], 43–56). On the nature and development of the dispute up to the time of Cicero, see Siegfried Sudhaus and Ludwig Radermacher, "Critolaus und die Rhetorik," *Phld. Rh.*, Suppl. (1895) V–XLII; Hans von Arnim, *Leben und Werke des Dio von Prusa. Mit einer Einleitung: Sophistik, Rhetorik, Philosophie in ihrem Kampf um die Jugendbildung* (Berlin: Weidmann, 1898), 87–114; Harry M. Hubbell, *The Rhetorica of Philodemus*, *Transactions of the Connecticut Academy of Arts and Sciences* 23 (1920): 364–82; Ferrario, "Frammenti del PHerc. 1669," 59–64; Jonathan Barnes, "Is Rhetoric an Art?" *D[iscourse] A[nalysis] R[esearch] G[roup] Newsletter* 2 (1986): 2–22; Brian Vickers, *In Defence of Rhetoric* (Oxford: Clarendon, 1988), 83–178.

[21] *Att.* 4.16.3; on this point, see Leeman, "The Structure of Cicero's *De oratore* I," *Ciceroniana: Hommages à Kazimierz Kumaniecki*, eds. Alain Michel and Raoul Verdière (Leiden: Brill, 1975), 140; *Ratio* 1:118.

standard view. First, it may be noted that the discussant entrusted with invention, Antonius, takes a cavalier view of the traditional mechanics of this part of the art, namely the analysis of disputable issues (or *status*) and the investigation of topics. Actually, he says, if one understands the case, the issue in dispute comes readily to mind (2.104). Likewise, the topics of argument, while certainly important, need not detain him long in presentation, since once they have been simply indicated, it is not art that is required for their application, but simply a moderate talent in the speaker (2.175). Second, Antonius nearly dismisses the importance of the subjects he treats—invention, arrangement, and memory, insofar as these compare with the subjects which fall to Crassus, style and delivery—"for if you wish for me to speak truly," he says, "I leave everything to you [Crassus]" (2.351). Finally, it seems quite significant that throughout *De oratore*, Crassus, Cicero's representative for the doctrine of style, frequently repeats the argument that while the speaker shares the material of discourse with the other arts, it is an eloquent expression that constitutes the peculiar property of the speaker (1.49, 50, 51, 54, 57; 3.143).

By the time of his composition of *Orator*, Cicero's break with the standard view was complete. Here he characterizes the parts of rhetoric as invention, arrangement, style, and delivery (54). But the omission of memory is hardly his most significant innovation. For when he provides accounts of invention and arrangement, he makes it quite obvious that he no longer holds these in their former esteem. Invention and arrangement are to be treated briefly, he says, because they are notable not so much for the highest praise as for their being unavoidable (44). And despite their absolute importance, when compared with expression, they offer less scope for art and effort (51). Accordingly, in this work Cicero dispenses with invention and arrangement in 8 sections (43–50); and afterwards, he devotes six sections to delivery (55–60) and 180 to style (51–54, 61–236). Admittedly, the proportions of treatment in *Orator* are to some extent distorted by the task which Cicero sets for himself in the work, namely to describe the style of the ideal orator (2–3, 54). Still, as Cicero's explicit comments make indisputable, the order of importance ascribed to the parts of rhetoric is significantly different from that which we find in treatises less than half a century older.

The kinds of rhetorical speaking are treated by Cicero a little differently in *De oratore* and *Orator*, but the main features of the two accounts are quite comparable. Within *De oratore* he approaches the subject of rhetorical genera through an inquiry regarding the scope of rhetoric. Here he initially observes that the province of the orator includes both general and particular matters (2.41–42). In the latter category we would expect him to offer the usual three-fold analysis of kinds; but, in fact, he does not. Rather, he insists that the theory of speaking only recognizes two kinds of discourse: forensic and deliberative (2.43). There is a third, laudatory, kind, he says, but it is less essential and besides there is no need for special principles for this kind, since panegyric is only one among many varieties of discourse that are expected of orators, but for which the principles that guide forensic and deliberative speaking will easily suffice (2.44–47). In what follows, Cicero extends this reasoning quite explicitly to giving evidence (2.48), composing official dispatches (2.49), rebuking (2.50), encouraging (2.50, 64), comforting (2.50, 64), teaching (2.64), admonishing (2.64), writing history (2.51–64), and even treating general matters (2.65). The upshot is that while Cicero recognizes a large number of forms of discourse that are rhetorical, he limits the art and principles of rhetoric to the forensic and deliberative types only. And lest we misunderstand, he is quick to explain (2.69–70):

> [T]o prevent any surprise at my omitting to lay down any regulations on so many highly important subjects, I make this declaration: . . . I hold that in this oratory, . . . he who has acquired such power as to be able to sway at his pleasure the minds of hearers invested with authority to determine some issue concerning the State, or questions of fact, or the parties he may be attacking or defending, will on any other oratorical topic whatever be no more at a loss for words than famous Polyclitus, when modeling his "Hercules," was at a loss how to model the wild beast's skin or the water-serpent, even though he had never been taught to fashion these subjects in isolation.[22]

In *Orator* Cicero comes to account for the kinds of rhetorical discourse as part of his consideration of what constitutes the best type of eloquence. Here again he omits theoretical treatment of all but forensic and deliberative speaking, giving the name epideictic to the whole class of speeches excluded—a class comprising at least eulogies, descriptions, histories, and certain forms of exhortation (37, 69, 207). His rationale in this connection is very telling. Epideictic speeches are ruled out, he says, because they are remote from contention in

---

[22] Edward William Sutton and Harris Rackham, trans., *De oratore*, books I and II, LCL (Cambridge: Harvard University Press, 1942).

the forum (37); likewise, forensic and deliberative speeches are ruled
in, because they pertain to the speaker who can speak in the forum
on legal and civic matters so as to teach, please, and move (69, 207).
Now, I submit that this rationale resonates in a significant way with
Cicero's explanation of the relation between kinds of speaking selected
and not selected for treatment in De oratore. For both accounts feature
the fact that forensic and deliberative speeches attempt to sway audiences in legal and political contention. Accordingly, out of De oratore
and Orator, I believe we may understand Cicero's mature position to
be that, although there are a large number of forms of rhetorical
speaking, forensic and deliberative speaking are distinguished for artistic treatment inasmuch as they aim at persuasion in public venues.[23]

Cicero's conception of the relation of rhetoric to other disciplines
is one of the major themes in both De oratore and Orator. In De oratore, his position is announced early on and prosecuted throughout
the work: "In my view," he says, "no one will be able to be a
speaker consummate in every excellence, unless he will have gained
knowledge of all important matters and arts" (1.20). On behalf of
this position, Cicero argues that just claiming the mantle of speaker
requires that the claimant be prepared to speak on any subject with
knowledge and grace (1.59, 64). Likewise, he insists that apart from
knowledge of the subject matter, human nature, and the liberal arts,
the speaker will find intellectual respectability, effectiveness, and
expressive sophistication completely inaccessible (1.48–50, 53, 60, 72).
No wonder, then, that the speaker must grasp every ars et magna res.
In Orator, Cicero's requirements of the speaker are little changed,
though because of the nature of the work, he does not so much
argue as simply stipulate that the ideal speaker must possess training
in the great arts (4), dialectic (113), and all the topics of philosophy,

---

[23] The fact that Cicero multiplied the kinds of rhetorical discourse in De or. did
not escape the notice of Quintilian, who chides him for excess (Inst. 3.4.2; Ludwig
Radermacher, ed., and Vinzenz Buchheit, corr., M. Fabi Quintiliani Institutionis oratoriae libri XII, 2 vols. [Leipzig: B. G. Teubner, 1965–71]): verum et tum leviter est
temptatum, cum apud Graecos quosdam tum apud Ciceronem in libris de Oratore,
et nunc maximo temporum nostrorum auctore prope inpulsum, ut non modo plura
haec genera, sed paene innumerabilia videantur. ("Still a feeble attempt has been
made by certain Greeks and by Cicero in his de Oratore, to prove that there are
not merely more than three, but that the number of kinds is almost past calculation: and this view has almost been thrust down our throats by the greatest authority of our own times;" Harold Edgeworth Butler, trans., The Institutio Oratoria of
Quintilian, 4 vols., LCL [Cambridge: Harvard University Press, 1920]).

natural science, civil law, and history (118–20). Across the two works, Cicero makes plain that success in practical speaking requires not only rhetorical mastery, but equally, knowledge of a wide range of instrumental and substantive matters.

To the extent that the foregoing is acceptable, I believe that we are now in a position to identify at least a few of the developments characteristic of rhetorical theory in the latter part of the first century B.C.E. Particularly within the mature works of Cicero we may note four significant innovations. First, in a departure from simply assuming that rhetoric is an art, we may observe a deliberate consideration of the "art problem," which preserves the artistic status of rhetoric through a bifurcation of the conception of art. Second, as opposed to a theoretical focus on invention as the chief element of rhetoric, we see a shift of emphasis to presentational aspects of rhetoric, particularly style. Third, in contrast to a simple division of speaking into three kinds, we see a multiplication of discourse types, this marked by distinction of such types according to their level of concern with practical persuasion. Fourth, as compared with a conception of rhetoric as largely independent of other disciplines, we find an insistence that rhetoric is inherently dependent upon the contribution of many subjects and arts.

Rhetoric in Philodemus

I now turn to the final part of my argument, namely an attempt to prove my contention that Philodemus' account of rhetoric exemplifies the sorts of theoretical developments that were current in his day. In this connection, my procedure will simply be to address each of the developments just identified.

First, then, what is Philodemus' position on the artistic status of rhetoric? Given that Philodemus says more about the art problem than anyone ever, it would probably be foolish of me to go on about the deliberateness of his consideration of the issue, particularly since Philodemus' treatise is a philosophical investigation and the art problem was one of the central concerns in the Epicurean philosophy of rhetoric[24] However, it is hardly beside the point to inquire whether

---

[24] This much seems clear from the frequency with which the disciplinary qualifications of rhetoric are entertained in the surviving rhetorical fragments of the founding Masters of the School (οἱ καθηγεμόνες), namely, Epicurus (frs. 20.1, 20.3,

Philodemus offers a complicated conception of art and thereby finds it possible to make more subtle arguments about rhetoric. As regards the complexity of Philodemus' conception of art, it has for a long time been understood that he recognized art as having two types: exact art and conjectural art.[25] One basis for this understanding is Philodemus' definition of art at *Rh.* 2, *P. Herc.* 1674 col. 38.2–15:

νοεῖται τοίνυν καὶ λέγεται | [τ]έχνη παρὰ τοῖ[ς] Ἕλληι[5]σι[ν ἕ]ξις ἢ
διάθ[ε]σι[ς] ἀπὸ | παρ[α]τηρή[σ]εω[ς] τιν]ῶν|κοινῶν|καὶ
[σ]τοι[χειω] [[ν]] |δῶν, ἃ διὰ πλειόν[ω]ν διήκει τῶν ἐπὶ μέ[ρ]ο[υς],
καὶ[10] ταλαμβάνουσά [τ]ι καὶ | [σ]υντελοῦσα τοιοῦτον, | οἷον ὁμοίως
τῶν μὴ | μαθόντων ἔ[νιοι], ἑστη|κοτως καὶ βε[βαί]ως [ἢ |[15] τ]ε
στοχαστι[κῶς].[26]

20.6, 21.4), Graziano Arrighetti, ed., *Epicuro. Opere*, nuova ed. (Turin: Giulio Einaudi, 1973); Metrodorus (frs. 1, 2, 10, 11), Francesca Longo Auricchio, "Testimonianze dalla 'Retorica' di Filodemo sulla concezione dell'oratoria nei primi maestri Epicurei," *CErc.* 15 (1985): 31–61; cf. frs. 20–22, 25, A. Körte, *Metrodori Epicurei fragmenta, JCPH,* Suppl. 17 (1890): 521–97 (Körte does not include fr. 11 Longo Auricchio); Hermarchus (frs. 35, 36), Longo Auricchio, ed., *Ermarco. Frammenti,* La scuola di Epicuro: Collezione di testi ercolanesi diretta da Marcello Gigante 6, Frammenti dei Katheghemones 1 (Naples, Bibliopolis, 1988); and Polyaenus (fr. 43), Adele Tepedino Guerra, ed., *Polieno. Frammenti,* La scuola di Epicuro: Collezione di testi ercolanesi diretta da Marcello Gigante 11, Frammenti dei Katheghemones 2 (Naples: Bibliopolis, 1991). On the identity and authority of οἱ καθηγεμόνες, see Longo Auricchio, "La scuola di Epicuro," *CErc.* 8 (1978): 21–31.

[25] Cf. Hubbell, *Rhetorica* 258; G. M. A. Grube, *The Greek and Roman Critics* (London: Methuen, 1965), 202; Margherita Isnardi Parente, *Techne. Momenti del pensiero greco da Platone ad Epicuro* (Florence: La Nuova Italia, 1966), 389–90; Marcello Gigante, "Philodème: Sur la liberté de parole," *Actes du VIIIe Congrès, Association Guillaume Budé. Paris 5–10 avril 1968* (Paris: Les Belles Lettres, 1969), 203–05; Barnes, "Is Rhetoric an Art?" 7; cf. Doreen C. Innes, "Philodemus," *The Cambridge History of Literary Criticism,* ed. George A. Kennedy, 2 vols. (Cambridge: Cambridge University Press, 1989), 1: 218.

[26] I here follow the Longo Auricchio text (123) except that I restore [ἢ | τ]ε at lines 14–15 instead of [οὐὶδ]ὲ, which Longo Auricchio adopts following Sudhaus 1:70 (I first suggested this reading in my communication "Philodemus on the Artistic Status of Rhetoric," International Society for the History of Rhetoric, Göttingen, 1989). The inspiration for this restoration derives from Barnes, "Is Rhetoric an Art?" 21–22 n. 55, where Barnes argues that ἢ καί captures the sense required at lines 14–15. Citing a number of passages where "Philodemus seems straightforwardly to endorse the existence of stochastic τέχναι" (*Rh.* 2, PHerc. 1674 cols. 2.15–24, 5.34–6.19 [Longo Auricchio 47, 53–55]; PHerc. 1079 fr. 18.10–18 [Sudhaus 2:120]; cf. *Rh.* 2, PHerc. 1674 cols. 30.19, 39.8, 21 [Longo Auricchio 107, 125]), Barnes concludes the argument as follows: "I have suggested ἢ καί for οὐδέ. This disagrees with the reported epsilon, and it may be an emendation rather than a reading. But it is an emendation hard to resist: I cannot believe that Philodemus, alone among ancient philosophers and against his own defense of rhetoric, would have denied the existence of conjectural τέχναι (and have done so in his very definition of τέχνη). And there is a clinching argument: at 2, xxx 12–19 = <I 59> Philodemus plainly foreshadows the definition he will later offer. The text there

Now, art is considered and called by the Greeks a skill or disposition from observation of certain general and elementary principles which extend over the majority of cases to particulars, and an art comprehends something and accomplishes the sort of thing, such as few of those not knowing the art accomplish likewise, doing so firmly and surely or conjecturally.[27]

In relation to this definition, Philodemus later goes on to explain that conjectural arts are distinctive, because their methods are "not for achieving the end of the art in every case, but rather for achieving it in the majority of cases or at least more often than persons untrained in the art."[28] Having established art as a bifurcated notion, Philodemus exploits the notion in two ways. First, as an orthodox Epicurean, Philodemus felt the need to demonstrate that all non-Epicurean thinking on every subject was flawed.[29] Accordingly, in *On Rhetoric* 1 and 2, he opposes a large number of arguments concerning the art problem, refuting them essentially one by one. Some arguments claimed that rhetoric was an art. To these Philodemus was wont to apply the stringent criteria for exact art, criteria he knew practical rhetoric— which aimed at persuasion—could never meet.[30] Other arguments

---

reads as follows: θεωρεῖται γὰρ ἐμ μεθόδωι τοῦτο καί τινι παραδόσει κοινῶν τινων διατεινόντων ἐπὶ τὰ κατὰ μέρος, ἄ[ν]τ᾽ οὖν ἦι τῶν παγίων [ἐπι]στημῶν ἄντε τῶν στ[ο]χασ-τικῶν. The last clause runs parallel to the last clause of the definition: οὐδέ is therefore impossible in the definition" (20–21). The restoration proposed is designed to incorporate Barnes' insight while preserving the papyrological evidence (i.e., the epsilon legible in the papyrus before στοχαστι[κῶς]). These objectives are achieved equally well, and perhaps with greater felicity, by [ἤ ǀ γ]ε, which was recently suggested to me by Richard Janko.

[27] My translation supplies τέχνη at line 9 and τὴν τέχνην at line 13 on analogy with Philodemus' language at *Rh.* 2, PHerc. 1674 col. 20.16–19 (Longo Auricchio 85; see note 30 below). Cf. David Blank, *Sextus Empiricus. Against the Grammarians* (Oxford: Clarendon, 1998) xxxii, and "Philodemus on the Technicity of Rhetoric," *Philodemus and Poetry: Poetic Theory and Practice in Lucretius, Philodemus, and Horace*, ed. Dirk Obbink (New York: Oxford University Press, 1995), 179; Barnes, "Is Rhetoric an Art?" 6.

[28] *Rh.* 2, PHerc. 1674 cols. 38.30–39.24 (Longo Auricchio 123–25).

[29] This is something of an overstatement; still, polemic against opposing schools is a feature characteristic of Philodemus' technical writings and Epicurean philosophy in general; cf. Gigante, *Filodemo* 21 (= *Philodemus in Italy* 17); Phillip Howard De Lacy and Estelle Allen De Lacy, eds., trans., and comm., *Philodemus: On Methods of Inference*, rev. ed. with the collaboration of Marcello Gigante, Francesca Longo Auricchio, and Adele Tepedino Guerra, La Scuola di Epicuro, 1 (Naples: Bibliopolis, 1978) 153–54; Philippson, "Philodemos," 2454).

[30] Cf. *Rh.* 2, PHerc. 1674 cols. 20.16–21.1 (Longo Auricchio 85–87); here Philodemus' refutative comment, ὁ μὴ μαθὼ[ν] τ[ὴ]ν τέ[χνην] ἀδυνατεῖ τ[ὰ τῆ]ς ǀ τέχνη[ς] ἔργα συντελεῖν ("the one who does not know the art is incapable of accomplishing the results [or functions] of the art"), must certainly exploit criteria for exact art or science, since he is elsewhere committed to the fact that laymen achieve the

claimed that rhetoric was not an art. To these Philodemus was ready to apply the criteria for conjectural art, realizing that practical rhetoric could be defended as artistic in this sense, since trained speakers achieved their aim more often than those who were not trained.[31] Second, Philodemus also exploits the distinction to express his philosophical commitments. Prior to Philodemus' composition of *On Rhetoric*, his teacher, Zeno, had been attacked in the Epicurean school for saying that one kind of rhetoric—namely sophistic rhetoric—was artistic.[32] The attacker had insisted that the leaders of the school did not recognize any sort of rhetoric as meeting their criteria for art.[33] Wishing to defend the view held by Zeno and himself, Philodemus realized that the defense would have either to refute the attacker's interpretation of the leaders' view or, otherwise, show that sophistic rhetoric met the standards set down for art by the leaders of the school. Philodemus undertook both strategies, but it is the latter that is of interest to us here.[34] For he constructively defends the artistic

---

[31] *Rh.* 2, PHerc. 1674 col. 2.15–18; cf. *Rh.* 1, PHerc. 1427 fr. 2.13–23 [Longo Auricchio 47, 5]). The same criterion seems to be at stake *Rh.* 3, PHerc. 1426 7a.2–7 (= PHerc. 1506 53.14–18; Hammerstaedt 32–33), where the ability to read and write is denied to those who have not studied grammar (an exact art, see below, notes 35 and 36).

[31] *Rh.* 2, PHerc. 1674 cols. 5.31–6.19 (Longo Auricchio 53–55): πᾶς τεχνίτ[ης ἐ]πα[γ] ‖γέλλεται τὸ τέλ[ος] πο[ιη] Ιΐσειν, ὁ δὲ ῥήτωρ [οὐκ] ἐπα[γ] Ιγέλλεται πείσει[ν. οὐ] πᾶς ‖³⁵ τεχνί[τ]ης ἐὰν ἔχ[ηι] φρέ ‖ νας, [ἐπα]νγέλλεται τὸ Ι τέλ[ος] διὰ παντὸς π[οι] Ιήσειν. οὔτε γὰρ ἰατρὸ[ς οὔ] Ιτε κυβερνήτης οὔ[τε το] ‖⁵ξότης οὔτε ἁπλῶς ὅσοι Ι τὰς ἐπιστήμας οὐ παγίους ἔ[χ]ου[σ]ι[ν ἀλ]λὰ στοχαστικάς. ὥστ᾽ ἢ καὶ ταύτας οὐ ῥητέον εἶναι τέχν[ας Ι¹⁰ ἢ καὶ τὴν ῥητορικήν. ἐπαγγέλεταί τε καὶ ὁ Ι ῥήτωρ τὸ τέλος ποιήσειν. Ι ἐστὶ δ᾽ αὐτοῦ τὸ τέλος Ι ὃ φέρει τῶν πραγ[μάτων] Ι¹⁵ ἡ φύσις, οὔτε διὰ παντὸς Ι κεί[με]νον οὐδέ, μὰ Δία, καΙτὰ τὸ ᾽[πλεῖστ]ον. ἀλλὰ πολὺ μᾶ[λλο]ν τῶν μὴ ῥητό|ρων [τὸ] ἔργ|ον π]οιεῖ. ("[Opponent:] 'Every artist professes to achieve the end <of the art>, but the speaker does not profess to persuade.' [Philodemus:] Not every artist, if he has good sense, professes to achieve his end always. For neither the doctor, nor the pilot, nor the archer, nor generally as many as possess sciences that are not exact, but conjectural, <profess to achieve the end always>. So either it is necessary to say these are not arts, or that rhetoric <is an art>. And the speaker does profess to persuade. But his end, which the nature of the circumstances produces, is posited neither always nor, by Zeus, for the most part. Rather <the speaker> achieves the result (or function) <of the art> more often than non-speakers."); cp. *Rh.* 6 (?), PHerc. 1004, col. 46.8–11 (Cappelluzzo 73). An obvious implication of this line of reasoning is that Philodemus considered practical rhetoric, i.e., the sort(s) of rhetoric which aimed at persuasion, to be artistic in the conjectural sense.

[32] For the general basis of the dispute, see *Rh.* 2, PHerc. 1674 cols. 52.11–53.14 (Longo Auricchio 151–153); that the status of sophistic rhetoric was the central issue of controversy is clear from *Rh.* 2, PHerc. 1674 cols. 57.17–58.2 (Longo Auricchio 161–63).

[33] *Rh.* 2, PHerc. 1674 54.10–56.9 (Longo Auricchio 155–59).

[34] Philodemus attempts to refute his Epicurean opponent's interpretation by offering

status of sophistic rhetoric by arguing that it shares its form with elementary grammar and sculpture,[35] exact arts that must surely have met the standards for art set down by the leaders of the school.[36] Much more could be said here, but I believe it is already clear that Philodemus found a complication of the concept of art a useful tool in meeting his theoretical objectives in *On Rhetoric*. By recognizing arts at two levels, he was prepared to defend the artistic status of sophistic rhetoric at one level and practical rhetoric at the other; he was likewise prepared to overturn the arguments of those who claimed unreservedly that rhetoric was an art. In all this, I propose, Philodemus demonstrates knowledge and control of one of the major developments of rhetorical theory in the mid-first century B.C.E.

---

several passages that he believes support the contention that the Masters of the school accepted sophistic rhetoric as an art. These passages are presented at *Rh.* 2, PHerc. 1674 cols. 43.26–52.10 (Longo Auricchio 133–51); Philodemus explains their relation to his dispute with the Epicurean opponent at *Rh.* 2, PHerc. 1674, col. 57.13–58.2 (Longo Auricchio 161–63). A very useful account of Philodemus' position in the dispute has been offered by David Sedley, "Philosophical Allegiance in the Greco-Roman World," *Philosophia Togata: Essays in Philosophy and Roman Society*, ed. Miriam Griffin and Jonathan Barnes (Oxford: Clarendon, 1989), 97–119.

[35] *Rh.* 2, PHerc. 1674 cols. 42.33–43.17 (Longo Auricchio 131–133): φεύ|γον[τ]ες γὰρ ἅπασαν οὐ πρα¹³⁵γμα[τι]κὴν ἀμφισβήτη|σιν [μ]εταληψόμεθα τὰς | ὀνο[μ]ασί[α]ς, καὶ ταύτας ‖ ἃς νῦν φαμεν εἶ[ν]αι τέ|χνας, τὸ τοιοῦτ' ἔχειν | εἶδος ἐροῦμεν ὧ[ς] ἥ | γραμματικὴ καὶ ⌜πλ⌝ [ασ]|⁵τική, ταύτας δ', ἃς οὐ [τέ] |χνας, τὰς [ἐσ]τερημέ[νας] | τοῦ τοιούτο, παρατηρ[η] |τικὸν δ' [ἔ]χειν εἶδος, οἷον | ἀρ]τίως ἐξηριθμησά¹¹⁰με[θ]α, παραπλήσιον [καὶ] | φθ[ο]νήσομεν αὐταῖς. [εἴ] |δη ⟨δὲ⟩ τοιαῦτα καὶ τὰς ῥ[η] |τορικὰς ἐναρμόττο[ν] |τες, τὴν [μ]ὲν σοφιστικ[ὴν] |¹⁵ τέχνη[ν ἀ]ποφαινόμ[ε] |θα, [τ]ὴν δὲ πολιτικὴν [οὐ] | τέχνην. ("Avoiding all possible non-substantive dispute, we will interpret the expressions, and those which we now say are arts, we will say have the sort of form such as elementary grammar and sculpture have, and those which we say are not arts, which are deprived of this sort of form, and have the observational form, such as we have just reckoned, we will not grant a similar status to them. If indeed we apply these sorts of considerations to the rhetorical disciplines, then we declare that while sophistic rhetoric is an art, political science is not an art.") I have translated γραμματική in 43.4 with "elementary grammar" consistent with Blank's observation that the reference must certainly be to γραμματιστική, since in the preceding argument, the text has γρα[μμ]ατισ|τικῆι at 38.32–33 and γραμματιστής at 41.12 ("Technicity," 179). Philodemus may be using γραμματική in the same sense at *Rh.* 3, PHerc. 1426 7a.2–7 (= PHerc. 1506 53.14–18; Hammerstaedt 32–33), since he associates the term with instruction in writing and reading, a standard function of γραμματιστική (Sext. Emp. *Math.* 1.49). Philodemus' identification of the form of sophistic rhetoric with elementary grammar and sculpture suggests that he considered sophistic rhetoric to be an exact art.

[36] Philodemus commits himself to the status of elementary grammar and sculpture as exact arts at *Rh.* 2, PHerc. 1674 cols. 38.30–39.6 (Longo Auricchio 123–25). That elementary grammar (γραμματιστική) was considered an art by Epicurus is suggested at Sext. Emp. *Math.* 1.49–53.

I now turn to Philodemus' estimation of the parts of rhetoric. And here we face a little difficulty. The philosophical objectives that motivate *On Rhetoric* are largely polemical; accordingly, within the work, Philodemus is not at pains to offer a constructive theory for the parts of rhetoric. Still, it may be observed that near the end of book four, Philodemus indicates that one objective for the book has been to examine "all things, which some say are parts and precepts of rhetoric."[37] Now if we look into the materials which Philodemus employs in carrying out this examination, what we find is that they are apparently organized in five segments. The first four are devoted to expression (φράσις), delivery (ὑπόκρισις), the management of subjects through the parts of speeches (σχεδὸν πᾶν σκέμμα διὰ τούτων . . . διοικεῖται), and invention (εὕρεσις).[38] The last segment treats "problems that are judicial, deliberative, and concerned with praise and blame (τῶν προβλημάτων τὰ μέν ἐστιν δικανικά, τὰ δὲ συμβουλευτικά, [τὰ] δὲ περὶ τοὺς ἐπαίνους καὶ ψόγους).[39] For the present I would like to focus on the first four segments; these appear to discuss parts of rhetoric.[40] And given Philodemus' stated objective in discussing them, I conclude that they comprise a self-conscious handling of such parts as at least some had said belonged to rhetoric. Of course, if this much is true, then it seems quite legitimate to infer that Philodemus' discussion of these subjects represents, though it may not exhaust, his thinking on each of the parts discussed. For my purposes here, I believe this is all that is needed to gauge Philodemus' estimation of the parts of rhetoric. Consider that Philodemus treats the parts entirely out of their usual order, beginning with expression and delivery and postponing invention to end. Consider as well that in book four as we have it, Philodemus devotes fifty-four columns to expression,

---

[37] *Rh.* 4, PHerc. 1007/1673 col. 42a.4–8: ἀποτεθεωρημένων[5] τοιγαροῦν, ὦ Γάϊε Πάν᾿σ᾿α, πάν[των, ἃ μέρη φασί τινες καὶ διδάγματα τῆς ῥητορικῆς ǀ ὑπάρχειν, . . . (I here follow the text of this passage as recently corrected by Tiziano Dorandi, "Gaio bambino," *ZPE* 111 [1996] 41; cp. Sudhaus 1:222).

[38] Expression, *Rh.* 4, PHerc. 1423 cols. 1.1–20.28, PHerc. 1007/1673 cols. 1.1–24.25, 1a.1–11a.12; delivery, *Rh.* 4, PHerc. 1007/1673 cols. 11a.12–20a.12; management of subjects through the parts of speeches, *Rh.* 4, PHerc. 1007/1673 cols. 20a.12–22a.16; invention, *Rh.* 4, PHerc. 1007/1673 cols. 22a.16–30a.19 (Sudhaus 1: 147–93, 193–201, 201–04, 204–12).

[39] *Rh.* 4, PHerc. 1007/1673 cols. 30a.19–42a.4 (Sudhaus 1:212–22).

[40] Sudhaus, *Phld. Rh.* 1: XXXVII–XXXIX; Wilhelm Schneidewin, *Studia Philodemea* (Göttingen: Officina Academica Dieterichiana, 1905) 6; cp. Walter Scott, *Fragmenta Herculanensia. A Descriptive Catalogue of the Oxford Copies of the Herculanean Rolls* (Oxford: Clarendon, 1885), 85; Hubbell, *Rhetorica* 294.

ten to delivery, three to management or arrangement, and nine to invention. Whatever the contents of these discussions, my understanding from this order and scope of treatments is that Philodemus considered expression and delivery to be subjects more worthy of extended handling than invention and arrangement. But this pattern of emphasis, as I have argued, is much more typical of rhetorical theory around the mid-first century B.C.E. than earlier on. Accordingly, I would argue that Philodemus is once again demonstrating a commitment to theoretical interests that were quite current at the composition of *On Rhetoric*.

In the matter of Philodemus' conception of the kinds of rhetorical speaking we have considerable information, particularly in books 1–4.[41] The standard view of this information is that Philodemus recognized exactly three rhetorical genera, σοφιστική or epideictic rhetoric, ῥητορική or political and legal rhetoric, and πολιτική or political science.[42] I will not be following this view for two reasons. First, Philodemus sharply distinguishes rhetoric from political science throughout *On Rhetoric* book 3; in fact, he explicitly denies both that rhetoric is identical to political science and that rhetoric includes political science.[43] Second, Philodemus fairly frequently treats sophistic rhetoric,

---

[41] See Dorandi, "Filodemo sulla Retorica," 68–71, as well as Knut Kleve and Francesca Longo Auricchio, "Honey from the Garden of Epicurus," *Papiri letterari Greci e Latini*, Papyrologica Lupiensia 1, ed. Mario Capasso (Galatina: Cogendo, 1992), 211–26.

[42] For this view, see Hubbell, "Isocrates and the Epicureans," *CP* 11 (1916): 408–409, *Rhetorica* 254–55, 267, n. 6; Jane Isabella Marie Tait, *Philodemus' Influence on the Latin Poets*, Diss. Bryn Mawr, 1941 (Ann Arbor: Edwards Bros., 1941) 91.

[43] On the question whether rhetoric is the same as political science, cf., PHerc. 1506 col. 47.6–10 (= PHerc. 1426 col. A.6–10; Hammerstaedt 22) where Philodemus remarks: ⸤ο⸥[ὕτω]ς ο⸢ὔ⸥[τε τ]⸤ὴ⸥ν ῥητορικὴ[ν λέγο]⸤μεν κ⸥αὶ πολιτ[ικ]⸤ὴ⸥ν ὑπάρ⸤χ⸥ειν οὐδ' ὅλως ἀ⸤π⸥οτελεῖν⸥ |¹⁰ πολιτ⸢ι⸣κούς. (". . . so we say that neither is rhetoric also political science nor does rhetoric generally produce statesmen.") Whether rhetoric includes political science is discussed at PHerc. 1426 cols. 10a.25–11a.14 (= PHerc. 1506 col. 55.21–37; Hammerstaedt 38–41): ὅταν δὲ | γελοίους εἶναι φῶσι | τοὺς ἀφαιρουμέγους ⸤τ⸥ὴν πολειτικὴν δύναμ⸢ιν⸣ τ⸤ῆς⸥ ⸤τε⸢λ⸣ε⸣ίας ῥητορικῆς ἐμ|³⁰περιειλημμένην ἐγ | τῇ ⸤ι⸥' προλήψει καθάπερ | τοὺς τῆς ἰατρ⸢ι⸣κ⸢ῆ⸣ς τὴν εἴδησιν τῶν ὑ⸢γι⸣ ⸤ει⸥[ν]ῶν || καὶ νοσηρῶν, ἡδονῆς | εἰσιν ʽἀν᾽ ἄμεστοι. πῶς γὰρ | ἡ μὴ συγχωρουμένη πειριποιεῖν τὴν πολειτι⁵κὴν ἐμπεριειλη[φ]έναι | κατὰ τὴν πρόληψ[ι]ν δο|θήσεται τὴν πολει[τ]ικήν . . .; ("When they say those are absurd who exclude the political faculty from the complete rhetoric, on the ground that the political faculty is included in the preconception of rhetoric, just as those of the medical art have knowledge of the healthy and unhealthy, they are amusing. For how will that [i.e., rhetoric] which is not conceded to possess political science be granted to include political science by preconception . . .?")

political rhetoric, and legal rhetoric as a kind of theoretical unit;[44] and he also makes clear that these were envisioned as distinct and roughly comparable categories by members of his School whom he considers authoritative.[45] Accordingly, in what follows, I shall take it that Philodemus recognized at least sophistic, political, and legal rhetoric as types of speaking.[46] Now, regarding this set, my claim is that Philodemus recognized a theoretical distinction among its members based on the fact that political and legal rhetoric attempted to persuade audiences in practical contention, whereas sophistic rhetoric did not. My argument for this claim involves two sorts of evidence. One sort is direct. Philodemus argues that the end or object of

---

[44] See *Rh.* 2, PHerc. 1674 col. 22.5–12, 21–29; col. 37.22–27 (= Longo Auricchio 89–91, 121); *Rh.* 3, PHerc. 1506 col. 35.12–24 (Sudhaus 2:234–35); *Rh.* 4, PHerc. 1007/1673 col. 41a.6–22 (Sudhaus 1:222).

[45] See *Rh.* 2, PHerc. 1674 col. 21.17–23; cols. 21.30–22.2; cols. 23.30–24.9 (Longo Auricchio 87–89, 93–95), PHerc. 1672 col. 21.10–17 (Longo Auricchio 215); *Rh.* 3, PHerc. 1426 cols. 3a.7–5a.6 (= PHerc. 1506 cols. 50.22–52.8; Hammerstaedt 26–31). In PHerc. 1672 col. 21.13–15, I interpret the phrase τῆς ἐμπράκτ[ου] | καὶ πολειτικῆς ῥητορι|15κῆς as synonymous with "legal and political rhetoric." This is consistent with Philodemus' reference in what immediately follows to τ [α] ύτην ⌐τὴ⌐ [ν τοῦ] ⌐δ⌐η⌐μ⌐η| γ⌐ο⌐ρεῖν καὶ [δίκ]ας λέγειν || ἐμπειρίαν ("the experience with speaking in the assembly and pleading court cases") (PHerc. 1672 cols. 21.37–22.1; Longo Auricchio 215–17); cf. *Rh.* 1, PHerc. 1427 col. 5.30–33: τὴν | πολειτικὴν καὶ τὴν | ἔμπρακτον ῥητορι|κήν, where Longo Auricchio (17) translates "la retorica politica e quella forense."

[46] It has been suggested by Sudhaus, *Phld. Rh.*, 2:358 (Index, s.v. σοφιστική), Hubbell, *Rhetorica* 281, and argued by Tait, *Influence* 91, and G. M. A. Grube, *Critics* 201, that the sort of coequality I propose here is ruled out by Philodemus' comment that "sophistic rhetoric . . . is not a part of rhetoric" in book 2 (PHerc. 1674 col. 58.4–8 [= Sudhaus 1:98; Suppl. 47–48). However, I do not believe the comment actually supports this conclusion. The text of the passage at stake reads as follows (*Rh.* 2, PHerc. 1674 col. 58.4–16; Longo Auricchio 163): . . . ⌐καὶ [δι⌐ότι τέχ⌐[νην] |5 τὴν σοφισ⌐τικὴν⌐ καλο[υ]μένην ⌐ῥητορικὴν⌐ [λέγο]|μεν οὐ⌐χὶ τῆς ῥητορι⌐κῆ⌐ς⌐ | μέ⌐ροις. οὐ γάρ ἐστιν τῆς⌐ | ῥητορικῆς μέρος τὸ πα⌐|10νηγυ⌐ρικὸν κα⌐[ὶ] ⌐τὸ⌐ πολ⌐ει⌐τικὸν καὶ ⌐τὸ δικαν⌐ικό⌐ν⌐, | ὅν τρόπον ⌐αὐτὸς οἴετ⌐αι | κατὰ τὴν ⌐ἅπασαν γρα⌐|φή⌐ν⌐, ὥσ⌐π⌐ερ⌐ [οὐ]⌐δὲ τοῦ⌐ [κυ] |15⌐νὸς⌐ μέρος τὸ θαλάττιον⌐ |⌐ζῷον καὶ τὸ χερσαῖον⌐ . . . (". . . and we say that sophistic rhetoric is an art and although it is called 'rhetoric,' it is not a part of 'rhetoric.' For, it is not the case that the panegyric, political, and dicanic forms of rhetoric are parts of 'rhetoric,' as he supposes in his entire work, just as it is not the case that the sea-animal [i.e. dogfish] and the land-animal [i.e. canine] are parts of 'dog' . . ."). Philodemus here responds to an opponent who wished to apply Epicurus' observations on "rhetoric" to "sophistic rhetoric," since the opponent thought that sophistic rhetoric must be a part of rhetoric (this position is reported at *Rh.* 2, PHerc. 1674 col. 53.15–25; Longo Auricchio 153). Philodemus' point seems to be that forms of rhetoric are no more parts of the name applied to them, ῥητορική, than sharks and dogs are parts of their name, κύων. Accordingly, Philodemus' argument is more linguistic than theoretical and does nothing to discredit the possibility that sophistic, political, and legal rhetoric are types of rhetorical speaking.

rhetoric, in some conventional sense, is persuasion by means of a speech.[47] And he frequently associates a persuasive aim with speaking in political and legal venues.[48] Yet, he never attributes persuasion to sophistic rhetoric as an object and he actually dismisses the idea that sophistic rhetoric might be effective for political and legal speaking.[49]

Now for the indirect evidence. We know Philodemus argues that the leaders of his school conceived of sophistic rhetoric as an art.[50] But we also know that these same leaders insisted that there could be no art of persuading multitudes.[51] Accordingly, unless he wished to attribute a contradiction to the leaders of the School, Philodemus had to recognize something other than persuasion as the aim of sophistic rhetoric.[52] For these reasons, I believe that Philodemus' conception of rhetorical genera exhibits another feature characteristic to mid-first century B.C.E. rhetoric on types of speaking, namely an important distinction between types based on whether or not they aimed at persuading audiences.

This brings me to my final consideration, Philodemus' conception of the relation of rhetoric to other disciplines. Within *On Rhetoric* this is a fairly complicated subject; therefore, I hope I will be forgiven if I limit my remarks to the several ways in which Philodemus understands that speakers are dependent upon other arts for success in

---

[47] *Rh.* 1, PHerc. 1427 col. 3.30–33; *Rh.* 2, PHerc. 1674 col. 1.31–34 (Longo Auricchio 13, 45).

[48] Cf. *Rh.* 2, PHerc. 408 frs. 7.1–3, 11.2–18 (Sudhaus 2:83, 85–86); *Rh.* 5 (?), PHerc. 1015/832 cols. 21.4–22, 24.0–16 (Sudhaus 2:15, 18–19); *Rh.* 6 (?), PHerc. 1004 cols. 15.3–20, 76.4–13 (Sudhaus 1:332–33, 363–65); *Rh.* 7 (?), PHerc. 220 fr. 6.3–16 (Sudhaus 2:136); cf. *Rh.* 2, PHerc. 1674 col. 11.17–34 (Longo Auricchio 65).

[49] Cf. *Rh.* 2, PHerc. 1674, cols. 10.24–11.31 (after Epicurus), 17.8–13 (Longo Auricchio 63–65, 77); *Rh.* 3, PHerc. 1506 cols. 46.23–32, 48.13–17; PHerc. 1426 cols. 3a.7–5a.4 (after Epicurus) (= PHerc. 1506, cols. 50.22–52.6; Hammerstaedt 22, 23, 26–31); *Rh.* 7 (?), PHerc. 220, fr. 5.28–34 (Sudhaus 2:135).

[50] See *Rh.* 1, PHerc. 1427 col. 7.9–29; *Rh.* 2, PHerc. 1674 cols. 43.26–52.10; cf. col. 57.13–58.2 (Longo Auricchio 21, 133–51, 161–62).

[51] See, e.g., *Rh.* 2, PHerc. 1674 cols. 54.32–55.11; PHerc. 1672 col. 9.11–14 (Longo Auricchio 135–37, 167).

[52] The object of sophistic rhetoric is nowhere specified in *On Rhetoric*; rather Philodemus merely describes sophistic rhetoric as an art concerned with making displays and composing speeches, both written and extemporaneous *Rh.* 2, PHerc. 1672 col. 22.28–36 (Longo Auricchio 219); cf. PHerc. 1674 cols. 23.34–24.9, 37.22–25 (Longo Auricchio 93–95, 121). The notion that the epideictic speaker does not aim at persuasion about the subject matter of the speech is perhaps suggested at Arist. *Rh.* 1.3.2 (1358b2–5, Rudolf Kassel, *Aristotelis Ars rhetorica* [Berlin: Walter De Gruyter, 1976]), where Aristotle describes the audience member for an epideictic speech as a θεωρός (spectator), but characterizes the audience member for a deliberative speech as a κριτής (judge) of the future and that for a legal speech as a κριτής of the past.

their speaking. Let me begin with the relation of arts to Philodemus' conception of rhetorical genera. The available evidence suggests that for Philodemus, types of rhetorical speaking are associated with characteristic activities. We know, for example, that he associates sophistic rhetoric with "making displays," political rhetoric with "speaking in the assembly," and legal rhetoric with "pleading causes."[53] In this connection, we also know that Philodemus conceived the ability to carry out these characteristic activities with success as deriving, not from rhetoric, but from an associated discipline.[54] In the case of political and legal rhetoric, he is explicit: the associated discipline is politics.[55] In the case of sophistic rhetoric he is less clear, but the associated discipline is almost certainly philosophy, for Philodemus aligns the activity of "making displays" with praise and blame,[56] and these, he says, can be carried out properly only by those who know the causes of every good and harm and the nature of true virtue and vice.[57] Such persons would appear to be those who are trained in philosophy, and this identification is clenched, I think, by Philodemus' disclosure that he has undertaken a philosophical work related to these matters, a work entitled *On Praise* (Περὶ ἐπαίνου).[58] Accordingly, for Philodemus, it is clear that even to engage in speechmaking immediately involves speakers with other disciplines. However there are other relations as well. Philodemus argues, for instance, that extra-rhetorical assistance is required for the discovery and judgment of arguments in rhetorical invention.[59] He likewise insists that the principles of speech arrangement and delivery differ by discipline.[60]

---

[53] *Rh.* 2, PHerc. 1674 cols. 21.7–27, 23.33–24.9, 28.22–27, PHerc. 1672 cols. 21.10–22.7, 22.29–36 (Longo Auricchio 87, 93–95, 103, 215, 217–19), *Rh.* 3, PHerc. 1426 col. 6a.14–31 (= PHerc. 1506 col. 52.37–53.12; Hammerstaedt 30–33).

[54] Philodemus seems to locate the competence for "speaking in the assembly" and "pleading causes" outside the realm of rhetoric at *Rh.* 3, PHerc. 1426 col. 7a.8–23 (= PHerc. 1506 col. 53.18–31; Hammerstaedt 32–35). He likewise questions the competence of those trained in rhetoric—particularly sophists—to "make displays" throughout the latter part of *Rh.* 4 (PHerc. 1007/1673 cols. 32a.21–39a.3; Sudhaus 1:214–19).

[55] *Rh.* 2, PHerc. 1672 cols. 21.36–22.19 (Longo Auricchio 215–17).

[56] *Rh.* 4, PHerc. 1007/1673 col. 36a.6–15 (Sudhaus 1: 217); cf. PHerc. 1007/1673 col. 32a.6–26 (Sudhaus 1:213–14), where Philodemus associates praise and blame with the sophistic type of speech (τὸ σοφιστικὸν γένος).

[57] *Rh.* 4, PHerc. 1007/1673 cols. 33a.19–24, 36a.15–37a.4, 37a.4–19 (Sudhaus 1: 214–15, 217–18); cf. Elizabeth Asmis, "Philodemus' Epicureanism," *ANRW* II 36, 4:2402.

[58] *Rh.* 4, PHerc. 1007/1673 cols. 38a.15–39a.1 (Sudhaus 1:219).

[59] *Rh.* 4, PHerc. 1007/1673 cols. 24a.26–26a.7; see Robert N. Gaines, "Philodemus on the Three Activities of Rhetorical Invention," *Rhetorica* 3 (1985) 156–59.

[60] *Rh.* 4, PHerc. 1007/1673 cols. 19a.16–26; 21a.10–22a.13 (Sudhaus 1:201,

In fact, within *On Rhetoric*, Philodemus' conception of rhetoric is shot through with dependence upon disciplines other than rhetoric. And this I would argue, represents one more way that his work is connected with mid-first century B.C.E. rhetorical thought.

Conclusion

To the extent that the foregoing is acceptable, then I think I have shown that Philodemus' *On Rhetoric* reflects theoretical tendencies that arose significantly after the turn of the first century B.C.E. Particularly, along with Cicero in his mature works, Philodemus addresses the art problem with a complicated conception of art, emphasizes presentational parts of rhetoric over their substantive counterparts, divides his rhetorical genera into two sets, using the aim of practical persuasion as criterion, and makes rhetoric dependent upon other disciplines for its successful practice. Clearly, Philodemus was no idle bystander as rhetorical theory developed around him; rather, he was an active participant in the developments that shaped late Hellenistic rhetorical theory. Accordingly, my conclusion is that, however we may choose to theorize about the changes that were characteristic to rhetoric in the latter half of the first century B.C.E., Philodemus' *On Rhetoric* constitutes an intellectual event that is relevant to their explanation.[61] For this reason alone, I would argue, the work achieves inherent significance as an object of historical inquiry.[62]

202–04); see Gaines, "Activities," 162. Among the parts of rhetoric treated in some way by Philodemus, only expression seems independent of contributions from extra-rhetorical disciplines; this may be a consequence of Philodemus' view that there existed a single form of expression that was beautiful by nature (*Rh.* 4, PHerc. 1423 col. 7.6–14; Sudhaus 1:151): Ἔ[πει] ǀτ᾿ εἰ μὲν μηδὲ εἷς ἦν φ[υ]ǀσικῶς καλ[ὸ]ς λόγος, ἴσως ἂν ἦ[ν] ἀναγκαῖον ǀ[10] ἀγαπᾶ[ν τὸ]ν κατὰ θέǀμα· νῦν δ᾿ ὑπάρχοντος, ǀ ἄθλιον τὸ παριένǀτας αὐτὸν [ἐ]π᾿ ἐκεῖνον καταντ[ᾶ]ν. ("Next, if there were not one naturally beautiful expression, perhaps it would be necessary to be content with the arbitrarily determined beautiful expression; but since there is one, it is pitiful that those disregarding it have recourse to that arbitrarily determined one.")

[61] That is, because Philodemus' *On Rhetoric* reflects the unique developments in late Hellenistic rhetoric, it necessarily becomes a source of evidence about those developments. On the importance of systematic study of sources in rational history, cf. Lionel Gossman, *Towards a Rational Historiography*, Transactions of the American Philosophical Society, 79:3 (Philadelphia: American Philosophical Society, 1989), 61–68, and Arthur Marwick, "'A Fetishism of Documents'? The Salience of Source-based History," *Developments in Modern Historiography*, ed. Henry Kozicki (New York: St. Martin's, 1993), 107–38.

[62] The research reported in this essay was supported by a grant to the Philodemus

Appendix: The Date and Influence of Philodemus' On Rhetoric

The date of *On Rhetoric* is a thorny problem and several arguments have arisen to address it. Robert Philippson dated *Rh.* in the 70's B.C.E., believing that Philodemus' reference to Zeno of Sidon (i.e., *Rh.* 2, PHerc. 1674 cols. 52.11–53.11 [= Sudhaus Suppl. 44–45]) indicated Zeno was alive when the work was composed (*Horaz' Verhältnis zur Philosophie* [Madgeburg: n.p., 1911] 8–9; cf. Hubbell, *Rhetorica* 259). Philippson ("Zu Philodem und Horaz," *PhW* 49 [1929] 894, and "Philodemos," *RE* 19:2 [1938] 2445) supplemented this argument with the proposal of C. Calpurnius Piso Frugi as the apparent dedicatee of *Rh.* 4 at PHerc. 1007/1673 col. 42a.5 (i.e., Γάϊε παῖ; Sudhaus 1:223), a proposal which also recommended a date in the 70's (cf. Walter Allen, Jr., and Phillip H. De Lacy, "The Patrons of Philodemus," *CP* 34 [1939] 64–65, who proposed Gaius Memmius as dedicatee with similar consequences). Working from paleographical evidence, Guglielmo Cavallo suggested that *Rh.* was composed over a number of years, with the first three books completed during an initial period of activity, perhaps 75–50, and the last four datable sometime between 50 and 25 (*Libri scritture scribi a Ercolano, CErc* 13, suppl. 1 [1983] 63–64).

Recent scholarship has called all these arguments into question. Jakob Wisse has demonstrated that the references to Zeno in *Rh.* need not be read in the "real" present tense and so furnish no evidence for Zeno being alive at the time of the work's composition ("The presence of Zeno: The date of Philodemus' *On Rhetoric* and the Use of the 'Citative' and 'Reproducing' Present in Latin and Greek," *On Latin: Linguistic and Literary Studies in Honour of Harm Pinkster*, eds. Rodie Risselada, Jan R. De Jong, and A. Machtelt Bolkestein [Amsterdam: J. C. Gieben, 1996] 173–202, esp. 196–99). Likewise, Tiziano Dorandi has shown that the dedication of *Rh.* 4 actually reads, ὦ Γάϊε Πάν᾽ σ᾽α, making the dedicatee Gaius Vibius Pansa Caetronianus, a figure whose notoriety is associated with the 50's and early 40's ("Gaio bambino," 41–42). Finally, P. J. Parsons has argued that Cavallo's dating of Herculanean papyri, including those in *Rh.*, should be used

Translation Project from the National Endowment for the Humanities and by an award from the Graduate School General Research Board of the University of Maryland at College Park. An early version of the essay was presented at the Conference on the Text of Philodemus' Rhetoric, University of Texas at Austin, 21 April 1995.

with caution, not least because he proceeds using periods shorter than the productive life of a single scribe (Rev. of *Libri scritture scribi a Ercolano*, *CR* 39 [1989] 358–60). Still, Dorandi's reading of the dedication of *Rh.* 4 would seem to place a *terminus ante quem* in 43 for this segment of the work. And given the consistency of Dorandi's discovery with Cavallo's paleographical arguments, I have chosen to follow Cavallo's dating for *Rh.*, at least as a rough guide.

Determining the influence of *Rh.* also poses difficulties. A number of studies have cited affinities of *Rh.* with approximately contemporary literature, including Cicero's theoretical and historical works concerning oratory (but outside the technical corpus, Gigante, *Philodemus in Italy*, 32–35), Cicero's *De oratore* (Leeman, Pinkster, and Wisse, *De or. Komm.*, 4:148–49); Cicero's *Orator* (Augusto Rostagni, "Risonanze dell'estetica di Filodemo in Cicerone," *A&R*, n.s. 3 [1922] 28–44); Cicero's epistolary corpus (Daniel Delattre, "Philodème dans la «Correspondance» de Cicéron," *BAGB* [1984] 27–39), Dionysius of Halicarnassus' *Isocrates* (P. Costil, "L'esthétique littéraire de Denys d'Halicarnasse" [Thèse Paris, 1949] 369; Germaine Aujac, ed. *Denys d'Halicarnasse, Opuscules rhétoriques*, 5 vols. [Paris: Société D'Édition «Les Belles Lettres», 1978–1992] 1:193–95; and Dorandi, "Varietà Ercolanesi," *CErc.* 21 [1991] 106), and Sextus Empiricus' *Against the Professors* 2 (Longo Auricchio, "Epicureismo e Scetticismo sulla retorica," *Atti del XVII Congresso Internazionale di Papirologia* [*Napoli, 19–26 maggio 1983*] 3 vols. [Naples: Centro internazionale per lo studo dei papiri Ercolanesi, 1984] 2:453–72). But the fact remains, as Sedley has observed, "no doctrinal treatise by Philodemus is ever cited in any ancient source" ("Philosophical Allegiance," 104).

REMEMBERING THE GARDEN: THE TROUBLE WITH WOMEN IN THE SCHOOL OF EPICURUS[1]

PAMELA GORDON

Abstract

Readers of Philodemus are well aware of the difficulties posed by the fragmentary state of the charred papyri. The premise of this paper is that similar but often unacknowledged obstacles confront us when we read almost any text about Epicureanism, even if the text happens to be relatively well preserved. The problem is that most of our sources—in addition to being late, fragmentary, and highly partisan—are already engaged in the process of reconstructing the first generation of the Garden. Hostile writers are eager to document what they portray as the immoral sensualism of Epicurus. Friendly sources take an apologetic stance against such polemics but may sometimes incorporate hostile material unwittingly. To illustrate the problem, this essay focuses upon the issue of Epicurean women. Ancient and modern authorities seem to agree that the Garden included many female members, but a second look reveals that the sources are not as reliable as has been assumed. In fact, most of what the ancient texts say about Epicurean women is bound up—sometimes inextricably—with the twenty-three-hundred-year-old tradition of anti-Epicurean polemic and apologetic response. To generations of Greeks and Romans, the presence of women and slaves in the Garden was emblematic—for good or for ill—of the nature of Epicureanism.

Athenian philosophical schools did not in general welcome women and slaves, but a wide range of authorities, ancient and modern, assures us that Epicureanism was different. When followers of Epicurus gathered in the Garden in the late fourth century B.C.E., Epicurus

---

[1] I presented earlier versions of this work to audiences at Bryn Mawr College, Oberlin College, and the University of Oklahoma, and at the annual meetings of the Classical Association of the Middle West and South (April 1994) and the Society of Biblical Literature (November 1994). Translations are my own except where indicated. This work was supported by the Graduate Research Fund of the University of Kansas, the Hall Center for the Humanities, and the American Council of Learned Societies.

and the other free men were apparently joined by a male slave
named Mys and a sizable group of women, slave and free. Although
philosophizing women and slaves are not unheard of in the histories of the other Greek and Roman schools, the Garden stands out
both because so many women are associated with its founding generation, and because these women serve as a focal point for the considerable animosity directed against the school for the next several
centuries.[2] This essay examines the way hostility against the Epicureans
is couched in heavily gendered terms and suggests that this discourse
both is and is not "literally about gender itself."[3] My conviction is
that outsiders were indeed offended by the presence of women and
slaves in the Garden, but even more important, that the outside
world seized upon this issue largely because it suspected that there
was something fundamentally womanish—and therefore unmanly—
about the Garden itself.

A Garden of Hetairai

Perhaps the most salient feature of the ancient sources that list the
names of Epicurean women is that they identify the women as persons of less than respectable status. The Greek texts that name the
women of the first generation of the Garden (including Leontion,
Themista, Boidion, Erotion, Hedeia, Mammarion, and Nikidion) label
most of these women as *hetairai* (literally, "female companions"). The
term *hetaira* is difficult to translate across historical and cultural boundaries, but is generally regarded as a euphemism for a type of prostitute and in implication may be roughly equivalent to "geisha" or
"courtesan." In Cicero's Latin, Leontion appears as an outright *meretricula*, or "little prostitute" (*Nat. D.* 1. 93). The assertion that Leontion
and her associates were *hetairai* has survived for over two millennia
and appears even in modern studies that attempt to assign these
women a serious place in Epicurean history.

---

[2] On attitudes toward women philosophers in other schools see Michèle Le Dœff,
The Philosophical Imaginary (London: Athlone, 1989), 102; Richard Hawley, "The
Problem of Women Philosophers in Ancient Greece," *Women in Ancient Societies: An
Illusion of the Night*, ed. Leonie Archer, Susan Frishler, and Maria Wyke (New York:
Routledge, 1994), 70–87.
[3] Louis Montrose, "The Work of Gender in the Discourse of Discovery," *Repre-
sentations* 33 (1991): 1, who cites Joan Wallach Scott, *Gender and the Politics of History*
(New York: Columbia University Press, 1988), 45.

Lacking early Epicurean texts that discuss the philosophical bases for the education of women or slaves, sympathetic modern readers have linked the presence of women in the Garden to the broader Epicurean world view. To many of us, it seems reasonable that Epicureanism—a system that understands both nature and culture as developments in the atoms and void—might question the rightness of social conventions. Jane Snyder, for example, identifies Epicureanism as an ancient philosophical system that "advocated the emancipation of women," and asserts:

> The members of the Garden included not only full Athenian citizens like Epicurus himself but also several women and slaves, who, within the context of Athenian society at large, enjoyed few legal rights or privileges. Within the enclosure of the Garden, however, all members of the group—male and female, free and slave—were entitled to the benefits and responsibilities of the Epicurean school.[4]

Snyder acknowledges that no surviving texts explain the unprecedented openness she describes, but she argues that it harmonizes with the Epicurean rejection of teleology. Since Epicurean social theory rejected the notion that the status quo was part of a divinely-created natural order, it makes sense that the Epicureans would reject traditional Greek attitudes toward all social hierarchies, including gender roles and slavery. As Snyder puts it, Epicurus' belief that the world was not divinely created would lead him to assert that "man was not created to serve anyone, nor woman to serve man."[5] Snyder also points out that the Epicurean teaching that personal happiness depends upon ἀταραξία (tranquillity, or lack of turmoil) has ramifications for the lives of women and slaves:

> [A]n individual's marital status, family connections, political influence, or amount of wealth were all considered of little or no value to—or in some cases actually detrimental to—one's true happiness. This focus on individual rather than families or political groups, meant that both sexes were left free to develop their intellectual understanding of the universe through the study of atomic theory, instead of following gender-defined roles designed for economy in attaining material success.[6]

---

[4] Jane Snyder, *The Woman and the Lyre: Women Writers in Classical Greece and Rome* (Carbondale, Ill.: Southern Illinois University Press, 1989), 101–102.
[5] Snyder 102.
[6] Snyder 102–3.

Snyder does not deny that the Epicurean women were courtesans; in fact she asserts that "their position as *hetairai* seems to be confirmed by the typically suggestive meanings of their names: Hedeia ('Sweety'), Mammarion ('Tits'), Boidion ('Ox-eyes,' or something to that effect), Demetria ('Ceres'), and Erotion ('Lovey')."[7] Thus Snyder's idyllic portrayal of life in the Garden tentatively accepts the ancient claim that Leontion and Hedeia were *hetairai* but rejects the ancient assumption that a *hetaira* cannot study philosophy.[8]

Although I find much of Snyder's approach both attractive and defensible, I believe that a closer look at our sources reveals that the textual foundations for this agreeable description of the Garden are unstable and prone to sudden shifts. Most of what the ancient texts say about Epicurean women and slaves is tightly intertwined with the twenty-three-hundred-year-old tradition of anti-Epicurean polemic and apologetic response. There is a potential here for the recovery of an ancient tradition of women philosophers, but that history can be unfolded only as part of a broader inquiry into the ancient and modern notoriety of the Garden.

Why There Were Women in the Garden, According to the Hostile Sources

In antiquity, outsiders who heard tales of women in the Garden ignored the social theory behind the Epicureans' radical conduct and fixed instead upon the notion that the women were present simply to offer erotic pleasure to the men. Centuries after the Garden was founded, Plutarch (c. 46–c. 120 C.E.), for example, finds it self-evident that Leontion, Boidion, Hedeia, and Nikidion must have been "young and attractive" (εὐπρεπεῖς καὶ νέας, *Non Posse* 1097d–e); and he seldom mentions Epicurean women without also alluding to wine, perfumes, or banquets. This hackneyed association between women and other "Epicurean" sources of bodily pleasures appears throughout Plutarch's *Moralia* (see also 1089c, 1099b, and 1129b) as well as in the rhetorical and philosophical works of Cicero (106–43 B.C.E.).[9]

---

[7] Snyder 105.

[8] See also André Jean Festugière, *Epicurus and his Gods*, trans. C. W. Chilton (Oxford: Blackwell, 1955), 30.

[9] Plutarch knew better, of course; elsewhere he records ridicule of Epicurus' proposal that sex ought not to be mixed with food or drink (*Quaest. conv.* 3.6).

Cicero linked all Epicurean dinner parties with sexual debauchery whether the host was a refined personage who supplied the finest game, fish, and wine (Cic. *Fin.* 2.23), or a cheapskate who offered nothing but large quantities of bad wine and rancid meat (*Pis.* 67). This collocation of women, food, and wine is likely to have appeared also in a non-extant tract sardonically titled *Delights* (Τὰ Εὐφραντά) by Timocrates, the brother of Metrodorus and a contemporary of Epicurus.[10] According to Diogenes Laertius, this Timocrates was a renegade Epicurean who wrote *Delights* as an exposé of the Epicureans' alleged intemperance and what he called "those nighttime philosophies" of the Garden (τὰς νυκτερινὰς ἐκείνας φιλοσοφίας, Diog. Laert. 10.6). Also traceable back to Timocrates is the tradition of calling most of the Epicurean women *hetairai* (see Diog. Laert. 10.7).

Given the context (a culture that viewed philosophy as a masculine pursuit), there is a certain logic to the assumption that the feminine component of the Garden was there for the benefit of male pleasure. When Epicureans themselves respond to such charges, they seem to acknowledge the rationale of associating sex with food: "For it is not endless drinking, and parties, and the enjoyment of boys, women, and fish, and the other things supplied by a rich table, that produce a pleasant life, but sober reasoning . . ." (Epicurus, *Ep. Men.* 132). Similarly, the second-century C.E. Epicurean philosopher Diogenes of Oenoanda includes rich food and "the pleasures of exotic sexual activity" (ἀφροδεισίων ἐγλελεγμένων ἡδοναί, Smith Fr. 29) in his list of coveted possessions that are erroneously considered necessary for happiness.[11] Although Epicurus disapproved of illicit sex and considered erotic pleasure to be problematic, it is not entirely absurd for uninformed outsiders to assume that the Epicureans were wildly promiscuous.[12] Epicurean tenets such as "No pleasure is in itself evil" (*KD* 8) had often led detractors to view Epicurus as a dissolute sensualist. Detractors of course suppressed the second half of the saying, which warns: "but things producing certain pleasures involve

[10] For the importance of Timocrates, see David Sedley, "Epicurus and his Professional Rivals," *Etudes sur l'épicurisme antique*, eds. Jean Bollack and André Laks (Lille: Publications de l'Université de Lille III, 1976), 119–59.
[11] Pamela Gordon, *Epicurus in Lycia: The Second-Century World of Diogenes of Oenoanda* (Ann Arbor: University of Michigan Press, 1996), 88.
[12] For Epicurean disapproval of illicit sex (phrased as advice to men) see Diog. Laert. 10.118.

troubles many times greater than their pleasures." The less informed
may not have known that Epicurus praised a diet of bread and
water, that he regarded sexual activity as natural but "unnecessary,"
and that he warned his students that sex could in fact be harmful.[13]

Thus the most obvious complaint against Epicurean women emerges
as a misrepresentation of Epicurean hedonism. The point is to censure and ridicule the Epicureans' alleged devotion to the pleasures
of the flesh: the women represent a sort of food for the proverbial
Epicurean glutton. A closer look at the prevailing polemic against
the Garden, however, reveals a much deeper hostility toward Epicureanism. This deeper animosity has less to do with sex, but much
to do with gender.

"Live Unknown:" A Slogan for Cinaedi

Plutarch's polemic does not stop at the claim that flocks of Epicurean
women were brought to the Garden simply to feed the appetites of
Epicurean voluptuaries. (The pun "flocks" is of course Plutarch's
own: he describes Leontion, Boidion, and two other women as
"grazing" in the Garden, ἐνέμοντο περὶ τὸν κῆπον, *Non Posse* 1097d.)
In Plutarch's imagination, the women of the Garden, far from being
"co-philosophers," cannot even be dismissed as mere instruments of
physical pleasure.[14] Rather, the women are both emblem and proof
of the fact that Epicureanism is a disreputable and dangerous cult
that has no right to be ranked as a philosophy.

According to Plutarch, the Epicureans have given up all worthy
pursuits—including intellectual endeavors—for the mindless pursuit
of sensual pleasures. Instead of reading Aristotle or Homer or staying up late with the historical love stories that educated men esteem,

---

[13] On Epicurean attitudes toward sex, see Tad Brennan, "Epicurus on Sex,
Marriage, and Children," *CP* 91 (1996): 346–352. Brennan offers an important cor-
rective to Jeffrey S. Purinton, "Epicurus on the Telos," *Phronesis* 38 (1993): 281–320.
On the reliability (or not) of Cicero see: M. Stokes, "Cicero on Epicurean Pleasures,"
Cicero the Philosopher, ed. J. G. F. Powell (New York: Oxford University Press, 1995),
145–170. On Philodemus' attitudes toward sex and marriage see David Sider, *The
Epigrams of Philodemos: Introduction, Text, and Commentary* (New York: Oxford University
Press, 1997), 34–36 (with further bibliographical references). On the temperate
lifestyle of the Garden see Diog. Laert. 10.11.

[14] In Diogenes Laertius, Epicurus is praised for the fact that his slaves were his
co-philosophers (συνεφιλοσόφουν αὐτῷ, 10.10).

the ignorant Epicurean climbs into bed with a beautiful woman (*Non Posse* 1093c). As a poor substitute for Archimedes' famous triumphant cry of εὕρηκα ("Eureka!" or "I have found it!"), Plutarch implies, the Epicurean can only yell: βέβρωκα or πεφίληκα ("I have 'eaten!'" or "I have 'kissed!'" *Non Posse* 1094c). The joke is of course a distortion of Epicurean hedonism, which valued spiritual or cerebral pleasures over the physical, once essential bodily needs (food and shelter) had been met.[15]

The picture of the Epicurean who abandons the reading of literature and the pursuit of knowledge (two fundamentally masculine prerogatives in Greek and Roman culture) brings into focus the deeper significance of Plutarch's parody. These lampoons of the Epicureans' supposed disdain for erudition progress from criticizing Epicurus' alleged sexual intemperance to impugning his virility.[16] Plutarch's original readers would see no great conceptual leap here, for Greek culture commonly describes devotion to pleasure as a feminine vice.[17] Love of the body or excessive attention to its demands is thus construed as effeminacy.[18] This explains why the philosopher Epictetus calls Epicurus a *cinaedologos*, "a preacher of effeminacy," or "a pervert-professor" (Diog. Laert. 10.7).[19] If one takes *cinaedus* exclusively as a term for a "passive homosexual," Epictetus' name-calling seems random and inapposite. Although Epicurus was ridiculed for his attachment to "pretty Pythocles" (a male student, Diog. Laert. 10.5), polemicizers generally give him female lovers. Recent studies,

---

[15] See Diog. Laert. (10.137), who contrasts pleasures of the body (σάρξ and σῶμα) with the greater pleasures of the mind or spirit (ψυχή). This report is consistent with Epicurus' *Ep. Men.* 132. For discussion see J. C. B. Gosling and C. C. W. Taylor, *The Greeks on Pleasure* (Oxford: Oxford University Press, 1982), 349–354; and Anthony A. Long, "Pleasure and Social Utility: The Virtues of Being Epicurean," *Aspects de la philosophie hellénistique*, eds. I. G. Kidd, Hellmut Flashar, Olof Gigon (Geneva: Fondation Hardt, 1986).

[16] On Epicurean education and attitudes toward literature see Asmis, "Epicurean Economics," in this volume and Asmis, "Epicurean Poetics," *Philodemus and Poetry*, ed. Dirk Obbink (New York: Oxford University Press, 1995), 15–34.

[17] Catherine Edwards cites many Roman texts that also construe pleasure as feminine; *The Politics of Immorality* (Cambridge: Cambridge University Press, 1993), esp. 63–97 and 174 n. 1.

[18] As Page duBois puts it: "Women are hopelessly tied up with the body in ancient Greek culture" (*Sappho is Burning* [Chicago: University of Chicago Press, 1995], 95).

[19] For a more technical meaning of the term κιναιδολόγος, see "cinaedic poetry," *OCD³*.

however, have drawn attention to the wide connotations of the word
cinaedus, which overlap only fractionally with the implications of pejorative words for homosexuals in English. In calling Epicurus a *cinaedo-
logus*, Epictetus meant to match his barb to his target: the *cinaedus* is
a she-man who is above all licentious, and his interest in pleasure
is doubly suspect because he desires to teach pleasure to others.[20]

According to Plutarch, a man with any shame would hide such
a reprehensible lack of virility. This is the theme of *De Latenter Vivendo*
("Is 'Live Unknown' a Wise Precept?"), a treatise in Plutarch's *Moralia*
that travesties the Epicurean adage λάθε βιώσας, "Live Unknown."
This maxim urges withdrawal from public life and the renunciation
of the competitive values of the culture at large.[21] Those friendly to
Epicureanism would understand it as a call to renounce ostentation
and the desire for fame, wealth, and power. For Plutarch, however,
the appeal "Live unknown" warns the Epicurean to hide what is
shameful, "as he would his grave-robbing" (*De lat. viv.* 1128c).

In the *De Latenter Vivendo* Plutarch presents two poles: the public
glory of intellectual, political, and military achievement on one side;
and the shady, woman-filled disrepute of the Garden on the other.
Throughout the treatise, Plutarch associates the "rites" of Epicureanism
(τὰ τέλη, 1129b) with women, darkness, nighttime, and oblivion, and
contrasts this characterization of the Garden with the noble, light-
filled, virtuous world of the men he views as the true philosophers
and best generals and statesmen of Greece and Rome. Here Plutarch
is exploiting traditional Hellenic distinctions between public and private realms, which in Athenian culture are divided along gender
lines. As David Cohen puts it:

> They thought of public space in terms of places where *men* gathered:
> the agora, the Assembly, the courts, the baths, athletic grounds, and
> so on ... Private space in this narrow sense is largely female space,
> enclosed, hidden, guarded, dark. Public space, on the other hand, is

---

[20] Maud Gleason describes the Greek view thus: "A man who aims to please—
any one, male or female—in his erotic encounters is ipso facto effeminate" (*Making
Men* [Princeton: Princeton University Press, 1995], 65, with bibliography). Although
the Epicurean *telos* is the attainment—and not the giving—of pleasure, outsiders
tended to merge these ideas and to portray Epicurus as a (pleasure-giving) flatterer
(Diog. Laert. 10.4–5).

[21] Cf. Epicurus KD 7; SV 58, Diog. Laert. 10.119, Lucr. 5.1117–1132. See also
Arthur W. H. Adkins, *From the Many to the One* (London: Constable, 1970), 257 and
Long, "Pleasure and Social Utility," 287–89.

associated with men and with the public activities through which men pursue reputation and honor.[22]

The paradigm is prescriptive as well as descriptive: "The politics of reputation required a man to lead a public life."[23]

Although Plutarch identified primarily with the Greek elite, he was a great admirer of Roman "virtue" and Roman military might.[24] (Many Romans themselves identified "fighting and morality" as Rome's two great possessions.)[25] The following quotation from Seneca (first century c.e.) illustrates how Plutarch's characterization of the Garden engages Roman notions of the virility of moral probity as well as Hellenic notions of gendered realms. The context of this passage is Seneca's critique of the supposedly effeminate Garden, which he contrasts with the virility of the Stoa:

> Virtue is something lofty, exalted and regal, unconquered, untiring. Pleasure is something low, slavish, weak, decrepit, whose place and home are the brothels and taverns. Virtue you will find in the temple, in the forum, in the senate house, defending the city walls, dusty and sunburnt, hands callused. Pleasure you will find most often seeking out darkness, lurking around the baths and sweating rooms and places that fear the magistrates; soft, languid, reeking of wine and perfume, pallid or else painted and made up like a corpse. (Sen. *De vita beata* 7.3)

Plutarch also associates the pursuit of pleasure with death, for he develops the male/female contrast yet further: the masculine pole offers not just sunlight and fame but life itself. For the best of men the masculine world even offers immortality, not just in the form of lasting fame, but through attainment of an afterlife among the blessed. In contrast, the womanish Garden is aligned with mold, decay, and death. This death is not the simple cessation of life taught by Epicurean philosophy, but consignment to the deepest and most forgotten realm of the abyss (*De lat. viv.* 1129f–1130e).

---

[22] David Cohen, *Law, Sexuality, and Society: The Enforcement of Morals In Classical Athens* (Cambridge: Cambridge University Press, 1991), 73. Roman discourse usually allotted the baths to the feminine realm (see quotation from Seneca, below).

[23] Cohen 74.

[24] Jacques Boulogne, *Plutarque: un aristocrate grec sous l'occupation romaine* (Lille: Presses Universitaires de Lille, 1994); Simon Swain, *Hellenism and Empire: Language, Classicism, and Power in the Greek World a.d. 50–250* (Oxford: Oxford University Press, 1996), 135–186.

[25] Edwards 1.

Plutarch protests that Epicurus' supposed advice to hide in the shadows of the Garden would make weak, ill, or evil people even worse, for when people conceal their disorders they embed their vices yet deeper. Then he continues:

> On the other hand, if it is to good men that you tender this advice to go unnoticed and unknown, then you are telling Epaminondas not to be general, Lycurgus not to frame laws, Thrasybulus to slay no tyrants, Pythagoras not to teach, Socrates not to converse, and yourself to begin with, Epicurus, not to write to your friends in Asia, not to enlist recruits from Egypt, not to cultivate the youth of Lampsacus, not to circulate books to every man and every woman in which you advertise your wisdom, and not to leave instructions for your funeral (1128f–1129a).[26]

Ostensibly Plutarch is simply summing up the masculine achievements that the teachings of the Garden would ban while pointing out the inherent contradiction: the famous philosopher urges his followers to shun fame.

The reappearance of Epicurean women (and foreigners, who are so often feminized in Greek ideology) in this passage is especially significant, however. Plutarch's derisive allusion to Epicurus' habit of sending books "to every man and woman" (πᾶσι καί πάσαις, *De Lat. Viv.* 1129; cf. *Non Posse* 1094d) comes close to an acknowledgment that the Epicurean women were actually students or philosophers themselves. The point of this and most other gender-inclusive references to Epicurus' circle, however, is to dismiss Epicurus as a fraud, a non-philosopher, a *cinaedologos*. The ridicule of Leontion by Cotta, the Academic interlocutor in Cicero's *Natura Deorum*, has a similar tone. Leontion is denounced for being so forward as to write a treatise against Theophrastus. Although Cotta acknowledges the excellence of Leontion's prose, he calls her *meretricula*, "little prostitute" and condemns her audacity: "She writes in fine Attic Greek style, but really! What dissolution the Garden allowed!"[27] Cicero employs similar strategies when he ridicules Epicurus for contaminating his philosophical prose with references to a mere woman named Themista, an aberration he associates with the failure of the Epicureans to pay

---

[26] Benedict Einarson and Phillip H. De Lacy, trans., *Plutarch's Moralia*, vol. 7, LCL (Cambridge: Harvard University Press, 1927), 327–29.

[27] *Nat. D.* 1.93; trans. Snyder 103.

homage to Solon, Themistocles, and the other great Greek statesmen (*Fin.* 2.21.68).

Plutarch would agree with Cicero's claim that it is impossible to
remember any man who lived for pleasure: such men simply sink
into oblivion (Cic. *Fin.* 2.63; 2.67). Plutarch's characterization of pleasure differs, however, from that of Seneca and Cicero in a way that
may be due to a difference between Hellenic and Roman views.
Although Cicero and Seneca describe pleasure as exclusively feminine, Plutarch does not abolish pleasure entirely from the male
realm.[28] Instead, he claims certain higher pleasures as the exclusive
property of manly success. This is one of the main assertions of
Plutarch's *Non Posse* ("That Epicurus Actually Makes a Pleasant Life
Impossible"). In this treatise he describes, for example, the pleasure
felt by the Theban general Epaminondas when his parents had the
opportunity to gaze upon the trophy set up for his victory at Leuctra.
Plutarch contrasts the pride of the general's mother to the chagrin
of Epicurus' mother, who had to look at Epicurus and Polyaenus
"making babies in the little garden with [Hedeia] the *hetaira* from
Cyzicus" (*Non Posse* 1098).[29]

Elsewhere Plutarch presents disdain for Epicureans as a sign of
Roman strength. In the *Pyrrhus*, for example, when Fabricius hears
for the first time about the womanish teachings of the Garden (which
was founded just a few decades before the supposed time of this
story), he exclaims: "May Pyrrhus and the Samnites cherish these
notions as long as they are at war with us!" (*Pyrrh.* 20.7)

Revisionist Readings of the Hostile Sources

In the 1950's Norman De Witt, a scholar who was very friendly to
Epicureanism, published a description of the Garden in which the
male slaves of the Garden provided the labor force for Epicurean
book production, the young courtesans offered pleasant companion-
ship, the female slaves waited on the courtesans, and the entire

---

[28] On the Roman sources see Edwards 200 and footnote 17, above. Since most
of our sources on Epicureanism date to the era of the late Roman Republic and
Empire, it is difficult to sort Roman from Hellenic attitudes, even if the text is in
Greek.

[29] Plutarch derisively uses the diminutive κηπίδιον (*kepidion*) for κῆπος (*kepos*), thus
dubbing the Garden "the Gardenette."

community was kept in order by a strict hierarchy headed by Epicurus the patriarch.[30] More recently, Bernard Frischer has presented the novel thesis that the Garden recruited its members by setting up statues of a fatherly-looking bearded Epicurus in strategic locations throughout the Greek cities. According to Frischer's scenario, slaves and prostitutes—people who were especially in need of a good father figure to protect them—flocked to the Garden to sit at Epicurus' feet.[31] Several other modern studies have, however, caught glimpses of various degrees of Epicurean egalitarianism in the pages of (for example) Cicero, Diogenes Laertius, and Plutarch. I began this essay by describing the work of Jane Snyder; at this point I shall turn briefly to an early article by David Sedley and then to the work of Martha Nussbaum (to which I shall return more than once).

Sedley's re-reading of the ancient testimonia to a non-extant treatise by Epicurus called *On Occupations* lends support to the interpretations proposed by both Snyder and Frischer, while adding another slant.[32] Our polemical sources are not concerned with the distinctions between prostitutes, courtesans, and wanton women; to Plutarch and Cicero the words *hetaira* and *meretricula* seem to have all those connotations. Setting aside any judgment on their morality, we may wonder whether there were women who joined the Epicureans in order to flee a life in which they had to offer their bodies (and artistic talents; Greek *hetairai* were often expected to dance or play the flute) in return for economic subsistence. Sedley's reading of the fragments of *On Occupations* supplies evidence for the possibility that the Garden offered these women refuge. The extant references to this treatise show that it discussed the originally low status of certain eminent philosophers. Protagoras, for example, is said to have worked as a common laborer until his ingenious device for carrying logs attracted the notice of Democritus, and Aristotle supposedly worked in the drug-trade. The standard interpretation of these references is

---

[30] In De Witt's scenario, the work of male and female slaves is under the supervision of Mys and Phaedrium, respectively; *Epicurus and his Philosophy* (St. Paul: University of Minnesota Press, 1954), 95–96.

[31] Bernard Frischer *The Sculpted Word: Epicureanism and Philosophical Recruitment in Ancient Greece* (Berkeley and Los Angeles: University of California Press, 1982). Frischer's understanding of this Epicurean hierarchy seems to be based upon De Witt's reading of Philodemus' *On Frank Criticism*; "Organization and Procedure in Epicurean Groups," *CP* 31 (1936): 205–211.

[32] Sedley 119–59.

that *On Occupations* was a polemic against Epicurus' predecessors. Sedley, however, suggests that the purpose of these stories was not to condemn Protagoras or Aristotle, but to inspire others. Sedley offers the following modern parallel: "A New York art school used to advertise its course with a poster which read, 'At the age of thirty-five Gaugin worked in a bank'. The point was not, of course, to mock Gaugin as a bank-clerk."[33] Sedley also suggests that later stories about the advancement of Mys (from slave to philosopher) and Leontion (from courtesan to philosopher) have affinities with *On Occupations*, which may have been addressed to Leontion and Mys or others like them.

So perhaps Leontion and the others actually were courtesans before they turned to the life of philosophy. Ancient gossip, however, usually presented Leontion simply as a philosopher's consort, or denied that Leontion ever changed. In Athenaeus' *Deipnosophistae* (late second century C.E.), a character at the table claims that Leontion never gave up her wanton ways:

> Did not Epicurus have as his lover Leontion, who was notorious for being a *hetaira*? She did not stop being a *hetaira* when she became a philosopher, but had sex with all the Epicureans in the Garden, even in front of Epicurus, causing him great distress. (13.588b).

In Alciphron's fictional "Letters of Courtesans" (second or third century C.E.), Leontion complains that she is expected to play Xanthippe to Epicurus, while this pseudo-Socrates also keeps Pythocles as his Alcibiades (Alciphron 2.2.3). It is difficult to say whether the tradition of painting portraits of Leontion "in meditation" (Plin. *HN* 35.144; cf. 35.99) represents an alternate tradition (one that regarded her as a bona fide philosopher) or whether the point was to portray a beautiful *hetaira* who could also philosophize.

Martha Nussbaum's *Therapy of Desire* also considers the possibility that the hostile sources may contain some evidence for a radical stand on the education of *hetairai* among the Epicureans. This recent presentation of Hellenistic ethics traces the footsteps of an imaginary female pupil as she seeks wisdom and healing in the various Greek and Roman philosophical schools. Nussbaum's choice for the role of this pupil is not Leontion, but Nikidion, a "perhaps historical and

---

[33] Sedley 126.

probably fictitious"[34] woman of the Garden mentioned by Diogenes
Laertius (10.7) and Plutarch (*Non Posse* 1097d–e). Nussbaum takes
the name Nikidion ("little victory") as a *hetaira* name, but points out
that *hetairai* "would be more likely than other women to be literate,
and to have the freedom to move around at their own discretion."[35]
When Nikidion studies with Aristotle (in Nussbaum's fictional account),
she must disguise herself as a man even to gain admission, but among
the Epicureans she is welcome as herself. Although Nussbaum does
not see Epicurus "as a complete social radical," she asserts that "[t]he
radical step Epicurus took in opening his school to the real Nikidions
of the world both influenced and was influenced by his conception
of what philosophy should be."[36] In Nussbaum's analysis, however,
the result of the Garden's apparently progressive attitude toward
women seems ultimately to be a step backward, for Epicurus' conception of what philosophy "should be" also required the passivity
and intellectual submission of the pupil.

But an *Epicurean* hetaira *named "Pleasant?"*

While Sedley and Snyder rehabilitate Leontion the *meretricula* and
Hedeia the *hetaira*, others question the historicity of all or most of
the Epicurean *hetairai*. Despite her interest in Nikidion as a potential pupil of the Garden, Martha Nussbaum, for example, looks
askance at names like "Tit" (Mammarion) and "Sweety-Pie" (Hedeia),
and writes: "The authenticity of all the names is highly questionable, clearly; and we see that the beginnings of female philosophizing
went hand in hand with the beginnings of sexist 'humour' about the
character of the women concerned."[37] To my ear, the name Hedeia
(literally, "Sweet," or "Pleasant") seems especially suspect because it
sounds like a punning burlesque on Epicurean hedonism. Sifting fact
from polemic is not simple, however, and there is always the danger

---

[34] Nussbaum, *The Therapy of Desire: Theory and Practice in Hellenistic Ethics* (Princeton: Princeton University Press, 1994), 45.

[35] Nussbaum 53.

[36] Nussbaum 117, and 117 n. 32.

[37] Martha Nussbaum, "Therapeutic Arguments: Epicurus and Aristotle," *The Norms of Nature: Studies in Hellenistic Ethics*, ed. Malcolm Schofield and Gisela Striker (Cambridge: Cambridge University Press, 1986), p. 38 n. 10. See also Hawley ("The Problem of Women Philosophers"), and Nussbaum, *Therapy of Desire*.

that the names sound suspicious only if we harbor erroneous notions of respectable names for fourth-century Greek women.

This much is certain, however: epigraphical evidence proves that the most dubious-sounding Epicurean women's names are in fact genuine Greek names. Until recently, there also seemed to be significant evidence to suggest that those names belonged in fact to women from the Garden. The apparent confirmation comes from two epigraphical sources: names that match those of four of the Epicurean *hetairai* appear in third- or fourth-century B.C.E. inscriptions from Attic healing sanctuaries. One inscription in particular has led Catherine Castner to suggest that three Epicurean women (Nikidion, Hedeia, and Boidion) made a pilgrimage from the Garden to the temple of Amphiaraos at Oropos, and that Hedeia also made an offering (this time in the company of Mammarion) at the temple of Asclepius in Athens.[38]

Castner's study does not focus upon an analysis of the epigraphical sources that might lead to such a conclusion, but concentrates instead upon the theological issue: since Epicurus denied that the gods are interested in human affairs, would he have allowed the women to visit the temples? Citing sources such as Philodemus' *On Piety* (93), Castner acknowledges that Epicureanism allowed for traditional worship, but concludes that the *quid pro quo* of the healing cults was antithetical to Epicurean teachings. For Castner, the special allowances made for errant female students in Philodemus' *On Frank Criticism* (to which I shall return below) supplies the solution: "Once the women had made the dedications, they would have found indulgence and forgiveness on the return to the Kepos."[39]

Recent work on the temple archives, however, demonstrates that the appearance of the women's names (among dozens of others) on the same stone means very little: the temple inventories were taken so sporadically that the records demonstrate only that offerings made by women with "Epicurean" names were present in the temples during two particular inventories. As Sara Aleshire makes clear in her discussion of the inscription from the Asclepieum on the slopes of the Acropolis, "the putative proximity of the dedications does not

---

[38] Catherine Castner, "Epicurean Hetairai As Dedicants to Healing Divinities?" *GRBS* 60 (1982): 51–57.

[39] Castner 56.

exist: not only are [the names] separated by a break of unknown dimension (at least 23 lines in height) thus destroying their supposed close arrangement in the temple, but even the proximity of dedications as listed in this ἐξετασμός indicates nothing about the chronological sequence when those dedications were made."[40] Years or even decades may have intervened between the women's offerings, and the inscriptions themselves are not securely dated to the first generation of the Garden. (Aleshire dates the inventory from the Asklepieum shortly before 274/3 B.C.E., around 25 years later than Castner's date of 301/0.) It is important to note also that the name Hedeia, which seems at first to provide a link between the two inscriptions, is in fact a very common name: a recent lexicon lists twenty-two occurrences of the name Hedeia for Attica alone.[41] Thus the inscriptional evidence establishes only that the names themselves are real names, not that they belonged to women who visited the temple together, nor that the women had come from the Garden.

It may be significant that the two Epicurean women's names with the best authority (both appearing in the writings of Epicurus) are also the least sexually suggestive: Themista and Leontion. Although it was not uncommon to give animal names to prostitutes, and although the related name Leaina ("Lioness") may evoke a sexual position, Leontion's name ("Little Lioness") is not necessarily erotic.[42] Cicero's allusion (via Cotta in *Nat. D.* 1.93) to Leontion's philosophical writings makes clear that she must have been at the very least a disciple of the Garden (and not simply a "companion").[43]

---

[40] Sara Aleshire, *The Athenian Asklepieion: The People, Their Dedications, and the Inventories* (Amsterdam: J. C. Gieben, 1989), 67. Having seen this inscription (for which I owe thanks to Harry Kritzas, curator of the National Epigraphical Museum at Athens), I can confirm that the printed editions make the text appear more compact and less damaged than it actually is. Although Aleshire's published work treats mainly the Asclepieum, her judgment is also relevant for the temple of Amphiaraos.

[41] M. J. Osborne and S. G. Bryne, eds., *A Lexicon of Greek Personal Names* Vol. II: *Attica* (Oxford: Clarendon Press, 1987). Two of these 22 citations are those discussed by Aleshire and Castner; a third is Diogenes Laertius 10.7.

[42] For a recent discussion of the "lioness" position and *hetairai* named Leaina, see Andrew Stewart, "Reflections," *Sexuality in Ancient Art*, ed. Natalie Kampen (Cambridge: Cambridge University Press, 1996), 136–154; and Andrew Stewart, *Art, Desire, and the Body in Ancient Greece* (Cambridge: Cambridge University Press, 1997), 159–162.

[43] Christian Jensen once suggested that a text from Herculaneum listed Leontion as a director of the Garden, but his reading has not found support. Christian Jensen, "Ein neuer Brief Epikurs," *Abhandlungen der Gesellschaft der Wissenschaften zu Göttingen*, Philologisch-Historische Klasse, III 5 (1933): 1–94.

Themista ("Righteous"), who is not labeled as a *hetaira* in the ancient texts, seems—as Cicero's testimony tells us (*Fin.* 2.21.68)—to have figured in some of Epicurus' philosophical writings. Cicero's reference to his enemy Piso's being "wiser than Themista" is apparently another contemptuous allusion to Themista's reputed philosophical expertise (*Pis.* 63), and she appears as a genuine Epicurean philosopher in Clement of Alexandria (*Strom.* 4.19) and Lactantius (*Div. Inst.* 3.25.15). Perhaps Leontion and Themista were the only women of the early Garden, and there were no *hetairai* involved until Timocrates invented them in his exposé. If we discount Timocrates' report on the Epicurean lifestyle, however, and excise the erotic-sounding names from our lists of first-generation Epicureans, we are left with very few women. This may be the safest path for the historian, but later Epicureans were not so inhospitable. They seem instead to have welcomed Hedeia and Mammarion as their own.

Hedeia et aliae in Later Epicurean Circles

Whether there really were women in the Garden with names like "Erotion" and "Hedeia," or whether the names were invented by anti-Epicurean pamphleteers, the stories endured. To generations of outsiders, Epicurus' relations with these women, together with the stories of Epicurus' over-indulgence in food and wine, epitomized his immoral doctrine of pleasure. Epicurus was not only rumored to have associated with *hetairai*; he also supposedly kept up a salacious correspondence with them. In Alciphron's "Letters of Courtesans," Leontion is made to complain to the famous *hetaira* Lamia about a lecherous Epicurus who will not stop sending her "interminable" letters (Alciphron 2.2.1–3 = Epicurus fr. 142 US).[44] The foes of Epicurus could easily imagine such letters, or they could fabricate them. In fact, Diogenes Laertius tells us of a collection of dirty letters "from Epicurus" that Diogenes claims were actually composed by Diotimus the Stoic (Diog. Laert. 10.3). An Epicurean letter that appears in the second-century C.E. inscription of Diogenes of Oenoanda responds

---

[44] Part of the joke here seems to be that Lamia's correspondent is Leontion (Little Lioness) rather than Leaina (Lioness). Leaina and Lamia were famous *hetairai* who associated with the tyrant Demetrius Poliorketes; the sources seem to treat these women as a familiar pair (Athenaeus 13.577).

to such defamation by replacing the popular view of Epicurus with
a more favorable portrayal. I regard this text, which is known as
the *Letter to Mother*, as a fictional portrayal of the founding sage of
the Garden.[45] Rejecting the dominant tradition, *The Letter to Mother*
documents another Epicurus: a man who wrote helpful letters to his
mother, teaching her how to seek Epicurean ἀταραξία (tranquillity).
The letter not only demonstrates that Epicurus cared for his mother
(perhaps the ultimate character reference), but, by depicting him
engaged in philosophical discussion with her, it suggests that his interest in welcoming women to the Garden was completely honorable.
In Plutarch's imagination Epicurus was a source of shame to his
mother, but the text from Oenoanda demonstrates instead that
Epicurus brought her joy and wisdom.

While rumors spread among outsiders, the Epicureans seem not
to have refuted the stories about *hetairai*, but instead responded
obliquely: they either affirmed that women can indeed engage in
philosophy (as in the *Letter to Mother*), or criticized the dominant culture's attitudes toward erotic love (as in book 4 of Lucretius). While
outsiders viewed Hedeia and the other women as proof of Epicurean
depravity, later Epicureans added them to their lists of forebears.
Thus Hedeia, Nikidion, Mammarion, and Demetria appear in a text
of Philodemus (*PHerc.* 1005).[46] Most of the known names are also
recorded (without any denial that the women belonged to Epicurus'
circle) by Diogenes Laertius, who was certainly a great supporter of
Epicureanism if he was not an official member of a particular
Epicurean group.[47] Considering Diogenes' regard for Epicureanism,
it is noteworthy that he records that Leontion became the concu-
bine (παλλακή, Diog. Laert. 10.23) of Metrodorus, although she
appears in a fragment of Seneca as his wife (*uxor*; Haase, fr. 45).

Philodemus acknowledges that there were complaints about erotic
encounters in the Garden when he writes that a certain man "griped
repeatedly that Leontion and a certain *hetaira* are mentioned in the
Epicurean *Pragmateia* (ἐν τῆι πραγματείαι) and that Nikidion was the
lover of Idomeneus, Mammarion of Leonteus, Demetria of Hermar-

---

[45] See Gordon 66–93.
[46] Anna Angeli, *Agli amici di scuola (PHerc. 1005)*. La scuola di Epicuro 7 (Naples: Bibliopolis, 1988), 191.
[47] Gordon 51; Jaap Mansfeld, *Studies in the Historiography of Greek Philosophy* 348 (Assen: Van Gorcum, 1990).

chus, and about what kind of 'paedagogue' Polyaenus was to Pythocles ..." (PHerc. 1005, fr. 117.2).[48] Some scholars have supposed
that the man to whom Philodemus here refers must be an outsider
(perhaps a Stoic), or a defector like our Timocrates. Recent work on
this text, however, shows that the complainer is in fact an Epicurean
who does not have his facts straight.[49] He knows a few Epicurean
texts but his knowledge is superficial, and he is profoundly confused
about the lives of the first Epicureans. Anna Angeli suggests that
Philodemus implies that this grumbling Epicurean had learned some
of his Epicurean history from spurious sources, perhaps even from
fake letters such as those by Diotimus the Stoic.[50] Although the text
breaks off just after the apparent allegation of an erotic relationship
between Pythocles and Polyaenus (quoted above), it seems that
Philodemus is criticizing the wayward Epicurean for believing bad
things about the first generation of the Garden, not for believing in
Epicurean *hetairai* who did not exist.

A few other texts of Philodemus suggest that he was indeed unper-
turbed by the notion that a woman could have a voice in philosophical discourse. Perhaps the most tantalizing (but inconclusive)
evidence comes from Philodemus' epigrams in the Greek Anthology,
a corpus that is seldom read as an integral part of Philodemus'
Epicurean writings.[51] These epigrams present fleeting images of a
woman named Xanthippe who is not only conversant with Epicurean
thought, but more knowledgeable than her male companion (Epigram
3).[52] Even more interesting is David Sider's observation that Xanthippe,
the lover and wife of "Philodemus" in some of the poems is also
portrayed as his "Epicurean friend" (e.g. in Epigram 7).[53] Even the
combination—lover, spouse, and friend—is startling: the idea that a

---

[48] The *Pragmateia* may be a document on Epicurean history or Epicurean discipline; Anna Angeli translates: "negli scritti dottrinari dottrinari," Angeli 191.

[49] Angeli 26, 271–277.

[50] Angeli 272.

[51] For a sustained assessment of the Epicurean stance of Philodemus' poems, see
Sider's edition of the *Epigrams*, which makes frequent reference also to the work of
Gigante. For the possibility that Philodemus' love poetry affirms that women can
be Epicurean philosophers see Sider, "The Love Poetry of Philodemus," *American
Journal of Philology* 108 (1987): 311–323, esp. 319.

[52] Sider, *Epigrams* 68. See also Sider's essay in this volume.

[53] Sider, *Epigrams*, 36. In Sider's reading, the woman's name suggests that the
"Philodemus" of the poems is playing Socrates to her Xanthippe.

man might desire his own wife appears only rarely in Greek, the notorious exception being the story of Candaules (Hdt. 1.8.1). But given the importance of friendship among Epicureans, the apparent inclusion of a woman "as a 'friend' in the special sense used within the Garden"[54] is even more significant. And yet the evidence from the poems is too slight to allow a full treatment of Philodemus' attitudes toward female Epicureans.

Another scrap of evidence comes to us from the papyrus text of Philodemus' *On Frank Criticism*, an incomplete and sometimes perplexing work that—according to the current consensus—offers "a fairly good picture of later Epicurean psychagogy and communal pedagogy."[55] The main topic of this text is the candid criticism of moral error among Epicurean friends, and the papyrus indicates that Philodemus is recording the wisdom of the Epicurean scholarch Zeno, whose lectures Philodemus heard in Athens. Thus it is notable that the discussions of various modes of speech for different sorts of students (or Epicurean friends) include references to the teacher's need to make adjustments not only for the student's age and status, but also for the student's gender: "just as a lad differs from a woman and old men will differ from [<women>] and youngsters alike" (VIa).[56] Later the text also cautions that women have difficulty accepting criticism because "they assume rather that they are being reviled and they are all the more crushed by the disgrace" (XXIIa) and tend to burst into tears (XXIIb). While this is not strong evidence for the existence of leading Epicurean women philosophers, Philodemus certainly implies here that an Epicurean community would include serious female practitioners or students. A decided lack of sympathy for the Epicurean woman is apparent, however, in his comments that woman are suspicious of their teachers, and that they are "too impulsive and too vain and too fond of their [reputation]" (XXIIa).

Other papyrus texts of Philodemus also provide further indication that Philodemus or his teachers may have been uneasy with the presence of women in the early Garden. Philodemus frequently appeals to Epicurean authority, but for him the canonical texts are clearly

---

[54] Sider, *Epigrams* 89.
[55] David Konstan, Diskin Clay, Clarence E. Glad, Johan C. Thom, and James Ware, eds., *Philodemus: On Frank Criticism*, SBLTT (Altanta, Georgia: Scholars Press, 1998), 2.
[56] Translation from Konstan et al. 101.

not just those of Epicurus himself, but of a group he calls οἱ ἄνδρες ("the men"): Epicurus, Metrodorus, Hermarchus, and Polyaenus.[57] These three companions to Epicurus are of course well known from the texts of Diogenes Laertius and others, but it was only with the discovery of the papyri of Philodemus that a tradition of four Founding Fathers was revealed.[58] My suspicion is that this is a case of an "invention of tradition" and that first-century Epicureans call the founders "the men" (rather than, say, "the four") advisedly. The evidence is too slight to pin down the date or author of such an invention, but my own candidate is Philodemus' teacher Zeno. According to Cicero (who also heard Zeno lecture), Zeno habitually ridiculed the Stoic Chrysippos by calling him *Chrysippa* (in the feminine; *Nat. D.* 1.93). This suggests some name-calling exchanges between Stoics and Epicureans in which Zeno responded in kind to the pervasive anti-Epicurean rhetoric. Outsiders could call the Garden womanish, but this new tradition of Founding Fathers asserts its manliness.

Perhaps the impulse that gave the Garden "the men" also made it hostile toward female disciples. The Garden survived for several hundred years, but most of the women whose names appear in our sources belong to the first generation only. It is hard to say whether this is due only to the backward-looking glance of both Epicureans and outsiders, or whether there simply were no women in the Garden through much of its history. During the second century c.e. when Epicureanism enjoyed a widespread revival, some women attached themselves to the school—including Plotina (wife of the emperor Trajan) and at least one woman in Rhodes (see Diogenes of Oenoanda, who mentions the friendly ministrations of this woman in a badly damaged fragment, Smith fr. 122). I imagine that these women saw themselves as the successors of Leontion and Themista, as well as of Mammarion, Hedeia, and Erotion.

---

[57] Sedley, "Philosophical Allegiance in the Greco-Roman World," *Philosophia Togata: Essays on Philosophy and Roman Society*, ed. Miriam Griffin and Jonathan Barnes (Oxford: Oxford University Press, 1989), 105–6; and Francesca Longo Auricchio, "La suola di Epicuro," *CErc* 8 (1978): 21–37.

[58] Seneca may be alluding to this tradition when he writes that the three became *magnos viros* through their association with Epicurus (Sen. *Ep.* 6.6). Plutarch also makes sardonic use of "the men" as a title throughout the *Non Posse* (1087A, 1087B, 1088D, 1096E, and passim).

A Suggestion in Lieu of a Conclusion

While some modern scholarship continues (in the Timocratean tradition) to treat the Epicureans as unreflective pleasure-seekers, several studies have come to the Garden's defense. In this essay I have given serious consideration to Jane Snyder's confident description of gender equality in the Garden. In stark opposition is the work of Norman De Witt, who argued that Epicurean circles maintained a strict hierarchy with Epicurus as patriarch. An uneasy middle ground is now occupied by Martha Nussbaum, who holds that women and slaves did indeed study in the Garden, but who questions the intellectual value of Epicureanism itself. To illustrate her view Nussbaum quotes an ancient Greek joke in which the sage Arcesilaus is asked why students from various schools can move to the Garden, but no Epicureans ever go over to the other schools. Arcesilaus replies: "Because men can become eunuchs, but eunuchs never become men" (Diog. Laert. 4.43).[59] To Nussbaum, this quip offers an apt assessment of the analytical inadequacies of Epicurean training, but I would shift the focus back to the sexual slur. Surely the eunuch joke refers not just to the alleged intellectual inferiority of the Garden, but also to the gender issues raised in this essay.

Male Epicureans were notorious not only for withdrawing to the Garden in the company of women, but also for their subversion of conventional notions of what it means to be a Greek (or a Roman) and a man. To return to the metaphorical use of women as a sign for the Epicurean character and to complaints about Epicureans not making good generals or politicians: can we not concede that Plutarch is sometimes right? Instead of siding with Plutarch, Cicero, and others who ridicule the Epicureans for not being *real men*, current readers can take the polemics as evidence that Epicureanism deserves to be taken seriously as a critique of Greek and Roman society. The final suggestion I would offer to students of Epicureanism is to test this paradigm shift whenever any joke or anecdote about the Epicureans is encountered: the Garden was notorious not because it promoted licentious behavior (as its enemies claimed), but because it was critical of the dominant culture. Although it will always be difficult to

---

[59] Nussbaum, "Therapeutic Arguments," 73–4; also Nussbaum, *The Therapy of Desire*, 139.

rewrite the history of Epicureanism, our inquiries will be most fruit-
ful if we grant that it is no coincidence that the Garden, which is
arguably the least respected and most maligned of the Greek and
Roman philosophical schools, is also the one that is most often cited
as the school that harbored women and slaves.

CALL ME FRANK: LUCIAN'S (SELF-)DEFENSE OF FRANK SPEAKING AND PHILODEMUS' Περὶ Παρρησίας

Glenn S. Holland

Abstract

The satirist Lucian of Samosata provides valuable insights into the popular estimation of the philosophical schools, their teachings, and their adherents in the second century C.E. In his dialogue, *The Dead Come to Life, or the Fisherman*, Lucian's alter ego, Παρρησιάδης (Frank Talk), is accused by the shades of the great philosophers of slandering them in his satires. Frank Talk wins acquittal by claiming that his satiric attacks are in fact an exercise of the philosophical virtue of frank criticism, exercised against the charlatans who claim to follow the great philosophers, but who by their hypocrisy bring the founders of their philosophical schools into disrepute. Although much of what Lucian says in the character of Frank Talk is consistent with the exercise of παρρησία as Philodemus describes it, Lucian in fact extends the mandate for frank criticism beyond brotherly correction within the philosophical community to cover satiric attacks carried out in public for educated but non-philosophical audiences in search of amusement.

New Testament scholars have long recognized the satiric works of Lucian of Samosata as a helpful resource for illuminating certain aspects of the New Testament,[1] and they are beginning to recognize the writings of the Epicurean philosopher Philodemus of Gadara as a similar resource.[2] Lucian mentions Christians in passing a few times

---

[1] The most significant study in this regard is that of Hans Dieter Betz, *Lukian von Samosata und das Neue Testament: religionsgeschichtliche und paränetische Parallelen*, Beitrag zum Corpus Hellenisticum Novi Testamenti (Berlin: Akademie-Verlag, 1961). The passages in Lucian most often cited as a source of information about Christianity appear in *The Passing of Peregrinus*, describing that philosopher's brief fling with Christianity (*De Morte Peregrini* [Περὶ τῆς Περεγρίνου τελευτῆς] 11–16). As early as the turn of the last century, one scholar was able to write, "The attitude of Lucian towards Christianity has been the subject of more discussion than that of any other heathen writer;" W. Lucas Collins, *Lucian* (Philadelphia: Lippincott, n.d.) 168; see his chapter "Lucian and Christianity," 167–80.

[2] A major example in this case is Clarence E. Glad's *Paul and Philodemus: Adaptability*

while Philodemus obviously does not, but both authors provide insights into the Hellenistic culture of their times, and especially into dominant attitudes and systems of value among the intellectual elites.[3] But it might also prove instructive, to New Testament scholars as well as to classicists, to compare what these two authors have to say on a specific subject they both discuss at length: the philosophical virtue of παρρησία, frank criticism.[4]

There are two primary reasons for asking whether the views of a Syrian satirist of the second century c.e. are relevant to a modern understanding of Philodemus' first century b.c.e. treatise *On Frank Criticism* (Περὶ παρρησία). The first is, as one scholar has put it, "... [Lucian] had the misfortune of living in the second century a.d., which has too often been regarded as bearing much the same relation to classical and archaic culture as postnatal depression does to birth."[5] The second is, Lucian *was* a satirist, someone whose primary purpose was not to present an accurate picture of his contemporaries and his culture but to produce humor through ridicule.[6] One might reasonably wonder whether Lucian can be trusted to provide an accurate account of what was considered in his time a primarily philosophical and political virtue.

---

in Epicurean and Early Christian Psychagogy (Leiden: Brill, 1995); see also the introduction to this volume by John T. Fitzgerald.

[3] Among the major works on Lucian are: Francis G. Allinson, *Lucian: Satirist and Artist* (Boston: Marshall Jones, 1926), Graham Anderson, *Studies in Lucian's Comic Fiction* (Leiden: Brill, 1976), idem, *Lucian: Theme and Variation in the Second Sophistic* (Leiden: Brill, 1976), Barry Baldwin, *Studies in Lucian* (Toronto: Hakkert, 1973), Robert Bracht Branham, *Unruly Eloquence: Lucian and the Comedy of Traditions* (Cambridge: Harvard University Press, 1989), Jennifer Hall, *Lucian's Satire*, Monographs in Classical Studies (New York: Arno, 1981), Christopher Prestige Jones, *Culture and Society in Lucian* (Cambridge: Harvard University Press, 1986). Studies that concentrate on Lucian's influence on subsequent ages include David Marsh, *Lucian and the Latins: Humor and Humanism in the Early Renaissance* (Ann Arbor: University of Michigan Press, 1998), Christiane Lauvergnat-Gagnière, *Lucien de Samosate et le Lucianisme en France au XVIe Siècle: Athéisme et Polémique* (Geneva: Librairie Droz, 1988), Christopher Robinson, *Lucian and His Influence in Europe* (Chapel Hill: University of North Carolina Press, 1979).

[4] According to the context, in this essay παρρησία will be translated variously as "frank criticism" (specifically in reference to Philodemus' treatise, Περὶ παρρησία), "frank speaking," or, particularly in regard to Lucian's assumed character Παρρησιάδης in *The Dead Come to Life*, "frank talk."

[5] Branham, *Unruly Eloquence* 12.

[6] For the definition and intention of satire, cf. the short study by Arthur Pollard, *Satire*, The Critical Idiom (London: Methuen, 1970), who focuses primarily on Augustan satirists such as Swift, Dryden, and Pope. For a more comprehensive

But Lucian's value for our purposes lies precisely in his role as a satirist. Lucian made his living, as he himself tells us, as an orator who traveled from place to place giving public performances of his satiric dialogues.[7] We are justified in making the following assumptions, as have most of those who have written about Lucian:

> Those for whom he wrote and performed were not the unlettered public but the "cultured," "those who pursue letters." It is to be expected that when he talks of contemporary culture and society he does so from the vantage point of a practiced observer: not an otherworldly "artist," still less a "journalist," but a man in touch with his time.[8]

But what guarantee can we have that the work of a satirist such as Lucian accurately reflects the philosophical ideas of either the classical past or his own era? It is generally conceded that Aristophanes, for example, in his satire of Socrates in *The Clouds*, draws more upon the figure of the Sophist than upon the character of Socrates himself.[9] Lucian makes philosophers a frequent target of his satire, most notably in *Vitarum Auctio* (*Philosophies for Sale* [Βίων Πρᾶσις]) and its

---

account, with some specific attention to Lucian, see Gilbert Highet, *The Anatomy of Satire* (Princeton: Princeton University Press, 1962), esp. 3–44; Ronald Paulson, *The Fictions of Satire* (Baltimore: Johns Hopkins, 1967), esp. 31–42; Dustin Griffin, *Satire: A Crticial Reintroduction* (Lexington: University Press of Kentucky, 1994), esp. 6–34.

[7] Cf. *Zeuxis or Antiochus* (Ζεῦξις ἢ Ἀντίοχος) 1, where Lucian describes the aftermath of one of his lectures; *Piscator* (*The Dead Come to Life* [Ἀναβιοῦντες ἢ ἁλιεύς]) 25, where the shade of Diogenes describes Lucian's professional activities in his indictment of Frank Talk; and *Bis accusatis* (*The Double Indictment* [Δὶς κατηγορούμενος]) 25–35, where the subject is Lucian's innovative combination of oratory and comic dialogue. For an outline of Lucian's career as a satiric orator, see Jones 9–15 and Hall 16–44.

[8] Jones 23.

[9] Ar. *Nu.* 218–509, 627–790; Socrates himself makes this complaint in *Apol.* 19c1–5, and scholars generally support it, at least to the extent that they feel it is necessary to explain the discrepancy between Aristophanes' portrayal and that of Plato and Xenophon. W. K. C. Guthrie reviews a number of such explanations in his *Socrates* (Cambridge: Cambridge University Press, 1971) 39–55, but argues that there are points of contact between Socrates in the *Clouds* and in Plato's dialogues, 50–52; Kenneth J. Dover suggests that Aristophanes was ridiculing a type, "the intellectual," a pretentious blowhard who holds forth on a variety of highfalutin topics; see the introduction to *Aristophanes: Clouds*, ed. and trans. Kenneth J. Dover (Oxford: Clarendon, 1968) xxxii–lvii, and a revised version, "Socrates in the *Clouds*," in *The Philosophy of Socrates: A Collection of Critical Essays*, ed. Gregory Vlastos (Notre Dame: University of Notre Dame Press, 1971) 50–77. The stock character of "the intellectual" Aristophanes parodied in *Clouds* has comedic descendants in "the doctor" of Commedia dell'Arte and "the professor" in twentieth-century comedy, including characters created by Sid Caesar and Groucho Marx.

"sequel," *Piscator* (*The Dead Come to Life, or the Fisherman* ['Αναβιοῦντες ἢ ἁλιεύς]). Even his apparently sincere description of his own search for true philosophy, placed in the mouth of his alter ego Παρρησιάδης in *The Dead Come to Life* 11–12, is not entirely what it seems. It is, rather, "Lucian's parody of a standard pattern of narrative used to describe philosophical searches, for example by the Christian Justin, and again it may be in part a literary device of which the aim is to palliate his attacks on modern philosophers."[10]

But in spite of these satirical attacks, Lucian repeatedly presents himself as a friend of philosophy. As C. P. Jones notes, ". . . As would be expected of a cultured man of letters in the second century, [Lucian's] acquaintance with philosophy and philosophers was not merely superficial. In his own words, he was 'bred up to culture and moderately conversant with philosophy.'"[11] If Lucian sometimes mocks certain groups, particularly the Stoics, he declares solidarity with others and in his writings often uses philosophers as the spokesmen for his own (satiric) point of view. He seems most sympathetic to the Epicureans, perhaps because they, like Lucian, viewed religious claims with a healthy skepticism, and were often vociferous opponents of religious charlatans.[12] He also favors the milder sort of Cynics, like Demonax, and makes the Cynic Menippus of Gadara his spokesman in such works as *Dialogues of the Dead*.

But even if Lucian were demonstrably opposed to philosophy and philosophers *per se*, the evidence his work provides about the meaning and use of a popular philosophical concept such as παρρησία could not be dismissed out of hand. The comic effect of Lucian's satire depended on his audience's familiarity with the contemporary manifestations of an inherited conglomerate of Hellenistic culture as well as Lucian's ability to evoke that culture and draw attention to its contradictions in his own day. As Arthur Pollard notes,

---

[10] Jones 25; he cites Justin Martyr's *Dialogue with Trypho* 2. For a careful discussion of the scholarly debate over Lucian's relationship to philosophy and the extent to which he himself might be styled a philosopher, see Hall 151–93.

[11] Jones 26; the words are said of Lycinus by Crato in *De saltatione* (*On the Dance* [Περὶ ὀρχησέως]) 2.

[12] Jones treats the agreements between Lucian and the Epicureans in some detail, *Culture and Society*, 26–28. He writes, ". . . Lucian brings conventional charges against the Epicureans, their gluttony and hedonism, their apparent hypocrisy in observing conventional religion. But these jabs are very gentle compared to his treatment of other schools" (27).

Satire is always acutely conscious of the difference between what things are and what they ought to be . . . For [the satirist] to be successful his society should at least pay lip-service to the ideals he upholds . . . He is then able to exploit more fully the differences between appearance and reality and especially to expose hypocrisy.[13]

This was the situation Lucian addressed. He was

a seriocomic sophist who engages his audience in a playful reappraisal of the contemporary value of its celebrated cultural past, a reappraisal made necessary by the simple historical fact that the significance of ancient Hellenic traditions and institutions for an audience of the second century A.D. could no longer be that of the classical and archaic periods in which the cultural matrix took on its original shape. Indeed, this ongoing process of selective imitation and reinterpretation is the surest sign that authentic continuity with the past was still possible.[14]

Christopher Robinson argues that Lucian's audiences were made up of an intellectual elite:

A Lucianic satire relies on the previous existence of myths, romance, tragedy, comedy, the novella, all of which it absorbs into its own pattern. It belongs to an esoteric tradition, in that only the cognoscenti— those who can identify the ingredients and thus appreciate the assimilation—will fully appreciate the art.[15]

Since Lucian addressed an educated, intelligent audience, he may reasonably be expected to reveal a reliable indication of how the concept of frank criticism, so thoroughly expounded in terms of Epicurean philosophy by Philodemus some two centuries before, was understood by the educated elite of the second century C.E.

In fact, Lucian depended not only on his audience's familiarity with the teachings of the philosophical schools of his time but also on its knowledge of the characteristics of their professed adherents. This dependence is particularly clear in *Philosophies for Sale* and *The Dead Come to Life, or the Fisherman*.[16] It is in the latter satire that Lucian

---

[13] Pollard 3.

[14] Branham 7.

[15] Robinson 44. He qualifies the term "cognoscenti" by comparing Lucian's audience to the modern audience of Ken Russell's film, "The Boy Friend," whose members must have a broad range of reference if they are to fully appreciate Russell's comic intentions (ibid.). This term must also be understood in the light of Robinson's earlier assertion that Lucian's career took him only to what were "hardly the most fashionable parts of the empire" (ibid., 3).

[16] There have been few specialized studies of *Piscator*; it has generally been con-

himself appears under the guise of the character Παρρησιάδης (for our purposes, "Frank Talk"). His appropriation of παρρησία as this character's defining characteristic assumes both that παρρησία is a widely-admired virtue and that his audience will accept Lucian's (self-) characterization as a valid one. Not surprisingly, it is in this dialogue that we find Lucian's most thorough treatment of this philosophical virtue and so also the best source of useful information regarding the prevailing ideas about παρρησία among the educated elite in Lucian's day.[17]

The essential plot of *The Dead Come to Life* is the trial of Lucian's alter ego Frank Talk on the charge of slandering the great philosophers of the past, and his eventual acquittal. Frank Talk is the target of a violent attack by the shades of the great philosophers, who are temporarily on leave from Hades for the very purpose of hunting him down. They accuse Frank Talk of slandering their reputations and their teachings in his satires and plan to do him bodily harm. Frank Talk protests that he is really his accusers' greatest friend and defender, and asks for the opportunity to prove as much in a fair trial. Since the philosophers are wary of Frank Talk's abilities as a forensic orator, he suggests that Philosophy herself serve as judge, and that the shades of the philosophers serve as both prosecutors and jury.

Frank Talk and the philosophers intercept Philosophy and her entourage during her daily stroll to the Stoa. Philosophy and several of her attendants agree to participate in the trial, with Diogenes taking the role of prosecutor on the philosophers' behalf.[18] His case is that Frank Talk, having tired of the courtroom, has made his

---

sidered within the larger context of Lucian relationship to philosophy and philosophers;" cf. Alice S. Alexiou, "Philosophers in Lucian" (Ph.D. diss., Fordham University, 1990).

[17] The concept of παρρησία also provides the pretext for the extended invective of *Pseudologista* (*The Would-Be Critic*) 1; cf. Branham, *Unruly Eloquence*, 29–32.

[18] Diogenes is most likely assigned this role because he was viewed as a paradigm of philosophical παρρησία, frank speaking, as well as ἐλευθερία, free action; see Branham, "Defacing the Currency: Diogenes' Rhetoric and the Invention of Cynicism" in *The Cynics: The Cynic Movement in Antiquity and Its Legacy*, ed. Branham and Marie-Odile Goulet-Cazé, Hellenistic Culture and Society 23 (Berkeley and Los Angeles: University of California Press, 1996) 81–104, esp. 96–104. As we will see is the case with Lucian, Diogenes exercised παρρησία not for the benefit of the one he addressed, but for the instruction and amusement of an audience, Branham 100–103.

living by ridiculing philosophers as cheats and frauds. But worse, he has maligned Philosophy herself, inciting laughter among the crowds, who like to jeer at what is most noble and worthy. Frank Talk is worse than Aristophanes, who at least could claim the protection of the license granted by the Dionysia.[19] Frank Talk claims to be serving Philosophy, but Diogenes charges he has in fact seduced Dialogue and even enlisted Menippus, who is notably not among his accusers, in his cause. Frank Talk's most recent outrage, Diogenes continues, is the satire *Philosophies for Sale*, which presents Diogenes himself being sold for the measly sum of two obols. Frank Talk must be punished, Diogenes argues, so that others will heed the warning and respect both Philosophy and her faithful devotees, the philosophers.

Frank Talk's self-defense will be examined in some detail below, but it is based on the power of satire to expose and ridicule those who falsely present themselves as philosophers and who, by so doing, bring into disrepute the very doctrines they claim to uphold. Truth herself attests to the veracity of Frank Talk's self-defense. Plato and Diogenes, on behalf of the dead philosophers, withdraw the charges and declare Frank Talk to be their friend. He is acquitted, and Philosophy admits him as a member of her household.

In the second part of the dialogue, Frank Talk encourages the shades of the philosophers to prosecute the frauds whose failings and hypocrisies have discredited them. He gathers the fraudulent philosophers for arraignment by loudly proclaiming an offer of gifts. Hordes of philosophers gather from all directions, but when they learn Frank Talk's true intention, they scatter, leaving behind only those few true philosophers who have nothing to fear from a trial. Frank Talk then "fishes" for philosophers belonging to the different schools, each of whom is denounced by his school's founder.

Finally, Philosophy empowers Frank Talk to distinguish the frauds from the sincere by testing them with the help of Investigation (ὁ Ἔλεγχος), ordering him to brand the frauds and crown the sincere with olive branches.[20] That settled, Philosophy and her entourage

---

[19] The Dionysia was an Athenian festival in honor of Dionysius Eleuthereus that included performances of both tragedies and comedies.

[20] The verb (ἐλέγχω) appears in Phild. *De lib. dic.* XVIb.7–8, in reference to exposing those who only feign their love for παρρησία: "But when the rebuke comes, they have their pretense exposed . . ."; as in *Pisc.*, there is the idea of searching out and exposing those who are not faithful to the philosophical ideals they confess.

return to their stroll, the dead philosophers return to Hades, and Frank Talk and Investigation begin their work, knowing that, wherever they go, they will need "plenty of brands and very few wreaths."[21]

The key to understanding the idea of παρρησία that underlies Lucian's theory of satire comes in Frank Talk's self-defense (*Pisc.* 29–37).[22] He begins by noting that Diogenes could have included among the list of Frank Talk's "offenses" many other, more serious criticisms he has leveled against his targets. But he also asks his accusers to consider who his real targets were. Frank Talk then begins a somewhat stereotyped account of his career as a follower of Philosophy. Originally, he says, he was a law-court orator but, having become disgusted with the many vices that seem to accompany forensic rhetoric, he left the law and turned to the ideals espoused by Philosophy (*Pisc.* 29). He came to admire deeply not only those ideals but also those who had espoused them, the same great philosophers of the past who are now his accusers. These are the "founding fathers of the good life," who have "the finest and most useful counsel to offer—provided someone had the power and tenacity to adhere to it!" (*Pisc.* 30).

But, Frank Talk continues, he quickly became aware of the many philosophical charlatans who are mere caricatures of the great philosophers of the past. Although they present the appearance well enough, their lives contradict everything they profess to believe. All of this hypocrisy and pretense fueled Frank Talk's indignation, which he compares to the indignation one might feel if an effeminate actor were to play the part of one of the great heroes of the past, and so make a woman of him.

But since the great philosophers are dead, most people think that these philosophical frauds are true philosophers. Frank Talk has seen how people lay the blame for the vices of these charlatans on Philosophy herself, or on the founders of the schools to which they claim to belong. Frank Talk argues that he took the only course of action he could: in order to defend the great philosophers of the past, he had to expose the philosophic charlatans of his own day

---

[21] English quotations from Lucian's work are taken from *Selected Satires of Lucian*, ed. and trans. Lionel Casson (Garden City, NY: Anchor Books, 1962) 334–61.
[22] Numbers in parentheses refer to sections of *The Dead Come to Life* in the LCL edition of Lucian's works, ed. and trans Austin Morris Harmon (New York: Putnam, 1921) 3:1–81.

for the frauds they are, lest anyone confuse them with the genuine article.

What makes this task all the more difficult, however, is that the frauds know all their masters' works and say all the right things. But their behavior is almost exactly the opposite of the doctrines they teach—and teach for a good price. These charlatans are the ones who hold Philosophy up to ridicule. People notice the contradiction between what the false philosophers say and what they do, and they hold Philosophy to scorn "for producing such scum" (εἰ τοιαῦται καθάρματα εκτρέφει (*Pisc.* 34); cp. 1 Cor. 4:13, περικαθάρματα).

The grossest offense of the charlatans is their obsession with money, in spite of their teaching that "Wealth should be shared" and "Money is a matter of 'indifference'" (*Pisc.* 35). They value money above everything else and are quick to borrow but reluctant to lend to those in need, despite their praise of friendship (φιλία).[23] The truth is, they practice friendship and virtue until money is at stake, and then their true nature becomes apparent. "They act like a pack of hounds who have had a bone tossed in their midst—making a simultaneous leap, they snap away at each other and howl at the one who's quick enough to grab it" (*Pisc.* 36).

Frank Talk considers it his duty to expose and ridicule such frauds, but he would never speak against the philosophers of the past who are his accusers, or against their sincere followers—for such true devotees do exist. Indeed, what charge could he bring against the true philosophers? Do his accusers wish to claim that they have anything in common with the wretches he attacks?

This is Frank Talk's defense. His basic argument is that he has, in the name of Philosophy and on behalf of the great philosophers of the past, attacked the frauds and charlatans of his day who falsely call themselves philosophers and in so doing bring that noble profession into disrepute. The frank talk (παρρησιάδης) that characterizes his work and gives him his name is simply a matter of calling a spade a spade. He cannot allow fraud to go unexposed, and feels it is his duty to bring the true nature of those who pose as philosophers to the attention of the public.

---

[23] For one example of Lucian's ironic presentation of the virtue of φιλία, see Richard I. Pervo, "With Lucian: Who Needs Friends?: Friendship in the *Toxaris*," *Greco-Roman Perspectives on Friendship*, ed. John T. Fitzgerald (Atlanta: Scholars, 1997) 163–80.

The argument Frank Talk offers draws upon both political and philosophical traditions regarding the use of and justification for παρρησία, and depends upon those traditions for its logical force. But the argument also expands upon the traditional mandate for frank speaking to provide a defense of satire as another form of socially beneficial παρρησία.

Παρρησία is first of all a political virtue, one exercised by free men for the public good.[24] Within the Athenian assembly, each citizen had the right to speak his mind frankly about whatever problems the city faced and how best to address them. As David Fredrickson notes, this proposition provided a pretext for orators to retain their audiences' sympathy and attention even in the act of calling their actions to account: "When orators admonished their audiences for some civil ill, they relied upon the city's reputation for loving frank speech and asked for toleration of their plain speaking in light of its beneficent aim."[25]

Indeed, the exercise of παρρησία was so closely bound up with the rights and obligations of citizenship that it marks the boundary between a free man and a slave.[26] If one were not allowed to exercise παρρησία for some reason, one's practical status would be no better than that of a slave, and slaves were denied citizenship. A slave had no right to speak frankly, even for the benefit of his betters. What is more important, however, is that those who were the objects of παρρησία, those who submitted to and benefited from frank talk, were also free men. One did not speak frankly to slaves, because slaves were not equipped to appreciate or respond to its benefits.

Given this context, it is notable that Lucian portrays Plato complaining that Frank Talk has treated his victims like slaves, having put them up for auction in *Philosophies for Sale*. Plato objects that the dead philosophers are in fact wise men and, more important, free

---

[24] See the relevant remarks in the essays in this volume by David Sider, Ben Fiore, and J. Paul Sampley.

[25] David E. Fredrickson, "Paul's Bold Speech in the Argument of 2 Cor 2:14–7:16" (Ph.D. dissertation, Yale University, 1990) 69. I am throughout indebted to Fredrickson's thorough treatment of παρρησία as a political and philosophical concept. See also his essay, "Παρρησία in the Pauline Epistles," in *Friendship, Flattery, and Frankness of Speech*, ed. John T. Fitzgerald, NovTSup 82 (Leiden: Brill, 1996) 163–83.

[26] Fredrickson, "Paul's Bold Speech," 68–70.

men (ἐλευθέρους; *Pisc.* 4). He chastises Frank Talk: "So, on top of everything, we're supposed to thank you for your slanders, eh? You really think you're dealing with slaves, don't you? All the insults and sodden rant in your dialogues you're going to put under the heading of doing us a service, eh?" (*Pisc.* 5).

In fact, Frank Talk's very use of παρρησία indicates he regards the philosophers as free men who can benefit from his frankness. Truly free men, Lucian implies, would regard Frank Talk's words as a service. At the same time, Plato's insistence on the dead philosophers' status as free men betrays an ironic misreading of their situation. In point of fact, they're dead, and as a result they are "bound" by Hades as their master. Indeed, they have had to ask Hades for a furlough from the underworld in order to attack Frank Talk (*Pisc.* 14).

Lucian himself makes the connection between political liberty and frank speaking explicit in this dialogue by placing personifications of these two virtues among the followers of Philosophy. When Philosophy agrees to act as judge and asks Truth to accompany her, Truth enlists the aid of her two handmaids Freedom and Frankness (Ἐλευθερία καὶ Παρρησία), saying, "We have to see if we can save this poor man who loves us so dearly" (*Pisc.* 17).

Moreover, there was already a link between παρρησία and the comic license exercised by the satirist. In his accusation, Diogenes charges that Frank Talk's ridicule of the philosophers is worse than Aristophanes' and Eupolis' mockery of Socrates, especially since Frank Talk ridicules philosophers without the sanction of the Dionysia (*Pisc.* 25–26). Although even Diogenes seems to admit there is some right of παρρησία in satire, he apparently would insist it be restricted to a particular divinely-sanctioned time and place. Even then what the comic poets claim to be παρρησία may in reality amount to no more than regrettable buffoonery (*Pisc.* 25).[27]

In this dialogue, Lucian appears to be attempting to expand the license already granted the comic poets in order to validate his own satires as a means of exposing all sorts of social ills, including the follies of the fraudulent philosophers. Lucian bases his argument for such license not only on the political right to speak frankly, but also on the παρρησία granted philosophers themselves.

---

[27] Fredrickson comments on παρρησία and comic license and cites considerable evidence for the moral philosophers' rejection of any real value in comic παρρησία, "Paul's Bold Speech" 70, n. 18.

Παρρησία was the distinguishing mark of the philosopher as one who enjoys moral freedom. This freedom is similar to the freedom of the citizen, except that it derives not from one's social or political standing, but from one's moral standing. The philosopher is his own master and, more important, master over himself. The philosopher exercises and exhibits self-control (σωφροσύνη) in his pursuit of wisdom. He is the only truly free man, irrespective of exile, slavery, or other conditions imposed by human beings. His self-control grants him moral freedom, which in turn allows him to speak frankly regardless of circumstances.

Fredrickson has demonstrated this connection between moral freedom and παρρησία.[28] He notes, "The philosopher's παρρησία resides not in his political status but in his freedom from fear, and the ability to make all things depend upon himself. Moral freedom has replaced political freedom as the basis of παρρησία."[29] Indeed, to some extent it is speaking frankly that demonstrates the philosopher's moral freedom; Musonius Rufus makes this point by citing Diogenes' example as well as his own:

> But tell me, my friend, when Diogenes was in exile at Athens, or when he was sold by pirates and came to Corinth, did anyone, Athenian or Corinthian, ever exhibit greater freedom of speech [παρρησίαν] than he? And again, were any of his contemporaries freer than Diogenes? . . . Are you not aware that I am an exile? Well, then, have I been deprived of freedom of speech [ἐστέρημαι παρρησίας]? Have I been bereft of the privilege of saying what I think?[30]

In his Περὶ παρρησίας, Philodemus assumes both the right and the responsibility of the (Epicurean) philosopher to exercise frank criticism within the philosophical community. His whole purpose in writing the treatise is to assist the members of the Epicurean community to provide frank criticism to one another in as effective a manner as possible. In fact, the well-being of the community is presumed to depend on the rigorous practice of mutual παρρησία. The political virtue once exercised in the public forum has become a personal

---

[28] Fredrickson, "Paul's Bold Speech," 73–82.
[29] Fredrickson, "Paul's Bold Speech," 77–78.
[30] *Mus. Ruf.* 9; the translation is that of Cora Elizabeth Lutz, *Musonius Rufus: the Roman Socrates*, Yale Classical Studies 10 (New Haven: Yale University Press, 1947) 74–75, cited by Fredrickson, "Paul's Bold Speech," 78–79; 79, n. 38.

virtue to be practiced primarily within the confines of the Epicurean community.[31]

In this context, Lucian's adoption of the character of Παρρησιάδης, Frank Talk, as his representative constitutes a claim to be a free man in the philosophical sense. But because of the idea, fostered by Philodemus and the other Epicureans, that frank criticism is a philosophical responsibility as well as a right, in Lucian's hands παρρησία also becomes the basis for a right to what we might call "creative license," the freedom to say what is necessary to fulfill one's satiric intentions in a comic dialogue.

Satiric intention may easily be understood to be consistent both with Frank Talk's claims to be an admirer of Philosophy and with the tradition of philosophical παρρησία. The freedom to exercise frank criticism is not merely a means of demonstrating the moral superiority of the philosopher, although this was sometimes the case among the Cynics, as Fredrickson demonstrates.[32] Its primary intention was the moral improvement of those whom the philosopher addressed. Some philosophers, moreover, claimed to have taken on the job of exercising παρρησία at the behest of the gods; for them, frank criticism became a function of the philosopher's divinely-designated office. Both Epictetus and Dio Chrysostom, for example, repeatedly emphasize the divine nature of their calling.[33] This tradition goes back at least to Socrates, who in his defense presented before the Athenian assembly based his philosophical mission on the Delphic oracle's enigmatic reply to Chairephon (*Apol.* 20e9–23c1).[34]

In much the same way, in *The Dead Come to Life* Frank Talk repeatedly asserts that his own use of παρρησία (i.e., in satire) arises from his high regard for Philosophy, personified in this dialogue as a

---

[31] Cf. the frequent invocations of Epicurus in *On Frank Criticism* as an example, *De lib. dic.* 6.5, 15.9, 49.6, 49.10, 55.5, 73.3–4, T14.end.5, and as an authority, *De lib. dic.* 20.9, 45.8.

[32] Fredrickson, "Paul's Bold Speech," 83–93.

[33] Fredrickson, "Paul's Bold Speech," 94–105 cites cf. Epict. *Diss.* 3.22.3–4, 3.21.17 (96), 3.22.95–96 (99–100) and Dio Chrys. *Or.* 32.12 (104). Epictetus said that the divine call was what distinguished the true philosopher from the charlatan and in fact sanctioned his use of παρρησία (*Diss.* 3.22.19, 93); see Abraham J. Malherbe, *Paul and the Popular Philosophers* (Minneapolis: Fortress, 1989) 46–47.

[34] In the case of Socrates, the divine call was not only the origin of his philosophical mission of ἔλεγχος, but also of his philosophical irony; see Glenn Holland, *Divine Irony* (Selinsgrove, PA: Susquehanna University Press, 2000), ch. 4.

258

GLENN S. HOLLAND

goddess. Therefore the exercise of frank criticism takes on the connotations of a sacred duty to the goddess.[35] Moreover, Frank Talk compares his satiric assaults against the philosophical charlatans to the flogging an actor might receive for portraying a god in an unworthy way. The gods would not condemn such an action in defense of their honor, according to Frank Talk. Indeed, "I rather imagine the gods would get satisfaction out of the punishment" (33). In both cases, παρρησία becomes more than a philosophical responsibility; it is a sacred service to the gods.

Moreover, at the end of the dialogue, παρρησία becomes a tool for the fulfillment of a divine commission which is personified as Investigation (τὸν Ἔλεγχον). Frank Talk is to employ παρρσία at the behest of the goddess Philosophy to winnow the philosophers of his day and thereby determine which deserve an olive wreath and which deserve a brand (46, 52).

Within the context of philosophical communities, the exercise of παρρησία is most often tied to the mutual obligations of friendship as a means of promoting the moral improvement of one's comrades.[36] Philodemus makes the point that the one who employs frank criticism in the right way at the right time is a true friend to his friend (*De lib. dic.* 50.8), and friendship is the basis of Epicurean παρρησία in Philodemus' treatise *On Frank Criticism*.[37] It should come as no surprise that Lucian also plays upon the theme of philosophical friendship in *The Dead Come to Life*.

At the outset of the dialogue, Frank Talk protests that the philosophers are completely mistaken in their attacks against him:

> Gentlemen! Understand one thing—if you kill me, the man who has suffered so much on your behalf, you'll be killing the one person in the whole world who deserves your cheers, your kinsman who thinks and feels as you do, and—if it's not vulgar to bring it up—the agent of your best interests. Watch out that you don't behave like the philosophers of today and treat a benefactor with a display of ingratitude . . . [*Pisc.* 5]

---

[35] Plutarch implies a similar connection when he begins his "How to Tell a Flatter from a Friend" by citing the Delphic oracle's command to "know thyself" (γνῶθι σαυτόν; *Quomodo quis suos* 49B, cp. 65F).
[36] Fredrickson, "Paul's Bold Speech," 131–37.
[37] Cf. *De lib. dic.* 15.8–9, 50.5, col. XIIIa.10 (φίλος); 28.5 (φιλία); col. XIXb.6 (φιλικός).

In this speech, Frank Talk mentions several of the characteristics of a true friend—suffering on the friend's behalf, looking out for his best interests, providing benefits—to persuade his accusers that he is their friend (*Pisc.* 30–33, 37). Ultimately, his self-defense is successful, and Plato says on behalf of the philosophers, "Dismiss the complaint and declare him our friend and benefactor" (φίλον ἡμῖν καὶ εὐεργέτην).[38] Even Diogenes, who has led the prosecution as its spokesman, says, "He's a hero; he's my friend" (φίλον ποιοῦμαι αὐτὸν γενναῖον ὄντα; *Pisc.* 38). This assessment of Frank Talk is shared by Philosophy herself, who, after his acquittal, admits him to her household. This honor confirms not only Frank Talk's status as a "philosopher," or at least a friend of Philosophy, but also his right to exercise παρρησία, specifically among the members of the philosophical community.

To further emphasize the philosophical basis of Frank Talk's exercise of παρρησία, his self-defense is presented as an obvious and sometimes explicit parallel to Socrates' self-defense as it is presented in Plato's *Apology*. Like Socrates, Frank Talk claims that, despite the charges against him, he is in fact his accusers' greatest benefactor (εὐεργέτης; *Pisc.* 5, cp. *Apol.* 36b5–d5). The philosophers are initially reluctant to bring Frank Talk to trial because they fear that his rhetorical skill, honed by years of experience as a forensic orator, will sway a judge and jury through rhetorical tricks (*Pisc.* 9).[39] In the *Apology*, Socrates imputes a similar fear of his own rhetorical skill to his accusers. He assures them he will not employ rhetoric, but he does lay claim to what he calls the chief virtue of the "true orator:" speaking the truth (*Apol.* 17a1–18a6). Not coincidentally, Frank Talk's own apology measures up to this test when Truth herself ('Αληθεία) testifies to the veracity of his self-defense (*Pisc.* 38).[40] Although Socrates'

---

[38] We find the idea of rendering a good work to the wise by employing παρρησία also in Philodemus: *De lib. dic.* 4.4–5 ([οἱ δ᾿εὐεργετ[ή]σαντες ἀπ[ὸ σ]εβασμοῦ τὸ[ν] σοφὸν εὐγεν[είας); 82.3–4 (ὁ σο]φὸς οὐκ ἐπὶ πάντων κ[ᾶι]τ᾿ εὐ[εργ]ετήσειν πέποιθεν).

[39] In *The Dead Come to Life*, it is Socrates who argues reluctantly that the philosophers must allow Frank Talk a fair trial, if only for the sake of their reputations: "What will we be able to say about my accusers Anytus and Meletus or the men who sat on my jury if this fellow here dies without getting his share of courtroom time?" (*Pisc.* 10). Socrates apparently doesn't mind if Frank Talk dies *after* receiving his share of courtroom time; it appears that, as far as Socrates is concerned, a guilty verdict is a foregone conclusion.

[40] Cp. Phild. *De lib. dic.* Col. XVb; in order to know the truth, it is necessary to examine oneself, but also to hear frank criticism from others.

protégé Plato at first rejects Frank Talk's claims of benevolence towards the philosophers in scorn (*Pisc.* 5), he later confirms the justness of the claim in the words cited above (*Pisc.* 38). This seal of approval from Socrates' primary disciple only adds luster to Frank Talk's "Socratic" self-defense.

Frank Talk does not aspire to full Socratic status, however. Rather, his reward from Philosophy after his acquittal is the job of testing contemporary philosophers to determine which are worthy imitators of Socrates's example. It is Truth who urges that Frank Talk, assisted by Investigation, be given the job. Here again there seems to be a clear parallel between Frank Talk and Socrates, who carried out his "divine commission" through elenchic dialogue (*Apol.* 20e9–23c1).[41] Truth adds a further stipulation to Frank Talk's task: "Whoever he finds is genuine he's to give a wreath of ivy and free meals for life at City Hall [the Prytaneum]" (*Pisc.* 46). This was the reward for Olympic champions who enhanced the city's standing among the other Greek states. But it was also what Socrates suggested as an appropriate sentence after his conviction, on the grounds that he had been a greater benefactor for Athens than any athlete had ever been (*Apol.* 36b3–37a1). Lucian appears to support the notion that a city's greatest claim to honor is the true philosophers among its citizens.

But the commission Frank Talk receives from Truth marks a shift in his role. He is ordered to use παρρησία, not as a method of promoting the welfare of others, but as a means of testing sincerity. Frank Talk shifts roles from a "Socratic" accused philosopher to a "Lucianic" accuser of philosophers. In so doing he in fact takes up the task, not of Socrates, but of those who brought him to trial, the task of distinguishing the true philosopher from the false. Frank Talk does so, however, with the permission and mandate not of the

---

[41] For the discussion of the relationship of Socrates' elenchic method to the oracle given to Chaerephon see Thomas G. West, *Plato's Apology of Socrates: An Interpretation, with a New Translation* (Ithaca: Cornell University Press, 1979) 104–126; Thomas C. Brickhouse and Nicholas D. Smith, *Socrates on Trial* (Princeton: Princeton University Press, 1989) 87–108; Michael C. Stokes, "Socrates' Mission," in *Socratic Questions: New essays on the Philosophy of Socrates and Its Significance*, eds. Barry S. Gower and Michael C. Stokes (New York: Routledge, 1992) 26–81; Thomas C. Brickhouse and Nicholas D. Smith, *Plato's Socrates* (New York: Oxford University Press, 1994) 30–45; and Holland, *Divine Irony*, ch. 4.

Athenian assembly, but of Philosophy herself, with Truth standing by to attest to the veracity of his charges.

Frank Talk's commission as a philosophical fraud-detector is in keeping with the satiric attack on philosophers that runs throughout the dialogue. The great philosophers of the past are portrayed as members of an angry, blood-thirsty mob who at first wish simply to annihilate Frank Talk. It is only gradually and grudgingly that they are brought around to granting him a trial, and so to live up to their own teachings about justice and temperance. As an author Lucian also ridicules individual philosophers in various small ways. Diogenes, whose Cynic school disdained worldly possessions, is obsessively concerned with the low price (two obols) he was portrayed fetching at auction in *Philosophies for Sale*. Chrysippus praises Plato's eloquence in terms so glowing that he makes Plato out to be more of a grandiloquent Sophist than a "plain-speaking" Socratic philosopher:

> A marvelously noble mind, a beautiful and wonderfully pure diction, charm that's so persuasive, understanding, precision, arguments that carry such conviction at the crucial moment—all these you have in abundance . . . Add a sprinkling of Socratic irony, give him those tricky, rapid-fire questions, and, if you think it's a good idea, stick in somewhere that line of yours about "Great Zeus who drives his winged chariot across the heavens" . . . [*Pisc.* 22].[42]

Even Socrates' opening exhortations to his fellow philosophers reflect the peculiarities of their respective schools. Epicurus and the hedonist Aristippus of Cyrene both have trouble keeping up with the others, presumably from over-indulgence and lack of exercise (*Pisc.* 1).[43] Aristotle, the first Peripatetic (i.e., "walking" philosopher), is encouraged by Socrates to hurry up: "Faster, Aristotle, faster!" (*Pisc.* 2). Although these are minor jests, they are part of Lucian's larger project of satirizing the great philosophers even while his alter ego, Frank Talk, claims only to revere them and to work to benefit them.

---

[42] Chrysippus' elaborate praise of Plato is of course ironic in view of his own career; although educated in part at the Academy, he converted to Stoicism and became its staunch defender against the Platonists.

[43] If this is indeed intended as a sly dig at the two philosophers, it reflects a popular, rather than an accurate, view of Aristippus and Epicurus. The real irony, of course, is that Epicurus, the quintessential materialist who taught that death is merely non-existence, is present among these shades at all.

Nor is such satire restricted only to the reputations of the "founding fathers." Frank Talk subtly denigrates the value of the philosophers' teaching, both on the grounds that they are difficult to follow (*Pisc.* 30), and that the philosophical frauds know all their masters' teachings perfectly (*Pisc.* 34). In a culture where knowledge of the Good was supposed inevitably to produce virtuous behavior,[44] this was a particularly telling criticism. Even at the most basic level, the implicit question is, if the great philosophers' teachings fail to produce virtuous behavior among their most vociferous followers, what good are those teachings after all?

In contrast to the philosophical theorists, Frank Talk presents himself as someone who makes philosophy practical—that is, likely to produce virtuous behavior—by selecting among the teachings of various philosophical schools and presenting them in a way that commends them to the public:

> Where have I gotten the very words I write if not from you [philosophers]? I draw them the way a bee does honey and display them to men; they applaud—but they know where and how I plucked each flower and whose it was originally. Ostensibly it's me they envy for the bouquets I've garnered, but actually it's you and your garden;[45] the blooms you have produced are of such beautiful and varied tints—if people only know how to pluck them and mix and arrange them so that one wouldn't clash with another! [*Pisc.* 6]

In other words, it only through the labors of someone like Frank Talk, a rhetorician and a Sophist, that the difficulties of contending philosophical schools can be clarified and their best teaching can be presented in a way that commends itself to the general public.

Frank Talk essentially presents himself as a Sophist in service to Philosophy who defends her by exposing fraudulent philosophers. His weapon is philosophical παρρησία, and by wielding this weapon effectively he becomes Lady Philosophy's most effective champion. The heroic service he performs on her behalf justifies in part the

---

[44] This is virtually the unanimous opinion of classical and Hellenistic philosophy. On this point see Albrecht Dihle, *The Theory of Will in Classical Antiquity*, Sather Classical Lecture 48 (Berkeley and Los Angeles: University of California Press, 1982), 21–66.

[45] I am assuming that there is no veiled reference here—a perilous thing when dealing with a satirist—to the Garden of Epicurus.

extension of Frank Talk's mandate for exercising παρρησία in other contexts than the comradely correction of a fellow philosopher. His mandate extends beyond what Philodemus among others had always envisioned as the proper scope of a philosopher's use of frank criticism, to include also what we might call "satiric παρρησία."

What is the nature of this mandate for satiric παρρησία? In the character of Frank Talk, Lucian provides a defense of himself and his satires that is entirely in keeping with the political idea of παρρησία that had been current in the Greek world since the classical era and with the philosophical virtue extolled by Philodemus. But Lucian's extension of the argument is that frank speaking in satire performs much the same function among the educated classes who made up his audiences as it did in the city council or the philosophical community. It could be argued that the educated classes formed something of a governing assembly of the cosmopolitan intellectual community, or something like a fellowship of those who are philosophers in the broad sense of those who approve what is good and true. Παρρησία has a place in either sort of gathering, and Lucian claims to provide it in plenty for the common good. When satiric παρρησία reveals philosophical charlatans for what they are, the argument goes, it restores the good reputation of the great philosophers of the past and those few of their contemporary followers who are worthy of public esteem.

But in the course of laying claim to the traditional mandate for παρρησία on behalf of his satiric dialogues, Lucian also widens and redirects the mandate. Most notably, it is no longer necessary that παρρησία be directed to those it is theoretically intended to benefit. Lucian did not read his satires before gatherings of philosophers, but in front of educated audiences seeking entertainment. His frank criticism is not intended to correct privately an erring fellow philosopher, but rather to ridicule publicly those who fail to live up to the standards of the great philosophers they claim to follow. This sort of παρρησία is not intended to foster the moral growth of the frauds whom he publicly and repeatedly denigrates and dismisses as rogues and cheats. He wants to expose these charlatans, not reform them.

Nor is this kind of frank criticism intended to foster the moral growth of the audience, except perhaps in fueling their indignation against the philosophical frauds. Satire is instead intended to ridicule and thereby solicit laughter, although it does depend on the satirist and the audience sharing a common set of moral and cultural values.[46] Despite Frank Talk's protestations that he is a champion and defender of the great philosophers of the past, if his satire provides any benefit for them at all, it is an indirect result of his primary purpose and to that extent beside the point. His profession is not philosophical apologist but satirist.

But παρρησία also serves an important function for the satirist: it allows him to probe and expose the evils that afflict society, and so to render them innocuous through laughter. By calling a spade a spade, the satirist prevents his audience from mistaking it for a spoon, a sword, or a topographical sculpturing device.

Frank Talk characterizes himself primarily as "fraud-hater, cheat-hater, lie-hater, humbug-hater," summing up with "I hate the whole damned breed" (*Pisc.* 20). Although he is also "truth-lover, beauty-lover, simplicity-lover" he adds, "I'm afraid I've already forgotten the one because I use it so little and have become an expert in the other" (*Pisc.* 20). The goddess Philosophy assures him they are "two sides of the same coin, as the saying goes" (ibid.). But it remains true that any positive effects of Lucian's satire are secondary to its primary intention, which is to ridicule what is fraudulent and vainglorious, and, in the effort, to inspire laughter.

In this respect, Lucian and his alter ego Frank Talk are the literary descendants of the authors of Old Comedy. Diogenes gets it half right: Frank Talk is indeed like authors such as Aristophanes, who mocked Socrates and other philosophers not for the moral improvement of the philosophers, but for the amusement of the crowd (*Pisc.* 25–26). But this is not the whole truth of the matter. Lucian was also concerned with exposing the absurdities of philosophical speculation and the glaring contradictions between what the contemporary philosophers taught and the way most of them behaved. He was interested not only in whatever laughter might be squeezed out of philosophers as comic figures, but also in presenting the many faces of fraud and hypocrisy. This is why Lucian's work continues

---

[46] Scholars generally agree that the satirist and the audience must share a common set of values if satire is to be successful. Cf. Robert C. Elliott, *The Power of Satire: Magic, Ritual, Art* (Princeton: Princeton University Press, 1960) 266; Paulson 9–20; Pollard 3–5; cp. Highet 18–21. For a full treatment of classical and contemporary theories of satire, see Griffin, esp. 6–34.

to amuse and instruct his audiences some eighteen centuries after it was first written.[47]

What can Lucian's second century C.E. (self-)defense of the use of παρρησία in satire tells us about the exercise of frank criticism as it is discussed by Philodemus in the first century B.C.E. or practiced by a New Testament author such as Paul in the mid-first century C.E.? In regard to Philodemus, the fact that Lucian is able to assume his audience's knowledge and approval of the various attributes and virtues of παρρησία, and to evoke them in terms that echo those used by the Epicurean philosopher, demonstrate the general acceptance of the ideas worked out and explained in his Περὶ παρρησίας. As a result, we are justified in assuming his theories would find general acceptance among the educated elite of his own time and the centuries that followed.

More specifically, both Lucian and Philodemus place a very high value on παρρησία as a central tool of their respective professions, different as those professions may be. Both also recognize that the exercise of παρρησία is likely to cause offense and therefore must be defended, primarily by invocation of its social benefits. But those benefits accrue to different groups. In the case of Philodemus, the beneficiaries are his fellow members of the Epicurean community; in the case of Lucian, the beneficiaries are the educated members of his audiences, who are amused and entertained by his attacks on the philosophical charlatans.

Moreover, Philodemus employs a similar form of satirical παρρησία when he attacks other philosophical schools, as in his *On the Stoics*.[48] These attacks are intended to benefit his fellow Epicureans by enhancing and supporting their common identity through the exposure of the failings and hypocrisies of the opposing schools. This common identity is also reinforced by Philodemus' frequent invocation of Epicurus; in the absence of any idea of a divine call, such as Frank Talk claimed to have received from Philosophy (*Pisc.* 46),

---

[47] The durability of satire, which allows it to find an appreciative audience long after its original targets are long gone and forgotten, is ample demonstration that satire's primary function is not moral instruction for those satirized, but the amusement of the audience. The idea that satire is primarily a moral endeavor intended to censure vice and praise virtue, is a product of "the moral obsession of literary criticism in later antiquity" and originally applied to Old Comedy (G. L. Hendrickson, "Satura Tota Nostra Est," *CP* 22 (1927): 46–60, 49, cited by Griffin 10).

[48] See the essay by Clay in this volume.

what binds the community together is their veneration of the Master and their conformity to his teachings: "and the encompassing and most important thing is, we shall obey Epicurus, according to whom we have chosen to live" (*De lib. dic.* 45.7–10). Although Lucian appears to have a high opinion of Epicurus and his followers as opponents of religious fraud and pious nonsense, he also makes use of the common stereotype of Epicureans as hedonists.[49]

At the same time, we also find a broadening of the mandate for the one who exercises παρρησία, a mandate that by the time of Lucian has come to include vilification and abuse of hypocrites and wrong-doers for the benefit of a third party. This fact should at least make those who read Paul's letters more aware of the possibility that his attacks on his opponents may include satiric exaggeration, invective, and irony. This possibility seems most likely in the case of the Paul's apology in 2 Cor. 10–13,[50] but should at least be entertained whenever Paul refers to his opponents; at the very least, his remarks about them should never be taken simply at face value.

In essence, Frank Talk's self-defense of his satirical exercise of παρρησία in *The Dead Come to Life* provides a philosophical justification for the business of mocking professional hypocrites. His apology is also an argument for the public usefulness of satire, based on the idea that satire makes it harder for frauds to prey upon the public. If the reputations of the great philosophers of the past and those of their sincere followers in the present are enhanced as a result, all the better. Even Philosophy herself acknowledges that such mockery is more likely to help true philosophers than to hurt them: ". . . You see, I know that jokes never do any harm. On the contrary, they'll make a thing of beauty gleam more brightly and stand out all the more, like gold hammered clean at the mint" (*Pisc.* 14).

This is ultimately Lucian's strongest argument. His satires delighted and enlightened his audiences, and little harm was done to the man of common sense who heard him or the sincere philosopher whose hypocritical brethren Lucian satirized. The man of common sense

---

[49] See above, nn. 10, 40.

[50] For an exposition of these chapters with an emphasis on their ironic content, see Holland, "Speaking Like a Fool: Irony in 2 Corinthians 10–13" in *Rhetoric and the New Testament: Essays from the 1992 Heidelberg Conference*, ed. Stanley E. Porter and Thomas H. Olbricht, JSNTSup 90 (Sheffield: Sheffield Academic Press, 1993) 250–64, and an expanded treatment in Holland, *Divine Irony*, ch. 5.

would enjoy his attacks and applaud them. The philosopher, because he was a wise man, would suffer fools gladly.[51] So a true philosopher could also reasonably be expected to suffer gladly the beneficial foolishness of Lucian's frank talk.

---

[51] John T. Fitzgerald has documented this philosophical principle in *Cracks in an Earthen Vessel: An Examination of the Catalogues of Hardships in the Corinthian Correspondence*, SBL Dissertation Series 99 (Atlanta: Scholars Press, 1988), 59–65, 103–107.

PART THREE

PHILODEMUS AND THE NEW TESTAMENT WORLD

THE PASTORAL EPISTLES IN THE LIGHT OF PHILODEMUS' "ON FRANK CRITICISM"

Benjamin Fiore, S.J.

Abstract

The Pastoral Epistles show a number of points of contact with Epicurean philosophical thought, both in agreement and disagreement. This is true to the extent that the Pastorals may plausibly be said to be in conversation with Epicurean thought. This general connection suggests a context for the striking parallels between Philodemus and the Pastorals on the proper use of frank speech. Although the Pastorals disagree with Philodemus' theory in significant ways, the two share the popular philosophical aim of moral improvement and also agree on the best measures to be taken to achieve their aim.

The excavation of Herculaneum's "Villa of the Papyri" in the eighteenth century led to the discovery of a library of Epicurean works, mostly by Philodemus.[1] The library's papyri rolls were badly charred and very fragile and included a roll of Philodemus' instructions Περὶ Παρρησίας, *On Frank Criticism*.[2] In the work there is no systematic elaboration of the subject since Philodemus' work seems to be comprised of lecture notes of his teacher Zeno of Sidon's treatment of παρρησία. Philodemus studied under Zeno at Athens and appears to have organized his material by first quoting a topic or question and then going on to give his teacher's elaboration of it.[3] In general, Philodemus describes the use of παρρησία, its aim and its pitfalls. Overall he sees it as a useful tool in the effort to promote moral

---

[1] Jane I. Tait, *Philodemus' Influence on the Latin Poets* (diss. Bryn Mawr, 1941), 4, notes that of the approximately 200 volumes contained in the library, Philodemus wrote over half and that three-fourths of the recovered papyri are his.

[2] *Philodemus: On Frank Criticism*, trans. David Konstan, Diskin Clay, Clarence E. Glad, Johan C. Thom, and James Ware, SBLTT 43 (Atlanta: Scholars Press, 1998).

[3] Clarence E. Glad, "Frank Speech, Flattery and Friendship in Philodemus," in *Friendship, Flattery, and Frankness of Speech: Studies on Friendship in the New Testament World*, ed. John T. Fitzgerald NovTSup 82 (Leiden: Brill, 1996), 30.

progress among friends. Frank speech is, in this sense, used by the wise person in correcting the deficiencies of disciples/friends. Philodemus and other Epicureans advocate mutual psychagogy through admission and correction of error as an aspect of friendship.[4]

Παρρησία was an esteemed concept and practice in classical antiquity. For Isocrates it meant to speak concisely and without reservation but with utmost frankness and without raising ire.[5] In its public and political dimension it was the privilege of free citizens (male) and the focus was therefore on the spoken word.[6] This contrasts with the understanding of παρρησία as a personal characteristic. In this case it refers to confidence or boldness, a usage commonly thought to be used by Paul in 2 Cor. 3:12.[7]

Philosophers such as Musonius Rufus saw παρρησία's basis to be not political status (citizenship) but inner autonomy and freedom, particularly freedom from fears, for which civic freedom is a metaphor.[8] Thus the Cynics relished using bold, even disconcerting words as an expression of their moral freedom from convention.[9] Epictetus speaks not just of the boldness arising from inner freedom but of frank speech as a tactic in a divinely appointed task.[10] While many Cynics saw it as a means to improve public morals and the common good,[11] Lucian's Demonax uses it to improve other individuals and to foster friendship. Φιλανθρωπία among the milder Cynics called for their benefiting others (ὠφέλεια) even with the application of painful, frank criticism.[12] This last attitude and practice parallels those of the

---

[4] Glad 30–31 and David Fredrickson, "*Parresia* in the Pauline Epistles," in Fitzgerald, ed., *Friendship* 168–69. See also Fredrickson 164–65, where he explains that χρῆσθαι παρρησία is "nearly synonymous" with νουθετεῖν, ἐπιτιμᾶν, ἐλέγχειν, and other words of moral reproof. Epicurus' *Principal Doctrines* 27 sees friendship as the greatest happiness that wisdom might provide. Philodemus, *De lib. dic.* fr. 25 refers to the mutual benevolence which inspires the use of frank speech.

[5] Fredrickson 168.

[6] Fredrickson 165 and nn. 16–17 and Giuseppe Scarpat, *"ΠΑΡΡΗΣΙΑ": Storia del termine e delle sue traduzioni in Latino* (Brescia: Paideia, 1964), 33. Scarpat goes on to note, 34–38, that metics, foreigners and slaves were excluded from exercising this privilege, as were citizens who lost civic rights through condemnation to τιμία.

[7] But Fredrickson effectively argues against this translation in his essay, 170–82.

[8] Fredrickson 166 and nn. 21–25.

[9] Fredrickson 166 and n. 26.

[10] Fredrickson 166–67 and n. 27, Epictetus *Diss.* 3.22.2, 8, 52.

[11] Fredrickson 167 and n. 34.

[12] Fredrickson 168–69 and also Scarpat 64, where he describes the aims of Cynic παρρησία to be moral freedom from passions, from the desire to possess and dominate, and from fear of the tyrant death.

Epicurean Philodemus. It also reflects a common opinion about the use of frank speech among moralists of various philosophical stripes such as Isocrates and Plutarch.[13]

Paul's undisputed letters reveal his acquaintance with and use of παρρησία in its public and popular philosophical meaning. In Philippians he refers to public speech in the proclamation of the gospel and contrasts it with shame (Phil. 1:20), a common juxtaposition.[14] In 2 Corinthians 10:9–10 he draws a contrast between his epistles with their bold expressions and his meek presence.[15] Nonetheless, in 2 Cor. 2:17–4:6, Paul vindicates his openness and unashamed confidence in a context of friendship. In 1 Thessalonians 2:3, Paul claims to have used it (ἐπαρρησιασάμεθα ἐν τῷ θεῷ ἡμῶν λαλῆσαι πρὸς ὑμᾶς) not as the harsh Cynics do, but gently (1 Thess. 2:7).[16] Rather he stresses the hortatory and comforting (nurse-like) aspects of his frankness, and he stresses the friendship and mutuality that provide the context for his παρρησία (1 Thess 2:9–12).[17] In Philemon 8–9 Paul finds his frankness grounded in Christ, as Dio and Epictetus see divine approval for theirs.[18] Paul's exercise of παρρησία is carried out in love, which turns his frankness away from the commanding (ἐπιτάσσειν) of the harsh Cynics to the encouraging (παρακαλεῖν) of the milder Cynics.[19] He avoids causing shame and maintains the context of friendship.[20] One might conclude from these texts a certain understanding of παρρησία as a reality in the πολιτεία of the church. It appears to be a right in the society of the church community, as παρρησία was in secular society. It was exercised by

---

[13] Fredrickson 168. Scarpat 59 sees in Isocrates' *Ad Nicoclem* 1.2–3 the belief that παρρησία, the ability openly to reprove one's friends, is an indispensable quality for true friendship. See also Troels Engberg-Pedersen, "Plutarch to Prince Philopappus," in Fitzgerald, *Friendship* 76.

[14] Fredrickson 172.

[15] Fredrickson 171–82.

[16] For the gentle approach of the milder Cynics, see esp. Abraham J. Malherbe, *Paul and the Popular Philosophers* (Minneapolis: Fortress, 1989), 35–48. Paul claims also not to have wanted to cause distress at 2 Cor. 2:4.

[17] Fredrickson 171, and Malherbe 58–60.

[18] Fredrickson 170, Dio Chrysostom, *Orations* 13.9, 32.12.

[19] Benjamin Fiore, S.J., *The Function of Personal Example in the Socratic and Pastoral Epistles*, Analecta Biblica 105 (Rome: Biblical Institute, 1986), 117–118, and Malherbe 130–131.

[20] Fredrickson 171.

persons and groups who were not in shameful positions, e.g. women and slaves, for shame inhibits παρρησία.[21]

Among the uses in the deutero-Pauline letters παρρησία is mentioned only at 1 Tim. 3:13. It is this last-mentioned use and its context in the Pastoral Epistles overall that will be the focus of the remainder of this study. Although the word appears just once, the hortatory concerns and recommendations in the Pastorals coincide with many of those voiced in Philodemus' description of the purpose and use of frank speech.

The parenetic features of the Pastoral Epistles that echo those described by Philodemus will be analyzed below. In addition to these, there are other aspects of the Pastorals that suggest an awareness of the world of Epicurean philosophy. In some respects the Pastorals seem to agree with the Epicureans, while in others they disagree with and reject Epicurean ideas. 1 Tim. 1:3 locates the addressee at Ephesus; 2 Timothy suggests the same with its reference to "everyone in Asia" and the presumed acquaintance of the addressee with Phygelus and Hermogenes at 2 Tim. 1:15, and with Onesiphorus' connection to Ephesus at 2 Tim. 1:18. There is also the salutatory greeting to him at 2 Tim. 4:19 as well as a greeting to Aquila and Priscilla, who are known to have been at Ephesus from Acts 18:19, 26 and 1 Cor. 16:19. Asia had long been Epicurean territory from Epicurus' own school at Colophon and with nearby Epicurean centers at Mytilene and Lampsacus.[22] The movement became a dominant philosophical force in both the Greek and Roman worlds through and even long after the New Testament period.[23] Epicurean concerns entered the consciousness of both the literary elite, e.g. Virgil and Cicero, and the populace at large. Ephesus would be a likely meeting point for Christianity and Epicureanism.[24]

Among the ideas shared by the Epicureans and the Pastoral Epistles, 1 Tim. 3:3 and Tit. 1:7 mention that a "bishop" should not be πλήκτης ("pugnacious," "a bully," or "given to blows").[25] The Epicureans were

---

[21] Jerome Neyrey, *Paul in Other Words: A Cultural Reading of His Letters* (Louisville, KY: Westminster/John Knox, 1990), 67.

[22] Norman W. De Witt, *St. Paul and Epicurus* (Minneapolis: University of Minnesota, 1954), 62.

[23] The durability and wide popularity of Epicureanism is attested by the third-century c.e. Diogenes Laertius 10.9–10, *OCD*[1] 285.

[24] De Witt 88–89.

[25] "A bully," *BAG*; "given to blows," De Witt 17.

opposed to the long-standing tradition of corporal punishment for slaves and this idea might well have been incorporated into the Pastorals' understanding of proper household management (1 Tim. 3:4). Instead, the "bishop" should be ἐπιεικής ("considerate," "forbearing," "gentle"), an Epicurean ideal.[26]

Concern for wisdom and the path to it runs throughout both the Pastoral Epistles and Epicurean writings. The Pastorals urge officials (1 Tim. 3:8, 11), older men (Tit. 2:2), and Christians generally (1 Tim. 2:2) to be "honorable" (σεμνός) and worthy of respect (Tit. 2:7), echoing Epicurus' urging of reverence for the wise.[27] The Epicurean virtuous wise persons, assuming free will to make moral choices, expose vices and contrasting virtues to their charges and admonish them to choose virtue. This is unlike the Aristotelian view of virtue as a mean between two extremes.[28] Philodemus himself wrote *On Vices and the Corresponding Virtues*. The Pastorals likewise follow the pattern of presenting vices and contrasting virtues in their moral admonition (1 Tim. 6:3–12; 2 Tim. 3:1–17; 4:3–5; Tit. 1:7–9; 2:3–5, 9–10, 11–12). Finally, both decry the deceptive allurement of riches and urge contentment with little.[29] In fact, the Pastorals refer to the ideal of αὐτάρκεια when it discusses riches, religion and real gain (1 Tim. 6:6). In addition to αὐτάρκεια, the Pastorals express another Epicurean virtue at 1 Tim. 6:18, where Timothy is urged to instruct the rich to be κοινωνικούς. The motive advanced for pursuing the path of sharing at 1 Tim. 6:19, while pointing to eternal life with God, is also expressed in an Epicurean-like way when it speaks of gathering a "treasure as a foundation for the future" and of "getting a hold on what is really life."

---

[26] "Considerate," De Witt; "gentle," *BAG*. Compare Philodemus' characterization of πασρρησία as ἐπιεικός at fr. 26, IV; cp. XVI.

[27] De Witt 30, 51.

[28] De Witt 82, 173.

[29] 1 Tim. 6:7–10 and De Witt 19; see also 172 where he quotes Epicurus who said, "Every man takes leave of life just as he was at the moment of birth" (SV 60) and compare 1 Tim. 6:7. See also De Witt 179 where he refers to Epicurus' image of a trap for the apparent good of an injurious desire and compare the use of the same image at 1 Tim. 6:9 for the temptation and ultimate injury of riches. In SV 44 Epicurus speaks of the wise man being accustomed to the bare necessities and of his discovery of the "treasure house of self-sufficiency" as translated by Eugene O'Connor, *The Essential Epicurus* (Buffalo: Prometheus, 1993), 81. SV 81 notes that possession of great riches does not relieve the soul's disturbance or lead to lasting joy. And the same deficiency holds true for honor, admiration of others, and any other unlimited desire.

Despite these and other areas of agreement mentioned below, the
two systems of belief and thought stood irreconcilably opposed on
other grounds. Traces of this opposition might be detected in the
Pastoral Epistles. Pleasure (ἡδονή) was the Epicurean goal[30] and the
task was to learn to discriminate correctly and with sober reasoning
and prudence (φρόνησις)[31] among desires in order to select those that
are natural and necessary and reject the injurious ones.[32] The Pastorals
also seem to accept the difference among desires (ἐπιθυμίαι) and
warn against those that are foolish, harmful and lead to ruin and
destruction (1 Tim. 6:9). Nonetheless, the only use of the word "pleasure" (ἡδονή) in the Pauline literature is found at Tit. 3:3, where it
appears among a list of vices.[33] Similarly, 2 Tim. 3:4 lists "loving
pleasure" (φιλήδονοι) among the unbridled, vice-filled attitudes of the
sinners in the final days.

The disparaging reference to pleasure in 2 Tim. 3:4 includes a
contrast to "loving God" (φιλόθεοι) as the alternative virtue. This
calls attention to another point of difference and conflict between
the writer of the Pastoral Epistles and the Epicureans. While the
Epicureans did not disbelieve in the gods' existence, they relieved
the gods of active concern for human affairs.[34] To support their hope
of pleasure in life they eliminated fear of divine punishment and,
ultimately, of death and its threat of final divine retribution for sin.
To accomplish this they posited the gods in a realm of unruffled
calm, indifferent to human wickedness, concerned with their own
virtues, receptive to those like themselves.[35]

---

[30] De Witt 179 and *Principal Doctrines* 5, 29, 31.

[31] *Letter to Menoeceus* 132, where Epicurus adds that prudence is the virtue from
which all others derive. A.-J. Festugière, *L'Ideal religieux des Grecs et l'evangile* (Paris:
Gabalda, 1981), 62 finds prudence to be the way to ταραξία of the soul and a
happy life, *Letter to Menoeceus* 62.12–15 and 64.21–25. KD 5 and 21 both speak of
the need for wisdom to know the limits of life and thereby how to achieve happiness.

[32] De Witt 179 and KD 5, 29, 31.

[33] De Witt 19. The other four New Testament uses of the word: Luke 8:14,
James 4:1, 3; 2 Peter 2:13, are all negative. Malherbe 82–84 details the use of the
beast image principally in Cynic and Stoic writings to characterize shameless pleasures, often associated with the Epicureans, and the virtuous struggle to purify one's
life of them. Interesting for the purposes of this study is the connection of the image
with Ephesus and Paul's struggles there (1 Cor. 15:32).

[34] KD 65 declares, "It is useless to ask the gods for what one is capable of obtain-
ing for oneself" (O'Connor 83).

[35] Philodemus *De dis.* bk. 3 col. 1.15–20 Diels says, "The gods are friends of the

In the Epicurean world of atomic materialism, the gods do not watch over humans nor do they give them special dominion any different from that of insects. Human civilization and supremacy over other beings is the fruit of humanity's own labor, pain and cumulative experience.[36] To place pleasure at the beginning and end of a happy life would effectively displace the Jewish-Christian God as Alpha and Omega, the beginning and end, of creation, as well as its sustaining power.[37] Epicurean theology stands in direct contrast to basic Christian ideas as developed in the Pastoral Epistles. For the Epicureans, the atom was the basic and indestructible building block of all reality, both of matter and of spirit. The gods were simply composed of extremely refined atoms.[38] The atom was unseen in itself.[39]

The Pastoral Epistles, on the other hand, see the one God as incorruptible, unseen and the only being who has immortality (1 Tim. 1:17; 6:16). It also comes as no surprise to find the Pastoral Epistles stress the active interest and intervention of God in human affairs, as well as God's providential direction of creation to its completion. Thus God commands apostolic and ministerial activity (1 Tim. 1:1, 11, 12–16; 2:7; 4:6; 2 Tim. 1:1, 6, 11; Tit. 1:1, 7) and God and Jesus Christ are the sources of their designees' strength (1 Tim. 1:12; 2 Tim. 1:7, 12–14; 2:1; 3:11; 4:17; Tit. 2:11–14, 3:4–7). God created the world (1 Tim. 2:13; 4:3; 6:13) and revealed the

---

wise and the wise are friends of the gods" (cf. De Witt 160). Festugière 63–64 finds that the Epicurean gods have no concern for the world, because it is beneath them, but live in unruffled ἀταραξία, referring to the *Letter to Herodotus* 29.3 and KD 1.71.3.

[36] De Witt 180.

[37] De Witt 182. The Epicureans, dispensing with belief in the afterlife, lived totally within the perspective of the present as noted by Malherbe 84, referring to Usener, fragments 336–341, 396–397. O'Connor 76–77 quotes the *Epistle to Herodotus* 76–77, where Epicurus rejects the idea of an immortal being who ordained and arranged the motions of heavenly bodies and other astronomical phenomena. The epistle (38–39, 73–74) also speaks of the eternity of the universe within which multiple worlds are created and destroyed spontaneously. Margherita Isnardi Parente, ed., *Opere di Epicuro* (Turin: Unione Tipografico, 1974), 332–33 cites Epiphanius, *Adversus haereses* 1.7–8 (589 Diels), where he explains the Epicurean teaching that the world is a spontaneous generation from atoms, into which it will eventually experience a fiery dissolution.

[38] Ettore Bignone, tr., *Epicuro: Opere, frammenti, testimonianze sulla sua vita* (Rome: "L'Erma" di Bretschneider, 1964), 237–238 and Festugière 63.

[39] De Witt p. 158.

plan for the world (οἰκονομία) which includes its consummation
(1 Tim. 1:4; 2:4; 4:1; 6:3, 14–16; 2 Tim. 1:9; 2:7; 3:16; 4:1; Tit.
1:2–3). God works with humans through the mediator Jesus Christ
(1 Tim. 2:5–6; 3:16; 6:13; 2 Tim. 1:10) and is susceptible to humans'
prayers (1 Tim. 2:1–3, 8; 4:5; 5:5; 2 Tim 1:16–18; 2:19). The opponents in the Pastorals are summarily dismissed as godless (1 Tim.
1:9) and irreligious (2 Tim. 3:5), charges commonly laid at the
Epicureans' door.[40] The interest of the God of the Pastoral Epistles
in human affairs leads to God being pleased or displeased by human
activity (1 Tim. 2:3; 5:4, 21; 2 Tim. 2:12–13, 15; 4:14) and to God's
bestowal of rewards/salvation and punishments (1 Tim. 1:1, 15; 2:6,
15; 4:10; 5:12; 6:18–19; 2 Tim. 1:18; 2:10, 25–26; 3:15; 4:1, 8).

Hope, too, is a topic of divergent views between the Epicureans
and the Pastoral Epistles. The Epicureans restricted hope to the
happy expectation of pleasures to come. When applied to the fundamental concern over health, Epicurus said, "The stable condition
of sound health in the flesh and the confident hope of this means
the height of pleasure and the best assurance of it for those who
are able to figure the problem out." Such hope for sound health is
crucial for a system in which human death means no more than
physical and spiritual dissolution into constituent atoms.[41] In the
Pastorals hope rests in Jesus Christ and God (1 Tim. 1:1; 4:10; 5:5;
6:17) and looks to the promise of everlasting life (1 Tim. 4:8; 6:12;
2 Tim. 1:10; 2:10–12; 4:18; Tit. 1:2; 3:7). In fact, self-indulgent
pleasure-seeking actually leads to "death," even for those still alive
(1 Tim. 5:6, 11).

Other Epicurean echoes in the Pastoral Epistles remain to be indicated. While Epicurus was a "savior" to his followers,[42] that title is
reserved for God and Jesus Christ in the Pastoral Epistles (1 Tim.
1:1; 2:3; 4:10; 2 Tim. 1:10; Tit. 1:3, 4; 2:10, 13; 3:4, 6). Epicureans

---

[40] Plutarch *Suav. Viv. Epic* 1086C–1107C (trans. Einarson and DeLacey LCL) and
see Benjamin Fiore, S.J., "Passion in Paul and Plutarch: I Corinthians 5–6 and the
Polemic Against Epicureans" in David Balch, Everett Ferguson, and Wayne A.
Meeks, eds., *Greeks, Romans, and Christians* (Minneapolis: Fortress, 1990), 141–43.

[41] De Witt 131–36 and see SV 47 and 48, *Letter to Menoeceus* 124–26 and KD 2.

[42] De Witt 5, 29, 67, 83 and Dieter Nestle, *Eleutheria. I Teil: Studien zum Wesen
der Freiheit bei den Griechen und im Neuen Testament* (Tübingen: J. C. B. Mohr [Paul
Siebeck], 1967), 119. Lucretius *De rerum natura* 3.9–13 refers to Epicurus as "our
father, the revealer of truth, the giver of fatherly precepts ... maxims of immortal
life" (Rackham trans. LCL).

cultivated gratitude for past benefits and pleasures,[43] while the Pastorals direct gratitude to God (1 Tim. 1:12; 2:1; 4:3, 4; 2 Tim. 1:3). The Epicureans passed on their formulation of Epicurus' *Authorized Doctrines*[44] while at the same time they ridiculed vain beliefs of other movements.[45] The Pastorals express concern for the integrity of doctrinal tradition (1 Tim. 4:6, 9, 6:3, 20; 2 Tim. 1:12, 14; 2:15; Tit. 1:9; 2:8) and take a dim view of scurrilous, pointless debate, ruinous teachings, and ridicule (1 Tim. 1:3; 2 Tim. 2:14–18; 3:2; Tit. 3:9). The quiet and tranquil life in the preserve of the Epicurean gods becomes accessible to the community of the Pastorals through prayer (1 Tim. 2:2) and not just by withdrawal from public life to the Epicurean "garden."[46] With their hope tied to the continual experience of pleasure, the Epicureans were particularly interested in health and the ministrations of doctors. Innovative remedies advanced by Epicureans included the use of wine for certain ailments, which 1 Tim. 5:23 applies to Timothy's digestive problems.[47]

While this survey of Epicurean themes reflected in the Pastoral Epistles might include some matters that are better explained in light of other contexts, the overall claim of a dialogue in the Pastorals with Epicurean thought, among other Hellenistic philosophical systems, seems to be plausible. This general connection suggests a context for the striking parallels between Philodemus and the Pastorals on the application of frank speech for moral improvement.

The only explicit use of the word παρρησία in the Pastoral Epistles appears in the list of qualifications for "deacons" at 1 Tim. 3:13. There the expected rewards for the good service of qualified deacons include καλὸν βαθμόν ("good standing"/"rank")[48] and πολλὴ

---

[43] De Witt 132–133 and SV 52 and 69.

[44] De Witt 17–18. O'Connor refers to these as "Principal Doctrines." SV 41 declares, "We must never cease proclaiming the sayings born of true philosophy."

[45] De Witt 51, 108, 178, 180. They especially decried dialecticians as corrupters of youth.

[46] The requirement of a good reputation among outsiders for candidates for "bishop" in 1 Tim. 3:7 implies that the Christians, unlike the Epicureans, continue an active life among the citizenry at large. The Epicurean withdrawal from everyday affairs and politics is urged by SV 58 and is expressed in the shorthand command of Epicurus, λάθε βιώσας fr. 86; cp. KD 14 (O'Connor 11). *Letter to Menoeceus* 135 declares that the sober enjoyment of pleasure under the guidance of prudent wisdom leads to a life "without disturbance, as a god among men" (O'Connor 68).

[47] De Witt 135.

[48] "Good standing," NRSV; "rank," BAG 130, *EDNT* 189–90.

παρρησία ("confidence" in relation to God, or "abundant confidence/ full redemptive trust in faith in Jesus Christ").[49] The *EDNT* reflects the caution of contemporary New Testament lexicographers who take into account the usage of words in the Greco-Roman context. While it still retains the theological emphasis of the earlier BAG, the *EDNT* tries to balance this with a secular sense. The merger of the two, however, remains rough and unexplained.

The παρρησία of deacons is different from that of the bishops and elders because the latter have the teaching function (1 Tim. 3:2, 5:17), while the deacons do not. Deacons do, however, speak in their ministerial service and are cautioned not to be δίλογοι (= "double-tongued" [RSV], "deceitful" [NAB], "insincere" [BAG]). That quality would contrast with their παρρησία (1 Tim. 3:13) as flattery versus frank speech. The wives of deacons or the women deacons are similarly cautioned not to misuse speech (μὴ διαβάλους, 1 Tim. 3:11). Nevertheless, good reputation supports the rank and standing of all (1 Tim. 3:2, 7, 13). For the deacons, men (and women?) (1 Tim. 3:11), this external reputation is balanced by an internal clear conscience about the adherence to the faith (1 Tim. 3:9). The external reputation finds a complement in παρρησία or frank speech. One area where this frankness comes into play is in the informal instruction involved in taking care of one's children and household (1 Tim. 3:12). With the conjunction γάρ the author makes the link between the deacons' qualities and practice in 3:8–12 and their result in 3:13. In this connection "Paul" recalls the instruction in scripture that Timothy received from infancy (2 Tim. 3:15; cp. 1:15) and entrusts younger women to older women for training in virtue (Tit. 2:3–5). These stand in contrast to the vice-laden false teachers who are unqualified in matters of faith (ἀδόκιμοι περὶ τὴν πίστιν, 2 Tim. 3:8), and with those self-interested teachers whose teachings upset entire households (Tit. 1:11). It is also important to keep in mind the close relationship between works and religious conviction in the Pastoral Epistles. The openly observable demeanor and actions verify or contradict religious claims of women (1 Tim. 2:9–10), official functions

---

[49] "Confidence" in relation to God, BAG 630–31; "abundant confidence/full redemptive trust in faith in Jesus Christ" inasmuch as it refers to "one's confident relationship to God (in prayer) and to candor in relation to other persons," *EDNT* 3:47.

of bishops (1 Tim. 3:7), Timothy's teaching (1 Tim. 4:15–16), widows' claims (1 Tim. 5:7–8, 14), the doctrine adhered to by slaves (1 Tim. 6:1), and the rich who hope for salvation (1 Tim. 6:18–19). Similarly, Titus 1:9 expresses a direct connection between the blameless virtue of the bishop and his ability (ἵνα δυνατὸς ᾖ) to exhort (παρακαλεῖν) and criticize (ἐλέγχειν). This relationship between virtue and its public manifestation is found in Philodemus' exposition of frank speech (fr. 16, πειθεῖν δὲ καὶ διὰ τὸν [ἔρ]γον). There is some reason, therefore, to associate the παρρησία referred to at 1 Tim. 3:13 with the frank speech in the work of moral development which Philodemus outlines and which the Pastoral Epistles urge on their addressees.

While the word παρρησία is used only once in the Pastoral Epistles, the directives given and the ministerial activities urged upon Timothy and Titus in the Pastoral Epistles relate to the philosophical exercise of frank speech, like that outlined by Philodemus. By the same token, the actions of the opponents and the community fit the profile of a misguided reaction to and application of παρρησία. Thus, while the explanation by Philodemus elaborates the nuances of the use of frank speech, the Pastoral Epistles provide examples of the aim and practice of the virtuous tactic[50] as it is elaborated by Philodemus. The paraenetic character of the Pastorals is thereby set in higher relief against the background of the directives on the proper use of frank speech.

Despite the focus on "sound teaching" in the Pastorals[51] and their inclusion of credal summaries,[52] the Pastoral Epistles are heavily concerned with paraenesis,[53] as demonstrated in their stress on behavior

---

[50] Marcello Gigante, *Ricerche Filodemee*, 2nd ed. (Naples: Macchiaroli, 1982), 62–65 argues that rather than a virtue opposed to the vice "flattery," frank speech in Philodemus is an ἦθος, a way of comporting oneself. It is a technique to aid in the acquisition of wisdom and happiness. He goes on to explain how, to Philodemus, παρρησία is a τέχνη στοχαστική, a "conjectural art," by which philosophers, through variable and provisional arguments, nudge their charges in the direction of the acquisition of what is useful in the philosophers' view. See also fr. 10 and 68 and Gigante 72–74.

[51] 1 Tim. 1:10; 4:6, 11, 13, 16; 5:17; 6:1–3; 2 Tim. 2:2; 3:10, 16; 4:2–3; Tit. 1:9; 2:1, 7, 10, 15.

[52] 1 Tim. 1:15; 2:5–6; 6:16; 2 Tim. 1:9–10; 2:11–13; Tit. 3:4–7.

[53] Fiore, *Use of Personal Example* p. 216 and παρακαλεῖν, 1 Tim. 1:3; 2:1; 2 Tim. 4:1; Tit. 2:6; παραγέλλειν, 1 Tim. 6:13; ἀναμιμνήσκειν, 2 Tim. 1:6.

(1 Tim. 3:5) and good works,[54] on virtuous qualities as qualifications
for ministry,[55] and on examples to be imitated.[56] Thus the false teaching of opponents, apostates, and misguided teachers and their followers and the true teaching of Paul, which Timothy has long followed
(1 Tim. 4:6; 2 Tim. 3:10–11), all have to do with action as well as
theory. Since truth is a concern in the letters, they often gauge the
truth of the teaching by the kind of vice or virtue it fosters (1 Tim.
1:9–11, 13; 4:1–3, 7–8; 6:3–10; 2 Tim. 1:13; 3:2–7, 10; Tit. 1:13–16;
2:7–8, 11–12). This concern rises to the top in the Epicurean discourse of Philodemus (fr. 40), who calls for the pupil to show his
teacher his errors (διαμαρ[τί]ας) forthrightly so that the teacher might
be a guide of right speech and action ([ὁ]δηγὸν ὀρθοῦ καὶ λ[ό]γου
κα[ὶ] <ἔργου>) and a savior (σωτῆρ[α]) through the treatment of
admonishment (θεραπε[ύ]ειν . . . [νουθετέσιν]).[57]

The context of the letters, too, is one of friendship. The household image for the community in its greatest extension would include
friends.[58] The letters express the teacher and father relationship with
which friendship is associated.[59] Their affectionate forms of address
(ἀγαπητὸς τέκνος, 2 Tim. 1:2; γνήσιος τέκνος, 1 Tim. 1:2, Tit. 1:4),
friendly salutary closings (2 Tim. 4:19–21; Tit. 3:15), friendly references to visiting back and forth,[60] to supplying goods and offering
support,[61] to ἀγάπη[62] and φιλεῖν (Tit. 3:15 and contrast φίλαυτος,
2 Tim. 3:2), and the dismay at the abandonment and bad treatment
by former associates (2 Tim. 1:15; 4:14–16) establish the philophro-
netic tone of the letters. Their concern is for the growth and improvement of the addressees (προκοπή, 1 Tim. 4:15), the pursuit, acquisition

[54] 1 Tim. 2:10; 3:1; 5:10, 25; 6:18; 2 Tim. 2:21; 3:17; Tit. 1:16; 2:7, 14; 3:1,
8, 14.
    [55] 1 Tim. 3:1–13; 4:7; 2 Tim. 2:21; 3:10–11; Tit. 1:6–9.
    [56] 1 Tim. 1:16; 4:12; 2 Tim. 1:18; Tit. 2:7.
    [57] On Frank Criticism 54–55. SV 54 equates true philosophy with true health. See
Scarpat 67, who finds a similar emphasis in the Cynic Diogenes.
    [58] 1 Tim. 3:5, 15; 5:1–2; 2 Tim. 2:20–21.
    [59] 1 Tim. 1:2, 18; 2 Tim. 1:2; 2:1; Tit. 1:4; and see Fiore, The Use of Personal
Example 32–34.
    [60] 1 Tim. 3:14; 2 Tim. 1:4; 4:9, 20; Tit. 3:15; Fitzgerald, ed. Friendship 74, 140,
236.
    [61] 1 Tim. 3:14; 2 Tim. 1:16; 4:9–13; Tit. 3:12–14; Fitzgerald, ed. Friendship 66–68,
234–35.
    [62] 1 Tim. 1:5; 2:15; 4:12; 6:11; 2 Tim. 1:7, 13; 2:22; 3:10; Tit. 2:2; Fitzgerald,
ed. Friendship 199, 234.

and expression of virtue,[63] the avoidance of vice,[64] and sorrow at the backsliding of others.[65] This sets the Pastoral Epistles in the context of the philosophical paraenetic effort that makes use of παρρησία as a tool.

Before going any further, however, it is important to state a basic difference between the background of the activity of παρρησία in the Pastorals and that in Philodemus. Philodemus' Epicurean philosophy has no room for the active intervention of gods in human affairs and so his παρρησία is grounded in the philosophy itself. It aims at the betterment of individuals in the circle of friends by their own efforts. The Pastorals find the ground, as Paul does, in God, and they aim at the exercise of virtue within the church community, comprised of people brought into a circle of relationship which appeals to faith in support of its ethical convictions.[66] Nonetheless, the Epicureans and Christians deal with each other and pursue the tasks associated with the life of virtue within the same cultural context and with all of its tools.

The aim of παρρησία for Philodemus is improvement in virtue,[67] as it is in 1 Tim. 4:15 (προκοπή). Philodemus (fr. 1 and passim) notes that virtue is often clouded by sin (μήτε συναισθάνεσθαι τὰς ἁμαρτίας), but παρρησία calls attention to sin in an effort to eradicate it. The diversion of people from the path of progress by sin is decried in the Pastorals in the case of the younger widows (ἔχουσαι κρίμα, 1 Tim. 5:11–12), of certain people (αἱ ἁμαρτίαι ... προάγουσαι εἰς κρίσιν, 1 Tim. 5:24), of women easily led captive by teachers in their homes (γυναικάρια σεσωρευμένα ἁμαρτίαις, 2 Tim. 3:6), and of the

---

[63] 1 Tim. 2:8–15; 4:7–8; 6:11–12, 17–18; 2 Tim. 2:22; Fitzgerald, ed. *Friendship* 87–89.

[64] 1 Tim. 1:8–11; 6:3–10; 2 Tim. 2:23; 3:1–5; Tit. 3:9–11; Glad 30–33.

[65] 1 Tim. 1:19–20; 5:15; 6:9–10; 2 Tim. 2:17–18, 25–26.

[66] Roland Schwarz, *Bürgeliches Christentum im Neuen Testament: eine Studie zu Ethik, Amt und Recht in den Pastoralbriefen*, ÖBS 4 (Klosterneuburg: Östereichisches katholisches Bibelwerk, 1983), 173–76.

[67] Fr. 1, ὁ συνφέρει διαγινώσκειν ("discern what is advantageous") and fr. 86, τοῖς ἀ[πα]θοῦ[σι θερ]απεύε[σ]θαι πο[ικί]λως [βο]ηθοῦντες [δια'] ἰατ[ρῶ]ν ("[subt]ly helping [through] doctors even those who are indifferent to being treated"). Glad 10, 25 notes the importance of psychagogy to Philodemus and his circle of Epicurean friends. Gigante, 74–75, calls attention to fr. 18 where Philodemus considers frank speech to be a type of assistance and the only appropriate nutriment (τροφ[ῆς ἰδι]α καὶ βοηθείας, "[suitable] food and assistance"). See also fr. 67 and 43 where sympathy for the wayward youths spurs the offer of aid.

apostates and wayward in the "latter days" (ἁμαρτωλοῖς, 1 Tim. 1:9; cp. 2 Tim. 3:1–5; Tit. 1:10). While Jesus saved sinners (ἁμαρτωλούς, 1 Tim. 1:15), the Pastorals spell out the details of the life of virtue and the path to it. Timothy and Titus are the agents of this salvific progress.

Philodemus is careful to discriminate among the recipients of criticism in the form of frank speech.[68] Thus, those giving instruction will not give in to anger over or give up on recalcitrant students (fr. 2–3).[69] The admonitor will have to deal with some whose progress is minimal and who are open to blame, while he will have "orderliness" with others (fr. 33). Philodemus notes (fr. 31) that some of the young become irritated when rebuked, especially when they are used to gentler treatment, that women (col. XXII) bear rebuke poorly, as contrary to what is due their weaker nature, and that older men need special attention (col. XXIV) because they think their age makes them wiser, because they are sensitive to any exploitation of their weakness, and because they too expect the honor enjoyed by some of their contemporaries.

In like manner the Pastorals recommend paraenetic approaches appropriate to the individuals being admonished. Thus Timothy is urged to treat younger men "like brothers" (1 Tim. 5:1; cp. Tit. 2:6) and to be careful in dealing with women, both older and younger (1 Tim. 5:2, 11, 14). Titus is even told to have older women instruct the younger ones (Titus 2:3–5). Furthermore, Titus is to encourage the sobriety, self-control, and dignity of older men (Tit. 2:2), while Timothy, urging them like "fathers," is not to rebuke (ἐπιπλήξῃς) them (1 Tim. 5:1) nor accept unsubstantiated accusations against elders (1 Tim. 5:19). In a similar vein, Timothy is cautioned to be gentle with all and tolerant.[70] The Pastorals also aim their corrective advice at the young Timothy and Titus themselves.[71] Thus, the

---

[68] Glad 33–35 describes Philodemus' distinction between two types of students: the "weak" and the "stubborn," each requiring tactics tailored to their temperaments. He goes on to find a variety of categories under the blanket term "young," whom the wise care for, as well as other persons of various classes and professions.

[69] Konstan et al., "Introduction," *On Frank Criticism* 14.

[70] 1 Tim. 6:11; 2 Tim. 2:22–25; cp. Tit. 3:2 and note the words πραϋπαθία, εἰρήνη, ἤπιος, ἀνεθίκακος, πραΰτης, ἐπιεικεῖς.

[71] 1 Tim. 3:15, ἵνα εἰδῇς πῶς δεῖ . . . ἀναστρέφεσθαι; 2 Tim 2:15, σεαυτὸν δόκιμον παραστῆσαι; 2:22, τὰς δὲ νεωτερικὰς ἐπιθυμίας φεῦγε; 4:5, νῆφε ἐν πᾶσιν; Tit. 2:7, σεαυτὸν παρεχόμενος τύπον καλῶν ἔργων.

people who are instructed in the techniques of frank speech are themselves the objects of it.[72]

Of course, frank speech is not always kindly received and the recalcitrant, with a low level of knowledge of themselves and of what is truly beneficial (τοῦ συμφέροντος), resist it (col. XX) and even insult, ridicule (βλασφημεῖν καὶ λυμαίνεσθαι) and mistreat the wise person (fr. 18). Similarly, the Pastorals encourage their addressees to resist contempt (1 Tim. 4:12, μηδείς σου τῆς νεότητος καταφρονείτω; Tit. 2:15, μηδείς σου περιφρονείτω) but to offer no occasion for accusation from quarters of opposition (Tit. 2:8, μηδὲν ... περὶ ἡμῶν φαῦλον).

Those who resist are incapable of reasonable argument (fr. 1, εὐ[λ]ογίαις), tend to be quarrelsome (fr. 19, πολεμοῦντα), and even abandon philosophy in their persistent waywardness (fr. 59, φιλοσ[ο]φίας ἀποστήσεται).[73] They are focused on "passions that puff one up" (τοῖς ἐκχαυνο[ῦ]σι πάθεσιν) and this preoccupation blocks the effect of the philosophical wise one's admonitions (fr. 65–66). In the Pastoral Epistles the wayward opponents have deviated from the truth and want to teach the law but know nothing about it (1 Tim. 1:6–7, ἐξετράπησαν εἰς ματαιολογίαν ... μὴ νοοῦντες; 2 Tim. 3:8–9, κατεφθαρμένοι τὸν νοῦν). Timothy and Titus are warned away from the opponents' ignorant babbling (1 Tim. 6:20, τὰς βεβήλους κενοφωνίας καὶ ἀντιθέσεις τῆς ψευδωνύμου γνώσεως). They are argumentative (2 Tim. 2:23, γεννῶσιν μάχας; Tit. 3:9, ἔρεις καὶ μάχας νομικάς) and are full of vain curiosity (2 Tim. 2:23 and Tit. 3:9, μωρὰς ... ζητήσεις; see 2 Tim. 4:3–4). It is quite often their misguided passions that have led them astray. Such was the case with the self-indulgent widows who were carried away from their Christian resolve by their sensuality (1 Tim. 5:11–12, καταστρηνιάσωσιν τοῦ Χριστοῦ); the rich who were led on by foolish desires (1 Tim. 6:9, ἐπιθυμίας πολλὰς ἀνοήτους καὶ βλαβεράς); women at home with passionate leanings (2 Tim. 3:6, ἀγόμενα ἐπιθυμίαις ποικίλαις), the unbridled people (Tit.

---

[72] Glad 30 describes "the participatory nature of late Epicurean psychagogy" in fr. 45.1–6, where Philodemus declares that teachers continue to admonish their pupils, even after the latter have acquired prominent positions in the community.

[73] Philip Mitsis, *Epicurus' Ethical Theory: The Pleasures of Invulnerability* (Ithaca: Cornell University Press, 1988), 73 describes the importance of λογισμός in Epicurean thought. "The more our beliefs begin to coincide with true doctrine and knowledge, the more stable and less changeable they become." Moreover, he notes (75) that Epicurus sees that the virtues of courage and temperance spring ultimately from φρόνησις and the calculation of one's own good (*Ad Menoec* 132).

1:10, φρεναπάται; 2 Tim. 3:2, φιλάργυροι ... βλάσφημοι ... ἀκρατεῖς ...
φιλήδονοι) who are deceived deceivers (2 Tim. 3:13, πλανῶντες καὶ
πλανώμενοι); so-called teachers in pursuit of sordid gain (Tit. 1:11,
αἰσχροῦ κέρδους χάριν); and community members themselves in the
past (Tit. 3:3, πλανώμενοι, δουλεύοντες ἐπιθυμίαις καὶ ἡδοναῖς ποικίλαις).

Consequently, Timothy and Titus are expected to select only candidates for office who are temperate, self-controlled,[74] gentle, not
contentious, aggressive or greedy.[75] The same quality of temperate-
ness is expected of the women and the widows in particular.[76] In
general the older men (νηφαλόυς ... σεμνούς ... σώφρονας), women
(σώφρονας), younger men (σωφρονεῖν) are to exhibit self-control (Tit.
2:1–6), following the promptings of the grace of God which taught
temperance as opposed to following worldly desires (Tit. 2:11–12,
ἀρνησάμενοι ... τὰς κοσμικὰς ἐπιθυμίας σωφρόνως ... ζήσωμεν).[77] Timothy
and Titus are to turn from youthful desires (2 Tim. 2:22, νεωτερικάς
ἐπιθυμίας φεῦγε), avoid debates and quarrels (2 Tim. 2:23, τάς δὲ
μωρὰς καὶ ἀπαιδεύτους ζητήσεις; Tit. 3:9, μωρὰς δὲ ζητήσεις καὶ γενεα-
λογίας καὶ ἔρεις καὶ μάχας νομικὰς περιΐστασο) and be self-possessed
(2 Tim. 4:5, νῆφε ἐν πᾶσιν).

Philodemus finds an effective technique in παρρησία in the admon-
itors' own admission that they too had been guilty of the faults in
their own youth (fr. 9, ποτ' ἐφ' ἑαυτὸν ὁ σοφός θ' ἁμάρτημ' ἄνετον ἐν
τ[ῆι] νεότητι γε[γ]ονέ[ν]αι, "Since the wise man will also transfer to
himself an intemperate error, {saying} that it occurred in his youth ..."),
but have since reformed and have made progress in dealing with
their own imperfections (fr. 46, πῶς γὰρ μισεῖν τὸν ἁμαρτάνοντα μὴ
ἀπογνώ[σ]ιμα μέλλει, γινώσκω[ν] αὐτον οὐκ ὄντα τέλε[ι]ον, "For how is

---

[74] Mitsis 81 focuses on ἀταραξία as the Epicurean conception of the good. He
explains that "for the Epicurean ... to guarantee that we achieve ἀταραξία and
ἀπονία, we must be capable of restricting our desires to those that are necessary
and easily satisfied." This presumes the ability "to control and limit our desires
rationally" (91). He finds that Philodemus' *On Anger* emphasizes the essential note
that our beliefs play on our πάθη (139–40). In Philodemus the passions are "so
sanitized and restructured by beliefs that little remains in them that is not amenable
to rational correction and control."

[75] 1 Tim. 3:2–7, νηφάλιον ... ἐπιεική ... ἀφιλάργυρον; Tit. 1:6–9, μὴ ἐν κατη-
γορίαι ἀσωτίας ... μὴ ὀργίλον ... μὴ αἰσχροκερδῆ ... ἐγκρατῆ; 1 Tim. 3:8–13,
σεμνούς ... μὴ αἰσχροκερδεῖς.

[76] 1 Tim. 3:11, σεμωάς ... νηφαλίους; 1 Tim. 5:5–7, ἡ δὲ σπαταλῶσα ζῶσα
τέθηκεν.

[77] See also Tit. 3:1–2, ἐπιεικεῖς, πᾶσαν ἐνδεικνυμένους πραΰτητα.

he going to hate the one who errs, though not desperately, when he knows that he himself is not perfect . . .?"). In view of this they present models worthy of imitation in their own successful imitation of the life of their chosen model Epicurus (fr. 43–46). This is important given the penchant of pupils to imitate their teachers, whether good or bad. Furthermore, such admission of former guilt demonstrates that former transgression is no cause for discredit (fr. 35), but rather shows how self-criticism helps the one corrected (fr. 51).

In this connection Glad finds that in the community of friends the position of admonitor does not come to a person in view of authority or attributed status.[78] Rather it is the result of "acquired status" or the individual's "function and ability to heal and admonish others." And so, while Timothy and Titus are placed in their positions by Paul (Tit. 1:5) and through a ceremony of official designation by the community,[79] they are still expected to incorporate their teaching into the practice of their own lives (1 Tim. 4:15, ἡ προκοπὴ φανερὰ ᾖ πᾶσιν). They are expected to follow Paul's example as a key element in this process (2 Tim. 3:10–11). They are also to acknowledge and surpass their own faults (see below) and become models of the exhortation for which they are designating other teachers (2 Tim. 2:2, Tit. 1:5).

In the Pastoral Epistles, just as the false teachers are leading others into their ways (2 Tim. 3:7, 4:3–4), so Timothy and Titus are urged to be examples fit for imitation (1 Tim. 4:12, 2 Tim. 4:5, Tit. 2:7). Paul himself unabashedly describes his own rescue from ignorance and sin through God's mercy and patience (1 Tim 1:13–16).[80] Thus, he can call attention to his own good example (2 Tim. 3:10–11). He generalizes the lesson at Tit. 2:14 (ἵνα λυτρώσηται ἡμᾶς) and 3:3 (ἦμεν γὰρ ποτε καὶ ἡμεῖς ἀνόητοι) by using the first person plural pronoun to include the audience among those who were cleansed for good works and freed from slavery to delusion, pleasures

---

[78] Glad 59. In this connection the Pastoral Epistles expect church officials to have demonstrated the qualities expected of office holders (1 Tim. 3:4–5, 10, 12; cp. Tit. 2:4). The Pastorals designate the office of bishop at 1 Tim. 3:1 as an ἔργον; cp. Philodemus, col. XIXb where he calls the friendly office of admonition an ἔργον.

[79] 1 Tim. 1:3, 18; 4:15; 2 Tim. 1:6, 13–14; 2:2; see 1 Tim. 6:20.

[80] Neyrey 222 emphasizes that "honor, shame and reputation were primary values of an individual" in first-century Mediterranean society. These, however, "could be lost when challenged." The Pastoral Epistles are acutely attuned to honor regained (by Paul) and acquired (by the addressees and their communities).

and hatefulness. The behavior expected of community members serves a similar purpose of embodying the lesson in a lived example (1 Tim. 6:1; Tit. 2:5, 8, 10). The same can be said of the recommendations to community officials and ministers (1 Tim. 3:13, 5:14).

Philodemus (fr. 16, πείθειν δὲ καὶ διὰ τῶν [ἔργ]ων) sees the force of deeds as supportive of frank criticism in the effort to improve others. The Pastorals, too, emphasize this positive proof that deeds offer (see above) for claims of θεοσέβεια (1 Tim. 2:10), as the content of witness (1 Tim. 5:10), as an effect of spiritual cleansing (2 Tim. 2:21, Tit. 2:14), as the acts of a competent man of God (2 Tim. 3:17), and as a confirmation of one's confession of God (Tit. 1:16).

Philodemus commends open and above-board admonition wherein errors are openly divulged (fr. 40–42), because no secret can permanently escape detection (fr. 41, π[λ]εῖον ο[ὐ]δὲν ἔσται κρύπτοντος οὐ γὰρ ἕν ἔλαθεν).[81] 1 Tim. 5:20–25 makes the same observation when it recommends public reprimand (τοὺς ἁμαρτάνοντας ἐνώπιον πάντων ἔλεγχε) and notes that ultimately one's sins will become known (τὰ ἄλλως ἔχοντα κρυβῆναι οὐ δύνανται). This openness contrasts with the sneaky infiltration by false teachers who make captives of silly, passionate women but whose foolishness will be plain to all (2 Tim 3:6–9, ἡ γὰρ ἄνοια αὐτῶν ἔκδηλος ἔσται πᾶσιν).[82]

Philodemus offers advice on the variety of ways in which frank criticism can be applied and the appropriate occasions for it: severe and intense in dealing with the strong and more needy (fr. 7, τῶι σκληρῶι . . . τῆς παρρησίας), more artful in most instances (fr. 10, διαφι[λ]οτεχν[ή]σει), not abusively, haughtily, angrily (fr. 37–38, [μ]ηδὲ σοβ[αρῶ]ς καὶ [δι]ατεταμένως . . . [μηδ᾽ ὑβριστικὰ] καὶ καταβλ[ητικά τινα μη]δὲ διασυρτικὰ), sparingly with friends (fr. 84, ὑ[περο]κνουμ[ένη]ν . . . ἀνε[λευθέ]ρως), in a variety of modes from cultivated to direct (col. I–IV).

The Pastoral Epistles foresee a similar diversity in the application of frank speech. The public reproof described at 1 Tim. 5:20 has

---

[81] This echoes KD 35, "If someone does a secret act in secret violation of compacts men make . . . right up to the day of death, it remains unclear whether he will escape detection," and SV 7.

[82] The Cynics likewise linked frank speech with open and public life. Because mystery religions were not public, the Cynics rejected them, according to Scarpat 64–65 who cites Lucian's *Demonax* 11. *Demonax* 12 goes on to characterize frank speech as typical of manliness rather than soft effeminacy.

been noted above. The preceding verse sets out the cautionary requirement of accepting an accusation only with the substantiation of witnesses. The Pastorals, like Philodemus, rule out haughtiness and abusiveness.[83]

The contexts of instruction, however, appear to be different. Whereas Philodemus describes the efforts of the wise individual in the community of friends, an informal position which results from progress made and recognized, the Pastoral Epistles address an evangelist with an official ministry in the church (2 Tim. 4:5). While Philodemus looks to one-on-one exhortation, occasionally with some communal criticism, among the friends in the community (fr. 40 and 42), the Pastoral Epistles presume a more structured, communal situation. They describe public reproof of officials before witnesses (1 Tim. 5:19–20),[84] regulation of widows' activities (1 Tim. 5:7) and slaves' conduct (1 Tim. 6:1–2), and instructions given by the addressees to the assembled brothers (1 Tim. 4:6), or to the Cretans (Tit. 1: 13). Nonetheless, they also recommend some individualized exhortation, differentiated according to its object. For example, an older man and other community members are to receive kind and familiar treatment (1 Tim 5:1–2); opponents (2 Tim. 2:24) and a heretic are to be given timely ultimatums (Tit. 3:10). The rich may also be expected to be admonished singly (1 Tim. 6:17) and similarly indeterminate is the object of the reminder not to dispute at 2 Tim. 2:14. The letters themselves, on the other hand, exemplify the one-on-one mode of exhortation, since they are presented as Paul's individualized advice to Timothy and Titus.

Philodemus cautions that the wise should apply frank speech at the opportune moment[85] (fr. 25, οὐδ' εἰς καιρὸν ἐνχρονίζειν, "nor . . . to dawdle up to the critical moment," and fr. 32, ἐπὶ τήν εἴ ποτε γένοιτο, [ν]ουθέτησιν, "to proceed {gradually} to admonishment, if it should ever occur"). The opportune time is the occasion for moral progress, which the wise may determine from astute observation of their disciples. In the Pastoral Epistles the opportune moment is not

---

[83] 1 Tim. 3:3, 5:1–2; 2 Tim. 2:24–25; Tit. 1:7.

[84] Philodemus affirms that the wise use frank speech with each other to change them for the better, Glad 42, 48 and cols. IIIa 3–5, VIIIb 6–13, IXa 1–8.

[85] Marcello Gigante, "Philodème: Sur la liberté de parole," in *Actes du Vllle Congrès Association Guillaume Budé* (Paris, 5–10 Avril 1980) (Paris: Société d'édition "Les Belles Lettres," 1969), 206 also refers to fr. 22.

one selected by Paul or by other teachers but by God as part of the plan of history. It is the time when God's word is revealed (Titus 1:3), the time when Christ ransomed humanity (1 Tim. 2:6), the time of Christ's parousia (1 Tim. 6:14–15). It denotes the final times when apostasy and heresy break out (1 Tim. 4:1; 2 Tim. 3:1, 4:3). The word καιρός is mostly plural but at 2 Tim. 4:3 it is singular, as it is in Philodemus. The meaning, however, in the Pastorals is consistent, except at 2 Tim. 4:6 where it refers to the time of Paul's death. Despite this basic difference in determining the opportune time, the reaction to it in both Philodemus and the Pastorals is the same. Both see it as a moment of high moral seriousness and opportunity. Both speak of the coming of the opportune time as an occasion for moral reformation and progress.

Philodemus uses medical imagery that presents frank speech as a cure for the ills of the soul, to be applied by the wise much as a doctor applies remedies for physical ailments (fr. 69). Some (fr. 86) even resist being healed and have need of the diverse curative measures of the wise. In fact, (fr. 39) the work of the wise is a *sine qua non* for acquiring spiritual soundness, just as the doctor's art is indispensable for physical well-being. The therapy involved the use of frank speech (fr. 40) to lead the young to recognize their errors and defects and see in the teacher their unique savior and guide to a cure.[86] The Pastoral Epistles also use the image of illness and curative measures[87] when they refer to the community's opponents and their gangrenous teaching (2 Tim. 2:17). The dissidents and apostates are also criticized for resistance to healthy/sound teaching,[88] for being pathologically argumentative (1 Tim. 6:4), seared/scarred

---

[86] Gigante, *Ricerche Filodemee* 75–78. See also fr. 8, 20, 23, 44, 64, 75, 79, col. XVII, XXI, tab XII M. Fredrickson 2 and nn. 15–16 calls attention to the parallel between the application of παρρησία "to treat moral failures" and the use of medical instruments to treat disease in Philodemus (fr. 64–65), Dio Chrysostom, *Or.* 77/78.45, Plutarch, *Quomodo adulator ab amico internoscatur* 73A–B and 71D.

[87] Both use the words ὑγιής, ὑγιαίνειν fr. 13, 1 Tim. 1:10; 6:3; 2 Tim. 1:13; 4:3; Titus 1:9, 13; 2:12. See Abraham J. Malherbe, "Medical Imagery in the Pastoral Epistles" in *Texts and Testaments: Essays on the Bible and the Early Christian Fathers*, ed. W.E. March (San Antonio: Trinity University Press, 1980), 19–35. The Pastoral Epistles, like the Stoics and Cynics and even the Middle Platonist Plutarch, who also used the image, see one cause of moral illness to be passions and indulgence in pleasures.

[88] 1 Tim. 1:10; 6:3; 2 Tim. 4:3; cp. Tit. 1:9 and 2:2.

in conscience (1 Tim. 4:2), wracked with pain (1 Tim. 6:10), and with itching ears (2 Tim. 4:3).[89]

As a consequence of success at directing disciples to moral progress and spiritual healing, the wise one is called "savior" (fr. 40, σωτῆρ[α]) and the successful effort salvation (fr. 4, σωτηρ[ίας; cp. fr. 36).[90] As noted above, the Pastorals restrict the title "savior" to God and Jesus Christ.[91] Paul and his church ministers, however, are instrumental in the acquisition of salvation (2 Tim. 2:10, 3:15). At 2 Tim. 3:15 Paul reminds Timothy that scripture is capable of giving "wisdom for salvation" and goes on (2 Tim. 3:16–17) to detail the ways it is used for that end. These include ἐλεγμόν, ἐπανόρθωσιν, παιδείαν τὴν ἐν δικαιοσύνῃ, so that the individual may be "competent" and "equipped for every good work" (NAB). These are hortatory means and ends comparable to those adopted by Philodemus.

In addition to the word παρρησία, Philodemus also uses a range of paraenetic vocabulary to nuance the admonitory work of correction and many of his words find an echo in the Pastoral Epistles. The language describes the parenetic effort, sometimes critical but always intended to foster moral development: ἐλεγμόν, ἐλέγχειν, ἐξελέγχειν;[92] ὑπόμνησις, ὑπομιμνήσκειν;[93] παράκλησις, παρακαλεῖν;[94] νουθεσία, νουθετησία, νουθετεία, νουθετέσις, νουθετεύω, νουθετεῖν;[95] ἐπιτίμησις, ἐπιτίμης, ἐπιτιμᾶν;[96] ἐπιπλήξις, ἐπιπλήσσειν, ἐπιπλήττω;[97]

---

[89] Contrast the reference to real illness at 2 Tim. 4:20. See Malherbe "Medical Imagery" for parallels to the medical imagery in Philo, Dio Chrysostom and Plutarch.

[90] For other passages where Philodemus uses σῴζω and its cognates in a similar way see fr. 34.5, 36.1–2, 40.8, 43.13, 77 (= 78N).3–4, 78.6–7, col. VIb 10–11, T2.D2.

[91] 1 Tim. 1:1, 2:3, 4:10; 2 Tim. 1:10; Tit. 1:3, 4; 2:10, 13; 3:4, 6.

[92] Fr. 42, col. XVIb, col. XXIIIa, tab III G; 1 Tim. 5:20; 2 Tim. 4:2; Titus 1:9, 13; 2:15.

[93] Fr. 38; 68; 93N; col. VIIIb; XIa; 2 Tim. 1:5, 2:14; Tit. 3:1. Malherbe, "Medical Imagery" 135 quotes Plutarch, *Progress in Virtue* 80BC where he distinguishes bellicosity from frankness. The former rises from a spirit of contention, rancor, arrogance, and quarreling and looks to win in conflict over debatable questions, as do the false teachers in the Pastoral Epistles. Plutarch, as do the Pastoral Epistles, recommends the use of reasonableness and mildness.

[94] Fr. 38, col. XVIb, XVIIa (2x); 1 Tim. 1:3; 2:1; 4:13; 5:1; 6:2; 2 Tim. 4:2; Tit. 1:9; 2:6, 15.

[95] Fr. 13, 20, 23, 26, 32, 35, 36, 38, 39, 40, 45, 61, 66, 73, 77, 84, 91N, XVIIa, XVIIIb, XIXb, XXIb, XXIIa, tab V; Tit. 3:10.

[96] Fr. 6, 30, 31, 38, 62, 75, 82, 84, 93N, col. IXb, XVb, XXIa, XXIIIa, XXIVb, tab IV I; 2 Tim. 4:2.

[97] Col. XVIa, XIXb; 1 Tim. 5:1.

παιδεία, παιδεύειν;[98] λαλεῖν.[99] The two also agree in their description of the problem to be remedied: διάβολος, διαβολή, διαβάλλειν;[100] ἁμαρτία, ἁμάρτημα, ἁμαρτωλός, ἁμαρτάνειν;[101] βλάσφημος, βλασφεμία, βλασφημεῖν.[102]

Both aim for comparable results: προκοπή,[103] ἐπίγνωσις, ἐπιγινώσκειν.[104] It goes without saying that each has its own unique vocabulary to describe the effort of exhortation by means of frank speech. The agreement noted here is nonetheless remarkable and reflects a common hortatory context.

Philodemus, ever the realistic idealist, recommends persistence even in the face of the not unexpected rejection of frank criticism (fr. 5–6, col. X, XII–XXI). The Pastorals also urge their addressees to keep at their task (1 Tim. 4:11–16) despite rejection and without losing patience (2 Tim. 4:2).

The rejection of frank criticism points to another, even broader similarity in the perspectives of Philodemus and the Pastoral Epistles. In the section of Philodemus that deals with "Whether wise men too will diverge from one another in respect to frankness" (col. IIIa), he describes the positive reaction of the wise to criticism (cols. VIIIa–Xb). This contrasts with the situation of the apostate and false teachers in the Pastoral Epistles. There some teachers are hypocritical, "with seared consciences" (1 Tim. 4:2). They "make a pretense of religion" and "oppose the truth" (2 Tim. 3:5–9) with "absurdities of so-called knowledge" (1 Tim. 6:20). In general, however, just as Philodemus believes the effort of frank speech will ultimately lead to a cure (col. VIII–XIV), so the Pastorals do not abandon hope for the wayward but advance the paradigm of the conversion of the once arrogant and blaspheming Paul (1 Tim. 1:13–16) as well as of the transformation of the ignorant, libidinous, deceived community (Tit. 3:3).

---

[98] Fr. 26; 1 Tim. 1:20; 2 Tim. 3:16; Tit. 2:12.

[99] Fr. 47, 48; col. XIVa, XVIIIa; Tit. 3:2.

[100] Fr. 17, 35, 50, 51; 1 Tim. 3:11; 2 Tim. 3:3; Tit. 2:3.

[101] Fr. 1, 6, 9, 46, 49, 55, 62, 63, 64, 76, 77, 79N, 79, 83, IIIb, VIb, IXb, XIa, XIIa. Xva, XVb, XVIIa, XVIIIb, XIXb, XXIa, XXIIIb, XXIVb; tab 2, 12M; 1 Tim. 5:20, 22, 24; 2 Tim. 3:6; Tit. 3:11.

[102] Fr. 13, 18; 1 Tim. 1:13, 20; 6:1, 4; 2 Tim. 3:2; Titus 2:5; 3:2.

[103] Fr. 10, 33; 1 Tim. 4:15.

[104] Of mutual perfection, col. IXa; of the truth, 1 Tim. 2:4, 4:3; 2 Tim. 2:25, 3:7; Tit. 1:1. See also fr. 88; col. XXa.

When read against the background of Philodemus, the Pastorals appear to be filled with concern for the proper application of frank criticism leading to the improvement of the Christian community in much the same way that the Epicurean philosopher was for his Epicurean followers. The Pastorals also seem to be in conversation with and to a significant degree condemnatory of the ἦθος of Epicurean philosophy. Despite their theoretical disagreements, however, the Pastoral Epistles and Philodemus share the popular philosophical aim of moral improvement and also agree on the best measures to be taken to achieve their aim.

PAUL'S FRANK SPEECH WITH THE GALATIANS AND THE CORINTHIANS

J. Paul Sampley

Abstract

This study examines four instances of Paul's frank speech—one in his letter to the Galatians and the other three reflected in the fragments that make up 2 Corinthians—and finds (1) that Paul uses frank speech according to the conventions embraced by Philodemus and Plutarch, (2) that Paul adjusts or varies the harshness of frank speech according to his appraisal of the circumstances he addresses, and (3) that Paul's frankness ranges from the gentlest "sting" in 2 Cor. 6:13, 7:2, to mixed frank speech in Galatians, to harsh frankness in 2 Cor. 10–13.

Philodemus situated frank speech (παρρησία)[1] in the social context of friendship. The person who speaks frankly is "performing the office of a friend" (φιλικὸν ἔργον; *De lib. dic.* [*On Frank Criticism*] col. XIXb).[2] Plutarch shared this perspective; for him, frank speech is a "fine art . . . it is the greatest and most potent medicine in friendship" (Plut., *Quomodo quis suos* [*How to Tell a Flatterer from a Friend*] 74D).[3] Friends keep "close watch" on one another "not only when they go

---

[1] Translating παρρησία presents a challenge. In Philodemus and in Plutarch παρρησία is always "frank" but it is not always "criticism." As translations "frank speech" and "frankness" honor the necessary frankness that is always present in παρρησία and the use of "frank speech" or "frankness" leaves open the question, to be decided in each context, just how much and how negative the explicit or implicit criticism is. So in this study we will generally use "frank speech" and "frankness" to translate παρρησία and will reserve "frank criticism" for the places where the παρρησία in question is harsh and more explicitly and exclusively connected with blame.

[2] All quotations of Philodemus are from the translation of David Konstan, Diskin Clay, Clarence E. Glad, Johan C. Thom, and James Ware, *Philodemus: On Frank Criticism*, SBLTT 43 (Atlanta: Scholars, 1998). On παρρησία as a "duty" of friendship, see Konstan, "Friendship, Frankness and Flattery," *Friendship, Flattery, and Frankness of Speech: Studies on Friendship in the New Testament World*, ed. John T. Fitzgerald (Leiden: Brill, 1996) 10; as a "sign of goodwill," see Glad, "Frank Speech, Flattery, and Friendship in Philodemus," *Friendship, Flattery, and Frankness*, 31–32.

[3] All translations of Plutarch, *Quomodo quis suos*, are from F. C. Babbitt (LCL).

wrong but also when they are right" (Plut., *Quomodo quis suos* 73D).
True friends will understand frank speech as a sign of "good will"
(τὴν εὔνοιαν; Phild., *De lib. dic.* cols. Xb, XIb, XVIIb); true friends
will also seek to "foster the growth of what is sound and to preserve
it" (Plut., *Quomodo quis suos* 61D). Analogies abound to the physician-
patient relationship: "the true frankness such as a friend displays
applies itself to errors that are being committed; the pain which it
causes is salutary and benignant, and, like honey, it causes the sore
places to smart and cleanses them too . . ." (Plut., *Quomodo quis suos*
59D). Though it is pleasant to have a friend "commend and extol
us," it is more difficult to find and probably more important to have
"a friend to take us to task, to be frank with us, and indeed to
blame us when our conduct is bad. For there are but few among
many who have the courage to show frankness rather than favor to
their friends" (Plut., *Quomodo quis suos* 66A). Self-correction and the
emendation of one's ways are facilitated by παρρησία properly delivered by a friend. Παρρησία is a vital instrument in an individual's
ability to stay on the right track and to keep perspective not only
on one's self, but also on surrounding matters and on events.[4]

Frank speech does not settle for the status quo; it seeks another
level of performance. In some cases it reaches for increased maturity
or, if the person in question has ventured onto a dubious path, it calls
for a change in direction. And the person who employs frankness
values those aspirations and goals highly enough to risk that the
recipient may reject not only the frank speech but the speaker as
well. That willingness to risk one's own standing with another for
the good of the other is why frank speech can only be understood
in the context of genuine friendship.[5]

As life's problems come in all degrees of difficulty, from the most
minor to the seemingly earth-shattering, so παρρησία varies in degree

---

[4] See Konstan, "Friendship" 7–19, for the history of the relationship of the title's
concepts in antiquity from Aristotle forward (cf. his *Friendship in the Classical World*
[Cambridge: University Press, 1997] 103–105, where he notes a "change from the
political to the moral sense . . ." 104). "Friends were imagined as constituting a network of mutual assistance . . ." (Konstan, "Friendship" 10). Cf. also Troels Engberg-
Pedersen, "Plutarch to Prince Philopappus on How to Tell a Flatterer From a
Friend," *Friendship, Flattery, and Frankness* 75–76. See Konstan's description of the "new"
understanding of friendship that was operative in Roman times, "Friendship" 7–10.
[5] The connection of παρρησία with friendship dates at least from Aristotle; see
Alfons Fürst, *Streit unter Freunden: Ideal and Realität in der Freundschaftslehre der Antike*
(Stuttgart: Tuebner, 1996), 133–34.

from gentle to harsh.[6] At one extreme lies harsh παρρησία (using a form of σκληρός as the descriptor, Phild. *De lib. dic.* frg. 7; or using a form of πικρός, frg. 60; Plutarch makes the same point with σθοδρὸν, "severe," *Quomodo quis suos* 69E) whose focus is on blame alone. It is the nearest neighbor to insult (λοιδορία; Phild. *De lib. dic.* frg. 60), something that is no longer παρρησία.[7] At the other extreme lies "mixed" (μικτή; Phild. *De lib. dic.* frg. 58),[8] "that is, compounded of reproof, generous praise and exhortation."[9] Its neighbor is flattery, which cannot pretend to be παρρησία.

Human relations and interchanges range on a continuum from insult to flattery. True παρρησία functions in varying degrees along but within that continuum, not reaching insult and falling short of flattery, and ranging from harsh/severe/simple criticism on the one extreme to what Philodemus calls "the gentlest of stings" (*De lib. dic.* col. VIIIb) and what he calls "mixed" παρρησία (κατὰ μικτὸν τρόπον, because it interlaces frank speech and praise) on the other (frg. 58). Simple, harsh frank speech is straightforward and direct, having no praise intermixed, but consisting simply of blame. Mixed παρρησία is a combination of frankness and praise. Between the extremes of contemptuousness and pure praise, παρρησία takes a supposedly infinite variety of configurations ranging from blame through less praise to more praise. Accordingly, if one wanted to assess just how harsh is the παρρησία in a given document, one could look for the amount of praise that accompanies the frank speech. The more praise one finds alongside the call for a change of conduct or for the avoidance of a contemplated course of action, the further to the right on the imaginary continuum one would place the document and its παρρησία.

When does one use harsher criticism? When does one employ only the slightest corrective? Philodemus is especially helpful as he addresses the problem of how to nurture his most obstinate young students whom

---

[6] Here I follow the interpretation of Norman W. De Witt, "Organization and Procedure in Epicurean Groups," *CP* 31 (1936) 205–11, and Glad, *Paul and Philodemus: Adaptability in Epicurean and Early Christian Psychagogy* (Leiden: Brill, 1995) 143–46. See also Glad, "Frank Speech" 35 n. 74. Though their interests are focused on Epicureans, a similar picture emerges in Plutarch, as we shall see.

[7] Peter Marshall, *Enmity in Corinth: Social Conventions in Paul's Relations with the Corinthians* (Tübingen: J. C. B. Mohr [Paul Siebeck], 1987) 79 n. 59: the "line between ridicule and reproach was a thin one indeed . . ."

[8] So also Plutarch: ". . . among the most useful helps is a light admixture of praise . . ." *Quomodo quis suos* 72C.

[9] De Witt, "Organization," 209.

he likens to horses/stallions (*De lib. dic.* frg. 71; cf. frg. 83 and Philo, *De agricultura* 34). The harshest criticism is employed with such people, as an ultimate measure, as an effort of last resort when all else has failed. The gentlest of correctives is applied between friends who have the highest regard for one another (Phild. *De lib. dic.* col. VIII).

One of the challenges facing the dispenser of frank speech is to make certain that the frankness is proportional to the crisis.

> In what circumstances, then, should a friend be severe, and when should he be emphatic in using frank speech? It is when occasions demand of him that he check the headlong course of pleasure or of anger or of arrogance, or that he abate avarice or curb inconsiderate heedlessness. (Plut. *Quomodo quis suos* 69E–F)

Philodemus intimates that the best of circumstances for the mildest παρρησία is between two sages. His irenic picture imagines two persons who are already attuned to high standards for themselves and who enjoy one another's company and mutual respect: ". . . they will be reminded pleasurably by one another in the ways we have made clear, as also by themselves, and they will sting each other with the gentlest of stings and will acknowledge gratitude [for the benefit]" (Phild. *De lib. dic.* col. VIIIb).

We now turn to an examination of four selected instances of παρρησία in Paul's correspondence.[10] Though I shall not make a detailed survey of Paul's use of the term παρρησία,[11] I shall note Paul's use of frank speech in Galatians and in three places in the letter fragments that compose 2 Corinthians.

Frank Speech in Galatians

Paul thinks that some believers in Galatia are courting disaster. His letter suggests that they are near what he considers a precipice and that they are deliberately moving away from Paul's gospel and toward the cliff. They have not yet done what Paul would construe as wrong,

---

[10] David E. Fredrickson, "ΠΑΡΡΗΣΙΑ in the Pauline Epistles," *Friendship, Flattery, and Frankness* 163–83, is interested in the occurrence of the term παρρησία and treats instances of frank speech not examined in this essay (e.g., Phlm. and 1 Thess.), but he considers only those places where the term παρρησία occurs, whereas my study will examine four examples of frank speech, whether the term παρρησία is found or not.

[11] Fredrickson, "ΠΑΡΡΗΣΙΑ" 163–84, does that.

so Paul warns them vigorously. Plutarch differentiates two uses of
frank speech. One "reclaim[s] a wrongdoer." The other "stir[s] a
man to action" (*Quomodo quis suos* 74A). In the former, one lightly
chides: "'You acted unbecomingly' rather than 'You did wrong' . . ."
(73F). In the latter "we should . . . ascribe their action to some unnatural or unbecoming motives" (74A). Because the Galatians have
not yet done "wrong" Paul pursues the course of questioning their
motives, as Plutarch suggests. How could they possibly "turn back
again to the weak and beggarly elemental spirits, whose slaves you
want to be once more?" (Gal. 4:8–11). He expresses astonishment
over them where they might have been expecting to hear a thanks-
giving (Gal. 1:6ff.). Twice he dubs them foolish or unthinking (ἀνόητοι;
Gal. 3:1, 3).

Effective frank speech requires a solid, respectable ἦθος, character, on the part of the speaker.[12] The stronger the frank speech, the
stronger the necessary ἦθος. In a letter the frank speaker is perforce
absent and ἦθος refurbishment will regularly be present in the letter. Frank speech draws upon the reservoir of good will built up by
a consistent life whose values govern the behavior of the one who
employs frankness. So it is in Galatians. By noting his past comportment and his on-going concern, Paul commends himself to the
Galatians and puts himself in a position to employ frankness with
them. His role as their community founder via his preaching is the
foundation on which his frankness ultimately stands.

The first two chapters of Galatians are a refinement of Paul's ἦθος
and an offering of himself as a model.[13] There, details of Paul's past
are selectively chosen and told in such a way as not only to encourage the Galatians' identification with Paul and his gospel but also
to recognize his consistency and dependability. Paul can sympathize

---

[12] Philodemus' treatise on παρρησία is part of his multi-volume work "Character
and Lives" (περὶ ἠθῶν καὶ βίων), signifying an interrelationship between frank speech
and ἦθος, character, one's fundamental identity. In antiquity, ἦθος is a comprehensive term describing an individual's total bearing or character or core identity;
his or her distinguishing hallmarks; those specific qualities that betoken who a person really is, particularly those moral qualities that are strongly developed and strik-
ingly displayed with an identifiable consistency. One's ἦθος is constantly being
formulated and refined, positively or negatively. All of one's actions and statements
contribute to one's ἦθος. See Mario M. DiCicco, *Paul's Use of Ethos, Pathos, and Logos
in 2 Corinthians 10–13* (Lewiston, NY: Mellen Biblical, 1995), 36–77.
[13] Cf. George Lyons, *Pauline Autobiography: Toward a New Understanding*, SBLDS 73
(Atlanta: Scholars, 1985), 123–164.

with those among the Galatians who have been subjected to the influence of others and are tempted to capitulate, but his own story, from his self-identification in 1:1 to his depiction of the Jerusalem conference (2:1–10), shows that he stood fast against such an influence and affirmed that God was the one in control of his life.

Like the Galatians, Paul also had experienced a radical change. They were "slaves to elemental spirits" and alienated from God (4:8–9); Paul used to oppose the gospel and persecute its advocates (1:13–14). Paul was called to be an apostle (1:1, 15); the Galatians were called (1:6). Coincidentally, the Galatians are now being pressured to change regarding the very same issue that Paul had to confront at the Jerusalem conference, namely circumcision. There some persons of eminent status, James, Cephas and John, pressed Paul on the very same issue. There Paul stood his ground; in the Galatians' circumstances, Paul thinks they should stand theirs. Further, all those great leaders *agreed* with Paul that circumcision was not necessary (2:9). Paul's leadership, constancy, and therefore his dependability, are reaffirmed and enhanced by his recounting the Jerusalem conference story to his readers. The encoded message, made explicit later in the letter, is that the Galatians who are tempted to undertake circumcision are out of step.

The next account in the letter, the Antioch story (2:11–21), refines and enhances his consistency of belief and comportment. The story is perfect for Paul's rhetorical purposes because it shows him, clear-headed about the heart of the gospel, resolutely standing firm against one even so prominent as Cephas,[14] in the presence of "those from James," and even with Barnabas' hypocrisy.[15] Others may lose their way regarding the gospel, but not Paul, not even for a moment.

Philodemus and Plutarch would have recognized immediately that in Paul we have someone eminently qualified as a true friend, tried and true through all the tests that life can provide. Paul shows he merits the Galatians' trust in "the truth of the gospel" and in the

---

[14] Lyons, *Pauline Autobiography*, 164–68, 170–76, 225–26, and Sampley, "Reasoning From the Horizons of Paul's Thought World: A Comparison of Galatians and Philippians," *Theology and Ethics in Paul and His Interpreters: Essays in Honor of Victor Paul Furnish*, ed. Eugene H. Lovering, Jerry L. Sumney (Nashville: Abingdon, 1996) 114–31.

[15] Paul heightens his consistency, a necessary base for frankness, by small notes in the larger account: he does not "build up again those things which I tore down" (Gal. 2:18) and he does not nullify (ἀθέτω; Gal. 2:21) God's grace because justification never came nor will ever come through circumcision.

comportment appropriate to it. His opening chapters position him as one eminently qualified to carry out the "work of friendship:" namely, to warn them of the dangers of their contemplated action. The Galatians' readiness to change again is set over against Paul's steadfastness and dependability. Paul and the Galatians already share a foundational change that brought them all into the faith; another radical shift is unthinkable and retrograde in Paul's view. Their first was a formative turning, a conversion; the second promises to be destructive. Accordingly, Paul structures much of the remainder of Galatians on a contrast between their good start and their present temptation. Praise is lavished on the former; warning is plastered onto the latter.

Paul does praise the Galatians. They began as they should have, namely with the Spirit (Gal. 3:3). With one of his beloved athletic metaphors, Paul declares, "You were running well," signifying that they not only got "out of the blocks" efficiently, but were moving along before they hit the hindrance introduced by the outsiders (Gal. 5:7). Praiseworthy also was their overwhelming response to him when he first preached the gospel to them (Gal. 4:14–15; to be examined more fully below). Paul's laudatory portraits of the Galatians' good start and enthusiasm should surely function rhetorically to have them yearn to be like their better selves (Plut. *Quomodo quis suos* 72D). Paul's concluding blessing—"peace and mercy upon them"—on those who "follow in the footsteps of this rule" (5:16) is designed to encourage conformity to him.

Paul's warnings and expressions of shame are preponderant in Galatians. The believers in Galatia are described as "deserting" God (Gal. 1:6). Though they started well with the Spirit, they threaten to "end up with the flesh" (Gal. 3:3), to have it come to nothing (Gal. 3:4). Now free, they are tempted to revert to slavery (Gal. 4:9). They venture to lose their "blessedness" (ὁ μακαρισμὸς ὑμῶν; Gal. 4:15). As if those cautions were not strong enough, Paul warns them with the same teaching he had given them earlier: those who do works of the flesh shall not inherit God's kingdom (Gal. 5:19–21). Warning against self-deception, Paul declares that God will repay people according to what they sow (Gal. 5:15, 26). And the proof of the pudding: Paul is not pleased with the way some Galatians are relating to others among them (Gal. 6:1–5).

At the letter's heart and at the epicenter of Paul's friendship and frankness with the Galatians lies a rich and crucial passage (Gal.

302   J. PAUL SAMPLEY

4:12–20) that can fully be appreciated only in the context of frank speech. The passage signals friendship from start to finish. First, Paul addresses them as ἀδελφοί, "brothers," a term indicating familiarity and used with great frequency (11 times) in this letter to reflect the resocialization of believers into a new family with God as Father (1:3). He implores (δέομαι) them (Gal. 4:12) to manifest the mutuality of friendship that is so proper to genuine friendship: brothers and sisters in Christ, like true friends, find their unity in becoming like one another. Paul's "become as I am" must carry the auditors' minds back to his exemplary performance depicted in the opening chapters and to the intervening passages where Paul has carefully told the common story of the origins of faith in such a way as to include himself in it with them. As he puts it in Gal. 4:12, he has "become as" them: "Before faith came *we* were confined under the law, *mutually* restrained [συγκλειόμενοι] until faith should be disclosed . . ." (Gal. 3:23; italics added). Then, when describing how the heir must reach majority before receiving the estate, he includes himself once again with his auditors: "Just so with *us*, when *we* were children, *we* were slaves to the elemental spirits of the cosmos . . . in order that *we* might receive sonship" (Gal. 4:3–5; italics added).

Paul's exculpatory declaration that the Galatians have done him no wrong (Gal. 4:12) clarifies that his frank speech is not in reprisal for something they have done to him, because that would not be an appropriate context for frankness (Plut. *Quomodo quis suos* 66F–67A). This is part of Paul's effort to make sure that the Galatians understand that his frank speech on either side of Gal. 4:12–20 is not self-servingly motivated—a charge he will readily lodge against the outsiders (Gal. 4:17; 6:12–13).[16] There σύγκρισις, comparison, serves Paul's purposes well and strengthens his ground for the frank speech of this letter.[17]

Gal. 4:12–20 is Paul's recounting of the foundational story for the Galatian churches. It is a story at once of God's grace and of the

---

[16] Cf. the rhetorical traditions concerning how one discredits opponents by impugning their motives, particularly by declaring that such persons serve their own self-interest: Sampley, "Paul, His Opponents in 2 Corinthians 10–13, and the Rhetorical Handbooks," *The Social World of Formative Christianity and Judaism: Essays in Tribute to Howard Clark Kee*, ed. Jacob Neusner, Peder Borgen, Ernest S. Frerichs, Richard Horsley (Philadelphia: Fortress, 1988) 162–77.

[17] Christopher Forbes, "Comparison, Self-Praise and Irony: Paul's Boasting and the Conventions of Hellenistic Rhetoric," *NTS* 32 (1986) 2–8. Cf. also Marshall, *Enmity* 53–55, 348–53.

inauguration of a strong friendship. Though Paul had not expected to preach among them, illness stopped him and he shared the gospel with them. Their response showed that they overcame whatever trial his illness was to them—an early sign of friendship on their side—and that their friendship flourished so that quickly they were ready to give of themselves for the well-being of their new friend, Paul (Gal. 4:14–15). He reminds them that they would have plucked out their eyes and given them to him—surely a metaphorical and rhetorically exuberant way of describing such a deep friendship that nothing matters more than the well-being of one's friend. What has changed, he asks in effect, since that foundational time of such great, good enthusiasm? Not himself. Not the gospel. Paul recounts the Galatians' early exuberance, which he calls "blessedness," an overflowing of God's love through them back to Paul. Paul asks them in effect why they need to do anything different, like seek circumcision, to add to the blessedness that was so rich and overflowing from early on.

Precisely in this context of recounted rich and genuine friendship Paul now lodges the question that bears directly on how the Galatians, receiving this letter, will respond to his frank speech. Paul employs that frank speech in various ways to call them to task for their wavering in face of the temptation to follow outsiders in seeking circumcision. Will they judge that his frank speech is not genuine, that it is not founded in a heartfelt and strong friendship? Will they view Paul as no friend at all, in fact as an enemy (ἐχθρός), because he has been dealing truly and candidly with them (Gal. 4:16)?[18] In the verse following this question Paul pictures, by contrast with himself, the outsiders in terms similar to those Plutarch uses to describe flatterers who praise others for the benefits they can receive from them (Gal. 4:17).

Paul then goes ahead to move the discourse to a level above and beyond friendship, namely maternity. Mother Paul directly and affectionately addresses the Galatians: "My little children [τέκνα μου], again I am in labor until Christ be formed in you" (Gal. 4:19). Just as their attachment to him made the Galatians ready to show extravagant signs of friendship to Paul, so now Paul escalates the sentiments to yet another level, namely the travail of childbirth where

---

[18] Cf. Marshall, *Enmity*, 35–51, for a good understanding of enmity at that time.

one suffers greatly over the delivery of the beloved children. Friendship and family overlap in Paul as they do in the culture of his time.[19]

The passage concludes with Paul's double-sided wish that he could be with them now and that he could change his tone or voice (φωνή) because he is perplexed with them (Gal. 4:20). Paul is passionately involved with them and with their well-being, as any genuine friend and good mother rightly would be. Plutarch would have thought Paul perfectly in line here to show passionate feeling about the Galatians' predicament: ". . . if it concern matters of greater moment, let feeling also be evident" (*Quomodo quis suos* 68C). Paul's frankness here passes the test of "weight and firmness" (*Quomodo quis suos* 59C). It also qualifies as mixing a little praise in with it (*Quomodo quis suos* 72C).

Paul has no alternative but to engage the Galatians with frank speech, and if they turn against him, as Gal. 4:16 ponders, he must proceed, even though the consequences of frank speech are well-known in his time: ". . . it is the duty of a friend to accept the odium that comes from giving admonition when matters of importance and of great concern are at stake" (Plut. *Quomodo quis suos* 73A); "the man who by chiding and blaming implants the sting of repentance is taken to be an enemy and an accuser . . ." (56A). As a friend, much less as an apostle/mother, Paul cannot allow the Galatians to go further down that road without challenge (*Quomodo quis suos* 64C).

What classification of frankness has Paul used in Galatians? Surely it is not simple frank criticism because some praise is scattered across the letter. The scattered praise within the frank speech shows that Paul believes that the Galatians are capable of being set right; they have not gone too far so that they could not turn back. The harshest frank speech, namely that with no praise included, was reserved for those who are more nearly beyond hope (Phild. *De lib. dic.* frg. 71). Our assessment of Galatians as mixed frank speech also fits Plutarch's conviction that frankness is best when the recipients are not down and out (*Quomodo quis suos* 69A–B). Paul's approach in the letter to the Galatians is mixed frank speech. From that fact we have further insight into Paul's estimate of them: he has good reason to expect his rhetoric to bring them around.

Paul's mixed frank speech in the letter calls for the Galatians to reevaluate themselves. His frankness engages those who are tempted

---

[19] See John T. Fitzgerald, "Friendship in the Greek World Prior to Aristotle," in *Greco-Roman Perspectives on Friendship* 16–22.

to follow the outsiders' suggestions that circumcision must be added to the faith and to the reception of the Spirit that is undeniably theirs. Paul's frank speech, with its ἦθος enhancement, is designed first to refresh the auditors' attachment to himself as the one who brought the gospel and in so doing became their Mother/Father/Apostle whose understanding of the gospel should be theirs. Second, his frank speech is intended to make sure that the Galatians understand the fullness of what the Spirit has already begun in their lives and will continue not only to provide but to enrich if they stay the course. Paul's frank speech calls for the Galatians to turn back from the precipice that lies directly ahead of them in the form of the outsider's understanding of circumcision and the law.

Frank Speech in the "Painful Letter" and in 2 Corinthians 1–7

The "painful letter" is the one written after what we call 1 Corinthians (mentioned in 2 Cor. 2:3–4, 9 and 7:8–12), after a "painful visit" where things went poorly between Paul and the Corinthians, and after a projected visit which Paul failed to make. It is often dubbed the "painful letter" because of the way in which Paul describes his disposition in writing: "For I wrote you out of great affliction and distress of heart, with many tears, not in order to grieve you but in order that you may know the overflowing love which I have toward you" (2 Cor. 2:4). Paul shares with Philodemus the supposition that λυπέω describes a possible *effect* of παρρησία (see 2 Cor. 2:4, 7:8, 9, and *De lib. dic.* frg. 61.1, 82.7).

We can know very little of the content of this letter, as it is lost.[20] Our access to the letter is limited to Paul's own reflections about it in 2 Cor. 1–7 and about the response it elicited from the Corinthians. What we can study is, first, Paul's own statements about his disposition and purpose when he wrote it and, second, Paul's understanding of the Corinthians' response.

Paul expresses four reasons for writing the painful letter: 1) he wrote in an effort to clear matters for a subsequent pain-free visit (2 Cor. 2:3); 2) he wrote to show his overflowing love for them (2 Cor. 2:4);

---

[20] See Victor Paul Furnish, *II Corinthians*, AB 32A (Garden City, NY: Doubleday, 1984) 37 for his argument that 2 Cor. 10–13 is not part of the painful letter, and 35–48 for his accounting of the sequence of the letter fragments of 2 Corinthians to which I subscribe.

3) he wrote "in order to know your tried-and-trueness,²¹ that is, if in everything you were obedient" (2 Cor. 2:9; see again in 2 Cor. 7:15); and 4) he wrote so that "your zeal for us might be revealed to you before God" (2 Cor. 7:12). Three times he assures them that his primary purpose was not to grieve or pain them (2 Cor. 2:4, 7:8–9). In the letter's exigency is some person who did wrong (2 Cor. 2:6–11; 7:12), who seems to have caused pain to Paul, and, Paul widens the impact, to the other Corinthians as well (2 Cor. 2:5). Paul has no need to describe what the wrong was; he and all the Corinthians know both it and the individual responsible for it. Probably in response to Paul's painful letter, the Corinthians have practiced the most forceful of frank speech with this wrong-doer and (we may assume publicly) rebuked him (the term is ἐπιτιμία, which though found nowhere else in Paul is used widely by Philodemus and Plutarch to describe a rebuke, a reproving, a censuring; 2 Cor. 2:6).²² Paul later describes the Corinthians' collective action against this person as ἐκδίκησις, a working out of justice (7:12),²³ though as 2 Cor. 2:7 and 7:10b suggest, Paul shares Plutarch's concern that a public rebuke can, because of its shame, harm an individual beyond restoration (*Quomodo quis suos* 70E–71A; cf. Philodemus, *De lib. dic.* frg. 71).

By his accounting, Paul is pleased with the results that the painful letter effected. Frank speech aims at a change of behavior or direction and it has worked in the painful letter. Titus confirmed it for Paul: the Corinthians responded with mourning, (2 Cor. 7:7), zeal (twice, 2 Cor. 7:7, 11), longing (twice, 2 Cor. 7:7, 11), and earnestness (2 Cor. 7:11)—all of which signal to Paul a restoration of relationship. And their other responses—eagerness to clear themselves, indignation, alarm, and a working out of justice—indicate to him that they have acquitted themselves with regard to the one who did the wrong (2 Cor. 7:11). As a result, Paul declares them ἁγνούς,

---

²¹ For Paul's understanding of δοκιμός and its related family, see Sampley, *Walking Between the Times: Paul's Moral Reasoning* (Minneapolis: Fortress, 1991) 65–66.

²² BAG² 302, 303. The term does not occur elsewhere in Paul (though ἐπιτιμάω does occur in 2 Tim. 4:2) or in Philodemus, but two cognates do: ἐπιτιμάω, frg. 6.8, 31.3, 38.7–8, 62.1, 93N.7; col. IXb.9, XVb.12–13, XVIa.9, XIXa.11–12, XXIa.7, XXIIIa.3, XXIVb.4–5; ἐπιτίμησις, frg. 30.11, 75.2, 82.1, 84.7; col. XXIa.3, XXIVa.1–2, T4.I.23.

²³ In his assessment of the Corinthian response, did Paul place too much emphasis on the righting of the wrong done by person whose identity we do not know, thinking *that* change signaled that all was restored and well and perhaps overlooking pockets of resentment that went on unabated?

guiltless, across the board (2 Cor. 7:11). Their own zeal (σπουδή) for Paul has been revealed to them and he finds comfort in it (2 Cor. 7:11, 12). Paul's earlier boast to Titus about the Corinthians had proved true—and he cannot resist nurturing his ἦθος just a bit on this point as well: "just as we spoke all things to you in truth" (2 Cor. 7:14).

Paul's recommendation concerning the wrong-doer is significant for understanding the limits of frank speech as Paul sees it. The pain of one person in the community belongs to all (2 Cor. 2:5; cf. 1 Cor. 12:26, Rom. 12:15), just as does the joy (2 Cor. 2:3). Paul is concerned not to lose one for whom Christ has died (Rom. 14:15; 1 Cor. 8:11), so frank speech, though it may certainly be employed, must ultimately be curbed by love.[24] Paul has not given up on the wrong-doer and hopes for the same kind of grief-to-repentance-to-salvation from the wrong-doer that he takes to be under way with the Corinthians (2 Cor. 7:9–10).[25] Paul distinguishes between a godly grief (κατὰ θεόν; 2 Cor. 7:9) and a worldly grief (τοῦ κόσμου; 2 Cor. 7:10). The former works through to repentance and finally into salvation; the latter works itself out into death. Paul calls a halt to the Corinthians' scornful rebuke of the wrong-doer: "Sufficient is the scorn [ἐπιτιμία] of such a one by the majority" (2 Cor. 2:6). They should now rather "forgive and comfort him" so he will not be crushed by overflowing grief (2 Cor. 2:7). Accordingly, Paul appeals (παρκάλω) that they confirm or decide in favor of (κυρῶσαι) love to him (2 Cor. 2:8).[26]

Paul does not simply rejoice that the frank speech of the painful letter has accomplished its desired goal; he also uses the Corinthians' reported wholesome response as an occasion for another instance of frank speech. But this time it takes the form of a gentle "sting" of encouragement: he calls for the Corinthians to "open their hearts" to him (2 Cor. 7:2a), an echo of his own declaration earlier that

---

[24] Cf. Glad's interpretation that Philodemus also finds it difficult to give up on anyone, no matter how recalcitrant or arrogant, "Frank Speech" 42.

[25] Cf. the same sort of hope held out for the man sleeping with his father's wife (1 Cor. 5:5).

[26] In his willingness to forgive anyone whom they forgive, he manifests the clemency that he thinks Christ has modeled (2 Cor 10:1) and, ready to practice what he preaches, insists that forgiveness and reconciliation are basic to the gospel of which he is proud to be ambassador (2 Cor 5:20). The same sequence (ἐπιτιμάω/παρακαλέω) appears in 2 Tim. 4:2. Note also Philodemus' concern that frankness not be used in anger (De lib. dic. frg. 38).

"our heart is wide open" (2 Cor. 6:11 NRSV) to them. Immediately he insists on his uprightness and fairness (2 Cor. 7:2b–d), topics which have been asserted in a variety of ways in the preceding chapters where he has been busily nurturing his ἦθος (cf. 2 Cor. 2:17, 4:2).

The amount of ἦθος enhancement in the letter fragment 2 Cor. 1–7 is extraordinary; it is found on every page of 2 Cor. 1–7. The opening chapter focuses on Paul's sufferings and afflictions, most recently in Asia (2 Cor. 1:8); his bid for their prayers (2 Cor. 1:11) is an open request for identification with Paul. His behavior in the world is mentioned in 2 Cor. 1:12 and will be elaborated by a whole series of assertions and depictions—many of them benefiting from σύγκρισις, comparison, with others—to follow. Paul is not a huckster of God's word, but a person of sincerity (2 Cor. 2:17; revisited in 4:2ff.); he does not need letters of recommendation (2 Cor. 3:1–3); his is a διακονία of the Spirit, of glory, not one of death (2 Cor. 3:7–4:1); though afflicted and beset by great challenges, even death (2 Cor. 4:16–5:5), he endures (2 Cor. 4:7–12; and again in 2 Cor. 6:3–10); he values proper boasting based on a person's heart and not on their public image (2 Cor. 5:12). And his special calling as an ambassador for Christ leads him to devote himself to reconciliation, as he is in fact seeking to practice, both in the painful letter and in 2 Cor. 1–7, in regard to the Corinthians who have wavered from his leadership.

The new issue he addresses gently with frank speech in 2 Cor. 1–7 itself is that the Corinthians do not reciprocate as fully as he would wish. His "mouth is open to you," that is, he has "spoken freely and openly" to them.[27] He has shown himself ready to do the "office of a friend" (Phild. *De lib. dic.* col. XIXb) with them, both in the painful letter and now here in 2 Cor. 1–7. His current assessment of them is not so favorable in one regard: "You are not restricted in us, but you are restricted in your affections" (2 Cor. 6:12). Paul addresses them as children who need his leadership and calls, in this newest use of frank speech, for them to be reciprocal (ἀντιμισθίας) by opening wide their own hearts (πλαντυνάθητε; note the emphatic ὑμεῖς, 2 Cor. 6:13).

A few verses later, he refines that appeal, and with it his frank speech, by returning to the topic and urging them to open their

---

[27] BAG² 71; cf. Ezek. 16:63, 29:21.

hearts to him (2 Cor. 7:2). He next discloses how they stand—and have stood ("I said before")—in his heart,[28] namely "to live together and to die together" (2 Cor. 7:3). The signs of friendship! To make common cause, to identify so fully with them that their fate is his. Paul's consistency of dedication and friendship is here emphatically reaffirmed precisely in the context where he asks for an alteration of their hearts to be more inclusive of him. With his next three statements (2 Cor. 7:4a–c), 1) Paul openly acknowledges, as only friends can do, what he has been doing and how he has been relating to them throughout this letter fragment, "Great is my frank speech toward you" (πολλή μοι παρρησία πρὸς ὑμᾶς; 7:4a);[29] 2) in 7:4b he telegraphs the note on which the section will end (2 Cor. 7:16), namely his considerable confidence in them; and 3) in 7:4c he declares that he is overflowing in comfort, the reason for which will be detailed in 7:5–15.

Just what varieties of frank speech have we encountered in the painful letter and in 2 Cor. 1–7? We are at a loss to specify the frank speech of the painful letter. We simply have too little evidence and we cannot truly tell how much if any praise there was in it. As to the variety of frank speech found in 2 Cor. 1–7 there can be no mistake that it is what Philodemus and Plutarch would have called "mixed" because there is a fair amount of praise salted into the text. That is just as one would expect because Paul's earlier frank speech, however severe it may have been, had turned the Corinthians onto a better course, one that pleased Paul greatly. But Paul is not completely satisfied with their response to his earlier frank speech, and appeals here, in yet another instance of frankness, for them to open their hearts and to express their affection more fully. Indeed, much of Paul's ἦθος nurturing in 2 Cor. 1–7 is designed to help bring the Corinthians closer to him, to reconcile them to him even more completely.

---

[28] Philodemus acknowledges that many fine things come from friendship, but "there is nothing so grand as having one to whom one will say what is in one's heart . . ." (Phild. *De lib. dic.* frg. 28).

[29] The phrase παρρησία χρῆσθαι "refers to a manner of speaking"—and that generally in the context of moral counsel (Fredrickson, "ΠΑΡΡΗΣΙΑ" 164–65). "Paul's candor is a sign of his friendship (7.3) with the Corinthians" (Fitzgerald, "2 Corinthians: Introduction and Notes," *The HarperCollins Study Bible* [New York: HarperCollins, 1993] 2173).

In 2 Cor. 1–7 Paul praises the Corinthians with strong declarations: "Our hope for you is unshaken . . ." (1:7); ". . . being persuaded about all of you that my joy is shared by all of you" (2:3); "You yourselves are our letter [of recommendation] . . ." (3:2–3); all of the descriptions, derived from Titus' report, of how moved and rededicated the Corinthians were to Paul after they received the painful letter (7:7, 11); and the concluding note, "I have confidence in you in all things" (7:16).[30]

Paul's frank speech worked for him in the painful letter. In the very letter where he celebrates the results of his earlier frank speech, Paul employs frank speech yet another time. If 2 Cor. 10–13, to which we now turn, is any indication, his frank speech in 2 Cor. 1–7 was not so efficacious and we will have occasion to reflect on that again later in this study.

The following observations are in order:

1) The painful letter was undoubtedly harsher in its use of παρρησία than 2 Cor. 1–7. The relief he expresses in the letter is not only a good indicator of the anxiety he had about the possible negative response but also probably an indicator of its harshness.

2) For Paul and Philodemus (and Plutarch), παρρησία elicits an emotional response. Philodemus seems mostly concerned with *anger* as a response (cf. *De lib. dic.* frg. 58, 71, 87; col. Xa). Anger may have been Paul's concern in the Corinthians' response to the painful letter and surely may be a factor in 2 Cor. 10–13. In his comments about the Corinthian use of frankness with the one who did wrong, however, Paul's main concern regarding a response seems to be not anger but grief (2 Cor. 2:4; 7:8, 9).

3) The Corinthians' use of παρρησία with the wrong-doer demonstrates that παρρησία is a communal activity, not an exclusively apostolic one. Moreover their exercise of παρρησία toward the man was apparently not mixed with any praise and Paul was worried that its effect would be destructive. His exhortation to reaffirm love (2 Cor. 2:8) is his attempt to make their speech "mixed."

Frank Speech in 2 Corinthians 10–13

2 Cor. 10–13 is notorious for the troubled relations it depicts between Paul and the Corinthians.[31] Paul sees a great distance between where

---

[30] For these and other statements of Pauline self-confidence, see S. N. Olson, "Epistolary Uses of Expressions of Self-Confidence," *JBL* 103 (1984) 585–97.

[31] I follow Furnish's reasoning about the sequence of this letter fragment; see *II Corinthians* 38–41.

the Corinthians are and where he thinks they should be. Somewhat reminiscent of his appeal in the earlier letter fragment (2 Cor. 6:11–12, 7:2), that they should open their hearts to him and not be so restricted in their affections, is the newly-expressed but continuing hope that his "sphere of action or influence"[32] (κανών) among them will flourish (2 Cor. 10:15). He openly expresses his fears that he may come and find them not as he wishes (2 Cor. 12:20). Making the same point eschatologically and theologically, he fears that when he next visits Corinth God may humble him because his followers, the Corinthians, will not have lived the lives in the gospel that they should have. This would manifest his failure as the one responsible for presenting them to Christ as a pure bride (2 Cor. 11:2). He depicts himself as the one who cares enough about the Corinthians' well-being that he would be shamed before God by his and their failure. He prays for their "being made complete"[33] (κατάρτισις; 2 Cor. 13:9). The letter-fragment closes with a powerful sententious appeal for change (2 Cor. 13:11).

The entire letter fragment (2 Cor. 10–13) is laced with frank speech in which Paul calls for the Corinthians to realign themselves with him and his gospel and challenges them to recognize how far off the mark they are. In fact this letter fragment, unlike every other example of frank speech in the Pauline corpus, has not one instance of Paul's praising the Corinthians.[34] This is frank speech without any admixture of praise: it is what Philodemus and Plutarch called "pure," "simple," "harsh," or "severe" frank speech.

What does that tell us about the relationship between Paul and the Corinthians at the time of this writing? Why has Paul resorted to pure, simple frank speech in 2 Cor. 10–13? "In what circumstances, then, should a friend be severe, and when should he be emphatic in using frank speech? It is when occasions demand of him that he check the headlong course of pleasure or of anger or of

---

[32] BAG[2] 403.

[33] BAG[2] 418.

[34] I readily grant that this is a letter fragment, so there may have been praise in parts of the letter unavailable to us, but nowhere else in the Pauline correspondence do we have four chapters without *some* praise. Certainly, when evaluated in terms of letter style, 2 Cor. 10–13, though a combination of frankness and appeal, is "an excellent example of a mixed letter type" (Fitzgerald, "Paul, the Ancient Epistolary Theorists, and 2 Corinthians 10–13: The Purpose and Literary Genre of a Pauline Letter," in *Greeks, Romans, and Christians: Essays in Honor of Abraham J. Malherbe*, ed. David L. Balch, Everett Ferguson, Wayne A. Meeks [Minneapolis: Fortress, 1990], 200).

arrogance, or that he abate avarice or curb inconsiderate heedless-
ness" (Plut. *Quomodo quis suos* 69E–F). 2 Cor. 10–13 is such frank
criticism, pure and simple. This is the παρρησία best reserved for
those "somewhat more in need of treatment . . . the strong who will
scarcely change [even] if they are shouted at . . ." (Phild. *De lib. dic.*
frg. 7).[35] Paul's employment of pure frank speech indicates that he
finds himself without any other available resources in his effort to
turn the Corinthians from what he sees as a disastrous direction.

Paul's frank speech climaxes in 2 Cor. 13 in two ways. First, Paul
lays down the guideline for their confrontation when he next arrives:
the Deuteronomic canon of two or three witnesses will be enforced
regarding any claim (2 Cor. 13:1; Deut. 19:15), and the Corinthians
should realize that in their relations to Paul they are dealing with
God's power (2 Cor. 13:3–4; 10:3, 8; 12:9, 12; 13:10). Second, he
calls for them to test themselves (πειράζετε) and reinforces it with
the parallel insistence that they examine themselves (δοκιμάζετε;
13:5–9). We will return to this last point below.

We expect ἦθος enhancement correlative to the degree of frankness. 2 Cor. 10–13 does not disappoint. We may describe his ἦθος
augmentation around three foci: the first is Paul's foundational work
in bringing them the gospel, the second Paul's consistency from that
first day forward, and the third new information about Paul. First, God
had apportioned the Corinthians to Paul (2 Cor. 10:13). Paul was
the one who extended himself "all the way" to them (ὑπερεκτείνομεν;
2 Cor. 10:14). He formally presented the Corinthians as a (supposedly) pure bride to Christ (2 Cor. 11:2). He preached the gospel
without a fee (2 Cor. 11:7), did not burden anyone (2 Cor. 11:9), and
performed the signs of a true apostle while with them (2 Cor. 12:12).

Second, consistency and dependability are the hallmarks of true
friendship and a requirement of a strong ἦθος sufficient to support
frank speech. Paul makes a persistent and strong case for himself in
this regard. One statement captures this point: "And what I do, so
shall I [continue to] do" (2 Cor. 11:12). Like a genuine friend, he
never took advantage of them (2 Cor. 11:20, 12:14); neither did
Titus as Paul's representative (2 Cor. 12:17). If he warns them now
he has warned them before (2 Cor. 13:2). He has always spoken the
truth to them; indeed he can do nothing else (2 Cor. 12:6; 13:8).

---

[35] For a description of the varied approaches designed for different types of students, see Glad, *Paul and Philodemus*, 137–52.

He has always preached the same Jesus, the same Spirit, and the same gospel (2 Cor. 11:4). While given the authority to build up or tear down (an *inclusio*, 2 Cor. 10:8; 13:10), he has always worked for their edification, but the implicit threat of his divinely-given power to destroy is not subtly brandished. He pictures himself as having always worked for their well-being as a true friend should.[36] Indications of his love for them punctuate the fragment: "God knows" Paul loves them (2 Cor. 11:11); Paul calls them his "beloved" (2 Cor. 12:19); and he wonders how it can be that he loves them more while they love him less (2 Cor. 12:15). In this particular, Paul is completely aligned with Philodemus who says that "when he is . . . very vehemently indicating his own annoyance, he will not, as he speaks, forget 'dearest' and 'sweetest' and similar things . . ." (*De lib. dic.* frg. 14).

Third, a new detail, probably hitherto unknown also to the Corinthians, is added to his ἦθος in this letter fragment.[37] Though the Corinthians already know him to be a person given to visions and revelations (1 Cor. 2:10, 14:6; 2 Cor. 13:7), they now hear of his extraordinary heavenly ascent and vision (2 Cor. 12:2–10), told in the rhetorically modest third person. In paradise, he heard "unspeakable words" (2 Cor. 13:4), but has never (before) boasted of this or used it as a boost to his authority; the Corinthians probably hear about it now because Paul's opponents must have made similar (but probably not as spectacular!) claims. Paul has eschewed making claims on the basis of that ecstatic experience "so that no one may think better of me than what is seen in me or heard from me . . ." (2 Cor. 12:6 NRSV).

Though we have seen frank speech across Paul's correspondence, this is the first instance of simple or pure frank speech, that is, without any praise intermingled. Unlike the doctors who are so often depicted as comparable to frank speakers, Paul has left his patients with no balm (Plut. *Quomodo quis suos* 74D).

We must note another feature present in this letter fragment. Paul now entertains the notion that this ultimate form of frank speech

---

[36] This strong picture is elaborated even more by the many texts of Paul's σύγκρισις with the outsiders whom he sometimes dubs "superlative apostles".

[37] Paul employs the irony of the self-portraits in 11:1–12:20 to elaborate his ἦθος. See Glenn Holland, "Speaking Like a Fool: Irony in 2 Corinthians 10–13" in *Rhetoric and the New Testament: Essays from the 1992 Heidelberg Conference*, ed. Stanley E. Porter and Thomas H. Olbricht, JSNTS 90 (Sheffield: Sheffield Academic Press, 1993) 252–64.

may fail, surely always a possibility: he reports his prayer to God that the Corinthians may not do wrong, that they may do right, *"even though we may seem to have failed"* (13:7 NIV; italics added). Matters with the Corinthians have come to a worrisome head. Paul seems to expect that his next visit will be a showdown. The explicit call for self-examination and self-testing, implicit or relatively more hidden in all frank speech but unmistakable in this example of pure frankness, is designed to provide a basis for their next meeting.[38] But we may rightly wonder just what sort of basis it provided because Plutarch cautions against ending an interview—and one may suppose the same would apply to a letter—on a "painful and irritating ... final topic of conversation" (*Quomodo quis suos* 74E) as Paul seems to have done in 2 Cor. 13.[39]

Could Paul's earlier efforts at frank speech (in the painful letter and in 2 Cor. 1–7) have contributed to the breakdown in relations that we see in 2 Cor. 10–13? Quite likely, though clearly there are other factors that have been detailed in previous studies.[40] People who think themselves wise (and we know some Corinthians do; cf. 1 Cor. 1:18–2:10) are annoyed by frankness, Philodemus tells us (*De lib. dic.* col. XXIVa). Philodemus also recognized that "those who are illustrious both in resources and reputations abide [frank criticism] less well [than others]" (col. XXIIb). Likewise, those who feel "they are ... in [a position of] honor" may be "annoyed" by frank speech (col. XVIIb). So the peculiar socio-economic makeup of the Corinthian congregation,[41] and what we may suppose is an even wider Corinthian aspiration to be considered wise apart from socio-economic background, may have contributed to more resistance to Paul's frank speech among its Corinthian recipients.[42]

---

[38] Frankness helps keep perspective as to what is important and what is indifferent; see *Quomodo quis suos* 59F.

[39] Not only Paul, but also the later redactor who compiled 2 Corinthians from fragments.

[40] See Furnish, *II Corinthians* 44–54.

[41] Cf. 1 Cor. 1:26 and Gerd Theissen, *The Social Setting of Pauline Christianity: Essays on Corinth*, ed. and trans. J. H. Schütz, (Philadelphia: Fortress, 1982) 69–119.

[42] John Fitzgerald has called to my attention M. Gigante's argument that παρρησία is for Philodemus a τέκνη στοχαστική, a "stochastic" or "conjectural" art (*Ricerche Filodemee*, 2nd ed. [Naples: Macchiaroli, 1982], 62–67). In doing this, Gigante is drawing on a distinction that Philodemus sometimes makes between "exact art" (with fixed principles) and "conjectural art" that is based on observation of what usually happens. Paul's uses of παρρησία demonstrate that the results of παρρησία necessarily vary from one situation to another, depending not only on the skill of the speaker to adapt his frankness to the person or group but also on the nature or character of the person or group.

We are now in a position to assess how Paul's repeated use of frank speech with the Corinthians may have affected Paul's relationship to them in the passages that we have analyzed here. Four factors about Paul's use of frank speech with the Corinthians probably contributed to the deterioration of his relationship with them. First, Plutarch recognizes that persistent use of frank speech, if not smoothed over, builds further and enduring problems in a relationship, and perhaps Paul has now become recipient of some negative fallout along these lines: "But the man who has been hard hit and scored by frankness, if he be left rough and tumid and uneven, will, owing to the effect of anger, not readily respond to an appeal the next time . . ." (*Quomodo quis suos* 74E). Paul may simply have gone to the well too often.

Second, and related, are the twinned facts that frank speech depends on sound ἦθος and that Paul's ἦθος had suffered some serious blows during the time covered by the examples of his frank speech to the Corinthians examined in this essay. I will note just a couple of the most devastating: Paul's projected but unrealized visit and the resulting charge of vacillation and lack of dependability (2 Cor. 1:15–2:1) and Paul's shame-producing refusal to accept the patronage of some at Corinth (2 Cor. 11:7–10).[43]

Third, Paul may well have received an unrealistic evaluation of the Corinthian response from Titus. Frank speech always risks building residual anger (Phild. *De lib. dic.* frg. 70). Even though Paul rejoices over the Corinthians' self-correction in response to his painful letter, it is reasonable to wonder whether there was not residual irritation, if not anger, among some of the Corinthians. Many factors may have contributed to Paul glossing over what he took as an end to Corinthian disaffection. Titus may have had an overly optimistic assessment of the Corinthian turn-around, or at least he may have communicated such to Paul. In his own eagerness to regain common ground with the Corinthians, Paul may have single-handedly inflated what could have been an accurate assessment of a lesser reconciliation from Titus, painting a rhetorically idealized picture in the hope that the Corinthians would make the positive portrait their own reality.

In any case, those persons who were still tender over the frank speech of the previous letter probably experienced increased resentment over

---

[43] Marshall, *Enmity*.

Paul's immediate, follow-up frank speech in 2 Cor. 6:11–13 and 7:2–4 (Phild. *De lib. dic.* frg. 71). By his repeated resorts to frank speech with the Corinthians, Paul may have contributed to a reservoir of resentment that not only provided fuel for opponents to use against him but which also makes it seem that Paul had used up too much of what Plutarch calls one's "supply of frankness" (*Quomodo quis suos* 73B). 2 Cor. 10–13, by its resort to pure frank speech, shows us Paul at a near impasse with the Corinthians. Too much resentment and an over-tapping of Paul's supply of frankness probably diminished the persuasive leverage Paul needed to accomplish what he would consider a righting of the Corinthian situation. If that was the case, Paul's earlier successes with frank speech sowed the seed of rancor toward any further frank speech.[44]

Fourth, and critically, in 2 Cor. 7:2–4, the second Corinthian example of frank speech examined in this essay, Paul used frank speech inappropriately to call for increased affection, which is of course an emotion and not the appeal to reason for which frank speech is suited. Frank speech employs "the thinking and reasoning powers," not the emotions (*Quomodo quis suos* 61E), and moves the hearer to a reevaluation of past or contemplated actions or behavior.[45]

We must be careful to distinguish an emotional response to frank speech, that is, the emotions that frank speech may indirectly elicit, such as anger or godly grief (2 Cor. 7:11; indignation, alarm, long-

---

[44] Though we cannot know the outcome of the show-down visit Paul projects in 2 Cor. 10–13, we can cite several indicators that suggest he likely had success in reclaiming the Corinthians in that encounter: (1) the letter fragment 2 Cor. 10–13 was preserved; (2) the Achaians (and therefore quite possibly the Corinthians) took part in the collection for the saints in Jerusalem (Rom. 15:26); (3) he wrote Romans, a subsequent letter, from Corinth where Gaius, one of Paul's first converts there (see 1 Cor. 1:14), is host to Paul "and to the whole church" (Rom. 16:23); (4) he sends the Romans greetings from Erastus, Corinth's treasurer (Rom. 16:23); and (5) Clement, the early second century bishop of Rome, identifies the Corinthian church with Paul (1 Clem. 47:3).

[45] Flattery plays to emotion, frank speech to "the thinking and reasoning powers" (*Quomodo quis suos* 61E). Frank speech calls for moral reasoning; it asks the recipient to engage in reflection, in deliberation, in the weighing of whether to continue in the present direction or to change. Frank speech provides the context for self-evaluation and suggests self-correction. Παρρησία does not force change. It does call for change, but the recipient must weigh the matter and decide what response is appropriate. When emotions such as anger assert themselves, deliberation is shunted aside or aborted. Although frank speech can prompt an emotional response, such as anger or grief, it does not, at its best, appeal for an emotional response (such as the affection Paul desires), but rather for the employment of reason in moral deliberation.

ing, zeal), from the response for which one directly appeals in one's frank speech. The emotions are always involved; Paul, Philodemus and Plutarch all recognized that. The goal of frank speech, however, is not the emotional response that may well be provoked but the change of comportment, of direction. Emotion, or affection as in Paul's case with the Corinthians, is not the proper object or goal of frankness; it may well accompany the desired result, but is not to be confused with the desired result itself. Similarly, frankness does not appeal for the show of emotion but for some deliberation and a resulting change of course or alteration of behavior, comportment, or, as in Paul's case again, allegiance.

Apart from all the other problems that contributed to the decline in Paul's relations with the Corinthians, and surely not intending to diminish their importance, we must now assert that two additional factors, namely Paul's repeated resort to frank speech with the Corinthians and his use of frank speech to enjoin greater affection, aggravated other problems Paul had with the Corinthians and led to the breakdown of relations that we see so clearly represented in 2 Cor. 10–13.

Conclusions

Paul knows and employs παρρησία, frank speech, within the conventions of his time, as a powerful tool of social transaction. Further, just as one would suspect from Philodemus and Plutarch, Paul varies the strength of the frank speech according to his appraisal of the circumstances he addresses.

If we consider these Pauline instances of frank speech with regard to 1) how much praise they intermingle with the call for an emendation of conduct or of contemplated action and 2) how harsh and fundamental is the "sting" they carry, we can make relative distinctions among the instances. Clearly the harshest frankness is found in the letter fragment 2 Cor. 10–13 where not a note of praise is heard. 2 Cor. 10–13 is unmitigated frank criticism. The gentlest sting of frank speech in this study is found in the letter fragment 2 Cor. 1–7. There Paul, happy that the frank speech of the previous letter has brought the Corinthians around in their relation to him, but unsatisfied because their response is not as full or whole-hearted as it could be, uses frank speech to ask for an increase of Corinthian affection for himself.[46] In between those two instances is the frank speech of Galatians, where the strong frank speech is mixed with some praise.

Without a clear understanding of frank speech, one might have reckoned the harshness of Galatians as equal to that of 2 Cor. 10–13, but now we see that the two, though related, are quite distinguishably different. Though 2 Cor. 10–13 sits very directly in the blame column and lacks praise, Galatians praises the recipients even while it has a very fundamental problem with what they, or more accurately some of them,[47] are tempted to do. Further, in 2 Cor. 10–13 we found a hint of fear that his frank speech efforts to correct the Corinthians might end in failure—Paul finds them about as incorrigible as Philodemus does his recalcitrant students—but in Galatians we find no such hint. In fact in Galatians Paul writes with such authority and power that he must assume that his leverage is adequate to bring them around.[48] So, to use the categories we derived from Philodemus and Plutarch, 2 Cor. 10–13 is simple, pure, harsh frank speech, what we can properly term frank criticism, while Galatians is an example of mixed frank speech.

The painful letter is much more difficult to rank with precision relative to the others because we do not have direct access to it. We do know that it contained rebuke because Paul celebrates the fact that his calling them to task had been effective, but we have no way of telling whether it was of a mixed or simple form of frank speech, since we do not know whether the letter also contained praise. By inference back from 2 Cor. 10–13, where things seem to be viewed by Paul as worse than ever, we could suppose that there might have

---

[46] Plutarch notes that a good time for "admonition [νουθεσίας] arises when people, having been reviled by others for their errors, have become submissive and downcast" (*Quomodo quis suso* 70D)—though in the Corinthian instance it has been Paul who has used the earlier frank speech.

[47] The *correctio* raises yet another possible distinction between 2 Cor. 10–13 and Galatians. May we not suppose that an ingredient in the harshness gradient between these two letters is that a higher percentage of the Corinthians than of the Galatians are tempted to stray from Paul and his understanding of the gospel?

[48] Though we could seek to advance this argument on several fronts, let this one suffice: in the middle parts of the letter νόμος is so problematic that Paul even insulates God from the direct giving of it by mentioning angels in the chain of mediation (Gal. 3:19), but later in the letter he dares to use νόμος in a positive way (Gal. 6:2), as if he supposes that his letter, by this late point, will have brought the wayward Galatians securely enough back into camp that he can employ the term in a way that serves his own sense of the gospel.

been some praise in the "painful letter" so that it would have to be considered mixed frank speech, but we cannot be certain.

Recognition of frank speech's indissoluble connection with the ἦθος of the speaker should occasion further reconsideration of previous scholarly treatment of Paul's self-references that occur alongside frank speech.[49] The idea of ἦθος as a limited, exhaustible currency (*Quomodo quis suso* 73B) should illuminate how better to read Paul's efforts to enhance his standing with his readers when he feels obligated to speak with frankness to them. The simpler and harsher the frank speech, the more likely it is that attention will be given to nurturing the speaker's ἦθος.

This study of frank speech as employed by Paul sheds additional light on Paul's understanding of community and on his sense that individuals within the community of faith have responsibilities toward one another.[50] Friendship is fundamental to community among believers despite the properly noted paucity of friendship terminology *per se*.[51] The study of Paul's appropriation of friendship terms and topoi is further complicated by the way, as we have seen in this study, Paul does not keep a clear distinction between categories of friendship and familial concepts. Friendship assumptions fade into family categories quite readily for Paul.

The commonplace assumptions of Paul's time that friends care for one another and sometimes show that concern for one another by frank speech are transposed into Paul's deliberations about the proper functioning of community: he thinks believers are responsible for one another as brothers and sisters for whom Christ died.[52] It is a theme found across Paul's letters: "If one member suffers, all suffer together with it; if one member is honored, all rejoice together with it" (1 Cor. 12:26 NRSV; cf. Rom. 12:15). And he practices what he preaches: "Who is led astray and I am not indignant?" (2 Cor. 11:29). Regarding the man who is sleeping with his father's wife, Paul's distress is not directed toward the man himself but toward the community, whose members, we may suppose, failed in their responsibilities to express

---

[49] I intend this suggestion to support, but now in the specific context of frank speech, the general reassessment that Lyon's *Pauline Autobiography* invites.

[50] The best study on this topic to date is Glad's *Paul and Philodemus*; see esp. 185–332.

[51] E. A. Judge, "Paul as a Radical Critic of Society," *Interchange* 16 (1974) 191–203.

[52] Glad, *Paul and Philodemus* 190–235.

the sort of proper care that friends, and so even more brothers and sisters in Christ, owe one another (1 Cor. 5:2a–b). One can suppose that if some one or more of the Corinthian believers had used earlier, more gentle frank speech with the man who was sleeping with his stepmother, the matter never would have gotten to the point where he needed to be removed from the fellowship.[53]

In regard to the same issue, this study suggests that Rom. 15:14, one of Paul's expressions of great confidence in the recipients of the letter in Rome, represents Paul's understanding of the obligation all believers have toward one another when it goes on to stress their capability to ἀλλήλους νουθετεῖν, to "admonish, warn, instruct" one another.[54] The problem of interpreting that verb (the NIV, RSV, NRSV all choose "instruct," while in Philodemus and Plutarch the term most frequently shades over into "admonish" or "warn") is one of understanding the extent of the believers' obligations to one another and responsibility for one another. "Instruct" is surely right to express one part of believers' responsibilities to each other, but so is "warn" and in some cases "admonish." The gentlest of frank speech's stings could almost be counted as instruction; harsher stings, though still using νουθετεῖν, can denote warning or admonishment and can even border on censure. Paul seems to expect a range of responses between and among believers, a range that he himself expresses in his epistolary responses to his readers: his own reactions extend from praise, commendation and encouragement on the one extreme—indirect speech, appeal, chiding, reproach fill in the middle ground—to removing an offender from the fellowship on the other.[55] Believers are expected to experience that same range of relationships between and among themselves. Frank speech encompasses part of that spectrum, beginning with some cases of appeal, all chiding, moving to reproach and, in extreme cases, to exclusion from fellowship.

Frank speech functions as part of the larger Pauline concern for keeping perspective, for self-testing, self-examination, and for distinguishing what is important from what does not matter. Frank speech, by its engagement with another believer or group of them, stimu-

---

[53] Removing someone from fellowship is surely frank speech carried to the extreme.
[54] BAG[2] 544.
[55] Plutarch has a similar scale which ranges as follows: commend (ἐπαινοῦντος), extol (κατευλογοῦντος), take to task (ἐλέγχοντος), be frank (παρρησιαζομένου), and blame (ψέγοντος; *Qumodo quis suos* 66A).

lates self-reflection. It appeals to reason. We do not intend by this observation to suggest any alienation between the heart or spirit and the mind in Paul's anthropology; in fact, as 1 Cor. 14:13–19 shows so powerfully, Paul models and expects an integrated and holistic spiritual life for himself and his followers. But integral to that holistic life and often underestimated in studies about Paul is the obligation of individuals to test where they are and how they stand with regard to God's unfolding story.[56] So frank speech is a helpful tool in the moral reasoning of believers and, when properly used, serves to enhance the health of the entire body of believers.

Finally, this study has also given occasion to see the risks and the potential for a downside to frank speech as Paul has employed it. The greatest and most obvious risk is the termination of the friendship, as Paul recognizes in writing the Galatians, as to speak frankly may generate enmity (Gal 4:16). Short of that, however, frank speech can lead to misunderstanding, to questions about the genuineness of the friendship, to perplexity about the motives of the one who speaks frankly, to residual anger that festers and draws to it other distresses and other persons who have their own difficulties with the frank speaker. As we have observed, Paul repeatedly used frank criticism with the Corinthians to achieve an end for which its use was ill-suited, namely to enhance affection, and in so doing contributed substantially to the breakdown of his relationship with them.

---

[56] See my *Walking Between the Times* 63–69, for a discussion of self-examination and self-testing as a part of the believers' spiritual discipline. The Lord's Supper is the foundational place of such self-examination (1 Cor. 11:28–32), but Paul's calls for self-assessment appear across the corpus (Gal. 6:4; 2 Cor. 13:5–10; cf. 1 Cor. 9:24–27).

PHILODEMUS AND PAUL ON
RHETORICAL DELIVERY (ὑπόκρισις)

BRUCE W. WINTER

Abstract

From their particular ideological perspectives Philodemus and Paul provide critiques of a contemporary preoccupation of orators with "rhetorical delivery" (ὑπόκρισις) that had consumed the public orators and audiences of their day. Philodemus had witnessed its "formal" introduction into the syllabus on rhetoric only to see it become its most important element. Paul, standing as he did in the early days of the Second Sophistic, saw the penchant for it in public declamations obscuring content for performance and hence denounced its use for Christian proclamation and teaching as 1 and 2 Corinthians demonstrates. His rhetorically able opponents denigrated him for his lack of this essential component in his public presentations. For both Epicureanism and Christianity rhetorical delivery would not effect the personal transformation which they sought in the life of their hearers although there was the predisposition of some for it.

Introduction

Philodemus' extensive work, *On Rhetoric*, is a much neglected but important treatise for New Testament scholars.[1] In it, he provides significant

---

[1] Part of the difficulty hindering its widespread use has been the lack of a satisfactory English text and translation. Harry M. Hubbell, "The Rhetorica of Philodemus," *Transactions of the Connecticut Academy of Arts and Sciences* 23 (1920): 243–382 tends in places to engage in substantial paraphrasing and at times leaves out major sections of the text rather than translating them. This is certainly the case in the section on delivery. For an Italian translation which to date covers Books 1–2 see Francesca Longo Auricchio, Φιλοδήμου Περὶ ῥητορικῆς, *Ricerche sui papiri ercolanesi* (Naples: Giannini, 1977), vol. 3. For details of more recent work on the text of *On Rhetoric* see Dirk Obbink, "Philodemus on Poetics, Music and Rhetoric: A Classified Bibliography," *Philodemus and Poetry: Poetic Theory and Practice in Lucretius, Philodemus and Horace*, ed. Dirk Obbink (Oxford: Oxford University Press, 1995), 276–78. The neglect of Philodemus' work on rhetoric is epitomized by the fact that a little over a page was devoted to Philodemus by George A. Kennedy in *The Art of Persuasion in Greece* (London: Routledge & Kegan Paul, 1963), 300–301. R. Dean Anderson Jr.

information and an extended critique of a contemporary development
in rhetoric that flourished also in Paul's day. In an era of New Testament scholarship where the discussion of rhetoric has far outstripped
the more measured approach of the end of the nineteenth century,[2]
Philodemus' work provides important correctives to some of the
uncritical discussion of the use of rhetoric in the New Testament
corpus—simply citing ancient handbooks for that purpose is insufficient.[3]
Paul, like Philodemus, not only used rhetoric, but also provided a
critique of a contemporary trend that each saw as deleterious to
Christianity and Epicureanism respectively. As this study will show,
the preoccupation with "rhetorical delivery" (ὑπόκρισις) in the eras
of both men had, in some circles, overwhelmed the significant aspects
of rhetoric. Philodemus' comments help us to understand the reason for Paul's reaction to his Corinthian opponents' counterattack
when they ridiculed him because of his deficiencies in rhetorical
delivery. Christian teachers who opposed Paul highlighted his deficiencies, apparently in retaliation for his stinging critique of this rhetorical convention, and they did so with the most damning criticism
that could be made of any public speaker.

Evidence from Philodemus also provides a cautionary note for
ancient historians interested in the Second Sophistic. His corpus
shows that Philostratus' statement in the third century, that this movement suddenly began with Nicetes who declaimed in the Principate
of Nero, cannot be taken at face value.[4] The sophistic movement
was well on the march in the time of Philo of Alexandria at the
beginning of the first century C.E.[5] He observed that the sophists
were "winning the admiration of city after city, and . . . drawing well-
nigh the whole world to honor them" (Agr. 143). Characteristics that
epitomized the Second Sophistic were present not only in Philo's day,
but were also thriving in the time of Philodemus. A compelling ques-

---

in *Ancient Rhetorical Theory and Paul*, Contributions to Biblical Exegesis and Theology
18, rev. ed. (Leuven: Peeters, 1998), 50–52 is also somewhat dismissive of the importance of Philodemus' work.

   [2] See for example Johannes Weiss, "Beiträge zur Paulinischen Rhetorik" in
Theologischen Studien B. Weiss (Göttingen: Vandenhoeck & Ruprecht, 1897), 165–247.

   [3] For an important critique of the direct application of rhetorical theory to the
Pauline letters see most recently Anderson, *Ancient Rhetorical Theory and Paul.*

   [4] Philostratus, *Lives of the Sophists* 511.

   [5] For a detailed discussion of Philo see my *Philo and Paul among the Sophists:
Alexandrian and Corinthian Responses to a Julio-Claudian Movement*, 2nd ed. (Grand Rapids,
MI: Eerdmans, 2002), ch. 3–5.

tion for those writing on this important phenomenon in the early empire is, "What was the difference between the activities of the sophists discussed by Philodemus and those who occupied the center stage in the unfolding of the Second Sophistic in the first century?" The "origins" of this great movement are not as clear as Philostratus would have us believe when he speculates on them in his third century c.e. work, *The Lives of the Sophists*.

Because delivery had long been given pride of place by the sophists and their audiences, we can also understand why the inhabitants of Roman Corinth, including Christians, would have been so enamoured of rhetorical delivery. Early Christianity arose at the time when the Second Sophistic was flowering,[6] if not in full bloom.[7] Philodemus' work on rhetoric can be put to good use, because in the next two centuries after his death in 44 b.c.e., some of the issues he addresses were still alive in the ongoing conflict between the philosophers and the sophists,[8] and, as this study will show, between early Christian teachers who were either in favor of or opposed to the use of rhetorical delivery.

This study is intended (1) to focus on one important aspect of rhetoric which is discussed in Philodemus' portion of Book IV *On Rhetoric*, namely the preoccupation in his day with delivery and its deleterious effects on the audience; (2) to discuss the implications of the denigration of Paul's performance in this area by his opponents in Corinth; and (3) to examine the reasons for Paul's renunciation of this rhetorical device because of the major hindrance it put in the way of Christian proclamation and ministry.

---

[6] *Contra* Stephen M. Pogoloff, *Logos and Sophia: The Rhetorical Situation of 1 Corinthians*, SBLDS 134 (Atlanta: Scholars, 1992), 65, who wrongly works on the assumption that "the Second Sophistic postdates Paul's Corinth by a century."

[7] Glen Warren Bowersock, *Greek Sophists in the Roman Empire* (Oxford: Clarendon, 1969) 9, rightly sees the origins going back into the first century b.c.e. I have suggested in *Philo and Paul among the Sophists* 23–4, 43–4, 243 that there were certain social and pecuniary factors in the first century c.e. that may have stimulated the growth of what was an existing movement. There was (1) conflict between Julio-Claudian and Flavian emperors and philosphers which resulted in their replacement by the virtuoso orators in public life and education, (2) the financial incentive provided by the lifting of the embargo on charging fees for professional services by forensic orators, and (3) Vespasian's exemption of teachers from taxes and the performances of liturgies.

[8] The problems had not abated two hundred years later; see Pamela Gordon, "A Philosopher among the Sophists," *Epicurus in Lycia: The Second Century World of Diogenes of Oenoanda* (Ann Arbor: University of Michigan Press, 1996), ch. 1, esp. 36–42.

Philodemus on Rhetorical Delivery

In the second section of Book IV of *On Rhetoric*, Philodemus devotes
a relatively short but extremely important section to "delivery." He
was not the first to have done so. Aristotle commented on this subject
when he discussed style and opined that delivery "is of the greatest
importance but has not yet been treated by any one." The reason
he gave for this comment was that discussion of delivery had only
recently appeared in relation to tragedy and rhapsody because, up
to this point, poets had acted their own tragedies. "It is clear, therefore, that there is something of the sort in rhetoric as well as in poetry."
Aristotle restricted delivery to the voice and mentions three aspects,
namely volume, harmony and rhythm. Those who made proper use
of these carried off the prizes in dramatic contests or, as actors, dominated performances. Aristotle added, "It is the same in political contests [i.e., the law courts and the public assembly] owing to the
corruptness of our forms of government." He reiterated that there
was no treatise on the subject and made the telling comments that
"rightly considered it is thought vulgar. But since the whole business
of rhetoric is to influence opinion, we must pay attention to it, not as
being right but necessary . . . nevertheless as we have just said, it is of
great importance owing to the corruption of the hearer . . . Now, when
delivery comes into fashion, it will have the same effect as acting."[9]

Although in a work entitled *Pathos* Thrasymachus "attempted to
say a few words" on the subject, it was Aristotle's associate and successor, Theophrastus, who was apparently the first to discuss the
theory of oratorical delivery. He considered not only the use of the
voice and its modulation but also added comments on facial expressions and gestures.[10]

Philodemus, in his discussion of rhetorical delivery, rehearses a
short history of the attitudes taken by ancient orators which reveals
the great importance they attached to it. He first lists Isocrates who
actually refrained from public appearances because he recognized
that he was deficient in rhetorical delivery. Hieronymus is reported
by him to have said of his orations that are "easy to read, but hard

---

[9] Aristotle, *"Art" of Rhetoric* 1403b–1404a.
[10] Aristotle, *"Art" of Rhetoric* 1404a. See Friedrich Solmsen, "The Aristotelian
Tradition in Ancient Rhetoric," *Rhetorika: Schriften zur aristotelischen und hellenistischen
Rhetorik*, ed. P. Steinmetz (Hildesheim: G. Olms, 1968), 322–3.

to deliver in public; there is no fire in them; everything is monoto-
nously smooth. He sounds like a boy speaking through a heroic mask"
(*Rhet.* 4 col. XVII.23). Isocrates' long sentences mitigated against ease
of delivery (*Rhet.* 4 col. XVI.9–13). Isocrates himself was to complain
that his discourses were read aloud by others "in the worst possible
manner," yet he admits how much more persuasive the discourse is
when it is spoken, for when read it is "robbed of the prestige of the
speaker, the tones of his voice, the variations which are made in the
delivery."[11] On his own admission, delivery was a crucial ingredient
in any oral presentation of his work. Isocrates was himself caught
up in his day in a vigorous debate between writing and extemporary orators, in which he was a noted representative of the former.[12]
While he objected to the premise of his opponents that they could
make the least gifted person into a public orator, his own deficiencies
in delivery would have forced him in any case to side with those
who argued in favor of the overall importance of written orations.

Demosthenes placed great store on delivery, according to Philodemus.
"Yea by Zeus, but (Νὴ Δί ἀλλὰ) Demosthenes used to say delivery
was the first thing in oratory, and the second, and the third" (*Rhet.*
4 col. XV.3–6). In this he agreed with Athenaeus who said that of
the parts of rhetoric "the most important is delivery" (*Rhet.* 4 col.
XI.12–16). Philodemus is highly critical of Demosthenes even though
he was seen as a first-rate orator[13]—"Notwithstanding [this reputa-
tion] he foolishly said that this element [delivery] which is of assistance to every work and presentation of treatises is of more importance
in rhetoric than in other prose writings" (XV.13–19).[14] That even

[11] Isocrates, *Panathenaicus* 17, *Philip* 25–6.
[12] On Alcidamas who opposed Isocrates see Ludwig Radermacher, "Alcidamas,"
Artium scriptores: Reste der voraristotelischen Rhetorik (Vienna: Rudolfe M. Rohrer, 1951),
no. 15, E.T. by La Rue van Hook, "Alcidamas versus Isocrates: The Spoken versus the Written Word," *CW* 12 (1918): 91–4. Isocrates' response is found in *Against
the Sophists* (391 B.C.E.) 9–10, 13 which was written as he commenced a career as
a teacher of rhetoric, having spent 403–392 B.C.E. as a speech writer (λογογράφος)
for Athenian law courts. See also his later work, *The Antidosis*, which shows how
firmly entrenched the view was that extemporary oratory was superior.
[13] Hubbell appears to have missed the point, apart from omitting lines 7–13 from
his paraphrase, that ἔλεγεν in line 14 refers back to line 4 where the subject of
that verb is Demosthenes, and the former sentence is resumptive Ὅμως μέντοι.
Hubbell later rightly picks up that the criticisms of Aeschines were directed against
Demosthenes even through the latter is not mentioned by name in lines 20–24.
[14] ὅτι τὸ πᾶσιν συνεργοῦν καὶ μεθοδερόμενον ἐν τοῖς ἰδίος ὑφ᾿ ἑκάστων πολὺ μεῖζον
ἐν τῇ ῥητορικῇ δρᾷ, μᾶλλον ἤ ταῖς ἄλλαις πεζολογίαις.

Demosthenes had surprisingly succumbed to the folly of those who believe that delivery was everything in oratory, surprised Philodemus.

Though Demosthenes was regarded as a great orator, he was criticized by his bitter opponent, Aeschines, because of the timbre of his voice which Aeschines said was shrill as well as loud. Demetrius of Phalerum also criticized him because he was too "artful and over-subtle in his delivery, not straightforward and did not use a good style" (*Rhet.* 4 col. XVI.9–13).[15] It is clear that the most devastating criticism one could make of any public orator was that he was deficient in rhetorical delivery.

Philodemus concluded, "Moreover most of the [ancient] sophists, judged by their writings, delivered in a wretched fashion" (ἀθλίω ὑποκεκρίσθαι). The reason given for this was that "their long sentences were bad for delivery, just as it was proposed by Demetrius concerning those of Isocrates" (*Rhet.* 4 col. XVI.9–13).[16] How should we take his comment, "Sophists of the present day have somewhat improved in delivery," when he subsequently noted that "The formal instruction in delivery is a product of recent foolishness" (*Rhet.* 4 col. XVIII.18)? This suggests that only recently had delivery come into its own as a recognized subject in the curriculum for the teaching of rhetoric, and that the formal teaching of techniques in rhetorical delivery was seen as a mistaken move. Philodemus is certainly seeking to diminish the stature of ancient and contemporary orators by drawing attention to their deficiencies in the very thing which had come to epitomize much of their activity and in which they clearly took so much pride, namely the professionalism of their delivery. At the same time Philodemus criticizes recent developments which they considered an improvement but which he brands as "foolish."

Does Philodemus, himself a philosopher, believe that there is a delivery appropriate to his profession? He commences his discussion of the topic by agreeing that delivery is important, for by it a person "exhibits a statesmanlike presence," "catches an audience's attention," and more than that, "makes the audience take notice of and

---

[15] Hubbell's paraphrase reads "too theatrical and not simple and noble in his delivery."

[16] Hubbell surprisingly translates "Their long periods are hard to pronounce, *teste Demetrio,*" and leaves out any reference to Isocrates in *Rhet.* 4 col. XVI.5–22. The relevant text reads πονηρὸν γὰρ εἰς ὑπόκρισιν αἱ μακραὶ περίοδοι, καθάπερ καὶ παρὰ Δημητρίῳ κεῖται περὶ τῶν Ἰσοκράτους.

recollect" what has been said, "even sways [the audience] emotion-
ally," and more than that "actually achieves these things" (*Rhet.* 4
col. XI.16–25).[17] "But if it is fitting for rhetoric to teach this [deliv-
ery] rather than dialectic or grammar, one would desire to learn it"
(*Rhet.* 4 col. XI.25–XII.4), he comments ironically.[18] Later he states
emphatically that there is no place for the teaching of delivery (*Rhet.*
4 col. XVII.18), for dialectic and grammar are sufficient. His reason for saying this is that dialectic aimed at teaching a person how
to argue and grammar enabled one to read (*Rhet.* 4 col. XII.5–8).
This is what was needed.

Reference is made at the very beginning of his discussion to a form
of delivery that Philodemus believed would be appropriate to the
sphere of philosophy. It is spelled out in terms of the apposite effects
which "philosophical delivery" would have upon an audience (*Rhet.*
4 col. XI.16–25). Later, he elaborates further when he states, "There
is a need of natural good proportions similar to the melody and
loftiness and tone and spirit of the voice, and the dignity and proportion and boldness of the face and the hands and the rest of the
body" (*Rhet.* 4 col. XIV.19–25).[19] Here we deduce that he not only
restricted "philosophical" delivery simply to the way in which the
voice is used. He also contended that it concerned the whole bearing, or presence, of the person who stood before the audience, as
well as the effects his delivery technique had upon them. One is
struck by the fact that, in certain aspects, Philodemus' response to
rhetorical delivery coalesces with that of Isocrates.[20]

If the assistance of rhetoricians has not been sought by actors for
whom delivery is a crucial element in their profession, then as a
philosopher, Philodemus believes that his discipline should be allowed
to lay down a "delivery appropriate to our own sphere." He is highly
critical of the rhetoricians for daring to suggest that they alone have

---

[17] Lines 23–24 have been reconstructed as ἄλλων [οὐχ ὁμ]οίως ταῦτα δρώντων,
but the negative rendering of the sentence makes little sense.

[18] The text is rendered thus, rather than Hubbell's translation, "But if it is more
the task of rhetoric to teach this than it is the task of dialectic or grammar one
would desire to learn it." See n. 21 concerning irony in Philodemus.

[19] καὶ φυσικῆς εὐκληρίας δεῖται, καθάπερ εὐμέλεια φωνῆς καὶ μελέθη καὶ τόνοι καὶ
πνεῦμα, καὶ προσώπου καὶ χειρῶν καὶ λοιποῦ σώματος ἀξίωμά τε καὶ ῥυθμοί, καὶ τόλμα.

[20] See Isocrates, *Antidosis*, 197–98 on natural ability over against the sophist's education which was guaranteed to be able to improve any person's ability to speak well.

formulated an art of delivery, for "poets and prose writers have a
theory of delivery even though they have never committed it to writing" (*Rhet.* 4 col. XIII.21–XIV.7). In a comment full of irony he
states emphatically, "Yes, by Zeus, if they [the sophists] claim that
delivery in drama comes under the aegis of rhetoric, then we con-
gratulate them for [their] intelligence" (*Rhet.* 4 col. XII.8–14).[21] As
a result of the sophists' teaching on delivery, Philodemus accuses
them of changing the use of voice and the body not for the better
but for the worse (*Rhet.* 4 col. XIV.8–12). He points to the "natural"
use of delivery by laymen as well as barbarians (*Rhet.* 4 col. XIV.13–17).

Philodemus reveals that "what the writers on the art of rhetoric
(οἱ τεχνογράφοι)[22] have done is to make plain what had been kept
secret by the politicians by the subordination of truth (τὸ κατ᾽ ἀλήθειαν
μὲν ὑπάρχον), which presented them as statesmen and public benefactors (σεμνοὶ καὶ καλοὶ κἀγαθοί),[23] and worse, to mislead the audience"
(*Rhet.* 4 col. XIX.3–10). The latter comment is, in my opinion, at the
heart of his concerns, namely the deleterious effects their delivery had
on the audience, whether it be the jury in the law court or citizens
in the public assembly. Contrast this with the criterion by which he
has already judged "appropriate" delivery, i.e., the beneficial effects
it has upon the audience who absorb what they were meant to learn.

The effect upon the hearers is clearly one, if not his major objection, to his naming "political" rhetoric, which included courtroom
speeches and those delivered in the assembly, as an art (τέχνη).[24]
This conclusion has puzzled scholars. The issue has been approached
by citing Philodemus' definition of what constitutes a τέχνη:

---

[21] David Sedley, "Philosophical Allegiance in the Greco-Roman World," *Philosophia
Togata: Essays on Philosophy and Roman Society*, ed. Miriam Griffin and Jonathan Barnes
(Oxford: Clarendon, 1989), 115, comments that the use of irony in Philodemus has
not been acknowledged in discussions of his work.

[22] The translation of the term as "the technocrats" while a literal rendering is
not apposite in this context, for it was used of the writers on the art of rhetoric;
cf. Aristotle, *"Art" of Rhetoric* 1354a.

[23] On the use of καλὸς καὶ ἀγαθός or καλὸς κἀγαθός for a civic benefactor who
operated in the public place see e.g. *OGIS* 215, *SIG* 307 and Arnold Wycombe
Gomme, "The Interpretation of ΚΑΛΟΙ ΚΑΓΑΘΟΙ in Thucydides 4.40.2," *CQ* (1953):
653 and G. E. M. De Ste. Croix, "Additional Notes on ΚΑΛΟΣ ΚΑΓΑΘΟΣ," *Origins
of the Peloponnesian War* (London: Duckworth, 1972), Appendix xxix.

[24] See Dirk Obbink's translator's note on sophistic and political rhetoric in Marcello
Gigante, *Philodemus in Italy: The Books of Herculaneum* The Body, In Theory: Histories
of Cultural Materialism (Ann Arbor: University of Michigan Press, 1995), 31–2.

a faculty or disposition arising from observation of certain common
and fundamental things which extend through most particular instances,
a faculty which grasps and produces an effect such as only a few who
have not learned the art can accomplish, and doing this firmly and
surely, rather than conjecturally.[25]

David Blank has commented, "On the basis of this definition, Philodemus comes to the remarkable conclusion that sophistic rhetoric
('speech or writing concerned purely with description or praise,
and ... encomiastic or epideictic rhetoric') of all things, is a *techne*,
while rhetoric proper (i.e., forensic) and political rhetoric are not."[26]
Blank proceeds next with an examination of "exact" arts such as
"grammatistic," music, painting, and sculpture and then states, "It
is clear, however, that the orator's ability to achieve the goal of persuasion with some regularity by applying rules is what makes sophistic rhetoric an art for Philodemus ... it is a transmissible method of
using this language to write clear treatises."[27] However, Blank has
ignored Philodemus' comments on delivery; I am suggesting here
that they make "the remarkable conclusion" less so, if still not explicable. The widespread use of rhetorical delivery and its unhelpful
effect upon the audience in the crucial arena of governing the city
may have provided one, if not the major reason, for the exclusion
of "political" rhetoric from Philodemus' definition of an "art."

The reason for suggesting this is that we have here once again
the age-old clash between the philosophers and the sophists. Whether
it was over the issue of charging fees or the use of sophisticated
forms of rhetorical showmanship such as was taught under the heading of delivery, the former were forced to mount a long defense,
while the latter continued to win the day in the field of education
(παιδεία) and public life (πολιτεία). As Dio Chrysostom was to remind
an audience, philosophers in his day had quit the field in their advice

---

[25] *Rhet.* 2 col. XXXVIII = p. 123 Longo..

[26] For a full discussion of the significance of Philodemus' view of the term "art"
as applied to rhetoric see David Blank, "Philodemus on the Technicity of Rhetoric,"
Philodemus and Poetry: Poetic Theory and Practice in Lucretius, Philodemus, and Horace, ed.
Dirk Obbink (Oxford: Oxford University Press, 1995), 179. See also Obbink in the
translator's note in Gigante, *Philodemus in Italy* 32, for the suggestion that Philodemus
excluded political rhetoric as an "art" because "it cannot be systematically mastered or taught (it is a 'knack' or matter of personal skill), because it does not
achieve results with reliable regularity. Therefore it does not qualify for treatment
by the philosopher and sage."

[27] Blank, "Philodemus on the Technicity of Rhetoric," 186–87.

to the δῆμος and that role had been usurped by the orators and
sophists (*Or.* 32.8). Furthermore in an age of declamation with its
megastar orators, parents had voted with their feet and were only
too anxious to enroll their sons in the sophists' schools. "The People"
not only paid to hear public declamations but employed the sophists
in the assemblies and on embassies.[28] Alas for the philosophers, they
no longer held center stage in the public's estimation.

It is important to be reminded at this point that Philodemus was
not dismissive of rhetoric *per se*. One has only to read the extant
portion of Section I of Book IV which discusses rhetorical "expression" to be aware of the importance he attached to the various categories discussed under this heading, namely "correctness," "clarity,"
"forcefulness," "brevity," "appropriateness" and "elaboration." A
speech must not flout the rules of rhetorical composition.[29]

For Philodemus the crux of the issue was that rhetorical delivery
(ὑπόκρισις) was now being developed by the teachers of oratory into
an "art" form, as if it were appropriate for the orator's podium or
court room rather than the actor's stage. It had become the master
and not the servant of rhetoric. Because it was not taught in any
other sphere, Philodemus states categorically in his conclusion, "This
system is not needed by any other artist, certainly not by philosophers. The fact is, each profession has its own peculiar delivery"
(*Rhet.* 4 col. XIX.11–16).

In the second century c.e. the Epicurean writer, Diogenes of
Oenoanda, wrote to Hermarchus, who as a young man had studied rhetoric. He pointed out the dichotomy facing rhetorically-edu-
cated young men who contemplated the royal route of philosophy.

> [At present you reject our philosophy; but later perhaps you will wish,
> when your hostility has been banished] to open the congenial entrance
> to our community, and you will veer away from the speeches of the
> rhetoricians in order to listen to some of our doctrines. And from then
> on it is our firm hope that you will come as quickly as you can to
> knock at the doors of philosophy.[30]

[28] For a discussion see my *Philo and Paul among the Sophists*, ch. 1 and 2.
[29] On this subject see Robert N. Gaines, "Qualities of Rhetorical Expression in
Philodemus," *TAPA* 112 (1982): 71–81 with some modification of his position in
I. Rutheford, "ΕΜΦΑΣΙΣ in Ancient Literary Criticism and *Tractatus Coislinianus* c. 7,"
Maia 40 (1988): 128–29.
[30] See Martin Ferguson Smith, *Diogenes of Oenoanda: The Epicurean Inscription* (Naples:
Bibliopolis, 1992), frg. 127 and his suggestion to whom the comment was made by
Diogenes, 415.

Diogenes and Philodemus knew only too well that the rhetorical delivery of orators was inappropriate for the purpose of the transformation of the followers of Epicureanism. What would its relationship with nascent Christianity be?

Paul's opponents on rhetorical delivery

In the year 44 B.C.E., probably a few years before Philodemus died, Julius Caesar undertook the important step of authorizing the refounding of the dismantled city of Corinth as a Roman colony. A century later a Christian community was established there as a result of Paul's evangelistic activities and drew converts from all walks of life.[31] Not only did the Christian message impact both Jews and Greeks, citizens and non-citizens, in what, by the Principate of Claudius, had become the most prestigious and certainly most prosperous Roman colony in Macedonia and Achaea,[32] but so too, after Paul's departure, secular mores began to reshape the thinking of some in the church concerning the presentation of the Christian message. It is easy to forget that early Christianity's uniqueness rested in the fact that it was not a cultic religion with sacrifices either in Corinth or Jerusalem, as was the case in Jerusalem with Judaism. This new "religion" was one in which proclamation and teaching played a highly central role. It should not therefore surprise us that conflict developed over the use of rhetoric in Christian preaching, apologetics and teaching. Those who engaged in such activities needed to revolve the "form" of delivery or presentation appropriate to the Christian message. (This issue will be discussed below.)

The love of public oratory in Corinth is well attested by Favorinus, a late first century C.E. sophist, who states that even "the women and children" in that city gathered to hear him declaim (*Or.* 37.33). Just as Favorinus was to fall foul of the rhetorically fickle Corinthians after his second visit to them, so too did Paul after his unsuccessful return visit. In the case of both men, the attack against them came from within. Favorinus incurred the displeasure of the city fathers

---

[31] D. W. J. Gill, "In Search of the Social Elite in the Corinthian Church," *Tyndale Bulletin* 44.2 (1993): 323–37.
[32] On the enormous prosperity of the colony from the Principate of Claudius see C. H. Williams II, "Roman Corinth as a Commercial Center," in Timothy E. Gregory (ed.), *The Corinthia in the Roman Period*, Supp. JRA 8 (Ann Arbor: Journal of Roman Archaeology, 1993), 31–46, esp. 45–6.

334 BRUCE W. WINTER

who overthrew his statue that had occupied a prominent place outside the city library (*Or.* 37.20). Paul experienced the derisory comments of Christian teachers who had come to Corinth after he left.

The best strategy for Paul's opponents to adopt in order to denigrate him in the eyes of the Corinthian Christian community was to attack his deficiencies as a public speaker. After all, he had been followed by the rhetorically-trained Apollos whose return had been requested by the Christian community but turned down (1 Cor. 16:12, cf. Acts 18:24–8).[33] The most damaging thing that could be said of Paul in the rhetorically-fastidious Roman colony of Corinth was that he was sadly deficient in his delivery. This is precisely the "charge" they brought against him: "For, people are saying,[34] on the one hand the letters are weighty and strong, but on the other, the bodily presence is weak and the speech is of no account" (ὅτι αἱ ἐπιστολαὶ μέν, φησίν, βαρεῖαι καὶ ἰσχυραί, ἡ δὲ παρουσία τοῦ σώματος ἀσθενὴς καὶ ὁ λόγος ἐξουθενημένος; 2 Cor. 10:10).

In regard to the two important components which made up ὑπόκρισις, Paul is declared to be found wanting. To mention the matter of Paul's "bodily presence" reminds the reader of the discussion which occurred early in the second century C.E. between a Corinthian student of rhetoric and the philosopher, Epictetus, on the issue of "personal adornment." The extent to which rhetorical delivery had become intertwined with personal appearance is demonstrated in the extremes to which this student of the sophists in Corinth had gone. Apart from wearing elaborate clothing, he had removed bodily hair by means of pitch plasters in order to appear god-like before an audience.[35]

Quintilian observed that "a good delivery is undoubtedly impossible for one who cannot remember what he has written, or lacks the quick faculty of speech required by sudden emergencies, or is hampered by incurable impediments of speech . . . physical uncouthness may be such that no art can remedy it, while a weak voice is incompatible with first-rate excellence in delivery" (*Instit.* 9.3, 12–13). Lucian in his *Lover of Lies*, 34 provides an interesting insight into the comment that Paul's bodily presence was weak (ἀσθενής). Lucian

---

[33] See *Philo and Paul among the Sophists* 174–75.

[34] See Ralph P. Martin, *2 Corinthians* (Waco: Word Books, 1986), 311 for the view that φησίν is an indefinite verb and should not be taken to mean that a particular person is saying these things; cp. BDF #130.3 where it is seen as a diatribe convention.

[35] See Epictetus "On Personal Adornment," IV.1. For a discussion see my "Epictetus and a Corinthian Student of the Sophists," *Philo and Paul among the Sophists*, ch. 6.

describes Pancrates as "wonderfully learned," familiar with all σοφία καὶ παιδεία. His friend, Arignotus, is surprised because he identifies him as speaking "imperfect Greek," as "flat-nosed with protruding lips and thinnish legs."[36] By the canons of delivery his appearance would be judged inadequate for public oratory. Arignotus clearly associates ὑπόκρισις with rhetorical connotations.[37]

What do we know of Paul's bodily presence? A subsequent generation preserved a tradition which supported the statement of Paul's detractors that he was "a man of little stature, baldheaded, crooked . . . with eye-brows meeting and a long nose."[38] He was hardly the god-like figure the public orator was meant to cut according to Philostratus.[39] Paul's opponents had clearly hit on a deficiency that, in spite of his letters being "weighty and strong," struck what was the Achilles' heel in public oratory. In terms of the division between the writing and speaking orators, Paul clearly falls into the category of the former, the reason being that was he was like Isocrates and not Alchimadas, for he did not possess bodily presence.[40] In the words of Philodemus he lacked "the dignity and proportion and boldness of the face and the hands and the rest of the body" (*Rhet.* 4 col. XIV.23–25). A much later observer was to note in the *Scholia* of Aristides: ὁ ῥήτωρ μᾶλλον ὁρώμενος πείθει, ἥπερ διὰ γραμμάτων.[41]

---

[36] Hans Dieter Betz in his *Der Apostel Paulus und die sokratische Tradition: eine exegetische Untersuchung zu seiner "Apologie" 2 Korinther 10–13* (Tübingen: Mohr [Siebeck], 1972), 45, 53–4, and "Rhetoric and Theology," in *L'Apôtre Paul: Personnalité, style et conception du ministère*, ed. Albert Vanhoye (Leuven: Leuven University Press, 1986), 41, believes that this is a reference to the Cynic concept of σχῆμα. Lucian does not use the term σχῆμα. Betz' choice of σχῆμα as the issue being discussed in 2 Cor. 10:10 falls short because σχῆμα has to do with personal appearance only. For a helpful discussion of the meaning of σχῆμα see Dio Chrysostom, Περὶ τοῦ σχήματος, *Or.* 72. It is not a synonym for ὑπόκρισις.

[37] Victor Paul Furnish in *II Corinthians*, AB 32A (Garden City, NY: Doubleday, 1984), 468, has suggested that Epictetus III.22.86–89 resembles 10.10b, that Epictetus argues that if a Cynic hopes to carry the day with his teaching, then he must be able to say "Look, both I and my body are witnesses of this." However, Epictetus discusses a Cynic who is "consumptive . . . pale and thin." He alone commends his message who extols the virtues of the plain and simple life style; this requires a person whose body is a μαρτυρία of the truth of Cynic philosophy. While it would be possible to describe the physical appearance of this debilitated Cynic as ἀσθενής, this is not what the term means in the sophistic movement as Lucian, *Lover of Lies*, 34 shows.

[38] "The Acts of Paul and Thecla," *Acta Apostolorum Apocrypha*, 1.237.

[39] On the audience's verbal approval of the dress and "perfect elegance" of the sophist Alexander of Seleucia, see Philostratus, *The Lives of the Sophists* 570–72.

[40] See n. 12.

[41] Wilhelm Dindorf, *Aristides*, 191.3 (Leipzig: Weidmann, 1829), 3.606.

To what were his detractors referring when they commented on
Paul's λόγος? It does not means "talk," otherwise it would be in the
plural and without the article. According to Liddell, Scott and Jones,
λόγος is used of a speech delivered in court, an assembly, etc.[42] They
cite Aristotle, *The "Art" of Rhetoric* 1358a38, where the speech is
divided into three parts, having referred in what immediately pre-
cedes to the hearers of "the speeches."[43] It could also be used of a
spoken, in contrast to a written, word (Plato, *Phdr.* 276a). In 2 Cor.
10:10, the first reference is to the judgment formed on how Paul's
letters were perceived, and the last statement refers to his spoken
word. What did the detractors intend when they used the pejorative term ἐξουθενημένος with reference to ὁ λόγος of Paul? The verb
means "to set at naught," i.e. "to despise" or "to hold contemptible"
and in this context it suggests that in presentation Paul's speech fails
miserably to measure up to what was expected of a public speaker.
This contrasts with the comments on his letters which are declared
to be "weighty and strong." Paul belonged to the writing orators
and not the extemporary ones: his detractors could say that he had
no choice, given his bodily presence and his λόγος that militated
against the requirements of rhetorical delivery of speeches.

In 2 Cor. 11:6 further information emerges about Paul when he
states, "And even if I am indeed a layman (ἰδιώτης) in speech, still
(ἀλλά) I am not in knowledge, but (ἀλλά) in every way we have
been manifested to you in all things." It would seem that it was
alleged that he is a "layman"—a term which could be used as an
antonym for a sophist, but also of a person who had been trained
in rhetoric but had not proceeded to become a practicing orator.[44]
If this understanding of Paul as a "layman" is correct, then it is
right to assume that in 2 Cor. 10:10 Paul was being disparaged on
the grounds that he could never really have practiced as a public
orator. He lacked the requisite attributes for what was judged to be
essential for rhetorical delivery. Even if this were so, why would
Paul's opponents have mounted such an attack on him?

---

[42] λόγος, LSJ 4:1058.
[43] Cf. 1358b where there is a reference to "rhetorical speeches" and 1420a where
he suggests that "the most appropriate style is that which has no connecting particles, in order that it may be a peroration [ἐπίλογος] but not an oration [ἀλλὰ μή
λόγος ᾖ]."
[44] See for example Isocrates, *Antidosis*, 201, 204 and Philo, *Agr.* 143, 159–60.

Paul's renunciation of rhetorical delivery

Just as Philodemus argued that Epicurean philosophy had a delivery that was suited to its discipline, so too Paul in 1 Corinthians defends his "delivery," which he saw was apposite for the Christian message. Paul's *apologia* for his *modus operandi* on his initial ministry in Corinth is spelled out succinctly in 1 Cor. 2:1–5. He argues that he consciously rejected the conventions surrounding the entry and delivery of the public orators on their initial visit to a city. He, like Philodemus, deliberately avoided rhetorical delivery in order to benefit their respective audiences, because Paul judged that, if he were to present his message according to its canons, it would not have the right effect of evoking belief in Christ.

An orator observed certain well-established procedures when he came to a city in order to secure his reputation in the πολιτεία and to make money by demanding exorbitant fees from students attending a school he would establish. Invitations were issued to attend a public lecture, preferably in a location where the acoustics enhanced the voice of the orator; a preliminary speech (προλαλιά or λαλιά) about himself and an *encomium* on the city were presented. The former was a sophisticated piece of boasting or self-commendation and the latter aimed to curry favor with the hearers by praising their city. These preliminaries were delivered seated in front of the audience and would be followed by an invitation to the audience to nominate any topic on which they wanted the orator to declaim. Once this was determined, an option to delay presentation for twenty-four hours could be taken up, or else the orator stood up to declaim immediately. The audience's reception determined the future of the orator in that particular city. If he passed the test, fame and wealth would follow; if rejected, he would have to try his fortunes in another place.[45]

---

[45] See Dio Chrysostom *Or.* 47.22 and Aristides, *Or.* 51.29-34 and the discussion in Donald Andrew Russell, *Greek Declamations* (Cambridge: Cambridge University Press, 1983), 76. It would seem that A. Duane Litfin, *St. Paul's Theology of Proclamation: An Investigation of 1 Corinthians 1–4 and Greco-Roman Rhetoric*, SNTSMS 79 (Cambridge: Cambridge University Press, 1994), 204–9, Anderson, *Ancient Rhetorical Theory and Paul* 239–48, and Michael A. Bullmore, *St. Paul's Theology of Rhetorical Style: An Examination of 1 Corinthians 2.1–5 in the Light of Graeco-Roman Rhetorical Culture* (San Francisco: International Scholars Publications, 1995), each of whom makes the passage central to his thesis, all fail to take account of the reference to "the entry" conventions to which Paul refers not only in 1 Cor. 2:1–5, but also in 1 Thess. 2:1–12; see my "The Entries and Ethics of Orators and Paul (1 Thessalonians 2:1–12)," *Tyndale Bulletin* 44.1 (May, 1993): 55–74.

How does Paul explain his entry? 1 Cor. 2:1–5 is preceded immediately by an important citation from Jeremiah 9:22–3, where the
prophet proscribes the wise man from boasting in his wisdom, as
well as the rich and the powerful leaders gaining their confidence
from the status arising from the abundance of their resources or
their success in politics. Rather they were to "boast" in the Lord
with whom they enjoyed a covenantal relationship, knowing that he
delighted in covenantal mercies and justice. So Paul's discussion of
his original coming to Corinth in 1 Cor. 2:1–5 is meant to demonstrate what boasting in the Lord in negative terms meant and what
the "wise" man boasting in his wisdom referred to in his day. Hence
Barrett translates κἀγώ in v. 1 as, "It was in line with this principle."[46] Paul undertakes his explanation by showing how he did not
come to them using the personal reference (κἀγώ) in verses 1 and
3, following this with an explanation as to why he acted as he did,
using a ἵνα purpose construction in verse 5.

He clearly wished to give emphasis not just to his actual coming
to Corinth, but to the manner of his coming to the Corinthians.
"And I myself, in coming to you, brothers, did not come in accordance with the superiority of speech or wisdom proclaiming the mystery of God" (κἀγὼ ἐλθὼν πρὸς ὑμᾶς, ἀδελφοί, ἦλθον οὐ καθ᾽ ὑπεροχὴν
λόγου ἢ σοφίας καταγγέλλων ὑμῖν τὸ μυστήριον τοῦ θεοῦ; 1 Cor. 2:1).
He then spells out how his "coming" did not conform to the conventions.[47] It was not in accordance with superior speech and clev-
erness[48] that he came proclaiming the doctrine of the mystery of
God. In fact, the topic had already been determined, and unlike the
orators who boasted that they could declaim on anything nominated
to them from the floor as a test of their prowess, Paul himself had
previously fixed the one topic upon which he was determined to
speak in Corinth, i.e. Jesus Christ and him crucified (1 Cor. 2:2).
How did he go on to describe his delivery? In verses 3–4 he discusses
his "presence" in terms of "weakness, fear and much trembling"
which is the antithesis of the studied, confident presence of the orators.[49] Concerning his speech and his message he declares that it was

---

[46] Charles Kingsley Barrett, *The First Epistle to the Corinthians* (London: A&C Black,
1973), 62.
[47] κατά, "in accordance with;" BAG[2] 407, II.5.b.β.
[48] When used in the context of rhetoric λόγος and σοφία can be translated thus.
See Dio Chrysostom, *Or.* 47.1.
[49] See Philo, *Det.* 35 where the strength of the sophists is contrasted with the
weakness of their opponents "at that sort of thing."

not delivered in the persuasiveness of rhetoric but in clear demonstration of the Spirit and power.[50] Paul's "demonstration" (ἀπόδειξις) was not that which had been recommended by Aristotle as one of the three means of persuasion (*Rhet.* 1356A)—the other two involved *ethos* and *pathos*, the former connected with acting the part and the latter with manipulating the emotions of the audience—but it was a demonstration of the "Spirit" and a demonstration of "power" (1 Cor. 2:4).[51]

In v. 5 Paul explains that his whole purpose of renouncing these conventions was designed to ensure that the Corinthians' "proof" (πίστις) or "faith" (perhaps a play on the Aristotelian traditional πίστεις or "proofs" in the art of persuasion) might not rest in the wisdom of men but in the power of God (2:5).

What Paul does in 1 Corinthians 2:1–5 is important because, in the judgment of E. A. Judge, he "plunders the Egyptians," using rhetorical terms but filling them with very different meanings. He further notes that Paul "was not willing to concede terms to his opponents. He stigmatizes what is invalid."[52] Paul describes his own ministry in terms that are chosen deliberately to show his rejection of rhetorical delivery[53] and reveals that the confidence of his converts would have been misplaced had he not operated thus in Corinth. Here Paul joins sides with Philodemus whose concerns for the audience were such that his delivery was determined by their need. Philodemus was seeking to have his audience anchor their confidence in Epicurean philosophy, while Paul ardently believed that their confidence in the gospel must be where the power of God could be made known (cf. Rom. 1:16).

This was not the first reference in Paul's letter to the Corinthians in which he made reference to the reason for speaking as he did. Earlier in the letter he indicates that he would not proclaim the gospel in the "wisdom of rhetoric" (σοφία λόγου), for if he did so the cross of Christ would be emptied of its power for the audience

---

[50] On πίστις as "proof," see Acts 17:31.

[51] On the use of *ethos* and *pathos* see Jakob Wisse, *Ethos and Pathos: From Aristotle to Cicero* (Amsterdam: Hakkert, 1989).

[52] E. A. Judge, "The Reaction against Classical Education in the New Testament," *Journal of Christian Education*, Paper 77 (July, 1983): 11, and "Paul's Boasting in Relation to Contemporary Professional Practice," *Australian Biblical Review* 16 (1968): 40, on plundering the Egyptians.

[53] L. Harman, "Some remarks on 1 Cor. 2:1–5," *Svensk Exegetisk Årsbok* 39 (1974): 120, speaks of Paul becoming "anti-rhetor."

who heard it (1 Cor. 1:17).[54] There was a form of delivery for this
message that Paul judged inappropriate, in the same way Philodemus
judged rhetorical delivery to be so for Epicurean philosophy.

With such an attack by Paul on rhetoric and, in particular, rhetorical delivery and its inadequacy for conveying the message of the
crucified God in 1 Cor. 1–2, it is explicable that his trenchant criticisms of rhetorical delivery would draw strong fire. "The wise among
you in this age," whom Paul cautions not to be deceived by "the
wisdom of this world" (1 Cor. 3:18–19), would have felt attacked.
His Christian opponents in 2 Cor. 10–13, who have every reason
to contest his critique of rhetorical delivery, would not have accused
Paul of a deficiency in this area if they themselves did not have
prowess in it. They threw Paul on the defensive (2 Cor. 10–12), no
doubt deriving great satisfaction from pointing out to the Corinthian
congregation that Paul's rejection of rhetorical delivery did not really
stem from his theological "objections." They would have been
acquainted with them for they now served as teachers in the church
in Corinth. His attack was, in fact, a theological rationalization for
his own personal inadequacies in the area of rhetorical delivery. As
has been noted, they conceded his ability in rhetoric as a letter
writer, but could very happily contrast it with his performances,
which they judged by the canons of delivery. Like many before him
he simply did not possess the requisite attributes and therefore could
not be the sort of teacher and preacher required in order to present the gospel by commanding the attention of the rhetorically fastidious Corinthians.

Conclusions

Although separated by over a century in time, Philodemus and Paul
confronted a common difficulty, namely the primacy of rhetorical
delivery (ὑπόκρισις) used by megastar orators of their day and the
part, if any, it might play in their respective movements. Philodemus
clearly did have a theory of a delivery that he considered appropriate for the Epicurean philosopher, i.e., "the presence" of the
speaker and modulation of the voice. He recognized that these did

---

[54] For a discussion of the connection between 1 Cor. 1:17 and 2:4–5 see Litfin
190–92.

make a difference in philosophical presentation.[55] However, his declaration that political rhetoric was not an "art" indicates the strength of his feelings based on the deleterious effect that rhetorical delivery had on the solemn task of informing and persuading the citizens where the "salvation" of their city lay.[56]

Paul argued that from the very beginning of his ministry in Corinth that he had renounced the techniques of rhetorical delivery (ὑπόκρισις) and his "rhetorical presence" for persuading the Corinthians to convert to Christianity. He believed that rhetorically-delivered presentations before rhetorically-sophisticated hearers would only draw attention to the rhetorical prowess of the messenger. It would deflect attention away from the content of the scandalous message of the crucified God in which their "salvation" lay.

In that Paul's primary concern was the distraction of the audience from the content and life-changing importance of the message because of the use of rhetorically polished deliveries, he shared similar concerns with Philodemus. He would also have agreed with Philodemus that each discipline has its own "art" (τέχνη) and "learning procedure" (μάθησις) and that those who practice it should alone invent the appropriate λόγοι and not be ruled by fashionable trends in rhetoric. Rhetoric had certainly exceeded its boundaries and nowhere had this been demonstrated more clearly than with rhetorical delivery (Rhet. 4 col. XXV.1–14; 1 Cor. 2:1–5).

Both men stood at moments in the history of the development of rhetoric where change was in the air. As a recent innovation Philodemus saw rhetorical delivery become a core or central part of the curriculum in Greek παιδεία. Paul witnessed the flowering of the Second Sophistic with its central emphasis on extemporary oratory and declamations which emphasized the prowess of virtuoso orators in rhetorical delivery. They both recognized the problem it created. Philodemus introduced an accommodation that would not distract his hearers. Paul defended his rejection of "rhetorical delivery" (ὑπόκρισις) in Corinth where both its inhabitants and members of the Christian community were so enamoured with it that even some fifty years later Favorinus was to record how the charm of his eloquence won the approval of its citizens along with their "women and children" (Or. 37.33).

---

[55] See above, 326–30.
[56] The term σωτηρία meant "health," "safety," or even "welfare" when used in the semantic field of πολιτεία.

Rightly used, *On Rhetoric* can provide important correctives to some of the more recent studies of the application of rhetoric to the New Testament.[57] It has always to be borne in mind that much water had passed under the bridge in the study of rhetoric by ancient authors after Aristotle's *The "Art" of Rhetoric*. In this New Testament field of study Philodemus' work provides an essential set of older snapshots, and the letters of Paul another. A comparative study of their shots of rhetorical delivery (ὑπόκρισις) has shown how mutually helpful they can be in illuminating aspects of their concerns and convictions and those of their contemporaries.

---

[57] For more measured treatments on Paul generally see Anderson, *Ancient Rhetorical Theory and Paul* and Philip H. Kern, *Rhetoric and Galatians: Assessing an Approach to Paul's Epistle*, SNTSMS 101 (New York: Cambridge University Press, 1998).

GADARA: PHILODEMUS' NATIVE CITY

John T. Fitzgerald

Abstract

Philodemus was a native of Gadara, a famous Hellenistic city in southern Syria. This essay, which draws heavily on the results of recent
excavations of the city, traces the history of Gadara from the Ptolemaic
period until the Roman period, when it reached its apex as as a cultural center.

According to the geographer Strabo (16.2.29), Philodemus the
Epicurean was born in the city of Gadara, as were also Meleager,
Menippus, and Theodorus. Because the other three individuals whom
Strabo associates with Gadara are well-attested natives of the Syrian
city, there is every reason to accept Strabo's testimony that Philodemus
also hailed from Gadara.[1] The same assessment cannot be made
about the site where Strabo locates the city. Whereas Gadara was
located to the east of the Jordan River, Strabo apparently confuses
it with Gazara (= Gezer, M.R. 142140),[2] which lay in the foothills
of the Judean range.[3] Strabo was not alone in confusing Gadara

---

[1] For a discussion, see Tiziano Dorandi, "La patria di Filodemo," *Philologus* 131
(1987): 254–56.

[2] For a convenient listing of grid reference numbers used to identify biblical and
other sites, see the *Student Map Manual: Historical Geography of the Bible Lands* (Jerusalem:
Pictorial Archive [Near Eastern History] Est., 1979).

[3] So Emil Schürer, *The History of the Jewish People in the Age of Jesus Christ (175
b.c.–a.d. 135)*, rev. ed., ed. G. Vermes and F. Millar, 3 vols. in 4 (Edinburgh: Clark,
1973–87), 1:191 n. 8, and 2:50. On the limitations of Strabo as a geographer, especially in regard to the ancient Near East, see Lee A. Maxwell, "Gadara of the
Decalopis" (Th.D. Diss., Concordia Seminary, 1990), 39–40. Ancient Gezer or
Gazara (Gazaris) is today a 33–acre mound (Tell Jezer = Tell el-Jazari) located
some 5 miles south-southeast of modern Ramleh. A powerful city during the Middle
Bronze Age (esp. 1800–1500 b.c.e.), it remained a crucial site during the days of
ancient Israel. By the end of the second century b.c.e., however, it had ceased to
be an important city and by the Herodian period the site was virtually deserted.
For a brief history of Gezer/Gazara in light of modern excavations, see William
G. Dever, "Gezer," *ABD* 2 (1992): 998–1003. See also the extremely valuable

with another city, for ancient writers often confused the Syrian city with other cities and towns that had similar or identical names. This confusion occurs in Jewish, Christian, and pagan material, as do other kinds of errors regarding the city and its natives.[4] Sometimes these errors appear to have originated with the authors of these texts, whereas in other cases scribal confusion is the likely explanation.

In Josephus, *J.W.* 1.170 and *Ant.* 14.91, for example, Gadara is almost certainly a mistake for Gazara,[5] Gadora,[6] or Adora.[7] Similarly, the reference in *J.W.* 4.413–419 and 428 to a Gadara that is "the capital of Perea" cannot be to Gadara of the Decapolis, which did not lie in Perea, but must be to the site elsewhere called Gedor, Gedora, and Gadora (= Tell Jedur, M.R. 220160).[8] Similarly, it is inconceivable that the Roman general Vespasian would destroy Gadara in Syria, which was pro-Roman. Josephus likely referred to Gabara, a city in Galilee, though all manuscripts of *J.W.* 3.132 read Gadara. Even where Josephus' references to the Decapolis city of Gadara appear to be correct, the manuscripts occasionally offer variants, as at *Ant.* 13.396, where Adara and Gazara are textual variants to Gadara.[9]

The same kind of textual confusion exists in the three New Testament accounts of Jesus' exorcising one or two demoniacs and sending the demons into a nearby herd of swine, who immediately

---

gazetteer compiled by Yoram Tsafrir, Leah Di Segni, and Judith Green, *Tabula Imperii Romani: Iudaea • Palaestina: Eretz Israel in the Hellenistic, Roman and Byzantine Periods* (Jerusalem: Israel Academy of Sciences and Humanities, 1994), 131.

[4] For a chronological error involving two natives of Gadara, see Diogenes Laertius 6.99, where Menippus and Meleager are wrongly made contemporaries.

[5] See the notes to these passages by H. St. J. Thackeray and Ralph Marcus in the LCL edition of Josephus. Unless otherwise noted, translations of Josephus are the LCL.

[6] Maxwell, "Gadara of the Decapolis," 65–66.

[7] Schürer, *The History of the Jewish People*, 1:268 n. 5.

[8] See the note on this passage by Thackeray in the LCL; Schürer, *The History of the Jewish People*, 1:498; 2:134; Diane I. Treacy-Cole, "Perea," *ABD* 5 (1992): 224–25. As Birgit Mershen and Ernst Axel Knauf, "From *Gadar* to *Umm Qais*," *ZDPV* 104 (1988): 128–45, esp. 130, point out, all "the vowels of Γάδαρα/*Gadar* [in the Decapolis] are short," in contrast to "Γάδαρα-Γάδωρα/*Gadār-Gadōr*," the ancient name of el-Salt in Perea.

[9] For another possible example of confusion in the manuscript tradition, see *Ant.* 13.375, where Gadara is perhaps either the name of an otherwise unknown village in southern Gaulanitis or an error for Garada. For a brief discussion of the problem, see Maxwell, "Gadara of the Decapolis," 55–56. See also *J.W.* 1.166 (cf. *Ant.* 14.88), where Gadara is one of several textual variants.

rush down a steep bank into the water (the Sea of Galilee = Lake
Tiberias) and drown (Matt 8:28–34; Mark 5:1–20; Luke 8:26–39).
The setting for this story is clearly Gentile rather than Jewish, as
the references to the pigs and the swineherds indicate, and the exor-
cism is depicted as occurring near the lake, in the countryside attached
to the town rather than in the city proper. Manuscripts of the
Synoptic Gospels give the names of three different towns as the one
in whose territory this exorcism occurred: Gadara, Gerasa (modern
Jerash, M.R. 234187),[10] and Gergesa (= Chorsia = modern Kursi,
M.R. 210248).[11] Of these,[12] Gergesa, which is located closest to the
Sea of Galilee and is not far from a steep cliff, best fits the details
of the narrative; yet it is the poorest attested reading and appears
to have arisen as a conjectural solution to the geographical difficulties
raised by both Gerasa and Gadara.[13] Mark (5:1), followed by Luke
(8:26, 37), most likely places the exorcism in the country of the
Gerasenes. Inasmuch as Gerasa is more than 30 miles southeast of
the Sea of Galilee, it is extremely unlikely that this reference is accurate. In changing the reference to the country of the Gadarenes,
Matthew (8:28) is probably making a connection between Gadara
and the Semitic deity Gad, who is rendered as δαίμων by the

---

[10] See esp. Carl H. Kraeling, ed., *Gerasa: City of the Decapolis* (New Haven: American
Schools of Oriental Research, 1938); Shimon Applebaum and Arthur Segal, "Gerasa,"
in *The New Encyclopedia of Archaeological Excavations in the Holy Land*, ed. E. Stern,
4 vols. (Jerusalem: The Israel Exploration Society & Carta; New York: Simon &
Schuster, 1993), 2:470–79; Fawzi Zayadine, ed., *Jerash Archaeological Project*, 2 vols.
(vol. 1: Amman: Department of Antiquities of Jordan, 1986; vol. 2: Paris: Librairie
Orientaliste Paul Geuthner, 1989); and Jacques Seigne, "Gerasa-Jerasch—Stadt der
1000 Säulen," in *Gadara—Gerasa und die Dekapolis*, ed. Adolf Hoffmann and Susanne
Kerner, Sonderbände der antiken Welt (Mainz: Zabern, 2002), 6–22.

[11] The M.R. number for the ancient Christian basilica is 211248. See esp. Vassilios
Tzaferis, "Kursi," in *The New Encyclopedia of Archaeological Excavations in the Holy Land*,
3:893–96. See also Tsafrir, Di Segni, and Green, *Tabula Imperii Romani*, 104.

[12] For the chief textual witnesses in support of these three readings and a brief
discussion, see Bruce M. Metzger, *A Textual Commentary on the Greek New Testament*,
2d ed. (Stuttgart: Deutsche Bibelgesellschaft, 1994), 18–19.

[13] Origen championed Gergesa and may well have been the first to propose it;
see esp. Tjitze Baarda, "Gadarenes, Gerasenes, Gergesenes and the 'Diatessaron'
Traditions," in *Neotestamentica et Semitica: Studies in Honour of Matthew Black*, ed. E. E.
Ellis and M. Wilcox (Edinburgh: Clark, 1969), 181–97. In view of the textual evidence, a compelling case for Gergesa as the original site for the story can only be
made by assuming that the name of the city was already confused with Gerasa (or
Gadara) during the period of oral transmission, and that the reading "Gergesa" is
a later scribal emendation designed to correct the received textual tradition.

Septuagint in Isa 65:11.[14] Matthew thus provides a more appropriate symbolic setting for Jesus' encounter with two δαίμονες (Matt 8:31), so that the exorcism of the Gadarene demoniacs takes place in the haunt of the daimon Gad and demonstrates Jesus' power over him. Simultaneously, Matthew also makes it comparatively easier, following the exorcism, for "the whole town" to make the five- to six-mile journey from Gadara to meet Jesus by the lake (8:34).[15]

Despite the uncertainty of particular references to Gadara, much can be said about Philodemus' native city, though the early history of the city is difficult to reconstruct. This difficulty is created by the paltry number of early literary references to the city and the scant archaeological evidence thus far uncovered for the earliest period. The task of describing Hellenistic and early Roman Gadara and of narrating its history during these periods is particularly daunting. As one of the city's excavators has noted,

> Nearly all buildings visible above the surface are from the late Roman and Byzantine times; earlier buildings were reused for a very long period, to the extent that only the foundation walls still exist, making it rather difficult to explore the earlier (Hellenistic and Early Roman) history of the city in any detail.[16]

Furthermore, a late Ottoman village was built over Gadara's ancient acropolis, covering the nucleus of the old Hellenistic city and ren-

---

[14] The Gadarenes themselves appear to have made the connection, for they honored Tyche, Gad's Greek counterpart, as the city-goddess. On this point, see below. On Isa 65:11 and its context, see now Joseph Blenkinsopp, *Isaiah 56–66: A New Translation with Introduction and Commentary*, AB 19B (New York: Doubleday, 2003), 273–79.

[15] There is another possibility. Matthew obviously thinks of "the country of the Gadarenes" as extending all the way to Lake Tiberias, and this appears to have been the case. Josephus, who shares Matthew's conviction, claims that Gadara had villages (κώμας) that "lay on the frontiers of Tiberias" (*Life* 42) and that Gadara's territory bordered on Galilee (*J.W.* 3.37). Therefore, Matthew could conceivably be thinking of one of these small villages that lay in the territory of Gadara rather than Gadara proper, in spite of the fact that he refers to the place as a *polis*. Flexibility in using the term *polis* would certainly not be unique to Matthew; the author of 1 Maccabees, for example, uses *polis* of both a village (2:15) and a fortified settlement (5:26–27; cf. Polybius 5.70.7). Whatever the merit of this suggestion, it does not answer the chief objection to "the country of the Gadarenes" as the original site of the story, viz., that whereas Matthew (8:32) refers to a steep bank, the terrain on the southeast shore of Lake Tiberias is quite flat.

[16] Susanne Kerner, "The German Protestant Institute for Archaeology and Other German Projects in Jordan," in *The Near East in Antiquity*, ed. Susanne Kerner, 4 vols. (Amman: At Kutba, 1990–94), 4:49–63, esp. 54.

dering it partly inaccessible and thus difficult if not impossible to excavate thoroughly. In the process of building the Ottoman village, moreover, the builders flattened large parts of the acropolis, not only making the task of excavation more difficult but also complicating the prospects for future analysis.[17] Furthermore, like residents of other cities, ancient Gadarenes were prone to recycle building materials, so that not much from the earliest period can be recovered, and even the late Roman and Byzantine structures were severely damaged by earthquakes, especially in the seventh and eight century.[18] All these factors as well as others combine to make the recovery of Gadara's history quite problematic.[19] Despite these limitations and the need at key points to rely on inference and conjecture rather than literary and material evidence, it is possible to trace the general outline of ancient Gadara's history and to note some aspects of the city's social, cultural, economic, and religious life. This depiction, which at points relies heavily on published results and interpretations of recent archaeological excavations, is necessarily tentative and subject to revision in light of the ongoing excavations at Gadara. In undertaking the task of providing this outline, it will be helpful to begin with the city's geographical location.

In terms of modern geography, the remains of the Greco-Roman city of Gadara are situated alongside the modern village of Umm Qeis (= Umm Qais = Umm Qays, M.R. 214229).[20] The ruins cover an

---

[17] Ibid.

[18] Susanne Kerner, "Umm Qais—Gadara: Recent Excavations," *ARAM* 4 (1992): 407–23, esp. 407–8.

[19] Another major difficulty is that the ancient literary references to Gadara vary significantly in quality and accuracy. On this point, see Maxwell, "Gadara of the Decalopis," 30, who also provides a fairly complete list of ancient and medieval literary references to Gadara and discusses each reference briefly (30–89).

[20] A medieval name for the site that appears in nineteenth- and early-twentieth-century literature is "Mkēs" (or "Mukēs"), which probably indicated the presence of a toll station (*maks* = "tax") there in later times. See Mershen and Knauf, "From Gadar to Umm Qais," 132, who discuss the history of the site and its various names. The identification of Umm Qeis as the site of ancient Gadara was made by Ulrich Jasper Seetzen, a German explorer, in 1806, and Gottlieb Schumacher did the first thorough survey of the site in 1886. Jordan's Department of Antiquities started work on the site in the 1930s, with various international teams beginning to participate in excavation and restoration projects as early as the 1970s. Teams from Germany have been at the forefront, viz., the German Protestant Institute for Archaeology (headed successively by Ute Wagner-Lux and Thomas Weber), the German Archaeological Institute in Berlin (Adolf Hoffmann), and the Liebighaus Museum (Gallery of Ancient Sculpture) in Frankfurt am Main (Peter Cornelius Bol), though a team

area of approximately 450 meters from north to south and about 1600
meters from east to west, with the Greco-Roman acropolis, as previously indicated, still partly buried beneath the late nineteenth century
Ottoman village.[21] Beginning from that acropolis in the east, the settlement expanded westward in several different phases, with the east-
west street (in Roman times the *decumanus maximus*) serving as the
backbone of the growing town.[22] Located on a flat plateau in northern
Jordan, the ancient site is perched about 350 meters above sea level[23]
and offers a panoramic view of the surrounding region, which includes
"the perennial Yarmouk River to the north, the forested hills of the
Ajlun range to the south, the fertile lands of the Irbid plateau to
the east and of the Jordan Valley to the west."[24] The name Gadara
is clearly Semitic,[25] which indicates its origin in the pre-Hellenistic

from Denmark (headed by Svend Holm-Nielsen) has made important contributions,
especially in regard to the Byzantine baths. For the history of exploration and excavation of the site to 1990, see Maxwell, "Gadara of the Decalopis," 90–125. See
also Thomas Weber, "One Hundred Years of Jordanian-German Fieldwork at Umm
Qais (1890–1990)," in *The Near East in Antiquity* 1:15–27.

[21] Thomas Weber, *Umm Qais, Gadara of the Decapolis: A Brief Guide to the Antiquities*,
At Kutba Jordan Guides (Amman: At Kutba, 1989), 12. On ancient Gadara, see
esp. Schürer, *The History of the Jewish People*, 2:132–36; Maxwell, "Gadara of the
Decapolis"; Svend Holm-Nielsen, Ute Wagner-Lux, and K. J. H. Vriezen, "Gadarenes,"
ABD 2 (1992): 866–68; and Adolf Hoffmann, "Topographie und Stadtgeschichte
von Gadara/Umm Qais," in *Gadara—Gerasa und die Dekapolis*, 98–124. To my great
regret, I have not been able to consult Thomas M. Weber, *Gadara Decapolitana:
Untersuchungen zur Topographie, Geschichte, Architektur und der Bildenden Kunst einer "Polis
Hellenis" im Ostjordanland*, vol. 1 of *Gadara—Umm Qēs*, Abhandlungen des Deutschen
Palästinavereins 30.1 (Wiesbaden: Harrassowitz, 2002). For the late nineteenth cen-
tury Ottoman village of Umm Qeis, see Seteney Shami, "Umm Qeis—A Northern
Jordanian Village in Context," in *Studies in the History and Archaeology of Jordan III*,
ed. A. Hadidi (Amman: Department of Antiquities; London: Routledge & Kegan
Paul, 1987), 211–13, and Susanne Kerner, "Gadara—Schwarzweisse Stadt zwischen
Adjlun und Golan," in *Gadara—Gerasa und die Dekapolis*, 125–36, esp. 125–28.

[22] Adolf Hoffmann, "The Monumental Gate extra muros in Gadara," in *The Near
East in Antiquity*, 1:95–103, esp. 96.

[23] The maximum altitude of the plateau is 378 meters above sea level; the sur-
face of Lake Tiberias is, by contrast, about 210 meters below sea level (Weber,
"One Hundred Years," 15).

[24] Weber, *Umm Qais*, 5. According to Eusebius, *Onom.* 32.16, Gadara was located
twelve miles southwest of Abila, another Decapolis city. Josephus occasionally mentions it together with Hippos, a Decapolis city located to the northwest on the eastern shore of Lake Tiberias (*Ant.* 15.217; 17.320; etc.). For Gadara's physical
environment, see esp. Maxwell, "Gadara of the Decapolis," 1–23, who discusses the
city's location, topography, geology, climate, hydrology, and land use.

[25] The ancient name of the site was apparently "Gadar." The Hellenistic name
"Gadara" is thus simply a transliteration of the Semitic name into Greek, with, as

period,[26] and the recent discovery of what appears to have been an
old "high place" may go back to this period and have been the site
of various sacrifices.[27] But by the time of Philodemus' birth about
the year 110 B.C.E. the city had acquired a number of Greek features[28]

---

was often the case with Semitic toponyms, the Greek locative ending -α added to
the Semitic stem. Etymologically, the name "Gadar" means "wall" (as is also the
meaning of both נדר and נדרה in Hebrew), and it is possible that the name originally referred to agricultural terracing on the upper slopes of a local wadi or in
the Yarmuk valley. In this case, the name "could have been used as early as the
Late Bronze Age" (Mershen and Knauf, "From Ğadar to Umm Qais," 129). Alternatively,
the name may suggest a fortification wall, linking the name to its use as a frontier
post (Weber, Umm Qais, 6). Etymology thus suggests that Gadara originated as either
a military or agricultural settlement. Needless to say, these two options are not
mutually exclusive.

[26] Mershen and Knauf, "From Ğadar to Umm Qais," 129, suggest that the site
was occupied as early as the fourteenth and thirteenth centuries B.C.E. The earliest
evidence of people at the site comes from Iron Age and Persian pottery found in
a survey; see Flemming G. Andersen and John Strange, "Bericht über drei Sondagen
in Umm Qēs, Jordanien, im Herbst 1983," ZDPV 103 (1987): 78–100, esp. 90–92.
For an orientation to Syria in the Early Bronze (ca. 3000–2000), Middle Bronze
(ca. 2000–1550), Late Bronze (ca. 1550–1200), Iron Age I (ca. 1200–1000), and
Iron Age II (ca. 1000–550 B.C.E.), see Rudolph H. Dornemann, "Bronze Age and
Iron Age Syria," ABD 6 (1992): 274–81. For possible but unlikely references to
Gadara in ancient Egyptian topographical lists, see Maxwell, "Gadara of the
Decapolis," 32–34.

[27] For a brief discussion of this possible old "high place," see Hoffmann, "Topographie und Stadtgeschichte," 108.

[28] As the finds at Lefkandi in Euboea prove, the Greeks had contacts with Cyprus
and the Levant at an early pre-colonial stage. According to Mervyn Popham, one
of its excavators, the burial grounds there have yielded "an extraordinary wealth
of Near Eastern imports which make it certain that the Syro-Palestinian region"
was a vital part of the Mediterranean exchange network in the late Protogeometric
period of ca. 950–900 B.C.E. See his "Precolonization: Early Greek Contact with
the East," in The Archaeology of Greek Colonisation: Essays Dedicated to Sir John Boardman,
ed. G. R. Tsetskhladze and F. De Angelis, Oxford University Committee for
Archaeology 40 (Oxford: Oxford University Committee for Archaeology, 1994),
11–34, esp. 17. Similarly, Mycenaean pottery has been found at Sabouni, a hill
town closely associated with the Iron Age port city of Al Mina. The latter, located
in the delta of the Orontes (the major river of western Syria), is usually viewed as
the site of the first Greek presence in Syria, perhaps as early as 825 B.C.E., though
the preponderance of Greek pottery found there dates to ca. 750. Al Mina has
been traditionally regarded as an important trading post where Greeks resided and
perhaps constituted a small colony, but some scholars regard it as devoid of any
real significance, "a mere funnel for the transmission of table-ware to the élites of
the more important administrative centres that lay inland." So A. M. Snodgrass,
"The Nature and Standing of the Early Western Colonies," in The Archaeology of
Greek Colonisation, 1–10, esp. 4–5. For discussion and a range of viewpoints, see
J. M. Cook, The Greeks in Ionia and the East, Ancient Peoples and Places 31 (London:
Thames and Hudson, 1962), 64–65; Rosalinde Kearsley, The Pendent Semi-Circle
Skyphos: A Study of Its Development and Chronology and an Examination of It as Evidence for

and no little renown.[29] Although Hellenistic influence in Syria goes back to the conquest of Alexander,[30] the beginnings of a Greek presence in Gadara itself likely go back only to the third century, when the Ptolemies appear to have fortified the town and settled a military garrison there.[31] The town at that point likely would have been

Euboean Acitivity at Al Mina, Bulletin of the Institute of Classical Studies 44 (London: University of London, Institute of Classical Studies, 1989); Jacques Y. Perreault, "Les *emporia* grecs du Levant: Mythe ou réalité?" in *L'Emporion*, ed. A. Bresson and P. Rouillard; Publications du Centre Pierre Paris 26; Paris: E. de Boccard, 1993), 59–83; Popham, "Precolonization," 26–27; and John Boardman, *The Greeks Overseas: Their Early Colonies and Trade*, 4th ed. (London: Thames and Hudson, 1999), 38–54, 270–71. Two other coastal sites in North Syria, located to the south of Al Mina, are also widely viewed as showing signs of a Greek presence from a slightly later period: Ras el Bassit ("Poseidon") and Tell Sukas. On the former, see esp. Paul Courbin, "Ras el Bassit, Al Mina et Tell Sukas," *Revue archéologique* (1974): 174–78; "Bassit," *Syria* 63 (1986): 175–220; and "Bassit-Posidaion in the Early Iron Age," in *Greek Colonists and Native Populations: Proceedings of the First Australian Congress of Classical Archaeology held in honour of Emeritus Professor A. D. Trendall*, ed. J.-P. Descœudres (Canberra: Humanities Research Centre; Oxford: Clarendon, 1990), 503–9. For the latter, see esp. P. J. Riis, *Sukas I: The North-East Sanctuary and the First Settling of Greeks in Syria and Palestine* (Copenhagen: Royal Danish Academy of Sciences and Letters, 1970), *Sukas VI: The Graeco-Phoenician Cemetery and Sanctuary at the Southern Harbor* (Copenhagen: Royal Danish Academy of Sciences and Letters, 1979), and *Sukas X: The Bronze and Early Iron Age Remains at the Southern Harbour* (Copenhagen: Royal Danish Academy of Sciences and Letters, 1996). These early contacts between Greece and the Levant played a role in fostering the so-called "orientalizing revolution" in archaic Greece; see Walter Burkert, *The Orientalizing Revolution: Near Eastern Influence on Greek Culture in the Early Archaic Age* (Cambridge: Harvard University Press, 1992).

[29] Meleager (fl. ca. 100 B.C.E.) calls it a "famous city" (κλεινὰ πόλις) in one of his autobiographical epigrams (*Anth. Pal.* 7.418).

[30] During the Roman period, the Transjordanian cities of Capitolias, Dium, Gerasa, and Pella claimed to have been founded by Alexander, but many scholars have been highly suspicious of these unproven claims, viewing them as foundation legends propagated in a later period. In any case, it should be noted that the region of northern Syria, where Antioch, Apamea, Seleucia, and Laodicea were located, "was the most intensively hellenised in the whole Orient," but southern Syria, where Gadara was located, was less affected during the third century. The key difference was that the Seleucids controlled northern Syria, whereas the Ptolemies controlled southern Syria. See Cook, *Greeks*, 169–70. For the activity of Seleucus I Nicator in founding Greek cities and creating a new Macedon, see Appian, *Syr.* 57. For the northern Syrian cities, see John D. Grainger, *The Cities of Seleukid Syria* (Oxford: Clarendon, 1990).

[31] George Syncellus (fl. ca. 800 C.E.) in his *Chronicle* (558–559 Dindorf = 355.7–10 Mosshammer) gives Gadara as one of several Macedonian ἀποικίαι conquered by Alexander Jannaeus, and Stephanus of Byzantium (early sixth century C.E.) in his *Ethnika* (s.v., Gadara) says that Gadara is the name of both a city in Coele Syria and a town in Macedonia, and also that it was also called Seleuceia. As A. H. M. Jones, *The Cities of the Eastern Roman Provinces*, 2nd ed., revised by M. Avi-Yonah

laid out in typical Ptolemaic fashion, with urban features concentrated on the acropolis, a simple asymmetrical street system, and fortifications forming geometrical lines around the summit.[32] The fortifications themselves may have consisted of a ring of standing towers about the city, with each isolated tower placed at a strategic

---

et al. (Oxford: Clarendon, 1971), 449 n. 16, notes, this late evidence has led some scholars to infer that Gadara was founded by Macedonians, who named the new city after the Macedonian village. Maurice Sartre, for example, contends that Gadara was founded by either Alexander or his lieutenant Perdiccas; see his "La Syrie à l'époque hellénistique," in *La Syrie de l'époque achéménide à l'avènement de l'Islam*, vol. 2 of *Archéologie et histoire de la Syrie*, ed. J.-M. Dentzer and W. Orthmann, Schriften zur vorderasiatischen Archäologie 1 (Saarbrücken: Saarbrücker Druckerei, 1989), 31–44, esp. 36. Similarly, Julius Beloch, "Die auswärtigen Besitzungen der Ptolemäer," *Archiv für Papyrusforschung und verwandte Gebiete* 2 (1902): 229–56, esp. 233, suggests that Gadara was founded by Antigonus I or his predecessors. Because of the toponym Seleuceia, one could also propose Seleucus I Nicator (312–281 B.C.E.)—who founded Seleuceia on the Tigris (ca. 305 B.C.E.)—as the founder of Gadara. Finally, Thomas Weber, "Gadara," in *RGG*⁴ 3 (2000): 449, gives Gadara as a Macedonian colony of the fourth century B.C.E.

In order to accept a Macedonian origin for Gadara, however, one must argue that Syncellus' information was gleaned from a reliable earlier source, and that Stephanus' attempt to link the Semitic name Gadara with a town in Macedonia was the result of confusion about the true explanation for Gadara's Macedonian descent. This is the approach taken, for example, by Bezalel Bar-Kochva, *The Seleucid Army: Organization and Tactics in the Great Campaigns*, Cambridge Classical Studies (Cambridge: Cambridge University Press, 1976), 35, 221–22 nn. 77–78. On the one hand, it is clear that Syncellus' source for his report about Alexander Jannaeus and his conquests is not dependent on Josephus, and that it helpfully specifies which Gadara was conquered; see Heinrich Gelzer, *Sextus Julius Africanus und die byzantinische Chronographie* (2 vols.; Leipzig: Hinrich, 1898; repr. New York: Burt Franklin, 1967), 1:256–58, and for Syncellus' use of his sources, see William Adler, *Time Immemorial: Archaic History and Its Sources in Christian Chronography from Julius Africanus to George Syncellus*, Dumbarton Oaks Studies 26 (Washington: Dumbarton Oaks, 1989), esp. 132–234. On the other hand, there is no archaeological evidence to connect Gadara to "the first Macedonians" (see Strabo 16.2.10, with regard to the founding of Pella). Consequently, as Hoffmann, "Topographie und Stadtgeschichte," 100, notes, the question whether Gadara had a Macedonian foundation still can not be answered.

In the absence of supporting archaeological evidence, it is best to follow those scholars who attribute the Hellenistic settlement at Gadara to the Ptolemies. They include A. Negev, "Gadara," in *The Princeton Encyclopedia of Classical Sites*, ed. R. Stillwell (Princeton: Princeton University Press, 1976), 341; Shami, "Umm Qeis," 211; Mershen and Knauf, "From *Gadar* to *Umm Qais*," 130; and Esti Dvorjetski, "Nautical Symbols on the Gadara Coins and their Link to the Thermae of the Three Graces at Hammat-Gader," *Mediterranean Historical Review* 9 (1994): 100–11, esp. 100.

[32] For these and other characteristic features of Ptolemaic urban forms, see Asem N. Barghouti, "Urbanization of Palestine and Jordan in Hellenistic and Roman Times," in *Studies in the History and Archaeology of Jordan I*, ed. A. Hadidi (Amman: Department of Antiquities, 1982), 209–29, esp. 213.

location.[33] Archaeological evidence from the second half of the third century B.C.E. indicates that Ptolemaic Gadarenes had a remarkably high standard of living, which is suggested by a large number of fine ceramic and glass pieces imported from Egypt, Greece, and Italy. These decorated vessels, terracotta figurines, and amphora handles indicate that Ptolemaic Gadara was no mere military outpost but a city of some affluence, and they also attest both the city's strong commercial links to the Greek islands and its strategic location along the supra-regional transportation network.[34] As military stations, moreover, Gadara and other fortified towns in the region would have functioned to maintain control of the inland caravan trade routes, to secure the area against rebellion by the indigenous population, and to protect the Ptolemies' northern border against incursions by the Seleucids.[35] The last of these was the role that Gadara played in the Fourth Syrian War (219–217 B.C.E.),[36] when it was regarded as the strongest town in that district (Polybius 5.71.3).[37]

---

[33] Hoffmann, "Topographie und Stadtgeschichte," 104, suggests that the great tower under the so-called *Bait Melkawi* (a modern archaeological station) could have belonged to the Ptolemaic defense system.

[34] Hoffmann, "Topographie und Stadtgeschichte," 99 and 101, and "The Monumental Gate," 96. The strategic importance of the site for commerce is also emphasized by Jones, *Cities of the Eastern Roman Provinces*, 251: "Abila and Gadara . . . must have grown up in the Persian and Ptolemaic periods, stimulated by the development of the Indian and South Arabian trade through Petra to Damascus and the Phoenician ports."

[35] For the Ptolemaic use of colonies as a military buffer, see Victor Tcherikover, *Hellenistic Civilization and the Jews* (Philadelphia: Jewish Publication Society of America, 1959), 106; Martin Hengel, *Judaism and Hellenism: Studies in their Encounter in Palestine during the Early Hellenistic Period*, 2 vols. (Philadelphia: Fortress, 1974), 1:14; and Mershen and Knauf, "From *Gadar* to *Umm Qais*," 130. For the Ptolemies' use of both military garrisons and military settlers in Syria and Phoenicia, see Roger S. Bagnall, *The Administration of the Ptolemaic Possessions Outside Egypt*, Columbia Studies in the Classical Tradition 4 (Leiden: Brill, 1976), 14–17.

[36] For the Fourth Syrian War, see Werner Huss, *Untersuchungen zur Aussenpolitik Ptolemaios' IV.*, Münchener Beiträge zur Papyrusforschung und antiken Rechtsgeschichte 69 (Munich: Beck, 1976), 20–87, and Édouard Will, *Histoire politique du monde hellénistique (323–30 av. J.-C.)*, 2 vols., 2d ed., Annales de l'Est 30, 32 (Nancy: Presses Universitaires de Nancy, 1979–82), 2:26–44. For particular attention to the role played by Jews in this conflict, see Dov Gera, *Judaea and Mediterranean Politics 219 to 161 B.C.*, Brill's Series in Jewish Studies 8 (Leiden: Brill, 1998), 9–20.

[37] Gadara was doubtless selected by the Ptolemies because of its strategic importance both militarily and commercially, and subsequent powers continued to occupy the site for the same reasons. It overlooked both the Sea of Galilee and the Golan Heights, and during the Roman period it lay directly on the way from Tiberias via Capitolias to Bosra in the Hauran (see, for example, the Peutinger Table).

Gadara's political orbit changed briefly in 218 when it was taken by the Seleucid king Antiochus (III) the Great (ca. 242–187),[38] but the Ptolemies quickly resumed control of Gadara after Ptolemy IV Philopator defeated Antiochus at Raphia the following year in what rightly has been called "one of the two greatest battles of the Hellenistic world."[39] Gadara doubtless rejoiced at this outcome, for it was a Ptolemaic city and, like Coele Syria in general, was more attached to the Ptolemies than to the Seleucids (Polybius 5.86.7–11). Yet Gadara's reprieve and rejoicing was to be quite brief. Ptolemaic power declined dramatically toward the end of Philopator's reign, so that when he died and the child king Ptolemy V Epiphanes acceded to the throne—perhaps in 204[40]—the Ptolemaic kingdom was the weakest that it had been in more than a century.[41] Antiochus the Great took full advantage of the situation, at least as much as his circumstances permitted. Having reached an accord with Philip V of Macedon (221–179),[42] he launched the Fifth Syrian War (202–198)

Mershen and Knauf, "From *Ǧadar* to *Umm Qais*," 134, note that "the strategically important plateau of *Umm Qais*" was "a perfect spot to erect some form of military installation to monitor both the activities of the other side of the Jordan and any traffic on the road to and from Tiberias."

[38] Polybius 5.71.3. On Antiochus III, see esp. Hatto H. Schmitt, *Untersuchungen zur Geschichte Antiochos' des Grossen und seiner Zeit*, Historia Einzelschriften 6 (Wiesbaden: F. Steiner, 1964), and Susan Sherwin-White and Amélie Kuhrt, *From Samarkhand to Sardis: A New Approach to the Seleucid Empire*, Hellenistic Culture and Society 13 (Berkeley and Los Angeles: University of California Press, 1993), 188–216. For the biblical depiction of the reign of Antiochus III, see Dan 11:10–19.

[39] E. Galili, "Raphia, 217 B.C.E., Revisited," *Scripta classica israelica* 3 (1976–1977): 52–126, esp. 52, with the other great battle being the one at Ipsus in 301 B.C.E. On the battle of Raphia, see also Huss, *Aussenpolitik Ptolemaios' IV*, 55–68; and Bar-Kochva, *The Seleucid Army*, 128–41.

[40] The date of Ptolemy IV Philopator's death and especially the year when Ptolemy V Epiphanes acceded to the throne have been much debated. For 204 as the year for both Philopator's death and Epiphanes' accession, see Gera, *Judaea and Mediterranean Politics*, 20–21. For 205 as the year of Philopator's death and 204 as the date of Epiphanes' accession, see Alan Edouard Samuel, *Ptolemaic Chronology*, Münchener Beiträge zur Papyrusforschung und antiken Rechtsgeschichte 43 (Munich: Beck, 1962), 106–14. For 204 as the year of Philopator's death and 203 as the date of Ptolemy's accession, see F. W. Walbank, "The Accession of Ptolemy Epiphanes: A Problem in Chronology," *JEA* 21 (1936): 20–34.

[41] John D. Grainger, *The Roman War of Antiochos the Great*, Mnemosyne Supplements 239 (Leiden: Brill, 2002), 17.

[42] On Philip V, see F. W. Walbank, *Philip V of Macedon* (Cambridge: Cambridge University Press, 1940), and N. G. L. Hammond, G. T. Griffith, and F. W. Walbank, *A History of Macedonia*, 3 vols. (Oxford: Clarendon, 1972–88), 3:367–487. The historicity of the secret pact between Philip and Antiochus has been fiercely contested,

by invading Coele Syria.[43] He apparently took Gadara in the first phase of the war, only to lose it during the second phase.[44] But after decisively defeating the Ptolemaic forces at Panion (Panium) in 200,[45] Antiochus quickly regained control of Gadara later that year (Polybius 16.39.3; Josephus, *Ant.* 12.136) and completed his occupation of the region in 198 (when Gaza fell), thereby extending Seleucid domination to the Sinai.[46]

Antiochus and his successors colonized the Jordan region, establishing new cities and re-founding old ones,[47] giving the latter Seleucid dynastic toponyms to signify their new foundations.[48] As a consequence, "Syria was covered with Greek cities,"[49] and Gadara received

---

with R. Malcolm Errington calling it "one of the most disputed problems of hellenistic history." See his *A History of Macedonia* (Berkeley and Los Angeles: University of California Press, 1990), 291 n. 18. Some scholars accept the pact as an agreement between Antiochus and Philip to divide the Ptolemaic lands between them, whereas others dismiss it as nothing more than Rhodian propaganda designed to heighten Roman suspicions about Philip; still others grant the pact's authenticity but contend that Polybius has misconstrued its terms. See, for example, the contrasting views of Schmitt, *Untersuchungen*, 237–61, and Errington, "The Alleged Syro-Macedonian Pact and the Origins of the Second Macedonian War," *Athenaeum* 49 (1971): 336–54.

[43] On the Fifth Syrian War, see Will, *Histoire politique du monde hellénistique*, 2:118–21. The inception of this war is usually dated to 202, but Gera, *Judaea and Mediterranean Politics*, 22–23, argues strongly for 201.

[44] Gera, *Judaea and Mediterranean Politics*, 24.

[45] It was likely the victory at Panion—the decisive battle of the war—that prompted Antiochus to lay claim to the title "Great King," i.e., the king of Asia; see John Ma, *Antiochos III and the Cities of Western Asia Minor* (New York: Oxford University Press, 1999), 73, 272–76. On the Battle of Panion, see Bar-Kochva, *The Seleucid Army*, 146–57.

[46] For a recent modern discussion of key events and negotiations during this period (202–198) of Antiochus' reign, see Grainger, *Roman War*, 15–29. On the support that Antiochus received from Ptolemy, the son of Thraseas, see Dov Gera, "Ptolemy Son of Thraseas and The Fifth Syrian War," *Ancient Society* 18 (1987): 63–73, and *Judaea and Mediterranean Politics*, 28–34. Antiochus' actions in regard to Gadara are noted by Edwyn Robert Bevan, *The House of Seleucus*, 2 vols. (London: E. Arnold, 1902), 1:317; 2:37; and Pierre Jouguet, *Macedonian Imperialism and the Hellenization of the East* (London: Kegan Paul, Trench, Trubner; New York: Knopf, 1928), 228.

[47] See, in general, Getzel M. Cohen, *The Seleucid Colonies: Studies in Founding, Administration and Organization*, Historia Einzelschriften 30 (Wiesbaden: Steiner, 1978).

[48] See esp. Edmond Frézouls, "Fondations et refondations dans l'Orient syrien: Problèmes d'identification et interpretation," in *Géographie historique au Proche-Orient (Syrie, Phénicie, Arabie, grecques, romaines, byzantines)*, ed. P.-L. Gatier, B. Helly, and Jean-Paul Rey-Coquais, Notes et monographies techniques 23 (Paris: Centre National de la Recherche Scientifique, 1988), 11–31, esp. 117–19.

[49] Jouguet, *Macedonian Imperialism*, 367.

the toponyms Seleuceia and Antioch (Stephanus of Byzantium, *Ethnika*, s.v. Gadara).[50] It was during the second century B.C.E., therefore, that the largely village society of Syria began to be more urbanized, and inasmuch as urbanization and Hellenization were inextricably linked, the city of Gadara soon acquired a more pronounced Hellenistic character.[51] Once the Seleucids were in control of Gadara, the city would have begun to acquire urban forms characteristic of the Seleucids, such as a street system based on major and minor thoroughfares, with the major thoroughfare running east-west, but having no necessary relation to the fortification walls.[52] Apparently replacing the Ptolemaic fortifications with their own, the Seleucids enclosed the entire acropolis with extremely well-built walls, thus making Gadara as secure as possible against attack.[53] They may also have used the occasion to expand the size of the city.[54] Be that as it may, already in the Hellenistic period people likely built houses beyond the safety of the city walls.[55]

---

[50] The reliability of Stephanus' testimony has been debated by scholars, with some regarding it as reflecting only a late foundation legend. Others, such as Tcherikover, *Hellenistic Civilization*, 98, regard Stephanus' statement as "credible although not yet confirmed by coins." Hoffmann, "Topographie und Stadtgeschichte," 101, believes that a fragmentary building inscription dating from 86/85 B.C.E. probably confirms the historicity of the toponyms. The credibility of Stephanus' testimony is certainly supported by the actions of Jason and other Jewish Hellenizers during the reign of Antiochus IV Epiphanes (175–164 B.C.E.). They wanted Jerusalem to be renamed Antioch and a citizen list established (2 Macc 4:9, on which see Tcherikover, *Hellenistic Civilization*, 161–62, 404–9, and Hengel, *Judaism and Hellenism*, 2:184 n. 134; see also 2 Macc 4:19).

[51] Jean-Paul Rey-Coquais, "Decapolis," *ABD* 2 (1992): 116–21, esp. 118. Gadara is usually viewed as having acquired its status and concomitant rights as a *polis* during the first half of the second century, during the reign of either Antiochus III (died 187 B.C.E.) or Antiochus IV Epiphanes (175–164 B.C.E.). For a second century B.C.E. intaglio found in the vicinity of Gadara that portrays a young Seleucid prince, see Martin Henig and Mary Whiting, *Engraved Gems from Gadara in Jordan: The Sa'd Collection of Intaglios and Cameos*, Oxford University Committee for Archaeology 6 (Oxford: Oxford University Committee for Archaeology, 1987), no. 274 (description on pp. 1, 28).

[52] For characteristic features of the Seleucid urban form, see Barghouti, "Urbanization," 215. See, however, Hoffmann, "Topographie und Stadtgeschichte," 106, who suggests that Gadara had an orthogonal system of streets directed toward the gates of the city.

[53] Hoffmann, "Topographie und Stadtgeschichte," 104.

[54] Ibid., 106.

[55] Ibid. The domestic quarters found south of the city may, however, go back only to the early Roman period. See Kerner, "Umm Qais—Gadara," 409.

Inasmuch as the Seleucids used the gymnasium as their chief institution to foster social stability and transmit cultural values, one may confidently posit the presence of one in Hellenistic Gadara and affirm that it would have been central to Greek life in the city and to the luxury that the city offered.[56] The same is true for an ephebeion, with which the gymnasium usually was closely allied and which would have been particularly important for the Greek Gadarene aristocracy.[57] They certainly built sanctuaries and temples,[58] as the recent discovery of a Hellenistic monumental sanctuary in the northeast section of the acropolis hill proves.[59] This particular temple, which has three well-preserved rooms as part of its substructure, was quite likely devoted to Zeus, who was popular both in Gadara and in the area.[60] Inasmuch as the building of the temple appears to have commenced about the middle of the second century, it may well have been begun or commissioned by Antiochus IV (Theos) Epiphanes (175–164 B.C.E.),[61] who not only adopted Zeus as his patron deity

[56] On the central importance of the gymnasium in the Hellenistic East, see Cohen, *The Seleucid Colonies*, 36–37 and 87. Fergus Millar notes the existence of gymnasia at Laodicea and Daphne near Antioch, and suggests that "Poseidonius' remarks on the luxury of life in Syria (*Ath.* 210e–f = 527e–f) imply that gymnasia were common." See his "The Problem of Hellenistic Syria," in *Hellenism in the East: The Interaction of Greek and Non-Greek Civilizations from Syria to Central Asia after Alexander*, ed. A. Kuhrt and S. Sherwin-White (Berkeley and Los Angeles: University of California Press, 1987), 110–33, esp. 117. That the pre-Hasmonean Jewish Hellenizers built a gymnasium in Jerusalem (1 Macc 1:14; 2 Macc 4:9) reflects their perception of its fundamental significance for Greek culture.

[57] See esp. 2 Macc 4:9, 12 for the coherence between the two institutions in Jerusalem. For the Hellenistic ephebeion as primarily the domain of the affluent, see A. H. M. Jones, *The Greek City from Alexander to Justinian* (Oxford: Clarendon, 1940), 224, and Tcherikover, *Hellenistic Civilization*, 162.

[58] For an orientation to sanctuaries in Syria and the religious life of the region, see the essays by Javier Teixidor ("Sur quelques aspects de la vie religieuse dans la Syrie à l'époque hellénistique et romaine"), Jean-Marie Dentzer ("Le sanctuaire syrien"), and Michel Gawlikowski ("Les temples dans la Syrie à l'époque hellénistique et romaine") in *La Syrie de l'époque achéménide à l'avènement de l'Islam*, vol. 2 of *Archéologie et histoire de la Syrie*, ed. J.-M. Dentzer and W. Orthmann, Schriften zur vorderasiatischen Archäologie 1 (Saarbrücken: Saarbrücker Druckerei, 1989), 81–95 (Teixidor), 297–322 (Dentzer), and 323–46 (Gawlikowski).

[59] Adolf Hoffmann, "Ein hellenistisches Heiligtum in Gadara," *TOΠOI: Orient-Occident* 9 (1999): 795–831. See also Hoffmann, "Topographie und Stadtgeschichte," 106–12.

[60] Seleucid sanctuaries of Zeus are attested at other Decapolis cities, such as Gerasa and Scythopolis, and the propylaeum of a Roman temple to Jupiter appears to have stood on the southern side of the *decumanus maximus*.

[61] The suggestion is that of Hoffmann, "Topographie und Stadtgeschichte," 109.

and gave himself the traditional Zeus epithet of Nikephoros but also minted coins of himself with an enthroned Zeus Nikephoros on the reverse. That a marble statue of an enthroned Zeus Nikephoros was found on the temple plateau and that Gadarene imperial coins often bear an image of Zeus Nikephoros seated in a tetrastyle temple give credence to this hypothesis.[62]

It is much more difficult to posit what other features of a traditional Greek *polis* Gadara would have had during this period because of insufficient archaeological and literary evidence.[63] That it, for example, had a theater is extremely doubtful, for no theaters are attested anywhere in Hellenistic Syria.[64] That it was organized and functioned like the traditional self-governing, free Greek cities of the Aegean world is debated, with one's position on that issue dependent on inferences drawn from other Hellenistic cities and one's overall assessment of the Hellenistic *polis*.[65]

Whatever its limitations in comparison with Greek cities located elsewhere in the ancient Mediterranean world, Gadara appears to have attained a conspicuous position within Syria by the beginning of the first century B.C.E. At that point Meleager, one of its natives,

---

[62] For the statute found in 1974 on the plateau beyond the so-called "northern" theater, see Thomas Weber, "A Survey of Roman Sculpture in the Decapolis: Preliminary Report," *ADAJ* 34 (1990): 351–55, esp. 352. Photographs of the statue appear in Weber, *Umm Qais*, 36, and Hoffmann, "Topographie und Stadtgeschichte," 111. Gadarene coins from the imperial period depict temples devoted to both Zeus and Tyche. For a list of these coins, see the index in Augustus Spijkerman, *The Coins of the Decapolis and Provincia Arabia*, ed. M. Piccirillo, Studii biblici Franciscani collectio maior 25 (Jerusalem: Franciscan Printing Press, 1978), 314–15.

[63] Pausanias (10.4.1) gives government offices, a gymnasium, a theater, an agora, and fountains as the minimal features necessary to be considered a *polis*, and Gadara probably lacked a theater (see main text and next note). But Hoffmann, "Topographie und Stadtgeschichte," 101, argues that a fragmentary building inscription dating from 86/85 B.C.E. proves that Gadara had developed into a true *polis* by that date.

[64] E. Frézouls, "Recherches sur les theaters de l'Orient syrien," *Syria* 36 (1959): 202–27, and David F. Graf, "Hellenisation and the Decapolis," *ARAM* 4 (1992): 1–48, esp. 28–29, reprinted in Graf's *Rome and the Arabian Frontier: From the Nabataeans to the Saracens*, Variorum Collected Studies Series: CS594 (Aldershot: Ashgate, 1997). Gadara during the imperial Roman period had three theaters, two in the city proper and a third at Hammat Gader.

[65] The older assumption that Gadara and the other cities of the Decapolis were city-states with a constitution patterned after the Greek model is represented, among others, by Spijkerman, *Coins of the Decapolis*, 14. For a challenge to this view, see esp. Graf, "Hellenisation and the Decapolis," 6–8, 28–29, and *passim*. For a possible *bouleterien* in Roman Gadara, see Hoffmann, "Topographie und Stadtgeschichte," 120.

could unabashedly refer to it as "an Attic fatherland among Syrians" (*Anth. Pal.* 7.417).[66] By comparing it "with the Hellenic world's undisputed centre of Classical arts, culture and science,"[67] Meleager was boasting that Gadara had a similar status in Syria.[68] Some two centuries later Josephus, writing about the city during the reign of Augustus, could call it without hesitation a "Greek city" (*J.W.* 2.97; *Ant.* 17.320), undoubtedly reflecting the claims of the Gadarenes themselves.[69] At the same time, it must be stressed that Gadara during the Seleucid and early Roman periods was not a demographically homogenous colony comprised of Greeks but a city with a decidedly mixed population and culture,[70] where Greeks were statistically the minority.[71] Nor was there any program aimed at the Hellenization of the non-Greek Gadarenes. "The hellenizing that did occur was a natural process and not one actively fostered by the [Seleucid] kings."[72] That Seleucid Gadara was a culturally diverse

---

[66] Compare Meleager's claim that Homer was a Syrian (Athenaeus, *Deipn.* 4.157b). For these and other examples of pride and patriotism in regard to the Greek cities, see Joseph Geiger, "Local Patriotism in the Hellenistic Cities of Palestine," in *Greece and Rome in Eretz Israel: Collected Essays*, ed. Aryeh Kasher, U. Rappaport, and G. Fuks (Jerusalem: Yad Izhak Ben-Zvi, 1990), 141–50.

[67] Weber, *Umm Qais*, 4.

[68] Its closest cultural rival would have been nearby Hippos, which, according to Rey-Coquais, "Decapolis," 119, "was considered the most cultivated city of southern Syria" during the second century B.C.E.

[69] Geiger, "Local Patriotism," 143.

[70] *Contra* Aryeh Kasher, *Jews and Hellenistic Cities in Eretz-Israel: Relations of the Jews in Eretz-Israel with the Hellenistic Cities during the Second Temple Period (332 B.C.E.–70 C.E.)*, TSAJ 21 (Tübingen: Mohr, 1990), 25 and 45, Meleager's poetry gives no indication that Gadara had a "Phoenician colony, populated by former denizens of Tyre." Kasher's claim is an attempt to find support for his thesis that the cultural affinity between Gadara and Phoenicia resided in their shared oriental paganism, which, he argues, was in strong historical continuity with ancient Canaanite and Philistine culture. For Kasher's problematic working assumptions, see the review by Daniel J. Harrington in *JBL* 111 (1992): 137–39.

[71] Cohen, *The Seleucid Colonies*, 37, notes that "heterogeneity of population was one of the distinguishing characteristics of the great Seleucid cities," and calls attention to Appian, *Syr.* 1, where Antiochus the Great is said to have re-founded Lysimacheia with a mixed population. Nor was this phenomenon entirely new; for cosmopolitanism as a characteristic of early western Greek settlements, marked by a high "degree of integration of indigenous and intrusive populations," see Snodgrass, "The Early Western Colonies," 2. As to the minority status of Greeks in "Greek cities" such as Gadara, Graf argues that "foreign settlers of the Decapolis cities in the Hellenistic period probably numbered in the hundreds at most, and were greatly dominated by the indigenous Arameans and Arabs." See his "Hellenisation and the Decapolis," 6.

[72] Cohen, *The Seleucid Colonies*, 88. See also Tcherikover, *Hellenistic Civilization*,

city was reflected in the particular urban form that it acquired during this period. Like other Greek cities in the region,[73] it was a mix-
ture of East and West:

> Outwardly, its physical aspect corresponds to the general principles
> developed in the Mediterranean West, but its essence and nature are
> Oriental. Urban arrangements in Syria during that period exhibit in
> many ways the interaction of the various elements of which the new
> culture was composed and show the development of the tradition which
> was shaped by these elements. Consequently, any consideration of
> urban arrangements in Syria has to be looked upon as part of the
> major development of Hellenistic culture, a Hellenistic harvest, in its
> various aspects. Therefore, the point is not the "ready-made" pat-
> terns... introduced to the area, rather it is the way in which they
> were applied and adapted according to the traditional and character-
> istic elements of the Syrian town.... Here it is enough to state the
> fact that religious tendencies, manifest in all Oriental material culture
> from its beginning, reveal themselves in sharp contrast to the princi-
> ples of the Graeco-Roman life. These tendencies guided the way in
> which foreign cultural aspects were accepted in Syria, giving the whole
> a distinctive and varied style.[74]

About the same time that Meleager was extolling the Greek character of his native city, its political status as a Seleucid city changed
dramatically. The Hasmonean ruler Alexander Jannaeus (103–76
B.C.E.) took Gadara at some point during his reign, though precisely

---

159–60, who emphasizes that the Seleucids did not seek "to Hellenize their subjects" but rather "saw in the Greek element of their kingdom the strongest prop
of their rule over the indigenous populations." Assessing the degree of Hellenization
in Syria is extremely problematic, especially in contrast to the situation in Judea,
where both the resistance to and the absorption of Greek culture can be clearly
seen in diverse kinds of material. The paucity of evidence for Syria's non-Greek
culture during both the pre-Hellenistic period and the Hellenistic period makes is
extraordinarily difficult to make a similar assessment for the impact of Hellenic culture on Syria during the Ptolemaic and Seleucid periods. On this problem, see esp.
Millar, "The Problem of Hellenistic Syria," 110–33.

[73] See, in general, Jean-Baptiste Yon, "The Greco-Roman Era: Cultural Fusion
in a Hellenistic Setting, 323 B.C.–337 A.D.," in *The Levant: History and Archaeology in
the Eastern Mediterranean*, ed. O. Binst (Cologne: Könemann, 2000), 80–139.

[74] Barghouti, "Urbanization," 211, 213. According to Rey-Coquais, "Decapolis,"
119, the eastern borrowing of the Decapolis cities served both to give them "a feeling of shared culture" and conferred on them "an originality noteworthy in this
part of the Orient." For the possible identification of a temple with a propylaeum
in Roman Gadara built according to local domestic traditions rather than Classical
and Hellenistic Greek forms, see Hoffmann, "Topographie und Stadtgeschichte,"
122.

when is a matter of debate.[75] The key text in the debate is Josephus, *Ant.* 13.356, a passage in which the Jewish historian writes as follows:

> Thereupon Alexander, being rid of his fear of Ptolemy,[76] at once marched on Coele-Syria[77] and took Gadara after a siege of ten months, and also took Amathūs, the greatest stronghold of those occupied beyond the Jordan, where Thedorus, the son of Zenon, kept his best and most valuable possessions. This man fell upon the Jews unexpectedly and killed ten thousand of them, and plundered Alexander's baggage.[78]

The majority opinion is that Josephus is referring to the Gadara that is the subject of this essay, later known as Gadara of the Decapolis (Umm Qeis).[79] If this is correct, Alexander would have launched his

---

[75] Gadara's relationship with the inhabitants of Judah during the second century can only be a matter of speculation and inference, for there are no texts that explicitly refer to Gadarene-Jewish relations during that period. One may readily assume that Gadara, as a Seleucid city, was neither supportive of the Hasmonean revolt nor sympathetic to the anti-Hellenistic elements within the independent Jewish state that subsequently emerged. Kasher's claim (*Jews and Hellenistic Cities*, 80) that Judas the Maccabee and Jonathan deliberately avoided the city because of its size and hostility is possible, yet problematic. It can only be sustained by anachronistically attributing to the Gadarenes of Judas' time the antagonistic feelings of those whose city was conquered by Jannaeus more than a half century later. Similarly, we have no evidence for Gadarene relations with Jannaeus' more immediate predecessors, though one may easily imagine that they were troubled by the expansionist policies of John Hyrcanus (134–104 B.C.E.) and Aristobulus (104–103 B.C.E.). Given those policies and the previous Hasmonean incursions into Idumea, Samaria, and Galilee, the Gadarenes should not have been surprised by Jannaeus' invasion of their territory. The Hasmonean policy of territorial expansion was dictated by a number of factors, including the need to provide land for the overcrowded Judean population. On this latter point, see esp. B. Bar-Kochva, "Manpower, Economics, and Internal Strife in the Hasmonean State," in *Armées et fiscalité dans le monde antique*, Colloques nationaux du Centre National de la Recherche Scientifique 936 (Paris: Éditions du Centre National de la Recherche Scientifique, 1977), 167–96.

[76] The reference is to Ptolemy IX Soter II (= Ptolemy Lathyrus ["Chickpea"]), who, in response to an entreaty from the city of Ptolemais, had invaded Judea and fought against Alexander Jannaeus in preparation for his invasion of Egypt and war against Cleopatra III, his mother. Lathyrus was ultimately unsuccessful in this attempt to defeat his mother and eventually returned to Cyprus. The conflict ultimately led to Jannaeus and Cleopatra forming an alliance (Josephus, *Ant.* 13.324–355). For the details, see Kasher, *Jews and Hellenistic Cities*, 139–51.

[77] In the section immediately preceding the one here quoted, Josephus locates Scythopolis in Coele Syria, though it lies west of the river Jordan (*Ant.* 13.355). Gadara and Amathus, by contrast, are located to the east, "beyond the Jordan." For the three different geographical connotations of Coele Syria in the Greco-Roman period, see Marcus' note in the LCL on Josephus, *Ant.* 11.25.

[78] See also Josephus, *J.W.* 1.86.

[79] This position is taken, for example, by Schürer, *The History of the Jewish People*, 1:221 n. 10.

campaign of 101 B.C.E. in northern Transjordan, with Gadara as his first and strategically most important target. "Jannaeus with great tactical wisdom first tried to capture Gadara . . . and its vicinity, for thereby he would obtain control of the natural and secure geographical border to the north of the Gilead—the Yarmuk River."[80] "Jannaeus apparently took its considerable advantages into account and realized that its occupation might well give him the key to expansion throughout Transjordan."[81] Therefore, according to this interpretation, Jannaeus' victory in 100 B.C.E. after a siege of ten months enabled him "to detach the first link in the chain of Hellenistic cities east of the Jordan."[82] With the powerful and heavily fortified Gadara subdued, he moved next against Amathus, "the greatest stronghold of those occupied beyond the Jordan" (*Ant.* 13.356).[83] With Gadara and Amathus thus under his control, Jannaeus would have two key bases from which to carry out his expansionist agenda.

The minority view identifies the Gadara of this narrative with the city that later was the capital of Perea.[84] It was located in the same

---

[80] Aryeh Kasher, *Jews, Idumaeans, and Ancient Arabs: Relations of the Jews in Eretz-Israel with the Nations of the Frontier and the Desert during the Hellenistic and Roman Era (332 B.C.E.–70 C.E.)*, TSAJ 18 (Tübingen: Mohr, 1988), 87.

[81] Kasher, *Jews and Hellenistic Cities*, 151.

[82] Kasher, *Jews, Idumaeans, and Ancient Arabs*, 87. Kasher (p. 86) also contends that Jannaeus's policy of conquest was designed to give him a firm grip on the two international highways in the region (the King's Highway and the *Via Maris*) and thus a share in the revenue generated by those who used them. Kasher's discussion of Gadara's occupation is intended as an illustration of this policy. In *Jews and Hellenistic Cities*, 144, he argues that Gadara and Amathus controlled an important segment of the King's Highway. But the situation is not nearly as clear as Kasher depicts it. Gadara certainly had strategic importance both militarily and economically, so it is easy to see why Jannaeus would have targeted it. But the city did not lie on either the King's Highway or the *Via Maris*, though a branch of the latter did pass through the Yarmuk Valley on the opposite slope, coming within about 5 km of Gadara. The King's Highway was even further away, about 30 km to the east of Gadara (see Maxwell, "Gadara of the Decapolis," 21). There is not, to my knowledge, any evidence that suggests that Gadara and Amathus jointly controlled a segment of this highway, and it is difficult to see how Jannaeus could hope to control segments of the two international highways without simultaneously controlling other key Decapolis cities, such as Abila, Hippos, and Pella.

[83] Kasher, *Jews, Idumaeans, and Ancient Arabs*, 87 n. 128, thinks that Jannaeus' attacks on Gadara and Amathus may have been simultaneous rather than sequential, attacking the two cities in pincer fashion.

[84] Advocates of this view include Jones, *Cities of the Eastern Roman Provinces*, 255 and 455 n. 39, and E. Mary Smallwood, *The Jews under Roman Rule: From Pompey to Diocletian*, SJLA 20 (Leiden: Brill, 1976), 15 n. 38.

general area as Amathus, against which Jannaeus also took action. Militarily, according to this interpretation, Jannaeus did not divide his energies by attacking cities in two different parts of Transjordan nor ignore Pella, an important city lying between Umm Qeis and Amathus. On the contrary, he concentrated his initial efforts in Perea and later switched from the east to the west, attacking cities on the southern part of the coast. He subsequently returned to middle and southern portions of Transjordan, avenging his defeat at Amathus by razing the fortress.[85] Consequently, it was only later in Jannaeus' reign, probably between 83 and 76 (especially 83–80), that he attacked and annexed Gadara, Pella, Hippos, and other inland Greco-Syrian cities that lay close to Perea and Galilee (which already had been successfully occupied by his father Aristobulus I [104–103 B.C.E.]). Furthermore, Josephus elsewhere (*J.W.* 4.413) describes Perean Gadara as a "strong" city that might indeed have taken ten months to subjugate.[86]

Of these two viewpoints, the one held by the majority of scholars is far more likely and has been bolstered by recent archaeological excavations that show that Gadara's walls were indeed destroyed,[87] almost certainly when the city fell to Alexander Jannaeus.[88] Yet Gadara's story may be considerably more complicated than the one that Josephus narrates. Gadara's Seleucid walls appear to have been destroyed in *two* stages, not one. That raises the possibility that the city walls were only partly destroyed when Jannaeus took the city, and that some years later, after the Gadarenes temporarily retook

---

[85] Josephus, *J.W.* 1.87–89; *Ant.* 13.357–374. Whether Josephus depicts Jannaeus as militarily involved in northern Transjordan during the early period of his reign depends in part on the interpretation of *J.W.* 1.90 and *Ant.* 13.375, where a conflict with the Nabataean king Obodas I (ca. 96–ca. 87 B.C.E.) is narrated. For a discussion and an affirmative answer, see Kasher, *Jews, Idumaeans, and Ancient Arabs*, 90–95.

[86] If the "Gadara" in Josephus, *J.W.* 1.170 and *Ant.* 14.91 is a reference to the city in Perea, this would be another instance of Josephus mentioning Amathus and Perean Gadara together. But most scholars identify this Gadara with Gazara (Gezer).

[87] For a comprehensive report on Gadara's walls, see Adolf Hoffmann, "Die Stadtmauern der hellenistisch-römischen Dekapolisstadt Gadara: Zusammenfassender Bericht über die seit 1991 durchgeführten Ausgrabungen und Untersuchungen," *Archäologischer Anzeiger* (2000): 175–233. See also his "Topographie und Stadtgeschichte," 103–5.

[88] Some scholars, such as Ya'akov Meshorer, *City-Coins of Eretz-Israel and the Decapolis in the Roman Period* (Jerusalem: The Israel Museum, 1985), 80, claim that the city was destroyed during the Jewish civil war between Hyrcanus II and Aristobulus II (67–63 B.C.E.), but I know of no evidence in support of this view.

the city and attempted to repair the walls, Jannaeus reclaimed the city and destroyed the walls completely. That is speculation,[89] but it would explain the archaeological evidence, and Jannaeus' defeat at the hands of the Nabataean king Obodas I (ca. 96–ca. 85 B.C.E.), perhaps near Hippos, and his subsequent withdrawal to Jerusalem would provide a suitable occasion for the Gadarenes to regain control of their city (*J.W.* 1.90; *Ant.* 13.375). If this hypothesis is correct, it would mean that Jannaeus' occupation of Gadara was not unlike that of Amathus, which he initially took, then lost, and finally razed to the ground (*J.W.* 1.86–89; *Ant.* 13.356, 374).

Because Gadara has not yet been fully excavated, it is impossible to calculate the extent of the damage that the city suffered at this point in time. Scholarly opinion on this issue varies, with some taking a minimalist view and others viewing the damage as constituting total devastation. According to the minimalist standpoint, most of the damage was restricted to the city walls, against which siegeworks had been employed (*Ant.* 13.356). The only other structures likely damaged or destroyed would have been the city's pagan temples.[90] Yet Josephus' language implies that the damage was much more catastrophic in scope than this. He not only says that Jannaeus forcibly "seized" (κρατεῖ: *J.W.* 1.86) and "took" (αἱρεῖ: *Ant.* 13.356) the city but also that he "destroyed" (κατεστραμμένην: *J.W.* 1.155)[91] and "demolished" (κατασκαφεῖσαν: *Ant.* 14.75)[92] it, so much so that it subsequently had to be rebuilt (ἀνέκτισε: *Ant.* 14.75; ἀνακτίζει: *J.W.* 1.155).[93] Such language evokes the image of massive destruction, not just damage to the city's fortifications and the destruction

---

[89] The hypothesis is that of Hoffmann, "Topographie und Stadtgeschichte," 104–5.

[90] So Kasher, *Jews and Hellenistic Cities*, 153.

[91] See esp. Josephus, *J.W.* 1.199: "to rebuild (ἀνακτίσαι) the ruined (κατεστραμμένα) walls." See also Amos 9:11 v.l. and Acts 15:16 v.l.

[92] See esp. Josephus, *Ant.* 4.313: Moses prophesied that "their land would be filled with the arms of enemies, their cities razed (κατασκαφῆναι), their temple burnt," and *Ant.* 8.128: God "would also raze their city to the ground (κατασκάψειν) by the hand of their enemies." See also Acts 15:16 (quoting Amos 9:11 LXX): "After this I will return, and I will rebuild the dwelling of David, which has fallen; from its ruins (κατεσκαμμένα) I will rebuild it, and I will set it up" (NRSV). For a brief discussion of the textual issues related to Acts 15:16 and its quotation of Amos 9:11, see Metzger, *A Textual Commentary*, 379.

[93] See esp. Josephus, *J.W.* 1.165: "restoring order in the cities which had escaped devastation, and rebuilding (ἀνακτίζων) those which he found in ruins (κατεστραμμένας)."

of specific structures within the city. On the other hand, Josephus may well have been exaggerating the devastation in order to vilify Jannaeus or to glorify those would rebuild Gadara and the other severely damaged Syrian cities. Indeed, the previously mentioned second-century Hellenistic temple to Zeus, which may have been finished only shortly before Jannaeus took Gadara, appears *not* to have been destroyed during the entire Hasmonean period.[94] Therefore, the damage done to Gadara by Jannaeus did not entail total devastation of the city, though it likely did render it in need of extensive repairs and selected rebuilding.

In any case, Gadara and many other Hellenistic cities situated east of the Jordan River suffered at the hands of the Hasmoneans and remained under their control for up to three and a half decades.[95] The general situation at this time is clear. For Gadarenes and the residents of other occupied cities, it was a time of political, social, economic, intellectual, and religious oppression.

> After a hellenized town had been sieged and taken, the rich politai [citizens] were normally expropriated and their lands on the *Chora* [country] were distributed to Jewish military colonists. Subversive elements of the population were either imprisoned or sold into slavery, opponent intellectuals were expelled from the cities, and spent the years of Hasmonean dominion in exile.[96]

Again,

> We will apparently not be wrong to state that the official Hasmonaean policy concerning the conquered Hellenistic cities was expressed in the suppression of idolatry, expulsion of the hostile pagan population to whatever degree possible, abolition of Hellenistic law and enforcement of the Biblical commandments, seizure of lands and property . . ., confiscation of other property owned by citizens (houses, shops, etc.), reduction of legal status, cutting off sources of income, etc.[97]

---

[94] Hoffmann, "Topographie und Stadtgeschichte," 109.

[95] Both Josephus (*Ant.* 13.396) and George Syncellus in his *Chronicle* (pp. 558–559 Dindorf = 355.7–11 Mosshammer) give a list of cities held by Alexander Jannaeus, and Syncellus makes clear that Gadara of the Decapolis was among them, doing so by referring to the hot springs in the vicinity.

[96] Thomas Weber, "Gadarenes in Exile: Two Inscriptions from Greece Reconsidered," *ZDPV* 112 (1996): 10–17, esp. 10.

[97] Kasher, *Jews and Hellenistic Cities*, 167. See also 142, where Kasher discusses Jannaeus' policy of Judaization and focuses on four elements of that policy. He does not believe that Jannaeus or the other Hasmoneans, as a matter of policy or practice, either "flooded the slave markets with captured citizens of devastated *poleis*" or impressed "various population groups into the service of the Jews." To the extent

Meleager and Philodemus, the two best know Gadarene intellectuals from this time period, are perhaps typical in this regard. Both
lived abroad while the Hasmoneans controlled the city, Meleager
residing in Tyre and Cos, and Philodemus in Athens and Campania.[98]
Their departures from the city may or may not have been occasioned by the Hasmonean occupation of the city, but it certainly
offered no incentive for them to return.[99]

The Hasmonean occupation of Gadara was brought to an end by
the Roman general Pompey, who "liberated" the city during his
incursion into Syria in 64/63 B.C.E.[100] As a favor to his freedman
Demetrius, a native of Gadara, Pompey re-founded (ἀνέκτισε) the
ruined city.[101] None of the other ruined cities received this benefac-
tion, which gave Gadara an enormous advantage over the other

---

that it occurred, "it was most probably marginal and local in scope" (166). Possible
counter-evidence is Pompey's freedman Demetrius, who hailed from Gadara, but
we do not know under what circumstances he either became or was born a slave.
Susan Treggiari, *Roman Freedmen during the Late Republic* (Oxford: Clarendon, 1969),
246, thinks it is possible that he was a prisoner of war. On Demetrius, see below.

[98] Weber, "Gadarenes in Exile," 14.

[99] In the case of Meleager, it is almost certain that he had left Gadara for Tyre
prior to the Hasmonean occupation of the city. His snide references to Jews and
Jewish practices (*Anth. Pal.* 5.160) are limited to sterotypes and can't be related
specifically to the Hasmonean occupation of Gadara, though the latter would hardly
have made him more sympathetic. Philodemus and his family, on the other hand,
are much more likely to have been affected by the city's loss of sovereignty and
status, and this is often given as a possible reason for his departure from the city;
see, e.g., Ernest Will, "L'urbanisation de la Jordanie aux époques hellénistique et
romaine: conditions géographiques et ethniques," in *Studies in the History and Archaeology
of Jordan II*, ed. A. Hadidi (Amman: Department of Antiquities; London: Routledge
& Kegan Paul, 1985), 237–41, esp. 240 n. 19.

[100] On Pompey in Syria, see Will, *Histoire politique du monde hellénistique*, 2:505–17.
Several intaglios dating from about the time of the Roman conquest have been
found at Gadara, and some of the Italic gems found there could have arrived with
Pompey's soldiers or as a result of trade; see Henig and Whiting, *Engraved Gems*, 1,
who point out that the nearest parallels to one intaglio (no. 267) are found on
Etruscan scarabs.

[101] For Pompey's action as evidence of Demetrius' pride in his native city, see
Geiger, "Local Patriotism," 146 n. 30. Demetrius' desire to see his native city rebuilt
was not unique; the same desire is attested for Aristotle in regard to Stagira (Dio
Chrysostom, *Or.* 2.79). Demetrius may have repaid this and other favors by building a monumental stone theatre on the Campus Martius and naming it after Pompey.
Cassius Dio (*Hist.* 39.38.6) says that he had heard the (likely false) rumor that the
famous "Theater of Pompey" (*theatrum Pompei*) "was not erected by Pompey, but by
one Demetrius, a freedman of his, with the money he had gained while making
campaigns with the general. Most justly, therefore, did he give his master's name
to the structure, so that Pompey might not incur needless reproach because of the

cities in the region (Josephus, *J.W.* 1.155; *Ant.* 14.75).[102] Its changed
economic situation is reflected in some of its pre-imperial coinage,
on which cornucopias appear as symbolic of its new wealth and
abundance.[103] Furthermore, if Gabinius, the proconsul of Syria in
57–55 B.C.E., did not—as is usually assumed on the basis of *J.W.*
1.166 and *Ant.* 14.88—undertake a massive rebuilding program for
the other ruined cities, Gadara had an even greater advantage over
its sister cities during the early years of Roman rule.[104] Be that as
it may, Pompey not only rebuilt Gadara but also assigned it and
the other Greek cities of that region to the Roman province of Syria
(Josephus, *J.W.* 1.155–157; *Ant.* 14.75–76).[105] Pompey appears also
to have laid the foundation for the subsequent organization, possibly on the basis of Hellenistic or even Persian precedents, of a number of prominent cities of the region into a geographical and
administrative unit later named the Decapolis, with Gadara included
in that group.[106] The relevant cities, inasmuch as they were attached

---

fact that his freedman had collected money enough to suffice for so huge an expen-
diture" (trans. E. Cary, LCL). On Demetrius, see also Plutarch, *Pom.* 40.1–5, and
Treggiari, *Roman Freedmen*, 184–85.

[102] It is surprising that the rebuilding of the city by Pompey apparently did not
involve the rebuilding of the walls, which appear to have been totally destroyed.
According to Hoffmann, "Topographie and Stadtgeschichte," 104, the walls were
not rebuilt until the second half of the first century C.E.

[103] See coins numbered 4–7 in the catalogue given by Spijkerman, *Coins of the
Decapolis*, 128–29. The coins are dated between 47/46 and 40/39 B.C.E. Cornucopias
also appear on Gadarene coins from the early Roman period; see coins numbered
12 (Tiberius), 17 (Claudius), 20 (Claudius), 25 (Nero), and 28 (Titus).

[104] Benjamin Isaac has raised considerable doubts about Gabinius' alleged building program. See his *The Limits of Empire: The Roman Army in the East* (Oxford:
Clarendon, 1990), 336–40.

[105] On Roman Syria, see esp. Rey-Coquais, "Syrie romaine, de Pompée à Diclé-
tien," *JRS* 68 (1978): 44–73, and also his "La Syrie, de Pompée à Diocétien: histoire
politique et administrative," in *La Syrie de l'époque achéménide à l'avènement de l'Islam*,
45–61.

[106] On the Decapolis, see Hans Bietenhard, "Die syrische Dekapolis von Pompeius
bis Traian," *ANRW* 2.8 (1977): 220–61; Rey-Coquais, "Decapolis," 116–21; and
Susanne Kerner, "Die Dekapolis-Städte: Der Versuch einer Zusammenfassung," in
Gadara—Gerasa und die Dekapolis, 146–47. For the possibility of a Hellenistic pre-
cursor to the Roman organization of the region, see Will, "L'urbanisation de la
Jordanie aux époques hellénistique et romaine," 239. For the related possibility that
"Coele Syria," the term that the cities used after the annexation of Arabia in 106
C.E., is "an older administrative term for the region, designating the former Ptolemaic
territories in Syria-Palestine, and perhaps originally the Greek equivalent for the
former Achaemenid Persian satrapy of 'Across the River' ('*abar naharâ*)," see Graf,
"Hellenisation and the Decapolis," 2–3.

to Syria, were placed under the jurisdiction of the Roman legate of that province (*J.W.* 1.155; *Ant.* 14.74) and likely administered by one of the legate's subordinates.[107]

Gadara and the other cities of the region welcomed this transition to Roman rule, viewing it as the dawning of a new era. "The enthusiasm of the Decapolis cities is not hard to understand, as the new regime signaled independence from the imperialistic schemes and religious intolerance of the Hasmoneans."[108] Needless to say, it provided the occasion for some of the Gadarenes living abroad to

---

[107] Although Pompey can rightly be said to have established the Roman province of Syria (Will, *Histoire politique du monde hellénistique*, 2:508–12), no ancient source credits him with creating the Decapolis. The frequent claim that he did so (see, e.g., Will, "L'urbanisation de la Jordanie aux époques hellénistique et romaine," 238), is a highly questionable inference drawn from the widespread use of the Pompeian era on Decapolis coins minted during the time of the Roman empire. Furthermore, S. Thomas Parker, "The Decapolis Reviewed," *JBL* 94 (1975): 437–41, correctly points out that there is no evidence that the Decapolis ever functioned as a league or confederation. What united the cities was their status as Greek cities within the same geographical region, and, as such, "shared common political, cultural, commercial and security interests" (Weber, "One Hundred Years," 16). Accordingly, the term "Decapolis" is used in the ancient sources primarily, though not exclusively, to describe a geographical region. Yet the significance of Pompey's action was almost certainly more than geographical, for implicit in the cities' attachment to Syria was the establishment of some means of administering the area. By the Flavian period at the end of the first century C.E., the Decapolis was an administrative unit annexed to the province of Syria, and this is very likely to have been true from an early period. See Benjamin Isaac, "The Decapolis in Syria: A Neglected Inscription," in his *The Near East Under Roman Rule: Selected Papers*, Mnemosyne Supplements 177 (Leiden: Brill, 1998), 313–21. Graf, "Hellenisation and the Decapolis," 23–24, suggests that the governor's (στρατηγός) deputy was called a sub-strategos (ὑποστράτηγος), a term that Josephus uses for one of Gabinius' subordinates (*J.W.* 1.172; *Ant.* 14.93). But he dates the organization of the Decapolis cities into a geographical unit to the Augustan era (26) and argues that it is anachronistic to use the term for the earlier period (34). Similarly, Hoffmann, "Topographie und Stadtgeschichte," 101–2, assigns the rise of the Decapolis to the first century C.E., but he thinks of it in terms of a league of independent cities, not a geo-administrative term. In any case, the New Testament provides the earliest evidence for the use of the term "Decapolis": Mark 5:20; 7:31 and Matt 4:25.

[108] David F. Graf, "The Nabateans and the Decapolis," in *The Defence of the Roman and Byzantine East*, 2 vols., ed. P. Freeman and D. L. Kennedy, BAR International Series 297 (Oxford: Hadrian Books, 1986), 785–96, esp. 789; reprinted in Graf's *Rome and the Arabian Frontier: From the Nabataeans to the Saracens*, Variorum Collected Studies Series: CS594 (Aldershot: Ashgate, 1997). Graf (785, 792–93) suggests that one of Pompey's chief purposes in freeing the Syrian cities was military, viz., to contain the Hasmoneans and check their expansionist ambitions. See also Weber, "One Hundred Years," 16, who argues that the Decapolis cities functioned as an effective check against expansion by both the Hasmoneans and the Nabataeans.

return home and for other people to move there for the first time.[109]
In celebration of this momentous transition and the reacquisition of
at least a certain degree of municipal autonomy, Gadara and most
other Decapolis cities abandoned the Seleucid era of dating and
inaugurated a new one, hailing the beginning of the Pompeian era.[110]
Coins issued by Gadara in the year 64/63 B.C.E. are dated "year
one of Rome,"[111] and one extant coin from that year depicts the
ram of a Roman galley,[112] most likely in honor of Pompey's victories over the pirates.[113] Later, in 161 C.E. the Gadarenes apparently
honored Pompey's foundation of the city and his naval victories by
holding a *naumachia* (a simulated sea battle).[114] The Gadarenes' continuing gratitude to Pompey is also reflected in imperial era coins
that designate the city "Pompeian Gadara."[115] Yet even as Gadarenes
embraced this transition to Roman power, they steadfastly maintained their connections with Greek culture. This continuity is seen
in numerous ways, especially in the realm of religion. Local Syrian

---

[109] Kasher, *Jews and Hellenistic Cities*, 175. The experience of Gadarenes living
abroad provides one reason for the discernible foreign influence on the city's funerary art; see Weber, "Gadarenes in Exile," 14.

[110] Of these, Gadara appears to have been the only city to have received permission to mint bronze coins; so Rey-Coquais, "Decapolis," 118. On coins issued
by Gadara from 64/63 B.C.E. to 240/241 C.E., see Spijkerman, *Coins of the Decapolis*,
126–55; for those from the Roman period, see Meshorer, *City-Coins of Eretz-Israel
and the Decapolis*, 80–83, 118. Meshorer (pp. 8, 80, 83) also points out that Gadara
had one of the largest municipal mints in the region, and that during the reign of
Caracalla (212–217 C.E.) it was granted the right to mint large silver coins; for the
latter, see Alfred R. Bellinger, *The Syrian Tetradrachms of Caracalla and Macrinus*, Numismatic Studies 3 (New York: American Numismatic Society, 1940), 90–92. At the
end of Gallienus' reign (268 C.E.), however, Rome cancelled the right of Gadara
and other cities to mint coins, thus bringing to an end more than three centuries
of almost continuous minting activity by Gadara.

[111] Spijkerman, *Coins of the Decapolis*, 15 n. 17, 128–29.

[112] Ibid., 128–29.

[113] The significance of the nautical imagery is fiercely contested, but the nautical imagery on Gadara's pre-imperial coins is most likely connected with the victories of Pompey and his troops. For the view that Gadarene imperial coins with
Roman galleys also signify Pompey's victories, see Meshorer, *City-Coins of Eretz-Israel
and the Decapolis*, 82.

[114] Ibid., 82–83.

[115] Πομπηιέων Γαδαρέων, "of the people of Pompeian Gadara." See Spijkerman,
Coins of the Decapolis, 127, 300–1, and Meshorer, *City-Coins of Eretz-Israel and the
Decapolis*, 80. The only other city in the region to take the name of Pompey was
Pella; see Kent J. Rigsby, *Asylia: Territorial Inviolability in the Hellenistic World*, Hellenistic
Culture and Society 22 (Berkeley and Los Angeles: University of California Press,
1996), 533 n. 9.

deities had long since been assimilated to their Greek counterparts; for example, Gad (גד), the Semitic deity of good luck, was most likely identified with Tyche, the Greek deity of good fortune, whom the residents of Gadara (גדר) honored as the city-goddess.[116] From their perspective, the honor was apt, since fortune had smiled on them through Pompey's generosity.[117] Busts of Tyche, Herakles,[118] and Athena[119] appear on pre-imperial Gadarene coinage[120] as well as on coins minted subsequently.[121] Throughout the Decapolis cities pairs of male military gods were routinely identified with the Dioscuri.[122] Furthermore, in an inscription found on Delos that probably dates from the late Hellenistic period, a Gadarene native named Ision

---

[116] On Gad the god of luck and the common equation of him with Tyche, the goddess of fortune, see Dominique Sourdel, *Les cultes du Hauran à l'époque romaine*, Bibliothèque archéologique et historique 53 (Paris: Imprimerie Nationale; Paris: Paul Geuthner, 1952), 49–52, and S. Ribichini, "Gad," in *Dictionary of Deities and Demons (DDD)*, ed. K. van der Toorn, B. Becking, and P. W. van der Horst, 2nd ed. (Leiden: Brill; Grand Rapids: Eerdmans, 1999), 339–41. The connection between the two terms appears also in Gen 30:11, where Leah's cry of "good fortune" (בגד) at the birth of Gad is translated by the LXX as ἐν τύχῃ. On the meaning of גד as "good fortune," see also *DCH* 2 (1995): 315. For Tyche as Gadara's city-goddess, see Meshorer, *City-Coins of Eretz-Israel and the Decapolis*, 80, and Weber, "One Hundred Years," 27. A larger-than-life-sized white marble statue of the seated goddess Tyche, likely weighing about three and a half tons, was found among the seats of Gadara's western theater, which dates from the Roman period. Weber, *Umm Qais*, 36, suggests that it originally stood in a shrine dedicated to the goddess. For a brief discussion and a photograph of the statute being removed from the theater, see Thomas Weber and Adolf Hoffmann, "Gadara of the Decapolis: Preliminary Report of the 1989 Season at Umm Qeis," *ADAJ* 34 (1990): 321–42, esp. 331, 342.

[117] For the quite different Jewish connection of Gad with the realm of the demonic, see Isa 65:1 LXX and the discussion above of Matt 8:28–34.

[118] Meshorer, *City-Coins of Eretz-Israel and the Decapolis*, 80, rightly infers from Herakles' presence on Gadarene coins that he was part of the city's pantheon. On the common equation of Herakles with Melqart ("king of the city"), see Sourdel, *Les cultes du Hauran*, 33–35, and D. E. Aune, "Heracles," and S. Ribichini, "Melqart," both in *DDD*, 402–5 (Aune), 563–5 (Ribichini).

[119] As the chief *polis* divinity in Greek religion, Athena naturally played an important role in Greek cities. In Syria, she was most often equated with the pre-Islamic Arab war-goddess Allat; see Sourdel, *Les cultes du Hauran*, 69–74, and Pau Figueras, "The Roman Worship of Athena-Allat in the Decapolis and the Negev," *ARAM* 4 (1992): 173–83.

[120] Spijkerman, *Coins of the Decapolis*, 128–29.

[121] See the index in Spijkerman, *Coins of the Decapolis*, 312–15. In several cases, as Meshorer, *City-Coins of Eretz-Israel and the Decapolis*, 83, points out, "a river-god, personifying the Yarmuk River, is shown swimming at Tyche's feet."

[122] Thomas Weber, "Karawanengötter in der Dekapolis," *Damaszener Mitteilungen* 8 (1995): 203–11.

gives thanks to Artemis Sosikolonos, "Artemis, the savior of colonies."[123] The inscription may well reflect not only a Gadarene's continuing devotion to the Greek gods but also his deep gratitude that, through Pompey, Artemis had saved his native city.[124]

Gadara's political situation changed several times in the decades following its incorporation into the Roman political orbit. When Sex. Julius Caesar was governor of Syria in 47–46 B.C.E., he appointed Herod (the Great) as strategos of Coele Syria (Josephus, *J.W.* 1.213; *Ant.* 14.180).[125] Inasmuch as Gadara was part of Coele Syria, it probably became temporarily subject to Herod. In the tumultuous period that followed Julius Caesar's assassination in 44 B.C.E., Syria as a whole was dramatically affected. It was under the administration of C. Cassius Longinus from 44 until 42 B.C.E., when Cassius and Brutus were defeated at Philippi. The control of Syria at this point passed to Mark Antony, who in 41 appointed a legate for the province (Cassius Dio 48.24.3) and named Herod and his brother Phasael joint tetrarchs of Judea (*J.W.* 1.244; *Ant.* 14.326). But later that year or in 40 the Parthians launched an invasion of Syria and conquered it (Cassius Dio 48.24.7–26.4), thereby gaining control of most of the province (Livy, *Epit.* 127). At this point Gadara and the other cities of the region would have been under Parthian control or at least threatened by that prospect. Herod fled to Rome, where, with the backing of both Antony and Octavian, the Senate declared him king of Judea in 40 (*J.W.* 1.282–285; *Ant.* 14.381–393). By 37 Herod had won his kingdom, having defeated the Hasmonean king Antigonus II, who had gained the throne as a Parthian protégé. But as long

---

[123] *Inscriptions de Délos* no. 2377, on which see Weber, "Gadarenes in Exile," 12–13.

[124] Marble fragments depicting Ephesian Artemis have been found in Gadara's so-called rectangular "nymphaeum"; see Weber, "One Hundred Years," 20, and Weber and Hoffmann, "Preliminary Report of the 1989 Season," 323. For a photograph of the statuette, see Weber, "Survey of Roman Sculpture," 354. On Artemis in Syria, see Sourdel, *Les cultes du Hauran*, 42, and at Gerasa, the essay by Roberto Parapetti, "Gerasa und das Artemis-Heiligtum," in *Gadara—Gerasa und die Dekapolis*, 23–35. On Artemis Ephesia, see Robert Fleischer, *Artemis von Ephesos und verwandte Kultstatuen aus Anatolien und Syrien*, EPRO 35 (Leiden: Brill, 1973), and G. Mussies, "Artemis," in *DDD* 91–97, esp. 93–96.

[125] On Sex. Julius Caesar, see Schürer, *The History of the Jewish People*, 1:248. Herod's father Antipater had previously appointed him strategos of Galilee, so Sex. Julius Caesar's appointment functioned to expand the area under Herod's control (Josephus, *J.W.* 1.203; *Ant.* 14.158).

as Antony was enamored of Cleopatra, Herod could have no hope
of regaining Gadara. Indeed, since Cleopatra sought to use her
influence over Antony to expand her kingdom, Herod was fortunate
in being able to retain Judea. As the powerbroker in the east, Antony
controlled the fate of Syria, though he did give Cleopatra a part of
Coele Syria (*Ant.* 15.79).

That situation changed in September of 31, when Octavian defeated
Antony and Cleopatra at Actium and became the new power-broker.[126]
Herod, who already had switched his allegiance from Antony to
Octavian (Plutarch, *Ant.* 71.1), wasted no time in acting: the following spring he went to see Octavian at Rhodes and was confirmed
by him as king (*J.W.* 1.386–393; *Ant.* 15.183–197). In the autumn
of that same year he once again visited Octavian, this time in Egypt,
and on this trip he finally succeeded in regaining Gadara as well as
a number of other cities (*J.W.* 1.396; *Ant.* 15.217). According to
Josephus, Herod obtained Gadara and the other cities as a result of
his hospitality to and friendship with Augustus, who recognized that
Herod's realm was insufficient and wished to enlarge its extent.[127] In
gratitude for the gift of Gadara and likely with Augustus' permission, Herod issued Gadarene coins in 30 B.C.E. with Augustus' portrait.[128] That city coins rarely bore Augustus' portrait is indicative of
Herod's appreciation for the acquisition of the city.[129]

---

[126] For the Roman Near East from the Battle of Actium to the death of Constantine,
see esp. Fergus Millar, *The Roman Near East, 31 B.C.–A.D. 337* (Cambridge: Harvard
University Press, 1993).

[127] For Herod's hospitality to Augustus and his soldiers and their recognition of
the limited extent of Herod's realm, see Josephus, *J.W.* 1.394–396. On Herod's
speaking to Augustus with frankness (παρρησία) as a sign of their friendship, see
Josephus, *Ant.* 15.217. For the role of hospitality in friendship and the connections
between frank speech and friendship, see John T. Fitzgerald, "Hospitality," in
Dictionary of New Testament Background, ed. C. Evans and S. Porter (Downers Grove:
InterVarsity, 2000), 522–25, and John T. Fitzgerald, ed., *Friendship, Flattery, and
Frankness of Speech: Studies on Friendship in the New Testament World*, NovTSup 82 (Leiden:
Brill, 1996). For the suggestion that Augustus' action in awarding Gadara to Herod
was a reward for his support at Pelusium, see Hoffmann, "Topographie und
Stadtgeschichte," 102; for the argument that it was a punitive measure taken against
Gadara on account of its perceived previous loyalty to Cleopatra, see Kasher, *Jews
and Hellenistic Cities*, 194.

[128] For the coins, see Spijkerman, *Coins of the Decapolis*, 130–31.

[129] Meshorer, *City-Coins of Eretz-Israel and the Decapolis*, 80: "From Augustus onwards,
imperial coins were struck in Gadara, including coins bearing his portrait, a feature uncommon on city-coins."

Most Gadarenes, however, were not thrilled with Herod's rule and subsequently sought relief, complaining about his tyrannical decrees, accusing him of violence and plunder, and charging him with razing their temples (*Ant.* 15.351, 354–358).[130] These were serious charges, especially the accusation that Herod had razed (κατασκαφὰς) Gadarene temples (*Ant.* 15.357). In making this charge, the Gadarenes were not only charging Herod with religious crimes but were probably also accusing Herod of showing contempt for Rome by violating its decree that Gadara was inviolable.[131] Despite the severity of these charges, Augustus viewed them as unfounded, acquitted Herod, and thus refused the city's petition to restore it to the province of Syria (*Ant.* 15.359). As a result, Gadara remained under Herod's control for the remainder of his reign.[132] When he died, the city once again asked to be annexed to Syria, and on this occasion it was finally successful (*J.W.* 2.97; *Ant.* 17.320).[133] To celebrate their regained freedom, the Gadarenes may have erected a new temple in gratitude to one of their gods.[134]

Consequently, Gadara belonged to the Roman province of Syria throughout the first century. Like the other Decapolis cities, it was

---

[130] According to Rey-Coquais, "La Syrie, de Pompée à Dioclétien," 50–51, the Gadarenes lost their municipal autonomy when they were given to Herod. Kasher, *Jews and Hellenistic Cities*, 195, thinks that their autonomy and sovereignty were only seriously curtailed, not forfeited entirely. Jones, *Cities of the Eastern Roman Provinces*, 271, infers from the Gadarenes' complaints against Herod that "the city enjoyed local self-government" and had not been assimilated to the general administrative structure of Herod's kingdom. In any case, Gadara's desire to escape Herodian rule indicates that it did not enjoy a privileged position vis-à-vis other sectors of Herod's kingdom; for this point, see Jack Pastor, "Herod, King of Jews and Gentiles: Economic Policy as a Measure of Evenhandedness," in *Jews and Gentiles in the Holy Land in the Days of the Second Temple, the Mishnah and the Talmud*, ed. M. Mor, A. Oppenheimer, J. Pastor, and D. R. Schwartz (Jerusalem: Yad Ben-Zvi Press, 2003), 152–64, esp. 161. On the Gadarenes' attempts to extricate themselves from Herod's control, see Kasher, *Jews, Idumaeans, and Ancient Arabs*, 157–60, and *Jews and Hellenistic Cities*, 195–97.

[131] See below. It is uncertain when Rome granted Gadara the status of inviolability, but the city's accusation against Herod would have had particular political poignancy if it already had achieved this status.

[132] Herod may have minted Gadarene coins in 20 B.C.E. depicting Augustus, doing so in gratitude for allowing Herod to retain Gadara. For this possibility, see Schürer, *The History of the Jewish People* 2:134 n. 249.

[133] See Smallwood, *The Jews under Roman Rule*, 105–10, and Kasher, *Jews and Hellenistic Cities*, 217–18.

[134] See Hoffmann, "Topographie und Stadtgeschichte," 108, who points to a recently discovered extra-mural temple located to the east of the city that was built about the beginning of the first century C.E.

apparently administered by an equestrian officer appointed by the legate of Syria.[135] At some point, either early in the first century C.E. or, as is much more likely, already during the first century B.C.E., Rome declared the city of Gadara "sacred (ἱερά) and inviolable (ἄσυλος)."[136] In making this declaration, Rome may well have been confirming a status granted the city by the Seleucids.[137] There has been much debate about the precise meaning and implications of such declarations of territorial inviolability in the Greco-Roman period, but it was most likely an honorific term designed to add prestige to a city and, above all, to its tutelary god.[138] Extant Gadarene coins from the second and third centuries C.E. bear these civic titles as well as that of "autonomous," another largely honorific title of even greater distinction.[139] Inasmuch as, with one exception, "the titles of inviolability always accompany an image of Zeus Nicephorus

---

[135] This was certainly true during the Flavian period, as *IGRom* 1.824 proves. On this inscription see Isaac, "The Decapolis in Syria," 313–17.

[136] Inasmuch as cities and their territories were typically declared inviolable when temples were located inside the city, this was quite likely the case at Gadara. For this general rule, first recognized by Louis Robert, see Rigsby, *Asylia*, 20. Rigbsy (532, 534) surmises that Gadara was the first of the Decapolis cities to be granted the status of inviolability, and he speculates that the status may date back to the time of Pompey or Gabinius. It was certainly granted this status prior to 22–23 C.E., when Rome became alarmed about the potential implications of this practice (2–4, 580–86).

[137] Some have seen in Meleager's (*Anth. Pal.* 7.419) reference to "Gadara's sacred soil" (ἱερὰ χθών) and to Tyre as "holy" (7.418) their status as "sacred and inviolable cities" during the Seleucid period (see, for example, Hengel, *Judaism and Hellenism*, 2:57 n. 209, in regard to Tyre). But this is the emotive language of poetry, "applied to cities by poets and orators from Homer . . . to the end of antiquity," and has nothing to do with Tyre's inviolable status, which is attested as early as 141/140 B.C.E. See Rigsby, *Asylia*, 8, 21, 533 n. 6. Consequently, there is no solid evidence to support my conjecture that Gadara first acquired this status during the Seleucid period. On the other hand, it is clear that the Seleucids, in fierce competition with rival monarchs for the allegiance of cities, did grant a large number of cities the status of inviolability. In Syria and Phoenicia they began to bestow this honor soon after 145 B.C.E., with this practice "accelerating toward the end of the second century B.C." (Rigsby, *Asylia*, 27). Given this situation, it would be remarkable if Gadara did not attain this honor. In any case, Gadara's inviolable status is certainly not Ptolemaic; the first known Ptolemaic declaration of inviolability is from 96 B.C.E. (Rigsby, *Asylia*, 21), by which time Gadara was in Hasmonean hands.

[138] Rigsby, *Asylia*, 14: "these declarations were first and foremost a religious gesture, increasing the honor of the god." For honor as the fundamental intention of the practice, see pp. 22–25.

[139] For "autonomous" as an honorific term reflecting privileged status rather than true political independence, see Graf, "Hellenisation and the Decapolis," 9. For its greater import than "sacred and inviolable," see Rigsby, *Asylia*, 28. Inasmuch as

seated in a tetrastyle temple," Rome's declaration of Gadara's inviolability likely functioned to extol Zeus, whose cult was highly prominent in this region.[140] Although the granting of this status to a city
was essentially honorific, Rome expected its decrees to be respected,
and any violation could be viewed seriously, not only as an affront
to Roman honor but also as a threat to the *pax Romana*.

The Roman peace was shattered in 66 C.E. by the outbreak of
the first Roman-Jewish War.[141] Gadara's inviolable status did not
exempt it from attack, and it is quite possible, indeed likely, that
Gadara was one of the Syrian cities whose unprovoked aggression
against Jews was a contributing factor in the outbreak of the war.[142]
In any case, the city was adversely affected when Jews from Tiberias,
responding to the savage massacre of the Jewish population of
Caesarea, attacked Gadara and other Hellenistic cities in Syria, burning the villages within their territories (*J.W.* 2.457–460; *Life* 42, 341,
410). Without walls to protect the city, Gadara was vulnerable, and
one likely casualty was the Hellenistic sanctuary of Zeus Nikephoros,
which on archaeological grounds appears to have been destroyed
about this time.[143] The Gadarenes and inhabitants of the other cities
responded predictably. In hatred and fear they slaughtered some of
the Jews in their midst—including some, such as infants, who posed
no threat to their own safety—and plundered their property, and
arrested other Jews whose only crime was that they sought to remain

---

Tyche "was a characteristic symbol of autonomous aspirations," a certain degree
of autonomy for Gadara may be evidenced by its frequent use of Tyche on its
coins (Hoffmann, "Topographie und Stadtgeschichte," 101). Gadarene coins as early
as 47/46 depict Tyche; see Spijkerman, *The Coins of the Decapolis*, 128–29.

[140] Rigsby, *Asylia*, 534. Among other Zeus sanctuaries, the one at Gerasa was
especially impressive; see J. Seigne, "Recherches sur le sanctuaire de Zeus à Jérash,"
in *Jerash Archaeological Project*, ed. F. Zayadine, 2 vols. (vol. 1: Amman: Department
of Antiquities; vol. 2: Paris: Librairie Orientaliste Paul Geuthner; 1986–89), 1:29–59.

[141] For Josephus' contradictory discussion of the hostilities between Jews and the
residents of Syria both prior to and at the beginning of the first Roman-Jewish
War, see Kasher, *Jews and Hellenistic Cities*, 268–87. For Gadara, see pp. 269–70,
276–77.

[142] See Josephus, *Life* 25: "The inhabitants of the surrounding cities of Syria proceeded to lay hands on and kill, with their wives and children, the Jewish residents
among them, without the slightest ground of complaint; for they had neither entertained any idea of revolt from Rome nor harboured any enmity or designs against
the Syrians." See also *J.W.* 2.461, where Josephus refers to previous acts of violence against Jews being done out of hatred rather than self-defense.

[143] Hoffmann, "Topographie und Stadtgeschichte," 109, 111.

politically neutral during the conflict (*J.W.* 2.461–465).[144] According to Josephus, "the people of Hippos and Gadara made away with the more daring of their enemies and kept the timid folk in custody" (*J.W.* 2.478). Nor, according to Josephus, were the city's reprisals restricted to Gadarene Jews. Alone of the Decapolis cities, Gadara joined forces with Gabara, Sogane, and Tyre to attack the Galilean city of Gischala.[145] The Gadarenes and their allies "mustered a large force, stormed and took Gischala, burnt and razed it to the ground, and returned to their homes" (*Life* 44). Their attack radicalized John of Gischala, turning him into one of the fiercest opponents of Rome and causing him to launch a counter-attack against the Gadarenes and their allies (*Life* 45).[146]

Given these conditions in Gadara, its Jewish inhabitants doubtless left the city if they were at all able to do so. Fleeing especially to Galilee, some of these Gadarene Jews and refugees from the other Decapolis cities joined in the war against Rome.[147] Of these, some were certainly killed whereas others were captured and brought before Vespasian, who had received complaints about the attack on Gadara's villages as soon as he had arrived in Ptolemais and begun planning Rome's attack on Galilee (*Life* 410).[148] Leniency was not deemed an

---

[144] Josephus depicts these atrocities as Syrian reprisals for the attacks by the Jews of Tiberias and their ringleader Justus. The Jewish attack on the Syrian villages not only changed the motive for attacking Jews but also enlarged its scope. What had previously been done by the Syrians out of pure hatred for the Jews was now done out of fear of attack, with even the very mildest among the Syrians taking part in the massacre of Jews (*J.W.* 2.461, 464). This depiction of events functions in part to castigate Justus—one of Josephus' adversaries—by showing that his rash actions had increased Jewish suffering (*Life* 40–41).

[145] Rey-Coquais, "Decapolis," 119, calls attention to the fact that "Gadara was the only city to organize an expedition against the Jews; the other Greek cities of the region do not seem to have sent any contingent."

[146] The story of Gadara's participation in this attack may well be wrong, the result of scribes confusing the Syrian city with another city that had a similar name. This possibility is strengthened by the fact that the names of Sogane and Tyre are not given in the manuscripts but are emendations of an obviously corrupt text. Furthermore, because Josephus does not supply here a motive for Gadara's participation in this attack, it is difficult to fathom why the Gadarenes would attack a Galilean city so far removed from their own area. For similar doubts, see Shaye J. D. Cohen, *Josephus in Galilee and Rome: His Vita and Development as a Historian*, Columbia Studies in the Classical Tradition 8 (Leiden: Brill, 1979), 4 n. 6.

[147] For the role of these Jewish refugees in radicalizing the town of Tarichaeae, see Kasher, *Jews and Hellenistic Cities*, 270–71.

[148] For Vespasian's arrival in Ptolemais and reception of a delegation from Sepphoris, see *J.W.* 3.29–34.

option. Vespasian had the old and unserviceable executed, the most robust of the youths sent to Corinth to work on the canal that Nero planned to dig across the isthmus, and the remainder sold as slaves (*J.W.* 3.532–542).

With the fall of Jerusalem in 70 C.E. and that of Masada a few years later, the *pax Romana* was restored to the region, and within this context Gadara enjoyed its greatest years, flourishing economically and reaching its cultural apex. It was during this post-war period of the last quarter of the first century C.E. that Gadara began a steady geographical expansion westward and the first Roman walls were erected, with gates placed where already existing paths and roads led to key regional destinations, such as Tiberias, Scythopolis, Hammat Gader, Capitolias, and Abila.[149] The next phase in its political history came in 106 C.E., when Rome established the province of Arabia and distributed the cities of the Decapolis among three different provinces. Gadara was apparently assigned to Judea (*Provincia Judaea*), though it and several of its sister Decapolis cities insisted on continuing their celebration of the imperial cult in the district of Coele Syria.[150] Furthermore, when the philhellene Roman emperor Hadrian visited the Roman East in 129–131 C.E., including the area around Gadara,[151] that visit undoubtedly provided a major new

---

[149] See Hoffmann, "Topographie und Stadtgeschichte," 112–14.

[150] For Gadara's probable assignment to Judea, see G. W. Bowersock, *Roman Arabia* (Cambridge: Harvard University Press, 1983), 91, and Hoffmann, "Topographie und Stadtgeschichte," 102. Gerasa and Philadelphia (modern Amman)—which were situated farther to the south—were definitely connected to the new Roman province of Arabia.. For the continuing affiliation of the Decapolis cities with Coele Syria and their participation in the imperial cult, see Rey-Coquais, "Philadelphie de Coelesyrie," *ADAJ* 25 (1981): 25–31, esp. 31, and "Decapolis," 120. See also Pierre-Louis Gatier, "Philadelphie et Gerasa du royaume nabatéen à la province d'Arabie," in *Géographie historique au Proche-Orient (Syrie, Phénicie, Arabie, grecques, romaines, byzantines)*, ed. P.-L. Gatier, B. Helly, and Jean-Paul Rey-Coquais, Notes et monographies techniques 23 (Paris: Centre National de la Recherche Scientifique, 1988), 159–70, esp. 164, who argues that the Greek cities, whether administratively attached to Judea (e.g., Gadara) or to Arabia (e.g., Philadelphia) continued even in the third century to recall their connection to Coele Syria. "They want to be Syrian," Gatier argues, "in spite of their attachment to other provinces; for them, it is a matter of recalling Alexander and the Seleucids, thus of being 'Greek' in the 'barbarian' provinces." Under Diocletian's reforms towards the end of the fourth century C.E., Gadara became part of *Palaestina Secunda* (Spijkerman, *Coins of the Decapolis*, 17, 42).

[151] For rabbinic evidence of Hadrian's presence at Hammat-Gader, see Dvorjetski, "Nautical Symbols on the Gadara Coins," 108, and Moshe David Herr, "The Historical Significance of the Dialogues between Jewish Sages and Roman Dignitaries,"

impetus toward Hellenization, accelerating trends and actualizing possibilities that had been present for centuries.[152] Consequently, the late first and the second century C.E. marked the "Golden Age of municipal expansion, architectural splendour, economic growth and artistic and cultural vitality," when "most of the standing Roman structures were built."[153] This naturally entailed a change in the physical layout of the city. Hellenistic Gadara was, first and foremost, a fortress, laid out according to an axial urban plan and having, like the Late Ottoman rural settlement that now covers it, a "squarish to trapezoidal layout."[154] The expanding Roman city inevitably began to look quite different from its Hellenistic predecessor, so that "the contrast between the defensive character of the Hellenistic architecture and the cultivated urban plan, which probably was adjusted to the taste and needs of the Italic citizens settled at Gadara by the Roman armed forces,"[155] became increasingly conspicuous. Many of the new buildings—and certainly the most important ones—during the Roman period were erected along the city's main street, the *decumanus maximus*. This colonnaded street was the city's civic and commercial heart, its central elongated organ to which and from which all its arteries flowed. In short, because Gadara did not build the kind of public square that characterized Roman cities in the West, its *decumanus maximus* served as its "linear forum."[156]

The city's vitality and growth during the Roman imperial period is indicated by four gates that lie on Gadara's western side, each marking a different phase in either the city's western expansion or the protective measures taken to safeguard that expanded area. The early Roman western gate was built as part of the city walls that gave Gadara renewed protection from its enemies and expanded the limits of the city approximately 1.7 kilometers to the west.[157] Further

---

in *Studies in Aggadah and Folk-Literature*, ed. J. Heinemann and D. Noy, ScrHier 22 (Jerusalem: Magnes Press, 1971), 123–50, esp. 123–24.

[152] Graf, "Hellenisation and the Decapolis," 31–33.

[153] Weber, *Umm Qais*, 8; see also his "One Hundred Years," 16. For the second and third centuries C.E. as the time when "the cities of the region attained their greatest economic development, accompanied by an unprecedented artistic flourishing which expressed itself in the fields of literature and monuments," see Spijkerman, *Coins of the Decapolis*, 17.

[154] Weber, "One Hundred Years," 17.

[155] Ibid.

[156] The phrase is that of Hoffmann, "Topographie und Stadtgeschichte," 122.

[157] Ibid., 112.

to the west a free-standing gate known today as the "Tiberias Gate"
was erected, so-called because it both resembled a structure that the
city of Tiberias erected during the first century c.e. and marked at
that time "the commencement of the road connection between Gadara
and the city of Tiberias at the western shore of the Galilean lake."[158]
Both gates likely functioned not only as welcoming centers for trav-
elers arriving at the outskirts of the city but also as border check
points and customs offices for the payment of duties on imported
goods.[159] Significantly, "both gate monuments were erected for one
and the same purpose, corresponding to each other not only by their
architectural concepts and features of detail, but also in their topographical settings."[160] The date of both gates is disputed, but the one
in Gadara most likely dates from the Flavian period, during the late
first or early second century c.e.[161] If the gate in Tiberias was built
at the same time, it would indicate that the two structures constituted a mutual building project carried out by both cities, and that
project would in turn give evidence of improved relations between
Gadara and Tiberias as well as increased trade for both cities.[162] In
any case, as an extra-mural structure, the Gadarene "Tiberias Gate"
was certainly not part of the city's defense system, though its imposing flanking towers would have signified its readiness to defend itself.[163]

A third gate was built later in the second century c.e. as part of
the city's walls. This late Roman western gate marked another stage
in the city's growth and westward expansion.[164] The "monumental

---

[158] Thomas Weber, "Gadara of the Decapolis: Tiberiade Gate, Qanawat el-
Far'oun and Bait Rusan: Achievements in Excavation and Restoration at Umm
Qais 1989–1990," in *The Near East in Antiquity*, ed. Susanne Kerner, 4 vols. (Amman:
At Kutba, 1990–94), 2:123–33, esp. 124.

[159] Ibid., 124–26. Weber notes the tax office at Capernaum (Mark 2:14) and
suggests that flanking structures on each side of the gates could have been used "as
offices or storages for customs clearance, one each for departures and arrivals."

[160] Ibid., 124.

[161] Ibid. See also Hoffmann, "Topographie und Stadtgeschichte," 114, who also
regards a Flavian date as likely.

[162] The gate located in Tiberias is usually dated to the period 18–26 c.e. (the
time of Herod Antipas) but could well be later. If it does date from the early first
century, Gadara's decision to build a matching gate would still give evidence of
improved relations between the two cities.

[163] Hoffmann, "Topographie und Stadtgeschichte," 114.

[164] For its location, see the topographical map in Weber and Hoffmann, "Preliminary
Report of the 1988 Season," 322. See also Weber, *Umm Qais*, 32, and Hoffmann,
"Monumental Gate," 102.

gate," which lies even farther to the west than the Tiberias Gate
and the late Roman western gate, was built during the late second
or early third century and marked the city's final plans in regard to
western urban expansion.[165] An extra-mural hippodrome (stadium)
that lies between the late Roman western gate and the monumental gate was part of this planned westward expansion, which likely
had already witnessed the erection of various extra-mural buildings.[166]
The monumental gate itself was probably modeled on and primarily inspired by the Hadrianic gate at Gerasa (Jerash). Unlike the latter, "a city wall in the line of the gate in Gadara was never planned,
but the towers, as *architecture parlante*, surely evoked the idea of a city
wall."[167] In short, as a reflection of the city's self-identity and as a
probative means of its public representation, the monumental gate
was designed to impress visitors who approached the city from the
Jordan Valley, announcing that they were about to enter a city of
both wealth and splendor, which by that point Gadara certainly
was.[168]

Finally, towards the end of the third or the beginning of the fourth
century, the city began the task of building walls to enclose many
of the buildings that had been erected to the west of the early Roman
walls. A new gate on the *decumanus maximus* was built as part of these
late Roman walls, and both the gate and the walls were placed
between the first western gate (which was part of the early Roman
walls) and the monumental gate. The building of these late Roman
walls and second western gate was probably occasioned by the growing threat posed by the Sassanids, who under Sapor (240–272 C.E.)
had begun making devastating incursions into Syria and had even
captured and humiliated the Roman emperor Valerian in 260. Unlike
the monumental gate and the Tiberias gate, this second gate was
designed for protection rather than propaganda.[169]

---

[165] Hoffmann, "Monumental Gate," 101, dates it "not earlier than the beginning
of the 3rd Century A.D." Weber, "Gadara of the Decapolis," 126, dates it to the
late second or early third century. See also Hoffmann's discussion in Weber and
Hoffmann, "Preliminary Report of the 1989 Season," 325, 328–31, and in "Topographie und Stadtgeschichte," 115–16.

[166] Because key parts of the hippodrome are missing, scholars debate whether it
was ever completed or fully used. See Weber, *Umm Qais*, 32–33.

[167] Hoffmann, "Monumental Gate," 100.

[168] Ibid., 100, 102–3. The gate at Tiberias had a similar propagandistic function;
see Weber, "Gadara of the Decapolis," 124.

[169] Hoffmann, "Topographie und Stadtgeschichte," 116.

It was during the Roman period, therefore, that the Hellenistic and Roman character of Gadara and other cities of the Decapolis became most prominent. That Gadara built two separate theaters during this period—a larger northen one during the early imperial period and a smaller western one during the middle imperial period—is vivid proof that the city had a lively and growing cultural life.[170] This development affected the lives of all their inhabitants and visitors, whether pagans, Jews,[171] or Christians.[172]

---

[170] On Gadara's northern and western Roman theaters, see Weber, *Umm Qais*, 20–21, and Hoffmann, "Topographie und Stadtgeschichte," 119–20.

[171] For Gadara as the site of a large Jewish community, see Meshorer, *City-Coins of Eretz-Israel and the Decapolis*, 80. For the synagogue at the hot springs near Gadara, see below.

[172] When and in what form Christianity first arrived in Gadara is unknown, but the church was firmly established there by the early fourth century. One of its deacons, Zacchaeus, was martyred in 303, and its bishop, Sabinus, took part in the Council of Nicea in 325 C.E. (Holm-Nielsen, Wagner-Lux, and Vriezen, "Gadarenes," 2:867). In the following century, Theodoros, the bishop of the Gadarene church, "was unable to sign the acts of the Ephesian Synod due to the fact that he was illiterate . . . On his behalf, the documents were ratified by the archdeacon Aitherios" (Weber, "One Hundred Years, 17). Some Gadarene Christians were buried in an underground "entrance hall," built during the first half of the fourth century C.E., that led to an older, completely intact Roman *hypogaeum* (underground mausoleum). In the Byzantine period this entrance hall, which was built with material quarried from the nearby Tiberias Gate, featured an impressive a floor mosaic. The mosaic mentions three of the interred Christians by name: Valentinianos, Eustathia, and Protogenia, with each name given on a separate line. In addition, an inscription on the lid of a lead sarcophagus found in front of a nearby *cryptoporticus* (a barrel-vaulted passageway) refers to a "Helladis the Diacon" (deaconess). See Weber, "Gadara of the Decapolis: A Summary of the 1988 Season at Umm Qeis," *ADAJ* 32 (1988): 349–52, 405, esp. 350–52; *Umm Qais*, 29–31; and "One Hundred Years," 20–25.

At least three churches have now been identified at Gadara, with a fourth church a distinct possibility. The first is a basilica with five aisles that was built over the underground mausoleum. This church, dating from the period 360–370 C.E., has now been thoroughly discussed by Mohammad al-Daire, *Die fünfschiffige Basilika in Gadara—Umm Qais, Jordanien: Studien zu frühchristlichen Sakralbauten des fünfschiffigen Typus im Orient* (Marburg: Tectum, 2001). He argues (100–34) that it was a pilgrimage church built in memory either of Jesus' exorcism of the two demoniacs who had encountered him after emerging from the tombs or of the local martyr Zacchaeus, who was very likely buried in the crypt beneath the church. On this issue see also Thomas Weber, "Wo trieb Jesus die Dämonen aus? Eine fünfschiffige Basilika frühchristlicher Zeit in Gadara," *Antike Welt* 31 (2000): 23–35. The second is a Byzantine "centralized church" (i.e., a church planned around a central point and having two axes at right angles), perhaps dating from the sixth century. It is sometimes referred to as an octagonal church because an octagonal stylobate enclosed the central part of the building. See Ute Wagner-Lux and Karel J. H. Vriezen, "A Preliminary Report on the Excavations at Gadara (Umm Qes) in Jordan from 1976

Whether Gadara ever became a Roman colony is debated but extremely doubtful. Inasmuch as Gadarene coins do not make any colonial claims, it is clear that this status had not been attained by the mid-third century C.E., when the city ceased to mint coins. A Latin inscription found at Byblos has often been understood to indicate that Gadara became a Roman colony during the reign of the emperor Valens (364–378 C.E.), but a new interpretation of that inscription, which assigns it to the first century C.E., casts significant doubt on that claim.[173] Another inscription, written in Greek but

---

to 1979," *ADAJ* 24 (1980): 157–61, 323; Weber, *Umm Qais*, 22–23; Holm-Nielsen, Wagner-Lux, and Vriezen, "Gadarenes," 2:866; and Karel J. H. Vriezen, "The Centralised Church in Umm Qais (Ancient Gadara)," *ARAM* 4 (1992): 371–86, esp. 372–75. For the terrace on which this centralized church was built, see Nicole F. Mulder and Robert Guinée, "Survey of the Terrace and Western Theatre Area in Umm Qais," *ARAM* 4 (1992): 387–406. The third church lies immediately to the southeast of the centralized church and was built as a three-aisled basilica. It appears to have been built in two phases, with the first phase dating perhaps to the later Byzantine period and the second to the middle of the seventh century. See Vriezen, "The Centralised Church in Umm Qais," 375–78, and Wagner-Lux, Vriezen, Nicole F. Mulder, and Robert L. J. J. Guinée, "Preliminary Report on the Excavations and Architectural Survey at Umm Qays (Ancient Gadara), Areas I and III (1997)," *ADAJ* 44 (2000): 425–31. Another three-aisled church, probably dating from the fifth century and located at the southwest corner of the acropolis, has now been tentatively identified. For this fourth possible church, see Hoffmann, "Topographie und Stadtgeschichte," 123–24.

After Islamic rule was established in north Jordan in the seventh century, Christians continued to live in Gadara. "A dedicaory inscription dated December 5, 662 A.D. recounts that the Umayyad Caliph Mu'awiya ordered the Christian Gadarene official John to restore the baths of Hammath for the sake of the Gadarenes." See Weber, *Umm Qais*, 11, and for the inscription itself, see Leah Di Segni, "Greek Inscriptions of the Bath-House in Hammath Gader," *ARAM* 4 (1992): 307–28, esp. 315–17.

Of the Christian gems found at Gadara, the most important is a Byzantine intaglio of the sixth or seventh century (no. 451) that depicts the story of Doubting Thomas (John 20:26–29). This glyptic predates by several centuries the earliest known (eleventh-century) illustrations of this scene but is somewhat similar in depiction to that found on a sixth-century ampulla from Jerusalem; see Henig and Whiting, *Engraved Gems*, 3 and 41.

[173] For the claim that Gadara was Roman colony during the late imperial period, see, for example, Thomas Leisten, "Gadara," in *Der Neue Pauly* 4 (1998): 729–30. This widespread opinion is based on Theodor Mommsen's restoration of a crucial line in the Byblos inscription: L(ucius) Philocalus, L. f(ilius) col(onia) Valen(tia) Gadara, "Lucius Philocalus, son of Lucius from the Valentian colony Gadara." This restoration and interpretation have been seriously challenged by Esti Dvorjetski and Rosa Last, "Gadara—Colony or Colline Tribe: Another Suggested Reading of the Byblos Inscription," *IEJ* 4 (1991): 157–62. They read: L(ucius) Philocalus, L(ucii) f(ilius) col(lina tribus) Valen(s), Gadara, "Lucius Philocalus, son of Lucius of the colline tribe of Valens, from Gadara." See also Maxwell, "Gadara of the Decapolis," 41–43, who dates the inscription to the first half of the first century C.E.

dating from the seventh century in the Umayyad period, does refer
to the city as a colony, but it does so with reference to Pompey's
liberation of the city in 64/63 B.C.E.[174] Rather than constituting evidence for Gadara as a Roman colony, it much more likely indicates
that Gadara during this period claimed to be a Macedonian colony
and interpreted Pompey's re-founding of the city "as the re-install-
ment of the Macedonian colony under Roman protection."[175]

It can safely be assumed that Greek was spoken in Gadara as
soon as it became a Hellenistic settlement, and that the language
was used for a variety of purposes. A particularly interesting example of popular poetry is provided by a Hellenistic papyrus from perhaps the first century B.C.E.; it contains a spell against fever that "is
ascribed to a 'Syrian woman' from *Gadara* and is composed in fault-
less hexameters."[176] At the same time, many of its residents doubtless were fluent or at least conversant in languages other than Greek.
Gadara, as we have seen, was a Hellenistic Syrian city, one that was
open to both western and eastern influence. Even at the level of
commerce, one may assume some facility in Greek on the part of
many of Gadara's local merchants, and, conversely, many of its native
Greek-speakers are likely to have had some acquaintance with the
other languages spoken in Gadara and elsewhere.[177]

The best example of a Gadarene knowing Semitic languages and
taking an interest in Judaism is the philosopher Abnimos. He is
depicted in Talmudic literature as knowing the Hebrew Bible well
enough to quote it from memory, to discuss it on equal terms with
Jewish rabbis, and to demand from the sages the biblical basis of

---

[174] The inscription was found embedded in a wall at the Roman baths of Hammat
Gader and is dated 662 C.E. See Judith Green and Yoram Tsafrir, "Greek Inscriptions
from Hammat Gader: A Poem by the Empress Eudocia and Two Building Inscriptions," *IEJ* 32 (1982): 77–96, esp. 94–96.

[175] Weber, "Gadarenes in Exile," 13, who also discusses an undated inscription
found on Delos (*Inscriptions de Délos* no. 2377), most likely from the late Hellenistic
period. In it a Gadarene exile gives thanks to Artemis Sosikolonos, "Artemis, the
savior of colonies," perhaps with reference to his native city. For the debate whether
Gadara was in fact a Macedonian colony, see note 31 above.

[176] Hengel, *Judaism and Hellenism*, 1:83. For the papyrus, see P. Maas, "The
Philinna Papyrus," *JHS* 62 (1942): 33–38. For an instance of the use of spells and
charms in the vicinity of Gadara, see Epiphanius, *Pan.* 30.8.10.

[177] Millar, "The Problem of Hellenistic Syria," 130, cites Plutarch, *Ant.* 41 as an
instance of a leading citizen of Antioch knowing Aramaic and perhaps Parthian.

their rulings.[178] Alhough the Talmudic Abnimos is largely a midrashic creation,[179] the depiction is grounded in the reality that some Gentiles, including those at Gadara, did take an interest in Judiasm.

Among other Gadarenes, the best candidate for knowing a number of other languages is Meleager, who may have been trilingual. In one of his autobiographical epigrams, written in the form of an epitaph, he addresses passing strangers in Syrian, Phoenician, and Greek.[180] He appears, however, to have taken little interest in Judaism.[181] Philodemus also *may* have been conversant in languages other than Greek, including Latin (from his later time in Italy)[182] and the local

---

[178] Menaham Luz, "Oenomaus and Talmudic Anecdote," *JSJ* 23 (1992): 42–80, esp. 54, 61–62, 65, 67, and 79.

[179] On Abnimos and his relation to Oenomaus, see below.

[180] *Anth. Pal.* 7.419, on which see esp. Menahem Luz, "Salam, Meleager!" *Studi italiani di filologia classica* 6 (1988): 222–31. Meleager was born in Gadara, reached manhood in Tyre, and spent his old age in Cos, where he died (*Anth. Pal.* 7.417–418). The three greetings that he uses in his sepulchral verse correspond to these three periods of his own life: "Salaam" to a Syrian (Gadara), "Naidios" (or "Audonis") to a Phoenician (Tyre), and "Chaire" to a Greek (Cos). How fluent Meleager was in the two Semitic languages is a matter of debate. Some (for example, Gilbert Murray, *The Literature of Ancient Greece*, 3d ed. [Chicago: University of Chicago Press, 1956], 394) have viewed Aramaic as his native language or have regarded the poet as at least quite conversant in it, whereas others have viewed his acquaintance with Semitic languages and culture as largely superficial. For example, Millar, "The Problem of Hellenistic Syria," 130, argues that Meleager's "epigrams are entirely Greek in spirit," and that "there is nothing in the quite extensive corpus of his poetry to show that he had deeply absorbed any non-Greek culture in his native city." In any event, Meleager's use of three languages in his epigram is not a claim to being trilingual (*contra* A. D. E. Cameron, "Meleager," *OCD*[3] [1996]: 953), but some degree of facility in all three languages is a distinct possibility. Furthermore, as Luz demonstrates, the epigram reflects a precise knowledge of Syrian (Aramaic) funerary conventions, which increases the likelihood of linguistic facility. In any case, while Meleager has a Greek name and exceptional facility in Greek, he calls himself—as well as Homer—a Syrian (*Anth. Pal.* 7.417; Athenaeus, *Deipn.* 4.157b) and proclaims his eastern origin on his epitaph. As such, he is one of a host of eastern expatriates who "were proud of their twin heritage in Hellenic and oriental culture" (Luz, "Salam," 226). On this latter point, see Millar," The Problem of Hellenistic Syria," 132.

[181] Meleager's only extant reference to Jewish practices (the observance of the Sabbath) is found in *Anth. Pal.* 5.160.

[182] David Armstrong, "The Addresses of the *Ars poetica*: Herculaneum, the Pisones and Epicurean Protreptic," *Materiali e discussioni per l'analisi de testi classici* 31 (1993): 185–230, esp. 196, infers from the discovery of a fragment of Ennius at Herculaneum that "Philodemus (unlike most Greek intellectuals of the period) was at least prepared to glance at Latin poetic texts."

Semitic tongue of Gadara,[183] but if he did, his writings apparently give no hint of that knowledge.

Many Gadarenes thought of their city as an intellectual and cultural center,[184] and they did not hesitate to make claims about it in this regard. Indeed, the epitaph of Apion of Gadara contains the patriotic boast: Γάδαρα χρηστομουσία, "Gadara, an excellent abode of learning," "the excellent dwelling-place of wisdom," "fond of the Muses," "devoted to good music."[185] The accomplishments and international fame of many of Gadara's native sons, such as Philodemus, naturally bolstered the city's reputation abroad and enhanced the sense of civic pride shared by its local residents,[186] even though almost all of these natives, including Philodemus, made their contributions

---

[183] For speculation that "Philodemus may have known Semitic languages well enough to amuse himself by reading the Aramaic and Hebrew prophecies that probably circulated in his time in both the Decapolis and in Italy," see Morton Smith, "On the History of ΑΠΟΚΑΛΥΠΤΩ and ΑΠΟΚΑΛΥΨΙΣ," in *Apocalypticism in the Mediterranean World and the Near East*, ed. D. Hellholm (Tübingen: Mohr, 1983), 9–20, esp. 13. Smith's speculation is based on the fact that Philodemus is apparently the first author to use the noun ἀποκάλυψις (in *On Vices* 22 [p. 38,15 Jensen]), and that "Gadara was both a center of Greek culture and a city where men acquainted with Greek literature might also be acquainted with the language of the Semitic world around them." But as Smith himself recognizes, Philodemus' use of the word concerns the uncovering of the head and has nothing to do with Jewish apocalyptic literature.

[184] On Gadara as an intellectual and cultural center, see Hengel, *Judaism and Hellenism*, 1:83–86, esp. 83, who argues that Gadara "acquired literary significance at a very early stage." Tcherikover, *Hellenistic Civilization*, 98, by contrast, argues that Gadara's reputation for Greek culture was particularly true for the Roman period (see also 115, for a similar judgment about the Greek cities of Palestine as a whole). Similarly, Graf, "Hellenisation and the Decapolis," 27–35, dates the emergence of Greek civic life in the Decapolis cities to the Augustan era and its flourishing to the reigns of Hadrian and the Antonines.

[185] The first translation is that given in the LSJ Supplement, 314 (s.v. χρηστομουσία); the second is that of Geiger, "Local Patriotism," 143; the third is that of Gilbert Murray in H. Porter, "A Greek Inscription from near Nazareth," *Palestine Exploration Fund* (1897): 188–89, esp. 189; the fourth is that of Rigsby, *Asylia*, 533. The noun is a *hapax legomenon* but the verb χρηστομουσέω occurs in Athenaeus, *Deipn.* 14.633b, where the context is music. Apion's point is that Gadara is a city that cultivates the fine arts, including good music, poetry, and rhetoric. For a similar judgment, see Schürer, *The History of the Jewish People*, 2:136 n. 255. On the epitaph of Apion see P. Perdrizet, "Syriaca," *RA* 35 (1899): 34–53, esp. 49–50; and Hengel, *Judaism and Hellenism*, 1:83. See also Charles Clermont-Ganneau, *Études d'archéologie orientale*, 2 vols., Bibliothèque de l'École pratique des hautes études 44, 113 (Paris: E. Bouillon, 1880–97), 2:141–43.

[186] Meleager (*apud Anth. Pal.* 7.417), for example, refers with pride to Menippus, his fellow Gadarene.

and achieved fame after leaving the city.[187] In terms of philosophy, the city was best known for its Cynics, beginning with Menippus in the third century B.C.E. and ending with Oenomaus in the second century C.E. The Jerusalem Talmud's depiction of Cynics may even be based in part on the Jewish sages' observations of Gadarene Cynics.[188] Other philosophical groups were almost certainly present in the city. The engraved gems from Gadara include a late Hellenistic bust of a philosopher as well as an early Roman portrait of Socrates.[189] That Epicureans were active in the city is a distinct possibility. There were certainly Epicureans in Syria,[190] and Menippus' attack on Epicurus as well as Oenomaus' criticisms of atomism could reflect the presence of an Epicurean tradition at Gadara.[191] In short, Philodemus' first exposure to Epicurean tenets could well have been in his native city.

By the third century C.E. the three Graces had become immensely important in Gadara.[192] Imperial tetradrachms bear their image as the emblem of the city,[193] civic coins from that period sometimes use depictions of the three Graces as a mint-mark, and a third-century C.E. ring found at Gadara features them standing in a temple, facts which suggest that their cult was widely practiced there.[194] An engraved gem from the first or second century C.E. even shows them wearing helmets,[195] possibly in honor of the Roman Tenth Legion Fretensis, which played a crucial military role in the history of both

---

[187] For Gadara's most famous native sons, see the discussion below.

[188] Menahem Luz, "A Description of the Greek Cynic in the Jerusalem Talmud," *JSJ* 20 (1989): 49–60, esp. 54. For knowledge of Gadara on the part of Jews in the Roman period, see Luz, "Oenomaus and Talmudic Anecdote," 50 n. 23, 55, 64.

[189] Henig and Whiting, *Engraved Gems*, 1, 29. The bust of the philosopher (no. 278) dates from the first century B.C.E. and the portrait of Socrates (no. 277) from either the first or the second century C.E.

[190] See esp. Wilhelm Crönert, "Die Epikureer in Syrien," *Jahreshefte des Österreichischen Archäologischen Institutes in Wien* 10 (1907): 145–52, and also W. Schmid, "Epikur," *RAC* 5 (1962): 681–819, esp. 758–61.

[191] Luz, "Oenomaus and Talmudic Anecdote," 46 n. 11.

[192] It should be recalled that the Gadarene Meleager's collection of miscellaneous essays on popular philosophical topics was entitled *Graces (Charities)*. See Athenaeus, *Deipn.* 4.157b and the introduction (which is printed without page numbers) of Peter Whigham and Peter Jay, trans., *The Poems of Meleager* (Berkeley and Los Angeles: University of California Press, 1975).

[193] Bellinger, *The Syrian Tetradrachms of Caracalla and Macrinus*, 90–92.

[194] Meshorer, *City-Coins of Eretz-Israel and the Decapolis*, 83.

[195] Henig and Whiting, *Engraved Gems*, 28 (no. 272).

Syria and Palestine and may at one point have been headquartered in Gadara.[196] Indeed, the nautical imagery that often appears on imperial Gadarene coins may reflect the legion's presence in the city and surrounding area.[197] In addition to soldiers on active duty as well as veterans during the Roman period,[198] Gadara at all times had no lack of slaves.[199]

As the Synoptic manuscript tradition of Jesus' exorcism of the Gadarene/Gerasene demoniac(s) near some tombs[200] indicates, each of the Decapolis cities was not simply an urban entity but had territory associated with it. These ten territories were apparently con-

---

[196] Dvorjetski, "Nautical Symbols on Gadara Coins," 109–10.

[197] Ibid., 105–11. Dvorjetski's article includes a comprehensive survey of the different theories in regard to nautical imagery on Gadara's coins. For these coins, see the index in Spijkerman, *Coins of the Decapolis*, 312–15.

[198] For inscriptions attesting the presence of Roman soldiers, centurions, and veterans at or from Gadara, see Isaac, *The Near East Under Roman Rule*, 196.

[199] For the Zenon papyri as evidence for the extensive slave trade in Hellenistic Syria, see Millar, "The Problem of Hellenistic Syria," 119–20. As Graf, "Hellenisation and the Decapolis," 10 n. 29, points out, two of Gadara's most famous natives were once slaves, viz., Menippus (Diogenes Laertius 6.99–101) and Theodorus (*Suda*, s.v. Theodorus). G. W. Bowersock, *Augustus and the Greek World* (Oxford: Clarendon, 1965), 35, suggests that Theodorus' parents were brought to Rome as prisoners of the Mithridatic Wars.

[200] Matthew indicates that the demoniacs encountered Jesus after emerging from the tombs where they lived (Matt 8:28; see also Mark 5:2–3, 5; Luke 8:27). There are numerous tombs and mausoleums in and around Gadara. For example, three family tombs to the east of the city have been excavated; they are the Tomb of the Germani, the Tomb of Modestus, and the Tomb of Chaireas, all of which likely date from the first century C.E.; see Weber, *Umm Qais*, 13–15. In addition, there are tombs to the east of the acropolis, and mausoleums have been found on the east, west, north, and south of the city, though the southern one appears to have been destroyed. The so-called "northern mausoleum" is located to the north of the *decumanus maximus* (Weber, *Umm Qais*, 28–29). A Greek inscription engraved on a lintel found near this mausoleum has the following epigram, in which the deceased speaks to passers-by: "To you I say, passer-by: As you are, I was; as I am you will be. Use life as a mortal!" See Fawzi Zayadine, "A Dated Greek Inscription from Gadara—Um Qeis," *ADAJ* 18 (1973): 78. There is also the previously mentioned Roman *hypogaeum*, which probably was built in the early Roman imperial period. The threshold of this underground mausoleum was originally guarded by two crouching Sphinx statuettes; see Weber, "Gadara of the Decapolis: A Summary of the 1986 and 1987 Seasons at Umm Qeis," *ADAJ* 31 [1987]: 531–33, 639–40, and *Umm Qais*, 30–31, and note 172 above. For these and other burial sites in and around Gadara, see Weber and Hoffmann, "Preliminary Report of the 1989 Season," 321–22, and Hoffmann, "Topographie und Stadtgeschichte," 114, 117–19. Finally, Epiphanius, *Pan.* 30.8.2 refers to caves near Hammat-Gader that were dug out in the rocks and which were called *polyandria*, i.e., common graves where "many men" were buried.

tiguous, forming a solid geographical block of landscape, so that one territory bordered on another and collectively formed a border to both Perea and Galilee.[201] The territory associated with the city of Gadara was famous in antiquity for three things: its fine wine, its abundant crops, and its hot mineral springs. The wine was produced in the Wadi Gadar (today known as Wādī l-ʿArab), a fertile area well suited for viticulture.[202] In terms of crop production, it rivaled some of the major agricultural centers of Italy and Africa. Varro (116–27 B.C.E.), who as the author of 150 books of *Menippean Satires* had a special interest in one of Gadara's most famous sons,[203] and who as Pompey's lieutenant had won the *corona navalis* for his heroics against the pirates, wrote a work on agriculture (*De re rustica*). In the latter he discusses the yields of certain crops such as wheat, noting that "the same seed in one district yields tenfold and in another fifteen-fold" (1.44.1). But the yield in certain places is much greater: "Around Sybaris in Italy the normal yield is said to be even a hundred to one, and a like yield is reported near Gadara in Syria, and for the district of Byzacium in Africa" (1.44.2). In short, Gadara was famous for its bumper crops, and Jesus' reference to "seed yielding a hundredfold" (Matt 13:8; Mark 4:8; Luke 8:8), if not an oblique reference to the fecundity of Gadarene land, was at least grounded in a local agricultural reality.[204]

The hot springs were those at Hammat Gader (= Hammatha = Emmatha = el-Hamme, M.R. 212232), a suburb of Gadara which was located six kilometers north of the main city and about eight kilometers southeast of Lake Tiberias.[205] The thermo-mineral baths built there during the Roman period were one of the largest such baths in the Roman world, with the excavated part of the building covering more than 6000 meters, and they had the reputation of

---

[201] Jones, *Cities of the Eastern Roman Provinces*, 259. For the Decapolis as a geographical region, see esp. Parker, "The Decapolis Reviewed," 437–41. See also the map in Kasher, *Jews and Hellenistic Cities*, 47.

[202] Mershen and Knauf, "From *Gadar* to *Umm Qais*," 131–32.

[203] See Jean-Pierre Cèbe, ed. and trans., *Varron, Satires Ménippées*, 13 vols., Collection de l'École française de Rome 9 (Paris: École française de Rome, 1972–99).

[204] For Gadara's advanced hydraulic technology that made possible field irrigation and its agricultural success, see note 206 below.

[205] For ancient references to "the hot waters of Gadara" (e.g., Strabo 16.2.45) and key modern bibliography, see Tsafrir, Di Segni, and Green, *Tabula Imperii Romani*, 138.

being inferior only to the celebrated baths at Baia in the Bay of Naples.[206] The Empress Eudocia Augusta (421–460 C.E.), the wife of Theodosius II, wrote a paean to the hot springs of Hammat Gader and to their marvelous healing power.[207] According to the scandal-monger Epiphanius of Salamis (ca. 315–403 C.E.), an annual health festival was held at the thermal waters, with men and women bathing together—a practice that he viewed as utterly diabolical.[208]

---

[206] The Roman bath-house at Hammat Gader was likely first built towards the middle of the second century C.E., but important changes were made later, especially in the fifth century. On the grand reputation of the Gadarene baths and hot springs, see Eunapius, *Vit. phil.* 459. For the site and the Roman baths, see esp. Yizhar Hirschfeld, *The Roman Baths of Hammat Gader: Final Report* (Jerusalem: Israel Exploration Society, 1997); see also Hirschfeld and Erez Cohen, "The Reconstruction of the Roman Baths at Hammat Gader," *ARAM* 4 (1992): 283–306; Hirschfeld and Michael Avi-Yonah, "Hammat Gader," in *The New Encyclopedia of Archaeological Excavations in the Holy Land*, ed. E. Stern, 4 vols. (Jerusalem: The Israel Exploration Society & Carta; New York: Simon & Schuster, 1993), 2:565–73; and Fikret Yegül, *Baths and Bathing in Classical Antiquity* (New York: Architectural History Foundation; Cambridge: MIT Press, 1992), 121–24. In addition to the baths at Hammat Gader, there were also at least two Roman baths (*thermae*) located in the lower portion of Gadara proper. The smaller of the two is known, after the donor, as the Baths of Herakleides; located about 100 meters north of the *decumanus maximus*, they date from the third century (Weber, *Umm Qais*, 28). The larger of the two is a complex located along the south side of the *decumanus maximus*, with the main building 30 × 50 m in size. These baths went through three periods. Built originally during the first half of the fourth century, the bath was a magnificent structure. "Its highly developed and efficient heating and water systems were of a high technical standard and well able to satisfy a fastidious taste. The town must have been especially prosperous to be able to build and maintain a Bath of that standard." So Svend Holm-Nielsen, Inge Nielsen, and Flemming Gorn Andersen, "The Excavation of Byzantine Baths in Umm Qeis," *ADAJ* 30 (1986): 219–32, 468–72, esp. 227. The first baths were destroyed ca. 400–450 C.E., perhaps by a fire or an earthquake. In its second phase the structure was again used as a bath, but on a smaller scale, a fact which may reflect a slight decline in economic conditions. During the third phase the building was used for residential and perhaps industrial purposes. See also Holm-Nielsen, Wagner-Lux, and Vriezen, "Gadarenes," 2:866–67, and esp. Nielsen, Andersen, and Holm-Nielsen, *Die byzantinischen Thermen*, vol. 3 of *Gadara— Umm Qēs*, Abhandlungen des Deutschen Palästinavereins 17 (Wiesbaden: Harrassowitz, 1993). For the possible existence of a third bath, see Weber, *Umm Qais*, 28. For Gadara's water system, which would have been crucial for the effective operation of the baths, see Weber, *Umm Qais*, 5, and "Gadara of the Decapolis," 127–29, and Kerner, "Umm Qais—Gadara," 409–12; "German Protestant Institute," 56–61; and "Gadara—Schwarzweisse Stadt zwischen Adjlun und Golan," 129–35.

[207] For the Eudocia inscription, see Green and Tsafrir, "Greek Inscriptions," 77–91.

[208] Epiphanius, *Pan.* 30.7.5. Epiphanius' source for this story is Joseph the *comes* (*Pan.* 30.4.1–5.8), a Jewish convert to Christianity, who told him how a licentious young Jewish patriarch in the bath deliberately rubbed his side against that of a gorgeous woman, who happened to be both married and a Christian, and how the

Because of the thermal baths and their medicinal value, the site became a therapeutic center as well as a vacation resort,[209] attracting hordes of visitors to this Syrian spa. The site was thus simultaneously sacred and secular. In classical antiquity, baths and bathing normally belonged to the secular sphere, so that those who came there to enjoy the thermal waters and fine wines of the region would have had a largely secular experience. But those who came for curative bathing and in hopes of healing would have viewed the site from a religious perspective:[210]

> Classical civilization explained the wondrous phenomenon of cold and hot springs and the magical qualities of thermal baths as manifestations of divine powers. These thermal sources and the bathing centers that grew around them were placed under the protection of nymphs and other deities of nature. For the individual who sought a cure at one of these centers, acts of homage to and worship of the nymphs and other tutelary deities of the waters were a necessary and normal part of treatment in the same manner as they were for patients who became suppliants of the god of medicine at an Aesculapium.[211]

Hammat Gader was especially popular with lepers. Antoninus of Placentia, writing in the sixth century C.E., gives the following account:

---

youth subsequently tried, without success, to seduce her, even resorting to magic (*Pan.* 30.7.5–8.10). On the phenomenon of nude mixed bathing in the Roman baths, see Roy Bowen Ward, "Women in Roman Baths," *HTR* 85 (1992): 125–47.

[209] During the Roman period a theater was erected near the baths, which enhanced the cultural and recreational appeal of the resort. Excavations have also revealed the presence of inns and private houses; see Di Segni, "Greek Inscriptions," 307.

[210] Of the approximately seventy Greek inscriptions discovered at the Roman bath-house, most use a fixed formula that underscores the importance of the *thermae* as a place of healing. The same formula is attested in both synagogues and churches of the period. See Di Segni, "Greek Inscriptions," 309.

[211] Yegül, *Baths and Bathing*, 125. The Roman baths at Hammat Gader probably contained images of Aesclepius and Sarapis; see Thomas Weber, "Thermalquellen und Heilgötter des Ostjordanlandes in römischer und byzantinischer Zeit," *Damaszener Mitteilungen* 11 (1999): 433–51. The city of Gadara had a nymphaeum that was ca. 36 meters broad and located to the north of the *decumanus maximus*; see Hoffmann, "Topographie und Stadtgeschichte," 121. Another structure, also north of the *decumanus maximus* but situated ca. 100 meters further to the west, has sometimes been identified as a second nymphaeum, but that identification is problematic. Its identity remains debated, though it may have been a monumental platform with steps ascending to an altar. See Weber, "Summary of the 1988 Season," 349–50; *Umm Qais*, 27–28; "One Hundred Years," 19–20; Weber and Hoffmann, "Preliminary Report of the 1989 Season," 323–24; and Hoffmann, "Topographie und Stadtgeschichte," 121–22.

Lepers are cleansed there and have their meals at the inn at public expense. The baths fill in the evening. In front of the basin there is a large tank. When it is full, all gates are closed, and they are sent in through a small door with lights and incense and sit in the tank all night. They fall asleep, and the person who is going to be cured sees a vision. When he has told it, the springs do not flow for a week. In one week, he is cleansed.[212]

Among those who visited Hammat Gader was the Neoplatonic philosopher Iamblichus of Chalcis in Coele Syria. The biographical tradition about Iamblichus presents him as a thaumaturge, and of the various wondrous deeds attributed to him, one is said to have taken place at the hot springs:

> Now he [Iamblichus] happened to be bathing and the others [his disciples] were bathing with him, and they were using the same insistence, whereupon Iamblichus smiled and said: "It is irreverent to the gods to give you this demonstration, but for your sakes it shall be done." There were two hot springs smaller than the others but prettier, and he bade his disciples ask the natives of the place by what names they used to be called in former times. When they had done his bidding they said: "There is no pretence about it, this spring is called Eros, and the name of the one next to it is Anteros." He at once touched the water with his hand—he happened to be sitting on the ledge of the spring where the overflow runs off—and uttering a brief summons he called forth a boy from the depth of the spring. He was white-skinned and of medium height, his locks were golden and his back and breast shone; and he exactly resembled one who was bathing or had just bathed. His disciples were overwhelmed with amazement, but Iamblichus said, "Let us go to the next spring," and he rose and led the way, with a thoughtful air. Then he went through the same performance there also, and summoned another Eros like the first in all respects, except that his hair was darker and fell loose in the sun. Both the boys embraced Iamblichus and clung to him as though he were genuinely their father. He restored them to their proper places and went away after his bath, reverenced by his pupils. After this the crowd of his disciples sought no further evidence, but believed everything from the proofs that had been revealed to them, and hung on to him as though by an unbreakable chain.[213]

---

[212] Antoninus of Placentia, *Itinerarium* 7. The translation is that of Yegül, *Baths and Bathing*, 124.

[213] Eunapius, *Vit. phil.* 459, trans. W. C. Wright, LCL. On Iamblichus, see esp. John M. Dillon, "Iamblichus of Chalcis," *ANRW* 2.36.2 (1987): 863–78; Henry J. Blumenthal and E. Gillian Clark, eds., *The Divine Iamblichus: Philosopher and Man of*

During the Roman period there appears to have been a large Jewish community that resided in the vicinity,[214] and numerous Jews flocked there to enjoy the springs, making it "the Miami Beach of its day."[215] Indeed, one part of the Roman baths appears to have been named after the prophet Elijah[216] and another part may have been nicknamed after a young Jewish patriarch.[217] The visitors to the area certainly included numerous rabbis, such as Rabbi Judah the Patriarch, who even laid down laws for traveling to and from the resort on the Sabbath.[218] In order to accommodate both the residents and the visitors to the recreational site, a synagogue was built near the thermal baths, at a prominent site about 7.5 kilometers southeast of Lake Tiberias.[219] Given the status of the hot springs as a tourist attraction, it is not surprising that some of the donations for the erection

---

Gods (Bristol: Bristol Classical Press, 1993); Gregory Shaw, *Theurgy and the Soul: The Neoplatonism of Iamblichus*, Hermeneutics: Studies in the History of Religions (University Park: Pennsylvania State University Press, 1995); and Emma C. Clarke, *Iamblichus' De Mysteriis: A Manifesto of the Miraculous* (Aldershot: Ashgate, 2001).

[214] Smallwood, *The Jews under Roman Rule*, 357, includes Gadara in a list of cities with a large Jewish minority at the time of the first Roman-Jewish war (66–70 C.E.).

[215] Hershel Shanks, *Judaism in Stone: The Archaeology of Ancient Synagogues* (New York: Harper & Row; Washington: Biblical Archaeology Society, 1979), 115. Di Segni, "Greek Inscriptions," 307, points out that many devout Jews would likely have preferred the hot springs at Hammat Gader to those near Tiberias because the numerous tombs associated with the latter created a problem for those seeking to maintain ritual purity. See Josephus, *Ant.* 18.36–38.

[216] Green and Tsafrir, "Greek Inscriptions," 88. Furthermore, as Green and Tsafrir also point out (pp. 84, 88), in the sixth century C.E. a companion of Antoninus Placentius says that the hot springs as a whole were called "the baths of Elijah" (*thermae Heliae*). In later Arabic tradition, the springs were connected instead with King Solomon, the son of David. See E. L. Sukenik, *The Ancient Synagogue of El-Hammeh (Hammath-by-Gadara): An Account of the Excavations Conducted on Behalf of the Hebrew University, Jerusalem* (Jerusalem: Rubin Mass, 1935), 22–23. To the testimonia regarding Hammat-Gader collected by Sukenik (pp. 18–23), add *SEG* 32.1502 (cited by Rigsby, *Asylia*, 533 n. 7).

[217] Ephrat Habas (Rubin), "A Poem by the Empress Eudocia: A Note on the Patriarch," *IEJ* 46 (1996): 108–19. See note 208 above.

[218] For Judah the Prince and Hammat Gader, see Sukenik, *The Ancient Synagogue of El-Hammeh*, 19, and Stuart S. Miller, "R. Hanina bar Hama at Sepphoris," in *The Galilee in Late Antiquity*, ed. L. I. Levine (New York: Jewish Theological Seminary of America, 1992), 175–200, esp. 190–91. For bibliography on Judah (R. Yehudah ha-Nasi), see H. L. Strack and G. Stemberger, *Introduction to the Talmud and Midrash*, 2d ed. (Minneapolis: Fortress, 1996), 81.

[219] The synagogue was discovered in 1932 and the results of the initial excavation were published in 1935 by Sukenik, *The Ancient Synagogue of El-Hammeh*. More recent discussions include Erwin R. Goodenough, *Jewish Symbols in the Greco-Roman*

of the synagogue were made by Jewish benefactors who resided in other localities.[220] Excavations of the synagogue conducted in 1982 revealed that the building likely had gone through three stages.[221] The first structure, probably erected during the third century C.E., was a rectangular public building, paved with a simple white mosaic floor. The mosaic floor, which had the remains of a black-and-red frame in its center, was 1.4 meters below the third stage's floor.[222] During the second stage of the synagogue's history, probably during the fourth century, the plan of the building was modified. The resulting structure was a rectangular building with a *bema* (platform), facing Jerusalem, attached to the center of the southern wall. The floor of the building was paved with flagstones (*opus sectile*). This structure was perhaps severely damaged by an earthquake during the fourth century. During the synagogue's third and final stage, which was during the fifth or sixth century, the flagstone floor was replaced with a mosaic one in the nave and aisles, and an apse was added in the southern small room of the building. Architecturally, this kind of synagogue design—a basilical type with an apse—represented an

---

Period, 13 vols., Bollingen Series 37 (New York: Pantheon Books, 1953–68), 1:239–41; Michael Avi-Yonah, "Hammat Gader," in *Encyclopedia of Archaeological Excavations in the Holy Land*, ed. M. Avi-Yonah, 4 vols. (Englewood Cliffs: Prentice-Hall, 1975–78), 2:469–73; Frowald Hüttenmeister, *Die jüdischen Synagogen, Lehrhäuser und Gerichtshöfe*, vol. 1 of *Die antiken Synagogen in Israel* by Frowald Hüttenmeister and G. Reeg, Beihefte zum Tübinger Atlas des Vorderen Orients, Reihe B, Geisteswissenschaften, 12.1 (Wiesbaden: Reichert, 1977), 152–59; Shanks, *Judaism in Stone*, esp. 115–20; Gideon Foerster, "The Ancient Synagogues of the Galilee," in *The Galilee in Late Antiquity*, 289–319, esp. 308, and "Dating Synagogues with a 'Basilical' Plan and an Apse," in *Ancient Synagogues: Historical Analysis and Archaeological Discovery*, ed. D. Urman and P. V. M. Flesher, 2 vols., StPB 47 (Leiden: Brill, 1995), 1:87–94, esp. 1:90–91; and Hirschfeld and Avi-Yonah, "Hammat Gader," 2:566–69.

[220] For the inscriptions that specify the donors, their provenance, and the amounts of their contributions, see Sukenik, *The Ancient Synagogue of El-Hammeh*, 39–57. As Lee I. Levine, *The Ancient Synagogue: The First Thousand Years* (New Haven: Yale University Press, 2000), 349, points out, the donors came from Arbel, Capernaum, Emmaus, Sepphoris, and Kefar 'Aqavia. In a similar way, other structures near the hot springs were built or restored by non-resident benefactors. See Hirschfeld and Avi-Yonah, "Hammat Gader," 2:566.

[221] Hirschfeld and Avi-Yonah, "Hammat Gader," 2:568–69. Similarly, Foerster, "Dating Synagogues," 1:90, gives three stages in the synagogue's history, but in "Ancient Synagogues," 308, he indicates that the first stage is uncertain.

[222] Hirschfeld and Avi-Yonah, "Hammat Gader," 2:568, and Foerster, "Dating Synagogues," 1:90. On the basis of *j. Qidd.* 64d, 13f., Hüttenmeister, *Die jüdischen Synagogen*, 159, suggests that a *bet ha-midrash* (House of Study) may be attested at Hammat Gader at the beginning of the third century C.E.

adaptation of church architecture, with the apse replacing the niche as the place where the Torah scrolls were kept.[223]

Relations between the residents of Gadara and those of Hammat Gader were not always cordial. The Babylonian Talmud contains the following conversation, which deals with the question why Rabbi Judah the Patriarch "permitted" the inhabitants of Gadara to go down to Hammat Gader on the Sabbath, but did not permit the latter to ascend to Gadara:

> When R. Dimi came, he explained, "The people of Geder [Gadara] would bother the people of Hametan [Hammat Gader], and 'permitted' means 'ordained.' And how come the Sabbath was distinguished from other days [that only on that day were they not permitted to make the trip]? It is because on that day there's a lot of drunkenness."
> Wouldn't the people of Geder bother them [the people of Hammat Gader] when they came there [to Hammat Gader]?
> Not at all, 'a dog that's new in town doesn't bark for seven years.'[224]
> Well, anyhow, won't the people of Hametan bother those of Geder? The latter are not such total wimps as that![225]

Philodemus was one of eight (or seven) Gadarenes who became famous in the ancient world by making important contributions to the intellectual life and literature of Greece and Rome.[226] The others were (1) Menippus the Cynic (early third century B.C.E.), whose satires were put to good use by his fellow Syrian Lucian several centuries later;[227] (2) Meleager (fl. ca. 100 B.C.E.), whose amatory epigrams

---

[223] Foerster, "Dating Synagogues," 1:89–91, and "Ancient Synagogues," 308.

[224] As Israel W. Slotki notes, R. Dimi is clearly quoting a proverb here. See the note to his translation of 'Erubin in the Soncino edition of *The Babylonian Talmud*, ed. I Epstein (London: Soncino Press, 1938), 427 n. 14.

[225] *b. 'Erub.* 61a. As Slotki, *'Erubin*, 427 n. 17, notes, the last two lines mean that the Gadarenes visiting in Hammat Gader will not initiate conflict with the local residents, but they will respond if attacked by them. The translation is a modified version of that given by Jacob Neusner, trans., *The Talmud of Babylonia: An American Translation. Volume III.C: Erubin, Chapters 5 and 6*, BJS 278 (Atlanta: Scholars Press, 1993), 45.

[226] For this emphasis, see Moses Hadas, *Hellenistic Culture: Fusion and Diffusion* (Morningside Heights, NY: Columbia University Press, 1959), 105–14, esp. 109–14, and "Gadarenes in Pagan Literature," *Classical Weekly* 25 (1931): 25–30. See also J. Geiger, "Athens in Syria: Greek Intellectuals of Gadara," *Kathedra* 35 (1985): 3–16 (in Hebrew).

[227] For the ancient tradition concerning Menippus, see esp. Diogenes Laertius 6.99–101; see also Donald R. Dudley, *A History of Cynicism: From Diogenes to the 6th Century A.D.* (London: Methuen, 1937), 69–74, and Joel C. Relihan, "Menippus the

inspired several Latin poets, including Ovid;[228] (3) Theodorus, who wrote on rhetoric, founded a rhetorical school that bore his name ("The Theodoreans"), wrote a work on Coele Syria (*FGHist* 850 T 1), and served as the emperor Tiberius' teacher (Suetonius, *Tib.* 57.1);[229] (4) Oenomaus, the second century C.E. Cynic[230] who sometimes has been suspected of being a Hellenized Jew[231] because of his

---

Cynic in the Greek Anthology," *Syllecta Classica* 1 (1989) 58–61; idem, "Menippus the Cur from Crete," *Prometheus* 16 (1990): 217–24; idem, "Menippus in Antiquity and the Renaissance," in *The Cynics: The Cynic Movement in Antiquity and Its Legacy*, ed. R. Bracht Branham and Marie-Odile Goulet-Cazé, Hellenistic Culture and Society 23 (Berkeley and Los Angeles: University of California Press, 1996), 265–93. On the relationship between Menippus and Lucian, the study of Rudolf Helm, *Lucian und Menipp* (Leipzig: Teubner, 1906) remains indispensable. For more recent treatments, see Jennifer Hall, *Lucian's Satire*, Monographs in Classical Studies (New York: Arno, 1981), esp. 64–150, and Joel C. Relihan, "Vainglorious Menippus in Lucian's *Dialogues of the Dead*," *Illinois Classical Studies* 12 (1987): 185–206, and *Ancient Menippean Satire* (Baltimore: Johns Hopkins University Press), esp. 39–48 (Menippus) and 103–18 (Lucian).

[228] Meleager, who is sometimes called "the Greek Ovid," is usually dated ca. 130–ca. 70 B.C.E. Alan Cameron, *The Greek Anthology from Meleager to Planudes* (Oxford: Clarendon, 1993), 49–56, persuasively dates Meleager's *Garland* (a collection of epigrams) to ca. 102–90 B.C.E. For a discussion of the biographical information about Meleager and the arrangement of his *Garland*, see Kathryn J. Gutzwiller, *Poetic Garlands: Hellenistic Epigrams in Context* (Hellenistic Culture and Society 28; Berkeley: University of California Press, 1998), 276–332. See also Lisa Loft Anderson Cox, "A Critical Study of the Love Poetry of Meleager of Gadara" (Ph.D. Diss., Boston University, 1988). For the epigrams themselves, see A. S. F. Gow and D. L. Page, eds., *The Greek Anthology: Hellenistic Epigrams*, 2 vols. (Cambridge: Cambridge University Press, 1965), 1:214–53 (text), 2:591–680 (commentary); Whigham and Jay, *The Poems of Meleager*, and Jerry Clack, *Meleager: The Poems* (Wauconda, IL: Bolchazy-Carducci, 1992).

[229] On Theodorus, see Martin Schanz, "Die Apollodoreer und die Theodoreer," *Hermes* 25 (1890): 36–54; Willy Stegemann, "Theodoros (39)," *RE* 5A (1934): 1847–59; G. M. A. Grube, "Theodorus of Gadara," *AJP* 80 (1959): 337–65; Bowersock, *Augustus and the Greek World*, 35–36; and George Kennedy, *The Art of Rhetoric in the Roman World, 300 B.C.–A.D. 300* (Princeton: Princeton University Press, 1972), 340–42. An inscription on the base of an Athenian statue most likely refers to him; see Eugene Vanderpool, "An Athenian Monument to Theodoros of Gadara," *AJP* 80 (1959): 366–68. For his work on Coele Syria and his attitude toward his native city, see Geiger, "Local Patriotism," 147.

[230] Oenomaus is traditionally dated to the time of Hadrian, ca. 120 C.E., though his exact date is far from certain, and some scholars have dated him to the third century. See Dudley, *History of Cynicism*, 162–70, and esp. Jürgen Hammerstaedt, "Der Kyniker Oenomaus von Gadara," *ANRW* 2.36.4 (1990): 2834–65, and "Oenomaus," in *Encyclopedia of Classical Philosophy*, 356–57.

[231] This possibility is mentioned by several scholars, including John L. Moles, "Oenomaus," *OCD³* (1996): 1062–63, and Diskin Clay, "Diogenes and His Gods," in *Epikureismus in der späten Republik und der Kaiserzeit*, ed. M. Erler, Philosophie der Antike 11 (Stuttgart: F. Steiner, 2000), 76–92, esp. 88.

fierce criticism of Greek oracles, denunciation of divination, and arguments against superstition.[232] In addition to exposing charlatans (*The Swindlers Unmasked*) and likely serving as a literary influence on his younger contemporary Lucian,[233] Oenomaus wrote a number of other works, including one *On Philosophy according to Homer*, which is somewhat similar in title to Philodemus' *On the Good King according to Homer*;[234] (5) Abnimos (Abnomos), a pagan philosopher who had a sympathetic attitude toward the Jewish community and was the friend of the second century C.E. *tanna*, R. Meir of Tiberias (ca. 135 C.E.).[235] Several anecdotes are told about him in rabbinic sources, one in which R. Abba bar Kahana, a late third century Palestinian *amora*,[236] compares the philosopher favorably to the prophet Balaam of Num 22, doing so because of the sage counsel that Abnimos gave his fellow Gentiles when they wanted to attack the Jewish people. Because

---

[232] Oenomaus' criticisms of oracles were quoted extensively by Eusebius in his *Praeparatio evangelica*. See esp. Jürgen Hammerstaedt, *Die Orakelkritik des Kynikers Oenomaus*, Athenäums Monograpfien, Altertumswissenschaft 188 (Frankfurt am Main: Athenaum, 1988). Translations of the fragments are provided by Léonce Paquet, trans., *Les Cyniques grecs: Fragments et témoignages*, 2nd ed., Collection Philosophica 35 (Ottawa: Les Presses de l'Université d'Ottawa, 1988), 239–70, and Georg Luck, trans., *Die Weisheit der Hunde: Texte der antiken Kyniker in deutscher Übersetzung mit Erläuterungen* (Stuttgart: Alfred Kröner, 1997; repr. Darmstadt: Wissenschaftliche Buch- gesellschaft, 2002), 406–29.

[233] His *The Swindlers Unmasked (The Charlatans Exposed)* is usually viewed as identical to his *Against the Oracles*, though some scholars, such as Heinrich Niehues-Pröbsting, *Der Kynismus des Diogenes und der Begriff des Zynismus*, 2d ed., Suhrkamp-Taschenbuch Wissenschaft 713 (Frankfurt am Main: Suhrkamp, 1988), 98, treat them as two separate works. For the literary affinities between Oenomaus and Lucian, see esp. I. Bruns, "Lucian und Oenomaus," *Rheinisches Museum* 44 (1889): 374–96, and Hammerstaedt, "Der Kyniker Oenomaus," 2860–62. See also Luck, *Die Weisheit der Hunde*, 405.

[234] Other works attributed to Oenomaus include *The Dog's Own Voice* (probably = *On Cynicism*); *On Crates, Diogenes, and the Other Cynics; The Republic*; and tragedies. For his *On Philosophy according to Homer*, see Hammerstaedt, "Der Kyniker Oenomaus," 2851–52, who notes the similarity of the title to Philodemus' work.

[235] R. Meir, who was a student of both R. Ishmael ben Elisha and R. Aqiba ben Joseph, belonged to the third generation of Tannaites (ca. 130–160 C.E.). According to rabbinic tradition, he was the descendant of proselytes—a circumstance that may have played a role in his friendship with a gentile philosopher. For bibliography and a brief discussion, see Strack and Stemberger, *Introduction to the Talmud and Midrash*, 76.

[236] R. Abba bar Kahana belonged to the third generation of Amoraim and was a student of the famous R. Yohanan bar Nappaha (who was born at Sepphoris and taught both there and at Tiberias). See Strack and Stemberger, *Introduction to the Talmud and Midrash*, 91.

of his Gadarene provenance and his date of activity in the first half
of the second century, he is considered by many scholars to be identical to Oenomaus.[237] While there may indeed be a connection
between Oenomaus and Abnimos,[238] a simple identification of the
two figures is highly problematic. It overlooks or minimizes the fact
that Oenomaus' condemnation of prophecy would also apply to the
Hebrew prophets and that the rabbinic depiction of Abnimos has
been shaped by midrashic concerns and is based, not so much on
the historical Oenomaus, but on the type of philosopher that Oenomaus was believed to represent;[239] (6) Valerius Apsines, an early third-
century c.e. rhetorician (perhaps ca. 190–250) whose *Technē* provides
a good example of how the art of rhetoric was taught during the
Second Sophistic;[240] and, finally, (7) Philo the mathematician (probably third century c.e.), who not only was the teacher of Sporus of
Nicaea but also improved on Archimedes' attempt to give an exact
numerical expression of mathematical pi.[241]

---

[237] See esp. S. J. Bastomsky, "Abnimos and Oenomaus: A Question of Identity,"
Apeiron 8 (1974): 57–61; see also Hengel, *Judaism and Hellenism*, 2:56 n. 189, who
considers the identity of the two figures "very probable."

[238] For a discussion of this possibility and some of the difficulties and solutions
involved, see Hammerstaedt, "Der Kyniker Oenomaus," 2836–39, and Menahem
Luz, "Abnimos, Nimos, and Oenomaus: A Note," *JQR* 77 (1986–87): 191–95.

[239] See esp. Luz, "Oenomaus and Talmudic Anecdote," 42–80. For the problem
of misunderstanding in the rabbinic depiction of Greek philosophers, see Luz's "A
Description of the Greek Cynic in the Jerusalem Talmud," 49–60.

[240] For text and translation, see Mervin R. Dilts and George A. Kennedy, eds.
and trans., *Two Greek Rhetorical Treatises from the Roman Empire: Introduction, Text, and
Translation of the Arts of Rhetoric attributed to Anonymous Seguerianus and to Apsines of Gadara*,
Mnemosyne Supplements 168 (Leiden: Brill, 1997), esp. ix–x, xv–xix, xxii–xxvi,
75–239. See also Kennedy, *Art of Rhetoric in the Roman World*, 633–34. A contemporary of Philostratus, Apsines was especially interested in declamation and the
rhetorical techniques employed by Demosthenes. According to the *Suda*, he studied
rhetoric in Smyrna with Heracleides and in Nicomedia with Basilicus. He later
taught in Athens, where he may have held a chair of rhetoric. An inscription found
at Athens indicates that he married into a prominent Athenian family and thus was
well-connected socially; see James H. Oliver, "Greek and Latin Inscriptions," *Hesperia*
10 (1941): 237–61, esp. 260–61, no. 65 ("Wife of the Sophist Apsines").

[241] Information on Philo appears to be confined to a single reference made to
him in Eutocius of Ascalon's (ca. 480–540) commentary on Archimedes' *Measurement
of a Circle* (3.258.25 Heiberg). The relevant portion of the text is translated by Sir
Thomas Heath in his *A History of Greek Mathematics*, 2 vols. (Oxford: Clarendon,
1921), 1:234. Gregor Damschen, "Philon von Gadara," in *Der Neue Pauly* 9 (2000):
857, conjectures a second century date for Philo, but his role as the teacher of
Sporus (usually dated ca. 240–ca. 300) suggests that he was active in the mid-third
century. Sporus himself was the teacher of Pappus of Alexandria (ca. 290–ca. 350),

In conclusion, Gadara was already a famous city when Philodemus was born in ca. 110 B.C.E., and his activities as a poet and philosopher added to his native city's renown. Yet he spent most of his life abroad. Like many Gadarenes both before and after him, Philodemus spent time in Athens.[242] For a Gadarene intellectual, that was almost to be expected. After all, inasmuch as Gadara considered itself "an Attic fatherland among Syrians" (Meleager *apud Anth. Pal.* 7.417), it was natural for its natives to want to spend time in Attica itself. Although Philodemus apparently never returned to his native city, his life coincided with some of the city's most dramatic vicissitudes. He was born when Gadara was a Hellenistic city under Seleucid control, but for approximately half of his life, his native land was under Hasmonean control. Philodemus would have been in his mid-40s when Pompey liberated and began to rebuild the city, and for the rest of his life, Gadara was part of the Roman province of Syria and its fluctuating fortunes. He likely died not too long after the year 40 B.C.E., thus before Augustus gave Gadara to Herod the Great. But long after he died, he was still considered one of that city's greatest natives.

---

who was the last of the great Greek geometers. See now Serafina Cuomo, *Pappus of Alexandria and the Mathematics of Late Antiquity*, Cambridge Classical Studies (Cambridge: Cambridge University Press, 2000).

[242] For other Gadarenes in Attica, see *IG* II/III, nos. 8448a–8449; Vanderpool, "An Athenian Monument to Theodoros of Gadara," 366–68; and Weber, "Gadarenes in Exile," 10–12.

INDEX OF ANCIENT AUTHORS AND TEXTS

The abbreviations used for the citation of primary texts follow, in general, the guidelines of the Society of Biblical Literature as published in the *Journal of Biblical Literature* 107 (1988) 579–96. Where no abbreviation has been recommended by the SBL, preference in the citation of ancient authors and texts is given to the abbreviations employed by N. G. L. Hammond and H. H. Scullard (eds.) in *The Oxford Classical Dictionary*, 2nd ed. (Oxford: Clarendon, 1970). Other abbreviations are self-evident.

NOTE: n = footnote(s). If the same page of this volume contains a reference in both the text and the footnotes to the same passage or author, only the reference in the text is indicated in the following index.

1. HEBREW BIBLE (OLD TESTAMENT)

Gen
30:11	369n
30:11 LXX	369n

Num
22	395

Deut
19:15	312

Isa
65:11	346n
65:11 LXX	346, 369n

Jer
9:22–23	338

Ezek
16:63	308n
29:21	308n

Amos
9:11 LXX	363n

Dan
11:10–19	353n

2. APOCRYPHA AND PSEUDEPIGRAPHA

1 Macc
1:14	356n
2:15	346n
5:26–27	346n

2 Macc
4:9	355n, 356n
4:12	356n
4:19	355n

3. JOSEPHUS AND PHILO

Josephus [Joseph.]	351n, 362, 364, 374n

AJ
4.313	363n
8.128	363n
11.25	360n
12.136	354
13.324–355	360n
13.355	360n
13.356	360, 361, 363
13.357–374	362n
13.374	363
13.375	344n, 362n, 363
13.396	344, 364n
14.74	367
14.75	363, 366

14.75–76	366	1.386–393	371
14.88	344n, 366	1.394–396	371n
14.91	344, 362n	1.396	371
14.93	367n	2.97	358, 372
14.158	370n	2.457–460	374
14.180	370	2.461	374n, 375n
14.326	370	2.461–465	375
14.381–393	370	2.464	375n
15.79	371	2.478	375
15.183–197	371	3.29–34	375n
15.217	348n, 371	3.37	346n
15.351	372	3.132	344
15.354–358	372	3.532–542	376
15.357	372	4.413	362
15.359	372	4.413–419	344
17.320	348n, 358, 372	4.428	344
18.36–38	391n		

Vit.

		25	374n
BJ		40–41	375n
1.86	360n, 363	42	346n, 374
1.86–89	363	44	375
1.87–89	362n	45	375
1.90	362n, 363	341	374
1.155	363, 366, 367	410	374, 375
1.155–157	366		
1.165	363n		
1.166	344n, 366	*Philo*	
1.170	344, 362n	*Agr.*	
1.172	367n	34	298
1.199	363n	143	324, 336
1.203	370n	159–160	336
1.213	370		
1.244	370	*Det.*	
1.282–285	370	35	338

4. The Talmud

The Babylonian Talmud [b.] · *The Jerusalem Talmud* [j.]
'Erubin ['Erub.] · *Qiddušin* [Qidd.]

61a	393n	64d, 13f.	392n

5. New Testament

Matt	346n	13:8	387
4:25	367n	19:21	196
5:3	196	19:29	195
5:3–11	194		
8:20	194	*Mark*	
8:28	345, 386n	2:14	378n
8:28–34	196n, 345, 369n	4:8	387
8:31	346	5:1	345
8:32	346n	5:1–20	345
8:34	346	5:2–3	386n
11:5	196	5:5	386n
11:6	196n	5:20	367n

7:31	367n
10:21	196
10:29	195

Luke
6:20	196
6:20–26	194
7:22	196
8:8	387
8:14	276n
8:26	345
8:26–39	345
8:27	386n
8:37	345
9:58	194
14:13	196
16:19–31	196
16:20	196
18:22	196
18:29	195

John
20:26–29	381n

Acts
15:16	363n
17	17
17:31	339n
18:19	274
18:24–28	334
18:26	274
26	17

Rom
1:16	339
12:15	307, 319
14:15	307
15:14	320
15:26	316n
16:23	316n

1 Cor
	323
1–2	340
1:14	316
1:17	340
1:18–2:10	314
2:1	338
2:1–5	337, 338, 339, 341
2:2	338
2:4	339
2:4–5	340n
2:5	339
2:10	313
3:18–19	340

4:13	253
5:2a–b	320
5:5	307n
8:11	307
9:19–22	16
9:19–23	17
9:19b–23	15
9:24–27	321n
11:28–32	321n
12:26	307, 319
14:13–19	321
15:32	276n
16:12	334
16:19	274

2 Cor
	323
1–7	305, 308, 309, 310, 314, 317
1:7	310
1:8	308
1:11	308
1:12	308
1:15–2:1	315
1:26	314n
2:3	305, 307, 310
2:3–4	305
2:4	273n, 305, 306, 310
2:5	306, 307
2:6	306, 307
2:7	306, 307
2:6–11	306
2:8	307, 310
2:9	305, 306
2:17	308
2:17–4:6	273
3:1–3	308
3:2–3	310
3:7–4:1	308
3:12	272
4:2	308
4:2ff.	308
4:7–12	308
4:10–11	49
4:16–5:5	308
5:12	308
5:20	307n
6:3–10	308
6:11	308
6:11–12	311
6:12	308
6:11–13	316
6:13	295, 308
7:2	295, 309, 311
7:2a	307

7:2b–d	308	13:2	312
7:2–4	316	13:3–4	312
7:3	309	13:4	313
7:4a	309	13:5–9	312
7:4a-c	309	13:5–10	321n
7:4b	309	13:7	313, 314
7:4c	309	13:8	312
7:5–15	309	13:9	311
7:7	306, 310	13:10	312, 313
7:8	305, 310	13:11	311
7:8–9	306		
7:8–12	305	*Gal*	298
7:9	305, 307, 310	1:1	300
7:9–10	307	1:3	302
7:10	307	1:5	300
7:10b	306	1:6	300, 301
7:11	306, 307, 310, 316	1:6ff	299
7:12	306, 307	1:13–14	300
7:14	307	2:1–10	300
7:15	306	2:9	300
7:16	309, 310	2:11–21	300
10–12	340	218	300n
10–13	266, 295, 305n, 310, 311,	2:21	300n
	312, 314, 316, 317, 318,	3:1	299
	340	3:3	299, 301
10:1	307n	3:4	301
10:3	312	3:19	318n
10:8	312, 313	3:23	302
10:9–10	273	4:3–5	302
10:10	334, 335n, 336	4:8–9	300
10:13	312	4:9	301
10:14	312	4:8–11	299
10:15	311	4:12	302
11:2	311	4:12–20	302
11:4	313	4:14–15	301
11:6	336	4:15	301
11:7	312	4:16	304, 321
11:7–10	315	4:17	302
11:9	312	4:20	304
11:11	313	5:7	301
11:12	312	5:15	301
11:20	312	5:16	301
11:29	319	5:19–21	301
12:2–10	313	5:26	301
12:6	312, 313	6:1–5	301
12:9	312	6:2	318n
12:12	312	6:4	321n
12:14	312	6:12–13	302
12:15	313		
12:17	312	*Phil*	
12:19	313	1:20	273
12:20	311		
13	312, 314	*1 Thess*	298n
13:1	312	2:3	273

2:7	273
2:1–12	337n
2:9–12	273

1 Tim

1:1	277, 278, 291n
1:2	282
1:3	274, 279, 281n, 287n, 291n
1:4	278
1:5	282n
1:6–7	285
1:8–11	283n
1:9	278, 284
1:9–11	282
1:10	281n, 290n
1:11	277
1:12	277, 279
1:12–16	277
1:13	282, 292n
1:13–16	287, 292
1:15	278, 281n, 284
1:16	282n
1:17	277
1:18	287n
1:19–20	283n
1:20	292n
2:1	279, 281n, 291n
2:1–3	278
2:2	275, 279
2:3	278, 291n
2:4	278, 292n
2:5–6	278, 281n
2:6	278
2:7	277, 280
2:8	278
2:8–15	283n
2:9–10	280
2:10	282n, 288
2:13	277, 280
2:15	278, 282n
3:1	282n, 287n
3:1–13	282n
3:2	280
3:2–7	286n
3:3	274, 289n
3:4	275
3:4–5	287n
3:5	282
3:7	279n, 281
3:8	275
3:8–12	280
3:8–13	286n
3:9	280
3:10	287n
3:11	275, 280, 286n, 292n
3:12	280, 287n
3:13	274, 279, 280, 281, 288
3:14	282n
3:15	282n, 284n
3:16	278
4:1	278, 290
4:1–3	282
4:2	291, 292
4:3	277, 279, 292n
4:4	279
4:5	278
4:6	277, 279, 281n, 282, 289
4:7	282n
4:7–8	282, 283n
4:8	278
4:9	279
4:10	278, 291n
4:11	281n
4:11–16	292
4:12	282n, 285, 287
4:13	281n, 291n
4:15	283, 287, 292n
4:15–16	281
4:16	281n
5:1	284, 291n
5:1–2	282n, 289
5:2	284
5:4	278
5:5	278
5:5–7	286n
5:6	278
5:7	289
5:7–8	281
5:10	282n, 288
5:11	278, 284
5:11–12	283, 285
5:12	278
5:14	281, 284, 288
5:15	283n
5:17	280
5:19	284
5:19–20	289
5:20	288, 291n, 292n
5:20–25	288
5:21	278
5:22	292n
5:23	279
5:24	283, 292n
5:25	282n
6:1	281, 288, 292n
6:1–2	289
6:1–3	281n
6:2	291n

6:3	278, 279, 290n	2:17–18	283n
6:3–10	282, 283n	2:20–21	282n
6:3–12	275	2:21	282n, 288
6:4	290, 292n	2:22	282n, 283n, 284n, 286
6:6	275	2:23	283n, 285, 286
6:7	275n	2:24	289
6:7–10	275n	2:24–25	289n
6:9	275n, 276, 285	2:25	292n
6:9–10	283n	2:25–26	278, 283n
6:10	291	3:1	290
6:11	282n, 284n	3:1–5	283n, 284
6:11–12	283n	3:1–17	275
6:12	278	3:2	279, 282, 286, 292n
6:13	277, 278, 281n	3:2–7	282
6:14–15	290	3:3	292n
6:14–16	278	3:4	276
6:16	277, 281n	3:5	278
6:17	278, 289	3:5–9	292
6:17–18	283n	3:6	285, 292n
6:18	275, 282n	3:6–9	288
6:18–19	278, 281	3:7	287, 292n
6:19	275	3:8	280
6:20	279, 285, 287n, 292	3:8–9	285
		3:10	281n, 282n
2 Tim		3:10–11	282, 287
1:1	277	3:11	277
1:2	282	3:13	286
1:3	279	3:15	278, 280, 284n, 291
1:4	282n	3:16	278, 281n, 292n
1:6	277, 281n, 287n	3:16–17	291
1:7	277, 282n	3:17	282n, 288
1:9	278	4:1	278, 281n
1:9–10	281n	4:2	291n, 292, 307n
1:10	278, 291n	4:2–3	281n
1:11	277	4:3	290, 291
1:12	279	4:3–4	285, 287
1:12–14	277	4:3–5	275
1:13	282, 290n	4:5	284n, 286, 287, 289
1:13–14	287n	4:6	290
1:14	279	4:8	278
1:15	274, 280, 282	4:9	282n
1:16	282n	4:9–13	282n
1:18	274, 278, 282n	4:14	278
2:1	277, 282n	4:14–16	282
2:2	281n, 287	4:17	277
2:7	278	4:18	278
2:10	278, 291	4:19	274
2:10–12	278	4:19–21	282
2:11–13	281n	4:20	282n, 291n
2:12–13	278		
2:14	289	*Tit*	
2:14–18	279	1:1	277, 292n
2:15	278, 279, 284n	1:2	278
2:17	290	1:2–3	278

1:3	278, 290, 291n	2:9–10	275
1:4	278, 282, 291n	2:10	278, 281n, 288, 291n
1:5	287	2:11–12	275, 282, 286
1:6–9	282n, 286n	2:11–14	277
1:7	274, 277, 289n	2:12	290n, 292n
1:7–9	275	2:13	278, 291n
1:9	278, 281, 290n, 291n	2:14	282n, 287, 288
1:10	284, 285, 286	2:15	281n, 285, 291n
1:11	280, 286	3:1	282n, 291n
1:13	289, 291n	3:1–2	287n
1:13–16	282	3:2	284n, 292n
1:16	282n, 288	3:3	276, 286, 292
1:19	290n	3:4	278, 291n
2:1	281n	3:4–7	277
2:1–6	286	3:6	278, 291n
2:2	275, 282n, 284, 290n	3:7	278
2:3	292n	3:8	282n
2:3–5	275, 280, 284	3:9	278, 285, 286
2:4	287n	3:9–11	283n
2:5	288, 292n	3:10	289, 291n
2:6	281n, 284, 291n	3:11	292n
2:7	275, 281n, 282n, 284n, 287	3:12–14	282n
		3:14	282n
		3:15	282
2:7–8	282	*Phlm*	
2:8	278, 285, 288	8–9	298n / 273
		Jas	
		4:1	276n
		4:3	276n
		2 Pet	
		2:13	276n

6. Other Early Christian Literature to the End of the 5th Century c.e.

Acts of Paul and Thecla		30.7.5	388n
1.237	335n	30.7.5–8.10	389n
		30.8.2	386n
1 Clement [*1 Clem.*]		30.8.10	382n
47.3	316n		
		Eudocia Augusta 388	
Clement of Alexandria [Clem. Al.]			
Strom.		Eusebius of Caesarea	
4.19	237	*Onom.*	
		32.16	348n
Epiphanius of Salamis	388		
Adv. Haer.		*Praep. ev.*	395n
1.7–8	277n		
		Justin Martyr	
Pan.		*Dial. Tryph.*	
30.4.1–5.8	388n	2	248n

Origen   345n
Comm. In Matth.
  15.15   195n

Tertullian [Tert.]
Adv. nat.
  2.2   82

7. Classical, Late Antique, and Byzantine Sources

Abnimos
  [Abnomos]   382, 383,
                       395, 396

Aelius Aristides
  [Aristid. Rhetor]
Or.   124n, 335
  51.29–34   337

Alciphron [Alciphr.]
Ep.
  2.2.1–3   237
  2.2.3   233

Antigonus of Carystus [Antig. Car.]
Lives   66

Antipater of Tarsus   154

Antoninus of
  Placentia   389, 390
Itinerarium
  7   390n

Appian
Syrian Wars [*Syr.*] (Book 11 of his
  Historia romana)
  1   358n
  57   350n

Apsines, Valerius   396
Technē   396

Archimedes   396
Measurement of a Circle 396n

Aristophanes [Ar.]
Nub.
  218–509   247
  627–790   247
Thesm.
  540–41   90

Aristotle [Arist.]
  Eth. Nic.   145n
Pol.
  1.9 (1257b19–1258a18)   143n
  5.3 (1303b15)   184n

  7.3 (1324b14–23)   169
  7.9 (1329a25–26)   172n
  7.10 (1330a25–26)   172

Rh.   94n, 342
  1.1 (1354a)   330n
  1.1 (1356a)   339
  1.3 (1358a38)   336
  1.3 (1358b)   336n
  1.3 (1358b2–5)   216n
  3   100
  3.1 (1403b–1404a)   326
  3.1 (1404a)   326n
  3.19 (1420a)   336n

On Philosophy   9n

Asconius   5

Athenaeus [Ath.]
Deipnosophistae [*Deipn.*]
  4.157b   358n,
                           383n,
                           385n
  5.210e–f   356n
  12.527e–f   356n
  13.588b   233
  13.577   237n
  14.633b   384n

Bion of Borysthenes   9n, 10n

Bromius   3n

Caecilius Statius
The Money-Lender   12

Carmen de bello Actiaco   11, 12
(*Aegyptiaco*)
  col. 6   12n

Carneiscus   8
Philistas   8n

Cassius Dio
Historia romana [*Hist.*]
  39.38.6   365n
  48.24.3   370
  48.24.7–26.4   370

Catullus [Catull.]	4	2.64	206
13	107n	2.65	206
14	107n	2.69–70	206
47	88n	2.99–349	204
61	11n	2.104	205
82	107n	2.175	205
		2.350–367	204
Chrysippus	11	2.351	205
Logical Questions	11n	3.19–212	204
On Providence	11n	3.143	205
Untitled work	11n	3.213–227	204
		Fin.	10
Cicero [Cic.]	1	1	5, 142
Acad. Post.		1.16	104
1.5	191n	1.65	135
Att.		2.7	136n
4.13.2	203n	2.12	141
4.16.3	204n	2.21.68	231, 237
Brut.		2.23	225
25–26	203	2.29	144n
69	203	2.63	231
151	203	2.67	231
265	11n	2.68	153n
291	203	2.91	146
De Or.	197, 203, 220	2.98	136
1.5	203n	2.101	108n, 140n
1.20	207	2.119	4n, 5
1.42–44	199	5.3	138n
1.46	199	*Inv. Rhet.*	199, 201, 203n
1.48–50	207	1.1	202
1.49	205	1.5	200
1.50	205	1.6	202
1.51	205	1.7	200, 201
1.53	207	1.8	200, 201
1.54	205	1.9	200, 201
1.57	205	1.16	200
1.59	207	1.33	202
1.60	207	1.50	200
1.64	207	1.77	202
1.72	207	1.86	202
1.85–86	199	2.5	200
1.107–109	204	2.6	200
1.141	199	2.7	200
1.142	199	2.8	200
1.145	199	2.11	200
2.29–33	204	*Nat. D.*	5n, 73n
2.32–33	204	1	5, 142
2.41–42	206	1.25–41	5
2.43	206	1.54	51n
2.44–47	206	1.59	5
2.48	206	1.93	222, 230, 236, 241
2.49	206	*Off.*	
2.50	206	3.36	124n
2.51–64	206	3.84	124n

Orat.	197, 203, 204, 220
2–3	205
4	207
37	206, 207
43–50	205
44	205
51	205
51–54	205
54	205
55–60	205
61–236	205
69	206, 207
113	203n, 207
118–120	208
122	203n
145	203n
147	203n
162	203n
174	203n
207	206, 207
Part Or.	199
3	200n
4	200n
5–8	200n, 201
5–26	200n
9	201n
9–15	201
16–24	200n
16–26	201
25	200n
26	200n
27–60	200n, 201
48	200
61–68	200n
61–138	200n, 201
62–67	201
68	201n
68–138	200n
69–82	201
83–97	201
98–138	201
137	200
139	200, 202
140	202
Pis.	
63	237
67	225
68	5n, 105
68–70	1n
68–72	5, 56
70–71	56n
85	105n
Prov. Cons.	
6–7	105n

Rhet. Her. (see under *Rhetorica*	
ad Herennium)	
Sest.	
94	105n
Tusc.	
1.82	22n
2.6–8	141n
3.38	5, 104
4.6–7	141, 164n
5.93	146n
Colotes of Lampsacus	8
Against Plato's Euthydemus	8n
Against Plato's Lysis	8n
Cornelius Severus	
Res Romanae	12n
Demetrius Lacon	3n, 9
PHerc. 1055	75
PHerc. 1786	109
On Fickleness	10n
On Geometry	10n
On Poems	10n
On the Form of God	
(= *On the Gods*)	10n
On the Puzzles of Polyaenus	10n
On the Size of the Sun	10n
Quaestiones convivales	10n
Untitled works	10n
Dio Cassius [Dio Cass.]	
Hist.	
55.7	107n
Dio Chrysostom [Dio Chrys.]	
Or.	
2.79	365n
13.9	273n
32.8	332
32.12	257n, 273n
47.1	338n
47.22	337n
72	335n
77	290n
78.45	290n
Diodorus Siculus [Diod. Sic.]	
13.103.4	59n
15.6	70n
16.92.3	47n
Diogenes Laertius [Diog. Laert.]	
1.47	95

4.43	242
5.37	138n
6.21	187n
6.23	187n
6.32	187
6.38	187
6.71	187n
6.74	187n
6.80	188, 195
6.83	195
6.87–88	195n
6.93	195n
6.99	344n
6.99–101	386n, 393n
6.104	185
7.6–9	63n
7.121	153n, 166n
7.130	163n
7.173	63n
7.181	60n
10.3	56n, 59, 237
10.4–5	228n
10.5	227
10.6	225
10.7	136n, 137n, 225, 227, 234, 236
10.8	184
10.9–10	274n
10.10	136n, 174n, 226n
10.11	137n, 139n, 226n
10.15	140n
10.17	63
10.17–19	136n
10.18	108n, 138n
10.19	186n
10.20–21	136n
10.22	44n, 136n
10.23	238
10.24	8n
10.25	9n
10.26	164n
10.27	195
10.31	50n
10.117	54, 134n
10.118	144n, 225n
10.119	54, 148, 162n, 166n, 228n
10.119–120	184
10.120	134n, 148, 151n, 161n, 162n, 171n
10.130	185n
10.137	227n

Diogenes of Oenoanda
A letter to mother	237, 238
Frag.	
29	225
122	241
127	332

Dionysius of Halicarnassus
[Dion. Hal.]
Comp.	
24	197
Isoc.	220

Donatus
Schol. Ad. Verg. Ecl.	
6.10	88n
6.13	88n
Vita Verg.	
11	88n
79	106n

Ennius
Ann.	
6	12, 109n

Epictetus
Diss.	
1.23	166n
3.1	334
3.7.19	166n
3.21.17	257n
3.22.2	272
3.22.8	272
3.22.52	272
3.22.3–4	257n
3.22.19	257n
3.22.86–89	335n
3.22.95–96	257n

Epicurus [Epicur.]
Epistulae [Ep.]	7n, 8n
Letter to Herodatus	
(Ep. Her.)	75
29.3	277n
36	50n
38–39	277n
61	47n
73–74	277n
75f	42
76–77	277n
83	47n, 50n
Letter to Menoceus	
(Ep. Men.)	
62,12–15	276n

64.21–25	276n
122	133
124	54
124–126	278n
128	151n
128–129	143n
129–130	144n
130	144n, 145, 148
131	145n, 148
132	225, 227n, 276n, 285n
135	279n

Fragmenta [U] (ed. Usener)

20	135n
45.7–10	92
117	134
135	147
141	138n
146	136n
163	134
164	134n
169	135n
181	139n
182	139
183	139
187	134n
202	147n
226	134n
408–428	143n
429–39	144n
456	144n, 146n
469	145
470	146n
471	146n, 147n
477	147n
526	166
551	139n

Fragments (ed. Arrighetti)

20.1	208n
20.3	208n
20.6	209n
21.4	209n
22.1	48n

On Nature	7n, 78n, 109

Ratae sententiae [KD]
(Κύριαι Δόξαι)   73n, 279

1	277n
2	278n
3	143n
5	276n
7	228n
8	225
14	279n
15	145

18	143n
19	23n
21	145n, 276n
27	272n
29	145n, 276n
30	144n
31	276n
32	134n
35	288n
40	89

Sententiae Vaticanae [SV]
(Vatican Sayings)

7	288n
22	23n
25	146
29	134n
33	23n
41	142, 279n
44	147, 275n
45	134n
47	278n
48	278n
52	279n
54	282n
58	148, 228n, 279n
60	275n
66	89
67	147
69	279n
77	147n
81	134n, 147n, 275n

Eunapius

Vit. phil.

459	388n, 390n

Euripides [Eur.]
Bacch.

668	90n

Eutocius of Ascalon	396n

Favorinus
Or.

37.20	334
37.33	333, 341

Fragmente der griechischen Historiker [FGrHist]
[ed. Jacoby]

850 T 1	394

Hermarchus
Frag.
  35   209n
  36   209n

Herodotus
Histories
  1.8.1   240
  1.30–33   69
  4.46.3   188

Homer [Hom.]
Il.
  8.306–308   25
  9.448–493   95

Horace [Hor.]   4
Carm. (*Odes*)
  1.1.1   107n
  1.6   106n
  1.20   107n, 108n
  2.17   107n
  3.29.41–48   44
Epist.
  1.1   107n
Epod.
  1.1   107n
  1.16   52, 107n
Sat.
  1.10.43f   106n
  1.2.121   4n

Iamblichus of Chalcis   390

Isidorus [Isid.]
Etym.
  8.6   82
  8.18   82
  8.21   82n
Isocrates [Isoc.]
Ad Nic.
  1.2–3   273n
Antidos.   327n
  197–198   329n
  201   336n
  204   336n
Contr. Soph.
  9–10   327n
  13   327n
Phil.
  25–26   327n
Panath.
  17   327n

Lactantius [Lactant.]
Div. Inst.
  3.25.15   237

Livy
Epit.
  127   370

Lucian   394n, 395
Bis acc.
  25–35   247n
Demon.
  11   288n
Dial. Mort.   248
Peregr.   245n
Philops.   335n
  34   334
Pisc.   245, 246n, 248, 249,
                                250, 251n, 257
  1   261
  2   261
  4   255
  5   255, 258, 259, 260
  6   262
  10   259n
  14   255, 266
  17   255
  20   264
  22   261
  25   247n, 255
  25–26   255, 264
  29   252
  29–37   252
  30   252, 262
  30–33   259
  33   258
  34   253, 262
  35   253
  36   253
  37   259
  38   259, 260
  46   258, 260, 265
  52   258
Pseudol.   250n
Salt.   248n
Vit. Auct.   247, 249, 251,
                                254, 261
Zeux.   247n

Lucretius [Lucr.]   9
De rerum nat.   5, 75, 105, 142
  2.1044–1047   51n
  3 53, 106n
  3.9–13   278n

3.41–93	27
3.830–1094	21n
3.904–911	89
4 238	
5 83	
5.1117–1132	228
5.1301	106n
5.1509	106n
Martial	5n
Maximus of Tyre [Max. Tyr.]	
Or.	
36	187n
Meleager	343, 344n, 357, 358, 365, 383, 393, 394
Garland	394n
Graces (Charities)	385n
apud Anth. Pal.	
5.160	365n, 383n
7.417	358, 383n, 384n, 397
7.417–418	383n
7.418	350n, 373n
7.419	373n, 383n
apud Athenaeus, *Deipn.*	
4.157b	358n, 383n, 385n
Menippus	343, 344n, 385, 386n, 393
Metrodorus of Lampsacus	8, 186n
Frag. (ed. Koerte)	
20–22	209n
25	209n
45	64n
Against the Dialecticians	8n
Against the Sophists	8n
Letters	8n
On Wealth	8n
Musonius Rufus [Mus. Ruf]	256
Or.	
14	195n
Nicander [Nic.]	
Alex.	93
Oenomaus	385, 394, 395, 396
Against the Oracles	395n
The Dog's Own Voice	395n
On Crates, Diogenes, and the Other Cynics	395n
On Cynicism	395n
On Philosophy according to Homer	395
Republic	395n
The Swindlers Unmasked (= The Charlatans Exposed)	395
tragedies	395n
Ovid	4, 394
Palatine Anthology [Anth. Pal.]	
5.160	365n, 383n
7.417	358, 383n, 384n, 397
7.417–418	383n
7.418	350n, 373n
7.419	373n, 383n
Pausanias	
Description of Greece	
10.4.1	357n
PHerc.	
124	10n
128	10n
176	11n
188	10n
200	8n
208	8n
307	11n
col. 1–2	11n
col. 9.7–12	11n
312	4n
frag. 1. col. 4	106
336	9n
440	8n
817	12n
831	10n
996	7n
1006	10n
1012	10n
col. 44	9n
1013	10n
1014	10n
1020	11n
col. 1	11n
col. 4	11n
1027	8n
1032	8n
1038	11n

1055	10n	5.112 (= Sider 5)	88
1061	10n	9.512 (= Sider 29)	86, 87, 89, 92,
1065	3n		94, 101, 108n
1083	10n	9.570 (= Sider 3)	86, 88, 89, 92,
1115	8n		94, 101, 239
1150	9n	11.34 (= Sider 6)	88
1258	10n	11.41 (= Sider 4)	52, 88
1389	3n	11.44 (= Sider 27)	107n, 140
1418	7n	11.44.7–8	107–108
col. 20	8n	*De adulatione [Adul.]*	58, 112n
1421	11n	[PHerc. 222, 223, 1089, 1457, 1675]	
1429	10n	(*On Flattery*)	
1471	3n	*De arrogantia [Arrog.]*	112n
1475	11n	[PHerc 1008] (*On Arrogance*)	
1520	9n	*De avaritia*	112n
1642	10n	[PHerc. 465, 1613] (*On Greed*)	
1647	10n	*De bono rege secundum*	
1786	10n	*Homerum*	80n, 105, 124,
1822	10n		151n, 395

Philo the
    [PHerc. 1507] (*On the Good King*
    Mathematician   396   *according to Homer*)

		De calumnia	106, 111
Philodemus [Phld.]		[PHerc. Paris 2] (*On Calumny*)	
Academicorum Historia	68, 79, 109n	*De dis*	75, 82
(ed. Dorandi)		(*On Gods*)	
Columns		Book 3	5
Y.3–1,7	60	Columns	
4.25–col. 15	66n	1.15–20	276n
8	65n	2.23–27	51
9	65n	*De garulitate*	109, 111n
10.11–15	65	[PHerc 1082]	
13.10–18	67	Columns	
13.20–27	67	1.1–7	109n
13–18	65n	11.1–7	106n
14.41–45	66	*De insania*	111, 112
22.35–23.7	67	*De ira*	27, 39–40, 58,
23.8	66		75, 109, 110,
24.9–12	60		111–112, 112n,
26.35–44	68n		116n, 286n
27.1–12	68n	[PHerc. 182] (*On Anger*)	
27.32–28.16	68n	Columns	
28.35–29.16	68n	1–2	17n
29.39–30.11	68n	1–8.8	26
30.1–12	68n	4.4–24	26
31.15–19	60	4.16	26
31.34–32.10	68n	8.20–31.24	26
32.14–16	68n	12.26–29	64n
36.4–5	67	18.34–21.40	28
36.19	59	18.35–21	17n
72.5	65n	36.24f	17n
Anth. Pal.		39.31–33	40n
5.4.5 (= Sider 7)	92, 239	39–40	42
5.46 (= Sider 20)	87n	67	42

De libertate dicendi
  [*De lib. dic.*]   16, 17, 55, 58, 61,
                           63, 66, 67, 68, 75,
                           78, 85, 86, 103,
                           104, 109, 111, 112,
                           113, 116, 129n,
                           235, 246, 271
  [PHerc. 1471] (*On Frank Criticism*)
    (ed. Olivieri)
  Fragments
    1   283, 285, 292n
    2–3   284
    2.3   141
    4   291
    4.4–5   259n
    5–6   292
    5.6–8   68n
    6   291n, 292n
    6.5   257n
    6.8   306n
    7   17n, 288, 297, 312
    8   290n
    8.6–7   141
    9   286, 292n
    9.6–9   96
    9–11   17n
    10   281n, 288, 292n
    10.3–7   91
    13   291n, 292n
    14   313
    15   92
    15.8–9   258n
    15.9   257n
    16   275n, 281
    17   292n
    18   285, 292n
    19   285
    20   290n, 291n
    20.4   257n
    22   289n
    23   290n, 291n
    24.8–12   70
    25   272n, 289
    25.6–7   141
    26   291n, 292
    26.4   275n
    28   309n
    28.5   258n
    30   291n
    30.11   306n
    31   91, 284, 291n
    31.3   306n
    32   289, 291n
    33   284, 292n

    34.5   291n
    35   287, 291n, 292n
    36   291
    36.1–2   291n
    37–38   288
    38   291n, 307n
    38.7–8   306n
    38.7–10   98
    39   290, 291n
    40   282, 289, 290, 291
    40.8   291n
    40–42   288
    41   92, 288
    42   289, 291n
    42.10   141
    43   283n
    43.13   291n
    43–46   287
    44   290n
    45   291n
    45.1–6   285n
    45.1–11   70
    45.7–10   92, 266
    45.8   257n
    46   286, 292n
    47   292n
    48   292n
    49   292n
    49.6   257n
    49.10   257n
    50   292n
    50.3–8   92
    50.5   258n
    51   287, 292n
    53.2–6   68n
    54–55   282n
    55   139n, 292n
    55.5   257n
    58   297, 310
    60   297
    60.4–7   91
    61   291n
    61.1   305
    62   291n, 292n
    62.1   306n
    63   292n
    64   290n, 292n
    64–65   290n
    64.5–7   91n
    65–66   285
    66   291n
    67   283n
    67.9–11   68n
    68   281n, 291n

69	290
70	315
70.5–7	68n
71	298, 304, 306, 310, 316
72	91
73	291n
73.3–4	257n
74.3–10	68n
75	291n
75.2	306n
76	292n
77	291n, 292n
78.6–7	291n
79	290n
81.1–4	68n
82	291n
82.1	306n
82.7	305
83	292n, 298
84	288, 291n
84.7	306n
86	283n, 290
87	310
88	292n
88.1–4	68n
T2	292n
T2.D2	291n
T3G	291n
T4.1	291n
T4.1.23	306n
T5	291n
T12	290n
T12M	292n
T14.end.5	257n
Columns	
1–4	288
1–24	116, 117, 118, 119, 120, 122
1a.1–4	68n
2–3	117
2b	91–92
3a	292
3a.3–5	68n, 69, 289n
3b	292n
4	275n
5a	64, 66
5b	64
5b.2	69
6a	64, 240
6b	292n
6b.10–11	291n
7b	118, 121
8	298
8a–10b	292
8b	291n, 297, 298
8b.6–13	289n
9a	291n, 292n
9a.1–8	289n
9b	291n, 292n
9b.9	306n
10	292
10a	310
10b	296
11a	292n
11b	296
12–21	292
12a	292n
13–14	292
13a.10	258
14a	292n
14a.7–9	68n
15a	292n
15b	69, 259n, 291n, 292n
15b.12–13	306n
15b–16a	65
16	275n
16a	291n
16a.1–5	70
16a.9	306n
16b	291n
16b.7–8	251
17	290n
17a	291n, 292n
17b	296, 314
18a	292n
18b	291n, 292n
19a.5–8	68n
19a.11–12	306n
19b	287n, 291n, 292n, 295, 308
19b.6	258n
20	285
20a	292n
20b.1–5	64
21	290n
21a	291n, 292n
21a.1–5	68n
21a.3	306n
21a.7	306n
21b	291n
21b.12–15	68n
21b–22b	91
22b.10–13	68n, 69
22	20n, 284
22a	240, 291n
22b	240, 314

22b–24a	91
23a	291n
23a.3	306n
23b	117n, 292n
24	91, 115, 117, 118, 284
24a	117n, 314
24a.1–2	306n
24b	117, 291n, 292n
24b.4–5	306n
Apographs	
N. 77	114
N. 79	114, 292n
N. 84	114
N. 87	114
N. 91	114, 291n
N. 93	114, 291n
N. 93.7	306n
De morte [*Mort.*]	4n, 5, 15, 18, 19, 26n, 27, 56, 75, 88, 106n, 111n, 116n
[PHerc. 1050] (*On Death*)	
Book 4	112n
Columns	
1–3	22
1–9	18n
3.30–4.1	22–23
3.32–39	35n
3–18	36–37
4	78n
4–10	22
8	23
8.1–9.14	25
8.6–10	25
8.30–10.14	25
8.32	25n, 26n
9	24
9.8	26n
11	22
12–20.1	36
12–36	44
12–39	22
13	36, 37
13.36–14.14	37, 38
17.32–18.16	38, 39
19	31
19.33–20.1	31
25.2–10	40
25.37–26.6	41
25.38	41n
36.1	41n
27	41
28–29	43
29.10–12	30

29–30	43
30.3	30n
30–33	43
31.1	30
32.24–31	30
33.36–34.1	43
33fin–35	43
34.1–3	30n
34–35	28
34.37–35.30	29, 30
35.36	43
35fin–36	43
35.36–39	33
35.39–36.8	34
35–36	33
36.17–25	34
37.1–12	45, 46, 47, 48
37–39	18n
39.7	49
39.15–27	49, 50
De musica	2n, 56, 110n
[PHerc. 1497] (*On Music*)	
4	27
De oeconomia [*Oec.*]	78, 112n, 133, 142, 161, 164, 178, 179, 193
[PHerc. 1424] [= Book 9 of *Vit.*]	
(*On Household Management*)	
Columns	
1–7.37	154
1.4–21	165n
1.5–8	195
1.5–10	188
2.8–12	189
2.17	160n
5.4–14	117n
7.37–12.2	154
7.45–8.18	167n
9.1–3	166n
9.7–9	167n
9.16–20	167n
9.26–10.28	175
10.43–44	160n
11.16–17	164n
11.18–19	160n
12.2–5	189
12.2–16.12	189
12.5–12	165n
12.5–17	189
12.5–25	155, 158n
12.5–22.16	150, 155
12.6–7	190
12.15–25	165n
12.17–25	190

12.17–13.29	186	17.5	160n
12.18–19	184n	17.14–40	158
12.19–22	149	17.15	160n
12.25ff.	179n	17.21–31	160n
12.25–41	190	17.29–30	160n
12.29	160n	17.31	160n
12.29–38	155	17.38	160n
12.41–43	190	18.2–7	157n
12.44–13.3	190	18.2–21.35	158n
12.45–21.35	186	18.5	160n
12.46	160n	18.6–7	174
13.3	160n	18.7–20	158
13.3–8	190	18.34–35	157n, 174
13.3–11	155	18.40	160n
13.8–11	190	19	160n
13.11–19	156n	19.4–19	158
13.15–19	190	19.19	160n
13.19–29	190	19.44	160n
13.29–35	190	20.13	160n
13.34	160n	20.16–32	165n
13.34–14.5	156n	20.33	160n
13.35–39	190	20.45–21.12	165n
13.39–44	190	20.45–21.35	186
13.44–14.2	191	21.1–3	189
14.2–5	191	21.28	165n
14.5	160n	21.28–35	189
14.5–9	156, 191	21.28–22.6	158n
14.8–9	151	21.34–35	169n
14.9–15	191	22.6–26	159, 167–68
14.9–23	156	22.17–23.36	168
14.15–17	191	22.17–fin	155
14.17–23	191	22.28	160n
14.23–30	191	22.28–41	169
14.23–46	157n	22.36–37	160n
14.30–37	191	22.41	160n
14.37–15.3	191	23.1–7	169
14.38	160n	23.7–11	169
15.3–6	191	23.11–18	170
15.6	174	23.18–22	170
15.6–14	191	23.23–36	170
15.14–21	192	23.36–27.20	173
15.20	184n	23.42–24.11	174
15.21–26	157n, 184n, 192	24.11–29	174n
15.26–31	192	24.35	174n
15.31–37	192	24.41	174
15.37–45	192	24.41–25.54	175
15.44–16.12	192	25.4–26.1	175
15.45–16.6	157	25.32	174n
16.2	195n	25.38	151
16.5–6	195	25.44	175
16.8–10	157	26.1–9	175
16.44–17.2	157	26.9–18	175
17.2–6	158	26.18–29	175
17.2–18.2	158n	26.28–34	175

27.5–9	175	18.1	61n
27.20	150	18.5	61n
27.20–29	176	18–21	61
27.23–29	186	22.5–10	61
27.30–35	176	*De vitiis*	4n
27.35–46	176	[PHerc. 253]	
27.42–47	189	Fragments	
28.3–5	189	12.4–5	106n
De pietate	5, 11n, 56, 75,	22	384n
	78n, 80, 82, 104n,	*Epigrams*	
	116n, 235	(ed. Sider)	
[PHerc. 1428] (*On Piety*)		3 (= *Anth. Pal.* 9.570)	86, 88, 89,
Part I			92, 94, 101,
61–72	110n		239
76	110n	4 (= *Anth. Pal.* 11.41)	52, 88
640–57	81n	5 (= *Anth. Pal.* 5.112)	88
705–706	80n	6 (= *Anth. Pal.* 11.34)	88
790–840	135	7 (= *Anth. Pal.* 5.4.5)	92, 239
1402–12	139n	20 (= *Anth. Pal.* 5.46)	87n
2260–65	81n	27 (= *Anth. Pal.* 11.44)	107n, 140
Columns		29 (= *Anth. Pal.* 9.512)	86, 87, 89,
5	81n		92, 94, 101,
8–11	81n		108n
10	81n	36	239n
75.2175–76	109n	68	239n
De poematis	4, 56, 82, 124n	*Index Academicorum*	82n
(*On Poems*)		[PHerc. 164 and 1021]	
Book 5	27, 82n, 93, 116	*On Character and Life*	111, 113n,
Columns		see also *De libertate*	299n
5.6–18	93	*dicendi* [*De lib. dic.*],	
26.5–8	94	above	
26.20	170n	[*On Choices and*	
34.28–29	170n	*Avoidances*]	21, 75n
35.17	170n	[PHerc. 1251]	
De signis	3, 19, 56, 78,	Columns	
[PHerc. 1065]	104n, 109,	17–23	27
(*On Signs/On the*	111n, 112n	23.9–12	27
Methods of Inference)		*On Not Living According to*	
Fragments		*Chance*	112n
1	50n	[PHerc. 168]	
27	3n	*On Passions*	112n,
45	3n		127n
Columns		*On Vices and the Opposing Virtues*	
2.15–18	109n	[*Vit.*]	78, 112,
De stoicis	55, 56, 58,		127n, 179,
	60, 62, 265		275
[PHerc. 155, 339] (*On the Stoics*)		*On Wealth*	111, 133,
Columns			142, 149,
3.6–8	61		150, 51,
3.13	62		160–61, 178,
13.24	61n		179, 193
14.21–22	61n	[PHerc. 97]	
14.23	61n	Fragments	
15.2	61n	2.9–10	180, 185

Columns

24.35	150n
27	180, 185
34.4–9	180
36.12–14	152n
37.11–15	150n
40.6–16	180
41.5	150n
41.9–14	152
41.10–15	180, 184
41.12–13	150n
41.32–34	152n
41.32–39	180–81
41.35–37	152
42.14	181
42.26–35	179n, 184
42.31–43.7	151
43.1–8	179n, 181, 184
43.4–8	184
45.15	177
45.15–38	151
45.15–40	181, 184, 194
46.26–34	182, 184, 185
46.30–34	194
46.31–34	151
47.9–11	151n, 182, 194
47.26–35	184
47.34	150n
48.18–24	151, 182
49.5–12	182, 184
50.5	182, 184
50.7	179n
50.30–38	182, 185
51.2–10	151n
51.2–11	182–83, 185
51.27–30	152
52.27–31	183
53.2–5	180n, 183, 185
53.3–5	152
54.4–10	183, 185
54.7–10	152
55.4–14	183
55.10	152n
56.2–9	183
56.4–8	152
58.3–9	183, 185
58.4–9	153
58.26–30	183
PHerc. 1003	3n, 111
Pragmateiai or *Negotia*	7n, 8n, 58
[PHerc 310 and 1418]	
(*Works on the Records of Epicurus and Some Others/Philosophy in Action*)	

Columns

12	140n
30	139
Rhetorica [Rh.]	20, 26, 56, 109n, 110, 171n, 197, 198, 210, 211, 212, 214, 218, 323, 342
Volume 1 (ed. Sudhaus)	
pp. xxvii–xxxix	213n
p. 70	209n
p. 98	215n
pp. 147–93	213n
p. 151	218n
pp. 193–201	213n
p. 201	217n
pp. 201–204	213n
pp. 202–204	218n
pp. 204–12	213n
pp. 212–22	213n
pp. 213–14	217n
pp. 214–15	217n
p. 217	216n
pp. 217–18	217n
p. 219	217n
p. 222	213n, 215n
pp. 265–67	30n
pp. 332–33	216n
pp. 363–65	216n
Volume II (ed. Sudhaus)	
p. 1	109n
p. 15	216n
pp. 18–19	216
pp. 83	216n
pp. 85–86	216n
p. 120	209n
p. 135	216n
p. 136	216n
p. 226	93
pp. 234–35	215n
Book 1	
[PHerc. 1427]	
Fragments	
2.13–23	211n
Columns	
3.30–33	216n
5.30–33	215n
7.9–29	216n
Book 2	
[PHerc. 408]	
Fragments	
7.1–3	216n
11.2–18	216n

[PHerc. 1079]
Fragments
18.10–18   216n
[PHerc. 1672]
Columns
9.11–14   216n
21.10–17   215n
21.10–22.7   217n
21.13–15   215n
21.36–22.19   217n
21.37–22.1   215n
22.28–36   216n
22.29–36   217n
[PHerc. 1674]
Columns
1.31–34   216n
2.15–18   211n
2.15–24   209n
5.31–6.19   211n
5.34–6.19   209n
10:24–11.31   216n
11.17–34   216n
17.8–13   216n
20.16–21.1   210n
21.7–27   217n
21.12–15   93
21.17–23   215n
21.30–22.2   215n
22.5–12   215n
22.21–29   215n
23.30–24.9   215n, 217n
23.34–24.9   216n
30.12–19   209n, 210n
30.19   209n
37.22–25   216n
37.22–27   215n
38   331n
38.2–15   209
38.30–39.6   212n
38.30–39.24   210n
38.32–33   212n
39.8   209n
39.21   209n
41.12   212n
42.37–43.17   212n
43.4   212n
43.26–52.10   212n, 216n
52.11–53.11   219
52.11–53.14   211n
53.15–25   215n
54.10–56.9   211n
54.32–55.11   216n
57.13–58.2   212n, 216n
57.17–58.2   211n

58.4–8   215n
58.4–16   215n
Book 3
[PHerc. 1426]
Columns
A.6–10   214n
3a.7–5a.4   216n
3a.7–5a.6   216n
6a.14–31   217n
7a.2–7   211n, 212n
7a.8–23   217n
10a.25–11a.14   214n
[PHerc. 1506]
Columns
35.12–24   215n
46.23–32   216n
47.6–10   214n
48.13–17   216n
50.22–52.6   216n
50.22–52.8   215n
52.37–53.12   217n
53.14–18   211n, 212n
55.21–37   214n
Book 4   325, 326
[PHerc. 1007, 1673]
Columns
1.1–24.25   213n
1a.1–11a.12   213n
11a.12–20a.12   213n
19a.16–26   217n
20a.12–22a.16   213n
21a.10–22a.13   217n
22a.16–30a.19   213n
24a.26–26a.7   217n
30a.19–42a.4   213n
32a.6–26   217n
32a.21–39a.3   217n
33a.19–24   217n
36a.6–15   217n
36a.15–37a.4   217n
37a.4–19   217n
38a.15–39a.1   217n
41a.6–22   215n
42a.4–8   213n
[PHerc. 1423]
Columns
1.1–20.282   13n
7.6–14   218n
9.16–25   329
11.12–16   327
11.16–25   329
11.25–12.4   329
12.5–8   329
12.8–14   330

13.21–14.7	330
14.8–12	330
14.13–17	330
14.19–25	329
14.23–25	335
15.3–6	327
15.13–19	327
16.5–22	328n
16.9–13	327, 328
17.18	329
17.23	327
18.18	328
19.3–10	330
19.11–16	332
25.1–14	341

Book 5 (?)
  [PHerc. 1015, PHerc. 832]
  Columns

21.4–22	216n
24.0–16	216n

Book 6 (?)
  [PHerc. 1004]
  Columns

15.3–20	216n
46.8–11	211n
76.4–13	216n

Book 7 (?)
  [PHerc. 220]
  Fragments

5.28–34	216n
6.3–16	216n

Stoicorum Historia	68
(ed. Dorandi)	
Columns	
4.4–5	62
4.5–7	62
6	62
7	62
8	62
8.2	63
10.8–10	60, 62
10.48	70n
13–16	62
16.2	65n
22–23	63
24.1–3	64
24.3–9	63
29,5	70n
68	63
69.4–5	68n
76.6–7	60
78.3	60
Syntaxis philosophorum	55, 56, 57
(*The Ordering of the Philosophers*)	

To Friends of the School	238
[PHerc. 1005]	
2.8–17	164n

Philostratus [Philostr.]

VS	325
2.1	100n
511	324n
570–72	335n

Pindar [Pind.]

Ol.	
1.4	96n
Pyth.	
3.61	96

Plato [Pl.]

Ap.	
17a1–18a6	259
19c1–5	247n
20e9–23c1	257, 260
36b5–d5	259, 260
Cri.	
50a	99
50b	99
50c	99
54d	99
Hp. Maj.	
286a	98
Leg.	
731d–e	124n
Letters	
7.337e	69
Phd.	
99d	69
Phdr.	99
240d	90n
276a	336
Phlb.	
19c	69
Prt.	
310a	100
328b–c	124n
361a	99
362a	99
Resp.	
557b	90
Soph.	
231d	67
Statesman	
300c	69
Symp.	
201cd	99
201e	99n
222c	90n

Ti.
  81e   22n

Plautus [Plaut.]
Asin.
  11   47n
Mi.
  211   47n
Tri.
  19   47n

Pliny
Ep.
  5.3.5   11n
HN
  35.5   138n
  35.99   233
  35.144 233

Plutarch [Plut.]
Mor.
Quaest. conv.
  3.6   224n
  7.52F   69
An seni
  18.814D   65n
  26.67C–D 70n
  26.67C–E 69

Quomodo adulator ab amico
  48E–74E 124n
  49B   258
  55C   64
  56A   304
  56E–F   124n
  59C   304
  59D   296
  59F   314n
  61D   298
  61E   316
  64C   304
  65F   258
  66A   296, 320n
  68C   304
  69A–B   304
  69E   297
  69E–F   298, 312
  70D   318n
  70E–71A 306
  71D   290
  72C   297n, 304
  72D   301
  73A   304
  73A–B   290
  73B   316, 319

  73D   296
  73F   299
  74A   299
  74D   295, 313
  74E   314

De prof. virt.
  80BC   291n

Conv. sept. sap.
  155a   187n

De Stoic repugn.
  1043B–C 163n
  1043E–44A 163n
  1043E   163n
  1047E   153

An vit. ad infel. suff.
  499D   195n

Non poss. suav. viv. sec. Epic.
  1086C–1107C 278n
  1087A   241
  1087B   241
  1088D   241
  1089C   224
  1093C   227
  1094C   227
  1094D   230
  1096E   241
  1097D   226
  1097D–E 224, 234
  1098   231
  1099B   224
Adv. Colotem 8n
  1118C   188n
De lat. viv.
  1128C   228
  1128f–1129A 230
  1129   230
  1129A   137
  1129B   224, 228
  1129F–1130E 229
Vit.
Ant.
  41   382n
  71.1   371
Pyrrh.
  20.7   231

Polyaenus
  Frag. 43   209n
  Polybius 354n
Hist.
  5.70.7   346n
  5.71.3   352, 353n

5.86.7–11	353
16.39.3	354
Polystratus	8, 9n
On Irrational Contempt	9n
col. 5b9–7a8	9n
col. 23.26–26.23	9n
On Philosophy	9n
Posidonius (Poseidonius)	
apud Athenaeus, *Deipn.*	
5.210e–f	356n
12.527e–f	356n
POxy.	
54.3724	3n
Praxiphanes	8n
Propertius	4
Ps.-Demetrius	
De elocutione	
287–94	100
Ps.-Socrates	187n
Ps.-Xenophon	
Ath.	90n
Quintilian [Quint.]	
Instit.	
1.pr.11–17	199
1.6.18	203n
2.2.24	197n
2.17.2	199
2.17.15	197n
3.1.20	203n
3.3.1	199
3.3.14–4.1	199
3.4.2	207n
3.6.60	203n
4.12–16	199
9.2.66f	100n
9.3	334
9,12–13	334
Rabirius, Gaius	12n
Rhetorica ad Herennium	
[*Rhet. Her.*]	199
1.1	200, 202
1.2	201
1.3	200, 202
1.3–3.15	201
1.16	200
2.1	200, 201
2.7	200
3.1	200
3.16	200
3.16–90	201
3.17	200
4.1	200
4.1–69	201
4.3	200
4.4	200
4.6	200
4.7	200
4.8	200
4.10	200
4.69	200, 202
Sappho	
1	96, 97, 98
Seneca [Sen.]	5
De vita beata	
7.3	229
21–22	153n
Ep.	
6.6	137, 241
18.9	139, 180n
66.48	52
77.20	52
87.38	152
87.38–39	181n
[*On Leisure*]	
3.2	162
Fr. (ed. Haase)	
45	238
Servius	
In Ecl. Verg.	106n
Sextus Empiricus [Sext. Emp.]	
Math.	220
1.49	212n
1.49–53	212n
49	134n
Pyr.	
1.14.153	195n
Sophocles [Soph.]	
Aias.	100
1142	94n
1147	94n
1150	94n
1152–1153	94n

Ant.
688–700   94n

Stephanus of
  Byzantium   351n, 355n
Ethnika
  Gadara   350n, 355

Stobaeus [Stob.]
Ecl.
  2   163n
  7   163n

Strabo   343
Geographica
  16.2.10   351n
  16.2.29   343
  16.2.45   387n

Suda
  Apsines   396n
  Theodorus   386n

Suetonius

Stoicorum Veterum Fragmenta [*SVF*]
(ed. von Arnim)
  1, p. vi   11n
  2, frg. 131   11n
  2, frg. 298a   11n
  3.54   152
  3.138   153
  3.645   153n

Suetonius [Suet.]
Tiberius [*Tib.*]
  57.1   394
Vita Hor.   107n
Vit. Verg.
  13   107n
  18   107n

Syncellus, George   351n
Chronicle
  355.7–10 Mosshammer   350n
  355.7–11 Mosshammer   364n
  558–559 Dindorf   350n, 364n

Tacitus [Tac.]
Ann.
  15.63   23n
  16.35   23n
Dial.
  30–32   203n

Teles
  4A   187n, 195n

Theodorus   343, 386n,
                        394

Thrasymachus
Pathos   326

Tibullus   5n

Torquatus, Lucius
  Manlius   9, 11n
Varius Rufus, Lucius   4n, 12n
De mor.   4n, 106

Varro
De re rustica   387
  1.44.1   387
  1.44.2   387
Menippean Satires   387

Velleius Paterculus [Vell. Pat.]
Hist.
  2.88   107n

Vergil [Verg.]   4
Catal.
  5.2   106n
  8   106n
Ecl.
  9.35f   106n
G.
  1.1   107n

Xenophon [Xen.]
Mem.
  1.5.6   187n
  1.5–6   194
Oec.   154, 164
  1   165
  2   165
  1.2–4   188
  1.4   189
  2.1–4   146n
  5.1–17   169
  6.8–11   169
  6.9   172
Symp.
  3.8   195
  4.34   185
  4.34–44   187n
  4.43   185n

Zeno of Citium   3, 5, 9n, 11n   Zenon Papyri   386n

8. Busts, Inscriptions, and Maps

Apion of Gadara   *Inscriptions de Délos*
Epitaph   384   no. 2377   370n, 382n

Corpus inscriptionum latinarum [*CIL*]   Naples Museum Inventory
  10.1423f   7n   no. 5468   11n

Inscriptiones graecae [*IG*]   The Peutinger
II/III   Table   352n
  no. 8448a   397n
  no. 8449   397n   *Supplementum epigraphicum Graecum*
                                             [*SEG*]
Inscriptiones graecae ad res Romanas pertinentes   32.1502   391n
[*IGRom*]
  1.824   373n

INDEX OF MODERN SCHOLARS

Achard, Guy   199n, 201n
Adkins, Arthur W. H.   228n
Adler, William   351n
al-Daire, Mohammad   380n
Aleshire, Sara   235–36
Alexiou, Alice S.   250n
Allen, Walter, Jr.   219
Allinson, Francis G.   246n
Ancona, R.   16n
Andersen, Flemming Gorn   349n, 388n
Anderson, Graham   246n
Anderson, R. Dean, Jr.   323n, 324n, 337n, 342n
Angeli, Anna   3n, 8n, 10n, 11n, 30n, 104n, 188n, 238n, 239
Applebaum, Shimon   345n
Armstrong, David   4n, 16n, 20n, 88n, 105n, 106n, 108n, 383n
Arnim, H. F. A. von   11n
Arrighetti, Graziano   5n, 8n, 58, 209n
Asmis, Elizabeth   3n, 56n, 57n, 85n, 93n, 105n, 106n, 108n, 111n, 127n, 151n, 177n, 178n, 181n, 186n, 188n, 217n, 227n
Aujac, Germaine   220
Aune, David E.   369n
Auvray-Assayas, C.   5n
Avi-Yonah, Michael   350n, 388n, 392n

Baarda, Tjitze   345n
Bagnall, Roger S.   352n
Bailey, Cyril   48n, 50n, 51n
Balch, David L.   193n, 195n
Baldwin, Barry   246n
Balty, Jean Ch.   7n
Bardon, Henry   12n
Barghouti, Asem N.   351n, 355n, 359n
Barker, Ethel Ross   1
Bar-Kochva, Bezalel   351n, 353n, 354n, 360n
Barnes, Jonathan   11n, 204n, 209n
Barrett, Charles Kingsley   338n
Barwick, Karl   200n
Bassi, Domenico   18n, 36n, 37n, 39n, 41n

Bastomsky, S. J.   396n
Becking, B.   369n
Bellinger, Alfred R.   368n, 385n
Beloch, Julius   351n
Benario, Herbert W.   12n
Betz, Hans Dieter   179n, 193n, 194, 195, 245n, 335n
Bevan, Edwyn Robert   354n
Bietenhard, Hans   366n
Bignone, E.   10n
Billerbeck, Margarethe   187n
Binst, O.   359n
Blank, David   210n, 212n, 331
Blenkinsopp, Joseph   346n
Bloch, Herbert   105n
Blumenthal, Henry J.   390n
Boardman, John   350n
Bol, Peter Cornelius   347n
Bollack, Jean   2n, 143n, 166n
Booth, Joan   4n
Bornkamm, Günther   16n
Boulogne, Jacques   229n
Bowersock, Glen Warren   325n, 376n, 386n, 394n
Branham, R. Bracht   187n, 195n, 246n, 249n, 250n, 394n
Bremer, J. M.   96n
Brennan, Tad   226n
Bresson, A.   350n
Brickhouse, Thomas C.   260n
Brueckner, Anthony L.   32n
Bruns, I.   395n
Bullmore, Michael A.   337n
Burkert, Walter   139n, 350n

Calboli, Gualtiero   199n
Cameron, Alan   3n, 86n, 383n, 394n
Cappelluzzo, Maria Giustina   197n
Capasso, Mario   4n, 7n, 8n, 9n, 113n, 115n, 116n, 126n
Cary, E.   366n
Castaldi, F.   160n
Castner, Catherine J.   2n, 4n, 11n, 235, 236n
Cataudella, Q.   93n
Cavallo, Guglielmo   110, 111, 112, 113, 115n, 116, 117n, 124n, 126n, 127n, 130n, 219n, 220

Cèbe, Jean-Pierre   387n
Cirillo, S.   180n, 181n
Clack, Jerry   394n
Clark, E. Gillian   390n
Clarke, Emma C.   391n
Classen, Carl Joachim   9n, 26n
Clay, Diskin   26n, 55n, 58, 71n, 76n,
    80n, 82n, 137, 138, 240, 265n,
    284n, 394n
Clermont-Ganneau, Charles   384n
Cohen, David   228–29
Cohen, Erez   388n
Cohen, Getzel M.   354n, 356n, 358n
Cohen, Shaye J. D.   12n, 375n
Colaizzo, Maria   3n
Cole, Thomas   9n
Collins, W. Lucas   245n
Comparetti, Domenico   1, 7n, 11n,
    55n, 57, 59
Concolino Mancini, Adele   8n
Cook, J. M.   349n, 350n
Costil, P.   220
Courbin, Paul   350n
Courtney, Edward   4n, 12n
Cox, Lisa Loft Anderson   394n
Craig, E.   4n
Croisille, Jean-Michel   7n
Crönert, Wilhelm   8n, 9n, 11n, 55n,
    111n, 385n
Cuomo, Serafina   397n

d'Amelio, M.   160n
Damschen, Gregor   396n
Daube, David   15n
De Angelis, F.   349n
De Falco, Vittorio   10n, 75n
De Lacy, Estelle Allen   9n, 210n
De Lacy, Phillip Howard   8n, 9n,
    210n, 219
De Petra, Giulio   1, 7n, 11n
De Witt, Norman W.   4n, 93n, 76n,
    136n, 137n, 139n, 141n, 142n, 231,
    232, 242, 274n, 275n, 276n, 277n,
    278n, 279n, 297n
Deiss, Joseph Jay   178n
Delattre, D.   5n, 220n
Denniston, John Dewar   87n
Dentzer, Jean-Marie   351n, 356n
Descœudres, J.-P.   350n
De Ste. Croix, G. E. M.   330n
Dever, William G.   343n
Di Cicco, Mario   299n
Diels, Hermann   39n, 82n
Dihle, Albrecht   262n

Dindorf, Wilhelm   335n
Di Segni, Leah   344n, 345n, 381n,
    387n, 389n, 391n
Dillon, John M.   390n
Dilts, Mervin R.   396n
Dorandi, Tiziano   10n, 18n, 55n, 56,
    57, 58, 59, 61n, 65n, 68n, 80n,
    83n, 105n, 149n, 197n, 213n, 214n,
    219, 220, 343n
Dornemann, Rudolph H.   349n
Douglas, A. E.   199n
Dover, Kenneth J.   247n
Downing, F. Gerald   193n
Drummond, William   74n
duBois, Page   227n
Dudley, Donald R.   393n, 394n
Dvorjetski, Esti   351n, 376n, 381n,
    386n

Edwards, Catherine   227n, 229n, 231n
Elliott, Robert C.   264n
Ellis, E. Earle   345n
Empson, William   52n
Engberg-Pederson, Troels   59n, 273n,
    296n
Epstein, I.   393n
Erler, Michael   2n, 3n, 4n, 5n, 6n,
    8n, 9n, 11n, 57n, 60n, 139n, 141n,
    161n, 178n, 180n, 184n, 186n, 394n
Errington, R. Malcolm   354n
Essler, Holger   75n
Evans, C.   371n

Fanon, Frantz   196n
Farrington, Benjamin   136
Feinberg, Joel   32n
Feldman, Fred   32n
Ferguson, Everett   12n
Ferguson, John   2n, 106n, 107n, 127n
Ferguson, William Scott   80n, 138n
Ferrario, Matilde   10n, 150n, 179n,
    198n, 204n
Festugière, André Jean   224n, 276n,
    277n
Figueras, Pau   369n
Fiore, Benjamin   254n, 273n, 278n,
    281n, 282n
Fischel, Henry A.   76n
Fischer, John Martin   32n
Fitzgerald, John T.   1, 12n, 49n,
    246n, 267n, 304n, 311n, 343, 371n
Flashar, H.   2n
Fleischer, Robert   370n
Flesher, P. V. M.   392n

Foerster, Gideon   392n, 393n
Forbes, Christopher   302n
Fowler, D. P.   6n, 162n
Frazer, A.   7n
Fredrickson, David E.   90n, 254,
    255n, 256, 257n, 258n, 272n, 273n,
    290n, 298n, 309n
Freeman, P.   367n
Freudenburg, Kirk   4n
Frézouls, Edmond   354n, 357n
Friedrich, G.   88n
Frischer, Bernard   232
Fritz, Kurt von   3n
Fuks, G.   358n
Furley, David   32n
Furnish, Victor Paul   18n, 305n,
    310n, 314n, 335n
Fürst, Alfons   296n

Gaines, Robert N.   200n, 204n, 217n,
    218n, 332n
Gaiser, Konrad   55n, 66n, 68n,
Galili, E.   353n
Gargiulo, Tristano   58n
Garuti, Giovanni   12n
Gatier, Pierre-Louis   354n, 376n
Gawlikowski, Michel   356n
Geiger, Joseph   358n, 365n, 384n,
    393n, 394n
Gelzer, Heinrich   351n
Gera, Dov   352n, 353n, 354n
Gercke, Alfred   11n
Giannantoni, Gabriele   2n, 195n
Gigante, Marcello 2n, 4n, 5n, 6, 7n,
    9n, 10n, 12n, 19n, 21n, 22n, 23n,
    25n, 35n, 45n, 47n, 48n, 53n, 56n,
    57, 59, 66n, 74n, 76n, 104, 105n,
    106n, 107, 108n, 109n, 110n, 111,
    112n, 113n, 114, 118n, 119n, 120,
    126n, 129n, 130n, 141n, 149n,
    162n, 178n, 179n, 184n, 198n,
    209n, 210n, 220, 281n, 283n, 289n,
    290n, 314n, 330n, 331n
Gildersleeve, B. L.   96n
Gill, D. W. J.   333n
Gilleland, Brady B.   119n
Glad, Clarence E.   12n, 15, 16,
    17–18, 55n, 58n, 59n, 91n, 104n,
    108n, 109n, 124n, 179n, 240n,
    245n, 271n, 272n, 283n,
    284n, 285n, 287, 289n, 295n, 297n,
    307n, 312n, 319n
Glannon, Walter   32n
Gleason, Maud   228n

Gomme, Arnold Wycomb   330n
Gomperz, Theodor   25n, 45n, 57
Goodenough, Erwin R.   391n
Gordon, Pamela   2n, 73n, 136n,
    225n, 238n, 325n
Gosling, J. C. B.   143n, 229n
Gossman, Lionel   218n
Goulet-Cazé, Marie-Odile   187n,
    195n, 394n
Gow, Andrew Sydenham. Farrar
    20n, 87, 88, 394n
Graf, David F.   357n, 358n, 366n,
    367n, 373n, 377n, 384n, 386n
Grainger, John D.   350n, 353n, 354n
Green, Judith   344n, 345n, 382n,
    387n, 388n, 391n
Green, O. H.   32n
Griffin, Dustin   247n, 264n, 265n
Griffin, Miriam   61n
Griffith, G. T.   353n
Grube, G. M. A.   26n, 209n, 215n,
    394n
Guinée, Robert L. J. J.   381n
Guthrie, W. C. K.   247n
Gutzwiller, Kathryn J.   394n

Habas (Rubin), Ephrat   391n
Hadas, Moses   5n, 393n
Hadidi, A.   348n, 351n, 365n
Hainsworth, John Bryan   96n
Haji, Ishtiyaque   32n
Hall, Jennifer   246n, 247n, 394n
Halperin, David   99n
Hammerstaedt, Jürgen   197n, 394n,
    395n, 396n
Hammond, N. G. L.   353n
Harman, L.   339n
Harrington, Daniel J.   358n
Hartung, Johann Adam   179n
Hawley, Richard   222n, 234n
Hayter, John   25n
Heath, Thomas, Sir   396n
Heinemann, J.   377n
Helly, B.   354n, 376n
Helm, Rudolf   394n
Henderson, M. I.   199n
Hendrickson, G. L.   265n
Hengel, Martin   12n, 179n, 352n,
    355n, 373n, 382n, 384n, 396n
Henig, Martin   355n, 365n, 381n,
    385n
Henrichs, Albert   82n
Herr, Moshe David   376n
Hershbell, Jackson P.   2n

Heschel, Susannah 193n, 194n
Highet, Gilbert 247n, 264n
Hirschfeld, Yizhar 388n, 392n
Hirzel, Rudolf 5n
Hock, Ronald 187n
Hoffmann, Adolf 345n, 347n, 348n,
 349n, 351n, 352n, 355n, 356n,
 357n, 359n, 362n, 363n, 364n,
 366n, 367n, 369n, 370n, 371n,
 372n, 374n, 376n, 377n, 378n,
 379n, 380n, 381n, 386n, 389n
Holland, Glenn S. 257n, 260n, 266n,
 313n
Holm-Nielsen, Svend 348n, 380n,
 381n, 388n
Hubbard, Thomas K. 96n
Hubbell, Harry M. 199n, 204n,
 209n, 213n, 214n, 215n, 219, 323n,
 327n, 328n, 329n
Hüttenmeister, Frowald 392n
Huss, Werner 352n, 353n

Indelli, Giovanni 8n, 9n, 21, 27n,
 75n, 112n
Innes, Doreen C. 209n
Isaac, Benjamin 366n, 367n, 373n,
 386n

Jacoby, Felix 60n
Jahn, Otto 203n
Janko, Richard 3n, 4n, 7n, 82n, 113n
Jay, Peter 385n, 394n
Jensen. Christian 150n, 179n, 188,
 191n, 236n
Jones, A. H. M. 350n, 352n, 356n,
 361n, 372n, 387n
Jones, Christopher Prestige 246n,
 247n, 248
Jouguet, Pierre 354n
Judge, E. A. 319n, 339

Kaibel, Georg 53n, 87, 88
Kamm, F. M. 32n
Käsemann, Ernst 196n
Kasher, Aryeh 358n, 360n, 361n,
 362n, 363n, 364n, 368n, 371n,
 372n, 374n, 375n, 387n
Kearsley, Rosalinde 349n
Kennedy, D. L. 367n
Kennedy, George A. 197n, 199n,
 202n, 209n, 323n, 394n, 396n
Kern, Philip H. 342n
Kerner, Susanne 345n, 346n, 347n,
 348n, 355n, 366n, 378n, 388n

Kleve, Knut 11n, 12n, 82n, 106n,
 109n, 214n
Kloss, Gerrit 12n
Knauf, Ernst Axel 344n, 347n, 349n,
 351n, 352n, 353n, 387n
Konstan, David 55n, 59n, 240n,
 284n, 295n, 296n
Körte, Alfred 1n, 4n, 8n, 10n, 209n
Kraeling, Carl H. 345n
Kroll, Wilhelm 197n, 199n, 200n,
 201n, 203n
Krueger, David 61n
Kuhrt, Amélie 353n, 356n
Kuiper, Taco 18n, 19n, 22n, 23n,
 34n, 39n, 41n, 53n, 75n

Laks, André 2n
Lana, I. 187n
Landolfi, L. 4n
Lane, Eugene N. 11n
Lasserre, François 70n
Last, H. M. 109n, 127n
Last, Rosa 381n
Lauvergnat-Gagnière, Christiane
 246n
Laurenti, Renato 150n, 160n, 168,
 179n, 181n, 184n, 186n, 187n,
 188n
Leach, Eleanor Winso 7n
Le Dœff, Michèle 222n
Leeman, Anton Daniel 199n, 203n,
 204n, 220
Lehmeier, Karin 192n
Leisten, Thomas 381n
Levine, Lee I. 391n, 392n
Litfin, A. Duane 337n, 340n
Lodge, Gonzalez 47n
Long, A. A. 9n, 11n, 51n, 140n,
 187n, 195n, 227n, 228n
Longo Auricchio, Francesca
 58n, 113n, 137n, 141n, 164n, 181n,
 197n, 209n, 214n, 220, 241n, 323n
Lorenz, Thuri 6n
Luck, Georg 395n
Luper-Foy, Steven 32n
Luz, Menahem 383n, 385n, 396n
Lyne, R. O. A. M. 16n
Lyons, George 299n, 300n, 319n

Ma, John 354n
Maas, P. 382n
Mace, Sarah Tolle 98n
MacKendrick, Paul 5n
Mahaffy, John Pentland, Sir 1

Malherbe, Abraham J. 12n, 16n, 76n, 184n, 193n, 257n, 273n, 276n, 277n, 290n, 291n
Mangoni, Cecilia 56n, 82n
Mansfeld, Jaap 238n
Marcus, Ralph 344n, 360n
Marrone, Livia 11n
Marsh, David 246n
Marshall, Bruce A. 5n
Marshall, Peter 297n, 302n, 303n, 315n
Martin, Ralph P. 336n
Martin, Richard P. 187n, 188
Marwick, Arthur 218n
Matthes, Dieter 200n
Maxwell, Lee A. 343n, 344n, 347n, 348n, 349n, 361n, 381n
Mayor, Joseph B. 5n
McIlwaine, I. C. 6n
McKirahan, Richard 18n
Meeks, Wayne A. 193n
Mekler, Siegfried 55n, 57, 59
Méndez, Eduardo Acosta 30n
Mershen, Birgit 344n, 347n, 349n, 351n, 352n, 353n, 387n
Meshorer, Yaʿakov 362n, 368n, 369n, 371n, 380n, 385n
Methner, R. 48n
Metzger, Bruce M. 345n, 363n
Michels, Agnes Kirsopp 93n
Militello, C. 60n, 75n, 139n
Millar, Fergus 32n, 343n, 356n, 359n, 371n, 382n, 383n, 386n
Miller, Stuart S. 391n
Mitsis, P. 32n, 85n, 89n, 143n, 285n, 286n
Moles, John L. 394n
Momigliano, Arnaldo 142n
Mommsen, Theodor 381n
Montrose, Louis 222n
Mor, M. 372n
Mueller, Reimar 160n
Mulder, Nicole F. 381n
Mullach, Friedrich Wilhelm August 185n
Münzer, F. 11n
Murray, Gilbert 383n, 384n
Mussies, G. 370n

Nagel, Thomas 32n, 34n
Natali, Carlo 167n
Nauck, August 48n
Negev, A. 351n
Nestle, Dieter 278n

Neudecker, Richard 6n, 7n
Neusner, Jacob 393n
Neyrey, Jerome 274n, 287n
Niehues-Pröbsting, Heinrich 395n
Nielsen, Inge 388n
Noy, D. 377n
Nussbaum, Martha 31n, 32n, 77n, 136n, 137n, 232, 233, 234, 242

Obbink, Dirk 3n, 4n, 5n, 7n, 19n, 23n, 27n, 53n, 56, 75n, 79n, 83n, 104n, 110n, 113n, 116n, 118n, 198n, 323n, 330n, 331n
Oberhelman, Steven 4n, 106n
Olbricht, Thomas H. 12n
Oliver, James H. 396n
Olivieri, Alexander 69, 114, 115n, 116n, 117n, 118, 119, 120, 121, 129n, 130n
Olson. S. N. 310n
Oppenheimer, A. 372n
Orthmann, W. 351n, 356n
Osiek, Carolyn 193n

Pace, Nicola 10n
Pagano, Mario 185n
Page, Denys Lionel 20n, 56n, 87, 88, 98, 394n
Pandermalis, Dimitrios 6n, 7n, 11n
Paquet, Léonce 395n
Parapetti, Roberto 370n
Parente, Margherita Isnardi 209n, 277n
Parker, S. Thomas 367n, 387n
Parsons, Peter J. 3n, 219–20
Partridge, Ernest 32n
Pastor, Jack 372n
Paulson, Ronald 247n, 264n
Perdrizet, P. 384n
Perreault, Jacques Y. 350n
Pervo. Richard I. 253n
Philippson, Robert 9n, 10n, 19n, 69, 105n, 114, 118n, 119n, 120n, 121n, 122n, 203n, 219
Piccirillo, M. 357n
Pinkster, Harm 199n, 203n, 204n, 220
Pitcher, George 32n
Pogoloff, Stephen M. 325n
Pohlenz, Max 22n
Pollard, Arthur 246n, 248, 264n
Pomeroy, Sarah B. 179n
Popham, Mervyn 349n, 350n
Porter, H. 384n

Porter, James
Porter, S. 371n
Praechter, Karl 2n
Procopé, John 42
Puglia, Enzo 9n, 10n
Purinton, Jeffrey S. 226n

Raalflaub, Kurt 90n
Radermacher, Ludwig 204n, 207n, 327n
Rappaport, U. 358n
Rasche, Wilhelm 87n
Rawson, Elizabeth 197n, 198n
Reeg, G. 392n
Reginos, Alice Swift 70n
Reiche, H. 76n
Relihan, Joel C. 393n, 394n
Renna, Enrico 10n
Rey-Coquais, Jean-Paul 354n, 355n, 358n, 359n, 366n, 368n, 372n, 375n, 376n
Ribichini, S. 369n
Rich, Audrey N. M. 149n
Richardson, Peter 16n
Richter, Gisela M. A. 11n
Rigsby, Kent J. 368n, 373n, 374n, 384n, 391n
Riis, P. J. 350n
Rilke, Rainer Maria 178
Rist, John M. 11n, 143n
Robert, Louis 373n
Robinson, Christopher 246n, 249
Robinson, James 194n
Romano, David Gilman 178n
Romeo, Costantina 9n, 10n, 82n
Rorty, Amélie 32n
Rosenbaum, Stephen 32n
Rostagni, Augusto 220
Rouillard, P. 350n
Rubin (Habas), Ephrat 391n
Russell, Donald Andrew 337n
Rutherford, I. 332n

Samuel, Alan Edouard 353n
Sampley, J. Paul 254n, 300n, 302n, 306n, 321n
Santoro, Mariacarolina 10n
Sartre, Maurice 351n
Sauron, Gilles 6n
Scarpat, Guiseppe 272n, 273n, 282n, 289n
Schanz, Martin 394n
Schmid, Wolfgang 53n, 67n, 87n, 385n

Schmidt, F. G. 48n
Schmitt, Hatto H. 353n, 354n
Schottroff, Luise 193n
Schürer, Emil 343n, 344n, 348n, 360n, 370n, 372n, 384n
Schumacher, Gottlieb 347n
Schwartz, D. R. 372n
Schwarz, Roland 283n
Scodel, Ruth 96
Scott, Joan Wallach 222n
Scott, Walter 18n, 39n, 213n
Sedley, David N. 8n, 9n, 11n, 51n, 68n, 70n, 73, 74, 76–77, 78, 79, 80n, 81, 141n, 142n, 212n, 220, 225n, 232, 233, 234, 241n, 330n
Seetzen, Ulrich Jasper 347n
Segal, Arthur 345n
Segal, Charles 21n, 36, 88n
Seigne, Jacques 345n, 374n
Shami, Seteney 348n, 351n
Shanks, Hershel 391n, 392n
Shaw, Gregory 391n
Sherwin-White, Susan 353n, 356n
Shoobridge, Leonard 1n
Sider, David 3n, 4n, 20n, 52, 53n, 56n, 79n, 85n, 87n, 88, 89n, 92n, 93n, 98n, 107n, 226n, 239, 240n, 254n
Silverstein, Harry 32n
Slater, William J. 96
Slotki, Israel W. 393n
Smallwood, E. Mary 361n, 372n, 391n
Smith, Martin Ferguson 332n
Smith, Morton 384n
Snell, Bruno 48n
Snodgrass, A. M. 349n, 358n
Snyder, Jane 223, 224, 232, 234, 242
Solmsen, Friedrich 200n, 326n
Sourdel, Dominique 369n, 370n
Spijkerman, Augustus 357n, 366n, 368n, 369n, 371n, 374n, 376n, 377n, 386n
Spina, Luigi 58n
Spinelli, Emidio 8n
Squires, Simon 5n
Stanford, W. B. 16n
Steckel, Horst 137n, 138n
Stegemann, Willy 394n
Stemberger, G. 391n, 395n
Stern, E. 345n
Stewart, Andrew 236n
Stillwell, R. 351n
Stocks, John L. 197n, 198n

Stokes, Michael C.   226n, 260n
Strack, H. L.   391n, 395n
Strange, John   349n
Sudhaus, Siegfried   30n, 155n, 168,
    186, 197n, 204n, 213n, 215n
Sukenik, E. L.   391n, 392n
Susemihl, Franz   1n, 4n
Swain, Simon   229n
Syme, Ronald   7n

Tait, Jane Isabella Marion
    4n, 93n, 214n, 215n, 271n
Talbert, Charles   18n
Tarn, William Woodthorpe
    63n
Taylor, C. C. W.   143n, 227n
Tcherikover, Victor   352n, 355n,
    356n, 358n, 384n
Teixidor, Javier   356n
Tepedino Guerra, Adele   3n, 8n,
    141n, 149n, 150n, 164n, 177n,
    179n, 180n, 181n, 182n, 184n,
    185n, 186n, 209n
Thackeray, H. St. J.   344n
Theissen, Gerd   193n, 314n
Thom, Johan C.   55n, 240n, 284n
Thompson, Edward M., Sir   12n
Thrall, Margaret E.   192n
Toorn, K. van der   369n
Traversa, Augusto   55n, 59
Treacy-Cole, Diane I.   344n
Treggiari, Susan   365n, 366n
Trevelyan, Raleigh   2n
Treves, Piero   2n, 3n, 4n
Tsafrir, Yoram   344n, 345n, 382n,
    387n, 388n, 391n
Tsakiropoulou-Summers, Anastasia
    4n
Tsetskhladze, G. R.   349n
Tsouna-McKirahan, Voula   21, 27,
    75n, 150n, 186, 187
Tzaferis, Vassilios   345n

Überweg, Friedrich   2n
Urman, D.   392n

van der Horst, P. W.   369n
Vander Waerdt, Paul A.   8n, 83n
Vanderpool, Eugene   394n, 397n
van Hook, La Rue   327n
Vermes, G.   343n
Vickers, Brian   204n
Vlastos, Gregory   3n
von Arnim, Hans   204n

von Spengel, Leonhard   179n
von Wilamowitz-Möllendorff, Ulrich
    185n
Vriezen, Karel J. H.   348n, 380n,
    381n, 388n

Wagner-Lux, Ute   347n, 348n, 380n,
    381n, 388n
Walbank, F. W.   353n
Waldstein, Charles   1n
Wallach, Barbara Price   19n, 26n, 88n
Wallach, L.   3n
Walpole, Robert   74n
Ward, Roy Bowen   389n
Warden, F. Gregory   178n
Ware, James   55n, 240n, 284n
Weber, Thomas M.   347n, 348n,
    349n, 351n, 357n, 358n, 364n,
    365n, 367n, 368n, 369n, 370n,
    377n, 378n, 379n, 380n, 381n,
    382n, 386n, 388n, 389n, 397n
Wehrli, Fritz   8n, 65n
Weiss, Johannes   324n
West, Thomas G.   260n
Westman, Rolf   8n
Whigham, Peter   385n, 394n
White, L. Michael   12n
Whtie, S.   77n
Whiting, Mary   355n, 365n, 381n, 385n
Wigodsky, Michae   193n
Wilcox, M.   345n
Wilke, C.   112n
Will, Édouard   352n, 354n, 365n, 367n
Will, Ernest   365n, 366n, 367n
Williams, Bernard   32n, 77n
Williams, C. H.   333n
Willis, W.   16n
Wimmel, Walter   4n, 106n
Winkler, John J.   98n
Winter, Bruce W.   324n, 325n, 332n,
    336n, 337n
Wisse, Jakob   199n, 219, 220,
    339n
Wojcik, Maria Rita   6n, 7n
Wright, W. C.   390n
Wycherley, R. E.   135n

Yegül, Fikret   388n, 389n, 390n
Yon, Jean-Baptiste   359n
Young, David C.   96n, 100
Yourgrav, Palle   32n

Zayadine, Fawzi   345n, 374n, 386n
Zeyl, D. J.   2n

SUPPLEMENTS TO NOVUM TESTAMENTUM

ISSN 0167-9732

69. Newman, C.C. *Paul's Glory-Christology*. Tradition and Rhetoric. 1992.
    ISBN 90 04 09463 6
70. Ireland, D.J. *Stewardship and the Kingdom of God*. An Historical, Exegetical, and
    Contextual Study of the Parable of the Unjust Steward in Luke 16: 1-13. 1992.
    ISBN 90 04 09600 0
71. Elliott, J.K. *The Language and Style of the Gospel of Mark*. An Edition of C.H. Turner's
    "Notes on Marcan Usage" together with other comparable studies. 1993.
    ISBN 90 04 09767 8
72. Chilton, B. *A Feast of Meanings*. Eucharistic Theologies from Jesus through Johannine
    Circles. 1994. ISBN 90 04 09949 2
73. Guthrie, G.H. *The Structure of Hebrews*. A Text-Linguistic Analysis. 1994.
    ISBN 90 04 09866 6
74. Bormann, L., K. Del Tredici & A. Standhartinger (eds.) *Religious Propaganda and
    Missionary Competition in the New Testament World*. Essays Honoring Dieter Georgi.
    1994. ISBN 90 04 10049 0
75. Piper, R.A. (ed.) *The Gospel Behind the Gospels*. Current Studies on Q. 1995.
    ISBN 90 04 09737 6
76. Pedersen, S. (ed.) *New Directions in Biblical Theology*. Papers of the Aarhus Conference,
    16-19 September 1992. 1994. ISBN 90 04 10120 9
77. Jefford, C.N. (ed.) *The* Didache *in Context*. Essays on Its Text, History and Trans-
    mission. 1995. ISBN 90 04 10045 8
78. Bormann, L. *Philippi – Stadt und Christengemeinde zur Zeit des Paulus*. 1995.
    ISBN 90 04 10232 9
79. Peterlin, D. *Paul's Letter to the Philippians in the Light of Disunity in the Church*. 1995.
    ISBN 90 04 10305 8
80. Jones, I.H. *The Matthean Parables*. A Literary and Historical Commentary. 1995.
    ISBN 90 04 10181 0
81. Glad, C.E. *Paul and Philodemus*. Adaptability in Epicurean and Early Christian
    Psychagogy. 1995. ISBN 90 04 10067 9
82. Fitzgerald, J.T. (ed.) *Friendship, Flattery, and Frankness of Speech*. Studies on Friend-ship
    in the New Testament World. 1996. ISBN 90 04 10454 2
83. Tilborg, S. van. *Reading John in Ephesus*. 1996. 90 04 10530 1
84. Holleman, J. *Resurrection and Parousia*. A Traditio-Historical Study of Paul's Escha-
    tology in 1 Corinthians 15. 1996. ISBN 90 04 10597 2
85. Moritz, T. *A Profound Mystery*. The Use of the Old Testament in Ephesians. 1996.
    ISBN 90 04 10556 5
86. Borgen, P. *Philo of Alexandria - An Exegete for His Time*. 1997. ISBN 90 04 10388 0
87. Zwiep, A.W. *The Ascension of the Messiah in Lukan Christology*. 1997.
    ISBN 90 04 10897 1
88. Wilson, W.T. *The Hope of Glory*. Education and Exhortation in the Epistle to the
    Colossians. 1997. ISBN 90 04 10937 4
89. Peterson, W.L., J.S. Vos & H.J. de Jonge (eds.) *Sayings of Jesus: Canonical and Non-
    Canonical*. Essays in Honour of Tjitze Baarda. 1997. ISBN 90 04 10380 5

90. Malherbe, A.J., F.W. Norris & J.W. Thompson (eds.) *The Early Church in Its Context*. Essays in Honor of Everett Ferguson. 1998. ISBN 90 04 10832 7

91. Kirk, A. *The Composition of the Sayings Source*. Genre, Synchrony, and Wisdom Redaction in Q. 1998. ISBN 90 04 11085 2

92. Vorster, W.S. *Speaking of Jesus*. Essays on Biblical Language, Gospel Narrative and the Historical Jesus. Edited by J. E. Botha. 1999. ISBN 90 04 10779 7

93. Bauckham, R. *The Fate of Dead*. Studies on the Jewish and Christian Apocalypses. 1998. ISBN 90 04 11203 0

94. Standhartinger, A. *Studien zur Entstehungsgeschichte und Intention des Kolosserbriefs*. 1998. ISBN 90 04 11286 3

95. Oegema, G.S. *Für Israel und die Völker*. Studien zum alttestamentlich-jüdischen Hintergrund der paulinischen Theologie. 1999. ISBN 90 04 11297 9

96. Albl, M.C. *"And Scripture Cannot Be Broken"*. The Form and Function of the Early Christian *Testimonia* Collections. 1999. ISBN 90 04 11417 3

97. Ellis, E.E. *Christ and the Future in New Testament History*. 1999. ISBN 90 04 11533 1

98. Chilton, B. & C.A. Evans, (eds.) *James the Just and Christian Origins*. 1999. ISBN 90 04 11550 1

99. Horrell, D.G. & C.M. Tuckett (eds.) *Christology, Controversy and Community*. New Testament Essays in Honour of David R. Catchpole. 2000. ISBN 90 04 11679 6

100. Jackson-McCabe, M.A. *Logos and Law in the Letter of James*. The Law of Nature, the Law of Moses and the Law of Freedom. 2001. ISBN 90 04 11994 9

101. Wagner, J.R. *Heralds of the Good News*. Isaiah and Paul "In Concert" in the Letter to the Romans. 2002. ISBN 90 04 11691 5

102. Cousland, J.R.C. *The Crowds in the Gospel of Matthew*. 2002. ISBN 90 04 12177 3

103. Dunderberg, I., C. Tuckett and K. Syreeni. *Fair Play: Diversity and Conflicts in Early Christianity*. Essays in Honour of Heikki Räisänen. 2002. ISBN 90 04 12359 8

104. Mount, C. *Pauline Christianity*. Luke-Acts and the Legacy of Paul. 2002. ISBN 90 04 12472 1

105. Matthews, C.R. *Philip: Apostle and Evangelist*. Configurations of a Tradition. 2002. ISBN 90 04 12054 8

106. Aune, D.E., T. Seland, J.H. Ulrichsen (eds.) *Neotestamentica et Philonica*. Studies in Honor of Peder Borgen. 2002. ISBN 90 04 126104

107. Talbert, C.H. *Reading Luke-Acts in its Mediterranean Milieu*. 2003. ISBN 90 04 12964 2

108. Klijn, A.F.J. *The Acts of Thomas*. Introduction, Text, and Commentary. Second Revised Edition. 2003. ISBN 90 04 12937 5

109. Burke, T.J. & J.K. Elliott (eds.) *Paul and the Corinthians*. Studies on a Community in Conflict. Essays in Honour of Margaret Thrall. 2003. ISBN 90 04 12920 0

110. Fitzgerald, J.T., T.H. Olbricht & L.M. White (eds.) *Early Christianity and Classical Culture*. Comparative Studies in Honor of Abraham J. Malherbe. 2003. ISBN 90 04 13022 5

111. Fitzgerald, J.T., D. Obbink & G.S. Holland (eds.) *Philodemus and the New Testament World*. 2004. ISBN 90 04 11460 2

112. Lührmann, D. *Die Apokryph gewordenen Evangelien*. Studien zu neuen Texten und zu neuen Fragen. 2004. ISBN 90 04 12867 0